Formulas

W9-AWJ-978

1. *Amdahl's Law: Speedup* = $\dfrac{1}{(1-\text{Fraction}_{\text{enhanced}}) + \dfrac{\text{Fraction}_{\text{enhanced}}}{\text{Speedup}_{\text{enhanced}}}}$ (page 8)

2. *CPU time* = Instruction count * Clock cycles per instruction * Clock cycle time (page 36)

3. *Average memory-access time* = Hit time + Miss rate * Miss penalty (page 405)

4. *Means*—arithmetic(AM), weighted arithmetic(WAM), harmonic(HM) and weighted harmonic(WHM):

$$\text{AM} = \frac{1}{n}\sum_{i=1}^{n}\text{Time}_i, \ \text{WAM} = \sum_{i=1}^{n}\text{Weight}_i * \text{Time}_i, \ \text{HM} = \frac{n}{\displaystyle\sum_{i=1}^{n}\frac{1}{\text{Rate}_i}}, \ \text{WHM} = \frac{1}{\displaystyle\sum_{i=1}^{n}\frac{\text{Weight}_i}{\text{Rate}_i}}$$

where Time_i is the execution time for the *i*th program of a total of *n* in the workload, Weight_i is the weighting of the *i*th program in the workload, and Rate_i is a function of $1/\text{Time}_i$ (page 51).

5. *Cost of integrated circuit* = $\dfrac{\text{Cost of die + Cost of testing die + Cost of packaging}}{\text{Final test yield}}$ (page 55)

6. *Die yield* = Wafer yield * $\left\{1 + \dfrac{\text{Defects per unit area * Die area}}{\alpha}\right\}^{-\alpha}$

where Wafer yield accounts for wafers that are so bad they need not be tested and α corresponds to the number of masking levels critical to die yield (usually $\alpha \geq 2.0$, page 59).

7. *Pipeline speedup* = $\dfrac{\text{Clock cycle time}_{\text{no pipelining}}}{\text{Clock cycle time}_{\text{pipelined}}} * \dfrac{\text{Ideal CPI * Pipeline depth}}{\text{Ideal CPI + Pipeline stall cycles per instruction}}$

where Pipeline stall cycles accounts for clock cycles lost due to pipeline hazards (page 258).

8. *System performance:*

$$\text{Time}_{\text{workload}} = \frac{\text{Time}_{\text{CPU}}}{\text{Speedup}_{\text{CPU}}} + \frac{\text{Time}_{\text{I/O}}}{\text{Speedup}_{\text{I/O}}} - \frac{\text{Time}_{\text{overlap}}}{\text{Maximum}(\text{Speedup}_{\text{CPU}}, \text{Speedup}_{\text{I/O}})}$$

where Time_{CPU} means the time the CPU is busy, $\text{Time}_{\text{I/O}}$ means the time the I/O system is busy, and $\text{Time}_{\text{overlap}}$ means the time both are busy. This formula assumes the overlap scales linearly with speedup (page 506).

Rules of Thumb

1. *Amdahl/Case Rule*: A balanced computer system needs about 1 megabyte of main memory capacity and 1 megabit per second of I/O bandwidth per MIPS of CPU performance (page 17).
2. *90/10 Locality Rule*: A program executes about 90% of its instructions in 10% of its code (pages 11–12).
3. *DRAM-Growth Rule*: Density increases by about 60% per year, quadrupling in 3 years (page 17).
4. *Disk-Growth Rule*: Density increases by about 25% per year, doubling in 3 years (page 17).
5. *Address-Consumption Rule*: The memory needed by the average program grows by about a factor of 1.5 to 2 per year; thus, it consumes between 1/2 and 1 address bit per year (page 16).
6. *90/50 Branch-Taken Rule:* About 90% of backward-going branches are taken while about 50% of forward-going branches are taken (page 108).
7. *2:1 Cache Rule*: The miss rate of a direct-mapped cache of size X is about the same as a 2-way–set-associative cache of size X/2 (page 421).

Computer Architecture
A
Quantitative
Approach

Computer
Architecture
A
Quantitative
Approach

David A. Patterson
UNIVERSITY OF CALIFORNIA AT BERKELEY

John L. Hennessy
STANFORD UNIVERSITY

With a Contribution by
David Goldberg
Xerox Palo Alto Research Center

MORGAN KAUFMANN PUBLISHERS, INC.
SAN MATEO, CALIFORNIA

Sponsoring Editor Bruce Spatz
Production Manager Shirley Jowell
Technical Writer Walker Cunningham
Text Design Gary Head
Cover Design David Lance Goines
Copy Editor Linda Medoff
Proofreader Paul Medoff
Computer Typesetting and Graphics Fifth Street Computer Services

Library of Congress Cataloging-in-Publication Data
Patterson, David A.
    Computer architecture : a quantitative approach / David A.
  Patterson, John L. Hennessy
      p.   cm.
    Includes bibliographical references
    ISBN 1-55860- 069-8
    1. Computer architecture. I. Hennessy, John L. II. Title.
QA76.9.A73P377 1990
004.2'2--dc20   89-85227
                                                        CIP

Morgan Kaufmann Publishers, Inc.
Editorial Office: 2929 Campus Drive. San Mateo, CA 94403
Order from: P.O. Box 50490, Palo Alto, CA 94303-9953

ADVICE, PRAISE, & ERRORS: Any correspondence related to this publication or intended for the authors should be addressed to the editorial offices of Morgan Kaufmann Publishers, Inc., Dept. P&H APE. Information regarding error sightings is encouraged. Any error sightings that are accepted for correction in subsequent printings will be rewarded by the authors with a payment of $1.00 (U.S.) per correction upon availability of the new printing. Electronic mail can be sent to bugs3@vsop.stanford.edu. (Please include your full name and permanent mailing address.)

INSTRUCTOR SUPPORT: For information on classroom software and other instructor materials available to adopters, please contact the editorial offices of Morgan Kaufmann Publishers, Inc. (415) 578-9911.

Third printing

To Andrea, Linda, and our four sons

Trademarks

The following trademarks are the property of the following organizations:

Alliant is a trademark of Alliant Computers.

AMD 29000 is a trademark of AMD.

TeX is a trademark of American Mathematical Society.

AMI 6502 is a trademark of AMI.

Apple I, Apple II, and Macintosh are trademarks of Apple Computer, Inc.

ZS-1 is a trademark of Astronautics.

UNIX and UNIX F77 are trademarks of AT&T Bell Laboratories.

Turbo C is a trademark of Borland International.

The Cosmic Cube is a trademark of California Institute of Technology.

Warp, C.mmp, and Cm* are trademarks of Carnegie-Mellon University.

CP3100 is a trademark of Conner Peripherals.

CDC 6600, CDC 7600, CDC STAR-100, CYBER-180, CYBER 180/990, and CYBER-205 are trademarks of Control Data Corporation.

Convex, C-1, C-2, and C series are trademarks of Convex.

CRAY-3 is a trademark of Cray Computer Corporation.

CRAY-1, CRAY-1S, CRAY-2, CRAY X-MP, CRAY X-MP/416, CRAY Y-MP, CFT77 V3.0, CFT, and CFT2 V1.3a are trademarks of Cray Research.

Cydra 5 is a trademark of Cydrome.

CY7C601, 7C601, 7C604, and 7C157 are trademarks of Cypress Semiconductor.

Nova is a trademark of Data General Corporation.

HEP is a trademark of Denelcor.

CVAX, DEC, DECsystem, DECstation, DECstation 3100, DECsystem 10/20, fort, LP11, Massbus, MicroVAX-I, MicroVAX-II, PDP-8, PDP-10, PDP-11, RS-11M/IAS, Unibus, Ultrix, Ultrix 3.0, VAX, VAXstation, VAXstation 2000, VAXstation 3100, VAX-11, VAX-11/780, VAX-11/785, VAX Model 730, Model 750, Model 780, VAX 8600, VAX 8700, VAX 8800, VS FORTRAN V2.4, and VMS are trademarks of Digital Equipment Corporation.

BINAC is a trademark of Eckert-Mauchly Computer Corporation.

Multimax is a trademark of Encore Computers.

ETA 10 is a trademark of the ETA Corporation.

SYMBOL is a trademark of Fairchild Corporation.

Pegasus is a trademark of Ferranti, Ltd.

Ferrari and Testarossa are trademarks of Ferrari Motors.

AP-120B is a trademark of Floating Point Systems.

Ford and Escort are trademarks Ford Motor Co.

Gnu C Compiler is a trademark of Free Software Foundation.

M2361A, Super Eagle, VP100, and VP200 are trademarks of Fujitsu Corporation.

Chevrolet and Corvette are trademarks of General Motors Corporation.

HP Precision Architecture, HP 850, HP 3000, HP 3000/70, Apollo DN 300, Apollo DN 10000, and Precision are trademarks of Hewlett-Packard Company.

S810, S810/200, and S820 are trademarks of Hitachi Corporation.

Hyundai and Excel are trademarks of the Hyundai Corporation.

432, 960 CA, 4004, 8008, 8080, 8086, 8087, 8088, 80186, 80286, 80386, 80486, iAPX 432, i860, Intel, Multibus, Multibus II, and Intel Hypercube are trademarks of Intel Corporation.

Inmos and Transputer are trademarks of Inmos.

Clipper C100 is a trademark of Intergraph.

IBM, 360, 360/30, 360/40, 360/50, 360/65, 360/85, 360/91, 370, 370/135, 370/138, 370/145, 370/155, 370/158, 370/165, 370/168, 370-XA, ESA/370, System/360, System/370, 701, 704, 709, 801, 3033, 3080, 3080 series, 3080 VF, 3081, 3090, 3090/100, 3090/200, 3090/400,

3090/600, 3090/600S, 3090 VF, 3330, 3380, 3380D, 3380 Disk Model AK4, 3380J, 3390, 3880-23, 3990, 7030, 7090, 7094, IBM FORTRAN, ISAM, MVS, IBM PC, IBM PC-AT, PL.8, RT-PC, SAGE, Stretch, IBM SVS, Vector Facility, and VM are trademarks of International Business Machines Corporation.

FutureBus is a trademark of the Institute of Electrical and Electronic Engineers.

Lamborghini and Countach are trademarks of Nuova Automobili Ferrucio Lamborghini, SPA.

Lotus 1-2-3 is a trademark of Lotus Development Corporation.

MB8909 is a trademark of LSI Logic.

NuBus is a trademark of Massachusetts Institute of Technology.

Miata and Mazda are trademarks of Mazda.

MASM, Microsoft Macro Assembler, MS DOS, MS DOS 3.1, and OS/2 are trademarks of Microsoft Corporation.

MIPS, MIPS 120, MIPS/120A, M/500, M/1000, RC6230, RC6280, R2000, R2000A, R2010, R3000, and R3010 are trademarks of MIPS Computer Systems.

Delta Series 8608, System V/88 R32V1, VME bus, 6809, 68000, 68010, 68020, 68030, 68882, 88000, 88000 1.8.4m14, 88100, and 88200 are trademarks of Motorola Corporation.

Multiflow is a trademark of Multiflow Corporation.

National 32032 and 32x32 are trademarks of National Semiconductor Corporation.

Ncube is a trademark of Ncube Corporation.

SX/2, SX/3, and FORTRAN 77/SX V.040 are trademarks of NEC Information Systems.

NYU Ultracomputer is a trademark of New York University.

VAST-2 v.2.21 is a trademark of Pacific Sierra.

Wren IV, Imprimis, Sabre, Sabre 97209, and IPI-2 are trademarks of Seagate Corporation.

Sequent, Balance 800, Balance 21000, and Symmetry are trademarks of Sequent Computers.

Silicon Graphics 4D/60, 4D/240, and Silicon Graphics 4D Series are trademarks of Silicon Graphics.

Stellar GS 1000, Stardent-1500, and Ardent Titan-1 are trademarks of Stardent.

Sun 2, Sun 3, Sun 3/75, Sun 3/260, Sun 3/280, Sun 4, Sun 4/110, Sun 4/260, Sun 4/280, SunOS 4.0.3c, Sun 1.2 FORTRAN compiler, SPARC, and SPARCstation 1 are trademarks of Sun Microsystems.

Synapse N+1 is a trademark of Synapse.

Tandem and Cyclone are trademarks of Tandem Computers.

TI 8847 and TI ASC are trademarks of Texas Instruments Corporation.

Connection Machine and CM-2 are trademarks of Thinking Machines.

Burroughs 6500, B5000, B5500, D-machine, UNIVAC, UNIVAC I, UNIVAC 1103 are trademarks of UNISYS.

Spice and 4.2 BSD UNIX are trademarks of University of California, Berkeley.

Illiac, Illiac IV, and Cedar are trademarks of University of Illinois.

Ada is a trademark of the U.S. Government (Ada Joint Program Office).

Weitek 3364, Weitek 1167, WTL 3110, and WTL 3170 are trademarks of Weitek Computers.

Alto, Ethernet, PARC, Palo Alto Research Center, Smalltalk, and Xerox are trademarks of Xerox Corporation.

Z-80 is a trademark of Zilog.

Foreword

by C. Gordon Bell

I am delighted and honored to write the foreword for this landmark book.

The authors have gone beyond the contributions of Thomas to Calculus and Samuelson to Economics. They have provided the definitive text and reference for computer architecture *and design*. To advance computing, I urge publishers to withdraw the scores of books on this topic so a new breed of architect/ engineer can quickly emerge. This book won't eliminate the complex and errorful microprocessors from semicomputer companies, but it will hasten the education of engineers who can design better ones.

The book presents the critical tools to analyze uniprocessor computers. It shows the practicing engineer how technology changes over time and offers the empirical constants one needs for design. It motivates the designer about function, which is a welcome departure from the usual exhaustive shopping list of mechanisms that a naive designer might attempt to include in a single design.

The authors establish a baseline for analysis and comparisons by using the most important machine in each class: mainframe (IBM 360), mini (DEC VAX), and micro/PC (Intel 80x86). With this foundation, they show the coming mainline of simpler pipelined and parallel processors. These new technologies are shown as variants of their pedagogically useful, but highly realizable, processor (DLX). The authors stress technology independence by measuring work done per clock (parallelism), and time to do work (efficiency and latency). These methods should also improve the quality of research on new architectures and parallelism.

Thus, the book is required *understanding* for anyone working with architecture or hardware, including architects, chip and computer system engineers, and compiler and operating system engineers. It is especially useful for software engineers writing programs for pipelined and vector computers. Managers and marketers will benefit by knowing the Fallacies and Pitfalls sections of the book. One can lay the demise of many a computer—and, occasionally, a company—on engineers who fail to understand the subtleties of computer design.

The first two chapters establish the essence of computer design through measurement and the understanding of price/performance. These concepts are applied to the instruction set architecture and how it is measured. They discuss the implementation of processors and include extensive discussions of techniques for designing pipelined and vector processors. Chapters are also devoted to memory hierarchy and the often-neglected input/output. The final chapter presents the opportunities and questions about machines and directions of the future. Now, we need their next book on how to build these machines.

The reason this book sets a standard above all others and is unlikely to be superseded in any foreseeable future is the understanding, experience, taste, and *uniqueness* of the authors. They have stimulated the major change in architecture by their work on RISC (Patterson coined the word). Their university research leading to product development at MIPS and Sun Microsystems established important architectures for the 1990s. Thus, they have done the analysis, evaluated the trade-offs, worked on the compilers and operating systems, and seen their machines achieve significance in use. Furthermore, as teachers, they have seen that the book is pedagogically sound (and have solicited opinions from others through the unprecedented Beta testing program). I know this will be the book of the decade in computer systems. Perhaps its greatest accomplishment would be to stimulate other great architects and designers of higher-level systems (databases, communications systems, languages and operating systems) to write similar books about their domains.

I've already enjoyed and learned from the book, and surely you will too.

—C. Gordon Bell

Contents

Preface

I started in 1962 to write a single book with this sequence of chapters, but soon found that it was more important to treat the subjects in depth rather than to skim over them lightly. The resulting length has meant that each chapter by itself contains enough material for a one semester course, so it has become necessary to publish the series in separate volumes...

Donald Knuth, *The Art of Computer Programming,*
Preface to Volume 1 (of 7) (1968)

Why We Wrote This Book

Welcome to this book! We're glad to have the opportunity to communicate with you! There are so many exciting things happening in computer architecture, but we feel available materials just do not adequately make people aware of this. This is not a dreary science of paper machines that will never work. No! It's a discipline of keen intellectual interest, requiring balance of marketplace forces and cost/performance, leading to glorious failures and some notable successes. And it is hard to match the excitement of seeing thousands of people use the machine that you designed.

Our primary goal in writing this book is to help change the way people learn about computer architecture. We believe that the field has changed from one that can only be taught with definitions and historical information, to one that can be studied with real examples and real measurements. We envision this book as suitable for a course in computer architecture as well as a primer or reference for professional engineers and computer architects. This book embodies a new approach to demystifying computer architecture—it emphasizes a quantitative approach to cost/performance tradeoffs. This does not imply an overly formal approach, but simply one that is grounded in good engineering design. To accomplish this, we've included lots of data about real machines, so that a reader can understand design tradeoffs in a quantitative as well as qualitative fashion. A significant component of this approach can be found in the problem sets at the end of every chapter, as well as the software that accompanies the book. Such exercises have long formed the core of science and engineering education. With the emergence of a quantitative basis for teaching computer architecture, we feel the field has the potential to move toward the rigorous quantitative foundation of other disciplines.

Topic Selection and Organization

We have a conservative approach to topic selection, for there are many interesting ideas in the field. Rather than attempting a comprehensive survey of every architecture a reader might encounter today in practice or in the literature, we've chosen the core concepts of computer architecture that are likely to be included in any new machine. In making these decisions, a key criterion has been to emphasize ideas that have been sufficiently examined to be discussed in quantitative terms. For example, we concentrate on uniprocessors until the final chapter, where a bus-oriented, shared-memory multiprocessor is described. We believe this class of computer architecture will increase in popularity, but despite this perception it only met our criteria by a slim margin. Only recently has this class of architecture been examined in ways that allow us to discuss it quantitatively; a short time ago even this wouldn't have been included. Although large-scale parallel processors are of obvious importance to the future, it is our feeling that a firm basis in the principles of uniprocessor design is necessary before any practicing engineer tries to build a better computer of any organization; especially one incorporating multiple uniprocessors.

Readers familiar with our research might expect this book to be only about reduced instruction set computers (RISCs). This is a mistaken judgment about the content of this book. Our hope is that design principles and quantitative data in this book will restrict discussions of architecture styles to terms like "faster" or "cheaper," unlike previous debates.

The material we have selected has been stretched upon a consistent structure that is followed in every chapter. After explaining the ideas of a chapter, we include a "Putting It All Together" section that ties these ideas together by showing how they are used in a real machine. This is followed by a section, entitled "Fallacies and Pitfalls," that lets readers learn from the mistakes of others.We show examples of common misunderstandings and architectural traps that are difficult to avoid even when you know they are lying in wait for you. Each chapter ends with a "Concluding Remarks" section, followed by a "Historical Perspective and References" section that attempts to give proper credit for the ideas in the chapter and a sense of the history surrounding the inventions, presenting the human drama of computer design. It also supplies references that the student of architecture may want to pursue. If you have time, we recommend reading some of the classic papers in the field that are mentioned in these sections. It is both enjoyable and educational to hear the ideas from the mouths of the creators. Each chapter ends with Exercises, over 200 in total, which vary from one-minute reviews to term projects.

A glance at the Table of Contents shows that neither the amount nor the depth of the material is equal from chapter to chapter. In the early chapters, for example, we have more basic material to ensure a common terminology and background. In talking with our colleagues, we found widely varying opinions of the backgrounds readers have, the pace at which they can pick up new material, and even the order in which ideas should be introduced. Our assumption is that the reader is familiar with logic design, and has had some exposure to at least one instruction set and basic software concepts. The pace varies with the chapters, with the first half gentler than the last half. The organizational decisions were formed in response to reviewer advice. The final organization was selected to conveniently suit the majority of courses (beyond Berkeley and Stanford!) with only minor modifications. Depending on your goals, we see three paths through this material:

Introductory coverage: Chapters 1, 2, 3, 4, 5, 6.1–6.5, 8.1–8.5, 9.1–9.5, 10, and A.1–A.3.

Intermediary coverage: Chapters 1, 2, 3, 4, 5, 6.1–6.6, 6.9–6.12, 8.1–8.7, 8.9–8.12, 9, 10, A (except skip division in Section A.9), and E.

Advanced coverage: Read everything, but Chapters 3 and 5 and Sections A.1–A.2 and 9.3–9.4 may be largely review, so read them quickly.

Alas, there is no single best order for the chapters. It would be nice to know about pipelining (Chapter 6) before discussing instruction sets (Chapters 3 and 4), for example, but it is difficult to understand pipelining without understanding the full set of instructions being pipelined. We ourselves have tried a few different orders in earlier versions of this material, and each has its strengths. Thus, the material was written so that it can be covered in several ways. The organization proved sufficiently flexible for a wide variety of chapter sequences in the Beta test program at 18 schools, where the book was used successfully. Some of these syllabi are reproduced in the accompanying Instructor's Manual. The only restriction is that some chapters should be read in sequence:

Chapters 1 and 2

Chapters 3 and 4

Chapters 5, 6, and 7

Chapters 8 and 9

Readers should start with Chapters 1 and 2 and end with Chapter 10, but the rest can be covered in any order. The only proviso is that if you read Chapters 5, 6, and 7 before Chapters 3 and 4, you should first skim Section 4.5, as the instruction set in this section, DLX, is used to illustrate the ideas found in those three chapters. A compact description of DLX and the hardware description notation we use can be found on the inside back cover. (We selected a modified version of C for our hardware description language because of its compactness, because of the number of people who know the language, and because there is no common description language used in books that could be considered prerequisites.)

We urge everyone to read Chapters 1 and 2. Chapter 1 is intentionally easy to follow so that it can be read quickly, even by a beginner. It gives a few important principles that act as themes guiding the tradeoffs in later chapters. While few would skip the performance section of Chapter 2, some might be tempted to skip the cost section to get to the "technical issues" in the later chapters. Please don't. Computer design is almost always balancing cost and performance, and few understand how price is related to cost, or how to lower cost and price by 10% in a way that minimizes performance loss. The foundations laid in the cost section of Chapter 2 allow cost/performance to be the basis of all tradeoffs in the last half of the book. On the other hand, some subjects are probably best left as reference material. If the book is part of a course, lectures can show how to use the data from these chapters in making decisions in computer design. Chapter 4 is probably the best example of this. Depending on your background, you already may be familiar with some of the material, but we try to include a few new twists for each subject. The section on microprogramming in Chapter 5 will be review for many, for example, but the description of the impact of interrupts on control is rarely found in other books.

We also invested special effort in making this book interesting to practicing engineers and advanced graduate students. Advanced topics sections are found in:

Chapter 6 on pipelining (Sections 6.7 and 6.8, which are about half the chapter)

Chapter 7 on vectors (the whole chapter)

Chapter 8 on memory-hierarchy design (Section 8.8, which is about a third of Chapter 8)

Chapter 10 on future directions (Section 10.7, about a quarter of that chapter)

Those under time pressure might want to skip some of these sections. To make skipping easier, the Putting It All Together sections of Chapters 6 and 8 are independent of the advanced topics.

You might have noticed that floating point is covered in Appendix A rather than in a chapter. Since it is largely independent of the other material, our solution was to include it as an appendix as our surveys indicated that a significant percentage of the readers would be exposed to floating point elsewhere.

The remaining appendices are included both for reference purposes for the computer professional and for the Exercises. Appendix B contains the instruction sets of three classic machines: the IBM 360, Intel 8086, and the DEC VAX. Appendices C and D give the mix of instructions in real programs for these machines plus DLX, either measured by instruction frequency or time frequency. Appendix E offers a more detailed comparative survey of several recent architectures.

Exercises, Projects, and Software

The optional nature of the material is also reflected in the Exercises. Brackets for each question (<chapter.section>) indicate the text sections of primary relevance to answering the question. We hope this helps readers to avoid exercises for which they haven't read the corresponding section, as well as providing the source for review. We have adopted Donald Knuth's technique of rating the Exercises. The ratings give an estimate of how much effort a problem might take:

[10] 1 minute (read and understand)

[20] 15–20 minutes for full answer

[25] 1 hour for full written answer

[30] Short programming project: less than 1 full day of programming

[40] Significant programming project: 2 weeks of elapsed time

[50] Term project (2–4 weeks by two people)

[Discussion] Topic for discussion with others interested in computer architecture

To facilitate the use of this book in the college curriculum, the book is also accompanied by an Instructor's Manual and software. The software is a UNIX tar tape that includes benchmarks, cache traces, cache and instruction set simulators, and a compiler. Readers interested in obtaining the software will find it available by anonymous FTP via Internet from max.stanford.edu. Copies may also be obtained by contacting Morgan Kaufmann at (415) 578-9911 (duplication and handling charges will apply on these orders).

Concluding Remarks

You might see a masculine adjective or pronoun in a paragraph. Since English does not have gender-neutral pronouns or adjectives, we found ourselves in the unfortunate position of choosing among the standard, consistent use of the masculine, alternating between feminine and masculine, and the grammatically unworkable third person plural. We tried to reduce the occurrence of this problem, but when a pronoun is unavoidable we alternate gender chapter by chapter. Our experience is this practice hurts no one, unlike the standard solution.

If you read the following acknowledgement section you will see that we went to great lengths to correct mistakes. Since a book goes through many printings, we have the opportunity to make even more corrections. If you uncover any remaining resilient bugs, please contact the publisher by electronic mail (bugs2@vsop.stanford.edu) or low-tech mail using the address found on the copyright page. The first reader to report an error that is incorporated in a future printing will be rewarded with a $1.00 bounty.

Finally, this book is unusual in that there is no strict ordering of the authors' names. About half the time you will see Hennessy and Patterson, both in this book and in advertisements, and half the time you will see Patterson and Hennessy. You'll even find it listed both ways in bibliographic publications such as *Books in Print*. (When we reference the book, we will alternate author order.) This reflects the true collaborative nature of this book: Together, we brainstormed about the ideas and method of presentation, then individually wrote one-half of the chapters and acted as reviewer for every draft of the other. (In fact, the final page count suggests each of us wrote exactly the same number of pages!) We could think of no fair way to reflect this genuine cooperation other than to hide in ambiguity—a practice that may help some authors but confuses librarians. Thus, we equally share the blame for what you are about to read.

John Hennessy   David Patterson

January 1990

Acknowledgements

This book was written with the help of a great many people—so many, in fact, that some authors would stop here, claiming there are too many to name. We decline to use that excuse, however, because to do so would hide the magnitude of help we needed. Therefore, we name the 137 people and five institutions to whom our thanks go.

When we decided to add a floating-point appendix that featured the IEEE standard, we asked many colleagues to recommend a person who understood that standard and who could write well and explain complex ideas simply. **David Goldberg**, of Xerox Palo Alto Research Center, fulfilled all those tasks admirably, setting a standard to which we hope the rest of the book measures up.

Margo Seltzer of U.C. Berkeley deserves special credit. Not only was she the first teaching assistant of the course at Berkeley using the material, she brought together all the software, benchmarks, and traces that we are distributing with this book. She also ran the cache simulations and instruction set simulations that appear in Chapter 8. We thank her for her promptness and reliability in taking odds and ends of software and putting them together into a coherent package.

Bryan Martin and **Truman Joe** of Stanford also deserve our special thanks for rapidly reading the Exercises for early chapters near the deadline for the fall release. Without their dedication, the Exercises would have been considerably less polished.

Our plan to develop this material was to first try the ideas in the fall of 1988 in courses taught by us at Berkeley and Stanford. We created lecture notes, first trying them on the students at Berkeley (because the Berkeley academic year starts before Stanford), fixing some of the errors, and then exposing Stanford students to these ideas. This may not have been the best experience of their academic lives, so we wish to thank those who "volunteered" to be guinea pigs, as well as the teaching assistants **Todd Narter**, **Margo Seltzer** and **Eric Williams,** who suffered the consequences of this growth experience.

The next step of the plan was to write a draft of the book in the winter of 1989. We expected this to be turning the lecture notes into English, but our feedback from the students and the reevaluation that is part of any writing turned this into a much larger task than we expected. This "Alpha" version was sent out for reviews in the spring of 1989. Special thanks go to **Anoop Gupta** of Stanford University and **Forest Baskett** of Silicon Graphics who used the Alpha version to teach a class at Stanford in the spring of 1989.

Computer architecture is a field that has both an academic side and an industrial side. We relied on both kinds of expertise to review the material in this book. The academic reviewers of the Alpha version include **Thomas Casavant** of Purdue University, **Jim Goodman** of the University of Wisconsin at Madison, **Roger Kieckhafer** of the University of Nebraska, **Hank Levy** of the University of Washington, **Norman Matloff** of the University of California at Davis, **David Meyer** of Purdue University, **Trevor Mudge** of the University of Michigan, **Victor Nelson** of Auburn University, **Richard Reid** of Michigan State University, and **Mark Smotherman** of Clemson University. We also wish to acknowledge those who gave feedback on our outline in the fall of 1989: **Bill Dally** of MIT, and **Jim Goodman**, **Hank Levy**, **David Meyer**, and **Joseph Pfeiffer** of New Mexico State. In April of 1989, a variety of our plans were tested in a discussion group that included **Paul Barr** of Northeastern University, **Susan Eggers** of the University of Washington, **Jim Goodman** and **Mark Hill** of the University of Wisconsin, **James Mooney** of the University of West Virginia, and **Larry Wittie** of SUNY Stony Brook. We appreciate their helpful advice.

Before listing the industrial reviewers, special thanks go to **Douglas Clark** of DEC, who gave us more input on the Alpha version than all other reviewers combined, and whose remarks were always carefully written with an eye toward our sensitive natures. Other people who reviewed several chapters of the Alpha version were **David Douglas** and **David Wells** of Thinking Machines, **Joel Emer** of DEC, **Earl Killian** of MIPS Computer Systems Inc., and **Jim Smith** of Cray Research. **Earl Killian** also explained the mysteries of the Pixie instruction set analyzer and provided an unreleased version for us to collect branch statistics.

Thanks also to **Maurice Wilkes** of Olivetti Research and **C. Gordon Bell** of Stardent for helping us improve our versions of computer history at the end of each chapter.

In addition to those who volunteered to read many chapters, we also wish to thank those who made suggestions of material to include or reviewed the Alpha version of the chapters:

Chapter 1: **Danny Hillis** of Thinking Machines for his suggestion on assigning resources according to their contribution to performance.

Chapter 2: **Andy Bechtolsheim** of Sun Microsystems for advice on price versus cost and workstation cost estimates; **David Hodges** of the University of California at Berkeley, **Ed Hudson** and **Mark Johnson** of MIPS, **Al Marston** and **Jim Slager** of Sun, **Charles Stapper** of IBM, and **David Wells** of Thinking Machines for explaining chip manufacturing and yield; **Ken Lutz** of U.C. Berkeley and the **FAST chip service** of USC/ISI for the price quotes on chips; **Andy Bechtolsheim** and **Nhan Chu** of Sun Microsystems, **Don Lewine** of Data General, and **John Mashey** and **Chris Rowen** of MIPS who also reviewed this chapter.

Chapter 4: **Tom Adams** of Apple and **Richard Zimmermann** of San Francisco State University for their Intel 8086 statistics; **John Crawford** of Intel for reviewing the 80x86 and other material; **Lloyd Dickman** for reviewing IBM 360 material.

Chapter 5: **Paul Carrick** and **Peter Stoll** of Intel for reviews.

Chapter 7: **David Bailey** of NASA Ames and **Norm Jouppi** of DEC for reviews.
Chapter 8: **Ed Kelly** of Sun for help on the explanation of DRAM alternatives and **Bob Cmelik** of Sun for the SPIX statistics; **Anant Agarwal** of MIT, **Susan Eggers** of the University of Washington, **Mark Hill** of the University of Wisconsin at Madison, and **Steven Przybylski** of MIPS for the material from their dissertations; and **Susan Eggers** and **Mark Hill** for reviews.

Chapter 9: **Jim Brady** of IBM for providing references for quantitative data on response time and IBM computers and reviewing the chapter; **Garth Gibson** of the University of California at Berkeley for help with bus references and for reviewing the chapter; **Fred Berkowitz** of Omni Solutions, **David Boggs** of DEC, **Pete Chen** and **Randy Katz** of the University of California at Berkeley, **Mark Hill** of the University of Wisconsin, **Robert Shomler** of IBM, and **Paul Taysom** of AT&T Bell Laboratories for reviews.

Chapter 10: **C. Gordon Bell** of Stardent for his suggestion on including a multiprocessor in the Putting It All Together section; **Susan Eggers, Danny Hillis** of Thinking Machines, and **Shreekant Thakkar** of Sequent Computer for reviews.

Appendix A: The facts about IEEE REM and argument reduction in Section A.6, as well as the $p \leq (q-1)/2$ theorem (page A-29) are taken from unpublished lecture notes of **William Kahan** of U.C. Berkeley (and we don't know of any published sources containing a discussion of these facts). The SDRWAVE data is from **David Hough** of Sun Microsystems. **Mark Birman** of Weitek Corporation, **Merrick Darley** of Texas Instruments, and **Mark Johnson** of MIPS provided information about the 3364, 8847, and R3010, respectively. **William Kahan** also read a draft of this chapter and made many insightful comments. We also thank **Forrest Brewer** of the University of California at Santa Barbara, **Milos Ercegovac** of the University of California at Los Angeles, **Bill Shannon** of Sun Microsystems, and **Behrooz Shirazi** of Southern Methodist University for reviews.

The software that goes with this book was collected and examined by **Margo Seltzer** of the University of California at Berkeley. The following individuals volunteered their software for our distribution:

C compiler for DLX: **Yong-dong Wang** of U.C. Berkeley and the **Free Software Foundation**

Assembler for DLX: **Jeff Sedayo** of U.C. Berkeley

Cache Simulator (Dinero III): **Mark Hill** of the University of Wisconsin

ATUM traces: **Digital Equipment Corporation**, **Anant Agarwal,** and **Richard Sites**

The initial version of the simulator for DLX was developed by **Wie Hong** and **Chu-Tsai Sun** of U.C. Berkeley.

While many advised us to save ourselves some effort and publish the book sooner, we pursued the goal of publishing the cleanest book possible with the help of an additional group of people involved in the final round of review. This book would not be as useful without the help of adventurous instructors, teaching assistants, and willing students, who accepted the role of Beta test sites in the class-testing program; we made hundreds of changes as a result of the Beta testing. (In fact we are so happy with the feedback that we are continuing the error reporting and reward system; see the copyright page.) The Beta test site institutions and instructors were:

Carnegie-Mellon University	**Daniel Siewiorek**
Clemson University	**Mark Smotherman**
Cornell University	**Keshav Pingali**
Pennsylvania State University	**Mary Jane Irwin/Bob Owens**
San Francisco State University	**Vojin Oklobdzija**
Southeast Missouri State University	**Anthony Duben**
Southern Methodist University	**Behrooz Shirazi**
Stanford University	**John Hennessy**
State University of New York at Stony Brook	**Larry Wittie**
University of California at Berkeley	**Vojin Oklobdzija**
University of California at Los Angeles	**David Rennels**
University of California at Santa Cruz	**Daniel Helman**
University of Nebraska	**Roger Kieckhafer**
University of North Carolina at Chapel Hill	**Akhilesh Tyagi**
University of Texas at Austin	**Joseph Rameh**
University of Waterloo	**Bruno Preiss**
University of Wisconsin at Madison	**Mark Hill**
Washington University (St. Louis)	**Mark Franklin**

Special mention should be given to **Daniel Helman**, **Mark Hill**, **Mark Smotherman**, and **Larry Wittie** who were especially generous with their advice. The compilation of exercise solutions for course instructors was aided by contributions from **Evan Tick** of the University of Oregon, **Susan Eggers** of the University of Washington, and **Anoop Gupta** of Stanford University.

The classes at SUNY Stony Brook, Carnegie-Mellon, Stanford, Clemson, and Wisconsin supplied us with the greatest number of bug discoveries in the Beta version. To all of those who qualified for the $1.00 reward program by submitting the first notice of a bug: Your checks are in the mail. We'd also like to note that numerous bugs were hunted and killed by the following people: **Michael Butler**, **Rohit Chandra**, **David Cummings**, **David Filo**, **Carl Feynman**, **John Heinlein**, **Jim Quinlan**, **Andras Radics**, **Peter Schnorf**, and **Malcolm Wing**.

In addition to the class testing, we also asked our friends in industry for help once again. Special thanks go to **Jim Smith** of Cray Research for a thorough review and thoughtful suggestions of the full Beta text. The following individuals also helped us improve the Beta release, and our thanks go to them:

Ben Hao of Sun Microsystems for reviewing the full Beta Release.

Ruby Lee of Hewlett-Packard and **Bob Supnik** of DEC for reviewing several chapters.

Chapter 2: **Steve Goldstein** of Ross Semiconductor and **Sue Stone** of Cypress Semiconductor for photographs and the wafer of the CY7C601 (pages 57–58); **John Crawford** and **Jacque Jarve** of Intel for the photographs and wafer of the Intel 80486 (pages 56 and 58); and **Dileep Bhandarkar** of DEC for help with the VMS version of Spice and TeX used in Chapters 2–4.
Chapter 6: **John DeRosa** of DEC for help with the 8600 pipeline.

Chapter 7: **Corinna Lee** of University of California at Berkeley for measurements of the Cray X-MP and Y-MP and for reviews.

Chapter 8: **Steven Przybylski** of MIPS for reviews.

Chapter 9: **Dave Anderson** of Imprimis for reviews and supplying material on disk access time; **Jim Brady** and **Robert Shomler** of IBM for reviews, and **Pete Chen** of Berkeley for suggestions on the system performance formulas.

Chapter 10: **C. Gordon Bell** for reviews, including several suggestions on classifications of MIMD machines and **David Douglas** and **Danny Hillis** of Thinking Machines for discussions on parallel processors of the future.

Appendix A: **Mark Birman** of Weitek Corporation, **Merrick Darley** of Texas Instruments, and **Mark Johnson** of MIPS for the photographs and floor plans of the chips (pages A-54–A-55); and **David Chenevert** of Sun Microsystems for reviews.

Appendix E: This was added after the Beta version, and we thank the following people for reviews: **Mitch Alsup** of Motorola, **Robert Garner** and **David Weaver** of Sun Microsystems, **Earl Killian** of MIPS Computer Systems, and **Les Kohn** of Intel.

While we have done our best to eliminate errors and to repair those pointed out by the reviewers, we alone are responsible for those that remain!

We also want to thank the **Defense Advanced Research Projects Agency** for supporting our research for many years. That research was the basis of many ideas that came to fruition in this book. In particular, we want to thank these current and former program managers: **Duane Adams**, **Paul Losleben**, **Mark Pullen**, **Steve Squires**, **Bill Bandy**, and **John Toole**.

Thanks go to **Richard Swan** and his colleagues at DEC Western Research Laboratory for providing us a hideout for writing the Alpha and Beta versions, and to **John Ousterhout** of U.C. Berkeley, who was always ready (and even a little too eager) to act as devil's advocate for the merits of ideas in this book during this trek from Berkeley to Palo Alto. Thanks also to **Thinking Machines Corporation** for providing a refuge during the final revision.

This book could not have been published without a publisher. **John Wakerley** gave us valuable advice on how to pick a publisher. We selected Morgan Kaufmann Publishers, Inc., and we have not regretted that decision. (Not all authors feel this way about their publisher!) Starting with lecture notes just after New Year's Day 1989, we completed the Alpha version in four months. In the next three months we received reviews from 55 people and finished the Beta version. After class testing with 750 students in the fall of 1989 and more reviews from industry, we submitted the final version just before Christmas 1989. Yet the book was available by March, 1990. We are not aware of another publisher who could have kept pace with such a rigorous schedule. We wish to thank **Shirley Jowell** for learning about pipelining and pipeline hazards and seeing how to apply them to publishing. Our warmest thanks to our editor **Bruce Spatz** for his guidance and his humor in our writing adventure. We also want to thank members of the extended Morgan Kaufmann family: **Walker Cunningham** for technical editing, **David Lance Goines** for the cover design, **Gary Head** for the book design, **Linda Medoff** for copy and production editing, **Fifth Street Computer Services** for computer typesetting, and **Paul Medoff** for proofreading and production assistance.

We must also thank our university staff, **Darlene Hadding, Bob Miller**, **Margaret Rowland**, and **Terry Lessard-Smith**, for countless faxes and express mailings as well as holding down the fort at Stanford and Berkeley while we worked on the book. **Linda Simko** and **Kim Barger** of Thinking Machines also provided numerous express mailings during the fall.

Our final thanks go to our families for their suffering through long nights and early mornings of reading, typing, and neglect.

And now for something completely different.

Monty Python's Flying Circus

1 Fundamentals of Computer Design

1.1 | Introduction

Computer technology has made incredible progress in the past half century. In 1945, there were no stored-program computers. Today, a few thousand dollars will purchase a personal computer that has more performance, more main memory, and more disk storage than a computer bought in 1965 for a million dollars. This rapid rate of improvement has come both from advances in the technology used to build computers and from innovation in computer designs. The increase in performance of machines is plotted in Figure 1.1. While technological improvements have been fairly steady, progress arising from better computer architectures has been much less consistent. During the first 25 years of electronic computers, both forces made a major contribution; but for the last 20 years, computer designers have been largely dependent upon integrated circuit technology. Growth of performance during this period ranges from 18% to 35% per year, depending on the computer class.

More than any other line of computers, mainframes indicate a growth rate due chiefly to technology—most of the organizational and architectural innovations were introduced into these machines many years ago. Supercomputers have grown both via technological enhancements and via architectural enhancements (see Chapter 7). Minicomputer advances have included innovative ways to implement architectures, as well as the adoption of many of the mainframe's techniques. Performance growth of microcomputers has been the fastest, partly because these machines take the most direct advantage of improvements in integrated circuit technology. Also, since 1980, microprocessor technology has been the technology of choice for both new architectures and new implementations of older architectures.

Two significant changes in the computer marketplace have made it easier than ever before to be commercially successful with a new architecture. First, the virtual elimination of assembly language programming has dramatically reduced the need for object-code compatibility. Second, the creation of standardized, vendor-independent operating systems, such as UNIX, has lowered the cost and risk of bringing out a new architecture. Hence, there has been a renaissance in computer design: There are many new companies pursuing new architectural directions, with new computer families emerging—mini-supercomputers, high-performance microprocessors, graphics supercomputers, and a wide range of multiprocessors—at a higher rate than ever before.

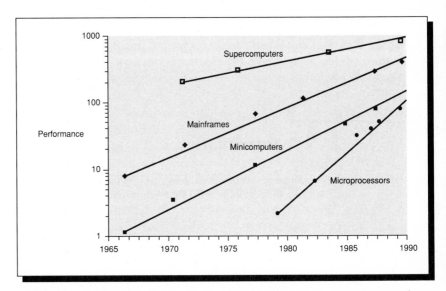

FIGURE 1.1 Different computer classes and their performance growth shown over the past ten or more years. The vertical axis shows relative performance and the horizontal axis is year of introduction. Classes of computers are loosely defined, primarily by their cost. *Supercomputers* are the most expensive—from over one million to tens of millions of dollars. Designed mostly for scientific applications, they are also the highest performance machines. *Mainframes* are high-end, general-purpose machines, typically costing more than one-half million dollars and as much as a few million dollars. *Minicomputers* are midsized machines costing from about 50 thousand dollars up to ten times that much. Finally, *microcomputers* range from small personal computers costing a few thousand dollars to large powerful workstations costing 50 thousand or more. The performance growth rates for supercomputers, minicomputers, and mainframes have been just under 20% per year, while the performance growth rate for microprocessors has been about 35% per year.

Starting in 1985, the computer industry saw a new style of architectures taking advantage of this opportunity and initiating a period in which performance has increased at a much more rapid rate. By bringing together advances in integrated circuit technology, improvements in compiler technology, and new architectural ideas, designers were able to create a series of machines that improved in performance by a factor of almost 2 every year. These ideas are now providing one of the most significant sustained performance improvements in over 20 years. This improvement was only possible because a number of important technological advances were brought together with a much better empirical understanding of how computers were used. From this fusion has emerged a style of computer design based on empirical data, experimentation, and simulation. It is this style and approach to computer design that are reflected in this text.

Sustaining the improvements in cost and performance of the last 25 to 50 years will require continuing innovations in computer design, and the authors believe such innovations will be founded on this quantitative approach to computer architecture. Hence, this book has been written not only to document this design style, but also to stimulate the reader to contribute to this field.

1.2 | Definitions of Performance

To familiarize the reader with the terminology and concepts of this book, this chapter introduces some key terms and ideas. Examples of the ideas mentioned here appear throughout the book, and several of them—pipelining, memory hierarchies, CPU performance, and cost measurement—are the focus of entire chapters. Let's begin with definitions of relative performance.

When we say one computer is faster than another, what do we mean? The computer user may say a computer is faster when a program runs in less time, while the computer center manager may say a computer is faster when it completes more jobs in an hour. The computer user is interested in reducing *response time*—the time between the start and the completion of an event—also referred to as *execution time* or *latency*. The computer center manager is interested in increasing *throughput*—the total amount of work done in a given time—sometimes called *bandwidth*. Typically, the terms "response time," "execution time," and "throughput" are used when an entire computing task is discussed. The terms "latency" and "bandwidth" are almost always the terms of choice when discussing a memory system. All of these terms will appear throughout the text.

Example   Do the following system performance enhancements increase throughput, decrease response time, or both?

1. Faster clock cycle time

2. Multiple processors for separate tasks (handling the airlines reservations system for the country, for example)

3. Parallel processing of scientific problems

Answer   Decreasing response time usually improves throughput. Hence, both 1 and 3 improve response time and throughput. In 2, no one task gets work done faster, so only throughput increases.

Sometimes these measures are best described with probability distributions rather than constant values. For example, consider the response time to complete an I/O operation to disk. The response time depends on a number of nondeterministic factors, such as what the disk is doing at the time of the I/O request and how many other tasks are waiting to access the disk. Because these values are not fixed, it makes more sense to talk about the average response time of a disk access. Likewise, the effective disk throughput—how much data actually goes to or from the disk per unit time—is not a constant value. For most of this text, we will treat response time and throughput as deterministic values, though this will change in Chapter 9 when we discuss I/O.

In comparing design alternatives, we often want to relate the performance of two different machines, say X and Y. The phrase "X is faster than Y" is used here to mean that the response time or execution time is lower on X than on Y for the given task. In particular, "X is $n\%$ faster than Y" will mean

$$\frac{\text{Execution time}_Y}{\text{Execution time}_X} = 1 + \frac{n}{100}$$

Since execution time is the reciprocal of performance, the following relationship holds:

$$1 + \frac{n}{100} = \frac{\text{Execution time}_Y}{\text{Execution time}_X} = \frac{\dfrac{1}{\text{Performance}_Y}}{\dfrac{1}{\text{Performance}_X}} = \frac{\text{Performance}_X}{\text{Performance}_Y}$$

Some people think of a performance increase, n, as the difference between the performance of the faster and slower machine, divided by the performance of the slower machine. This definition of n is exactly equivalent to our first definition, as we can see:

$$n = 100\left(\frac{\text{Performance}_X - \text{Performance}_Y}{\text{Performance}_Y}\right)$$

$$\frac{n}{100} = \frac{\text{Performance}_X}{\text{Performance}_Y} - 1$$

$$1 + \frac{n}{100} = \frac{\text{Performance}_X}{\text{Performance}_Y} = \frac{\text{Execution time}_Y}{\text{Execution time}_X}$$

The phrase "the throughput of X is 30% higher than Y" signifies here that the number of tasks completed per unit time on machine X is 1.3 times the number completed on Y.

Example

If machine A runs a program in 10 seconds and machine B runs the same program in 15 seconds, which of the following statements is true?

- A is 50% faster than B.
- A is 33% faster than B.

Answer

Machine A is n% faster than machine B can be expressed as

$$\frac{\text{Execution time}_B}{\text{Execution time}_A} = 1 + \frac{n}{100}$$

or

$$n = \frac{\text{Execution time}_B - \text{Execution time}_A}{\text{Execution time}_A} * 100$$

Thus,

$$\frac{15 - 10}{10} * 100 = 50$$

A is therefore 50% faster than B.

To help prevent misunderstandings—and because of the lack of consistent definitions for "faster than" and "slower than"—we will never use the phrase "slower than" in a quantitative comparison of performance.

Because performance and execution time are reciprocals, increasing performance decreases execution time. To help avoid confusion between the terms "increasing" and "decreasing," we usually say "improve performance" or "improve execution time" when we mean *increase* performance and *decrease* execution time.

Throughput and latency interact in a variety of ways in computer designs. One of the most important interactions occurs in pipelining. *Pipelining* is an implementation technique that improves throughput by overlapping the execution of multiple instructions; pipelining is discussed in detail in Chapter 6. Pipelining of instructions is analogous to using an assembly line to manufacture cars. In an assembly line it may take eight hours to build an entire car, but if there are eight steps in the assembly line, a new car is finished every hour. In the assembly line, the latency to build one car is not affected, but the throughput increases proportionally to the number of stages in the line if all the stages are of the same length. The fact that pipelines in computers have some overhead per stage increases the latency by some amount for each stage of the pipeline.

1.3 | Quantitative Principles of Computer Design

This section introduces some important rules and observations that arise time and again in designing computers.

Make the Common Case Fast

Perhaps the most important and pervasive principle of computer design is to make the common case fast: In making a design tradeoff, favor the frequent case over the infrequent case. This principle also applies when determining how to spend resources since the impact on making some occurrence faster is higher if the occurrence is frequent. Improving the frequent event, rather than the rare event, will obviously help performance, too. In addition, the frequent case is often simpler and can be done faster than the infrequent case. For example, when adding two numbers in the *central processing unit* (CPU), we can expect overflow to be a rare circumstance and can therefore improve performance by optimizing the more common case of no overflow. This may slow down the case when overflow occurs, but if that is rare, then overall performance will be improved by optimizing for the normal case.

We will see many cases of this principle throughout this text. In applying this simple principle, we have to decide what the frequent case is and how much performance can be improved by making that case faster. A fundamental law, called *Amdahl's Law*, can be used to quantify this principle.

Amdahl's Law

The performance gain that can be obtained by improving some portion of a computer can be calculated using Amdahl's Law. *Amdahl's Law* states that the performance improvement to be gained from using some faster mode of execution is limited by the fraction of the time the faster mode can be used.

Amdahl's Law defines the speedup that can be gained by using a particular feature. What is speedup? Suppose that we can make an enhancement to a machine that will improve performance when it is used. *Speedup* is the ratio

$$Speedup = \frac{\text{Performance for entire task using the enhancement when possible}}{\text{Performance for entire task without using the enhancement}}$$

Alternatively:

$$Speedup = \frac{\text{Execution time for entire task without using the enhancement}}{\text{Execution time for entire task using the enhancement when possible}}$$

Speedup tells us how much faster a task will run using the machine with the enhancement as opposed to the original machine.

Example

Consider the problem of going from Nevada to California over the Sierra Nevada mountains and through the desert to Los Angeles. You have several types of vehicles available, but unfortunately your route goes through ecologically sensitive areas in the mountains where you must walk. Your walk over the mountains will take 20 hours. The last 200 miles, however, can be done by high-speed vehicle. There are five ways to complete the second portion of your journey:

1. Walk at an average rate of 4 miles per hour.

2. Ride a bike at an average rate of 10 miles per hour.

3. Drive a Hyundai Excel in which you average 50 miles per hour.

4. Drive a Ferrari Testarossa in which you average 120 miles per hour.

5. Drive a rocket car in which you average 600 miles per hour.

How long will it take for the entire trip using these vehicles, and what is the speedup versus walking the entire distance?

Vehicle for second portion of trip	Hours for second portion of trip	Speedup in the desert	Hours for entire trip	Speedup for entire trip
Feet	50.00	1.0	70.00	1.0
Bike	20.00	2.5	40.00	1.8
Excel	4.00	12.5	24.00	2.9
Testarossa	1.67	30.0	21.67	3.2
Rocket car	0.33	150.0	20.33	3.4

FIGURE 1.2 The speedup ratios obtained for different means of transport depend heavily on the fact that we have to walk across the mountains. The speedup in the desert—once we have crossed the mountains—is equal to the rate using the designated vehicle divided by the walking rate; the final column shows how much faster our entire trip is compared to walking.

Answer We can find the answer by determining how long the second part of the trip will take and adding that time to the 20 hours needed to cross the mountains. Figure 1.2 shows the effectiveness of using the enhanced mode of transportation.

Amdahl's Law gives us a quick way to find speedup, which depends on two factors:

1. The fraction of the computation time in the original machine that can be converted to take advantage of the enhancement. In the example above, the fraction is $\frac{50}{70}$. This value, which we will call Fraction$_{enhanced}$, is always less than or equal to 1.

2. The improvement gained by the enhanced execution mode; that is, how much faster the task would run if *only* the enhanced mode were used. In the above example this value is given in the column labeled "speedup in the desert." This value is the time of the original mode over the time of the enhanced mode and is always greater than 1. We call this value Speedup$_{enhanced}$.

The execution time using the original machine with the enhanced mode will be the time spent using the unenhanced portion of the machine plus the time spent using the enhancement:

$$\text{Execution time}_{new} = \text{Execution time}_{old} * \left((1 - \text{Fraction}_{enhanced}) + \frac{\text{Fraction}_{enhanced}}{\text{Speedup}_{enhanced}} \right)$$

The overall speedup is the ratio of the execution times:

$$\text{Speedup}_{overall} = \frac{\text{Execution time}_{old}}{\text{Execution time}_{new}} = \frac{1}{(1 - \text{Fraction}_{enhanced}) + \dfrac{\text{Fraction}_{enhanced}}{\text{Speedup}_{enhanced}}}$$

Example Suppose that we are considering an enhancement that runs 10 times faster than the original machine but is only usable 40% of the time. What is the overall speedup gained by incorporating the enhancement?

Answer $\text{Fraction}_{enhanced} = 0.4$

$\text{Speedup}_{enhanced} = 10$

$$\text{Speedup}_{overall} = \frac{1}{0.6 + \dfrac{0.4}{10}} = \frac{1}{0.64} \approx 1.56$$

Amdahl's Law expresses the law of diminishing returns: The incremental improvement in speedup gained by an additional improvement in the performance of just a portion of the computation diminishes as improvements are added. An important corollary of Amdahl's Law is that if an enhancement is only usable for a fraction of a task, we can't speed up the task by more than the reciprocal of 1 minus that fraction.

A common mistake in applying Amdahl's Law is to confuse "fraction of time converted to use an enhancement" and "fraction of time after enhancement is in use." If, instead of measuring the time that **could use** the enhancement in a computation, we measure the time **after** the enhancement is in use, the results will be incorrect! (Try Exercise 1.8 to see how wrong.)

Amdahl's Law can serve as a guide to how much an enhancement will improve performance and how to distribute resources to improve cost/performance. The goal, clearly, is to spend resources proportional to where time is spent.

Example

Suppose we could improve the speed of the CPU in our machine by a factor of five (without affecting I/O performance) for five times the cost. Also assume that the CPU is used 50% of the time, and the rest of the time the CPU is waiting for I/O. If the CPU is one-third of the total cost of the computer, is increasing the CPU speed by a factor of five a good investment from a cost/performance viewpoint?

Answer

The speedup obtained is

$$\text{Speedup} = \frac{1}{0.5 + \dfrac{0.5}{5}} = \frac{1}{0.6} = 1.67$$

The new machine will cost

$$\frac{2}{3} * 1 + \frac{1}{3} * 5 = 2.33 \text{ times the original machine}$$

Since the cost increase is larger than the performance improvement, this change does not improve cost/performance.

Locality of Reference

While Amdahl's Law is a theorem that applies to any system, other important fundamental observations come from properties of programs. The most important program property that we regularly exploit is *locality of reference*: Programs tend to reuse data and instructions they have used recently. A widely held rule of thumb is that a program spends 90% of its execution time in only 10% of the code. An implication of locality is that based on the program's recent past, one can predict with reasonable accuracy what instructions and data a program will use in the near future.

To examine locality, several programs were measured to determine what percentage of the instructions were responsible for 80% and for 90% of the instructions executed. The data are shown in Figure 1.3, and the programs are described in detail in the next chapter.

Locality of reference also applies to data accesses, though not as strongly as to code accesses. There are two different types of locality that have been observed. *Temporal locality* states that recently accessed items are likely to be accessed in the near future. Figure 1.3 shows one effect of temporal locality. *Spatial locality* says that items whose addresses are near one another tend to be referenced close together in time. We will see these principles applied later in this chapter, and extensively in Chapter 8.

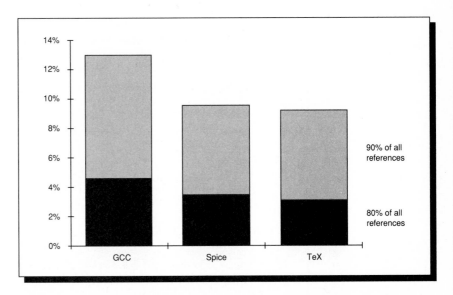

FIGURE 1.3 This plot shows what percentage of the instructions are responsible for 80% and for 90% of the instruction executions. For example, just under 4% of Spice's program instructions (also called the *static* instructions) represent 80% of the dynamically executed instructions, while just under 10% of the static instructions account for 90% of the executed instructions. Less than half the static instructions are executed even once in any one run—in Spice only 30% of the instructions are executed one or more times. Detailed descriptions of the programs and their inputs appear in Figure 2.17 (page 67).

1.4 | The Job of a Computer Designer

A computer architect designs machines to run programs. If you were going to design a computer, your task would have many aspects, including instruction set design, functional organization, logic design, and implementation. The implementation may encompass integrated circuit (IC) design, packaging, power, and cooling. You would have to optimize a machine design across these levels. This optimization requires familiarity with a very wide range of technologies, from compilers and operating systems to logic design and packaging.

Some people have used the term *computer architecture* to refer only to instruction set design. They refer to the other aspects of computer design as "implementation," often insinuating that implementation is uninteresting or less challenging. The authors believe this view is not only incorrect, but is even responsible for mistakes in the design of new instruction sets. The architect's or designer's job is much more than instruction set design, and the technical hurdles in the other aspects of the project are certainly as challenging as those encountered in doing instruction set design.

In this book the term *instruction set architecture* refers to the actual programmer-visible instruction set. The instruction set architecture serves as the boundary between the software and hardware, and that topic is the focus of Chapters 3 and 4. The implementation of a machine has two components: organization and hardware. The term *organization* includes the high-level aspects of a computer's design, such as the memory system, the bus structure, and the internal CPU design. For example, two machines with the same instruction set architecture but different organizations are the VAX-11/780 and the VAX 8600. *Hardware* is used to refer to the specifics of a machine. This would include the detailed logic design and the packaging technology of the machine. This book focuses on instruction set architecture and on organization. Two machines with identical instruction set architectures and nearly identical organizations that differ primarily at the hardware level are the VAX-11/780 and the 11/785; the 11/785 used an improved integrated circuit technology to obtain a faster clock rate and made some small changes in the memory system. In this book the word "architecture" is intended to cover all three aspects of computer design.

Functional Requirements

Computer architects must design a computer to meet functional requirements as well as price and performance goals. Often, they also have to determine what the functional requirements are, and this can be a major task. The requirements may be specific features, inspired by the market. Application software often drives the choice of certain functional requirements by determining how the machine will be used. If a large body of software exists for a certain instruction set architecture, the architect may decide that a new machine should implement an existing instruction set. The presence of a large market for a particular class of applications might encourage the designers to incorporate requirements that would make the machine competitive in that market. Figure 1.4 (see page 15) summarizes some requirements that need to be considered in designing a new machine. Many of these requirements and features will be examined in depth in later chapters.

Many of the requirements in Figure 1.4 represent a minimum level of support. For example, modern operating systems use virtual memory and protection. This requirement establishes a minimum level of support, without which the machine would not be viable. Any additional hardware above such thresholds can be evaluated from the viewpoint of cost/performance.

Most of the attributes of a computer—hardware support for different data types, performance of different functions, and so on—can be evaluated on the basis of cost/performance for the intended marketplace. The next section discusses how one might make these tradeoffs.

Balancing Software and Hardware

Once a set of functional requirements has been established, the architect must try to optimize the design. Which design choices are optimal depends, of course, on the choice of metrics. The most common metrics involve cost and performance. Given some application domain, one can try to quantify the performance of the machine by a set of programs that are chosen to represent that application domain. (We will see how to measure performance and what aspects affect cost and price in the next chapter.) Other measurable requirements may be important in some markets; reliability and fault tolerance are often crucial in transaction processing environments.

Throughout this text we will focus on optimizing machine cost/performance. This optimization is largely a question of where is the best place to implement some required functionality? Hardware and software implementations of a feature have different advantages. The major advantages of a software implementation are the lower cost of errors, easier design, and simpler upgrading. Hardware offers performance as its sole advantage, though hardware implementations are not always faster—a superior algorithm in software can beat an inferior algorithm implemented in hardware. Balancing hardware and software will lead to the best machine for the applications of interest.

Sometimes a specific requirement may effectively necessitate the inclusion of hardware support. For example, a machine that is to run scientific applications with intensive floating-point calculations will almost certainly need hardware for floating-point operations. This is not a question of functionality, but rather of performance. Software-based floating point could be used, but it is so much slower that the machine would not be competitive. Hardware-supported floating point is a de facto requirement for the scientific marketplace. By comparison, consider building a machine to support commercial applications written in

Functional requirements	Typical features required or supported
Application area	Target of computer
Special purpose	Higher performance for specific applications (Ch. 10)
General purpose	Balanced performance for a range of tasks
Scientific	High-performance floating point (Appendix A)
Commercial	Support for COBOL (decimal arithmetic), support for data bases and transaction processing
Level of software compatibility	Determines amount of existing software for machine (Ch. 10)
At programming language	Most flexible for designer, need new compiler
Object code or binary compatible	Architecture is completely defined—little flexibility—but no investment needed in software or porting programs
Operating system (OS) requirements	Necessary features to support chosen OS
Size of address space	Very important feature (Ch. 8); may limit applications
Memory management	Required for modern OS; may be flat, paged, segmented (Ch. 8)
Protection	Different OS and application needs: page vs. segment protection (Ch. 8)
Context switch	Required to interrupt and restart program; performance varies (Ch. 5)
Interrupts and traps	Types of support impact hardware design and OS (Ch. 5)
Standards	Certain standards may be required by marketplace
Floating point	Format and arithmetic: IEEE, DEC, IBM (Appendix A)
I/O bus	For I/O devices: VME, SCSI, NuBus, Futurebus (Ch. 9)
Operating systems	UNIX, DOS or vendor proprietary
Networks	Support required for different networks: Ethernet, FDDI (Ch. 9)
Programming languages	Languages (ANSI C, FORTRAN 77, ANSI COBOL) affect instruction set

FIGURE 1.4 Summary of some of the most important functional requirements an architect faces. The left-hand column describes the class of requirement, while the right-hand column gives examples of specific features that might be needed. We will look at these design requirements in more detail in later chapters.

COBOL. Such applications make heavy use of decimal and string operations; thus, many architectures have included instructions for these functions. Other machines have supported these functions using a combination of software and standard integer and logical operations. This is a classic example of a tradeoff between hardware and software implementation, and there is no single correct solution.

In choosing between two designs, one factor that an architect must consider is design complexity. Complex designs take longer to complete, prolonging time to market. This means a design that takes longer will need to have higher performance to be competitive. In general, it is easier to deal with complexity in software than in hardware, chiefly because it is easier to debug and change software. Thus, designers may choose to shift functionality from hardware to software. On the other hand, design choices in the instruction set architecture and in the organization can affect the complexity of the implementation as well as the complexity of compilers and operating systems for the machine. The architect must be constantly aware of the impact of his design choices on the design time for both hardware and software.

Designing to Last Through Trends

If an architecture is to be successful, it must be designed to survive changes in hardware technology, software technology, and application characteristics. The designer must be especially aware of trends in computer usage and in computer technology. After all, a successful new instruction set architecture may last tens of years—the core of the IBM 360 has been in use since 1964. An architect must plan for technology changes that can increase the lifetime of a successful machine.

To plan for the evolution of a machine, the designer must be especially aware of rapidly occurring changes in implementation technology. Figure 1.5 shows some of the most important trends in hardware technology. In writing this book, the emphasis is on design principles that can be applied with new technologies and on accounting for ongoing technology trends.

These technology changes are not continuous but often occur in discrete steps. For example, DRAM (dynamic random-access memory) sizes are always increased by factors of 4 due to the basic design structure. Thus, rather than doubling every year or two, DRAM technology quadruples every three or four years. This stepwise change in technology leads to thresholds that can enable an implementation technique that was previously impossible. For example, when MOS technology reached the point where it could put between 25,000 and 50,000 transistors on a single chip, it became possible to build a 32-bit microprocessor on a single chip. By eliminating chip crossings within the CPU, a dramatic decrease in cost/performance was possible. This design was simply infeasible until the technology reached a certain point. Such technology thresholds are not rare and have a significant impact on a wide variety of design decisions.

The architect will also need to be aware of trends in software and how programs will use the machine. One of the most important software trends is the increasing amount of memory used by programs and their data. The amount of memory needed by the average program has grown by a factor of 1.5 to 2 per year! This translates to a consumption of address bits at a rate of 1/2 bit to 1 bit per year. Underestimating address-space growth is often the major reason why an instruction set architecture must be abandoned. (For a further discussion, see Chapter 8 on memory hierarchy.)

Another important software trend in the past 20 years has been the replacement of assembly language by high-level languages. This trend has resulted in a larger role for compilers and in the redirection of architectures toward the support of the compiler. Compiler technology has been steadily improving. A designer must understand this technology and the direction in which it is evolving since compilers have become the primary interface between user and machine. We will talk about the effects of compiler technology in Chapter 3.

A fundamental change in the way programming is done may demand changes in an architecture to efficiently support the programming model. But the emergence of new programming models occurs at a much slower rate than improvements in compiler technology: As opposed to compilers, which improve yearly, significant changes in programming languages occur about once a decade.

Technology	Density and performance trend
IC logic technology	Transistor count on a chip increases by about 25% per year, doubling in three years. Device speed increases nearly as fast.
Semiconductor DRAM	Density increases by just under 60% per year, quadrupling in three years. Cycle time has improved very slowly, decreasing by about one-third in ten years.
Disk technology	Density increases by about 25% per year, doubling in three years. Access time has improved by one-third in ten years.

FIGURE 1.5 Trends in computer implementation technologies show the rapid changes that designers must deal with. These changes can have a dramatic impact on designers when they affect long-term decisions, such as instruction set architecture. The cost per transistor for logic and the cost per bit for semiconductor or disk memory decrease at very close to the rate at which density increases. Cost trends are considered in more detail in the next chapter. In the past, DRAM (dynamic random-access memory) technology has improved faster than logic technology. This difference has occurred because of reductions in the number of transistors per DRAM cell and the creation of specialized technology for DRAMs. As the improvement from these sources diminishes, the density growth in logic technology and memory technology should become comparable.

When an architect has understood the impact of hardware and software trends on machine design, he can then consider the question of how to balance the machine. How much memory do you need to plan for the targeted CPU speed? How much I/O will be required? To try to give some idea of what would constitute a balanced machine, Case and Amdahl coined two rules of thumb that are now usually combined. The combined rule says that a 1-MIPS *(million instructions per second)* machine is balanced when it has 1 megabyte of memory and 1-megabit-per-second throughput of I/O. This rule of thumb provides a reasonable starting point for designing a balanced system, but should be refined by measuring the system performance of the machine when it is executing the intended applications.

1.5 | Putting It All Together: The Concept of Memory Hierarchy

In the "Putting It All Together" sections that appear near the end of every chapter, we show real examples that use the principles in that chapter. In this first chapter, we discuss a key idea in memory systems that will be the sole focus of our attention in Chapter 8.

To begin this section, let's look at a simple axiom of hardware design: *smaller is faster*. Smaller pieces of hardware will generally be faster than larger pieces. This simple principle is particularly applicable to memories for two different reasons. First, in high-speed machines, signal propagation is a major cause of delay; larger memories have more signal delay and require more levels to decode addresses. Second, in most technologies one can obtain smaller memories that are faster than larger memories. This is primarily because the designer can use more power per memory cell in a smaller design. The fastest memories are generally available in smaller numbers of bits per chip at any point in time, but they cost substantially more per byte.

Increasing memory bandwidth and decreasing the latency of memory access are both crucial to system performance, and many of the organizational techniques we discuss will focus on these two metrics. How can we improve these two measures? The answer lies in combining the principles we discussed in this chapter together with the rule that smaller is faster.

The principle of locality of reference says that the data most recently used is likely to be accessed again in the near future. Favoring accesses to such data will improve performance. Thus, we should try to keep recently accessed items in the fastest memory. Because smaller memories will be faster, we want to use smaller memories to try to hold the most recently accessed items close to the CPU and successively larger (and slower) memories as we move further away

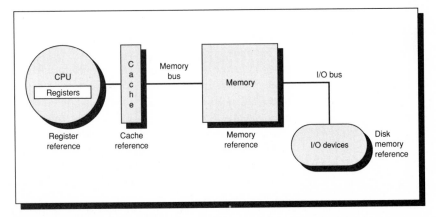

FIGURE 1.6   These are the levels in a typical memory hierarchy. As we move further away from the CPU, the memory in the level becomes larger and slower.

from the CPU. This type of organization is called a *memory hierarchy*. In Figure 1.6, a typical multilevel memory hierarchy is shown. Two important levels of the memory hierarchy are the cache and virtual memory.

A *cache* is a small, fast memory located close to the CPU that holds the most recently accessed code or data. When the CPU does not find a data item it needs in the cache, a *cache miss* occurs, and the data is retrieved from main memory and put into the cache. This usually causes the CPU to pause until the data is available.

Likewise, not all objects referenced by a program need to reside in main memory. If the computer has *virtual memory*, then some objects may reside on disk. The address space is usually broken into fixed-size blocks, called *pages*. At any time, each page resides either in main memory or on disk. When the CPU references an item within a page that is not present in the cache or main memory, a *page fault* occurs, and the entire page is moved from the disk to main memory. The cache and main memory have the same relationship as the main memory and disk.

Level	1	2	3	4
Called	Registers	Cache	Main memory	Disk storage
Typical size	< 1 KB	< 512 KB	< 512 MB	> 1 GB
Access time (in ns)	10	20	100	20,000,000
Bandwidth (in MB/sec.)	800	200	133	4
Managed by	Compiler	Hardware	Operating system	Operating system/user
Backed by	Cache	Main memory	Disk	Tape

FIGURE 1.7   The typical levels in the hierarchy slow down and get larger as we move away from the CPU. Sizes are typical for a large workstation or minicomputer. The access time is given in nanoseconds. Bandwidth is given in MB per second, assuming 32-bit paths between levels in the memory hierarchy. As we move to lower levels of the hierarchy, the access times increase, making it feasible to manage the transfer less responsively. The values shown are typical in 1990 and will no doubt change over time.

Machine	Register size	Register access time	Cache size	Cache access time
VAX-11/780	16 32-bit	100 ns	8 KB	200 ns
VAXstation 3100	16 32-bit	40 ns	1 KB on chip, 64 KB off chip	125 ns
DECstation 3100	32 32-bit integer; 16 64-bit floating point	30 ns	64 KB instruction; 64 KB data	60 ns

FIGURE 1.8   Sizes and access times for the register and cache levels of the hierarchy vary dramatically among three different machines.

Typical sizes of each level in the memory hierarchy and their access times are shown in Figure 1.7. While the disk and main memory are usually configurable, the register count and cache size are typically fixed for an implementation. Figure 1.8 shows these values for three machines discussed in this text.

Because of locality and the higher speed of smaller memories, a memory hierarchy can substantially improve performance.

Example

Suppose we have a computer with a small, high-speed memory that holds 2000 instructions. Assume that 10% of the instructions are responsible for 90% of the instruction accesses and that the accesses to that 10% are uniform. (That is, each of the instructions in the heavily used 10% is executed an equal number of times.) If we have a program with 50,000 instructions and we know which 10% of the program is most heavily used, what fraction of the instruction accesses can be made to go to high-speed memory?

Answer

Ten percent of 50,000 is 5000. Hence, we can fit 2/5 of the 90%, or 36% of the instructions fetched.

How significant is the impact of memory hierarchy? Let's do a simplified example to illustrate its impact. Though we will evaluate memory hierarchies in a much more precise fashion in Chapter 8, this rudimentary example illustrates the potential impact.

Example

Suppose a cache is five times faster than main memory, and suppose that the cache can be used 90% of the time. How much speedup do we gain by using the cache?

Answer

This is a simple application of Amdahl's Law.

$$\text{Speedup} = \cfrac{1}{(1 - \% \text{ of time cache can be used}) + \cfrac{\% \text{ of time cache can be used}}{\text{Speedup using cache}}}$$

$$\text{Speedup} = \cfrac{1}{(1 - 0.9) + \cfrac{0.9}{5}}$$

$$\text{Speedup} = \frac{1}{0.28} \approx 3.6$$

Hence, we obtain a speedup from the cache of about 3.6 times.

1.6 | Fallacies and Pitfalls

The purpose of this section, which will be found in every chapter, is to explain some commonly held misbeliefs or misconceptions that one could acquire. We call such misbeliefs *fallacies*. When discussing a fallacy, we try to give a counterexample. We also discuss *pitfalls*—easily made mistakes. Often pitfalls are generalizations of principles that are true in a limited context. The purpose of these sections is to help you avoid making these errors in machines that you design.

Pitfall: Ignoring the inexorable progress of hardware when planning a new machine.

Suppose you plan to introduce a machine in three years, and you claim the machine will be a terrific seller because it's twice as fast as anything available today. Unfortunately, the machine will probably not sell well, because the performance growth rate for the industry will yield machines of the same performance. For example, assuming a 25% yearly growth rate in performance, a machine with performance x today can be expected to have performance $1.25^3x=1.95x$ in three years. Your machine would have essentially no performance advantage! Many projects within computer companies are canceled, either because they do not pay attention to this rule or because the project slips and the performance of the delayed machine is below the industry average. While this phenomenon can occur in any industry, the rapid improvements in cost/performance make this a major concern in the computer industry.

Fallacy: Hardware is always faster than software.

While a hardware implementation of a well-defined and necessary feature is faster than a software implementation, the functionality provided by the hardware is often more general than the needs of the software. Thus, a compiler may be able to choose a sequence of simpler instructions that accomplishes the required work more efficiently than the more general hardware instruction. A good example is the MVC (move character) instruction in the IBM 360 architecture. This instruction is very general and will move up to 256 bytes of data between two arbitrary addresses. The source and destination may begin at any byte address—and may even overlap. In the worst case, the hardware must move one byte at a time; determining whether the worst case exists requires significant analysis when the instruction is decoded.

Because the MVC instruction is very general, it incurs overhead that is often unnecessary. A software implementation can be faster if it can eliminate this overhead. Measurements have shown that nonoverlapped moves are 50 times more frequent than overlapped moves and that the average nonoverlapped move is only 8 bytes long. In fact, more than half of the nonoverlapped moves move only a single byte! A two-instruction sequence that loads a byte into a register and then stores it in memory is at least twice as fast as MVC when moving a single byte. This illustrates the rule of making the frequent case fast.

1.7 | Concluding Remarks

The task the computer designer faces is a complex one: Determine what attributes are important for a new machine, then design a machine to maximize performance while staying within cost constraints. Performance can be measured as either throughput or response time; because some environments favor one over the other, this distinction must be borne in mind when evaluating alternatives. Amdahl's Law is a valuable tool to help determine what performance improvement an architectural enhancement can have. In the next chapter we will look at how to measure performance and what properties have the biggest impact on cost.

Knowing what cases are the most frequent is critical to improving performance. In Chapters 3 and 4, we will look at instruction set design and use, watching for common properties of instruction set usage. Based on measurements of instruction sets, tradeoffs can be made by deciding which instructions are the most important and what cases to try to make fast.

In Chapters 5 and 6 we will examine the fundamentals of CPU design, starting with a simple sequential machine and moving to pipelined implementations. Chapter 7 focuses on applying these ideas to high-speed scientific computation in the form of vector machines. Amdahl's Law will be our guiding light throughout Chapter 7.

We have seen how a fundamental property of programs—the principle of locality—can help us build faster computers by allowing us to make effective use of small, fast memories. In Chapter 8, we will return to memory hierarchies, looking in depth at cache design and support for virtual memory. The design of high-performance memory hierarchies has become a key component of modern computer design. Chapter 9 deals with a closely allied topic—I/O systems. As we saw when using Amdahl's Law to evaluate a cost/performance tradeoff, it is not sufficient to merely improve CPU time. To keep a balanced machine, we must also boost I/O performance.

Finally, in Chapter 10, we will look at current research directions focusing on parallel processing. How these ideas will affect the kinds of machines designed and used in the future is not yet clear. What is clear is that an empirical and experimental approach to designing new computers will be the basis for continued and dramatic performance growth.

1.8 | Historical Perspective and References

If ... history ... teaches us anything, it is that man in his quest for knowledge and progress, is determined and cannot be deterred.

John F. Kennedy, Address at Rice University, September 12, 1962.

A section of historical perspectives closes each chapter in the text. This section provides some historical background on some of the key ideas presented in the chapter. The authors may trace the development of an idea through a series of machines or describe some important projects. This section will also contain references for the reader interested in examining the initial development of an idea or machine or interested in further reading.

The First Electronic Computers

J. Presper Eckert and John Mauchly at the Moore School of the University of Pennsylvania built the world's first electronic general-purpose computer. This machine, called ENIAC (Electronic Numerical Integrator and Calculator), was funded by the United States Army and became operational during World War II, but was not publicly disclosed until 1946. ENIAC was a general-purpose machine used for computing artillery firing tables. One hundred feet long by eight-and-a-half feet high and several feet wide, the machine was enormous—far beyond the size of any computer built today. Each of the 20, 10-digit registers was two feet long. In total, there were 18,000 vacuum tubes.

While the size was two orders of magnitude bigger than machines built today, it was more than three orders of magnitude slower, with an add taking 200 microseconds. The ENIAC provided conditional jumps and was programmable, which clearly distinguished it from earlier calculators. Programming was done manually by plugging up cables and setting switches. Data was provided on punched cards. Programming for typical calculations required from a half-hour to a whole day. The ENIAC was a general-purpose machine limited primarily by a small amount of storage and tedious programming.

In 1944, John von Neumann was attracted to the ENIAC project. The group wanted to improve the way programs were entered and discussed storing programs as numbers; von Neumann helped crystalize the ideas and wrote a memo proposing a stored-program computer called EDVAC (Electronic Discrete Variable Automatic Computer). Herman Goldstine distributed the memo and put von Neumann's name on it, much to the dismay of Eckert and Mauchly, whose names were omitted. This memo has served as the basis for the commonly used term "von Neumann computer." The authors and several early inventors in the computer field believe that this term gives too much credit to von Neumann, who wrote up the ideas, and too little to the engineers, Eckert and Mauchly, who worked on the machines. For this reason, this term will not appear in this book.

In 1946, Maurice Wilkes of Cambridge University visited the Moore School to attend the latter part of a series of lectures on developments in electronic computers. When he returned to Cambridge, Wilkes decided to embark on a project to build a stored-program computer named EDSAC, for Electronic Delay Storage Automatic Calculator. The EDSAC became operational in 1949 and was the world's first full-scale, operational, stored-program computer [Wilkes, Wheeler, and Gill 1951; Wilkes 1985]. (A small prototype called the Mark I, which was built at the University of Manchester and ran in 1948, might be called the first operational stored-program machine.) The EDSAC was an accumulator-based architecture. This style of machine remained popular until the early 1970s, and the instruction sets looked remarkably similar to the EDSAC. (Chapter 3 starts with a brief summary of the EDSAC instruction set.)

In 1947, Eckert and Mauchly applied for a patent on electronic computers. The dean of the Moore School, by demanding the patent be turned over to the university, may have helped Eckert and Mauchly conclude they should leave. Their departure crippled the EDVAC project, which did not become operational until 1952.

Goldstine left to join von Neumann at the Institute for Advanced Study at Princeton in 1946. Together with Arthur Burks, they issued a report (1946) based on the memo written earlier. The paper led to the IAS machine built by Julian Bigelow at Princeton's Institute for Advanced Study. It had a total of 1024, 40-bit words and was roughly 10 times faster than ENIAC. The group thought about uses for the machine, published a set of reports, and encouraged visitors. These reports and visitors inspired the development of a number of new computers. The paper by Burks, Goldstine, and von Neumann was incredible for the period. Reading it today, one would never guess this landmark paper was written more than 40 years ago, as most of the architectural concepts seen in modern computers are discussed there.

Recently, there has been some controversy about John Atanasoff, who built a small-scale electronic computer in the early 1940s [Atanasoff 1940]. His machine, designed at Iowa State University, was a special-purpose computer that was never completely operational. Mauchly briefly visited Atanasoff before he built ENIAC. The presence of the Atanasoff machine, together with delays in filing the ENIAC patents (the work was classified and patents could not be filed until after the war) and the distribution of von Neumann's EDVAC paper, were used to break the Eckert-Mauchly patent [Larson 1973]. Though controversy still rages over Atanasoff's role, Eckert and Mauchly are usually given credit for building the first working, general-purpose, electronic computer [Stern 1980]. Another early machine that deserves some credit was a special-purpose machine built by Konrad Zuse in Germany in the late 1930s and early 1940s. This machine was electromechanical and, due to the war, was never extensively pursued.

In the same time period as ENIAC, Howard Aiken was building an electro-mechanical computer called the Mark-I at Harvard. He followed the Mark-I by a relay machine, the Mark-II, and a pair of vacuum tube machines, the Mark-III and Mark-IV. The Mark-III and Mark-IV were being built after the first stored-program machines. Because they had separate memories for instructions and data, the machines were regarded as reactionary by the advocates of stored-program computers. The term *Harvard architecture* was coined to describe this type of machine. Though clearly different from the original sense, this term is used today to apply to machines with a single main memory but with separate instruction and data caches.

The Whirlwind project [Redmond and Smith 1980] was begun at MIT in 1947 and was aimed at applications in real-time radar signal processing. While it led to several inventions, its overwhelming innovation was the creation of magnetic core memory. Whirlwind had 2048, 16-bit words of magnetic core. Magnetic cores served as the main memory technology for nearly 30 years.

Commercial Developments

In December 1947, Eckert and Mauchly formed Eckert-Mauchly Computer Corporation. Their first machine, the BINAC, was built for Northrop and was shown in August 1949. After some financial difficulties, they were acquired by Remington-Rand, where they built the UNIVAC I, designed to be sold as a general-purpose computer. First delivered in June 1951, the UNIVAC I sold for $250,000 and was the first successful commercial computer—48 systems were built! Today, this early machine, along with many other fascinating pieces of computer lore, can be seen at the Computer Museum in Boston, Massachusetts.

IBM, which earlier had been in the punched card and office automation business, didn't start building computers until 1950. The first IBM computer, the IBM 701, shipped in 1952 and eventually sold 19 units. In the early 1950s, many people were pessimistic about the future of computers, believing that the market and opportunities for these "highly specialized" machines were quite limited.

Several books describing the early days of computing have been written by the pioneers [Wilkes 1985; Goldstine 1972]. There are numerous independent histories, often built around the people involved [Slater 1987; Shurkin 1984], as well as a journal, *Annals of the History of Computing,* devoted to the history of computing.

The history of some of the computers invented after 1960 can be found in Chapters 3 and 4 (the IBM 360, the DEC VAX, the Intel 80x86, and the early RISC machines), Chapter 6 (the pipelined processors, including the CDC 6600), and Chapter 7 (vector processors including the TI ASC, CDC Star, and Cray processors).

Computer Generations—
A Capsule Summary of Computer History

Since 1952, there have been thousands of new computers, using a wide range of technologies and having widely varying capabilities. In an attempt to get a perspective on the developments, the industry has tended to group computers into generations. This classification is often based on the implementation technology used in each generation, as shown in Figure 1.9. Typically, each computer generation is eight to ten years in length, though the length and start times—especially of recent generations—is debated. By convention, the first generation is taken to be commercial electronic computers, rather than the mechanical or electromechanical machines that preceded them.

Generation	Dates	Technology	Principal new product	New companies and machines
1	1950-1959	Vacuum tubes	Commercial, electronic computer	IBM 701, UNIVAC I
2	1960-1968	Transistors	Cheaper computers	Burroughs 6500, NCR, CDC 6600, Honeywell
3	1969-1977	Integrated circuit	Minicomputer	50 new companies: DEC PDP-11, Data General Nova
4	1978-199?	LSI and VLSI	Personal computers and workstations	Apple II, Apollo DN 300, Sun 2
5	199?-	Parallel processing?	Multiprocessors?	??

FIGURE 1.9 Computer generations are usually determined by the change in dominant implementation technology. Typically, each generation offers the opportunity to create a new class of computers and for new computer companies to be created. Many researchers believe that parallel processing using high-performance microprocessors will be the basis for the fifth computer generation.

Development of Principles Discussed in This Chapter

What is perhaps the most basic principle was originally stated by Amdahl [1967] and concerned the limitations on speedup in the context of parallel processing:

A fairly obvious conclusion which can be drawn at this point is that the effort expended on achieving high parallel processing rates is wasted unless it is accompanied by achievements in sequential processing rates of very nearly the same magnitude. [p. 485]

Amdahl stated his law focusing on the implications of speeding up only a portion of the computation. The basic equation can be used as a general technique for measuring the speedup and cost-effectiveness of any enhancement.

Virtual memory first appeared on a machine called Atlas, designed in England in 1962 [Kilburn, et al. 1982]. The IBM 360/85, introduced in the late 1960s, was the first commercial machine to use a cache, but it seems that the idea was discussed for several machines being built in England in the early 1960s (see the discussion in Chapter 8).

Knuth [1971] published the original observations about program locality:

Programs typically have a very jagged profile, with a few sharp peaks. As a very rough approximation, it appears that the nth most important statement of a program from the point of view of execution time accounts for about $(a-1)a^{-n}$ of the running time, for some 'a' and for small 'n'. We also found that less than 4 per cent of a program generally accounts for more than half of its running time. [p. 105]

References

AMDAHL, G. M. [1967]. "Validity of the single processor approach to achieving large scale computing capabilities," *Proc. AFIPS 1967 Spring Joint Computer Conf. 30* (April), Atlantic City, N.J., 483–485.

ATANASOFF, J. V. [1940]. "Computing machine for the solution of large systems of linear equations," Internal Report, Iowa State University.

BELL, C. G. [1984]. "The mini and micro industries," *IEEE Computer* 17:10 (October) 14–30.

BURKS, A. W., H. H. GOLDSTINE, AND J. VON NEUMANN [1946]. "Preliminary discussion of the logical design of an electronic computing instrument," Report to the U.S. Army Ordnance Department, p. 1; also appears in *Papers of John von Neumann,* W. Aspray and A. Burks, eds., The MIT Press, Cambridge, Mass. and Tomash Publishers, Los Angeles, Calif., 1987, 97–146.

GOLDSTINE, H. H. [1972]. *The Computer: From Pascal to von Neumann,* Princeton University Press, Princeton, N.J.

KILBURN, T., D. B. G. EDWARDS, M. J. LANIGAN, AND F. H. SUMNER [1982]. "One-level storage system," reprinted in D. P. Siewiorek, C. G. Bell, and A. Newell, *Computer Structures: Principles and Examples* (1982), McGraw-Hill, New York.

KNUTH, D. E. [1971]. "An empirical study of FORTRAN programs," *Software Practice and Experience,* Vol. 1, 105–133.

LARSON, JUDGE E. R. [1973]. "Findings of Fact, Conclusions of Law, and Order for Judgment," File No. 4–67, Civ. 138, *Honeywell v. Sperry Rand and Illinois Scientific Development,* U.S. District Court for the District of Minnesota, Fourth Division (October 19).

REDMOND, K. C. AND T. M. SMITH [1980]. *Project Whirlwind—The History of a Pioneer Computer,* Digital Press, Boston, Mass.

SHURKIN, J. [1984]. *Engines of the Mind: A History of the Computer*, W. W. Norton, New York.

SLATER, R. [1987]. *Portraits in Silicon,* The MIT Press, Cambridge, Mass.

STERN, N. [1980]. "Who invented the first electronic digital computer," *Annals of the History of Computing* 2:4 (October) 375–376.

WILKES, M. V. [1985]. *Memoirs of a Computer Pioneer,* The MIT Press, Cambridge, Mass.

WILKES, M. V., D. J. WHEELER, AND S. GILL [1951]. *The Preparation of Programs for an Electronic Digital Computer*, Addison-Wesley Press, Cambridge, Mass.

E X E R C I S E S

1.1 [10/10/10/12/12/12] <1.1,1.2> Here are the execution times in seconds for the Linpack benchmark and 10,000 iterations of the Dhrystone benchmark (see Figure 2.5, page 47) on VAX models:

Model	Year shipped	Linpack execution time (seconds)	Dhrystone execution time (10,000 iterations) (seconds)
VAX-11/780	1978	4.90	5.69
VAX 8600	1985	1.43	1.35
VAX 8550	1987	0.695	0.96

a. [10] How much faster is the 8600 than the 780 using Linpack? How about using Dhrystone?

b. [10] How much faster is the 8550 than the 8600 using Linpack? How about using Dhrystone?

c. [10] How much faster is the 8550 than the 780 using Linpack? How about using Dhrystone?

d. [12] What is the average performance growth per year between the 780 and the 8600 using Linpack? How about using Dhrystone?

e. [12] What is the average performance growth per year between the 8600 and the 8550 using Linpack? How about using Dhrystone?

f. [12] What is the average performance growth per year between the 780 and the 8550 using Linpack? How about using Dhrystone?

1.2–1.5 For the next four questions, assume that we are considering enhancing a machine by adding a vector mode to it. When a computation is run in vector mode it is 20 times faster than the normal mode of execution. We call the percentage of time that could be spent using vector mode the *percentage of vectorization.*

1.2 [20] <1.3> Draw a graph that plots the speedup as a percentage of the computation performed in vector mode. Label the y axis "Net Speedup" and label the x axis "Percent Vectorization."

1.3 [10] <1.3> What percent of vectorization is needed to achieve a speedup of 2?

1.4 [10] <1.3> What percentage of vectorization is needed to achieve one-half the maximum speedup attainable from using vector mode?

1.5 [15] <1.3> Suppose you have measured the percentage of vectorization for programs to be 70%. The hardware design group says they can double the speed of the vector rate with a significant additional engineering investment. You wonder whether the compiler crew could increase the use of vector mode as another approach to increasing performance. How much of an increase in the percentage of vectorization (relative to current usage) would you need to obtain the same performance gain? Which investment would you recommend?

1.6 [12/12] <1.1, 1.4> There are two design teams at two different companies. The smaller and more aggressive company's management demands a two-year design cycle for their products. The larger and less aggressive company's management settles for a four-year design cycle. Assume that today the market they will be selling to demands 25 times the performance of a VAX-11/780.

a. [12] What should the performance goals for each product be, if the growth rates need to be 30% per year?

b. [12] Suppose that the companies have just switched to using 4-megabit DRAMS. Assuming the growth rates in Figure 1.5 (page 17) hold, what DRAM sizes should be planned for use in these projects? Note that DRAM growth is discrete, with each generation being four times larger than the previous generation.

1.7 [12] <1.3> You are considering two alternative designs for an instruction memory: using expensive and fast chips or cheaper and slower chips. If you use the slow chips you can afford to double the width of the memory bus and fetch two instructions, each one word long, every two clock cycles. (With the more expensive fast chips, the memory bus can only fetch one word every clock cycle.) Due to spatial locality, when you fetch two words you often need both. However, in 25% of the clock cycles one of the two words you fetched will be useless. How do the memory bandwidths of these two systems compare?

1.8 [15/10] <1.3> Assume—as in the Amdahl's Law example at the bottom of page 10— that we make an enhancement to a computer that improves some mode of execution by a factor of 10. Enhanced mode is used 50% of the time, measured as a percentage of the execution time when the enhanced mode is in use, rather than as defined in this chapter: the percentage of the running time **without** the enhancement.

a. [15] What is the speedup we have obtained from fast mode?

b. [10] What percentage of the original execution time has been converted to fast mode?

1.9 [15/15] <1.5> Assume we are building a machine with a memory hierarchy for instructions (don't worry about data accesses!). Assume that the program follows the 90-10 rule and that accesses within the top 10% and bottom 90% are uniformly distributed; that is, 90% of the time is spread evenly over 10% of the code and the other 10% of the time is spread evenly over the other 90% of the code. You have three types of memory for use in your memory hierarchy:

Memory type	Access time	Cost per word
Local, fast	1 clock cycle	$0.10
Main	5 clock cycles	$0.01
Disk	5,000 clock cycles	$0.0001

You have exactly 100 programs, each is 1,000,000 words, and all the programs must fit on disk. Assume that only one program runs at a time, and that the whole program must be loaded in main memory. You can spend $30,000 dollars on the memory hierarchy.

a. [15] What is the optimal way to allocate your budget assuming that each word must be statically placed in fast memory or main memory?

b. [15] Ignoring the time for the first loading from disk, what is the average number of cycles for a program to make a memory reference in your hierarchy? (This important measure is called the average memory-access time in Chapter 8.)

1.10 [30] <1.3,1.6> Find a machine that has both a fast and slow implementation of a feature—for example, a system with and without hardware floating point. Measure the speedup obtained when using the faster implementation with a simple loop that uses the feature. Find a real program that makes some use of the feature and measure the speedup. Using this data, compute the percentage of the time the feature is used.

1.11 [Discussion] <1.3,1.4> Often ideas for speeding up processors take advantage of some special properties that certain classes of applications have. Thus, the speedup obtained by an enhancement may be available to only certain applications. How would you decide to make such an enhancement? What factors would be most relevant in the decision? Could these factors be measured or estimated reasonably?

Remember that time is money.

Ben Franklin, *Advice to a Young Tradesman*

2 Performance and Cost

2.1 Introduction

Why do engineers design different computers? Why do people use them? How do customers decide on one computer versus another? Is there a rational basis for their decisions? If so, can engineers use that basis to design better computers? These are some of the questions this chapter addresses.

One way to approach these questions is to see how they have been used in another design field and then apply those solutions by analogy to our own. The automobile, for example, can provide a useful source of analogies for explaining computers: We could say that CPUs are like engines, supercomputers are like exotic race cars, and fast CPUs with slow memories are like hot engines in poor chassis.

Standard measures of performance provide a basis for comparison, leading to improvements of the object measured. Races helped determine which car and driver were faster, but it was hard to separate the skills of the driver from the performance of the car. A few standard performance tests eventually evolved, such as

- Time until the car reaches a given speed, typically 60 miles per hour

- Time to cover a given distance, typically 1/4 mile

- Top speed on a level surface

Standard measures allow designers to select between alternatives quantitatively, which enables orderly progress in a field.

Make and model	Month tested	Price (as tested)	Sec (0-60)	Sec (1/4 mi.)	Top speed	Brake (80-0)	Skidpad g	Fuel MPG
Chevrolet Corvette	2-88	$34,034	6.0	14.6	158	225	0.89	17.5
Ferrari Testarossa	10-89	$145,580	6.2	14.2	181	261	0.87	12.0
Ford Escort	7-87	$5,765	11.2	18.8	95	286	0.69	37.0
Hyundai Excel	10-86	$6,965	14.0	19.4	80	291	0.73	29.9
Lamborghini Countach	3-86	$118,000	5.2	13.7	173	252	0.88	10.0
Mazda Miata	7-89	$15,550	9.2	16.8	116	270	0.83	25.5

FIGURE 2.1   Quantitative automotive cost/performance summary. These data were taken from the October 1989 issue of Road and Track, page 26. "Road Test Summary" is found in every issue of the magazine.

Cars proved so popular that magazines were developed to feed the interest in new cars and to help readers decide which car to purchase. While these magazines have always carried articles describing the impressions of driving a new car—the qualitative experience—over time they have expanded the quantitative basis for comparison, as Figure 2.1 illustrates.

Performance, cost of purchase, and cost of operation dominate these summaries. Performance and cost also form the rational basis for deciding which computer to select. Thus, computer designers must understand both performance and cost if they want to design computers people will consider worth selecting.

Just as there is no single target for car designers, so there is no single target for computer designers. At one extreme, *high-performance design* spares no cost in achieving its goal. Supercomputers from Cray as well as sports cars from Ferrari and Lamborghini fit into this category. At the other extreme is *low-cost design*, where performance is sacrificed to achieve lowest cost. Computers like the IBM PC clones along with their automotive equivalents, such as the Ford Escort and the Hyundai Excel, belong here. In between these extremes is *cost/performance design* where the designer balances cost versus performance. Examples from the minicomputer or workstation industry typify the kinds of tradeoffs with which designers of the Corvette and Miata would feel comfortable.

It is on this middle ground, where neither cost nor performance is neglected, that we will focus our discussion. We begin by looking at performance, the measure of the designer's dream, before going on to describe the accountant's agenda—cost.

2.2 | Performance

Time is the measure of computer performance: the computer that performs the same amount of work in the least time is the fastest. Program *execution time* is measured in seconds per program. Performance is frequently measured as a rate of some number of events per second, so that lower time means higher performance. We tend to blur this distinction and talk about performance as either time or a rate, reporting refinements as improved performance rather than using adjectives higher (for rates) or lower (for time).

But time can be defined in different ways depending on what we count. The most straightforward definition of time is called wall-clock time, response time, or *elapsed time*. This is the latency to complete a task, including disk accesses, memory accesses, input/output activities, operating system overhead—everything. However, since with multiprogramming the CPU works on another program while waiting for I/O and may not necessarily minimize the elapsed time of one program, there needs to be a term to take this activity into account. *CPU time* recognizes this distinction and means the time the CPU is computing **not** including the time waiting for I/O or running other programs. (Clearly the response time seen by the user is the elapsed time of the program, not the CPU time.) CPU time can be further divided into the CPU time spent in the program, called *user CPU time*, and the CPU time spent in the operating system performing tasks requested by the program, called *system CPU time*.

These distinctions are reflected in the UNIX time command, which returned the following:

```
90.7u 12.9s 2:39 65%
```

User CPU time is 90.7 seconds, system CPU time is 12.9 seconds, elapsed time is 2 minutes and 39 seconds (159 seconds), and the percentage of elapsed time that is CPU time is (90.7+12.9)/159 or 65%. More than a third of the elapsed time in this example was spent waiting for I/O or running other programs or both. Many measurements ignore system CPU time because of the inaccuracy of operating systems' self-measurement and the inequity of including system CPU time when comparing performance between machines with differing system codes. On the other hand, system code on some machines is user code on others and no program runs without some operating system running on the hardware, so a case can be made for using the sum of user CPU time and system CPU time.

In the present discussion, a distinction is maintained between performance based on elapsed time and that based on CPU time. The term *system performance* is used to refer to elapsed time on an **unloaded** system, while *CPU performance* refers to **user** CPU time. We will concentrate on CPU performance in this chapter.

CPU Performance

Most computers are constructed using a clock running at a constant rate. These discrete time events are called ticks, clock ticks, clock periods, clocks, cycles, or *clock cycles*. Computer designers refer to the time of a clock period by its length (e.g., 10 ns) or by its rate (e.g., 100 MHz).

CPU time for a program can then be expressed two ways:

$$\text{CPU time} = \text{CPU clock cycles for a program} * \text{Clock cycle time}$$

or

$$\text{CPU time} = \frac{\text{CPU clock cycles for a program}}{\text{Clock rate}}$$

Note that it wouldn't make sense to show elapsed time as a function of CPU clock cycle time since the latency for I/O devices is normally independent of the rate of the CPU clock.

In addition to the number of clock cycles to execute a program, we can also count the number of instructions executed—the instruction path length or *instruction count*. If we know the number of clock cycles and the instruction count we can calculate the average number of *clock cycles per instruction* (CPI):

$$\text{CPI} = \frac{\text{CPU clock cycles for a program}}{\text{Instruction count}}$$

This CPU figure of merit provides insight into different styles of instruction sets and implementations.

By transposing instruction count in the above formula, clock cycles can be defined as instruction count * CPI. This allows us to use CPI in the execution time formula:

$$\text{CPU time} = \text{Instruction count} * \text{CPI} * \text{Clock cycle time}$$

or

$$\text{CPU time} = \frac{\text{Instruction count} * \text{CPI}}{\text{Clock rate}}$$

Expanding the first formula into the units of measure shows how the pieces fit together:

$$\frac{\text{Instructions}}{\text{Program}} * \frac{\text{Clock cycles}}{\text{Instruction}} * \frac{\text{Seconds}}{\text{Clock cycle}} = \frac{\text{Seconds}}{\text{Program}} = \text{CPU time}$$

As this formula demonstrates, CPU performance is dependent upon three characteristics: clock cycle (or rate), clock cycles per instruction, and instruction count. You can't change one of these in isolation from others because the basic technologies involved in changing each characteristic are also interdependent:

Clock rate—Hardware technology and organization

CPI—Organization and instruction set architecture

Instruction count—Instruction set architecture and compiler technology

Sometimes it is useful in designing the CPU to calculate the number of total CPU clock cycles as

$$\text{CPU clock cycles} = \sum_{i=1}^{n}(\text{CPI}_i * \text{I}_i)$$

where I_i represents number of times instruction i is executed in a program and CPI_i represents the average number of clock cycles for instruction i. This form can be used to express CPU time as

$$\text{CPU time} = \sum_{i=1}^{n}(\text{CPI}_i * \text{I}_i) * \text{Clock cycle time}$$

and overall CPI as

$$\text{CPI} = \frac{\sum_{i=1}^{n}(\text{CPI}_i * \text{I}_i)}{\text{Instruction count}} = \sum_{i=1}^{n}\left(\text{CPI}_i * \frac{\text{I}_i}{\text{Instruction count}}\right)$$

The latter form of the CPI calculation multiplies each individual CPI_i by the fraction of occurrences in a program.

CPI_i should be measured and not just calculated from a table in the back of a reference manual since it must include cache misses and any other memory system inefficiencies.

Always bear in mind that the real measure of computer performance is time. Changing the instruction set to lower the instruction count, for example, may lead to an organization with a slower clock cycle time that offsets the improvement in instruction count. When comparing two machines, you must look at all three components to understand relative performance.

Example

Suppose we are considering two alternatives for our conditional branch instructions, as follows:

CPU A. A condition code is set by a compare instruction and followed by a branch that tests the condition code.

CPU B. A compare is included in the branch.

On both CPUs, the conditional branch instruction takes 2 cycles, and all other instructions take 1 clock cycle. (Obviously, if the CPI is 1.0 for everything but branches in this simple example we are ignoring losses due to the memory system in this decision; see the fallacy on page 72.) On CPU A, 20% of all instructions executed are conditional branches; since every branch needs a compare, another 20% of the instructions are compares. Because CPU A does not have the compare included in the branch, its clock cycle time is 25% faster than CPU B's. Which CPU is faster?

Answer   Since we are ignoring all systems issues, we can use the CPU performance formula: CPI_A is $((.20*2) + (.80*1))$ or 1.2 since 20% are branches taking 2 clock cycles and the rest take 1. Clock cycle time$_B$ is $1.25 *$ Clock cycle time$_A$ since A is 25% faster. The performance of CPU A is then

$$CPU\ time_A = Instruction\ count_A * 1.2 * Clock\ cycle\ time_A$$

$$= 1.20 * Instruction\ count_A * Clock\ cycle\ time_A$$

Compares are not executed in CPU B, so 20%/80% or 25% of the instructions are now branches, taking 2 clock cycles, and the remaining 75% of the instructions take 1. CPI_B is then $((.25*2) + (.75*1))$ or 1.25. Because CPU B doesn't execute compares, Instruction count$_B$ is $.80*$Instruction count$_A$. The performance of CPU B is

$$CPU\ time_B = (.80*Instruction\ count_A) * 1.25 * (1.25*Clock\ cycle\ time_A)$$

$$= 1.25 * Instruction\ count_A * Clock\ cycle\ time_A$$

Under these assumptions, CPU A, with the shorter clock cycle time, is faster than CPU B, which executes fewer instructions.

Example   After seeing the analysis, a designer realized that by reworking the organization the difference in clock cycle times can easily be reduced to 10%. Which CPU is faster now?

Answer   The only change from the answer above is that Clock cycle time$_B$ is now $1.10 *$ Clock cycle time$_A$ since A is just 10% faster. The performance of CPU A is still

$$CPU\ time_A = 1.20 * Instruction\ count_A * Clock\ cycle\ time_A$$

The performance of CPU B is now

$$CPU\ time_B = (.80*Instruction\ count_A) * 1.25 * (1.10*Clock\ cycle\ time_A)$$

$$= 1.10 * Instruction\ count_A * Clock\ cycle\ time_A$$

With this improvement CPU B, which executes fewer instructions, is now faster.

Example

Suppose we are considering another change to an instruction set. The machine initially has only loads and stores to memory, and then all operations work on the registers. Such machines are called *load/store* machines (see Chapter 3). Measurements of the load/store machine showing the frequency of instructions, called an *instruction mix*, and clock cycle counts per instruction are given in Figure 2.2.

Operation	Frequency	Clock cycle count
ALU ops	43%	1
Loads	21%	2
Stores	12%	2
Branches	24%	2

FIGURE 2.2 An example of instruction frequency. The CPI for each class of instruction is also given. (This frequency comes from the GCC column of Figure C.4 in Appendix C, rounded up to account for 100% of the instructions.)

Let's assume that 25% of the *arithmetic logic unit* (ALU) operations directly use a loaded operand that is not used again.

We propose adding ALU instructions that have one source operand in memory. These new *register–memory instructions* have a clock cycle count of 2. Suppose that the extended instruction set increases the clock cycle count for branches by 1, but it does not affect the clock cycle time. (Chapter 6, on pipelining, explains why adding register–memory instructions might slow down branches.) Would this change improve CPU performance?

Answer

The question is whether the new machine is faster than the old machine. We use the CPU performance formula since we are again ignoring systems issues. The original CPI is calculated by multiplying together the two columns from Figure 2.2:

$$\text{CPI}_{old} = (.43*1 + .21*2 + .12*2 + .24*2) = 1.57$$

The performance of CPU_{old} is then

$$\text{CPU time}_{old} = \text{Instruction count}_{old} * 1.57 * \text{Clock cycle time}_{old}$$

$$= 1.57 * \text{Instruction count}_{old} * \text{Clock cycle time}_{old}$$

Let's give the formula for CPI_{new} first and then explain the components:

$$\text{CPI}_{new} =$$

$$\frac{(.43 - (.25*.43))*1 + (.21 - (.25*.43))*2 + (.25*.43)*2 + .12*2 + .24*3}{1 - (.25*.43)}$$

25% of ALU instructions (which are 43% of all instructions executed) become register–memory instructions, changing the first 3 components of the numerator. There are (.25∗.43) fewer ALU operations, (.25∗.43) fewer loads, and (.25∗.43) new register–memory ALU instructions. The rest of the numerator remains the same except the branches take 3 clock cycles instead of 2. We divide by the new instruction count, which is .25∗43% smaller than the old one. Simplifying this equation:

$$CPI_{new} = \frac{1.703}{.893} = 1.908$$

Since the clock cycle time is unchanged, the performance of the new CPU is

CPU time$_{new}$ = (.893 ∗ Instruction count$_{old}$) ∗ 1.908 ∗ Clock cycle time$_{old}$

= 1.703 ∗ Instruction count$_{old}$ ∗ Clock cycle time$_{old}$

Using these assumptions, the answer to our question is no: It's a bad idea to add register–memory instructions, because they do not offset the increased execution time of slower branches.

MIPS and What Is Wrong with Them

A number of popular measures have been adopted in the quest for a standard measure of computer performance, with the result that a few innocent terms have been shanghaied from their well-defined environment and forced into a service for which they were never intended. The authors' position is that the only consistent and reliable measure of performance is the execution time of real programs, and that all proposed alternatives to time as the metric or to real programs as the items measured have eventually led to misleading claims or even mistakes in computer design. The dangers of a few popular alternatives to our advice are shown first.

One alternative to time as the metric is MIPS, or *million instructions per second*. For a given program, MIPS is simply

$$MIPS = \frac{Instruction\ count}{Execution\ time * 10^6} = \frac{Clock\ rate}{CPI * 10^6}$$

Some find this rightmost form convenient since clock rate is fixed for a machine and CPI is usually a small number, unlike instruction count or execution time. Relating MIPS to time,

$$Execution\ time = \frac{Instruction\ count}{MIPS * 10^6}$$

Since MIPS is a rate of operations per unit time, performance can be specified as the inverse of execution time, with faster machines having a higher MIPS rating.

The good news about MIPS is that it is easy to understand, especially by a customer, and faster machines means bigger MIPS, which matches intuition. The problem with using MIPS as a measure for comparison is threefold:

- MIPS is dependent on the instruction set, making it difficult to compare MIPS of computers with different instruction sets;

- MIPS varies between programs on the same computer; and most importantly,

- MIPS can vary inversely to performance!

The classic example of the last case is the MIPS rating of a machine with optional floating-point hardware. Since it generally takes more clock cycles per floating-point instruction than per integer instruction, floating-point programs using the optional hardware instead of software floating-point routines take less time but have a **lower** MIPS rating. Software floating point executes simpler instructions, resulting in a higher MIPS rating, but it executes so many more that overall execution time is longer.

We can even see such anomalies with optimizing compilers.

Example

Assume we build an optimizing compiler for the load/store machine described in the previous example. The compiler discards 50% of the ALU instructions, although it cannot reduce loads, stores, or branches. Ignoring systems issues and assuming a 20-ns clock cycle time (50-MHz clock rate), what is the MIPS rating for optimized code versus unoptimized code? Does the ranking of MIPS agree with the ranking of execution time?

Answer

From the example above $CPI_{unoptimized} = 1.57$, so

$$MIPS_{unoptimized} = \frac{50 \text{ MHz}}{1.57*10^6} = 31.85$$

The performance of unoptimized code is

$$CPU \text{ time}_{unoptimized} = \text{Instruction count}_{unoptimized} * 1.57 * (20*10^{-9})$$

$$= 31.4*10^{-9} * \text{Instruction count}_{unoptimized}$$

For optimized code

$$CPI_{optimized} = \frac{(.43/2)*1 + .21*2 + .12*2 + .24*2}{1 - (.43/2)} = \frac{.215 + .42 + .24 + .48}{.785} = 1.73$$

since half the ALU instructions are discarded (.43/2) and the instruction count is reduced by the missing ALU instructions. Thus,

$$\text{MIPS}_{\text{optimized}} = \frac{50 \text{ MHz}}{1.73 * 10^6} = 28.90$$

The performance of optimized code is

$$\text{CPU time}_{\text{optimized}} = (.785 * \text{Instruction count}_{\text{unoptimized}}) * 1.73 * (20 * 10^{-9})$$

$$= 27.2 * 10^{-9} * \text{Instruction count}_{\text{unoptimized}}$$

Optimized code is 13% faster, but its MIPS rating is lower!

As examples such as this one show, MIPS can fail to give a true picture of performance in that it does not track execution time. To compensate for this weakness, another alternative to execution time is to use a particular machine, with an agreed-upon MIPS rating, as a reference point. *Relative MIPS*—as distinguished from the original form, called *native MIPS*—is then calculated as follows:

$$\text{Relative MIPS} = \frac{\text{Time}_{\text{reference}}}{\text{Time}_{\text{unrated}}} * \text{MIPS}_{\text{reference}}$$

where

Time$_{reference}$ = execution time of a program on the reference machine

Time$_{unrated}$ = execution time of the same program on machine to be rated

MIPS$_{reference}$ = agreed-upon MIPS rating of the reference machine

Relative MIPS only tracks execution time for the given program and input. Even when they are identified, it becomes harder to find a reference machine on which to run programs as the machine ages. (In the 1980s the dominant reference machine was the VAX-11/780, which was called a 1-MIPS machine; see pages 77–78 in Section 2.7.) The question also arises whether the older machine should be run with the newest release of the compiler and operating system, or whether the software should be fixed so the reference machine does not get faster over time. There is also the temptation to generalize from a relative MIPS rating using one benchmark to relative execution time, even though there can be wide variations in relative performance.

In summary, the advantage of relative MIPS is small since execution time, program, and program input still must be known to have meaningful information.

MFLOPS and What Is Wrong with Them

Another popular alternative to execution time is *million floating-point operations per second*, abbreviated megaFLOPS or MFLOPS but always pronounced "megaflops." The formula for MFLOPS is simply the definition of the acronym:

$$\text{MFLOPS} = \frac{\text{Number of floating-point operations in a program}}{\text{Execution time} * 10^6}$$

Clearly, a MFLOPS rating is dependent on the machine and on the program. Since MFLOPS were intended to measure floating-point performance, they are not applicable outside that range. Compilers, as an extreme example, have a MFLOPS rating near nil no matter how fast the machine since compilers rarely use floating-point arithmetic.

This term is less innocent than MIPS. Based on operations rather than instructions, MFLOPS is intended to be a fair comparison between different machines. The belief is that the same program running on different computers would execute a different number of instructions but the same number of floating-point operations. Unfortunately, MFLOPS is not dependable because the set of floating-point operations is not consistent across machines. For example, the CRAY-2 has no divide instruction, while the Motorola 68882 has divide, square root, sine, and cosine. Another perceived problem is that the MFLOPS rating changes not only on the mixture of integer and floating-point operations but also on the mixture of fast and slow floating-point operations. For example, a program with 100% floating-point adds will have a higher rating than a program with 100% floating-point divides. The solution for both problems is to give a canonical number of floating-point operations in the source-level program and then divide by execution time. Figure 2.3 shows how the authors of the "Livermore Loops" benchmark calculate the number of normalized floating-point operations per program according to the operations actually found in the source code. Thus, the *native MFLOPS* rating is not the same as the *normalized MFLOPS* rating reported in the supercomputer literature, which has come as a surprise to a few computer designers.

Real FP operations	Normalized FP operations
ADD, SUB, COMPARE, MULT	1
DIVIDE, SQRT	4
EXP, SIN, ...	8

FIGURE 2.3 Real versus normalized floating-point operations. The number of normalized floating-point operations per real operation in a program used by the authors of the Livermore FORTRAN Kernels, or "Livermore Loops," to calculate MFLOPS. A kernel with one ADD, one DIVIDE, and one SIN would be credited with 13 normalized floating-point operations. Native MFLOPS won't give the results reported for other machines on that benchmark.

Example

The Spice program runs on the DECstation 3100 in 94 seconds (see Figures 2.16 to 2.18 for more details on the program, input, compilers, machine, and so on). The number of floating-point operations executed in that program are listed below:

ADDD	25,999,440
SUBD	18,266,439
MULD	33,880,810
DIVD	15,682,333
COMPARED	9,745,930
NEGD	2,617,846
ABSD	2,195,930
CONVERTD	1,581,450
TOTAL	109,970,178

What is the native MFLOPS for that program? Using the conversions in Figure 2.3, what is the normalized MFLOPS?

Answer

Native MFLOPS is easy to calculate:

$$\text{Native MFLOPS} \quad = \quad \frac{\text{Number of floating-point operations in a program}}{\text{Execution time} * 10^6}$$

$$\approx \frac{110M}{94 * 10^6} \approx 1.2$$

The only operation in Figure 2.3 that is changed for normalized MFLOPS and is in the list above is divide, raising the total of (normalized) floating-point operations, and therefore MFLOPS, almost 50%:

$$\text{Normalized MFLOPS} \approx \frac{157M}{94 * 10^6} \approx 1.7$$

Like any other performance measure, the MFLOPS rating for a single program cannot be generalized to establish a single performance metric for a computer. Since normalized MFLOPS is really just a constant divided by execution time for a specific program and specific input (like relative MIPS), MFLOPS is redundant to execution time, our principal measure of performance. And unlike execution time, it is tempting to characterize a machine with a single MIPS or MFLOPS rating without naming the program. Finally, MFLOPS is not a useful measure for all programs.

Choosing Programs to Evaluate Performance

Dhrystone does not use floating point. Typical programs don't ...

RICK RICHARDSON, *Clarification of Dhrystone*, 1988

This program is the result of extensive research to determine the instruction mix of a typical FORTRAN program. The results of this program on different machines should give a good indication of which machine performs better under a typical load of FORTRAN programs. The statements are purposely arranged to defeat optimizations by the compiler.

Anonymous, from comments in the Whetstone benchmark

A computer user who runs the same programs day in and day out would be the perfect candidate to evaluate a new computer. To evaluate a new system he would simply compare the execution time of his *workload*—the mixture of programs and operating system commands that users run on a machine. Few are in this happy situation, however. Most must rely on other methods to evaluate machines and often other evaluators, hoping that these methods will predict performance for their usage of the new machine. There are four levels of programs used in such circumstances, listed below in decreasing order of accuracy of prediction.

1. *(Real) Programs*—While the buyer may not know what fraction of time is spent on these programs, he knows that some users will run them to solve real problems. Examples are compilers for C, text-processing software like TeX, and CAD tools like Spice. Real programs have input, output, and options that a user can select when running the program.

2. *Kernels*—Several attempts have been made to extract small, key pieces from real programs and use them to evaluate performance. Livermore Loops and Linpack are the best known examples. Unlike real programs, no user would run kernel programs, for they exist solely to evaluate performance. Kernels are best used to isolate performance of individual features of a machine to explain the reasons for differences in performance of real programs.

3. *(Toy) Benchmarks*—Toy benchmarks are typically between 10 and 100 lines of code and produce a result the user already knows before he runs the toy program. Programs like Sieve of Erastosthenes, Puzzle, and Quicksort are popular because they are small, easy to type, and run on almost any computer. The best use of such programs is beginning programming assignments.

4. *Synthetic Benchmarks*—Similar in philosophy to kernels, synthetic benchmarks try to match the average frequency of operations and operands of a large set of programs. Whetstone and Dhrystone are popular synthetic benchmarks. (Figures 2.4 and 2.5 on pages 46 and 47 show pieces of the benchmarks.) Like their cousins, the kernels, no user runs synthetic benchmarks

because they don't compute anything a user could use. Synthetic benchmarks are, in fact, even further removed from reality because kernel code is extracted from real programs, while synthetic code is created artificially to match an average execution profile. Synthetic benchmarks are not even **pieces** of real programs, while all the others might be.

If you're not sure how to classify a program, first check to see if there is any input or very much output. A program without input calculates the same result every time it is invoked. (Few buy computers to act as copying machines.) While some programs, notably simulation and numerical analysis applications, use negligible input, every real program has some input.

```
          I = ITER
          ...
          N8 = 899 * I
          ...
          N11 = 93 * I
          ...
          X = 1.0
          Y = 1.0
          Z = 1.0
          IF (N8) 89,89,81
81        DO 88 I = 1, N8, 1
88            CALL P3(X,Y,Z)
89        CONTINUE
          ...
          X = 0.75
          IF (N11) 119,119,111
111       DO 118 I = 1, N11, 1
118           X = SQRT(EXP(ALOG(X)/T1))
119       CONTINUE
          ...
          SUBROUTINE P3 (X,Y,Z)
          COMMON T, T1, T2
          X1 = X
          Y1 = Y
          X1 = T * (X1 + Y1)
          Y1 = T * (X1 + Y1)
          Z = (X1 + Y1) / T2
          RETURN
          END
          ...
```

FIGURE 2.4 Two loops of the Whetstone synthetic benchmark. Based on the frequency of Algol statements in programs submitted to a university batch operating system in the early 1970s, a synthetic program was created to match that profile. (See Curnow and Wichmann [1976].) The statements at the beginning (e.g., N8 = 899*I) control the number of iterations of each of the 12 loops (e.g., the DO loop at line 81). The program was later converted to FORTRAN and became a popular benchmark in marketing literature. (The line labeled 118 is the subject of a fallacy on pages 73–74 in Section 2.5.)

Because computer companies thrive or go bust depending on price/performance of their products relative to others in the marketplace, tremendous resources are available to improve performance of programs widely used in evaluating performance. Such pressures can skew hardware and software engineering efforts to add optimizations that improve performance of synthetic programs, toy programs, or kernels, but not real programs.

An extreme instance of such targeted engineering employed compiler optimizations that were benchmark sensitive. Rather than perform the analysis so that the compiler could properly decide if the optimization could be applied, a person at one startup company used a preprocessor that scanned the text for keywords to try to identify benchmarks by looking for the name of the author and the name of a key subroutine. If the scan confirmed that this program was on a predefined list, the special optimizations were performed. This machine made

```
...
for(Run_Index = 1; Run_Index<=Number_Of_Runs; ++Run_Index)
{
        Proc_5();
        Proc_4();
        Int_1_Loc = 2;
        Int_2_Loc = 3;
        strcpy(Str_2_Loc,"DHRYSTONE PROGRAMS, 2'ND STRING");
        ...
}
...
Proc_4()
{
        Boolean Bool_Loc;

        Bool_Loc = Ch1_1_Glob == 'A';
        Bool_Glob = Bool_Loc | Bool_Glob;
        Ch1_2_Glob = 'B';
} /* Proc_4 */

Proc_5()
{
        Ch1_1_Glob = 'A';
        Bool_Glob = false;
} /* Proc_5 */
...
```

FIGURE 2.5 A section of the Dhrystone synthetic benchmark. Inspired by Whetstone, this program was an attempt to characterize CPU and compiler performance for a typical program. It was based on the frequency of high-level language statements from a variety of publications. The program was originally written in Ada and later converted to C and Pascal (see Weicker [1984]). Note the small size and simple-minded nature of these procedures makes it trivial for an optimizing compiler to avoid procedure-call overhead by expanding them inline. The strcpy() on the eighth line is the subject of a fallacy on pages 73–74 in Section 2.5.

a sudden jump in performance—at least according to those benchmarks. Yet these optimizations were not only invalid to programs not on the list, they were useless to the identical code with a few name changes.

The small size of programs in the last three categories makes them vulnerable to such efforts. For example, despite the best intentions, the initial SPEC benchmark suite (page 79) includes a small program. 99% of the execution time of Matrix300 is in a single line (see SPEC [1989]). A minor enhancement of the MIPS FORTRAN compiler (which improved the induction variable elimination optimization—see Section 3.7 in Chapter 3) resulted in a performance increase of 56% on a M/2000 and 117% on an RC 6280. This concentration of execution time led Apollo down the path of temptation: The performance of the DN 10000 is quoted with this line changed to a call to a hand-coded library routine. If the industry adopts real programs to compare performance, then at least resources expended to improve performance will help real users.

So why doesn't everyone run real programs to measure performance? Kernels and toy benchmarks are attractive when beginning a design since they are small enough to easily simulate, even by hand. They are especially tempting when inventing a new machine because compilers may not be available until much later. Small benchmarks are also more easily standardized while large programs are difficult, hence there are numerous published results for small benchmark performance but few for large ones.

While there are rationalizations for use early in the design, there is no current valid rationale for using benchmarks and kernels to evaluate working computer systems. In the past, programming languages were inconsistent among machines, and every machine had its own operating system; so real programs could not be ported without pain and agony. There was also a lack of important software whose source code was freely available. Finally, programs had to be small because the architecture simulator had to run on an old, slow machine.

The popularity of standard operating systems like UNIX and DOS, freely distributed software from universities and others, and faster computers available today remove many of these obstacles. While kernels, toy benchmarks, and synthetic benchmarks were an attempt to make fair comparisons among different machines, use of anything less than real programs after initial design studies is likely to give misleading results and lead the designer astray.

Reporting Performance Results

The guiding principle of reporting performance measurements should be *reproducibility*—list everything another experimenter would need to duplicate the results. Let's compare descriptions of computer performance found in refereed scientific journals to descriptions of car performance found in magazines sold at supermarkets. Car magazines, in addition to supplying 20 performance metrics, list all optional equipment on the test car, the types of tires used in the performance test, and the date the test was made. Computer journals may have only seconds of execution labeled by the name of the program and the name and model of the computer—Spice takes 94 seconds on a DECstation 3100. Left to the reader's imagination are program input, version of the program, version of compiler, optimizing level of compiled code, version of operating system, amount of main memory, number and types of disks, version of the CPU—all of which make a difference in performance.

Car magazines have enough information about the measurement to allow readers to duplicate results or to question the options selected for measurements, but computer journals often do not.

Comparing and Summarizing Performance

Comparing performance of computers is rarely a dull event, especially when the designers are involved. Charges and countercharges fly across an electronic network; one is accused of underhanded tactics and the other of misleading statements. Since careers sometimes depend on the results of such performance comparisons, it is understandable that the truth is occasionally stretched. But more frequently discrepancies can be explained by differing assumptions or lack of information.

We would like to think that if we can just agree on the programs, the experimental environments, and the definition of "faster," then misunderstandings will be avoided, leaving the networks free for scholarly intercourse. Unfortunately, the outcome is not such a happy one, for battles are then fought over what is the fair way to summarize relative performance of a collection of programs. For example, two articles on summarizing performance in the same journal took opposing points of view. Figure 2.6, taken from one of the articles, is an example of the confusion that can arise.

	Computer A	Computer B	Computer C
Program 1 (secs)	1	10	20
Program 2 (secs)	1000	100	20
Total time (secs)	1001	110	40

FIGURE 2.6 Execution times of two programs on three machines. Taken from Figure I of Smith [1988].

Using our definition in Chapter 1 (page 6), the following statements hold:

A is 900% faster than B for program 1.

B is 900% faster than A for program 2.

A is 1900% faster than C for program 1.

C is 4900% faster than A for program 2.

B is 100% faster than C for program 1.

C is 400% faster than B for program 2.

Taken individually, any one of these statements may be of use. Collectively, however, they present a confusing picture—the relative performance of computers A, B, and C is unclear.

Total Execution Time: A Consistent Summary Measure

The simplest approach to summarizing relative performance is to use total execution time of the two programs. Thus

B is 810% faster than A for programs 1 and 2.

C is 2400% faster than A for programs 1 and 2.

C is 175% faster than B for programs 1 and 2.

This summary tracks execution time, our final measure of performance. If the workload consisted of running programs 1 and 2 an equal number of times, the statements above would predict the relative execution times for the workload on each machine.

An average of the execution times that tracks total execution time is the *arithmetic mean*

$$\frac{1}{n} \sum_{i=1}^{n} \text{Time}_i$$

where Time_i is the execution time for the ith program of a total of n in the workload. If performance is expressed as a rate (such as MFLOPS), then the average that tracks total execution time is the *harmonic mean*

$$\frac{n}{\sum_{i=1}^{n} \frac{1}{\text{Rate}_i}}$$

where Rate_i is a function of $1/\text{Time}_i$, the execution time for the ith of n programs in the workload.

Weighted Execution Time

The question arises what is the proper mixture of programs for the workload: Are programs 1 and 2 in fact run equally in the workload as assumed by the arithmetic mean? If not, then there are two approaches that have been tried for summarizing performance. The first approach when given a nonequal mix of programs in the workload is to assign a weighting factor w_i to each program to indicate the relative frequency of the program in that workload. If, for example, 20% of the tasks in the workload were program 1 and 80% of the tasks in the workload were program 2, then the weighting factors would be 0.2 and 0.8. (Weighting factors add up to 1.) By summing the products of weighting factors and execution times, a clear picture of performance of the workload is obtained. This is called the *weighted arithmetic mean*:

$$\sum_{i=1}^{n} \text{Weight}_i * \text{Time}_i$$

where Weight_i is the frequency of the ith program in the workload and Time_i is the execution time of that program. Figure 2.7 shows the data from Figure 2.6 with three different weightings, each proportional to the execution time of a workload with a given mix. The *weighted harmonic mean* of rates will show the same relative performance as the weighted arithmetic means of execution times. The definition is

$$\frac{1}{\sum_{i=1}^{n} \dfrac{\text{Weight}_i}{\text{Rate}_i}}$$

	A	B	C	W(1)	W(2)	W(3)
Program 1 (secs)	1.00	10.00	20.00	0.50	0.909	0.999
Program 2 (secs)	1000.00	100.00	20.00	0.50	0.091	0.001
Arithmetic mean :W(1)	500.50	55.00	20.00			
Arithmetic mean :W(2)	91.82	18.18	20.00			
Arithmetic mean :W(3)	2.00	10.09	20.00			

FIGURE 2.7 Weighted arithmetic mean execution times using three weightings. W(1) equally weights the programs, resulting in a mean (row 3) that is the same as the nonweighted arithmetic mean. W(2) makes the mix of programs inversely proportional to the execution times on machine B; row 4 shows the arithmetic mean for that weighting. W(3) weights the programs in inverse proportion to the execution times of the two programs on machine A; the arithmetic mean is given in the last row. The net effect of the second and third weightings is to "normalize" the weightings to the execution times of programs running on that machine, so that the running time will be spent evenly between each program for that machine. For a set of n programs each taking T_i time on one machine, the equal-time weightings on that machine are

$$w_i = \frac{1}{T_i * \sum_{j=1}^{n} \left(\dfrac{1}{T_j}\right)}.$$

Normalized Execution Time and the Pros and Cons of Geometric Means

A second approach to nonequal mixture of programs in the workload is to normalize execution times to a reference machine and then take the average of the normalized execution times, similar to the relative MIPS rating discussed above. This measurement gives a warm fuzzy feeling, because it suggests that performance of new programs can be predicted by simply multiplying this number times its performance on the reference machine.

Average normalized execution time can be expressed as either an arithmetic or *geometric* mean. The formula for the geometric mean is

$$\sqrt[n]{\prod_{i=1}^{n}\text{Execution time ratio}_i}$$

where *Execution time ratio$_i$* is the execution time, normalized to the reference machine, for the *i*th program of a total of *n* in the workload. Geometric means also have the nice property that

$$\frac{\text{Geometric mean}(X_i)}{\text{Geometric mean}(Y_i)} = \text{Geometric mean}\left(\frac{X_i}{Y_i}\right)$$

meaning that taking either the ratio of the means or the means of the ratios gets the same results. In contrast to arithmetic means, geometric means of normalized execution times are consistent no matter which machine is the reference. Hence, the arithmetic mean should **not** be used to average normalized execution times. Figure 2.8 shows some variations using both arithmetic and geometric means of normalized times.

| | Normalized to A | | | Normalized to B | | | Normalized to C | | |
	A	B	C	A	B	C	A	B	C
Program 1	100%	1000%	2000%	10%	100%	200%	5%	50%	100%
Program 2	100%	10%	2%	1000%	100%	20%	5000%	500%	100%
Arithmetic mean	100%	505%	1001%	505%	100%	110%	2503%	275%	100%
Geometric mean	100%	100%	63%	100%	100%	63%	158%	158%	100%
Total time	100%	11%	4%	910%	100%	36%	2503%	275%	100%

FIGURE 2.8 Execution times from Figure 2.6 normalized to each machine. The arithmetic mean performance varies depending on which is the reference machine—column 2 says B's execution time is 5 times longer than A's while column 4 says just the opposite; column 3 says C is slowest while column 9 says C is fastest. The geometric means are consistent independent of normalization—A and B have the same performance, and the execution time of C is 63% of A or B (100%/158% is 63%). Unfortunately total execution time of A is 9 times longer than B, and B in turn is about 3 times longer than C. As a point of interest, the relationship between the means of the same set of numbers is always harmonic mean ≤ geometric mean ≤ arithmetic mean.

Because weightings of weighted arithmetic means are set proportionate to execution times on a given machine, as in Figure 2.7, they are influenced not only by frequency of use in the workload, but also by the peculiarities of a particular machine and the size of program input. The geometric mean of normalized execution times, on the other hand, is independent of the running times of the individual programs, and it doesn't matter which machine is used to normalize. If a situation arose in comparative performance evaluation where the programs were fixed but the inputs were not, then competitors could rig the results of weighted arithmetic means by making their best performing benchmark have the largest input and therefore dominate execution time. In such a situation the geometric mean would be less misleading than the arithmetic mean.

The strong drawback to geometric means of normalized execution times is that they violate our fundamental principle of performance measurement—they do not predict execution time. The geometric means from Figure 2.8 suggest that for programs 1 and 2 the performance of machines A and B is the same, yet this would only be true for a workload that ran program 1 100 times for every occurrence of program 2 (see Figure 2.6 on page 49). The total execution time for such a workload suggests that machines A and B are about 80% faster than machine C, in contrast to the geometric mean, which says machine C is faster than A and B! In general there is **no workload** for three or more machines that will match the performance predicted by the geometric means of normalized execution times. Our original reason for examining geometric means of normalized performance was to avoid giving equal emphasis to the programs in our workload, but is this solution an improvement?

The ideal solution is to measure a real workload and weight the programs according to their frequency of execution. If this can't be done, then normalizing so that equal time is spent on each program on some machine at least makes the relative weightings explicit and will predict execution time of a workload with that mix (see Figure 2.7 on page 51). The problem above of unspecified inputs is best solved by specifying the inputs when comparing performance. If results must be normalized to a specific machine, first summarize performance with the proper weighted measure and then do the normalizing. Section 2.4 gives an example.

2.3 | Cost

While there are computer designs where costs tend to be ignored—specifically supercomputers—cost-sensitive designs are of growing importance. Textbooks have ignored the cost half of cost/performance because costs change, thereby dating books. Yet an understanding of cost is essential for designers to be able to make intelligent decisions about whether or not a new feature should be included in designs where cost is an issue. (Imagine architects designing skyscrapers without any information on costs of steel beams and concrete.) We therefore cover in this section fundamentals of cost that will not change for the life of the book and provide specific examples using costs that, though they may not hold up over time, demonstrate the concepts involved.

The rapid change in cost of electronics is the first of several themes in cost-sensitive designs. This parameter is changing so fast that good designers are basing decisions not on costs of today, but on projected costs at the time the product is shipped. The underlying principle that drives costs down is the *learning curve*—manufacturing costs decrease over time. The learning curve itself is best measured by change in *yield*—the percentage of manufactured devices that survive the testing procedure. Whether it is a chip, a board, or a system, designs that have twice the yield will have basically half the cost. Understanding how the learning curve will improve yield is key to projecting costs over the life of the product.

Lowering cost, however, does not necessarily lower price; it may just increase profits. But when the product is available from multiple sources and demand does not exceed supply, competition does force prices to fall with costs. For the remainder of this discussion we assume that normal competitive forces are at work with a reasonable balance between supply and demand.

As an example of the learning curve in action, the cost per megabyte of DRAM drops over the long term by 40% per year. A more dramatic version of the same information is shown in Figure 2.9, where the cost of a new DRAM chip is depicted over its lifetime. Between the start of a project and the shipping of a product, say two years, the cost of a new DRAM drops by nearly a factor of four. Since not all component costs change at the same rate, designs based on projected costs result in different cost-performance tradeoffs than those using current costs.

A second important theme in cost-sensitive designs is the impact of packaging on design decisions. A few years ago the advantages of fitting a design on a single board meant there was no backplane, no card cage, and a smaller and cheaper box—all resulting in much lower costs and even higher performance. In a few years it will be possible to integrate all the components of a system, except main memory, onto a single chip. The overriding issue will be making the system fit on the chip, thereby avoiding the speed and cost penalties of having multiple chips, which means more interfaces, more pins to interfaces, larger boards, and so forth. The density of integrated circuits and packaging technology determine the resources available at each cost threshold. The designer must know where these thresholds are—or blindly cross them.

Cost of an Integrated Circuit

Why would a computer architecture book have a section on integrated circuit costs? In an increasingly competitive computer marketplace where standard parts—disks, DRAMs, and so on—are becoming a significant portion of any system's cost, integrated circuit costs are becoming a greater portion of the cost that varies between machines, especially in the high volume, cost-sensitive portion of the market. Thus computer designers must understand the costs of chips to understand the costs of current computers. We follow here the American accounting approach to the cost of chips.

While the costs of integrated circuits have dropped exponentially, the basic procedure of silicon manufacture is unchanged: A *wafer* is still tested and chopped into *dies* that are packaged (see Figures 2.10a, b, and c). Thus the cost of a packaged integrated circuit is

$$\text{Cost of integrated circuit} = \frac{\text{Cost of die} + \text{Cost of testing die} + \text{Cost of packaging}}{\text{Final test yield}}$$

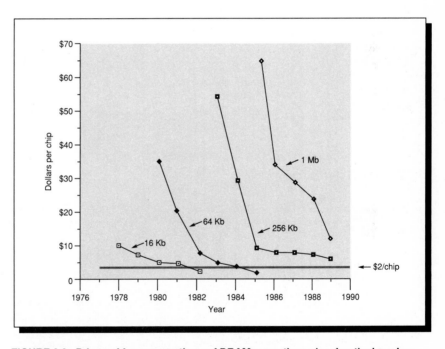

FIGURE 2.9   Prices of four generations of DRAMs over time, showing the learning curve at work. While the longer average is 40% improvement per year, each generation drops in price by nearly a factor of ten over its lifetime. The DRAMs drop to about $1 to $2 per chip over time, independent of capacity. Prices are **not** adjusted for inflation—if they were the graph would show an even greater drop in cost. For a time in 1987–1988, prices of both 256Kb and 1Mb DRAMs were higher than indicated by earlier learning curves due to what seems to have been a temporary excess of demand relative to available supply.

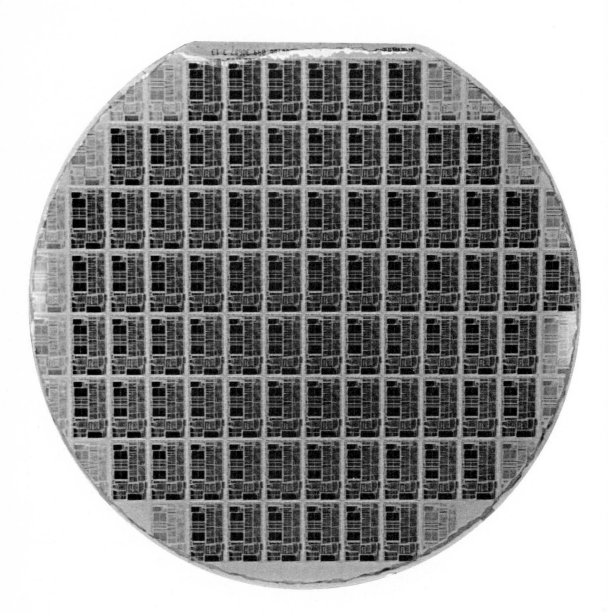

FIGURE 2.10a   Photograph of a 6-inch wafer containing Intel 80486 microprocessors. There are 80 1.6 cm x 1.0 cm dies, although four dies are so close to the edge that they may or may not be fully functional. There are no separate test dies; instead, the electrical and parametric test circuits are placed **between** the dies. The 80486 includes a floating point unit, a small cache, and a memory management unit in addition to the integer unit.

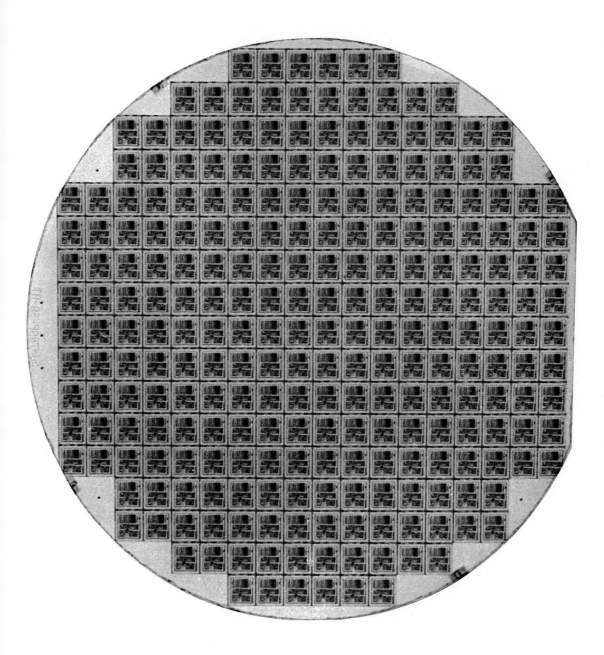

FIGURE 2.10b   Photograph of a 6-inch wafer containing Cypress CY7C601 microprocessors. There are 246 full 0.8 cm x 0.7 cm dies, although again four dies are so close to the edge it is hard to tell if they are complete. Like Intel, Cypress places the electrical and parametric test circuits between the dies. These test circuits are removed when the wafer is diced into chips. In contrast to the 80486, the CY7C601 contains the integer unit only.

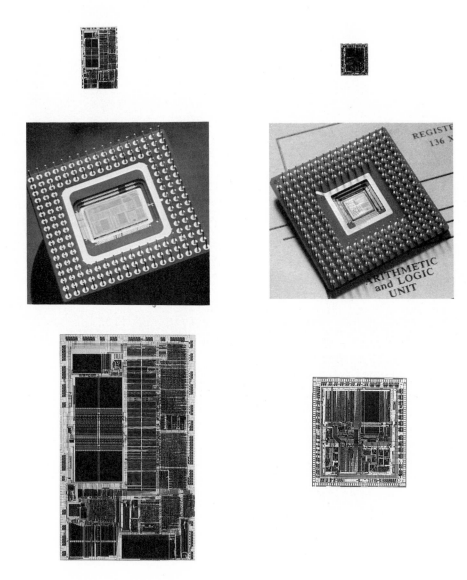

FIGURE 2.10c   At the top left is the Intel 80486 die, and the Cypress CY7C601 die is on the right, shown at their actual sizes. Below the dies are the packaged versions of each microprocessor. Note that the 80486 has three rows of pins (168 total) while the 601 has four rows (207 total). The bottom row shows a close-up of the two dies, shown in proper relative proportions.

Cost of Dies

To learn how to predict the number of good chips per wafer requires first learning how many dies fit on a wafer and then how to predict the percentage of those that will work. From there it is simple to predict cost:

$$\text{Cost of die} = \frac{\text{Cost of wafer}}{\text{Dies per wafer} * \text{Die yield}}$$

The most interesting feature of this first term of the chip cost equation is its sensitivity to die size, shown below.

The number of dies per wafer is basically the area of the wafer divided by the area of the die. It can be more accurately estimated by

$$\text{Dies per wafer} = \frac{\pi * (\text{Wafer diameter/2})^2}{\text{Die area}} - \frac{\pi * \text{Wafer diameter}}{\sqrt{2 * \text{Die area}}} - \text{Test dies per wafer}$$

The first term is the ratio of wafer area (πr^2) to die area. The second compensates for the "square peg in a round hole" problem–rectangular dies near the periphery of round wafers. Dividing the circumference (πd) by the diagonal of a square die is approximately the number of dies along the edge. The last term is for test dies that must be strategically placed to control manufacturing. For example, a 15-cm ($\approx$6-inch) diameter wafer with 5 test dies produces $3.14*225/4 - 3.14*15/\sqrt{2} - 5$ or 138 1-cm-square dies. Doubling die area—the parameter that a computer designer controls—would cut dies per wafer to 59.

But this only gives the maximum number of dies per wafer, and the critical question is what is the fraction or percentage of good dies on a wafer number, or the *die yield*. A simple model of integrated circuit yield assumes defects are randomly distributed over the wafer:

$$\text{Die yield} = \text{Wafer yield} * \left\{ 1 + \frac{\text{Defects per unit area} * \text{Die area}}{\alpha} \right\}^{-\alpha}$$

where *wafer yield* accounts for wafers that are completely bad and so need not be tested and α is a parameter that corresponds roughly to the number of masking levels critical to die yield. α depends upon the manufacturing process. Generally $\alpha = 2.0$ for simple MOS processes and higher values for more complex processes, such as bipolar and BiCMOS. As an example, wafer yield is 90%, *defects per unit area* is 2 per square centimeter, and die area is 1 square centimeter. Then die yield is $90\%*(1 + (2*1)/2.0)^{-2.0}$ or 22.5%.

The bottom line is the number of good dies per wafer, which comes from multiplying dies per wafer by die yield. The examples above predict $138*.225$ or 31 good 1-cm-square dies per 15-cm wafer. As mentioned above, both dies per wafer and die yield are sensitive to die size—doubling die area knocks die yield down to 10% and good chips per wafer to just $59*.10$, or 6! Die size depends on the technology and gates required by the function on the chip, but it is also limited by the number of pins that can be placed on the border of a square die.

A 15-cm-diameter wafer processed in two-level metal CMOS costs a semiconductor manufacturer about $550 in 1990. The cost for a 1-cm-square die with two defects per square cm on a 15-cm wafer is $550/(138∗.225) or $17.74.

What should a computer designer remember about chip costs? The manufacturing process dictates the wafer cost, wafer yield, α, and defects per unit area, so the sole control of the designer is die area. Since α is usually 2 or larger, die costs are proportional to the third (or higher) power of the die area:

$$\text{Cost of die} = f \ (\text{Die area}^3)$$

The computer designer affects die size, and hence cost, both by what functions are included on or excluded from the die and by the number of I/O pins.

Cost of Testing Die and Cost of Packaging

Testing is the second term of the chip-cost equation, and the success rate of testing (die yield) affects the cost of testing:

$$\text{Cost of testing die} = \frac{\text{Cost of testing per hour} * \text{Average die test time}}{\text{Die yield}}$$

Since bad dies are discarded, die yield is in the denominator in the equation—the good must shoulder the costs of testing those that fail. Testing costs about $150 per hour in 1990 and die tests take about 5 to 90 seconds on average, depending on the simplicity of the die and the provisions to reduce testing time included in the chip. For example, at $150 per hour and 5 seconds to test, the die test cost is $0.21. After factoring in die yield for a 1-cm-square die, the costs are $0.93 per good die. As a second example, let's assume testing takes 90 seconds. The cost is $3.75 per untested die and $16.67 per good die. The bill so far for our 1-cm-square die is $18.67 to $34.41, depending on how long it takes to test. These two testing-time examples illustrate the importance of reducing testing time in reducing costs.

Cost of Packaging and Final Test Yield

The cost of a package depends on the material used, the number of pins, and the die area. The cost of the material used in the package is in part determined by the ability to dissipate power generated by the die. For example, a *plastic quad flat pack* (PQFP) dissipating less than one watt, with 208 or fewer pins, and containing a die up to one cm on a side costs $3 in 1990. A ceramic *pin grid array* (PGA) can handle 300 to 400 pins and a larger die with more power, but it costs $50. In addition to the cost of the package itself is the cost of the labor to place a die in the package and then bond the pads to the pins. We can assume that costs $2. Burn-in exercises the packaged die under power for a short time to catch chips that would fail early. Burn-in costs about $0.25 in 1990 dollars.

We are not finished with costs until we have figured in failure of some chips during assembly and burn-in. Using the estimate of 90% for final test yield, the successful must again pay for the cost of those that fail, so our costs are $26.58 to $96.29 for the 1-cm-square die.

While these specific cost estimates may not hold, the underlying models will. Figure 2.11 shows the dies per wafer, die yield, and their product against the die area for a typical fabrication line, this time using programs that more accurately predict die per wafer and die yield. Figure 2.12 plots the change in area and cost as one dimension of a square die changes. Changes to small dies make little cost difference while 30% increases to large dies can double costs. The wise silicon designer will minimize die area, testing time, and pins per chip and understand the costs of projected packaging options when considering using more power, pins, or area for higher performance.

Cost of a Workstation

To put the costs of silicon in perspective, Figure 2.13 shows the approximate costs of components in a 1990 workstation. Costs of a component can be halved going from low volume to high volume; here we assume high-volume purchasing of 100,000 units. While costs for units like DRAMs will surely drop over time from those in Figure 2.13, units whose prices have already been cut, like displays and cabinets, will change very little.

The processor, floating-point unit, memory-management unit, and cache are only 12% to 21% of the cost of the CPU board in Figure 2.13. Depending on the options included in the system—number of disks, color monitor, and so on—the processor components drop to 9% and 16% of the cost of a system, as Figure 2.14 illustrates. In the future two questions will be interesting to consider: What costs can an engineer control? And what costs can a computer engineer control?

Cost Versus Price—Why They Differ and by How Much

Costs of components may confine a designer's desires, but they are still far from representing what the customer must pay. But why should a computer architecture book contain pricing information? Cost goes through a number of changes before it becomes price, and the computer designer must understand these to determine the impact of design choices. For example, changing cost by $1,000 may change price by $4,000 to $5,000. Without understanding the relationship of cost to price the computer designer may not understand the impact on price of adding, deleting, or replacing components.

Area (sq. cm)	Side (cm)	Die/ wafer	Die yield/ wafer	Cost of die	Cost to test die	Packaging costs	Total cost after final test
0.06	0.25	2778	79.72%	$0.25	$0.63	$5.25	$6.81
0.25	0.50	656	57.60%	$1.46	$0.87	$5.25	$8.42
0.56	0.75	274	36.86%	$5.45	$1.36	$5.25	$13.40
1.00	1.00	143	22.50%	$17.09	$2.22	$5.25	$27.29
1.56	1.25	84	13.71%	$47.76	$3.65	$52.25	$115.18
2.25	1.50	53	8.52%	$121.80	$5.87	$52.25	$199.91
3.06	1.75	35	5.45%	$288.34	$9.17	$52.25	$388.62
4.00	2.00	23	3.60%	$664.25	$13.89	$52.25	$811.54

FIGURE 2.11   Costs for several die sizes. Costs for a working chip are shown in columns 5 through 7. Column 8 is the sum of columns 5 through 7 divided by the final test yield. Figure 2.12 presents this information graphically. This figure assumes a 15.24-cm (6-inch) wafer costing $550, with 5 test die per wafer. The wafer yield is 90%, the defect density is 2.0 per square cm, and α is 2.0. It takes 12 seconds on average to test a die, the tester costs $150 per hour, and the final test yield is 90%. (The numbers differ a little from the text for a 1-cm-square die because the wafer size is calculated at the full 15.24 cm rather than rounded to 15 cm and because of the difference in testing time.)

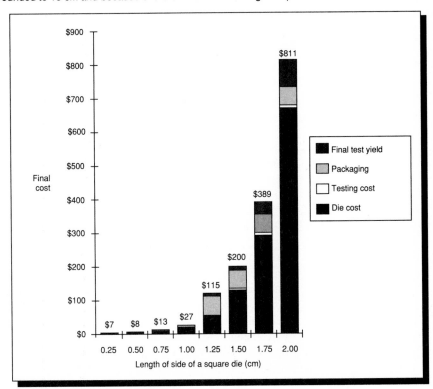

FIGURE 2.12   The costs of a chip from Figure 2.11 presented graphically. Using the parameters given in the text, packaging is a major percentage of the cost of dies of size 1.25-cm square and smaller, with die cost dominating final costs for larger dies.

		Rule of thumb	Lower cost	% Mono WS	Higher cost	% Color WS
CPU cabinet	Sheet metal, plastic		$50	2%	$50	1%
	Power supply and fans	$0.80/watt	$55	3%	$55	1%
	Cables, nuts, bolts		$30	1%	$30	1%
	Shipping box, manuals		$10	0%	$10	0%
	Subtotal		$145	7%	$145	3%
CPU board	IU, FPU, MMU, cache		$200	9%	$800	16%
	DRAM	$150/MB	$1200	56%	$2400	48%
	Video logic (frame buffer, DAC, mono/color) — Mono		$100	5%		
	Color				$500	10%
	I/O interfaces (SCSI, Ethernet, floppy, PROM, time-of-day clock)		$100	5%	$100	2%
	Printed circuit board	8 layers $1.00/sq. in.				
		6 layers $0.50/sq. in.	$50	2%	$50	1%
		4 layers $0.25/sq. in.				
	Subtotal		$1650	77%	$3850	76%
I/O devices	Keyboard, mouse		$50	2%	$50	1%
	Display monitor — Mono		$300	14%		
	Color				$1,000	20%
	Hard disk	100 MB	$400			
	Tape drive	150 MB	$400			
Mono workstation	(8 MB, Mono logic & display, keyboard, mouse, diskless)		$2,145	100%	$2,745	
Color workstation	(16 MB, Color logic & display, keyboard, mouse, diskless)		$4,445		$5,045	100%
File server	(16 MB, 6 disks+tape drive)		$5,595		$6,195	

FIGURE 2.13 Estimated cost of components in a 1990 workstation assuming 100,000 units. IU refers to integer unit of the processor, FPU to floating-point unit, and MMU to memory-management unit. The lower cost column refers to the least expensive options, listed as a Mono workstation in the third row from the bottom. The higher cost column refers to the more expensive options, listed as a Color workstation in the second row from the bottom. Note that about half the cost of the systems is in the DRAMs. Courtesy of Andy Bechtolsheim of Sun Microsystems, Inc.

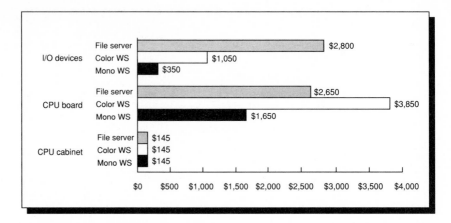

FIGURE 2.14 The costs of each machine in Figure 2.13 divided into the three main categories, assuming the lower cost estimate. Note that I/O devices and amount of memory account for major differences in costs.

The categories that make up price can be shown either as a tax on cost or as a percentage of the price. We will look at the information both ways. Figure 2.15 shows the increasing price of a product from left to right as we add each kind of overhead.

Direct costs refer to the costs directly related to making a product. These include labor costs, purchasing components, scrap (the leftover from yield), and warranty, which covers the costs of systems that fail at the customer's site during the warranty period. Direct cost typically adds 25% to 40% to component cost. Service or maintenance costs are not included because the customer typically pays those costs.

The next addition is called the *gross margin*, the company's overhead that cannot be billed directly to one product. This can be thought of as indirect cost. It includes the company's research and development (R&D), marketing, sales, manufacturing equipment maintenance, building rental, cost of financing, pretax profits, and taxes. When the component costs are multiplied by the direct cost and gross margin we reach the *average selling price*—ASP in the language of MBAs—the money that comes directly to the company for each product sold. The gross margin is typically 45% to 65% of the average selling price.

List price and average selling price are not the same. One reason for this is that companies offer volume discounts, lowering the average selling price. Also, if the product is to be sold in retail stores, as personal computers are, stores want to keep 40% of the list price for themselves. Thus, depending on the distribution system, the average selling price is typically 60% to 75% of the list price. The formula below ties the four terms together:

$$\text{List price} = \frac{\text{Cost} * (1 + \text{Direct costs})}{(1 - \text{Average discount}) * (1 - \text{Gross margin})}$$

Figure 2.16 demonstrates the abstract concepts of Figure 2.15 using dollars and cents by turning the costs of Figure 2.13 into prices. This is done using two business models. Model A assumes 25% (of cost) direct costs, 50% (of ASP) gross margin, and a 33% (of list price) average discount. Model B assumes 40% direct costs, 60% gross margin, and the average discount is dropped to 25%.

Pricing is sensitive to competition. A company striving for market share can therefore adjust to average discount or profits, but must live with its component cost and direct cost, plus the rest of the costs in the gross margin.

Many engineers are surprised to find that most companies spend only 8% to 15% of their income on R&D, which includes all engineering (except for manufacturing and field engineering). This is a well-established percentage that is reported in companies' annual reports and tabulated in national magazines, so this percentage is unlikely to change over time.

The information above suggests that a company uniformly applies fixed-overhead percentages to turn cost into price, and this is true for many companies. But another point of view is R&D should be considered an investment, and so an investment of 8% to 15% of income means every $1 spent on R&D must generate $7 to $13 in sales. This alternative point of view then suggests a different gross margin for each product depending on number sold and the size

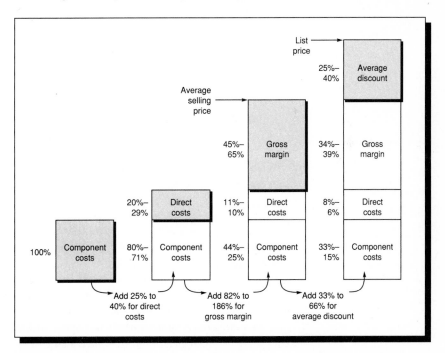

FIGURE 2.15 Starting with component costs, the price increases as we allow for direct costs, gross margin, and average discount, until we arrive at the list price. Each increase is shown along the bottom as a tax on the prior price. On the left of each column are shown the percentages of the new price for all elements.

	Model A	As % of costs	As % of list price	Model B	As % of costs	As % of list price
Component costs	$2,145	100%	27%	$2,145	100%	21%
Component costs + direct costs	$2,681	125%	33%	$3,003	140%	30%
Average selling price (adds gross margin)	$5,363	250%	67%	$7,508	350%	75%
List price	$8,044	375%	100%	$10,010	467%	100%

FIGURE 2.16 The diskless workstation in Figure 2.13 priced using two different business models. For every dollar of increased component cost the average selling price goes up between $2.50 and $3.50, and the list price increases between $3.75 and $4.67.

of the investment. Large expensive machines generally cost more to develop—a machine costing 10 times as much to manufacture may cost many times as much to develop. Since large expensive machines generally do not sell as well as small ones, the gross margin must be greater on the big machines for the company to maintain a profitable return on its investment. This investment model places large machines in double jeopardy—because there are fewer sold **and** they require larger R&D costs—and gives one explanation for a higher ratio of price to cost versus smaller machines.

2.4 | Putting It All Together: Price/Performance of Three Machines

Having covered performance and costs, the next step is to measure performance of real programs on real machines and list the costs of those machines. Alas, costs are hard to come by so prices are used instead. We start with the more controversial half of price/performance.

Figure 2.17 lists the programs chosen by the authors for performance measurement in this book. Two of the programs have almost no floating-point operations, and one has a moderate amount of floating-point operations. All three programs have input, output, and options—what you would expect from real programs. Each program has, in fact, a large user community that cares how fast these programs run. (In measuring performance of machines we would like to have a larger sample, but we keep the limit at three throughout the book to make tables and graphs legible.)

Figure 2.18 shows the characteristics of three machines we measure, including the list price as tested and the relative performance as calculated by marketing.

Figure 2.19 (page 69) shows the CPU time and elapsed time measured for these programs. We include total times and several weighted averages, with the weights shown in parentheses. The first weighted arithmetic mean is assuming a workload of just the integer programs (GCC and TeX). The second is the weightings for a floating-point workload (Spice). The next three weighted means give three workloads for equal time spent on each program on one of the machines (see Figure 2.7 on page 51). The only means that are significantly different are the integer and floating-point means for VAXstation 2000. The rest of the means for each machine are within 10% of each other, as can be seen in Figure 2.20 on page 69, which plots the weighted means.

Program name	Gnu C Compiler for 68000	Common TeX	Spice
Version	1.26	2.9	2G6
Lines	79,409	23,037	18,307
Options	-O	'&latex/lplain'	transient analysis, 200 ps steps, for 40 ns
Input	i*.c	bit-set.tex, compiler. tex,...	digsr - digital shift register
Lines/bytes of input	28,009/373,688	10,992/698,914	233/1294
Lines/bytes of output	47,553/664,479	758/524,728	656/4172
% floating-point operations (on the DECstation 3100)	0.01%	0.05%	13.58%
Programming language	C	C	FORTRAN 66
Purpose	Publicly licensed, portable, optimizing C compiler	Document formatting	Computer-aided circuit analysis

FIGURE 2.17   Programs used in this book for performance measurements. The Gnu C compiler is a product of the Free Software Foundation and, for reasons not limited to its price, is preferred by some users over the compilers supplied by the manufacturer. Only 9,540 of the 79,409 lines are specific to the 68000, and versions exist for the VAX, SPARC, 88000, MIPS, and several other instruction sets. The input for GCC are the source files of the compiler that begin with the letter "i." Common TeX is a C version of the document-processing program originally written by Prof. Donald Knuth of Stanford. The input is a set of manual pages for the Stanford SUIF compiler. Spice is a computer-aided circuit-analysis package distributed by the University of California at Berkeley. (These programs and their inputs are available as part of the software package associated with this book. The Preface mentions how to get a copy.)

	VAXstation 2000	**VAXstation 3100**	**DECstation 3100**
Year of introduction	1987	1989	1989
Version of CPU/FPU	μVAX II	CVAX	MIPS R2000A/R2010
Clock rate	5 MHz	11.11 MHz	16.67 MHz
Memory size	4 MB	8 MB	8 MB
Cache size	none	1 KB on chip, 64-KB second level	128 KB (split 64-KB instruction and 64-KB data)
TLB size	8 entries fully associative	28 entries fully associative	64 entries fully associative
Base list price	$4,825	$7,950	$11,950
Optional equipment	19" monitor, extra 10 MB	(model 40) extra 8 MB	19" monitor, extra 8 MB
List price as tested	$15,425	$14,480	$17,950
Performance according to marketing	0.9 MIPS	3.0 MIPS	12 MIPS
Operating system	Ultrix 3.0	Ultrix 3.0	Ultrix 3.0
C compiler version	Ultrix and VMS	Ultrix and VMS	1.31
Options for C compiler	-O	-O	-O2 -Olimit 1060
C library	libc	libc	libc
FORTRAN 77 compiler version	fort (VMS)	fort (VMS)	1.31
Options for FORTRAN 77 compiler	-O	-O	-O2 -Olimit 1060
FORTRAN 77 library	lib*77	lib*77	lib*77

FIGURE 2.18 The three machines and software used to measure performance in Figure 2.19. These machines are all sold by Digital Equipment—in fact, the DECstation 3100 and VAXstation 3100 were announced the same day. All three are diskless workstations and run the same version of the UNIX operating system, called Ultrix. The VMS compilers ported to Ultrix were used for TeX and Spice on the VAXstations. We used the native Ultrix C compiler for GCC because GCC would not run using the VMS C compiler. The compilers for the DECstation 3100 are supplied by MIPS Computer Systems. (The "-Olimit 1060" option for the DECstation 3100 tells the compiler not to try to optimize procedures longer than 1060 lines.)

The bottom line for many computer customers is the price they pay for performance. This is graphically depicted in Figure 2.21 (page 70), where arithmetic means of CPU time are plotted against price of each machine.

	VAXstation 2000		VAXstation 3100		DECstation 3100	
	CPU time	Elapsed time	CPU time	Elapsed time	CPU time	Elapsed time
Gnu C Compiler for 68000	985	1108	291	327	90	159
Common TeX	1264	1304	449	479	95	137
Spice	958	973	352	395	94	132
Arithmetic mean	1069	1128	364	400	93	143
Weighted AM—integer only (50% GCC, 50% TeX, 0% Spice)	1125	1206	370	403	93	148
Weighted AM—floating point only (0% GCC, 0% TeX, 100% Spice)	958	973	352	395	94	132
Weighted AM—equal CPU time on V2000 (35.6% GCC, 27.8% TeX, 36.6% Spice)	1053	1113	357	394	93	143
Weighted AM—equal CPU time on V3100 (40.4% GCC, 26.2% TeX, 33.4% Spice)	1049	1114	353	390	93	144
Weighted AM—equal CPU time on D3100 (34.4% GCC, 32.6% TeX, 33.0% Spice)	1067	1127	363	399	93	143

FIGURE 2.19   Performance of the programs in Figure 2.17 on the machines in Figure 2.18. The weightings correspond to integer programs only, and then equal CPU time running on each of the three machines. For example, if the mix of the three programs were proportionate to the weightings in the row "equal CPU time on D3100," the DECstation 3100 would spend a third of its CPU time running Gnu C Compiler, a third running TeX, and a third running Spice. The actual weightings are in parentheses, calculated as shown in Figure 2.7 on page 51.

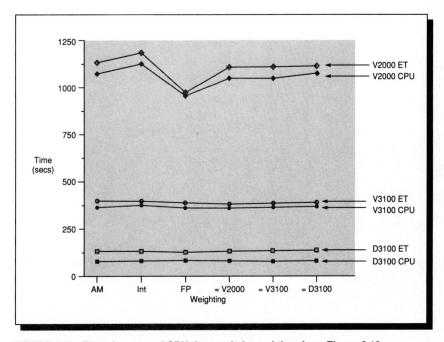

FIGURE 2.20   Plot of means of CPU time and elapsed time from Figure 2.19.

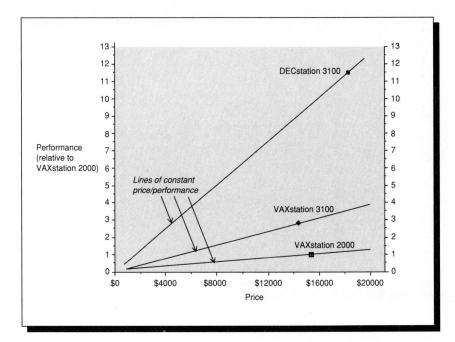

FIGURE 2.21   Price versus performance of VAXstation 2000, VAXstation 3100, and DECstation 3100 for Gnu C Compiler, TeX, and Spice. Based on Figures 2.18–2.19, this figure plots the list price **as tested** of a machine versus performance, where performance is the inverse of the ratio to the arithmetic mean of CPU time on a VAXstation 2000. The lines through the three machines show lines of constant price/performance. For example, a machine at the right end of the VAXstation 3100 line costs $20,000. Since it would cost 30% more, it must have 30% more performance than the VAXstation 3100 to have the same price performance.

2.5 Fallacies and Pitfalls

Cost/performance fallacies and pitfalls have ensnared many computer architects, including ourselves. For this reason, more space is devoted to the warning section in this chapter than in other chapters of this text.

Fallacy: Hardware-independent metrics predict performance.

Because accurately predicting performance is so difficult, the folklore of computer design is filled with suggested shortcuts. These are frequently employed when comparing different instruction sets, especially instruction sets that are paper designs.

One such shortcut is "Code Size = Speed," or the architecture with the smallest program is fastest. Static code size is important when memory space is at a premium, but it is not the same as performance. As we shall see in Chapter 6, larger programs composed of instructions that are easily fetched, decoded, and executed may run faster than machines with extremely compact instructions that are difficult to decode. "Code Size=Speed" is especially popular with compiler writers, for while it can be difficult to decide if one code sequence is faster than another, it is easy to see which is shorter.

Evidence of the "Code Size=Speed" fallacy can be found on the cover of the book *Assessing the Speed of Algol 60* in Figure 2.22. The CDC 6600's programs are over twice as big, yet the CDC machine runs Algol 60 programs almost six times **faster** than the Burroughs B5500, a machine designed for Algol 60.

Pitfall: Comparing computers using only one or two of three performance metrics: clock rate, CPI, and instruction count.

The CPU performance equation shows why this can mislead. One example is that given in Figure 2.22: The CDC 6600 executes almost 50% more instructions than the Burroughs B5500, yet it is 550% faster. Another example comes from increasing the clock rate so that some instructions execute fast—sometimes called *peak performance*—but making design decisions that also result in a high overall CPI that offsets the clock rate advantage. The Intergraph Clipper C100 has a clock rate of 33 MHz and a peak performance of 33 native MIPS. Yet the Sun 4/280, with half the clock rate and half the peak native MIPS rating, runs programs faster [Hollingsworth, Sachs, and Smith 1989, 215]. Since the Clipper's instruction count is about the same as Sun's, the former machine's CPI must be more than double that of the latter.

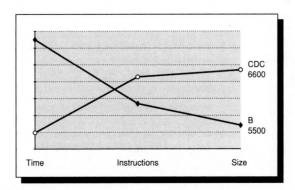

FIGURE 2.22 As found on the cover of *Assessing the Speed of Algol 60* by B. A. Wichmann, the graph shows relative execution time, instruction count, and code size of programs written in Algol 60 for the Burroughs B5500 and the CDC 6600. The results are normalized to a reference machine, with a higher number being worse. This book had a profound effect on one of the authors (DP). Seymour Cray, the designer of the CDC 6600, may not even have known of the existence of this programming language, while Robert Barton, architect of the B5500, designed the instruction set specifically for Algol 60. While the CDC 6600 executes 50% more instructions and has 220% larger code, the CDC 6600 is 550% faster than the B5500.

Fallacy: When calculating relative MIPS, the versions of the compiler and operating system of the reference machine make little difference.

Figure 2.19 shows the VAXstation 2000 taking 958 seconds of CPU time when running Spice with a standard input. Instead of Ultrix 3.0 with the VMS F77 compiler, many systems use Ultrix 3.0 with the standard UNIX F77 compiler. This compiler increases Spice CPU time to 1604 seconds. Using the standard evaluation of 0.9 relative MIPS for the VAXstation 2000, the DECstation 3100 is either 11 or 19 relative MIPS for Spice depending on the compiler of the reference machine.

Fallacy: CPI can be calculated from the instruction mix and the execution times of instructions found in the manual.

Current machines are too complicated to estimate performance from a manual. For example, in Figure 2.19 Spice takes 94 seconds of CPU time on the DECstation 3100. If we calculate the CPI from the DECstation 3100 manual—ignoring memory hierarchy and pipelining inefficiencies for this Spice instruction mix—we get 1.41 for the CPI. When multiplied by the instruction count and clock rate we get only 73 seconds. The missing 25% of CPU time is due to the estimate of CPI based only on the manual. The actual measured value, including all memory-system inefficiencies, is 1.87 CPI.

Pitfall: Summarizing performance by translating throughput into execution time.

The SPEC benchmarks report performance by measuring the elapsed time of each of 10 benchmarks. The sole dual processor workstation in the initial benchmark report ran these benchmarks no faster since the compilers didn't automatically parallelize the code across the two processors. The benchmarker's solution was to run a copy of each benchmark on each processor and record elapsed time for the two copies. This would not have helped if the SPEC release had only summarized performance using elapsed times, since the times were slower due to interference of the processors on memory accesses. The loophole was the initial SPEC release reported geometric means of performance relative to a VAX-11/780 in addition to elapsed times, and these means are used to graph the results. This innovative benchmarker interpreted ratio of performance to a VAX-11/780 as a **throughput** measure, so doubled his measured ratios to the VAX! Figure 2.23 shows the plots as found in the report for the uniprocessor and the multiprocessor. This technique almost doubles the geometric means of ratios, suggesting the mistaken conclusion that a computer that runs two copies of a program simultaneously has the same response time to a user as a computer that runs a single program in half the time.

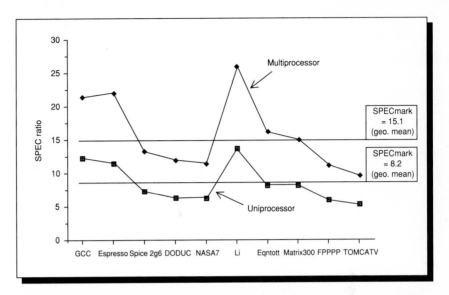

FIGURE 2.23 Performance of uniprocessor and multiprocessor as reported in SPEC Benchmark Press Release. Performance is plotted relative to a VAX-11/780. The ratio for the multiprocessor is really the ratio of elapsed time multiplied by the number of processors.

Fallacy: Synthetic benchmarks predict performance.

The best known examples of such benchmarks are Whetstone and Dhrystone. These are not real programs and, as such, may not reflect program behavior for factors not measured. Compiler and hardware optimizations can artificially inflate performance of these benchmarks but not of real programs. The other side of the coin is that because these benchmarks are not natural programs, they don't reward optimizations of behavior that occur in real programs. Here are some examples:

- Optimizing compilers can discard 25% of the Dhrystone code; examples include loops that are only executed once, making the loop overhead instructions unnecessary. To address these problems the authors of the benchmark "require" both optimized and unoptimized code to be reported. In addition, they "forbid" the practice of inline-procedure expansion optimization. (Dhrystone's simple procedure structure allows elimination of all procedure calls at almost no increase in code size; see Figure 2.5 on page 47.)

- All Whetstone floating-point loops make optimizations via vectorization essentially useless. (The program was written before computers with vector instructions were popular. See Chapter 7.)

■ Dhrystone has a long history of optimizations that skew its performance. The most recent comes from a C compiler that appears to include optimizations just for Dhrystone (Figure 2.5). If the proper option flag is set at compile time, the compiler turns the portion of the C version of this benchmark that copies a variable length string of bytes (terminated by an end-of-string symbol) into a loop that transfers a fixed number of words assuming the source and destination of the string is word-aligned in memory. Although it is estimated that between 99.70% to 99.98% of typical string copies could **not** use this optimization, this single change can make a 20% to 30% improvement in overall performance—if Dhrystone is your measure.

■ Compilers can optimize a key piece of the Whetstone loop by noting the relationship between square root and exponential, even though this is very unlikely to occur in real programs. For example, one key loop contains the following FORTRAN code (see Figure 2.4 on page 46):

$$\texttt{X = SQRT(EXP(ALOG(X)/T1))}$$

It could be compiled as if it were

$$\texttt{X = EXP(ALOG(X)/(2*T1))}$$

since

$$\texttt{SQRT(EXP(X))} = \sqrt[2]{e^X} = e^{X/2} = \texttt{EXP(X/2)}$$

It would be surprising if such optimizations were ever invoked except in this synthetic benchmark. (Yet one reviewer of this book found several compilers that performed this optimization!) This single change converts all calls to the square root function in Whetstone into multiplies by 2, surely improving performance—if Whetstone is your measure.

Fallacy: Peak performance tracks observed performance.

One definition of peak performance is performance a machine is "guaranteed not to exceed." The gap between peak performance and observed performance is typically a factor of 10 or more in supercomputers. (See Chapter 7 on vectors for an explanation.) Since the gap is so large, peak performance is not useful in predicting observed performance unless the workload consists of small programs that normally operate close to the peak.

As an example of this fallacy, a small code segment using long vectors ran on the Hitachi S810/20 at 236 MFLOPS and on the CRAY X-MP at 115 MFLOPS. Although this suggests the S810 is 105% faster than the X-MP, the X-MP runs a

	CRAY X-MP	Hitachi S810/20	Performance
A(i)=B(i)∗C(i)+D(i)∗E(i) (vector length 1000 done 100,000 times)	2.6 secs	1.3 secs	Hitachi 105% faster
Vectorized FFT (vector lengths 64, 32,…,2)	3.9 secs	7.7 secs	CRAY 97% faster

FIGURE 2.24 Measurements of peak performance and actual performance for the Hitachi S810/20 and the CRAY X-MP. From Lubeck, Moore, and Mendez [1985, 18-20]. Also see the pitfall in the Fallacies and Pitfalls section of Chapter 7.

Machine	Peak MFLOPS rating	Harmonic mean MFLOPS of the Perfect benchmarks	Percent of peak MFLOPS
CRAY X-MP/416	940	14.8	1%
IBM 3090-600S	800	8.3	1%
NEC SX/2	1300	16.6	1%

FIGURE 2.25 Peak performance and harmonic mean of actual performance for the Perfect Benchmarks. These results are for the programs run unmodified. When tuned by hand performance of the three machines moves to 24.4, 11.3, and 18.3 MFLOPS, respectively. This is still 2% or less of peak performance.

program with more typical vector lengths 97% faster than the S810. These data are shown in Figure 2.24.

Another good example comes from a benchmark suite called the Perfect Club (see page 80). Figure 2.25 shows the peak MFLOPS rating, harmonic mean of the MFLOPS achieved for 12 real programs, and the percentage of peak performance for three large computers. They achieve only 1% of peak performance.

While the use of peak performance has been rampant in the supercomputer business, recently this metric spread to microprocessor manufacturers. For example, in 1989 a microprocessor was announced as having the performance of 150 million "operations" per second ("MOPS"). The only way this machine can achieve this performance is for one integer instruction and one floating-point instruction to be executed each clock cycle **and** for the floating-point instruction to perform both a multiply operation and an add. For this peak performance to predict observed performance a real program would have to have 66% of its operations be floating point and no losses for the memory system or pipelining. In contrast to claims, typical measured performance of this microprocessor is under 30 "MOPS."

The authors hope that peak performance can be quarantined to the supercomputer industry and eventually eradicated from that domain; but in any case, approaching supercomputer performance is not an excuse for adopting dubious supercomputer marketing habits.

2.6 | Concluding Remarks

Having a standard of performance reporting in computer science journals as high as that in car magazines would be an improvement in current practice. Hopefully, that will be the case as the industry moves toward basing performance evaluation on real programs. Perhaps arguments about performance will even subside.

Computer designs will always be measured by cost and performance, and finding the best balance will always be the art of computer design. As long as technology continues to rapidly improve, the alternatives will look like the curves in Figure 2.26. Once a designer selects a technology, he can't achieve some performance levels no matter how much he pays and, conversely, no matter how much he cuts performance there is a limit to how low the cost can go. It would be better in either case to change technologies.

As a final remark, the number of machines sold is not always the best measure of cost/performance of computers, nor does cost/performance always predict number sold. Marketing is very important to sales. It is easier, however, to market a machine with better cost/performance. Even businesses with high gross margins need to be sensitive to cost/performance, otherwise the company cannot lower prices when faced with stiff competition. Unless you go into marketing, your job is to improve cost/performance!

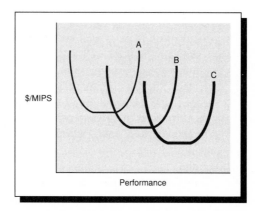

FIGURE 2.26 The cost per MIPS goes up on the y axis, and system performance increases on the x axis. A, B, and C are three technologies, let us say three different semiconductor technologies, to build a processor. Designs in the flat part of the curves can offer varieties of performance at the same cost/performance. If performance goals are too high for a technology it becomes very expensive, and too cheap a design makes the performance too low (cost per MIPS expensive for low MIPS). At either extreme it is better to switch technologies.

2.7 Historical Perspective and References

The anticipated degree of overlapping, buffering, and queuing in the [IBM 360] Model 85 [first computer with a cache] appeared to largely invalidate conventional performance measures based on instruction mixes and program kernels.

Conti, Gibson, and Pitkowsky [1968]

In the earliest days of computing, designers set performance goals—ENIAC was to be 1000 times faster than the Harvard Mark I, and the IBM Stretch (7030) was to be 100 times faster than the fastest machine in existence. What wasn't clear, though, was how this performance was to be measured. In looking back over the years, it is a consistent theme that each generation of computers obsoletes the performance evaluation techniques of the prior generation.

The original measure of performance was time to perform an individual operation, such as addition. Since most instructions took the same execution time, the timing of one gave insight into the others. As the execution times of instructions in a machine became more diverse, however, the time for one operation was no longer useful for comparisons. To take these differences into account, an *instruction mix* was calculated by measuring the relative frequency of instructions in a computer across many programs. The Gibson mix [1970] was an early popular instruction mix. Multiplying the time for each instruction times its weight in the mix gave the user the *average instruction execution time*. (If measured in clock cycles, average instruction execution time is the same as average CPI.) Since instruction sets were similar, this was a more accurate comparison than add times. From average instruction execution time, then, it was only a small step to MIPS (as we have seen, the one is the inverse of the other). MIPS has the virtue of being easy for the layman to understand, hence its popularity.

As CPUs became more sophisticated and relied on memory hierarchies and pipelining, there was no longer a single execution time per instruction; MIPS could not be calculated from the mix and the manual. The next step was benchmarking using kernels and synthetic programs. Curnow and Wichmann [1976] created the Whetstone synthetic program by measuring scientific programs written in Algol 60. This program was converted to FORTRAN and was widely used to characterize scientific program performance. An effort with similar goals to Whetstone, the Livermore FORTRAN Kernels, was made by McMahon [1986] and researchers at Lawrence Livermore Laboratory in an attempt to establish a benchmark for supercomputers. These kernels, however, consisted of loops from real programs.

The notion of relative MIPS came along as a way to resuscitate the easily understandable MIPS rating. When the VAX-11/780 was ready for announcement in 1977, DEC ran small benchmarks that were also run on an IBM 370/158. IBM marketing referred to the 370/158 as a 1-MIPS computer, and since the programs ran at the same speed, DEC marketing called the VAX-11/780 a 1-MIPS computer. (Note that this rating included the effectiveness of the compilers on both machines at the moment the comparison was made.) The popularity of the VAX-11/780 made it a popular reference machine for relative MIPS, especially since relative MIPS for a 1-MIPS computer is easy to calculate: If a machine was five times faster than the VAX-11/780, for that benchmark its rating would be 5 relative MIPS. The 1-MIPS rating was unquestioned for four years until Joel Emer of DEC measured the VAX-11/780 under a time-sharing load. He found that the VAX-11/780 native MIPS rating was 0.5. Subsequent VAXes that run 3 native MIPS for some benchmarks were therefore called 6-MIPS machines because they run 6 times faster than the VAX-11/780.

Although other companies followed this confusing practice, pundits have redefined MIPS as "Meaningless Indication of Processor Speed" or "Meaningless Indoctrination by Pushy Salespersons." At the present time, the most common meaning of MIPS in marketing literature is not native MIPS but "number of times faster than the VAX-11/780" and frequently includes floating-point programs as well. The exception is IBM, which defines MIPS relative to the "processing capacity" of an IBM 370/158, presumably running large system benchmarks (see Henly and McNutt, [1989, 5]). In the late 1980s DEC began using *VAX units of performance* (VUP), meaning ratio to VAX-11/780, so 6 relative MIPS became 6 VUPs.

The 1970s and 1980s marked the growth of the supercomputer industry, which was defined by high performance on floating-point–intensive programs. Average instruction time and MIPS were clearly inappropriate metrics for this industry, and hence the invention of MFLOPS. Unfortunately customers quickly forget the program used for the rating, and marketing groups decided to start quoting peak MFLOPS in the supercomputer performance wars.

A variety of means have been proposed for averaging performance. McMahon [1986] recommends the harmonic mean for averaging MFLOPS. Flemming and Wallace [1986] assert the merits of the geometric mean in general. Smith's reply [1988] to their article gives cogent arguments for arithmetic means of time and harmonic means of rates. (Smith's arguments are the ones followed in "Comparing and Summarizing Performance" under Section 2.2, above.)

As the distinction between architecture and implementation pervaded the computing community (see Chapter 1), the question arose whether the performance of an architecture itself could be evaluated, as opposed to an implementation of the architecture. A study of this question performed at Carnegie-Mellon University is summarized in Fuller and Burr [1977]. Three quantitative measures were invented to scrutinize architectures:

S   Number of bytes for program code

M   Number of bytes transferred between memory and the CPU during program execution for code and data (S measures size of code at compile time, while M is memory traffic during program execution.)

R   Number of bytes transferred between registers in a canonical model of a CPU

Once these measures were taken, a weighting factor was applied to them to determine which architecture was "best." Yet there has been no formal effort to see if these measures really matter—do the implementations of an architecture with superior S, M, and R measures outperform implementations of lesser architectures? The VAX architecture was designed in the height of popularity of the Carnegie-Mellon study, and by those measures it does very well. Architectures created since 1985, however, have poorer measures than the VAX, yet their implementations do well against the VAX implementations. For example, Figure 2.27 compares S, M, and CPU time for the VAXstation 3100, which uses the VAX instruction set, and the DECstation 3100, which doesn't. The DECstation 3100 is 200% to almost 400% faster even though its S measure is 35% to 70% worse and its M measure is 5% to 15% worse. The effort to evaluate architecture independent of implementation was a valiant one, it seems, if not a successful one.

	S (code size in bytes)		M (megabytes code + data transferred)		CPU Time (in seconds)	
	VAX 3100	**DEC 3100**	**VAX 3100**	**DEC 3100**	**VAX 3100**	**DEC 3100**
Gnu C Compiler	409,600	688,128	18	21	291	90
Common TeX	158,720	217,088	67	78	449	95
Spice	223,232	372,736	99	106	352	94

FIGURE 2.27   Code size and CPU time of the VAXstation 3100 and DECstation 3100 for Gnu C Compiler, TeX, and Spice. The programs and machines are described in Figures 2.17 and 2.18. Both machines were announced the same day by the same company and run the same operating system. The difference is in the instruction sets, compilers, clock cycle time, and organization. The M measure comes from Figure 3.33 (page 123) for smaller inputs than those in Figure 2.17 (page 67), but the relative performance is unchanged. Code size includes libraries.

A promising development in performance evaluation is the formation of the System Performance Evaluation Cooperative, or SPEC, group in 1988. SPEC contains representatives of many computer companies—the founders being Apollo/Hewlett-Packard, DEC, MIPS, and Sun—who have agreed on a set of real programs and inputs that all will run. It is worth noting that SPEC couldn't have happened before portable operating systems and the popularity of high-level languages. Now compilers, too, are accepted as a proper part of the performance of computer systems and must be measured in any evaluation. (See Exercises 2.8–2.10 on pages 83–84 for more on SPEC benchmarks.)

History teaches us that while the SPEC effort is useful with current computers, it will not be able to meet the needs of the next generation. An effort similar to SPEC, called the Perfect Club, binds together universities and companies interested in parallel computation [Berry et al. 1988]. Rather than being forced to run the existing sequential programs' code, the Perfect Club includes both programs and algorithms, and allows members to write new programs in new languages, which may be needed for the new architectures. Perfect Club members may also suggest new algorithms to solve important problems.

While papers on performance are plentiful, little is available on computer cost. Fuller [1976] wrote the first paper comparing price and performance for the Annual International Symposium on Computer Architecture. This was also the last price/performance paper at this conference. Phister's book [1979] on costs of computers is exhaustive, and Bell, Mudge, and McNamara [1978] describe the computer construction process from DEC's perspective. In contrast, there is a good deal of information on die yield. Strapper [1989] surveys the history of yield modeling, while technical details on the die-yield model used in this chapter are found in Strapper, Armstrong, and Saji [1983].

References

BELL, C. G., J. C. MUDGE, AND J. E. MCNAMARA [1978]. *A DEC View of Computer Engineering*, Digital Press, Bedford, Mass.

BERRY, M., D. CHEN, P. KOSS, D. KUCK [1988]. "The Perfect Club benchmarks: Effective performance evaluation of supercomputers," CSRD Report No. 827 (November), Center for Supercomputing Research and Development, University of Illinois at Urbana-Champaign.

CONTI, C. J., D. H. GIBSON, AND S. H. PITKOWSLI [1968]. "Structural aspects of the System/360 Model 85:I general organization," *IBM Systems J.* 7:1, 2–11.

CURNOW, H. J. AND B. A. WICHMANN [1976]. "A synthetic benchmark," *The Computer J.* 19:1.

FLEMMING, P. J. AND J. J. WALLACE [1986]. "How not to lie with statistics: The correct way to summarize benchmarks results," *Comm. ACM* 29:3 (March) 218–221.

FULLER, S. H. [1976]. "Price/performance comparison of C.mmp and the PDP-11," *Proc. Third Annual Symposium on Computer Architecture* (Texas, January 19–21), 197–202.

FULLER, S. H. AND W. E. BURR [1977]. "Measurement and evaluation of alternative computer architectures," *Computer* 10:10 (October) 24–35.

GIBSON, J. C. [1970]. "The Gibson mix," Rep. TR. 00.2043, IBM Systems Development Division, Poughkeepsie, N.Y. (Research done in 1959.)

HENLY, M. AND B. MCNUTT [1989]. "DASD I/O characteristics: A comparison of MVS to VM," Tech. Rep. TR 02.1550 (May), IBM, General Products Division, San Jose, Calif.

HOLLINGSWORTH, W., H. SACHS AND A. J. SMITH [1989]. "The Clipper processor: Instruction set architecture and implementation," *Comm. ACM* 32:2 (February), 200–219.

LUBECK, O., J. MOORE, AND R. MENDEZ [1985]. "A benchmark comparison of three super-computers: Fujitsu VP-200, Hitachi S810/20, and Cray X-MP/2," *Computer* 18:12 (December) 10–24.

MCMAHON, F. M. [1986]. "The Livermore FORTRAN kernels: A computer test of numerical performance range," Tech. Rep. UCRL-55745, Lawrence Livermore National Laboratory, Univ. of California, Livermore, Calif. (December).

PHISTER, M., JR. [1979]. *Data Processing Technology and Economics,* 2nd ed., Digital Press and Santa Monica Publishing Company.

SMITH, J. E. [1988]. "Characterizing computer performance with a single number," *Comm. ACM* 31:10 (October) 1202–1206.

SPEC [1989]. "SPEC Benchmark Suite Release 1.0," October 2, 1989.

STRAPPER, C. H. [1989]. "Fact and fiction in yield modelling," Special Issue of the *Microelectronics Journal* entitled *Microelectronics into the Nineties*, Oxford, UK; Elsevier (May).

STRAPPER, C. H., F. H. ARMSTRONG, AND K. SAJI, [1983]. "Integrated circuit yield statistics," *Proc. IEEE* 71:4 (April) 453–470.

WEICKER, R. P. [1984]. "Dhrystone: A synthetic systems programming benchmark," *Comm. ACM* 27:10 (October) 1013–1030.

WICHMANN, B. A. [1973]. *Algol 60 Compilation and Assessment*, Academic Press, New York.

EXERCISES

2.1 [20] <2.2> After graduating, you are asked to become the lead computer designer. Your study of usage of high-level–language constructs suggests that procedure calls are one of the most expensive operations. You have invented a scheme that reduces the loads and stores normally associated with procedure calls and returns. The first thing you do is run some experiments with and without this optimization. Your experiments use the same state-of-the-art optimizing compiler that will be used with either version of computer.

Your experiments reveal the following information:

- The clock cycle time of the unoptimized version is 5% faster.

- 30% of the instructions in the nonoptimized version are loads or stores.

- The optimized version executes 1/3 fewer loads and stores than the nonoptimized version. For all other instructions the dynamic execution counts are unchanged.

- All instructions (including load and store) take one clock cycle.

Which is faster? Justify your decision quantitatively.

2.2 [15/15/10] <2.2> Assume the two programs in Figure 2.6 on page 49 each execute 100,000,000 floating-point operations during execution.

a. [15] Calculate the (native) MFLOPS rating of each program.

b. [15] Calculate the arithmetic, geometric, and harmonic mean (native) MFLOPS for each machine.

c. [10] Which of the three means matches the relative performance of total execution time?

Questions 2.3–2.7 require the following information.

The Whetstone benchmark contains 79,550 floating-point operations, not including the floating-point operations performed in each call to the following functions:

- arctangent, invoked 640 times
- sine, invoked 640 times
- cosine, invoked 1920 times
- square root, invoked 930 times
- exponential, invoked 930 times
- and logarithm, invoked 930 times

The basic operations for a single iteration (not including floating-point operations to perform the above functions) are broken down as follows:

Add	37,530
Subtract	3,520
Multiply	22,900
Divide	11,400
Convert integer to fp	4,200
TOTAL	79,550

The total number of floating-point operations for a single iteration can also be calculated by including the floating-point operations needed to perform the functions arctangent, sine, cosine, square root, exponential, and logarithm:

Add	82,014
Subtract	8,229
Multiply	73,220
Divide	21,399
Convert integer to fp	6,006
Compare	4,710
TOTAL	195,578

Whetstone was run on a Sun 3/75 using the F77 compiler with optimization turned on. The Sun 3/75 is based on a Motorola 68020 running at 16.67 MHz, and it includes a floating-point coprocessor. (Assume the coprocessor does not include arctangent, sine, cosine, square root, exponential, and logarithm as instructions.) The Sun compiler allows the floating-point to be calculated with the coprocessor or using software routines, depending on compiler flags. A single iteration of Whetstone took 1.08 seconds using the coprocessor and 13.6 seconds using software. Assume that the CPI using the coprocessor was measured to be 10 while the CPI using software was measured to be 6.

2.3 [15] <2.2> What is the (native) MIPS rating for both runs?

2.4 [15] <2.2> What is the **total** number of instructions executed for both runs?

2.5 [8] <2.2> On the average, how many integer instructions does it take to perform each floating-point operation in software?

2.6 [18] <2.2> What is the native and normalized MFLOPS for the Sun 3/75 with the floating-point coprocessor running Whetstone? (Assume convert counts as a single floating-point operation and use Figure 2.3 for normalized operations.)

2.7 [20] <2.2> Figure 2.3 on page 43 suggests how many floating-point operations it takes to perform the six functions above (arctangent, sine, and so on). From the data above you can calculate the average number of floating-point operations per function. What is the ratio between the estimates in Figure 2.3 and the floating-point operation measurements for the Sun 3? Assume the coprocessor implements only Add, Subtract, Multiply, Divide, and Convert.

Questions 2.8–2.10 require the information in Figure 2.28.

The SPEC Benchmark Release 1.0 Summary [SPEC 89] lists performance as shown in Figure 2.28.

Program Name	VAX-11/780 Time	DECstation 3100 Time	Ratio	Delta Series 8608 Time	Ratio	SPARCstation 1 Time	Ratio
GCC	1482	145	10.2	193	7.7	138.9	10.7
Espresso	2266	194	11.7	197	11.5	254.0	8.9
Spice 2g6	23951	2500	9.6	3350	7.1	2875.5	8.3
DODUC	1863	208	9.0	295	6.3	374.1	5.0
NASA7	20093	1646	12.2	3187	6.3	2308.2	8.7
Li	6206	480	12.9	458	13.6	689.5	9.0
Eqntott	1101	99	11.1	129	8.5	113.5	9.7
Matrix300	4525	749	6.0	520	8.7	409.3	11.1
FPPPP	3038	292	10.4	488	6.2	387.2	7.8
TOMCATV	2649	260	10.2	509	5.2	469.8	5.6
Geometric mean	3867.7	381.4	10.1	496.5	7.8	468.5	8.3

FIGURE 2.28 SPEC performance summary 1.0. The four integer programs are GCC, Espresso, Li, and Eqntott, with the rest relying on floating-point hardware.The SPEC report does not describe the version of the compilers or operating system used for the VAX-11/780. The DECstation 3100 is described in Figure 2.18 on page 68. The Motorola Delta Series 8608 uses a 20-MHz MC88100, 16-KB instruction cache, and 16-KB data cache using two M88200s (see Exercise 8.6 in Chapter 8), the Motorola Sys. V/88 R32V1 operating system, the C88000 1.8.4m14 C compiler, and the Absoft SysV88 2.0a4 FORTRAN compiler. The SPARCstation 1 uses a 20-MHz MB8909 integer unit and 20-MHz WTL3170 floating-point unit, a 64-KB unified cache, SunOS 4.0.3c operating system and C compiler, and Sun 1.2 FORTRAN compiler. The size of main memory in these three machines is 16 MB.

2.8 [12/15] <2.2> Compare the relative performance using total execution times for the 10 programs versus using geometric means of ratios of the speed of the VAX-11/780.

a.   [12] How do the results differ?

b   [15] Compare the geometric mean of the ratios of the four integer programs (GCC, Espresso, Li, and Eqntott) versus the total execution time for these four programs. How do the results differ from each other and from the summaries of all ten programs?

2.9 [15/20/12/10] <2.2> Now let's compare performance using weighted arithmetic means.

   a. [15] Calculate the weights for a workload so that running times on the VAX-11/780 will be equal for each of the ten programs (see Figure 2.7 on page 51).

   b. [20] Using those weights, calculate the weighted arithmetic means of the execution times of the ten programs.

   c. [12] Calculate the ratio of the weighted means of the VAX execution times to the weighted means for the other machines.

   d. [10] How do the geometric means of ratios and the ratios of weighted arithmetic means of execution times differ in summarizing relative performance?

2.10 [Discussion] <2.2> What is an interpretation of the geometric means of execution times? What do you think are the advantages and disadvantages of using total execution times versus weighted arithmetic means of execution times using equal running time on the VAX-11/780 versus geometric means of ratios of speed to the VAX-11/780?

Questions 2.11–2.12 require the information in Figure 2.29.

Microprocessor	Size (cm)	Pins	Package	Clock rate	List price	Year available
Cypress CY7C601	0.8×0.7	207	Ceramic PGA	33 MHz	$500	1988
Intel 80486	1.6×1.0	168	Ceramic PGA	33 MHz	$950	1989
Intel 860	1.2×1.2	168	Ceramic PGA	33 MHz	$750	1989
MIPS R3000	0.8×0.9	144	Ceramic PGA	25 MHz	$300	1988
Motorola 88100	0.9×0.9	169	Ceramic PGA	25 MHz	$695	1989

FIGURE 2.29   Characteristics of microprocessors. List prices were quoted as of 7/15/89 at quantity 1000 purchases.

2.11 [15] <2.3> Pick the largest and smallest microprocessors from Figure 2.29, and use the values found in Figure 2.11 (page 62) for yield parameters. How many good chips do you get per wafer?

2.12 [15/10/10/15/15] <2.3> Let's calculate costs and prices of the largest and smallest microprocessors from Figure 2.29. Use the assumptions on manufacturing found in Figure 2.11 (page 62) unless specifically mentioned otherwise.

   a. [15] There are wide differences in defect densities between semiconductor manufacturers. What are the costs of untested dies assuming: (1) 2 defects per square cm; and (2) 1 defect per square cm.

   b. [10] Assume that testing costs $150 per hour and the smaller chip takes 10 seconds to test and the larger chip takes 15 seconds, what is the cost of testing each die?

   c. [10] Making the assumptions on packaging in Section 2.3, what is the cost of packaging and burn-in?

   d. [15] What is the final cost?

e. [15] Given the list price and the calculated cost from the questions above, calculate the gross margin. Assume the direct cost is 40% and average selling discount is 33%. What percentage of the average selling price is the gross margin for both chips?

2.13–2.14 A few companies claim they are doing so well that the defect density is vanishing as the reason for die failures, making wafer yield responsible for the vast majority. For example, Gordon Moore of Intel said in a talk at MIT in 1989 that defect density is improving to the point that some companies have been quoted as producing a 100% yield over the whole run. In fact, he has a 100% yield wafer on his desk.

2.13 [20] <2.3> To understand the impact of such claims, list the costs of the largest and smallest dies in Figure 2.29 for defect densities per square centimeter of 3, 2, 1, and 0. For the other parameters use the values found in Figure 2.11 (page 62). Ignore the costs of testing time, packaging, and final test.

2.14 [Discussion] <2.3> If the statement above becomes true for most semiconductor manufacturers, how would that change the options for the computer designer?

2.15 [10/15] <2.3,2.4> Figure 2.18 (page 68) shows the list price as tested of the DECstation 3100 workstation. Start with the costs of the "higher cost" model in Figure 2.13 on page 63, (assuming a color), workstation but change the cost of DRAM to $100/MB for the full 16 MB of the 3100.

a. [10] Using the average discount and overhead percentages of Model B in Figure 2.16 on page 66, what is the gross margin on the DECstation 3100?

b. [15] Suppose you replace the R2000 CPU of the DECstation 3100 with the R3000, and that this change makes the machine 50% faster. Use the costs in Figure 2.29 for the R3000, and assume the R2000 costs a third as much. Since the R3000 does not require much more power, assume that both the power supply and the cooling of the DECstation 3100 are satisfactory for the upgrade. What is the cost/performance of a diskless black-and-white (mono) workstation with an R2000 versus one with an R3000? Using the business model from the answer to part a, how much must the price of the R3000-based machine be increased?

2.16 [30] <2.2,2.4> Pick two computers and run the Dhrystone benchmark and the Gnu C Compiler. Try running the programs using no optimization and maximum optimization. (Note: GCC is a benchmark, so use the appropriate C compiler to compile both programs. Don't try to compile GCC and use it as your compiler!) Then calculate the following performance ratios:

1. Unoptimized Dhrystone on machine A versus unoptimized Dhrystone on machine B.

2. Unoptimized GCC on A versus unoptimized GCC on B.

3. Optimized Dhrystone on A versus optimized Dhrystone on B.

4. Optimized GCC on A versus optimized GCC on B.

5. Unoptimized Dhrystone versus optimized Dhrystone on machine A.

6. Unoptimized GCC versus optimized GCC on A.

7. Unoptimized Dhrystone versus optimized Dhrystone on B.

8.   Unoptimized GCC versus optimized GCC on B.

The benchmarking question is how well the benchmark predicts performance of real programs.

If benchmarks do predict performance, then the following equations should be true about the ratios:

(1) = (2) and (3) = (4)

If compiler optimizations work equally as well on real programs as on benchmarks, then

(5) = (6) and (7) = (8)

Are these equations true? If not, try to find the explanation. Is it the machines, the compiler optimizations, or the programs that explain the answer?

2.17 [30] <2.2,2.4> Perform the same experiment as in question 2.16, except replace Dhrystone by Whetstone and replace GCC by Spice.

2.18 [Discussion] <2.2> What are the pros and cons of synthetic benchmarks? Find quantitative evidence—such as data supplied by answering questions 2.16 and 2.17—as well as listing the qualitative advantages and disadvantages.

2.19 [30] <2.2,2.4> Devise a program in C or Pascal that gets the peak MIPS rating for a computer. Run it on two machines to calculate the peak MIPS. Now run GCC and TeX on both machines. How well do peak MIPS predict performance of GCC and TeX?

2.20 [30] <2.2,2.4> Devise a program in C or FORTRAN that gets the peak MFLOPS rating for a computer. Run it on two machines to calculate the peak MFLOPS. Now run Spice on both machines. How well do peak MFLOPS predict performance of Spice?

2.21 [Discussion] <2.3> Use the cost information in Section 2.3 as a basis for the merits of timesharing a large computer versus a network of workstations. (To determine the potential value of workstations versus timesharing, see Section 9.2 in Chapter 9 on user productivity.)

A n	Add the number in storage location n into the accumulator	
H n	Transfer the number in storage location n into the multiplier register.	
E n	If the number in the accumulator is greater than or equal to zero execute next the order which stands in storage location n; otherwise proceed serially.	
I n	Read the next row of holes on tape and place the resulting 5 digits in the least significant places of storage location n.	
Z	Stop the machine and ring the warning bell.	

Selection from the list of 18 machine instructions for the
EDSAC from Wilkes and Renwick [1949]

3 Instruction Set Design: Alternatives and Principles

3.1 | Introduction

In this chapter and the next we will concentrate on instruction set architecture—the portion of the machine visible to the programmer or compiler writer. This chapter introduces the wide variety of design alternatives with which the instruction set architect is presented. In particular, this chapter focuses on three topics. First, we present a taxonomy of instruction set alternatives and give some qualitative assessment of the advantages and disadvantages of various approaches. Second, we present and analyze some instruction set measurements that are largely independent of a specific instruction set. Finally, we address the issue of languages and compilers and their bearing on instruction set architecture. Before we discuss how to classify architectures, we need to say something about the instruction set measurement.

Throughout this chapter and the next, we will be examining a wide variety of architectural measurements. These measurements depend on the programs measured and on the compilers used in making the measurements. The results should not be interpreted as absolute, and you might see different data if you did the measurement with a different compiler or a different set of programs. The authors believe that the measurements shown in these chapters are reasonably indicative of a class of typical applications. The measurements are presented using a small set of benchmarks so that the data can be reasonably displayed, and so that the differences among programs can be seen. An architect for a new machine would want to analyze a **much larger** collection of programs to make his architectural decisions. All the measurements shown are *dynamic*—that is, the frequency of a measured event is determined by the number of times that event occurs during execution of the measured program rather than the number of static occurences in the code.

Now, we will begin exploring how instruction set architectures can be classified and analyzed.

3.2 | Classifying Instruction Set Architectures

Instruction sets can be broadly classified along the five dimensions described in Figure 3.1, which are roughly ordered by the role they play in distinguishing instruction sets.

The type of internal storage in the CPU is the most basic differentiation, so we will focus on the alternatives for this portion of the architecture in this section. As shown in Figure 3.2, the major choices are a stack, an accumulator, or a set of registers. Operands may be named explicitly or implicitly: The operands in a *stack architecture* are implicitly on the top of the stack; in an

Operand storage in the CPU	Where are operands kept other than in memory?
Number of explicit operands named per instruction	How many operands are named explicitly in a typical instruction?
Operand location	Can any ALU instruction operand be located in memory or must some or all of the operands be in internal storage in the CPU? If an operand is located in memory, how is the memory location specified?
Operations	What operations are provided in the instruction set?
Type and size of operands	What is the type and size of each operand and how is it specified?

FIGURE 3.1 A set of axes for alternative design choices in instruction sets. The type of storage provided for holding operands in the CPU, as opposed to in memory, is the major distinguishing factor among instruction set architectures. (All architectures known to the authors provide some temporary storage within the CPU.) The type of operand storage in the CPU sometimes dictates the number of operands explicitly named in an instruction. In one class of machines, the number of explicit operands may vary. Among recent instruction sets, the number of memory operands per instruction is another significant differentiating factor. The choice of what operations will be supported in instructions interacts less with other aspects of the architecture. Finally, specifying the data type and the size of an operand is largely independent of other instruction set choices.

accumulator architecture one operand is implicitly the accumulator. *General-purpose register architectures* have only explicit operands—either registers or memory locations. Depending on the architecture, the explicit operands to an operation may be accessed directly from memory or they may need to be first loaded into temporary storage, depending on the class of instruction and choice of specific instruction.

Temporary storage provided	Examples	Explicit operands per ALU instruction	Destination for results	Procedure for accessing explicit operands
Stack	B5500, HP 3000/70	0	Stack	Push and pop onto or from the stack
Accumulator	PDP-8, Motorola 6809	1	Accumulator	Load/store accumulator
Register set	IBM 360, DEC VAX	2 or 3	Registers or memory	Load/store of registers, or memory

FIGURE 3.2   Some alternatives for storing operands within the CPU. Each alternative means that a different number of explicit operands is needed for an instruction with two source operands and a result operand. Instruction sets are usually classified by this internal state as stack machine, accumulator machine, or general-purpose register machine. While most architectures fit cleanly into one or another class, some architectures are hybrids of different approaches. The Intel 8086, for example, is halfway between a general-purpose register machine and an accumulator machine.

Figure 3.3 shows how the code sequence C = A + B would typically appear on these three classes of instruction sets. The primary advantages and disadvantages of each of these approaches are listed in Figure 3.4 (page 92).

While most early machines used stack or accumulator-style architectures, every machine designed in the past ten years and still surviving uses a general-purpose register architecture. The major reasons for the emergence of general-purpose register machines are twofold. First, registers—like other forms of

Stack	Accumulator	Register
PUSH A	LOAD A	LOAD R1,A
PUSH B	ADD B	ADD R1,B
ADD	STORE C	STORE C, R1
POP C		

FIGURE 3.3   The code sequence for C = A + B for three different instruction sets. It is assumed that A, B, and C all belong in memory and that the values of A and B cannot be destroyed.

Machine type	Advantages	Disadvantages
Stack	Simple model of expression evaluation (reverse polish). Short instructions can yield good code density.	A stack cannot be randomly accessed. This limitation makes it difficult to generate efficient code. It's also difficult to implement efficiently, since the stack becomes a bottleneck.
Accumulator	Minimizes internal state of machine. Short instructions.	Since accumulator is only temporary storage, memory traffic is highest for this approach.
Register	Most general model for code generation.	All operands must be named, leading to longer instructions.

FIGURE 3.4   Primary advantages and disadvantages of each class of machine. These advantages and disadvantages are related to three issues: How well the structure matches the needs of a compiler; how efficient the approach is from an implementation viewpoint; and what the effective code size is relative to other approaches.

storage internal to the CPU—are faster than memory. Second, registers are easier for a compiler to use and can be used more effectively than other forms of internal storage. Because general-purpose register machines so dominate instruction set architectures today—and it seems unlikely that this will change in the future—it is only these architectures that we will consider from this point on. Yet even with this limitation, there is a large number of design alternatives to consider. Some designers have proposed the extension of the register concept to allow additional buffering of multiple sets of registers in a stack-like fashion. This additional level of memory hierarchy is examined in Chapter 8.

3.3 | Operand Storage in Memory: Classifying General-Purpose Register Machines

The key advantages of general-purpose register machines arise from effective use of the registers by a compiler, both in computing expression values and, more globally, in using registers to hold variables. Registers permit more flexible ordering in evaluating expressions than do either stacks or accumulators. For example, on a register machine the expression $(A*B) - (C*D) - (E*F)$ may be evaluated by doing the multiplications in any order, which may be more efficient due to the location of the operands or because of pipelining concerns (see Chapter 6). But on a stack machine the expression must be evaluated left to right, unless special operations or swaps of stack positions are done.

More important, registers can be used to hold variables. When variables are allocated to registers, the memory traffic is reduced, the program is sped up (since registers are faster than memory), and the code density improves (since a register can be named with fewer bits than can a memory location). Compiler writers would prefer that all registers be equivalent and unreserved. Many machines compromise this desire—especially older machines with many dedicated registers—effectively decreasing the number of general-purpose registers.

If the number of truly general-purpose registers is too small, trying to allocate variables to registers will not be profitable. Instead, the compiler will reserve all the uncommitted registers for use in expression evaluation.

How many registers are sufficient? The answer of course depends on how they are used by the compiler. Most compilers reserve some registers for expression evaluation, use some for parameter passing, and allow the remainder to be allocated to hold variables. To understand how many registers are sufficient, we really need to examine what variables can be allocated to registers and the allocation algorithm used. We deal with these in our discussion of compilers in Section 3.7 and examine measurements of register usage in that section.

There are two major instruction set characteristics that divide general-purpose register, or *GPR,* architectures. Both characteristics concern the nature of operands for a typical arithmetic or logical instruction, or ALU instruction. The first concerns whether an ALU instruction has two or three operands. In the three-operand format, the instruction contains a result and two source operands. In the two-operand format, one of the operands is both a source and a destination for the operation. The second distinction among GPR architectures concerns how many of the operands may be memory addresses in ALU instructions. The number of memory operands supported by a **typical** ALU instruction may vary from none to three. All possible combinations of these two attributes are shown in Figure 3.5, with examples of machines. While there are seven possible combinations, three serve to classify nearly all existing machines: *register–register* (also called *load/store*), *register–memory*, and *memory–memory*.

The advantages and disadvantages of each of these alternatives are shown in Figure 3.6 (page 94). Of course, these advantages and disadvantages are not absolutes. A GPR machine with memory–memory operations can easily be subsetted by the compiler and used as a register–register machine. The

Number of memory addresses per typical ALU instruction	Maximum number of operands allowed for a typical ALU instruction	Examples
0	2	IBM RT-PC
	3	SPARC, MIPS, HP Precision Architecture
1	2	PDP-10, Motorola 68000, IBM 360
	3	Part of IBM 360 (RS instructions)
2	2	PDP-11, National 32x32, part of IBM 360 (SS instructions)
	3	
3	3	VAX (also has two-operand formats)

FIGURE 3.5   Possible combinations of memory operands and total operands per ALU instruction with examples of machines. Machines with no memory reference per ALU instruction are called load/store or register–register machines. Instructions with multiple memory operands per typical ALU instruction are called register–memory or memory–memory, according to whether they have one or more than one memory operand.

Type	Advantages	Disadvantages
Register–register (0,3)	Simple, fixed-length instruction encoding. Simple code generation model. Instructions take similar numbers of clocks to execute (see Chapter 6).	Higher instruction count than architectures with memory references in instructions. Some instructions are short and bit encoding may be wasteful.
Register–memory (1,2)	Data can be accessed without loading first. Instruction format tends to be easy to encode and yields good density.	Operands are not equivalent since a source operand in a binary operation is destroyed. Encoding a register number and a memory address in each instruction may restrict the number of registers. Clocks per instruction varies by operand location.
Memory–memory (3,3)	Most compact. Doesn't waste registers for temporaries.	Large variation in instruction size, especially for three-operand instructions. Also, large variation in work per instruction. Memory accesses create memory bottleneck.

FIGURE 3.6 Advantages and disadvantages of the three most common types of general-purpose register machines. The notation (m, n) means m memory operands and n total operands. In general, machines with fewer alternatives make the compiler's task simpler since there are fewer decisions for the compiler to make. Machines with a wide variety of flexible instruction formats reduce the number of bits required to encode the program. A machine that uses a small number of bits to encode the program is said to have good *instruction density*—a smaller number of bits do as much work as a larger number on a different architecture. The number of registers also affects the instruction size.

advantages and disadvantages listed in the figure deal primarily with the impact both on the compiler and on the implementation. These advantages and disadvantages are qualitative and their actual impact depends on the compiler and implementation strategy. One of the most pervasive architectural impacts is on instruction encoding and the number of instructions needed to perform a task. In other chapters, we will see the impact of these architectural alternatives on various implementation approaches.

3.4 | Memory Addressing

Independent of whether the architecture is register–register (also called *load/store*) or allows any operand to be a memory reference, it must define how memory addresses are interpreted and how they are specified. We will deal with these two topics in this section. The measurements presented here are largely, but not completely, machine independent. In some cases the measurements are significantly affected by the compiler technology. These measurements have been made using an optimizing compiler since compiler technology is playing an increasing role. The measurements will probably reflect what we will be seeing in the future rather than what has been so in the past.

Interpreting Memory Addresses

How is a memory address interpreted? That is, what object is accessed as a function of the address and the length? All the machines discussed in this and the next chapter are byte addressed and provide access for bytes (8 bits), half-words (16 bits), and words (32 bits). Most of the machines also provide access for doublewords (64 bits).

There are two different conventions for ordering the bytes within a word, as shown in Figure 3.7. *Little Endian* byte order puts the byte whose address is "x...x00" at the least significant position in the word (the little end). *Big Endian* byte order puts the byte whose address is "x...x00" at the most significant position in the word (the big end). In Big Endian addressing, the address of a datum is the address of the most significant byte; while in Little Endian, the address of a datum is the least significant byte. When operating within one machine, the byte order is often unnoticeable—only programs that access the same locations as both words and bytes can notice the difference. However, byte order is a problem when exchanging data among machines with different orderings. (The byte orders used by a number of different machines are listed inside the front cover.)

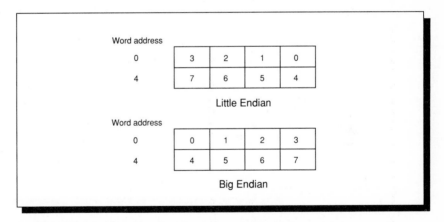

FIGURE 3.7   The two different conventions for ordering bytes within a word. The names "Big Endian" and "Little Endian" come from a famous paper by Cohen [1981]. The paper draws an analogy between the argument over which end to number the bytes from and the argument in Gulliver's Travels over which end of an egg to open. The DEC PDP-11/VAX and Intel 80x86 follow the Little Endian model, while the IBM 360/370 and Motorola 680x0, and others follow the Big Endian model. This numbering applies to bit positions as well, though only a few architectures supply instructions to access bits by their numbered position.

In some machines, accesses to objects larger than a byte must be aligned. An access to an object of size s bytes at byte address A is aligned if $A \bmod s = 0$. Figure 3.8 shows the addresses at which an access is aligned or misaligned.

Object addressed	Aligned at byte offsets	Misaligned at byte offsets
byte	0,1,2,3,4,5,6,7	(never)
halfword	0,2,4,6	1,3,5,7
word	0,4	1,2,3,5,6,7
doubleword	0	1,2,3,4,5,6,7

FIGURE 3.8   Aligned and misaligned accesses of objects. The byte offsets are specified for the low-order three bits of the address.

Why would someone design a machine with alignment restrictions? Misalignment causes hardware complications, since the memory is typically aligned on a word boundary. A misaligned memory access will, therefore, take multiple aligned memory references. Figure 3.9 shows what happens when an access occurs to a misaligned word in a system with a 32-bit-wide bus to memory: Two accesses are required to get the word. Thus, even in machines that allow misaligned access, programs with aligned accesses run faster.

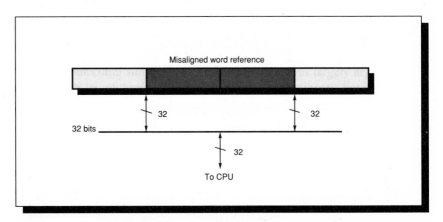

FIGURE 3.9   A word reference is made to a halfword (16-bit) boundary in a memory system that has a 32-bit access path. The CPU or memory system has to perform two separate accesses to get the upper and lower halfword. The two halfwords are then merged to obtain the entire word. With memory organized as independent byte-wide modules it is possible to access only the needed data, but this requires more complex control to supply a different address to each module to select the proper byte.

Even if data is aligned, supporting byte and halfword accesses requires an alignment network to align bytes and halfwords in registers. Depending on the instruction, the machine may also need to sign extend the quantity. On some machines a byte or halfword does not affect the upper portion of a register. For stores only the affected bytes in memory may be altered. Figure 3.10 shows the alignment network for loading or storing a byte from a word in memory into a register. While all the machines discussed in this chapter and the next permit byte and halfword accesses to memory, only the VAX and the Intel 8086 support ALU operations on register operands with a size shorter than a word.

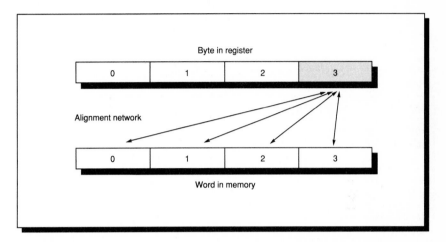

FIGURE 3.10 The alignment network to load or store a byte. The memory system is assumed to be 32 bits wide, and four alignment paths are required for bytes. Accessing aligned halfwords would require two additional paths to move either byte 0 or byte 2 in memory to byte 2 in the register. A 64-bit memory system would require twice as many alignment paths for bytes and halfwords, as well as two 32-bit alignment paths for word accesses. The alignment network only positions the bytes for a store—additional control signals are used to ensure that only the correct byte positions are written in memory. Rather than an alignment network, some machines use a shifter and shift the data only in those cases where alignment is required. This makes the access of a nonword object considerably slower, but eliminating the alignment network speeds up the more common case of accessing a word.

Addressing Modes

We now know what bytes to access in memory given an address. In this section we will look at addressing modes—how architectures specify the address of an object they will access. In GPR machines, an addressing mode can specify a constant, a register, or a location in memory. When a memory location is used, the actual memory address specified by the addressing mode is called the *effective address.*

Figure 3.11 shows all the data addressing modes that arise in the machines discussed in the following chapter. Immediates or literals are usually considered a memory addressing mode (even though the value they access is in the instruction stream), while registers are often separated. We have kept addressing modes that depend on the program counter, called *PC-relative addressing*, separate. PC-relative addressing is used primarily for specifying code addresses in control transfer instructions. The use of PC-relative addressing in control instructions is discussed in Section 3.5.

Figure 3.11 shows the most common names for the addressing modes, though the names differ among architectures. In this figure and throughout the book, we will use an extension of the C programming language as a hardware description notation. In this figure, only two non-C features are used. First, the left arrow ($\leftarrow$) is used for assignment. Second, the array M is used as the name for memory.

Addressing mode	Example instruction	Meaning	When used
Register	Add R4,R3	R4←R4+R3	When a value is in a register.
Immediate or literal	Add R4,#3	R4←R4+3	For constants. In some machines, literal and immediate are two different addressing modes.
Displacement or based	Add R4,100(R1)	R4←R4+M[100+R1]	Accessing local variables.
Register deferred or indirect	Add R4,(R1)	R4←R4+M[R1]	Accessing using a pointer or a computed address.
Indexed	Add R3,(R1 + R2)	R3←R3+M[R1+R2]	Sometimes useful in array addressing—R1=base of array; R2=index amount.
Direct or absolute	Add R1,(1001)	R1←R1+M[1001]	Sometimes useful for accessing static data; address constant may need to be large.
Memory indirect or memory deferred	Add R1,@(R3)	R1←R1+M[M[R3]]	If R3 is the address of a pointer p, then mode yields $*p$.
Auto-increment	Add R1,(R2)+	R1←R1+M[R2] R2←R2+d	Useful for stepping through arrays within a loop. R2 points to start of array; each reference increments R2 by size of an element, d.
Auto-decrement	Add R1,-(R2)	R2←R2−d R1←R1+M[R2]	Same use as autoincrement. Autoincrement/decrement can also be used to implement a stack as push and pop.
Scaled or index	Add R1,100(R2)[R3]	R1←R1+M[100+R2+R3*d]	Used to index arrays. May be applied to any base addressing mode in some machines.

FIGURE 3.11   Selection of addressing modes with examples, meaning, and usage. The extensions to C used in the hardware descriptions are defined above. In autoincrement/decrement and scaled or index addressing modes, the variable d designates the size of the data item being accessed (i.e., whether the instruction is accessing 1, 2, 4, or 8 bytes); this means that these addressing modes are only useful when the elements being accessed are adjacent in memory. In our measurements, we use the first name shown for each mode. A few machines, such as the VAX, encode some of these addressing modes as PC-relative.

Thus, M[R1] refers to the contents of the memory location whose address is given by the contents of R1. Later, we will introduce extensions for accessing and transferring data smaller than a word.

Addressing modes have the ability to significantly reduce instruction counts; they also add to the complexity of building a machine. Thus, the usage of various addressing modes is quite important in helping the architect choose what to include. While many measurements of addressing mode usage are machine dependent, others are largely independent of the machine architecture. Some of the more important machine-independent measurements will be examined in this chapter. But, before we look at this type of measurement, let's look at how often these various memory addressing modes are used.

Figure 3.12 shows the results of measuring addressing mode usage patterns in our benchmarks—Gnu C Compiler (GCC), Spice, and TeX—on the VAX, which supports all the modes shown in Figure 3.11. We will look at further measurements of addressing mode usage on the VAX in the next chapter.

As Figure 3.12 shows, immediate and displacement addressing dominate addressing mode usage. Let's look at some properties of these two heavily used modes.

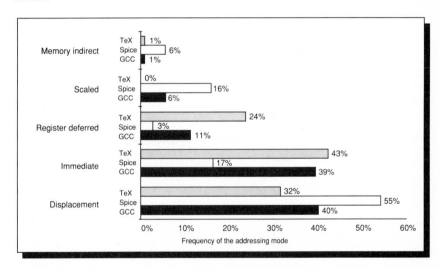

FIGURE 3.12 Summary of use of memory addressing modes (including immediates). The data were taken on a VAX using our three benchmark programs. Only the addressing modes with an average frequency of over 1% are shown. The PC-relative addressing modes, which are used almost exclusively for branches, are not included. Displacement mode includes all displacement lengths (8-, 16-, and 32-bit). Register modes, which are not counted, account for one-half of the operand references, while memory addressing modes (including immediate) account for the other half. The memory indirect mode on the VAX can use displacement, autoincrement, or autodecrement to form the initial memory address; in these programs, almost all the memory indirect references use displacement mode as the base. Of course, the compiler affects what addressing modes are used; we discuss this further in Section 3.7. These major addressing modes account for all but a few percent (0% to 3%) of the memory-accesses.

Displacement or Based Addressing Mode

The major question that arises for a displacement-style addressing mode is that of the range of displacements used. Based on the use of various displacement sizes, a decision of what sizes to support can be made. Choosing the displacement field sizes is important because they directly affect the instruction length. Measurements taken on the data access on a load/store architecture using our three benchmark programs are shown in Figure 3.13. We will look at branch offsets in the next section—data accessing patterns and branches are so different, little is gained by combining them.

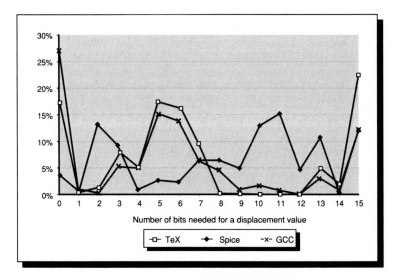

FIGURE 3.13   Displacement values are widely distributed. Though there is a large number of small values, there is also a fair number of large values. The wide distribution of displacement values is due to multiple storage areas for variables and different displacements used to access them. The different storage areas and their access patterns are discussed further in Section 3.7. The chart shows only the magnitude of the displacement and not the sign, which is heavily affected by the storage layout. The entry corresponding to 0 on the x axis shows the percentage of displacements of value 0. The vast majority of the displacements are positive, but a majority of the largest displacements (14+ bits) are negative. Again, this is due to the overall addressing scheme used by the compiler and might change with a different compilation scheme. Since this data was collected on a machine with 16-bit displacements, it cannot tell us anything about accesses that might want to use a longer displacement. Such accesses are broken into two separate instructions—the first of which loads the upper 16 bits of a base register. By counting the frequency of these "load immediate" instructions, which have limited use for other purposes, we can bound the number of accesses with displacements potentially larger than 16 bits. Such an analysis indicates GCC, Spice, and TeX may actually require a displacement longer than 16 bits for up to 5%, 13%, and 27% of the memory references, respectively. Furthermore, if the displacement is larger than 15 bits, it is likely to be quite a bit larger since most constants being loaded are large, as shown in Figure 3.15 (page 102).To evaluate the choice of displacement length, we might also want to examine a cumulative distribution, as shown in Exercise 3.3 (see Figure 3.35 on page 133).

Immediate or Literal Addressing Mode

Immediates can be used in arithmetic operations, in comparisons (primarily for branches), and in moves in which a constant is wanted in a register. The last case occurs for constants written in the code, which tend to be small, and for address constants, which can be large. For the use of immediates it is important to know whether they need to be supported for all operations or for only a subset. The chart in Figure 3.14 shows the frequency of immediates for the general classes of operations in an instruction set.

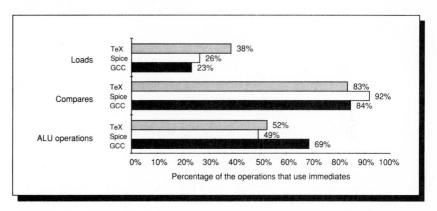

FIGURE 3.14   We see that for ALU operations about half the operations have an immediate operand, while for compares more than 85% of the occurrences use an immediate operand. (For ALU operations, shifts by a constant amount are included as operations with immediate operands.) For loads, the load immediate instructions load 16 bits into either half of a 32-bit register. These load immediates are not loads in a strict sense because they do not reference memory. In some cases, a pair of load immediates may be used to load a 32-bit constant, but this is rare. The compares include comparisons against zero that are done in conditional branches based on this comparison. These measurements were taken on a MIPS R2000 architecture with full compiler optimization. The compiler attempts to use simple compares against zero for branches whenever possible because these branches are efficiently supported in the architecture.

Another important instruction set measurement is the range of values for immediates. Like displacement values, the sizes of immediate values affect instruction lengths. As Figure 3.15 shows, immediate values that are small are most heavily used. However, large immediates are sometimes used, most likely in addressing calculations. The data in Figure 3.15 was taken on a VAX, which provides many instructions that have zero as an implicit operand. These include instructions to compare against zero and to store zero into a word. Because of the use of these instructions, the measurements show relatively infrequent use of zero.

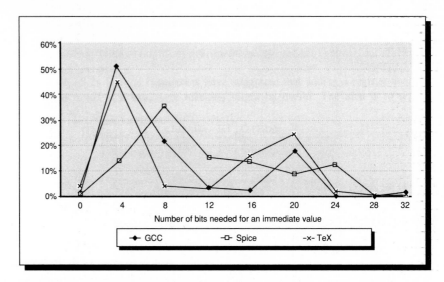

FIGURE 3.15 **The distribution of immediate values is shown.** The x axis shows the
number of bits needed to represent the magnitude of an immediate value—0 means the
immediate field value was 0. The vast majority of the immediate values are positive:
Overall, less than 6% of the immediates are negative. These measurements were taken on
a VAX, which supports a full range of immediates and sizes as operands to any instruction.
The measured programs are the standard set—GCC, Spice, and TeX.

Encoding of Addressing Modes

How the addressing modes of operands are encoded depends on the range of
addressing modes and the degree of independence between opcodes and modes.
For a small number of addressing modes or opcode/addressing mode combinations, the addressing mode can be encoded in the opcode. This works for the
IBM 360 with only five addressing modes and most operations offered in only
one or two modes. For a large number of combinations, typically a separate
address specifier is needed for each operand. The address specifier tells what
addressing mode the operand is using. In Chapter 4, we will see how these two
types of encodings are used in several real instruction formats.

When encoding the instructions, the number of registers and the number of
addressing modes both have a significant impact on the size of instructions. This
is because the addressing mode field and the register field may appear many
times in a single instruction. In fact, for most instructions many more bits are
consumed encoding addressing modes and register fields than in specifying the
opcode. The architect must balance several competing forces when encoding the
instruction set:

1. The desire to have as many registers and addressing modes as possible.

2. The impact of the size of the register and addressing mode fields on the average instruction size and hence on the average program size.

3. A desire to have instructions encode into lengths that will be easy to handle in the implementation. As a minimum, the architect wants instructions to be in multiples of bytes, rather than an arbitrary length. Many architects have chosen to use a fixed-length instruction to gain implementation benefits while sacrificing average code size.

Since the addressing modes and register fields make up such a large percentage of the instruction bits, their encoding will significantly affect how easy it is for an implementation to decode the instructions. The importance of having easily decoded instructions is discussed in Chapters 5 and 6.

3.5 | Operations in the Instruction Set

The operators supported by most instruction set architectures can be categorized, as in Figure 3.16. In Section 3.8, we look at the use of operations in a general fashion (e.g. memory references, ALU operations, and branches). In Chapter 4, we will examine the use of various instruction operations in detail for four different architectures. Because the instructions used to implement control flow are largely independent of other instruction set choices and because the measurements of branch and jump behavior are also fairly independent of other measurements, we examine the use of control-flow instructions next.

Operator type	Examples
Arithmetic and logical	Integer arithmetic and logical operations: add, and, subtract, or
Data transfer	Loads/stores (move instructions on machines with memory addressing)
Control	Branch, jump, procedure call and return, traps
System	Operating system call, virtual memory management instructions
Floating point	Floating-point operations: add, multiply
Decimal	Decimal add, decimal multiply, decimal-to-character conversions
String	String move, string compare, string search

FIGURE 3.16 Categories of instruction operators and examples of each. All machines generally provide a full set of operations for the first three categories. The support for system functions in the instruction set varies widely among architectures, but all machines must have some instruction support for basic system functions. The amount of support in the instruction set for the last three categories may vary from none to an extensive set of special instructions. Floating-point instructions will be provided in any machine that is intended for use in an application that makes much use of floating point. These instructions are sometimes part of an optional instruction set. Decimal and string instructions are sometimes primitives, as in the VAX or the IBM 360, or may be synthesized by the compiler from simpler instructions. Examples of instruction sets appear in Appendix B, while Appendix C contains measurements of typical usage. We will examine four different instruction sets and their usage in detail in Chapter 4.

Instructions for Control Flow

As Figure 3.17 shows, there is no consistent terminology for instructions that change the flow of control. Until the IBM 7030, control-flow instructions were typically called *transfers*. Beginning with the 7030, the name *branch* began to be used. Later, machines introduced additional names. Throughout this book we will use *jump* when the change in control is unconditional and *branch* when the change is conditional.

Machine	Year	"Branch"	"Jump"
IBM 7030	1960	All control transfers—addressing is PC-relative	
IBM 360/370	1965	All control transfers—no PC-relative	
DEC PDP-11	1970	PC-relative only, conditional and unconditional	All addressing modes; unconditional only
Intel 8086	1978		All transfers are jumps; conditional jumps are PC-relative only
DEC VAX	1978	Same as PDP-11	Same as PDP-11
MIPS R2000	1986	Conditional control transfer, always PC-relative	Unconditional jumps and call instructions

FIGURE 3.17   Machines, dates, and the names associated with control transfers in their architectures. These names vary widely based on whether the transfer is conditional or unconditional and on whether it is PC-relative or not. The VAX, PDP-11, and MIPS R2000 architectures allow only PC-relative addressing for branches.

We can distinguish four different types of control-flow change:

1. Conditional branches
2. Jumps
3. Procedure calls
4. Procedure returns

We want to know the relative frequency of these events, as each event is different, may use different instructions, and may have different behavior. The frequencies of these control-flow instructions for a load/store machine running our benchmarks is shown in Figure 3.18.

The destination address of a branch must always be specified. This destination is specified explicitly in the instruction in the vast majority of cases—procedure return being the major exception—since for return the target is not known at compile time. The most common way to specify the destination is to supply a displacement that is added to the *program counter*, or PC. Branches of this sort are called *PC-relative* branches. PC-relative branches are advantageous because the branch target is often near the current instruction, and specifying the position relative to the current PC requires fewer bits. Using PC-relative addressing also permits the code to run independent of where it is loaded. This property, called *position-independence*, can eliminate some work when the program is linked and is also useful in programs linked during execution.

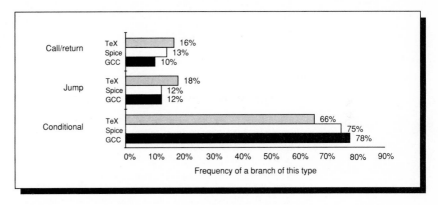

FIGURE 3.18 Breakdown of branches into three classes. Each branch is counted in one of three bars. Conditional branches clearly dominate. On average 90% of the jumps are PC-relative.

To implement returns and indirect branches in which the target is not known at compile time, a method other than PC-relative addressing is required. Here, there must be a way to specify the target dynamically, so that it can change at run-time. This may be as simple as naming a register that contains the target address. Alternatively, the branch may permit any addressing mode to be used to supply the target address.

A key question concerns how far branch targets are from branches. Knowing the distribution of these displacements will help in choosing what branch offsets to support and thus will affect the instruction length and encoding. Figure 3.19 (page 106) shows the distribution of displacements for PC-relative branches in instructions. About 75% of the branches are in the forward direction.

Since most changes in control flow are branches, deciding how to specify the branch condition is important. The three primary techniques in use and their advantages and disadvantages are shown in Figure 3.20 (page 106).

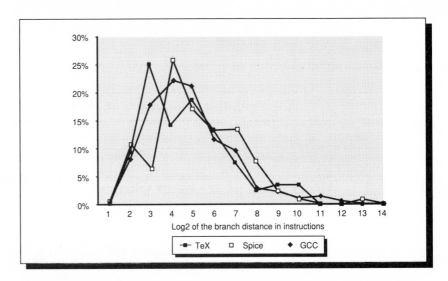

FIGURE 3.19 Branch distances in terms of number of instructions between the target and the branch instruction. The most frequent branches in Spice are to targets that are 8 to 15 instructions away (2^4). The weighted-arithmetic-mean branch target distance is 86 instructions (2^7). This tells us that short displacement fields often suffice for branches and that the designer can gain some encoding density by having a shorter instruction with a smaller branch displacement. These measurements were taken on a load/store machine (MIPS R2000 architecture). An architecture that requires fewer instructions for the same program, such as a VAX, would have shorter branch distances. Similarly, the number of bits needed for the displacement may change if the machine allows instructions to be arbitrarily aligned. A cumulative distribution of this branch displacement data is shown in Exercise 3.3 (see Figure 3.35 on page 133).

Name	How condition is tested	Advantages	Disadvantages
Condition code (CC)	Special bits are set by ALU operations, possibly under program control.	Sometimes condition is set for free.	CC is extra state. Condition codes constrain the ordering of instructions since they pass information from one instruction to a branch.
Condition register	Set arbitrary register with the result of a comparison.	Simple.	Uses up a register.
Compare and branch	Compare is part of the branch. Often compare is limited to subset.	One instruction rather than two for a branch.	May be too much work per instruction.

FIGURE 3.20 The major methods for evaluating branch conditions, their advantages, and disadvantages. Although condition codes can be set by ALU operations that are needed for other purposes, measurements on programs show that this rarely happens. The major implementation problems with condition codes arise when the condition code is set by a large or haphazardly chosen subset of the instructions, rather than being controlled by a bit in the instruction. Machines with compare and branch often limit the set of compares and use a condition register for more complex compares. Often, different techniques are used for branches based on floating-point comparison versus those based on integer comparison. This is reasonable since the number of branches that depend on floating-point comparisons is much smaller than the number depending on integer comparisons.

One of the most noticeable properties of branches is that a large number of the comparisons are simple equality or inequality tests, and a large number are comparisons with zero. Thus, some architectures choose to treat these comparisons as special cases, especially if a *compare and branch* instruction is being used. Figure 3.21 shows the frequency of different comparisons used for conditional branching. The data in Figure 3.14 said that a large percentage of the branches had an immediate operand (86%), and while not shown, 0 was the most heavily used immediate (83% of the immediates in branches). When we combine this with the data in Figure 3.21 we can see that a significant percentage (over 50%) of the compares in branches are simple tests for equality with zero.

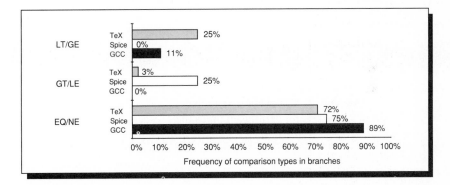

FIGURE 3.21 **Frequency of different types of compares in conditional branches.** This includes both the integer and floating-point compares in branches. Floating-point comparisons constitute 13% of the branch comparisons in Spice. Remember that earlier data in Figures 3.14 indicate that most comparisons are against an immediate operand. This immediate value is usually 0 (83% of the time).

Program	Percentage of backward branches	Percentage taken branches	Percentage of all control instructions that actually branch
GCC	26%	54%	63%
Spice	31%	51%	63%
TeX	17%	54%	70%
Average	25%	53%	65%

FIGURE 3.22 **Branch direction, branch-taken frequency, and frequency that the PC is changed.** The first column shows what percentage of all branches (both taken and untaken) are backward-going. The second column shows what percentage of all branches (remember that a branch is always conditional) are taken. The final column shows what percentage of all control-flow instructions actually cause a nonsequential transfer in the flow. This last column is computed by combining data from the second column and the data in Figure 3.18 (page 105).

We will say that a branch is *taken* if the condition tested by the branch is true and the next instruction to be executed is the target of the branch. All jumps, therefore, are taken. Figure 3.22 shows the branch-direction distribution, the frequency of taken (conditional) branches, and the percentage of control-flow instructions that change the PC. Most backward-going branches are loop branches, and typically loop branches are taken with about 90% probability.

Many programs have a higher percentage of loop branches, thus boosting the frequency of taken branches over 60%. Overall, branch behavior is application-dependent and sometimes compiler-dependent. Compiler dependencies arise because of changes to the control flow made by optimizing compilers to improve the execution time of loops.

Example

Assuming that 90% of the backward-going branches are taken, find the probability that a forward-going branch is taken using the averaged data in Figure 3.22.

Answer

The average frequency of taken branches is the sum of the backward-taken and forward-taken times their respective frequencies:

$$\% \text{ taken branches } = (\% \text{ taken backward} * \% \text{ backward}) + (\% \text{ taken forward} * \% \text{ forward})$$

$$53\% = (90\% * 25\%) + (\% \text{ taken forward} * 75\%)$$

$$\% \text{ taken forward } = \frac{53\% - 22.5\%}{75\%}$$

$$\% \text{ taken forward } = 40.7\%$$

It is not unusual to see the majority of forward branches be untaken. The behavior of forward-going branches often varies among programs.

Procedure calls and returns include control transfer and possibly some state saving; at a minimum the return address must be saved somewhere. Some architectures provide a mechanism to save the registers, while others require the compiler to generate instructions. There are two basic conventions in use to save registers. *Caller-saving* means that the calling procedure must save the registers that it wants preserved for access after the call. *Callee-saving* means that the called procedure must save the registers it wants to use. There are times when caller save must be used due to access patterns to globally visible variables in two different procedures. For example, suppose we have a procedure P1 that calls procedure P2, and both procedures manipulate the global variable x. If P1 had allocated x to a register it must be sure to save x to a location known by P2 before the call to P2. A compiler's ability to discover when a called procedure may access register-allocated quantities is complicated by the possibility of separate compilation, and situations where P2 may not touch *x,* but P2 can call another procedure, P3, that may access *x.* Because of these complications, most compilers will conservatively caller save **any** variable that **may be** accessed during a call.

In the cases where either convention could be used, some will be more optimal with callee-save and some will be more optimal with caller-save. As a result, the most sophisticated compilers use a combination of the two mechanisms, and the register allocator may choose which register to use for a variable based on the convention. Later in this chapter we will examine how well more sophisticated instructions match the needs of the compiler for this function, and in Chapter 8 we will look at hardware buffering schemes for supporting register save and restore.

3.6 | Type and Size of Operands

How is the type of an operand designated? There are two primary alternatives: First, the type of an operand may be designated by encoding it in the opcode—this is the method used most often. Alternatively, the data can be annotated with tags that are interpreted by the hardware. These tags specify the type of the operand, and the operation is chosen accordingly. Machines with tagged data, however, are extremely rare. The Burroughs' architectures are the most extensive example of tagged architectures. Symbolics also built a series of machines that used tagged data items for implementing LISP.

Usually the type of an operand—for example, integer, single-precision floating point, character—effectively gives its size. Common operand types include character (one byte), halfword (16 bits), word (32 bits), single-precision floating point (also one word), and double-precision floating point (two words). Characters are represented as either EBCDIC, used by the IBM mainframe architectures, or ASCII, used by everyone else. Integers are almost universally represented as two's complement binary numbers. Until recently, most computer manufacturers chose their own floating-point representation. However, in the past few years, a standard for floating point, the IEEE standard 754, has become the choice of most new computers. The IEEE floating-point standard is discussed in detail in Appendix A.

Some architectures provide operations on character strings, although such operations are usually quite limited and treat each byte in the string as a single character. Typical operations supported on character strings are comparisons and moves.

For business applications, some architectures support a decimal format, usually called *packed decimal.* Packed decimal is *binary-coded decimal*—four bits are used to encode the values 0–9, and two decimal digits are packed into each byte. Numeric character strings are sometimes called unpacked decimal, and operations—called packing and unpacking—are usually provided for converting back and forth between them.

Our benchmarks use byte or character, halfword (short integer), word (integer), and floating-point data types. Figure 3.23 shows the dynamic distribution of the sizes of objects referenced from memory for these programs. The frequency of access to different data types helps in deciding what types are most important to support efficiently. Should the machine have a 64-bit access path, or would taking two cycles to access a doubleword be satisfactory? How important is it to support byte accesses as primitives, which, as we saw earlier, require an alignment network? In Figure 3.23, memory references are used to examine the types of data being accessed. In some architectures, objects in registers may be accessed as bytes or halfwords. However, such access is very infrequent—on the VAX, it accounts for no more than 12% of register references, or roughly 6% of all operand accesses in these programs.

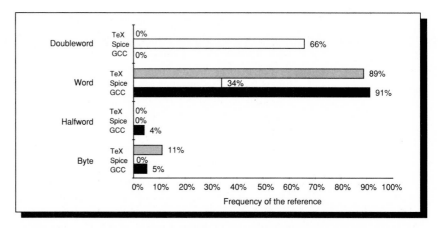

FIGURE 3.23 Distribution of data accesses by size for the benchmark programs. Access to the major data type (word or doubleword) clearly dominates. Reads outnumbered writes of data items by a factor of 1.6 for TeX to a factor of 2.5 for Spice. The doubleword data type is used solely for double-precision floating point in Spice. Spice makes only small use of single-precision floating point; most word references in Spice are to integers. These measurements were taken on the memory traffic generated on a load/store architecture.

In the next chapter we will look extensively at the differences in instruction mix and other architectural measurements on four very different machines. But before we do that, it will be helpful to take a brief look at modern compiler technology and its effect on program properties.

3.7 | The Role of High-Level Languages and Compilers

Today most programming is done in high-level languages. This means that since most instructions executed are the output of a compiler, an instruction set architecture is essentially a compiler target. In earlier times, architectural decisions were often made to ease assembly language programming. Because performance of a computer will be significantly affected by the compiler, understanding compiler technology today is critical to designing and efficiently implementing an instruction set. In earlier days it was popular to try to isolate the compiler technology and its effect on hardware performance from the architecture and its performance, just as it was popular to try to separate an architecture from its implementation. This is extremely difficult, if not impossible, with today's compilers and architectures. Architectural choices affect the quality of the code that can be generated for a machine and the complexity of building a good compiler for it. Isolating the compiler from the hardware is likely to be misleading. In this section we will discuss the critical goals in the instruction set primarily from the compiler viewpoint. What features will lead to high-quality code? What makes it easy to write efficient compilers for an architecture?

The Structure of Recent Compilers

To begin, let's look at what optimizing compilers are like today. The structure of recent compilers is shown in Figure 3.24.

A compiler writer's first goal is correctness—all valid programs must be compiled correctly. The second goal is usually speed of the compiled code. Typically, a whole set of other goals follow these first two, including fast compilation, debugging support, and interoperability among languages. Normally, the passes in the compiler transform higher-level, more abstract representations into progressively lower-level representations, eventually reaching the instruction set. This structure helps manage the complexity of the transformations and makes writing a bug-free compiler easier.

The complexity of writing a correct compiler is a major limitation on the amount of optimization that can be done. Although the multiple-pass structure helps reduce compiler complexity, it also means that the compiler must order and perform some transformations before others. In the diagram of the optimizing compiler in Figure 3.24, we can see that certain high-level optimizations are performed long before it is known what the resulting code will look like in detail. Once such a transformation is made, the compiler can't afford to go back and revisit all steps, possibly undoing transformations. This would be prohibitive, both in compilation time and in complexity. Thus, compilers make assumptions about the ability of later steps to deal with certain problems. For example, compilers usually have to choose which procedure calls to expand inline before they know the exact size of the procedure being called. Compiler writers call this problem the *phase-ordering problem*.

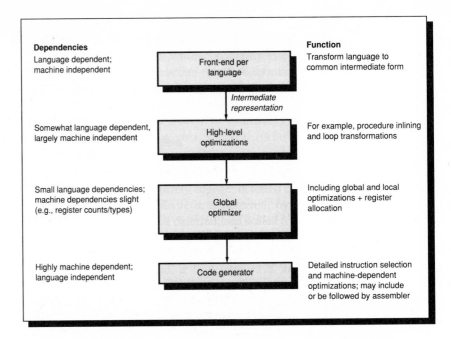

FIGURE 3.24 Current compilers typically consist of two to four passes, with more highly optimizing compilers having more passes. A *pass* is simply one phase in which the compiler reads and transforms the entire program. (The term "phase" is often used interchangeably with "pass.") The optimizing passes are designed to be optional and may be skipped when faster compilation is the goal and lower quality code is acceptable. This structure maximizes the probability that a program compiled at various levels of optimization will produce the same output when given the same input. Because the optimizing passes are also separated, multiple languages can use the same optimizing and code-generation passes. Only a new front end is required for a new language. The high-level optimization mentioned here, procedure inlining, is also called *procedure integration.*

How does this ordering of transformations interact with the instruction set architecture? A good example occurs with the optimization called *global common subexpression elimination.* This optimization finds two instances of an expression that compute the same value and saves the value of the first computation in a temporary. It then uses the temporary value, eliminating the second computation of the expression. For this optimization to be significant, the temporary must be allocated to a register. Otherwise, the cost of storing the temporary in memory and later reloading it may negate the savings gained by not recomputing the expression. There are, in fact, cases where this optimization actually slows down code when the temporary is not register allocated. Phase ordering complicates this problem, because register allocation is typically done near the end of the global optimization pass, just before code generation. Thus, an optimizer that performs this optimization **must** assume that the register allocator will allocate the temporary to a register.

Because of the central role that register allocation plays, both in speeding up the code and in making other optimizations useful, it is one of the most important—if not the most important—optimizations. Recent register allocation algorithms are based on a technique called *graph coloring*. The basic idea behind graph coloring is to construct a graph representing the possible candidates for allocation to a register and then to use the graph to allocate registers. As shown in Figure 3.25, each candidate for a register corresponds to a node in the graph, called an *interference graph*. The arcs between the nodes show where the ranges of usage for variables (called *live ranges*) overlap. The compiler then tries to color the graph using a number of colors equal to the number of registers available for allocation. In a graph coloring, no adjacent nodes may have the same color. This restriction is equivalent to saying that no two variables with overlapping uses may be allocated to the same register. However, nodes that are not connected by an arc may have the same color, allowing variables whose uses do not overlap to use the same register. Thus, a coloring of the graph corresponds to an allocation of the active variables to registers. For example, the four nodes in Figure 3.25 can be colored with two colors, meaning the code only needs two registers for allocation. Although the problem of coloring a graph is NP-complete, there are heuristic algorithms that work well in practice.

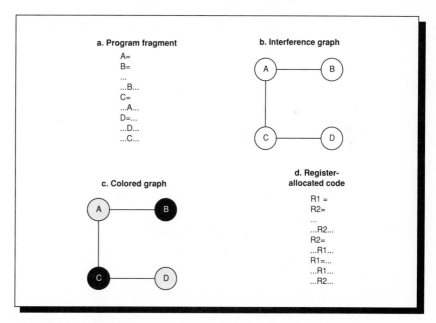

FIGURE 3.25   Graph coloring is used to allocate registers by constructing an interference graph that is colored heuristically using a number of colors corresponding to the register count. Part b shows the interference graph corresponding to the code fragment shown in part a. Each variable corresponds to a node, and the arcs show the overlap of the active ranges of the variables. The graph can be colored with two colors, as shown in part c, and this corresponds to the register allocation of part d.

Graph coloring works best when there are at least 16 (and preferably more) general-purpose registers available for global allocation for integer variables and additional registers for floating point. Unfortunately, graph coloring does not work very well when the number of registers is small because the heuristic algorithms for coloring the graph are likely to fail. The emphasis in the approach is to achieve 100% allocation of active variables.

Optimizations performed by modern compilers can be classified by the style of the transformation, as follows:

1. High-level optimizations—often done on the source with output fed to later optimization passes.

Optimization name	Explanation	Percent of the total number of optimizing transforms
High-level	**At or near the source level; machine-independent**	
Procedure integration	Replace procedure call by procedure body	N.M.
Local	**Within straightline code**	
Common subexpression elimination	Replace two instances of the same computation by single copy	18%
Constant propagation	Replace all instances of a variable that is assigned a constant with the constant	22%
Stack height reduction	Rearrange expression tree to minimize resources needed for expression evaluation	N.M.
Global	**Across a branch**	
Global common subexpression elimination	Same as local, but this version crosses branches	13%
Copy propagation	Replace all instances of a variable A that has been assigned X (i.e., $A=X$) with X	11%
Code motion	Remove code from a loop that computes same value each iteration of the loop	16%
Induction variable elimination	Simplify/eliminate array-addressing calculations within loops	2%
Machine-dependent	**Depends on machine knowledge**	
Strength reduction	Many examples, such as replace multiply by a constant with adds and shifts	N.M.
Pipeline scheduling	Reorder instructions to improve pipeline performance	N.M.
Branch offset optimization	Choose the shortest branch displacement that reaches target	N.M.

FIGURE 3.26   Major types of optimizations and examples in each class. The third column lists the static frequency with which some of the common optimizations are applied in a set of 12 small FORTRAN and Pascal programs. The percentage is the portion of the static optimizations that are of the specified type. These data tell us about the relative frequency of occurrence of various optimizations. There are nine local and global optimizations done by the compiler included in the measurement. Six of these optimizations are covered in the figure, and the remaining three account for 18% of the total static occurrences. The abbreviation "N.M." means that the number of occurrences of that optimization was not measured. Machine-dependent optimizations are usually done in a code generator, and none of those were measured in this experiment. The data are from Chow [1983], and were collected using the Stanford UCODE compiler.

2. Local optimizations—optimize code only within a straightline code fragment (called a *basic block* by compiler people).

3. Global optimizations—extend the local optimizations across branches and introduce a set of transformations aimed at optimizing loops.

4. Register allocation.

5. Machine-dependent optimizations—attempt to take advantage of specific architectural knowledge.

It is sometimes difficult to separate some of the simpler optimizations—local and machine-dependent optimizations—from transformations done in the code generator. Examples of typical optimizations are given in Figure 3.26. The last column of Figure 3.26 indicates the frequency with which the listed optimizing transforms were applied to the source program. Data on the effect of various optimizations on program run-time are shown in Figure 3.27. The data in Figure 3.27 demonstrate the importance of register allocation, which adds the largest single improvement. We will look at the overall effect of optimization on our three benchmarks later in this section.

Optimizations performed	Percent faster
Procedure integration only	10%
Local optimizations only	5%
Local optimizations + register allocation	26%
Global and local optimizations	14%
Local and global optimizations + register allocation	63%
Local and global optimizations + procedure integration + register allocation	81%

FIGURE 3.27 Performance effects of various levels of optimization. Performance gains are shown as what percent faster the optimized programs were compared to the unoptimized programs. When register allocation is turned off, data are loaded into, or stored from, the registers on every individual use. These measurements are also from Chow [1983] and are for 12 small FORTRAN and Pascal programs.

The Impact of Compiler Technology on the Architect's Decisions

The interaction of compilers and high-level languages significantly affects how programs use an instruction set. To better understand this interaction, three important questions to ask are:

1. How are variables allocated and addressed? How many registers are needed to allocate variables appropriately?

2. What is the impact of optimization techniques on instruction mixes?

3. What control structures are used and with what frequency?

To address the first questions, we must look at the three separate areas in which current high-level languages allocate their data:

- The *stack*—used to allocate local variables. The stack is grown and shrunk on procedure call or return, respectively. Objects on the stack are addressed relative to the stack pointer and are primarily scalars (single variables) rather than arrays. The stack is used for activation records, **not** as a stack for evaluating expressions. Hence values are almost never pushed or popped on the stack.

- The *global data area*—used to allocate statically declared objects, such as global variables and constants. A large percentage of these objects are arrays or other aggregate data structures.

- The *heap*—used to allocate dynamic objects that do not adhere to a stack discipline. Objects in the heap are accessed with pointers and are typically not scalars.

Register allocation is much more effective for stack-allocated objects than for global variables, and register allocation is essentially impossible for heap-allocated objects because they are accessed with pointers. Global variables and some stack variables are impossible to allocate because they are *aliased*, which means that there are multiple ways to refer to the address of a variable making it illegal to put it into a register. (All heap variables are effectively aliased.) For example, consider the following code sequence (where & returns the address of a variable and * dereferences a pointer):

```
p = &a       -- gets address of a in p
a = ...       -- assigns to a directly
*p = ...      -- uses p to assign to a
...a...       -- accesses a
```

The variable "a" could not be register allocated across the assignment to *p without generating incorrect code. Aliasing causes a substantial problem because it is often difficult or impossible to decide what objects a pointer may refer to. A compiler must be conservative; many compilers will not allocate **any** local variables of a procedure in a register when there is a pointer that may refer to **one** of the local variables.

After register allocation, memory traffic consists of five types of references:

1. Unallocated reference—a potentially allocatable memory reference that was not assigned to a register.

2. Global scalar—a reference to a global scalar variable not allocated to a register. These variables are usually sparsely accessed and thus rarely allocated.

3. Save/restore memory reference—a memory reference made to save or restore a register (during a procedure call) that contains an allocated variable and is not aliased.

4. A required stack reference—a reference to a stack variable that is required due to aliasing possibilities. For example, if the address of the stack variable were taken, then that variable cannot usually be register allocated. Also included in this category are any data items that were caller saved due to aliasing behavior—such as a potential reference by a called procedure.

5. A computed reference—any heap reference or any reference to a stack variable via a pointer or array index.

Figure 3.28 shows how these classes of memory traffic contribute to total memory traffic for GCC and TeX benchmark programs run with an optimizing compiler on a load/store machine and varying the number of registers used. The

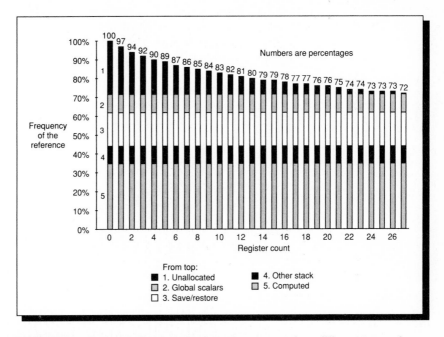

FIGURE 3.28 The percentage of memory references made to different types of variables as the register count increases. This data is averaged between TeX and GCC, which use only integer variables. The decreasing percentage represented by the top bar is the set of references that are candidates for allocation but are not actually allocated with the indicated number of registers. This data was collected for the DLX load/store machine described in the next chapter. The register allocator has 27 integer registers; the first seven integer registers capture about half of the references that can be allocated to registers. While each of the other four components contributes something to the remaining memory traffic, the dominant contribution is computed references to heap-based objects and array elements, which cannot be register allocated. Some small percentage of the required stack references may be contributed when the register allocator runs out of registers; however, from other measurements on the register allocator we know that this contribution is very small [Chow and Hennessy, 1990].

number of memory references to objects in categories 2 through 5 above is constant because they can never be allocated to registers by this compiler. (The save/restore references were measured with the full set of registers.) The number of allocatable references that are unallocated drops as the register count increases. References to objects that could be allocated but that are accessed only once are allocated by the code generator using a set of temporary registers. These references will be counted as required stack references; other allocation strategies might cause them to be treated as save/restore traffic.

The data in Figure 3.28 shows only the integer registers. The percentage of allocatable references with a given register count is computed by examining the frequency of access to registers with a compiler that generally tries to use as small a number of registers as possible. The percentage of the references captured in a given number of registers depends intimately on the compiler and its register-allocation strategy. This compiler cannot use more than the 27 integer registers available for allocating variables; additionally, some registers have a preferred use (such as those used for parameters). We cannot predict from this data how well the compiler might be able to use 100 registers. Given a substantially larger number of registers, the compiler could use the registers to reduce

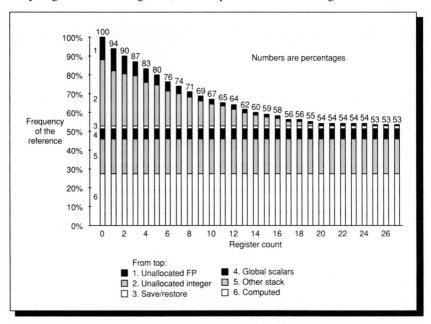

FIGURE 3.29 The percentage of references captured by the integer and floating-point register files for Spice increases to almost 50% with a full register set. Each increment on the x axis adds one integer register and one single-precision (SP), floating-point (FP) register. Thus, the point corresponding to a register count of 12 stands for 12 integer and 12 SP FP registers. Remember that most of the Spice FP data is double precision, which requires two FP registers per datum. As in Figure 3.28, about seven integer registers capture half of the integer references, but only about five registers are needed to capture half the FP references.

the save/restore memory references and the references for global scalars. However, neither class of memory references can be completely eliminated. In the past, compiler technology has made steady progress in its ability to use ever larger register sets, and we can probably expect this to continue, although the percentage of allocatable references may bound the value of larger register sets.

Figure 3.29 shows the same type of data, but this time for Spice, which uses both the integer and floating-point registers. The effect of register allocation is very different for Spice compared to GCC and TeX. First, the percentage of remaining memory traffic is smaller. This probably arises because the absence of pointers in FORTRAN makes register allocation more effective for Spice than for programs in C (i.e., GCC and TeX). Second, the amount of save/restore traffic is much lower. In addition to these differences, we can see that it takes fewer registers to capture the allocatable floating-point references. This is probably because a far smaller percentage of the FP references are allocatable, since the majority are to arrays.

Our second question concerns how an optimizer affects the mix of instructions executed. Figures 3.30 and 3.31 address this issue for the benchmarks used here. The data was taken on a load/store machine using full global optimization that includes all of the global and local optimizations listed in Figure 3.26 (page

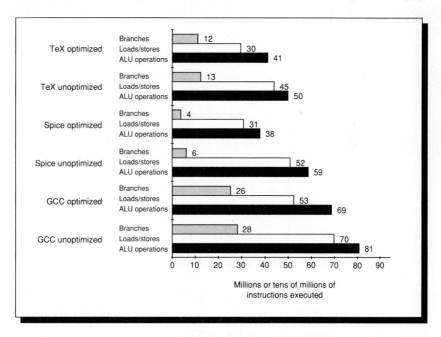

FIGURE 3.30 The effects of optimization in absolute instruction counts. The x axis is the number of instructions executed in millions for GCC and TeX and in tens of millions for Spice. The unoptimized programs execute 21%, 58%, and 30% more instructions for GCC, Spice, and TeX, respectively. This data was taken on a DECstation 3100 using −O2 optimization, as was the data in Figure 3.31. Optimizations that do not affect instruction count, but may affect instruction cycle counts, are not measured here.

114). Differences between optimized and unoptimized code are shown in both absolute and relative terms. The most obvious effect of optimization—besides decreasing the total instruction count—is to increase the relative frequency of branches by decreasing the number of memory references and ALU operations more rapidly than the number of branches (which are decreased only slightly). We show an example of how optimized and unoptimized code differ on a VAX in the Fallacies and Pitfalls section.

Finally, with what frequency are various control structures used? These are important numbers because branches are among the hardest instructions to make go fast and are very difficult to reduce with the compiler. The data in Figures 3.30 and 3.31 give us a good idea of the branch frequency—from 6.5 to 18 instructions are executed between two branches or jumps (including the branch or jump itself). Procedure calls occur about 12 to 13 times less frequently than branches, or in the range of once every 87 to 200 instructions for our programs. Spice has both the lowest percentage of branches and the fewest procedure calls per instruction by nearly a factor of two.

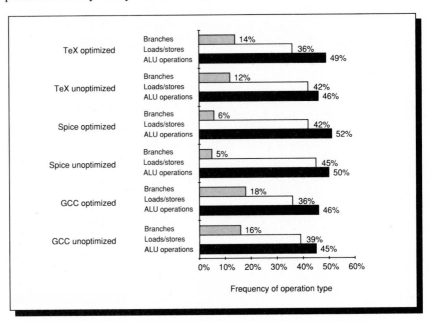

FIGURE 3.31   The effects of optimization on the relative mix of instructions for the data in Figure 3.30.

How the Architect Can Help the Compiler Writer

Today, the complexity of a compiler does not come from translating simple statements like A = B + C. Most programs are "locally simple," and simple translations work fine. Rather, complexity arises because programs are large and globally complex in their interactions, and because the structure of compilers means that decisions must be made about what code sequence is best, one step at a time.

Compiler writers often are working under their own corollary of a basic principle in architecture: "Make the frequent cases fast and the rare case correct." That is, if we know which cases are frequent and which are rare, and if generating code for both is straightforward, then the quality of the code for the rare case may not be very important—but it must be correct!

Some instruction set properties help the compiler writer. These properties should not be thought of as hard and fast rules, but rather as guidelines that will make it easier to write a compiler that will generate efficient and correct code.

1. *Regularity.* Whenever it makes sense, the three primary components of an instruction set—the operations, the data types, and the addressing modes—should be orthogonal. Two aspects of an architecture are said to be *orthogonal* if they are independent. For example, the operations and addressing modes are orthogonal if for every operation to which a certain addressing mode can be applied, all addressing modes are applicable. This helps simplify code generation and is particularly important when the decision about what code to generate is split into two passes in the compiler. A good counterexample of this property is restricting what registers can be used for a certain class of instructions. This can result in the compiler finding itself with lots of available registers, but none of the right kind!

2. *Provide primitives, not solutions.* Special features that "match" a language construct are often unusable. Attempts to support high-level languages may work only with one language, or do more or less than is required for a correct and efficient implementation of the language. Some examples of how these attempts have failed are given in Section 3.9.

3. *Simplify tradeoffs among alternatives.* One of the toughest jobs a compiler writer has is figuring out what instruction sequence will be best for every segment of code that arises. In earlier days, instruction counts or total code size might have been good metrics, but—as we saw in the last chapter—this is no longer true. With caches and pipelining, the tradeoffs have become very complex. Anything the designer can do to help the compiler writer understand the costs of alternative code sequences would help improve the code. One of the most difficult instances of complex tradeoffs occurs in a memory–memory architecture in deciding how many times a variable should be referenced before it is cheaper to load it into a register. This threshold is hard to compute and, in fact, may vary among models of the same architecture.

4. *Provide instructions that bind the quantities known at compile time as constants.* A compiler writer hates the thought of the machine interpreting at run time a value that was known at compile time. Good counterexamples of this

principle include instructions that interpret values that were fixed at compile time. For instance, the VAX procedure call instruction (CALLS) dynamically interprets a mask saying what registers to save on a call, but the mask is fixed at compile time, though in some cases it may not be known by the caller if separate compilation is used.

3.8 | Putting It All Together: How Programs Use Instruction Sets

What do typical programs do? This section will investigate and compare the behavior of our benchmark programs running on a load/store architecture and on a memory–memory architecture. The compiler technology for these two different architectures differs and these differences affect the overall measurements.

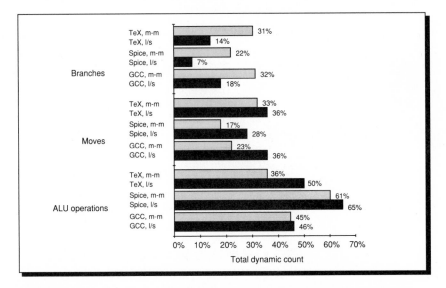

FIGURE 3.32 The instruction distributions for our benchmarks differ in straight forward ways when run on a load/store architecture (l/s) and on a memory–memory architecture (m–m). On the load/store machine, moves are loads or stores. On the memory–memory machine, moves include transfers between two locations; either of the operands may be a register or a memory location. However, the majority of the moves involve one register and a memory location. The load/store machine exhibits a higher percentage of moves because it is a load/store machine—for data to be operated on it must be moved into the registers. The lower relative frequency of branches is primarily a function of the load/store machine's use of more instructions in the other two classes. This data was measured with optimization on a VAXstation 3100 for the memory–memory machine and on DLX, which we discuss in detail in the next chapter, for the load/store machine. The input used is smaller than that in Chapter 2 to make it possible to collect the data on the VAX.

We can examine the behavior of typical programs by looking at the frequency of three basic operations: memory references, ALU operations, and control-flow instructions (branches and jumps). Figure 3.32 does this for a load/store architecture with one addressing mode (a hypothetical machine called DLX that we define in the next chapter) and for a memory–memory architecture with many addressing modes (the VAX). The load/store architecture has more registers, and its compiler places more emphasis on reducing memory traffic. Considering the enormous differences in the instruction sets of these two machines, the results are rather similar.

The same machines and programs are used in Figure 3.33, but the data represent absolute counts of instructions executed, instruction words, and data references. This chart shows a clear difference in instruction count: The load/store machine requires more instructions. Recall that this difference does not imply anything about the relative performance of machines based on these architectures.

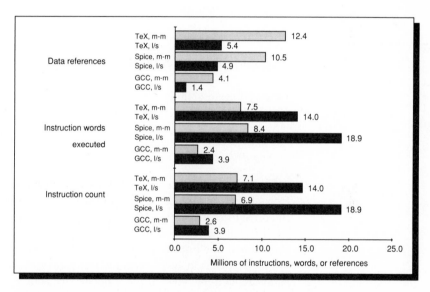

FIGURE 3.33 Absolute counts for dynamic events on a load/store and memory–memory machine. The counts are (from bottom to top) dynamic instructions, instruction words (instruction bytes divided by four), and data references (these may be byte, word, or doubleword). Each reference is counted once. Differences in the size of the register set and the compiler probably explain the large difference in the number of data references. In the case of Spice, the large difference in the total number of registers available for allocation is probably the basic reason for the large difference in total data accesses. This data was collected for the same programs, inputs, and machines as the data in Figure 3.32.

This chart also shows the number of data references made by each machine. From the data in Figure 3.32 and the instruction counts, we might guess that the total number of memory accesses made by the memory–memory machine would be much lower than the number made on the load/store machine. But the data in Figure 3.33 indicate that this hypothesis is false. The large difference in data references balances the difference in instruction references between the architectures, so that the load/store machine uses about the same memory bandwidth at the architectural level. This difference in data references probably arises because the load/store machine has many more registers, and its compiler does a better job of register allocation. For allocating integer quantities, the load/store machine has more than twice as many registers available. In total for integer and floating-point variables, more than four times as many registers are available for the compiler to use on the load/store architecture. This gap in register count combined with compiler differences is the most likely basis for the difference in data bandwidth.

We have seen how architectural measures can run counter to the designer's intuition, and that some of these measures do not directly relate to performance. In the next section we will see that architects' attempts to model machines directly after high-level software features can go awry.

3.9 | Fallacies and Pitfalls

Time and again architects have tripped on common, but erroneous, beliefs. In this section we look at a few of them.

Pitfall: Designing a "high-level" instruction set feature specifically oriented to supporting a high-level language structure.

Attempts to incorporate high-level language features in the instruction set have led architects to provide powerful instructions with a wide range of flexibility. But often these instructions do more work than is required in the frequent case or don't match the requirements of the language exactly. Many such efforts have been aimed at eliminating what in the 1970s was called the "semantic gap." While the idea is to supplement the instruction set with additions that bring the hardware up to the level of the language, the additions can generate what Wulf [1981] has called a "semantic clash":

... by giving too much semantic content to the instruction, the machine designer made it possible to use the instruction only in limited contexts. [p. 43]

More often the instructions are simply overkill—they are too general for the most frequent case, resulting in unneeded work and a slower instruction. Again, the VAX CALLS is a good example. CALLS uses a callee-save strategy (the registers to be saved are specified by the callee) **but** the saving is done by the call instruction in the caller. The CALLS instruction begins with the arguments pushed on the stack, and then takes the following steps:

1. Align the stack if needed.

2. Push the argument count on the stack.

3. Save the registers indicated by the procedure call mask on the stack (as mentioned in Section 3.7). The mask is kept in the called procedure's code—this permits callee-save to be done by the caller even with separate compilation.

4. Push the return address on the stack, then push the top and base of stack pointers for the activation record.

5. Clear the condition codes, which sets the trap enables to a known state.

6. Push a word for status information and a zero word on the stack.

7. Update the two stack pointers.

8. Branch to the first instruction of the procedure.

The vast majority of calls in real programs do not require this amount of overhead. Most procedures know their argument counts and a much faster linkage convention can be established using registers to pass arguments rather than the stack. Furthermore, the call instruction forces two registers to be used for linkage, while many languages require only one linkage register. Many attempts to support procedure call and activation stack management have failed to be useful either because they do not match the language needs or because they are too general, and hence too expensive to use.

The VAX designers provided a simpler instruction, JSB, that is much faster since it only pushes the return PC on the stack and jumps to the procedure (see Exercise 3.11). However, most VAX compilers use the more costly CALLS instructions. The call instructions were included in the architecture to standardize the procedure linkage convention. Other machines have standardized their calling convention by agreement among compiler writers and without requiring the overhead of a complex, very general procedure call instruction.

Fallacy: It costs nothing to provide a level of functionality that exceeds what is required in the usual case.

A far more serious architectural pitfall than the previous one was encountered by a few machines, such as the Intel 432, that provided only a high-overhead call instruction that handled the most rare cases. The call instruction on the Intel 432 always creates a new, protected context, and thus is fairly costly (see Chapter 8 for a further discussion on memory protection). However, most calls are within the same module and do not require a protected call. If a simpler call mechanism were available and used when possible, Dhrystone would run 20% faster on the 432 (see Colwell, et al. [1985]). When architects choose to have only a general and expensive instruction, compiler writers have no choice but to use the costly instruction, and suffer the unneeded overhead. A discussion of the experience of designers with providing fine-grain protection domains in hardware appears in the historical section of Chapter 8; the discussion further illustrates this fallacy.

Pitfall: Using a nonoptimizing compiler to measure the instruction set usage made by an optimizing compiler.

The instruction set usage of an optimizing and nonoptimizing compiler may be quite different. We saw some examples in Figure 3.31 (page 120). Figure 3.34 shows the differences in the use of addressing modes on a VAX for Spice, when it is compiled with the nonoptimizing UNIX F77 compiler and when it is compiled with DEC's optimizing FORTRAN compiler.

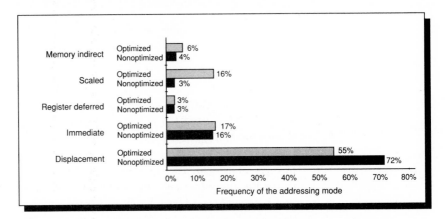

FIGURE 3.34 The address mode usage by an optimizing and nonoptimizing compiler can differ significantly. These measurements show the use of VAX addressing modes by Spice when it is compiled using a nonoptimizing compiler (f77) and an optimizing compiler (fort). In particular, the use of scaled mode is much higher for the optimizing compiler. The other VAX addressing modes account for the remaining 2-3% of the data memory references.

3.10 | Concluding Remarks

The earliest architectures were limited in their instruction sets by the hardware technology of that time. As soon as the hardware technology permitted, architects began looking for ways to support high-level languages. This search led to three distinct periods of thought about how to support programs efficiently. In the 1960s, stack architectures became popular. They were viewed as being a good match for high-level languages—and they probably were, given the compiler technology of the day. In the 1970s, the main concern of architects was how to reduce software costs. This concern was met primarily by replacing software with hardware, or by providing high-level architectures that could simplify the task of software designers. The result was both the high-level–language computer architecture movement and powerful architectures like the VAX, which has a large number of addressing modes, multiple data types, and a highly orthogonal architecture. In the 1980s, more sophisticated compiler technology and a renewed emphasis on machine performance has seen a return to simpler architectures, based mainly on the load/store style of machine. Continuing changes in how we program, the compiler technology we use, and the underlying hardware technology will no doubt make another direction more attractive in the future.

3.11 | Historical Perspective and References

One's eyebrows should rise whenever a future architecture is developed with a stack- or register-oriented instruction set.

Meyers [1978, 20]

The earliest computers, including the UNIVAC I, the EDSAC, and the IAS machines, were accumulator-based machines. The simplicity of this type of machine made it the natural choice when hardware resources were very constrained. The first general-purpose register machine was the Pegasus, built by Ferranti, Ltd. in 1956. The Pegasus had eight general-purpose registers, with R0 always being zero. Block transfers loaded the eight registers from the drum.

In 1963, Burroughs delivered the B5000. The B5000 was perhaps the first machine to seriously consider software and hardware-software tradeoffs. Barton and the designers at Burroughs made the B5000 a stack architecture (as described in Barton [1961]). Designed to support high-level languages such as ALGOL, this stack architecture used an operating system (MCP) written in a high-level language. The B5000 was also the first machine from a US manufacturer to support virtual memory. The B6500, introduced in 1968 (and discussed in Hauck and Dent [1968]), added hardware-managed activation records. In both the B5000 and B6500, the top two elements of the stack were kept in the CPU and the rest of the stack was kept in memory. The stack architecture yielded good code density, but only provided two high-speed storage locations. The authors of both the original IBM 360 paper [Amdahl et al. 1964] and the original PDP-11 paper [Bell et al. 1970] argue against the stack organization. They cite three major points in their arguments against stacks:

1. Performance is derived from fast registers, not the way they are used.

2. The stack organization is too limiting and requires many swap and copy operations.

3. The stack has a bottom, and when placed in slower memory there is a performance loss.

Stack-based machines fell out of favor in the late 1970s and essentially disappeared in the 1980s.

The term "computer architecture" was coined by IBM in 1964 for use with the IBM 360. Amdahl, Blaauw, and Brooks [1964] used the term to refer to the programmer-visible portion of the instruction set. They believed that a family of machines of the same architecture should be able to run the same software. Although this idea may seem obvious to us today, it was quite novel at that time. IBM, even though it was the leading company in the industry, had **five** different architectures before the 360. Thus, the notion of a company standardizing on a single architecture was a radical one. The 360 designers hoped that six different divisions of IBM could be brought together by defining a common architecture. Their definition of architecture was

... the structure of a computer that a machine language programmer must understand to write a correct (timing independent) program for that machine.

The term "machine language programmer" meant that compatibility would hold, even in assembly language, while "timing independent" allowed different implementations.

The IBM 360 was the first machine to sell in large quantities with both byte-addressing using 8-bit bytes and general purpose registers. The 360 also had register–memory and limited memory–memory instructions.

In 1964, Control Data delivered the first supercomputer, the CDC 6600. As discussed in Thornton [1964], he, Cray, and the other 6600 designers were the first to explore pipelining in depth. The 6600 was the first general-purpose, load/store machine. In the 1960s, the designers of the 6600 realized the need to simplify architecture for the sake of efficient pipelining. This interaction between architectural simplicity and implementation was largely neglected during the 1970s by microprocessor and minicomputer designers, but was brought back in the 1980s.

In the late 1960s and early 1970s, people realized that software costs were growing faster than hardware costs. McKeeman [1967] argued that compilers and operating systems were getting too big and too complex and taking too long to develop. Because of inferior compilers and the memory limitations of machines, most systems programs at the time were still written in assembly language. Many researchers proposed alleviating the software crisis by creating more powerful, software-oriented architectures. Tanenbaum [1978] studied the properties of high-level languages. Like other researchers, he found that most programs are simple. He then argued that architectures should be designed with this in mind and should optimize program size and ease of compilation. Tanenbaum proposed a stack machine with frequency-encoded instruction formats to accomplish these goals. However, as we have observed, program size does not translate directly to cost/performance, and stack machines faded out shortly after this work.

Strecker's article [1978] discusses how he and the other architects at DEC responded to this by designing the VAX architecture. The VAX was designed to simplify compilation of high-level languages. Compiler writers had complained about the lack of complete orthogonality in the PDP-11. The VAX architecture was designed to be highly orthogonal and to allow the mapping of a high-level–

language statement into a single VAX instruction. Additionally, the VAX designers tried to optimize code size because compiled programs were often too large for available memories. When it was introduced in 1978, the VAX was the first machine with a true memory–memory architecture.

While the VAX was being designed, a more radical approach, called *High-Level Language Computer Architecture* (HLLCA), was being advocated in the research community. This movement aimed to eliminate the gap between high-level languages and computer hardware—what Gagliardi [1973] called the "semantic gap"—by bringing the hardware "up to" the level of the programming language. Meyers [1982] provides a good summary of the arguments and a history of high-level–language computer architecture projects.

Smith, Rice, and their colleagues [1971] discuss the SYMBOL Project they started at Fairchild. SYMBOL became the largest and most famous of the HLLCA attempts. Its goal was to build a high-level–language, timesharing machine that would dramatically reduce programming time. The SYMBOL machine interpreted programs, written in its own new programming language, directly; the compiler and operating system were built into the hardware. The programming language was very dynamic—there were no variable declarations because the hardware interpreted every statement dynamically.

SYMBOL suffered from many problems, the most important of which were inflexibility, complexity, and performance. The SYMBOL hardware included the programming language, the operating system, and even the text editor. Programmers had no choice in what programming language they used, so subsequent advances in operating systems and programming languages could not be incorporated. The machine was also complicated to design and to debug. Because hardware was used for everything, rare and complex cases needed to be handled completely in hardware, as well as the simpler, more common cases.

Ditzel [1980] observed that SYMBOL had enormous performance problems. While exotic cases ran relatively fast, simple and common cases often ran slowly. Many memory references were needed to interpret a simple statement in a program. While the goal of eliminating the semantic gap seemed like a worthy one, any one of the three problems faced by SYMBOL would have been enough to doom the approach.

HLLCA never had a significant commercial impact. The increase in memory size on machines and the use of virtual memory eliminated the code-size problems arising from high-level languages and operating systems written in high-level languages. The combination of simpler architectures together with software offered greater performance and more flexibility at lower cost and lower complexity.

Studies of instruction set usage began in the late 1950s. The Gibson mix, described in the last chapter, was derived as a study of instruction usage on the IBM 7090. There were several studies in the 1970s of instruction set usage. Among the best known are Foster et al. [1971] and Lunde [1977]. Most of these early studies used small programs because the techniques used to collect data were expensive. Starting in the late 1970s, the area of instruction set measurement and analysis became very active. Because we use data from most of these papers in the next chapter, we will review the contributions there.

Other studies in the 1970s examined the usage of programming-language features. Though many of these studied only static properties, papers by Alexander and Wortman [1975] and Elshoff [1976] studied the dynamic properties of HLL programs. Interest in compiler utilization of instruction sets and interaction between compilers and architecture grew in the 1980s. A conference focusing on the interaction between software systems and hardware systems, called Architectural Support for Programming Languages and Operating Systems (ASPLOS), was created. Many papers on instruction set measurement and interaction between compilers and architectures have been published in this biannual conference.

In the early 1980s, the direction of computer architecture began to swing away from providing high-level hardware support for languages. Ditzel and Patterson [1980] analyzed the difficulties encountered by the high-level–language architectures and argued that the answer lay in simpler architectures. In another paper [Patterson and Ditzel 1980], these authors first discussed the idea of reduced instruction set computers (RISC) and presented the argument for simpler architectures. Their proposal was rebutted by Clark and Strecker [1980]. We will talk more about the effect of these ideas in the next chapter.

About the same time, other researchers published papers that argued for a closer coupling of architectures and compilers, rather than attempts to supplement compilers. These included Wulf [1981], and Hennessy and his colleagues [1982].

The early compiler technology developed for FORTRAN was quite good. Many of the optimization techniques in use in today's compilers were developed and implemented by the late 1960s or early 1970s (see Cocke and Schwartz [1970]). Because FORTRAN had to compete with assembly language, there was tremendous pressure for efficiency in FORTRAN compilers. However, once the benefits of HLL programming were obvious, focus shifted away from optimizing technology. Much of the optimization work in the 1970s was theoretically oriented rather than experimental. In the early 1980s, there was a new focus on developing optimizing compilers. As this technology stabilized, several researchers wrote papers examining the impact of various compiler optimizations on program execution time. Cocke and Markstein [1980] describe the measurements using the IBM PL.8 compiler; Chow [1983] describes the gain obtained with the Stanford UCODE compiler for a variety of machines. As we saw in this chapter, register allocation is the backbone of modern optimizing compilers. The formulation of register allocation as a graph-coloring problem was originally done by Chaitin and his colleagues [1982]. Chow and Hennessy [1984, 1990] extended the algorithm to use priorities in choosing the quantities to allocate. The progress in optimization and register allocation has led to more widespread use of optimizing compilers, and the impact of compiler technology on architectural tradeoffs has increased considerably in the past decade.

References

ALEXANDER, W. G. AND D. B.WORTMAN [1975]. "Static and dynamic characteristics of XPL programs," *Computer* 8:11 (November) 41–46.

AMDAHL, G. M., G. A. BLAAUW, AND F. P. BROOKS, JR. [1964]. "Architecture of the IBM System 360," *IBM J. Research and Development* 8:2 (April) 87–101.

BARTON, R. S. [1961]. "A new approach to the functional design of a computer," *Proc. Western Joint Computer Conf.,* 393–396.

BELL, G., R. CADY, H. MCFARLAND, B. DELAGI, J. O'LAUGHLIN, R. NOONAN, AND W. WULF [1970]. "A new architecture for mini-computers: The DEC PDP-11," *Proc. AFIPS SJCC,* 657–675.

CHAITIN, G. J., M. A. AUSLANDER, A. K. CHANDRA, J. COCKE, M. E. HOPKINS, AND P. W. MARKSTEIN [1982]. "Register allocation via coloring," *Computer Languages* 6, 47–57.

CHOW, F. C. [1983]. *A Portable Machine-Independent Global Optimizer—Design and Measurements,* Ph. D. Thesis, Stanford Univ. (December).

CHOW, F. C. AND J. L. HENNESSY [1984]. "Register allocation by priority-based coloring," *Proc. SIGPLAN '84 Compiler Construction (ACM SIGPLAN Notices 19:6* June) 222–232.

CHOW, F. C. AND J. L. HENNESSY [1990]. "The Priority-Based Coloring Approach to Register Allocation," *ACM Trans. on Programming Languages and Systems* 12:4 (October).

CLARK, D. AND W. D. STRECKER [1980]. "Comments on 'the case for the reduced instruction set computer', " *Computer Architecture News* 8:6 (October) 34–38.

COCKE, J., AND J. MARKSTEIN [1980]. "Measurement of code improvement algorithms," *Information Processing* 80, 221–228.

COCKE, J. AND J. T. SCHWARTZ [1970]. *Programming Languages and Their Compilers,* Courant Institute, New York Univ., New York City.

COHEN, D. [1981]. "On holy wars and a plea for peace," *Computer* 14:10 (October) 48–54.

COLWELL, R. P, C. Y. HITCHCOCK, III, E. D. JENSEN, H. M. B. SPRUNT, AND C. P. KOLLAR, [1985]. "Computers, complexity, and controversy," *Computer* 18:9 (September) 8–19.

DITZEL, D. R. [1981]. "Reflections on the high-level language Symbol computer system," *Computer* 14:7 (July) 55–66.

DITZEL, D. R. AND D. A. PATTERSON [1980]. "Retrospective on high-level language computer architecture," in *Proc. Seventh Annual Symposium on Computer Architecture,* La Baule, France (June) 97–104.

ELSHOFF, J. L. [1976]. "An analysis of some commercial PL/I programs," *IEEE Trans. on Software Engineering* SE-2 2 (June) 113–120.

FOSTER, C. C., R. H. GONTER, AND E. M. RISEMAN [1971]. "Measures of opcode utilization," *IEEE Trans. on Computers* 13:5 (May) 582–584.

GAGLIARDI, U. O. [1973]. "Report of workshop 4–software-related advances in computer hardware," *Proc. Symposium on the High Cost of Software,* Menlo Park, Calif., 99–120.

HAUCK, E. A., AND B. A. DENT [1968]. "Burroughs' B6500/B7500 stack mechanism," *Proc. AFIPS SJCC,* 245–251.

HENNESSY, J. L., N. JOUPPI, F. BASKETT, T. R. GROSS, AND J. GILL [1982]. "Hardware/software tradeoffs for increased performance," *Proc. Symposium on Architectural Support for Programming Languages and Operating Systems* (March), 2–11.

LUNDE, A. [1977]. "Empirical evaluation of some features of instruction set processor architecture," *Comm. ACM* 20:3 (March) 143–152.

MCKEEMAN, W. M. [1967]. "Language directed computer design," *Proc. 1967 Fall Joint Computer Conf.*, Washington, D.C., 413–417.

MEYERS, G. J. [1978]. "The evaluation of expressions in a storage-to-storage architecture," *Computer Architecture News* 7:3 (October), 20–23.

MEYERS, G. J. [1982]. *Advances in Computer Architecture*, 2nd ed., Wiley, N.Y.

PATTERSON, D. A. AND D. R. DITZEL [1980]. "The case for the reduced instruction set computer," *Computer Architecture News* 8:6 (October) 25–33.

SMITH, W. R., R. R. RICE, G. D. CHESLEY, T. A. LALIOTIS, S. F. LUNDSTROM, M. A. CHALHOUN, L. D. GEROULD, AND T. C. COOK [1971]. "SYMBOL: A large experimental system exploring major hardware replacement of software," *Proc. AFIPS Spring Joint Computer Conf.*, 601–616.

STRECKER, W. D. [1978]. "VAX-11/780: A virtual address extension of the PDP-11 family," *Proc. AFIPS National Computer Conf.* 47, 967–980.

TANENBAUM, A. S. [1978]. "Implications of structured programming for machine architecture," *Comm. ACM* 21:3 (March) 237–246.

THORNTON, J. E. [1964]. "Parallel operation in Control Data 6600," *Proc. AFIPS Fall Joint Computer Conf.* 26, part 2, 33–40.

WILKES, M. V. [1982]. "Hardware support for memory protection: Capability implementations," *Proc. Conf. on Architectural Support for Programming Languages and Operating Systems* (March) 107–116.

WILKES, M. V. AND W. RENWICK [1949]. *Report of a Conf. on High Speed Automatic Calculating Machines,* Cambridge, England.

WULF, W. [1981]. "Compilers and computer architecture," *Computer* 14:7 (July) 41–47.

EXERCISES

3.1 [15/10] <3.7> Use the data in Figures 3.30 and 3.31 (pages 119–120) for GCC for this problem. Assume the following CPIs:

ALU operation	1
Load/store	3
Branch	5

a.   [15] Find the CPI for the optimized and unoptimized versions of GCC.

b.   [10] How much faster is the optimized program than the unoptimized program?

3.2 [15/15/10] <3.8> Use the data in Figure 3.33 (page 123), in this problem. Assume that each instruction word and each data reference require one memory access.

a.   [15] Determine the percentage of memory accesses that are for instructions for each of the three benchmarks on the load/store machine.

b.   [15] Determine the percentage of memory accesses that are for instructions for each of the three benchmarks on the memory–memory machine.

c.   [10] What is the ratio of total memory accesses on the load/store machine versus the memory–memory machine for each benchmark?

3.3 [20/15/10] <3.3, 3.8> We are designing instruction set formats for a load/store architecture and are trying to decide whether it is worthwhile to have multiple offset lengths for branches and memory references. We will use average measurements for the three benchmarks to make this decision. We have decided that the offsets will be the same for these two classes of instructions. The length of an instruction would be equal to 16 bits + offset length in bits. ALU instructions will be 16 bits. Figure 3.35 contains the data from Figures 3.13 (page 100) and 3.19 (page 106) averaged and put in cumulative form. Assume an additional bit is needed for the sign on the offset.

For instruction set frequencies, use the data from the average of the three benchmarks for the load/store machine in Figure 3.32 (page 122).

Offset bits	Cumulative data references	Cumulative branches
0	16%	0%
1	16%	0%
2	21%	10%
3	29%	27%
4	32%	47%
5	44%	66%
6	55%	79%
7	62%	89%
8	66%	94%
9	68%	97%
10	73%	99%
11	78%	100%
12	80%	100%
13	86%	100%
14	87%	100%
15	100%	100%

FIGURE 3.35 The second and third columns contain the cumulative percentage of the data references and branches, respectively, that can be accommodated with the corresponding number of bits of magnitude in the displacement (i.e., the sign-bit is not included). This data is derived by averaging and accumulating the data in Figures 3.13 and 3.19.

a. [20] Suppose offsets were permitted to be 0, 8, or 16 bits in length including the sign-bit. Based on the dynamic statistics in Figure 3.32, what is the average length of an executed instruction?

b. [15] Suppose we wanted a fixed-length instruction and we chose a 24-bit instruction length (for everything, including ALU instructions). For every offset of longer than 8 bits, an additional instruction is required. Determine the number of instruction bytes fetched in this machine with fixed instruction size versus those fetched with a variable-sized instruction.

c. [10] What if the offset length were 16 and we never required an additional instruction? How would instruction bytes fetched compare to the choice of only an 8-bit offset? Assume ALU instructions will be 16 bits.

3.4 [15/10] <3.2> Several researchers have suggested that adding a register–memory addressing mode to a load/store machine might be useful. The idea is to replace sequences of

```
LOAD   R1,0(Rb)
ADD    R2,R2,R1
```

by

```
ADD    R2,0(Rb)
```

Assume the new instruction will cause the clock cycle to increase by 10%. Use the instruction frequencies for the GCC benchmark on the load/store machine from Figure 3.32 (page 122) and assume that two-thirds of the moves are loads and the rest are stores. The new instruction affects only the clock speed and not the CPI.

a. [15] What percentage of the loads must be eliminated for the machine with the new instruction to have at least the same performance?

b. [12] Show a situation in a multiple instruction sequence where a load of R1 followed immediately by a use of R1 (with some type of opcode) could not be replaced by a single instruction of the form proposed, assuming that the same opcode exists.

3.5 [15/20] <3.1–3.3> For the next two parts of this question, your task is to compare the memory efficiency of four different styles of instruction sets for two code sequences. The architecture styles are:

Accumulator

Memory–Memory—All three operands of each instruction are in memory.

Stack—All operations occur on top of the stack. Only push and pop access memory, and all other instructions remove their operands from stack and replace them with the result. The implementation uses a stack for the top two entries; accesses that use other stack positions are memory references.

Load/store—All operations occur in registers, and register-to-register instructions have three operands per instruction. There are 16 general-purpose registers, and register specifiers are 4 bits long.

To measure memory efficiency, make the following assumptions about all four instruction sets:

■   The opcode is always 1 byte (8 bits).

■   All memory addresses are 2 bytes (16 bits).

■   All data operands are 4 bytes (32 bits).

■   All instructions are an integral number of bytes in length.

There are no other optimizations to reduce memory traffic, and the variables A, B, C, and D are initially in memory.

Invent your own assembly language mnemonics and write the best equivalent assembly language code for the high-level–language fragments given.

a. [15] Write the four code sequences for

$$A = B + C;$$

For each code sequence, calculate the instruction bytes fetched and the memory-data bytes transferred. Which architecture is most efficient as measured by code size? Which architecture is most efficient as measured by total memory bandwidth required (code + data)?

b. [20] Write the four code sequences for

$$A = B + C;$$
$$B = A + C;$$
$$D = A - B;$$

For each code sequence, calculate the instruction bytes fetched and the memory-data bytes transferred (read or written). Which architecture is most efficient as measured by code size? Which architecture is most efficient as measured by total memory bandwidth required (code + data)? If the answers are different from part a, why are they different?

3.6 [20] <3.4> Supporting byte and halfword access requires an alignment network, as in Figure 3.10 (page 97). Some machines have only word accesses, so that a load of a byte or halfword takes two instructions (a load and an extract), and a partial word store takes three instructions (load, insert, store). Use the data for the TeX benchmark from Figure 3.23 (page 110) to determine what percentage of the accesses are to byte or halfwords, and use the data from TeX on the load/store machine from Figure 3.32 (page 122) to find the frequency of data transfers. Assume that loads are twice as frequent as stores independent of the data size. If all instructions on the machine take one cycle, what increase in the clock rate must we obtain to make eliminating partial word accesses a good tradeoff?

3.7 [20] <3.3> We have a proposal for three different machines, M_0, M_8, and M_{16}, that differ in their register count. All three machines have three operand instructions, and any operand can be either a memory reference or a register. The cost of a memory operand on these machines is six cycles and the cost of a register operand is one cycle. Each of the three operands has equal probability of being in a register.

The differences among the machines are described in the following table. The execution cycles per operation are in addition to the cost of operand access. The probability of an operand being in a register applies to each operand individually and is based on Figures 3.28 (page 117) and 3.29 (page 118).

Machine	Register count	Execution cycles per operation ignoring operand accesses	Probability of an operand being in a register as opposed to memory
M_0	0	4 cycles	0.0
M_8	8	5 cycles	0.5
M_{16}	16	6 cycles	0.8

What is the cycle count for an average instruction on each machine?

3.8 [15/10/10] <3.3, 3.7> One place where an architect can drive a compiler writer crazy is in making it difficult to tell if a compiler "optimization" may slow down a program on the machine.

Consider an access to A[*i*], where A is an array of integers and *i* is an integer offset in a register. We wish to generate code to use the value of A[*i*] as a source operand throughout this problem. Assume that all instructions take one clock cycle plus the cost of the memory addressing mode:

- Indexed addressing costs four clock cycles for the memory reference (for a total of five clock cycles for the instruction).

- Register indirect addressing costs three clock cycles for the memory reference (for a total of four clock cycles).

- Register-register instructions have no memory access cost, requiring only one cycle.

Assume that the value A[*i*] must be stored in memory at the end of the code sequence and that the base address of A is already in R1 and the value of *i* is in R2.

a. [15] Assume that the array element A[*i*] cannot be kept in a register, but the address of A[*i*] may be kept in a register once computed. Then, there are two different methods to access A[*i*]:

   (1) compute the address of A[*i*] into a register and use register indirect, and

   (2) use the indexed addressing mode.

   Write the code sequence for both methods. How many references to A[*i*] must occur for method 1 to be better?

b. [10] Suppose you choose method 1, but you ran out of registers and had to save the address of A[*i*] on the stack and restore it. How many references must occur now for method 1 to be better?

c. [10] Suppose that the value A[*i*] can be kept in a register (versus just the address of A[*i*]). How many references must occur to make this the best approach versus using method 2?

3.9 [Discussion] <3.2–3.8> What are the **economic** arguments (i.e., more machines sold) **for and against** changing instruction set architecture?

3.10 [25] <3.1–3.3> Find an instruction set manual for some older machine (libraries and private bookshelves are good places to look). Summarize the instruction set with the discriminating characteristics used in Figures 3.1 and 3.5 (pages 90 and 93). Does the machine fit nicely into one of the categories shown in Figures 3.4 and 3.6 (pages 92 and 94)? Write the code sequence for this machine for the statements in both parts of Exercise 3.5.

3.11 [30] <3.7, 3.9> Find a machine that has a powerful instruction set feature, such as the CALLS instruction on the VAX. Replace the powerful instruction with a simpler sequence that accomplishes what is needed. Measure the resultant running time. How do the two compare? Why might they be different? In the early 1980s, engineers at DEC did a quick experiment to evaluate the impact of replacing CALLS. They found a 30% improvement in run time on a very call-intensive program when the CALLS was simply replaced (parameters remained on the stack). How do your results compare?

The emphasis on performance rather than aesthetics is deliberate. Without an interest in performance the study of architecture is a sterile exercise, since all computable problems can be solved using trivial architectures, given enough time. The challenge is to design computers that make the best use of available technology; in doing so we may be assured that every increase in processing speed can be used to advantage in current problems or will make previously impractical problems tractable.

Leonard J. Shustek, *Analysis and Performance of Computer Instruction Sets* (1978)

4 Instruction Set Examples and Measurements of Use

4.1 Instruction Set Measurements: What and Why

In this chapter we will be examining some specific architectures and then detailed measurements of the architectures. Before doing so, however, let's discuss what we might want to measure and why, as well as how to measure it.

To understand performance, we are usually most interested in *dynamic measurements*—measurements that are made by counting the number of occurrences of an event during execution. Some measurements, such as code size, are inherently *static measurements,* which are made on a program independent of execution. Static and dynamic measurements may differ dramatically, as shown in Figure 4.1—using only the static data for this program would be significantly misleading. Throughout this text the data given is dynamic, unless otherwise specified. Exceptions are when only static measurements make sense (as with code size—the most important use of static measurement) and when it is interesting to compare static and dynamic measurements. As we will see in Fallacies and Pitfalls and the Exercises, the dynamic frequency of occurrence of two instructions and the time spent on those two instructions can sometimes be very different.

Our primary focus in this chapter will be on introducing the architectures and measuring instruction usage for each architecture. Although this suggests a concentration on opcodes, we will also examine addressing mode and instruction format usage.

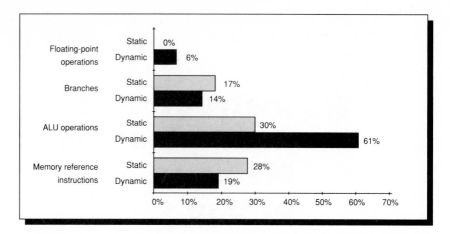

FIGURE 4.1 Data from a measurement of the IBM 360 FORTRAN benchmark, which we describe in detail in Section 4.6. The top 20 dynamically executed instructions have been broken into four wide classes, showing how different the static and dynamic occurrences can be. In the case of the dynamic measurements, these 20 instructions account for nearly 100% of the instruction executions, but only 75% of the static instruction occurrences.

The instruction set measurements in Section 4.6 can be used in two ways. At a high level, the measurements allow one to form broad approximations of the instruction usage patterns within each architectural approach. For example, we will see that "PC-changing" instructions for a powerful instruction set like the VAX average nearly 25% of all instruction executions. This tells us that techniques that try to optimize the fetching of the next sequential instruction (instruction prefetch buffers—discussed in Section 8.7 of Chapter 8) will be significantly limited because every fourth instruction is a branch. The data on the IBM 360 will show that the use of decimal and string instructions is almost nonexistent in programs written in languages other than COBOL. This leads us to conclude that support for such operations need not be included in a machine targeted at the scientific market. Measurements of the frequency of memory operands—about 40% of the operands on the 8086—can be used in the design of both the pipeline and the cache. This type of high-level, general measurement is background data that a computer architect will use on an almost daily basis.

The other purpose of such measurements is to serve as the knowledge data base that an architect would use in making detailed design tradeoffs. Such tradeoffs would be required in choosing what to include in an instruction set and what to omit, or in implementing a defined instruction set and choosing what cases to try to make fast. For example, the low frequency of use for the memory-indirect addressing modes on the VAX might encourage the architect to omit this addressing mode from a new architecture. If he was implementing a VAX, he would know that the performance penalty for disfavoring this complex addressing mode would be small. Another example that would use detailed information might be the evaluation of branching based on condition codes. By looking at the frequency of conditional branches and instructions whose only function is to set the condition code, we can evaluate the frequency with which the condition code is set implicitly (about 35% of the occurrences on the VAX). We could use this value to decide what kind of conditional branches to design in a new architecture, or we could use the data to optimize the implementation of conditional branches in a VAX. In this chapter and subsequent ones we will see many examples of how this data is applied to specific design problems.

We have chosen four machines to examine: the DEC VAX, the IBM 360, the Intel 8086, and a generic load/store machine called DLX. These architectures play a dominant role in the computer marketplace, and each has a set of unique and interesting characteristics. The Intel 8086 is the most popular general-purpose computer in the world; tens of millions of machines containing this microprocessor have been sold. The IBM 360 and DEC VAX represent architectures that have existed for long periods of time (25+ and 10+ years, respectively) and have each sold hundreds of thousands of units. DLX is representative of a new breed of machines that has become very popular since the late 1980s. These machines are also very different in architectural style, as we will see.

To try to simplify the reader's task, a common format is used for the syntax of instructions. This format puts the destination of a multiple-operand instruction first, followed by the first and second source operands. So, an instruction that subtracts R3 from R2 and puts the result in R1 is written as:

```
SUB    R1,R2,R3
```

This format follows the convention used on the Intel 8086, and is close to the convention on the 360. The only significant difference on the 360 is for store instructions, which place the source register first. While the VAX syntax always puts the source operands first and the destination last, we will show VAX code in our common format. Of course, this ordering is purely a syntactic convention and the architecture defines the encoding of operands in the binary instruction format.

The next four sections are summaries of the four architectures. Although these summaries are concise, the important attributes and most heavily used features are all discussed. Tables containing all the operations in the instruction sets are contained in Appendix B. To describe these architectures accurately, we need to introduce a few additional extensions to our C description language to explain the functions of the instructions. The additions are as follows:

- A subscript is appended to the symbol ← whenever the length of the datum being assigned might not be clear. Thus, $\leftarrow_n$ means transfer an n-bit quantity.

- A subscript is used to indicate selection of a bit from a field. Bits are labeled from the most significant bit starting at 0. The subscript may be a single digit (e.g., $R4_0$ yields the sign bit of R4) or a subrange (e.g., $R3_{24..31}$ yields the least significant byte of R3).

- A superscript is used to replicate a field (e.g., 0^{24} yields a field of zeros of length 24 bits).

- The variable M is used as an array that stands for main memory. The array is indexed by a byte address and may transfer any number of bytes.

- The symbol ## is used to concatenate two fields and may appear on either side of a data transfer.

A summary of the entire description language appears on the page preceding the back inside cover. As an example, assuming that R8 and R10 are 32-bit registers:

$$R10_{16..31} \leftarrow_{16} (M[R8]_0)^8 \# \# M[R8]$$

means that the byte at the memory location addressed by the contents of R8 is sign-extended to form a 16-bit quantity that is stored into the lower half of R10. (The upper half of R10 is unchanged.)

Following the instruction set architecture summaries in the next four sections, we examine and contrast dynamic use measurements of the four architectures.

4.2 | The VAX Architecture

The DEC VAX was introduced with its first model, the VAX-11/780, in 1977. The VAX was designed to be a 32-bit extension of the PDP-11 architecture. Among the goals of the VAX, two stand out as both important and having had a substantial impact on the VAX architecture.

First, the designers wanted to make the existing PDP-11 customer base feel comfortable with the VAX architecture and view it as an extension of the PDP-11. This motivated the name VAX-11/780, the use of a very similar assembly language syntax, inclusion of the PDP-11 data types, and emulation support for the PDP-11. Second, the designers wanted to ease the task of writing compilers and operating systems. This translated to a set of goals that included defining interfaces between languages, the hardware, and OS; and supporting a highly orthogonal architecture.

In terms of addressing modes and operations supported in instructions, the other architectures discussed in this chapter are largely subsets of the VAX. For this reason our discussion begins with the VAX, which will serve as a basis for comparison. The reader should be aware that there are entire books devoted to the VAX architecture as well as a number of papers reporting instruction set measurements. Our summary of the VAX instruction set—like the other instruction set summaries in this chapter—focuses on the general principles of the architecture and on the portions of the architecture most relevant to understanding the measurements examined here. A list of the full VAX instruction set is included in Appendix B.

The VAX is a general-purpose register machine with a large orthogonal instruction set. Figure 4.2 shows the data types supported. The VAX uses the name "word" to refer to 16-bit quantities, while in this text we use the convention that a *word* is 32 bits. Be careful when reading the VAX instruction mnemonics, as they often refer to the names of the VAX data types. Figure 4.2 shows the conversion between the data type names used in this text and the VAX names. In addition to the data types in Figure 4.2, the VAX provides support for fixed- and variable-length bit strings, up to 32 bits in length.

The VAX provides 16 general-purpose registers, but four registers are effectively claimed by the instruction set architecture. For example, R14 is the stack pointer and R15 is the PC (program counter). Hence, R15 cannot be used

Bits	Data type	Our name	DEC's name
8	Integer	Byte	Byte
16	Integer	Halfword	Word
32	Integer	Word	Long word
32	Floating point	Single precision	F_floating
64	Integer	Doubleword	Quad word
64	Floating point	Double precision	D_floating or G_floating
128	Integer	Quadword	Octa word
128	Floating point	Huge	H_floating
8n	Character string	Character	Character
4n	Binary-coded decimal	Packed	Packed
8n	Numeric string	Unpacked	Numeric strings: Trailing and leading separate

FIGURE 4.2 VAX data types, their lengths, and names. The first letter of the DEC type (B, W, L, F, Q, D, G, O, H, C, P, T, S) is often used to complete an opcode name. As examples, the move opcodes include MOVB, MOVW, MOVL, MOVF, MOVQ, MOVD, MOVG, MOVO, MOVH, MOVC3, MOVP. Each move instruction transfers an operand of the data type indicated by the letter following MOV. (There is no difference between moves of character and numeric strings, so only move character operations are needed.) The length fields that appear as *X*n indicate that the length may be any multiple of *X* in bits. The packed data type is special in that the length for operations on this type is always given in digits, each of which is four bits. The packed objects are still allocated and addressed in units of bytes. For any string data type the starting address is the low-order address of the string.

as a general-purpose register, and using R14 is very difficult because it interferes with instructions that manipulate the stack frame. Condition codes are used for branching and are set by all arithmetic and logical operations and by the move instruction. The move instruction transfers data between any two addressable locations and subsumes load, store, register–register moves, and memory–memory moves as special cases.

VAX Addressing Modes

The addressing modes include most of those we discussed in Chapter 3: literal, register (operand is in a register), register deferred (register indirect), autodecrement, autoincrement, autoincrement deferred, byte/word/long displacement, byte/word/long displacement deferred, and scaled (called "indexed" in the VAX architecture). Scaled addressing mode may be applied to any general addressing mode except register or literal. Register is an addressing mode no different from any other in the VAX. Thus, a 3-operand VAX instruction may include from zero to three operand memory references, each of which may be any of the memory addressing modes. Since the memory indirect modes require an additional memory access, up to 6 memory accesses may be required for a 3-operand instruction. When the addressing modes are used with R15 (the PC), only a few are defined, and their meaning is special. The defined addressing modes with R15 are as follows:

- *Immediate*—an immediate value is in the instruction stream; this mode is encoded as autoincrement on PC.

- *Absolute*—a 32-bit absolute address is in the instruction stream; this mode is encoded as autoincrement deferred with PC as the register.

- *Byte/word/long displacement*—the same as the general mode, but the base is the PC, giving PC-relative addressing.

- *Byte/word/long displacement deferred*—the same as the general mode, but the base is the PC, giving addressing that is indirect through a memory location that is PC-relative.

A VAX instruction consists of an opcode followed by zero or more operand specifiers. The opcode is almost always a single byte that specifies the operation, the data type, and the operand count. Almost all operations are fully orthogonal with respect to addressing modes—any combination of addressing modes works with nearly every opcode, and many operations are supported for all possible data types.

Operand specifiers may vary in length from one byte to many, depending on the information to be conveyed. The first byte of each operand specifier consists of two 4-bit fields: the type of address specifier and a register that is part of the addressing mode. If the operand specifier requires additional bytes to specify a displacement, additional registers, or an immediate value, it is extended in 1-byte increments. The name, assembler syntax, and number of bytes for each operand specifier are shown in Figure 4.3. The total instruction length and format are easy to state: Simply add up the sizes of the operand specifiers and include one byte (or rarely two) for the opcode.

Example

How long is the following instruction?

```
ADDL3 R1,737(R2),#456
```

Answer

The opcode length is 1 byte, as is the first operand specifier (R1). The second operand specifier has two parts: the first part is a byte that specifies the addressing mode and base register; the second part is the 2-byte long displacement. The third operand specifier also has two parts: the first byte specifies immediate mode, and the second part contains the immediate. Because the data type is long (ADDL3), the immediate value takes 4 bytes.

Thus, the total length of the instruction is 1 + 1 + (1+2) + (1+4) = 10 bytes.

Addressing mode	Syntax	Length in bytes
Literal	#value	1 (6-bit signed value)
Immediate	#value	1 + length of the immediate
Register	Rn	1
Register deferred	(Rn)	1
Byte/word/long displacement	Displacement (Rn)	1 + length of the displacement
Byte/word/long displacement deferred	@displacement (Rn)	1 + length of the displacement
Scaled (Indexed)	Base mode [Rx]	1 + length of base addressing mode
Autoincrement	(Rn)+	1
Autodecrement	− (Rn)	1
Autoincrement deferred	@(Rn)+	1

FIGURE 4.3 Length of the VAX operand specifiers. The length of each addressing mode is 1 byte plus the length of any displacement or immediate field that is in the mode. Literal mode uses a special 2-bit tag and the remaining 6 bits encode the constant value. The data we examined in Chapter 3 on constants showed the heavy use of small constants; the same observation motivated this optimization. The length of an immediate is dictated by the data type indicated in the opcode, not the value of the immediate.

Type	Example	Instruction meaning
Data transfers		**Move data between byte, halfword, word, or doubleword operands; * is the data type**
	MOV*	Move between two operands
	MOVZB*	Move a byte to a halfword or word, extending it with zeroes
	MOVA*	Move address of operand; data type is last
	PUSH*	Push operand onto stack
Arithmetic, logical		**Operations on integer or logical bytes, halfwords (16 bits), words (32 bits); * is the data type**
	ADD*_	Add with 2 or 3 operands
	CMP*	Compare and set condition codes
	TST*	Compare to zero and set condition codes
	ASH*	Arithmetic shift
	CLR*	Clear
	CVTB*	Sign extend byte to size of data type
Control		**Conditional and unconditional branches**
	BEQL, BNEQ	Branch equal/not equal
	BCS, BCC	Branch carry set, branch carry clear
	BRB, BRW	Unconditional branch with an 8-bit or 16-bit offset
	JMP	Jump using any addressing mode to specify target
	AOBLEQ	Add one to operand; branch if result ≤ second operand
	CASE_	Jump based on case selector
Procedure		**Call/return from procedure**
	CALLS	Call procedure with arguments on stack (see Section 3.9)
	CALLG	Call procedure with FORTRAN-style parameter list
	JSB	Jump to subroutine, saving return address
	RET	Return from procedure call
Bit-field character decimal		**Operate on variable-length bit fields, character strings, and decimal strings, both in character and BCD format**
	EXTV	Extracts a variable-length bit field into a 32-bit word
	MOVC3	Move a string of characters for given length
	CMPC3	Compare two strings of characters for given length
	MOVC5	Move string of characters with truncation or filling
	ADDP4	Add decimal string of the indicated length
	CVTPT	Convert packed-decimal string to character string
Floating point		**Floating-point operations on D, F, G, and H formats**
	ADDD_	Add double-precision D-format floating numbers
	SUBD_	Subtract double-precision D-format floating numbers
	MULF_	Multiply single-precision F-format floating point
	POLYF	Evaluate a polynomial using table of coefficients in F format
System		**Change to system mode, modify protected registers**
	CHMK, CHME	Change mode to kernel/executive
	REI	Return from exception or interrupt
Other		**Special operations**
	CRC	Calculate cyclic redundancy check
	INSQUE	Insert a queue entry into a queue

FIGURE 4.4 (Adjoining page) Classes of VAX instructions with examples. The asterisk stands for multiple data types—B, W, L, and usually D, F, G, H, and Q; remember how these VAX data types relate to the names used in the text (see Figure 4.2 on page 143). For example, a MOVW moves the VAX data-type word, which is 16 bits and is called a halfword in this text. The underline, as in ADDD_, means there are 2-operand (ADDD2) and 3-operand (ADDD3) forms of this instruction. The operand count is explicit in the opcode.

Operations on the VAX

What types of operators does the VAX provide? VAX operations can be divided into classes, as shown in Figure 4.4. (Detailed lists of the VAX instructions are included in Appendix B.) Figure 4.5 gives examples of typical VAX instructions and their meanings. Most instructions set the VAX condition codes according to their result; instructions without results, such as branches, do not. The condition codes are N (Negative), Z (Zero), V (oVerflow), and C (Carry).

Example assembly instruction	Length	Meaning
MOVL @40(R4),30(R2)	5	$M[M[40+R4]]\leftarrow_{32} M[30+R2]$
MOVAW R2,(R3)[R4]	4	$R2\leftarrow_{32} R3+(R4*2)$
ADDL3 R5,(R6)+,(R6)+	4	$i\leftarrow M[R6]; R6\leftarrow R6+4; R5\leftarrow i+M[R6]; R6\leftarrow R6+4$
CMPL -(R6),#100	7	$R6\leftarrow R6-4;$ Set the condition code using: $M[R6]-100$
CVTBW R10,(R8)	3	$R10_{16..31}\leftarrow_{16} (M[R8]_0)^8$ ## M[R8]
BEQL name	2	if equal(CC) {PC$\leftarrow$name} PC$-128 \leq$ name $<$ PC+128
BRW name	3	PC$\leftarrow$name PC$-32768 \leq$ name $<$ PC+32768
EXTZV (R8),R5,R6,-564(R7)	7	$t\leftarrow_{40} M[R7-564+(R5>>3)];$ $i\leftarrow R5$ & 7; $j\leftarrow$if R6>=32 then 32 else if R6<0 then 0 else R6; $M[R8]\leftarrow_{32} 0^{32-j}$ ## $t_{39-i-j+1..39-i};$
MOVC3 @36(R9),(R10),35(R11)	6	$R1\leftarrow 35+R11; R3\leftarrow M[36+R9];$ for (R0$\leftarrow$M[R10];R0!=0;R0--) {$M[R3]\leftarrow_8 M[R1]$; R1++; R3++} R2=0; R4=0; R5=0
ADDD3 R0,R2,R4	4	(R0##R1)$\leftarrow_{64}$ (R2##R3)+(R4##R5) register contents are type D floating point.

FIGURE 4.5 Some examples of typical VAX instructions. VAX assembly language syntax puts the result operand last; we have put it first for consistency with other machines. Instruction length is given in bytes. The condition equal(CC) is true if the condition-code setting reflects equality after a compare. Remember that most instructions set the condition code; the only function of compare instructions is to set the condition code. The names t, i, j are used as a temporaries in the instruction descriptions; t is 40 bits in length, while i and j are 32 bits. The EXTZV instruction may appear mysterious. Its purpose is to extract a variable-length field (0 to 32 bits) and zero extend it to 32 bits. The source operands to the EXTZV are the starting bit position (which may be any distance from the starting byte address), the length of the field, and the starting address of the bit string to extract the field from. The VAX numbers its bits from low order to high order, but we number bits in the reverse order. Thus, the subscripts adjust the bit offsets accordingly (which makes EXTV look more mysterious!). Although the result of the variable bit string operations are always 32 bits, the MOVC3 changes the values of registers R0 through R5 as shown (although any of R0, R2, R4, and R5 could be used to hold the count). A discussion of why MOVC3 uses the GPRs as working registers appears in Section 5.6 of the next chapter.

4.3 | The 360/370 Architecture

The IBM 360 was introduced in 1964. Its official goals included the following:

1. Exploit storage—large main storage, storage hierarchies (ROM used for microcode).

2. Support concurrent I/O—up to 5 MB/second with a standard interface on all machines.

3. Create a general-purpose machine with new OS facilities and many data types.

4. Maintain strict upward and downward machine-language compatibility.

The System/370, first introduced in 1970, was a successor to System/360. System/370 is fully upward compatible with System/360, even in system mode. The major extensions over the 360 included

- Virtual memory and dynamic address translation (see Chapter 8, Section 8.5)

- A few new instructions: synchronization support, long string instructions (long move and long compare), additional instructions for manipulating bytes in registers, and some additional decimal instructions

- Removal of data alignment requirements

In addition, several important implementation differences were introduced in the 370 implementations, including MOS main memory rather than core, and writeable control store (see Chapter 5).

In 1983, IBM introduced 370-XA, the eXtended Architecture. Until this extension, first used in the 3080 series, the 360/370 architecture had a 24-bit address space. Additional bits were added to the program status word so that the program counter could be extended. Unfortunately, it was common programming practice on the 360 to use the high-order byte of an address for status. Thus, old 24-bit programs cannot be run in 32-bit mode (actually a 31-bit address), while new and recompiled programs can take advantage of the larger address space. The I/O structure was also changed to permit higher levels of multiprocessing.

The latest extension to the architecture was ESA/370, introduced with the 3090 model in 1986. ESA/370 added additional instruction formats, called the Extended formats, with 16-bit opcodes. ESA/370 includes support for a Vector Facility (including a set of vector registers) and an extended (128-bit) floating-point format. The address space was extended by adding segments on top of the 31-bit address space (see Chapter 8, Sections 8.5 and 8.6); a new and more powerful protection model was added as well.

The remainder of this section surveys the IBM 360 architecture and presents measurements for the workload. First, let's examine the basics of the 360 architecture, then look at the instruction set formats and some sample instructions.

The 360/370 Instruction Set Architecture

The IBM System/360 is a 32-bit machine with byte addressability and support for a variety of data types: byte, halfword (16 bits), word (32 bits), doubleword (double-precision real), packed decimal, and unpacked character strings. The System/360 had alignment restrictions, which were removed in the System/370 architecture.

The internal state of the 360 has the following components:

- Sixteen 32-bit, general-purpose registers; register 0 is special when used in an addressing mode, where a zero is always substituted.

- Four double-precision (64-bit) floating-point registers.

- Program status word (PSW) holds the PC, some control flags, and the condition codes.

Later versions of the architecture extended this state with additional control registers.

Addressing Modes and Instruction Formats

The 360/370 has five instruction formats. Each format is associated with a single addressing mode and has a set of operations defined for that format. While some operations are defined in multiple formats, most are not. The instruction formats are shown in Figure 4.6 (page 150). While many instructions follow the paradigm of operating on sources and putting the result in a destination, other instructions (such as the control instructions BAL, BALR, BC) do not follow this paradigm, but use the same fields for other purposes. The associated addressing modes are as follows.

RR *(register–register)*—Both operands are simply contents of registers. The first source operand is also the destination.

RX *(register–indexed)*—The first operand and destination are a register. The second operand is the contents of the memory location given by the sum of a 12-bit displacement field D2, the contents of the register B2, and the contents of the register X2. This format is used when an index register is needed (and for most loads and stores).

RS *(register–storage)*—The first operand is a register that is the destination. The third operand is a register that is used as the second source. The second operand is the contents of the memory location given by the sum of the 12-bit displacement field D2 and the contents of the register B2. RS mode differs from RX in that a 3-operand form is supported, but the index register is eliminated. This instruction format is used for only a small number of instructions.

SI *(storage–immediate)*—The destination is a memory operand given by the sum of the contents of register B1 and the value of displacement D1. The second operand, an 8-bit immediate field, is the source.

SS *(storage–storage)*—The addresses of the two memory operands are the sum of the contents of a base register Bi and a displacement Di. The first operand is the destination. This storage-to-storage operation is used for decimal operations and for character strings. The length field can specify a single length of 1 to 256, or two lengths, each from 1 to 16. A single length is used for string instructions, while decimal instructions specify a length for each operand.

The displacement in the RS, RX, SI, and SS formats is 12 bits and is unsigned.

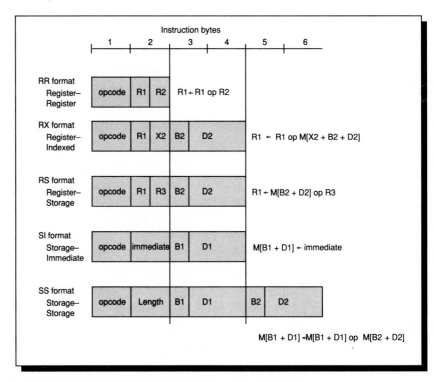

FIGURE 4.6 The 360/370 instruction formats. The possible instruction operands are a register (R1, R2, or R3), an 8-bit immediate, or a memory location. The opcode specifies where the operands reside and the addressing mode. The effective addresses for memory operands are formed using the sum of one or two registers (called B1, B2, or X2) and a 12-bit unsigned displacement field (called D1 or D2). In addition, the storage–storage instructions, which are all string-oriented, specify an 8-bit length field. Other instruction formats have been added in later architectural extensions. These formats allowed the opcode space to be extended and new data types to be added. For loads, stores, and moves only one source operand is used and the operation only moves the data (see Figure 4.8 on page 152). For SS instructions, the length is one greater than the value in the instruction.

Operations on the 360/370

Just as on the VAX, the instructions on the 360 can be divided into classes. Four basic types of operations on data are supported:

1. *Logical operations on bits, character strings, and fixed words.* These are mostly RR and RX formats with a few RS instructions.

2. *Decimal or character operations on strings of characters or decimal digits.* These are SS format instructions.

3. *Fixed-point binary arithmetic.* This is supported in both RR and RX formats.

4. *Floating-point arithmetic.* This is supported primarily with RR and RX instructions.

Branches use the RX instruction format with the effective address specifying the branch target. Since branches are not PC-relative, a base register may need to be loaded to specify the branch target. This has a rather substantial impact: in general, it means that there must be registers that point to every region containing a branch target. The condition codes are set by all arithmetic and logical operations. Conditional branches test the condition codes under a mask to determine whether or not to branch.

Some example instructions and their formats are shown in Figure 4.7. When an operation is defined for more than one format, separate opcodes are used to specify the instruction format. For example, the opcode AR (add register) says that the instruction type is RR; thus, the operands are in registers. The opcode A (add) says the format is RX; thus, one operand is in memory, accessed with the RX addressing mode. Figure 4.8 (page 152) has a longer listing of operations, including all the most common ones; a full table of instructions appears in Appendix B.

Type	Instruction example	Meaning
RR	AR R4,R5	R4← R4+R5
RX	A R4,10(R5,R6)	R4← R4+M[R5+R6+10]
RX	BC Mask,20(R5,R6)	if (CC & Mask)!=0 {PC← 20+R5+R6}
RS	STM 20(R14),R2,R8	for(i=2;i<=8;i++) {M[R14+20+(i-2)*4] ← $_{32}$ Ri}
SI	MVI 20(R5),#40	M[R5+20]← $_8$ 40
SS	MVC 10(R2),Len,20(R6)	for(i=0;i<Len+1;i++) {M[R2+10+i]← $_8$ M[R6+20+i]}

FIGURE 4.7   Typical IBM 360 instructions with their meanings. The MVC instruction is shown with the length as the second operand. The length field is a constant in the instruction; standard 360 assembly language syntax includes the length with the first operand. The variable i used in the MVC and STM is a temporary.

Class or instruction	Format	Instruction meaning
Control		**Change the PC**
BC_	RX,RR	Test the condition and conditionally branch
BAL_	RX,RR	Branch and link (address of next instruction is placed in R15)
Arithmetic, logical		**Arithmetic and logical operations**
A_	RX,RR	Add
S_	RX,RR	Subtract
SLL	RS	Shift left logical; shifts a register by an immediate amount
LA	RX	Load address—put effective address into destination
CLI	SI	Compare storage byte against immediate
NI	SI	AND immediate into storage byte
C_	RX,RR	Compare and set condition codes
TM	RS	Test under mask—perform a logical AND of the operand and an immediate field; set condition codes based on the result
MH	RX	Multiply halfword
Data transfer		**Moves between registers or register and memory**
L_	RX,RR	Load a register from memory or another register
MVI	SI	Store an immediate byte in memory
ST	RX	Store a register
LD	RX	Load a double-precision floating-point register
STD	RX	Store a double-precision floating-point register
LPDR	RR	Move a double-precision floating-point register to another
LH	RX	Load a halfword from memory into a register
IC	RX	Insert a memory byte into low-order byte of a register
LTR	RR	Load a register and set condition codes
Floating point		**Floating-point operations**
AD_	RX,RR	Double-precision floating-point add
MD_	RX,RR	Double-precision FP multiply
Decimal, string		**Operations on decimal and character strings**
MVC	SS	Move characters
AP	SS	Add packed-decimal strings, replacing first with sum
ZAP	SS	Zero and add packed—replace destination with source
CVD	RX	Convert a binary word to decimal doubleword
MP	SS	Multiply two packed-decimal strings
CLC	SS	Compare two character strings
CP	SS	Compare two packed-decimal strings
ED	SS	Edit—convert packed-decimal to character string

FIGURE 4.8 Most frequently used IBM 360 instructions. The underline means that the opcode is two distinct opcodes with an RX format and an RR format. For example A_ stands for AR and A. The full instruction set is shown in Appendix B.

4.4 | The 8086 Architecture

The Intel 8086 architecture was announced in 1978 as an upward-compatible extension of the then-successful 8080. Whereas the 8080 was a straightforward accumulator machine, the 8086 extended the architecture with additional registers. The 8086 fails to be a truly general-purpose register machine, however, because nearly every register has a dedicated use. Thus, its architecture falls somewhere between an accumulator machine and a general-purpose register machine. The 8086 is a 16-bit architecture; all internal registers are 16 bits. To obtain addressability greater than 16 bits the designers added segments to the architecture. This allowed a 20-bit address space, broken into 64-KB fragments. Chapter 8 discusses segmentation in detail, while this chapter will focus only on the implications for a compiler.

The 80186, 80286, 80386, and 80486 are "compatible" extensions of the 8086 architecture and are collectively referred to as the 80x86 processors. They are compatible in the sense that they all belong to the same architectural family. There are more instances of this architectural family than of any other in the world. The 80186 added a small number of extensions (about 16) to the 8086 architecture in 1981. The 80286, introduced in 1982, extended the 80186 architecture by creating an elaborate memory-mapping and protection model and by extending the address space to 24 bits (see Chapter 8, Section 8.6). Because 8086 programs needed to be binary compatible, the 80286 offered a real addressing mode to make the machine look just like an 8086.

The 80386 was introduced in 1985. It is a true 32-bit machine when running in native mode. Like the 80286, a real addressing mode is provided for 8086 compatibility. There is also a virtual 8086 mode that provides for multiple 20-bit 8086 address partitions within the 80386's memory. In addition to a 32-bit architecture with 32-bit registers and a 32-bit address space, the 80386 has a new set of addressing modes and additional operations. The added instructions make the 80386 nearly a general-purpose register machine—for most operations any register can be used as an operand. The 80386 also provides paging support (see Chapter 8). The 80486 was introduced in 1989 and added only a few new instructions, while substantially increasing performance.

Since 8086 compatibility mode is the dominant use of all 80x86 processors, we will take a detailed look in this section at the 8086 architecture. We will begin by summarizing the architecture and then discuss its usage by typical programs.

8086 Instruction Set Summary

The 8086 provides support for both 8-bit (byte) and 16-bit (called word) data types. The data type distinctions apply to register operations as well as memory accesses.

The address space on the 8086 is a total of 20 bits; however, it is broken into 64-KB segments addressable with 16-bit offsets. A 20-bit address is formed by taking a 16-bit effective address—as an offset within a segment—and adding it to a 16-bit segment base address. The segment base address is obtained by shifting the contents of a 16-bit segment register 4 bits to the left.

Class	Register	Purposes of class or register
Data		**Used to hold and operate on data**
	AX	Used for multiply, divide, and I/O; sometimes an implicit operand; AH and AL also have dedicated uses in byte multiply, divide, decimal arithmetic
	BX	Can also be used as address-base register
	CX	Used for string operations and loop instructions; CL is the dynamic shift count
	DX	Used for multiply, divide, and I/O
Address		**Used to form 16-bit effective memory addresses (within segment)**
	SP	Stack pointer
	BP	Base register—used in based-addressing mode
	SI	Index register, and also used as string source base register
	DI	Index register, and also used as string destination base register
Segment		**Used to form 20-bit real memory addresses**
	CS	Code segment—used with instruction access
	SS	Stack segment—used for stack references (SP) or when BP is base register
	DS	Data segment—used when a reference is not for code (CS used), to the stack (SS used), or a string destination (ES used)
	ES	Extra segment—used when operand is string destination
Control		**Used for status and program control**
	IP	Instruction pointer—provides the offset of the currently executing instruction (this is the lower 16-bits of the effective PC)
	FLAGS	Contains six condition code bits—carry, zero, sign, borrow, parity, and overflow—and three status control bits

FIGURE 4.9 The 14 registers on the 8086. The table divides them into four classes that have restricted uses. In addition, many of the individual registers are required for certain instructions. The data registers have an upper and lower half: xL refers to lower byte and xH to upper byte of register x.

The 8086 provides a total of 14 registers broken into four groups—data registers, address registers, segment registers, and control registers—as shown in Figure 4.9. The segment register for a memory access is usually implied by the base register used to form the effective address within the segment.

The addressing modes for data on the 8086 use the segment registers implied by the addressing mode or specified in the instruction with an override of the default mode. We will discuss how branches and jumps deal with segmentation in the section on operations.

Addressing Modes

Most of the addressing modes for forming the effective address of a data operand are among those discussed in Chapter 3. The arithmetic, logical, and data-transfer instructions are two-operand instructions that allow the combinations shown in Figure 4.10.

Source/destination operand type	Second source operand
Register	Register
Register	Immediate
Register	Memory
Memory	Register
Memory	Immediate

FIGURE 4.10 Instruction types for the arithmetic, logical, and data-transfer instructions. The 8086 allows the combinations shown. Immediates may be 8 or 16 bits in length; a register is any one of the 12 major registers in Figure 4.9 (not one of the control registers). The only restriction is the absence of memory–memory mode.

The memory addressing modes supported are absolute (16-bit absolute address), register indirect, based, indexed, and based indexed with displacement (not mentioned in Chapter 3). Although a memory operand can use any addressing mode, there are restrictions on what registers can be used in a mode. The registers usable in specifying the effective address are as follows:

- *Register indirect*—BX, SI, DI.

- *Based mode with 8-bit or 16-bit displacement*—BP, BX, SI, DI. (Intel gives two names to this addressing mode, Based and Indexed, but they are essentially identical and we combine them.)

- *Indexed*—address is sum of two registers. The allowable combinations are BX+SI, BX+DI, BP+SI, and BP+DI. This mode is called Based Indexed on the 8086.

■ *Based indexed with 8-bit or 16-bit displacement*—the address is sum of displacement and contents of two registers. The same restrictions on registers apply as in indexed mode.

Operations on the 8086

The 8086 operations can be divided into four major classes:

1. Data movement instructions, including move, push, and pop

2. Arithmetic and logic instructions, including logical operations, test, shifts, and integer and decimal arithmetic operations

3. Control flow, including conditional and unconditional branches, calls, and returns

4. String instructions, including string move and string compare

Instruction	Function
`JE   name`	`if equal(CC) {IP←name};` `IP-128 ≤ name < IP+128`
`JMP   name`	`IP←name`
`CALLF name,seg`	`SP←SP-2; M[SS:SP]←CS; SP←SP-2;` `M[SS:SP]←IP+5; IP←name; CS←seg;`
`MOVW   BX,[DI+45]`	`BX←`$_{16}$`M[DS:DI+45]`
`PUSH SI`	`SP←SP-2; M[SS:SP]←SI`
`POP   DI`	`DI←M[SS:SP]; SP←SP+2`
`ADD   AX,#6765`	`AX←AX+6765`
`SHL   BX,1`	`BX←BX`$_{1..15}$` ## 0`
`TEST DX,#42`	`Set CC flags with DX & 42`
`MOVSB`	`M[ES:DI]←`$_8$`M[DS:SI];` `DI←DI+1; SI←SI+1`

FIGURE 4.11   Some typical 8086 instructions and their functions. A list of the most frequent operations appears in Figure 4.12 (page 158). We use the abbreviation SR:X to indicate the formation of an address with segment register SR and offset X. This effective address corresponding to SR:X is (SR<<4)+X. The `CALLF` saves the IP of the next instruction and the current CS on the stack.

In addition, there is a repeat prefix that may precede any string instruction, which says that the instruction should be repeated using the value in the CX register for the number of repetitions. Figure 4.11 shows some typical 8086 instructions and their functions.

Control-flow instructions must be able to address destinations in another segment. This is handled by having two types of control-flow instructions: "near" for intrasegment (within a segment) and "far" for intersegment (between segments) transfers. In far jumps, which must be unconditional, two 16-bit quantities follow the opcode. One of these is used as the instruction pointer, while the other is loaded into CS and becomes the new code segment. Calls and returns work similarly—a far call pushes the return instruction pointer and return segment on the stack and loads both the instruction pointer and code segment. A far return pops both the instruction pointer and the code segment from the stack. Programmers or compiler writers must be sure to always use the same type of call **and** return for a procedure—a near return does not work with a far call, and vice versa.

Figure 4.12 (page 158) summarizes the most popular 8086 instructions. Many of the instructions are available in both byte and word formats. A full listing of instructions appears in Appendix B.

The encoding of instructions in the 8086 is complex, and there are many different instruction formats. Instructions may vary from one byte, when there are no operands, up to six bytes, when the instruction contains a 16-bit immediate and uses 16-bit displacement addressing. Figure 4.13 (page 159) shows the instruction format for several of the example instructions in Figure 4.11 (page 156). The opcode byte usually contains a bit saying whether the instruction is a word or byte instruction. For some instructions the opcode may include the addressing mode and the register; this is true in many instructions that have the form "register←register op immediate." For other instructions a "postbyte" or extra opcode byte contains the addressing mode information. This postbyte is used for many of the instructions that address memory. The encoding of the postbyte is shown in Figure 4.14 (page 160). Finally, there is a byte prefix that is used for three different purposes. It can override the default-segment usage of instructions, and it can be used to repeat a string instruction by a count provided in CX. (This latter function is useful for string instructions that operate on a single byte or word at a time and use autoincrement addressing.) Third, it can be used to generate an atomic memory access for use in implementing synchronization.

Instruction	Meaning
Control	**Conditional and unconditional branches**
JNZ, JZ	Jump if condition to IP + 8-bit offset; JNE (for JNZ), JE (for JZ) are alternative names
JMP, JMPF	Unconditional jump—8-bit or 16-bit offset intrasegment (near), and intersegment (far) versions
CALL, CALLF	Subroutine call—16-bit offset; return address pushed; near and far versions
RET, RETF	Pops return address from stack and jumps to it; near and far versions
LOOP	Loop branch—decrement CX; jump to IP + 8-bit displacement if CX $\neq 0$
Data transfer	**Move data between registers or between register and memory**
MOV	Move between two registers or between register and memory
PUSH	Push source operand on stack
POP	Pop operand from stack top to a register
LES	Load ES and one of the GPRs from memory
Arithmetic, logical	**Arithmetic and logical operations using the data registers and memory**
ADD	Add source to destination; register–memory format
SUB	Subtract source from destination; register–memory format
CMP	Compare source and destination; register–memory format
SHL	Shift left
SHR	Shift logical right
RCR	Rotate right with Carry as fill
CBW	Convert byte in AL to word in AX
TEST	Logical AND of source and destination sets flags
INC	Increment destination; register–memory format
DEC	Decrement destination; register–memory format
OR	Logical OR; register–memory format
XOR	Exclusive OR; register–memory format
String instructions	**Move between string operands; length given by a repeat prefix**
MOVS	Copies from string source to destination; may be repeated
LODS	Loads a byte or word of a string into the A register

FIGURE 4.12 Some typical operations on the 8086. Many operations use register–memory format, where either the source or the destination may be memory and the other may be a register or immediate operand.

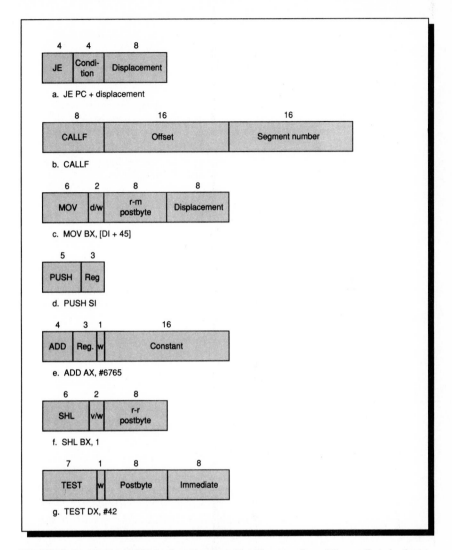

FIGURE 4.13 Typical 8086 instruction formats. The encoding of the postbyte is shown in Figure 4.14. Many instructions contain the 1-bit field w, which says whether the operation is a byte or word. Fields of the form v/w or d/w are a d-field or v-field followed by the w-field. The d-field in MOV is used in instructions that may move to or from memory and shows the direction of the move. The field v in the SHL instruction indicates a variable-length shift; variable-length shifts use a register to hold the shift count. The ADD instruction shows a typical optimized short encoding usable only when the first operand is AX. Overall instructions may vary from one to six bytes in length.

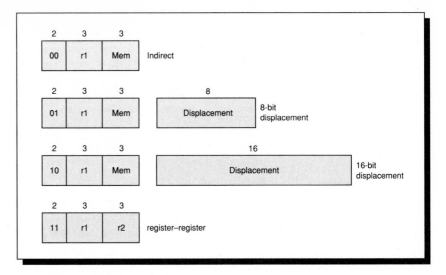

FIGURE 4.14 There are four postbyte encodings on the 8086 designated by a 2-bit tag. The first three indicate a register–memory instruction, where Mem is the base register. The fourth form is register–register.

4.5 | The DLX Architecture

In many places throughout this book we will have occasion to refer to a computer's "machine language." The machine we use is a mythical computer called "MIX." MIX is very much like nearly every computer in existence, except that is, perhaps, nicer … MIX is the world's first polyunsaturated computer. Like most machines, it has an identifying number—the 1009. This number was found by taking 16 actual computers which are very similar to MIX and on which MIX can be easily simulated, then averaging their number with equal weight:

$$\lfloor(360 + 650 + 709 + 7070 + U3 + SS80 + 1107 + 1604 + G20 + B220 + S2000 + 920 + 601 + H800 + PDP\text{-}4 + 11)/16\rfloor = 1009.$$

The same number may be obtained in a simpler way by taking Roman numerals.

Donald Knuth, *The Art of Computer Programming. Volume I: Fundamental Algorithms*

In this section we will describe a simple load/store architecture called DLX (pronounced "Deluxe"). The authors believe DLX to be the world's second polyunsaturated computer—the average of a number of recent experimental and commercial machines that are very similar in philosophy to DLX. Like Knuth, we derived the name of our machine from an average expressed in Roman numerals:

(AMD 29K, DECstation 3100, HP 850, IBM 801, Intel i860, MIPS M/120A, MIPS M/1000, Motorola 88K, RISC I, SGI 4D/60, SPARCstation-1, Sun-4/110, Sun-4/260) / 13 = 560 = DLX.

The architecture of DLX was chosen based on observations about the most frequently used primitives in programs. More sophisticated (and less performance-critical) functions are implemented in software with multiple instructions. In Section 4.9 we discuss how and why these architectures became popular.

Like most recent load/store machines, DLX emphasizes

- A simple load/store instruction set

- Design for pipelining efficiency (discussed in Chapter 6)

- An easily decoded instruction set

- Efficiency as a compiler target

DLX provides a good architectural model for study, not only because of the recent popularity of this type of machine, but also because it is an easy architecture to understand.

DLX—Our Generic Load/Store Architecture

In this section, the DLX instruction set is defined. We will use this architecture again in Chapters 5 through 7, and it forms the basis for a number of exercises and programming projects.

- The architecture has thirty-two 32-bit general-purpose registers (GPRs); the value of R0 is always 0. Additionally, there are a set of floating-point registers (FPRs), which can be used as 32 single-precision (32-bit) registers, or as even-odd pairs holding double-precision values. Thus, the 64-bit floating-point registers are named F0, F2, ..., F28, F30. Both single- and double-precision operations are provided. There are a set of special registers used for accessing status information. The FP status register is used for both compares and FP exceptions. All movement to/from the status register is through the GPRs; there is a branch that tests the comparison bit in the FP status register.

- Memory is byte addressable in Big Endian mode with a 32-bit address. All memory references are through loads or stores between memory and either the GPRs or the FPRs. Accesses involving the GPRs can be to a byte, to a halfword, or to a word. The FPRs may be loaded and stored with single-precision or double-precision words (using a pair of registers for DP). All memory accesses must be aligned. There are also instructions for moving between a FPR and a GPR.

- All instructions are 32 bits and must be aligned.

- There are also a few special registers that can be transferred to and from the integer registers. An example is the floating-point status register, used to hold information about the results of floating-point operations.

Operations

There are four classes of instructions: loads and stores, ALU operations, branches and jumps, and floating-point operations.

Example instruction	Instruction name	Meaning
LW R1,30(R2)	Load word	$R1 \leftarrow_{32} M[30+R2]$
LW R1,1000(R0)	Load word	$R1 \leftarrow_{32} M[1000+0]$
LB R1,40(R3)	Load byte	$R1 \leftarrow_{32} (M[40+R3]_0)^{24} \,\#\# \, M[40+R3]$
LBU R1,40(R3)	Load byte unsigned	$R1 \leftarrow_{32} 0^{24} \,\#\# \, M[40+R3]$
LH R1,40(R3)	Load halfword	$R1 \leftarrow_{32} (M[40+R3]_0)^{16} \,\#\#M[40+R3]\#\#M[41+R3]$
LHU R1,40(R3)	Load halfword unsigned	$R1 \leftarrow_{32} 0^{16} \,\#\#M[40+R3]\#\#M[41+R3]$
LF F0,50(R3)	Load float	$F0 \leftarrow_{32} M[50+R3]$
LD F0,50(R2)	Load double	$F0\#\#F1 \leftarrow_{64} M[50+R2]$
SW 500(R4),R3	Store word	$M[500+R4] \leftarrow_{32} R3$
SF 40(R3),F0	Store float	$M[40+R3] \leftarrow_{32} F0$
SD 40(R3),F0	Store double	$M[40+R3] \leftarrow_{32} F0; \; M[44+R3] \leftarrow_{32} F1$
SH 502(R2),R3	Store half	$M[502+R2] \leftarrow_{16} R3_{16..31}$
SB 41(R3),R2	Store byte	$M[41+R3] \leftarrow_{8} R2_{24..31}$

FIGURE 4.15 The load and store instructions in DLX. All use a single addressing mode and require that the memory value be aligned. Of course, both loads and stores are available for all the data types shown.

Any of the general-purpose or floating-point registers may be loaded or stored, except that loading R0 has no effect. There is a single addressing mode, base register + 16-bit signed offset. Halfword and byte loads place the loaded object in the lower portion of the register. The upper portion of the register is filled with either the sign extension of the loaded value or zeros, depending on the opcode. Single-precision floating-point numbers occupy a single floating-point register, while double-precision values occupy a pair. Conversions between single and double precision must be done explicitly. The floating-point format is IEEE 754 (see Appendix A). Figure 4.15 gives an example of the load and store instructions. A complete list of the instructions appears in Figure 4.18 (page 165).

All ALU instructions are register–register instructions. The operations include simple arithmetic and logical operations: add, subtract, AND, OR, XOR, and shifts. Immediate forms of all these instructions, with a 16-bit sign-extended immediate, are provided. The operation LHI (load high immediate) loads the top half of a register, while setting the lower half to 0. This allows a full 32-bit constant to be built in two instructions. (We sometimes use the mnemonic LI, standing for Load Immediate, as an abbreviation for an add immediate where one of the source operands is R0; likewise, the mnemonic MOV is sometimes used for an ADD where one of the sources is R0.)

There are also compare instructions, which compare two registers $(=,\neq,<,>,\leq,\geq)$. If the condition is true, these instructions place a 1 in the destination register (to represent true); otherwise they place the value 0. Because these operations "set" a register they are called set-equal, set-not-equal, set-less-than, and so on. There are also immediate forms of these compares. Figure 4.16 gives some examples of the arithmetic/logical instructions.

Control is handled through a set of jumps and a set of branches. The four jump instructions are differentiated by the two ways to specify the destination address and by whether or not a link is made. Two jumps use a 26-bit signed offset added to the program counter (of the instruction sequentially following the jump) to determine the destination address; the other two jump instructions specify a register that contains the destination address. There are two flavors of jumps: plain jump, and jump and link (used for procedure calls). The latter places the return address in R31.

Example instruction	Instruction name	Meaning
ADD R1,R2,R3	Add	R1←R2+R3
ADDI R1,R2,#3	Add immediate	R1←R2+3
LHI R1,#42	Load high immediate	R1←42##0^{16}
SLLI R1,R2,#5	Shift left logical	R1←R2<<5
SLT R1,R2,R3	Set less than	if (R2<R3) R1←1 else R1←0

FIGURE 4.16 Examples of arithmetic/logical instructions on DLX, both with and without immediates.

Example instruction	Instruction name	Meaning
J name	Jump	$PC \leftarrow name$; $((PC+4) - 2^{25}) \leq name < ((PC+4) + 2^{25})$
JAL name	Jump and link	$R31 \leftarrow PC+4$; $PC \leftarrow name$; $((PC+4) - 2^{25}) \leq name < ((PC+4) + 2^{25})$
JALR R2	Jump and link register	$R31 \leftarrow PC+4$; $PC \leftarrow R2$
JR R3	Jump register	$PC \leftarrow R3$
BEQZ R4,name	Branch equal zero	if (R4==0) $PC \leftarrow name$; $((PC+4) - 2^{15}) \leq name < ((PC+4) + 2^{15})$
BNEZ R4,name	Branch not equal zero	if (R4!=0) $PC \leftarrow name$; $((PC+4) - 2^{15}) \leq name < ((PC+4) + 2^{15})$

FIGURE 4.17 Typical control-flow instructions in DLX. All control instructions, except jumps to an address in a register, are PC-relative. If the register operand is R0, the branch is unconditional, but the compiler will usually prefer to use a jump with a longer offset over this "unconditional branch."

All branches are conditional. The branch condition is specified by the instruction, which may test the register source for zero or nonzero; this may be a data value or the result of a compare. The branch target address is specified with a 16-bit signed offset that is added to the program counter. Figure 4.17 gives some typical branch and jump instructions.

Floating-point instructions manipulate the floating-point registers and indicate whether the operation to be performed is single or double precision. Single-precision operations can be applied to any of the registers, while double-precision operations apply only to an even-odd pair (e.g., F4, F5), which is designated by the even register number. Load and store instructions for the floating-point registers move data between the floating-point registers and memory both in single and double precision. The operations MOVF and MOVD copy a single-precision (MOVF) or double-precision (MOVD) floating-point register to another register of the same type. The operations MOVFP2I and MOVI2FP move data between a single floating-point register and an integer register; moving a double-precision value to two integer registers require two instructions. Integer multiply and divide that work on 32-bit floating-point registers are also provided, as are conversions from integer to floating point and vice versa.

The floating-point operations are add, subtract, multiply, and divide; a suffix D is used for double precision and a suffix F is used for single precision (e.g., ADDD, ADDF, SUBD, SUBF, MULTD, MULTF, DIVD, DIVF). Floating-point compares set a bit in the special floating-point status register that can be tested with a pair of branches: BFPT and BFPF, branch floating point true and branch floating point false.

Figure 4.18 contains a list of all operations and their meaning.

Instruction type / opcode	Instruction meaning
Data transfers	**Move data between registers and memory, or between the integer and FP or special registers; only memory address mode is 16-bit displacement + contents of a GPR**
LB, LBU, SB	Load byte, load byte unsigned, store byte
LH, LHU, SH	Load halfword, load halfword unsigned, store halfword
LW, SW	Load word, store word (to/from integer registers)
LF, LD, SF, SD	Load SP float, load DP float, store SP float, store DP float
MOVI2S, MOVS2I	Move from/to GPR to/from a special register
MOVF, MOVD	Copy one floating-point register or a DP pair to another register or pair
MOVFP2I, MOVI2FP	Move 32 bits from/to FP registers to/from integer registers
Arithmetic / Logical	**Operations on integer or logical data in GPRs; signed arithmetics trap on overflow**
ADD, ADDI, ADDU, ADDUI	Add, add immediate (all immediates are 16 bits); signed and unsigned
SUB, SUBI, SUBU, SUBUI	Subtract, subtract immediate; signed and unsigned
MULT, MULTU, DIV, DIVU	Multiply and divide, signed and unsigned; operands must be floating-point registers; all operations take and yield 32-bit values
AND, ANDI	And, and immediate
OR, ORI, XOR, XORI	Or, or immediate, exclusive or, exclusive or immediate
LHI	Load high immediate—loads upper half of register with immediate
SLL, SRL, SRA, SLLI, SRLI, SRAI	Shifts: both immediate (S__I) and variable form (S__); shifts are shift left logical, right logical, right arithmetic
S__, S__I	Set conditional: "__" may be LT, GT, LE, GE, EQ, NE
Control	**Conditional branches and jumps; PC-relative or through register**
BEQZ, BNEZ	Branch GPR equal/not equal to zero; 16-bit offset from PC+4
BFPT, BFPF	Test comparison bit in the FP status register and branch; 16-bit offset from PC+4
J, JR	Jumps: 26-bit offset from PC (J) or target in register (JR)
JAL, JALR	Jump and link: save PC+4 to R31, target is PC-relative (JAL) or a register (JALR)
TRAP	Transfer to operating system at a vectored address; see Chapter 5
RFE	Return to user code from an exception; restore user mode; see Chapter 5
Floating point	**Floating-point operations on DP and SP formats**
ADDD, ADDF	Add DP, SP numbers
SUBD, SUBF	Subtract DP, SP numbers
MULTD, MULTF	Multiply DP, SP floating point
DIVD, DIVF	Divide DP, SP floating point
CVTF2D, CVTF2I, CVTD2F, CVTD2I, CVTI2F, CVTI2D	Convert instructions: CVTx2y converts from type x to type y, where x and y are one of I (Integer), D (Double precision), or F (Single precision). Both operands are in the FP registers
___D, ___F	DP and SP compares: "__" may be LT, GT, LE, GE, EQ, NE; sets comparison bit in FP status register

FIGURE 4.18 Complete list of the instructions in DLX. The formats of these instructions are shown in Figure 4.19. This list can also be found in the back inside cover.

Instruction Format

All instructions are 32 bits with a 6-bit primary opcode. Figure 4.19 shows the instruction layout.

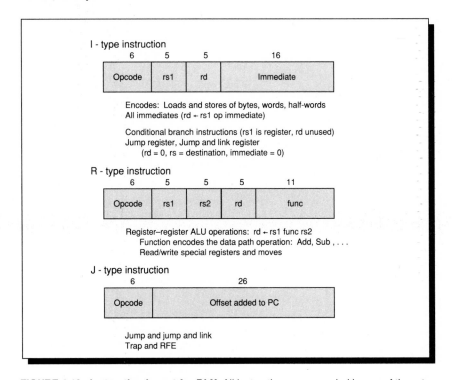

FIGURE 4.19   Instruction layout for DLX. All instructions are encoded in one of three types.

Machines Related to DLX

Between 1985 and 1990 many load/store machines were announced that are similar to DLX. Figure 4.20 describes the major features of these machines. All have 32-bit instructions and are load/store architectures; the figure lists their differences. These machines are all very similar—if you're not convinced, try making a table such as this one comparing these machines to the VAX or 8086.

DLX bears a close resemblance to all the other load/store machines shown in Figure 4.20. (See Appendix E for a detailed description of four load/store machines closely related to DLX.) Thus, the measurements in the next section will be reasonable approximations of the behavior of any of the machines. In fact, some studies suggest that compiler differences are more significant than architectural differences among these machines.

Machine	Registers	Addressing modes	Operations
DLX	32 integer; 16 DP or 32 SP FP	16-bit displacement; 16-bit immediates	See Figure 4.18.
AMD 29000	192 integer with stack cache; 8 DP FP	Register deferred only; 8-bit immediates	Integer multiply/divide trap to software. Branches =,≠ 0 only.
HP Precision Architecture	32 GPRs 32 DP or 64 SPFP	5-bit, 14-bit, and 32-bit displacements; scaled mode (load only); autoincrement; autodecrement	Every ALU operation can skip the next instruction. Many special bit-manipulation instructions. 32-bit immediates; decimal-support instructions: integer multiply/divide not single instructions. Stores of partial word. 64-bit addresses possible through segmentation.
Intel i860	32 integer; 16 DP or 32 SP FP	16-bit displacement; indexed mode; autoincrement; 16-bit immediates	Branch compares two registers for equality. Conditional traps are supported. FP reciprocal rather than divide. Some support for 128-bit loads and stores.
MIPS R2000 / R3000	32 integer; 16 FP	16-bit displacement; 16-bit immediates	Floating-point load/store moves 32 bits to upper or lower half of FP register. Branch condition can compare two registers. Integer multiply/divide in GPRs. Special instructions for partial word load/store.
Motorola 88000	32 GPRs	16-bit displacement; indexed mode	Special bit-manipulation instructions. Branches can test for zero and also test bits set by compares.
SPARC	Register windows with 32 integer registers available per procedure; 16 DP or 32 SP FP	13-bit offset and 13-bit immediates; indexed addressing mode	Branches use condition code, set selectively by instructions. Integer multiply/divide not instructions. No moves between integer and FP registers.

FIGURE 4.20 Comparison of the major features of a variety of recent load/store architectures. All the machines have a basic instruction size of 32 bits, though some provisions for shorter or longer are supported. For example, the Precision Architecture uses 2-word instructions for long immediates. Register windows and stack caches, which are used in the SPARC and AMD 29000 architectures, are discussed in Chapter 8. The MIPS R2000 is used in the DECstation 3100, the machine benchmarked in Chapter 2, and used as the load/store machine in Chapter 3. The number of double-precision floating-point registers is indicated if they are separate from the integer registers. Appendix E has a detailed comparative description of DLX, the MIPS R2000, SPARC, the i860, and the 88000 architectures. Both the MIPS and SPARC architectures have extensions that were not supported in hardware in the first implementation. These are discussed in Appendix E. In several of these machines R0=0, so they really have one less register available.

4.6 | Putting It All Together: Measurements of Instruction Set Usage

In this section we examine the dynamic use of the four instruction sets presented in this chapter. All instructions responsible for 1.5% or more of the instruction executions in a set of benchmarks are included in measurements of each architecture. In the interest of conciseness, fractional percents are rounded so that all entries in the graphs of opcode frequency will be at least 2%.

To facilitate comparisons among dynamic instruction set measurements, the measurements are organized by class of application. Figure 4.21 shows these application classes and the programs used to obtain instruction-use data on each of the machines discussed. We sometimes compare data for different architectures running the same type of application (e.g., a compiler) **but** different programs. The reader is cautioned that such comparisons must be made cautiously and with substantial limitations. Despite the fact that both programs may be the same type of application, differences in programming language, coding style, compilers, and so on, could substantially affect the results.

Machines	Compilers	Floating point	General integer	Business data processing
VAX	GCC	Spice	TeX	COBOLX
360	PL/I	FORTGO	PLIGO	COBOLGO
8086	Turbo C		Assembler	Lotus 1-2-3
DLX	GCC	Spice	TeX	US Steel

FIGURE 4.21 Programs used for reporting information about instruction mixes.
There are four types of workloads, and each workload type has a representation program—except that there is no floating-point program for the 8086. The inputs to GCC, Spice, and TeX used for the VAX were purposely shortened because the measurement process is very time intensive. (Readers who obtain measurements for the 360 or 8086 running GCC, Spice, or TeX and who are willing to share their data are asked to contact the publisher.)

In this section we present the instruction-mix measurements using a chart for each machine. The chart shows the average use of an instruction across the programs measured for that architecture. The detailed individual measurements for each program can be found in Appendix C. This appendix will be needed as a reference to do the exercises and examples in the chapter.

Remember that these measurements depend on the benchmarks chosen and the compiler technology used. While the authors feel that the measurements in this section are reasonably indicative of the usage of these four architectures, other programs may behave differently from any of the benchmarks here, and different compilers may yield different results. In doing a real instruction set study, the architect would want to have a much larger set of benchmarks, spanning as wide an application range as possible. He would also want to consider the operating system and its usage of the instruction set. Single-user benchmarks like those measured here do not necessarily behave in the same fashion as the operating system.

VAX Instruction Set Measurements

The data on VAX instruction set usage in this section come primarily from measurements on our three benchmark programs. We add the data reported in another study for COBOL when we discuss opcode distributions. For these measurements, Spice and TeX were compiled with the globally optimizing versions of the VAX compilers originally developed for VMS (called VCC and fort). GCC cannot be compiled by the vcc compiler and hence uses the standard VAX cc compiler, which performs only peephole optimization. Once compiled, these programs were run with the Trace bit turned on. This causes the program to trap on every instruction execution, allowing a measurement program to collect data. Because this slows the program down by a factor of between 1,000 and 10,000 times, smaller inputs were used for the programs GCC, TeX, and Spice.

Addressing Mode Usage

Let's begin by looking at the VAX addressing modes, since the choice addressing modes and operations are orthogonal. First, we break the references into three broad classes: register, immediate (including short literal), and memory addressing modes. Figure 4.22 shows the breakdown into these three classes for our benchmarks. In all three programs, more than half the operand references are to registers.

About one-third of the operands on the VAX are memory references. How are those memory locations specified? The VAX memory addressing modes fall

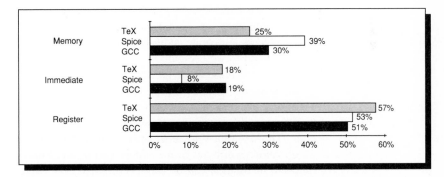

FIGURE 4.22 Breakdown of basic operand types for the three benchmarks on the VAX. The frequencies are very similar across programs, except for the low usage of immediates by Spice and its correspondingly higher use of memory operands. This probably arises because few floating-point constants are stored as immediates, but are instead accessed from memory. An operand is counted by the number of times it appears in an instruction, rather than by the number of references. Thus, the instruction ADDL2 R1,45(R2) counts as one memory reference and one register reference. The memory address modes in Figure 4.23 are counted in the same fashion. Wiecek [1982] reports that about 90% of the operand accesses are either a read or a write, and only about 10% of the accesses both read and write the same operand (such as R1 in the ADDL2).

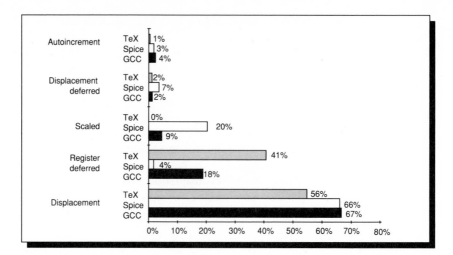

**FIGURE 4.23 Use of VAX memory addressing modes, which account for about 31%
of the operand references, in the three programs.** Spice again stands out because of
the low frequency of register deferred. In Spice, nonzero displacement values occur much
more frequently. The use of arrays rather than pointers probably influences this. Likewise,
Spice uses the scaled mode to access array elements. The displacement deferred mode is
used to access actual parameters in a FORTRAN subroutine. Remember that PC-based
addressing is not included here—use of PC-based addressing can be measured by branch
frequency.

into three separate classes: PC-based addressing, scaled addressing, and the
other addressing modes (sometimes called the general addressing modes). The
primary use of PC-based addressing is to specify branch targets, rather than data
operands; thus, we do not include this addressing mode here. Scaled mode is
counted as a separate addressing mode, and the based mode on which it is built
is counted as well. Figure 4.23 shows the use of addressing modes in the three
benchmark programs. Not surprisingly, displacement mode dominates. Taken
together, displacement and register deferred, which is essentially a special case
of displacement with a zero constant value, constitute from 70% to 96% of the
dynamically occurring addressing modes.

   The size of a VAX instruction is almost always one byte for the opcode plus
the number of bytes in the addressing modes. From these data the average size
of an instruction can be estimated. Architects often do this type of estimating
when they do not have exact measurements available. This is particularly true
when data collection is expensive. Collecting the VAX data in this chapter, for
example, took from one to several days of running time for each program.

Example   The average VAX instruction has 1.8 operands. Use this fact and the data on
displacement sizes in Figure 3.13 (on page 100 of Chapter 3) to estimate the
average size of a VAX instruction. Such an estimate is useful for determining
memory bandwidth per instruction, a critical design parameter.

Answer

From the above data we know that literal and register modes, which each take 1 byte, dominate the mix. The most heavily used addressing mode, displacement mode, can vary from 2 bytes to 5 bytes—the register byte plus 1 or more offset bytes. Based on the length information in Figure 3.13 we guess that the average displacement is 1.5 bytes, for a total size of 2.5 bytes for the addressing mode. For this example, we assume that literal, register, and displacement modes make up all the accesses.

This means there is 1 byte for the opcode, 1 byte for register or literal mode, and about 2.5 bytes for displacement mode. Using 1.8 operands per instruction and the average frequencies of accesses from Figure 4.22 (page 169), we obtain $1 + 1.8 * (0.54 + 0.15 + 0.31 * 2.5)$ or 3.64 bytes.

Wiecek [1982] measured 3.8 bytes per instruction. Direct measurements of our three programs showed the average sizes to be 3.6, 4.9, and 4.2 for GCC, Spice, and TeX, respectively.

Instruction Mixes

Now let's look at the distribution for instruction operations, using our three benchmarks plus the COBOLX program from the study published by Clark and Levy [1982]. COBOLX is a synthetic, internal DEC benchmark that was compiled by the VAX VMS COBOL compiler and uses decimal instructions. However, the new DEC compilers for the VAX avoid using the decimal instruction set, since most of that portion of the architecture is emulated in software—and is therefore much slower—on the newer VLSI-based VAXes.

The data in this section are presented in chart form, but detailed tables for each machine and benchmark appear in Appendix C. The data here focus on instruction frequency, but frequency distributions and time distributions do not always match. We will see an example of this in the next section. Appendix D contains a set of detailed measurements based on time-distribution measurements.

Figure 4.24 shows all instructions responsible for more than 1.5% of the dynamic instruction executions across all the benchmarks. Each complete bar shows an average instruction mix over the four programs, and how the programs make up that mix.

GCC and TeX are very similar in behavior; the largest difference is the higher frequency of data transfers in TeX. Spice and COBOLX look very different. Each of these executes more than 20% of its instructions using a portion of the instruction set that is essentially unused by the other benchmarks. Both COBOLX and Spice do many fewer integer arithmetic operations, instead using decimal or floating-point operations. COBOLX makes small use of the data transfer instructions (4% versus an average of 20% for the other three programs); instead, 38% of the instructions it executes are decimal or string instructions.

These 27 instructions in Figure 4.24 correspond to an average of 88% of the instructions executed in the four benchmarks. However, the tail of the

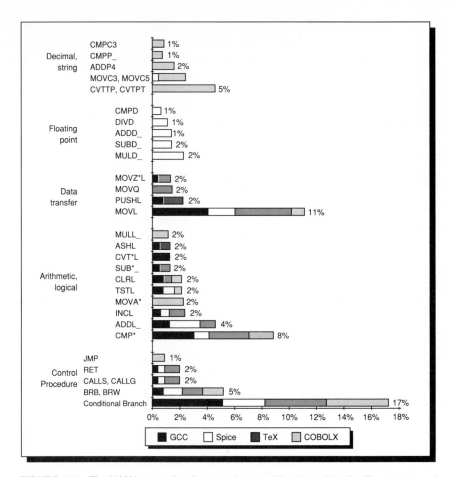

FIGURE 4.24   The VAX instruction frequencies combined graphically. The total size of each bar shows the behavior that would be seen on a machine that ran these four programs with equal frequency. The segments of the bar show what percentage of the usage of that instruction would come from each of the programs. This illustrates that some portions of the instruction set need to be there for only one class of applications. Overall, only a small number of instructions outside of the control, data transfer, and integer arithmetic instructions are heavily used.

distribution is long and there are many instructions executed with a frequency of 1/2 to 1%. In Spice, for example, the top 15 instructions make up 90% of the executions, and the top 26 make up 95%. However, there are 149 different VAX instructions executed at least once!

Measurements of 360 Instruction Set Usage

The measurements in this section are taken from those made by Shustek in his Ph.D. thesis [1978]. His work includes a study of the dynamic characteristics of seven large programs on the IBM 360 architecture. He collected his data by building an interpreter for the 360 architecture. The four programs described in Figure 4.25 are used in this section to examine characteristics of 360 instruction set usage.

Program	Benchmark class	Instruction count	Program function
COBOLGO	Business D.P.	3,559,533	COBOL usage report formatter
PLIGO	General integer	23,863,497	PL/I computer usage accounting
FORTGO	Floating point	11,719,853	FORTRAN linear systems solver
PLIC	Compiler	24,338,101	PL/I compile

FIGURE 4.25 Four programs used to measure the IBM 360. The suffix "GO" indicates an execution of a program, while the suffix "C" indicates a compile. We chose the PL/I compiler because it is the largest and most representative; it is also written in PL/I. Shustek's thesis used two FORTRAN executions. We chose to use LINSYS2 to represent the FORTRAN execution, since it is a more typical FORTRAN program; we refer to the execution of LINSYS2 as FORTGO.

Addressing Modes and Instruction Types

Figure 4.26 shows the frequency of data accesses by addressing mode. The COBOL program has a very high frequency of data accesses. Movements of character data and use of decimal data, which always reside in memory, probably account for this. FORTGO has a substantially lower number of memory references. This may arise because of allocation of variables to registers in the tight inner loops of the program.

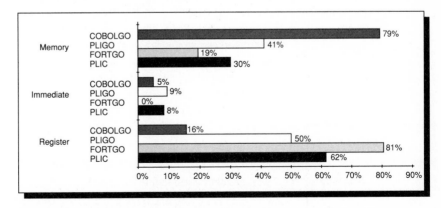

FIGURE 4.26 Distribution of operand accesses made by 360 instructions. Limited support for immediates is the chief reason that immediates see so little use.

There are only two memory addressing modes on the 360: base register + displacement (RS format, SI format, and SS format) and base register + displacement + index register (RX format). However, the operations available in the instructions that address memory typically appear in only one format. Therefore, it is probably most useful to look at instruction format usage, as shown in Figure 4.27. Most instructions are RX format with RR following behind that. The high usage of RX format should not lead you to conclude that the displacement + base register + index register addressing mode is heavily used, because in 85% of the RX instructions the index register is zero. COBOL displays a high percentage of SS-format instructions, and this is to be expected because the decimal and string instructions are all SS format. The FORTRAN execution displays a large percentage of RR format, 2-byte instructions. This makes sense in a program that makes heavy use of registers in its optimized inner loops.

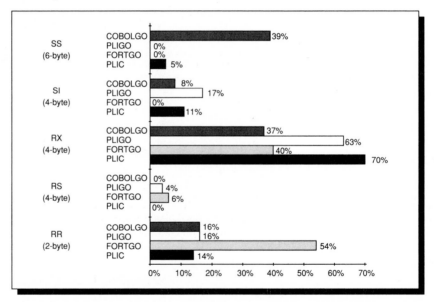

FIGURE 4.27 Percentage of 6-, 4-, and 2-byte instructions for the four 360 programs. The majority of the instructions are 4 bytes, and almost none are 6 bytes, except when running COBOLGO.

Example

Given the data in Figure 4.27 compute the average instruction length for the PLIGO program.

Answer

The average instruction length is

$$6 * \% \ SS + 4 * (\% \ RX + \% \ RS + \% \ SI) + 2 * \% \ RR$$
$$= 0 + 4 * (0.63 + 0.04 + 0.17) + 2 * 0.16 = 3.68 \text{ bytes}$$

Across all the four programs the average measured length is 3.7 bytes.

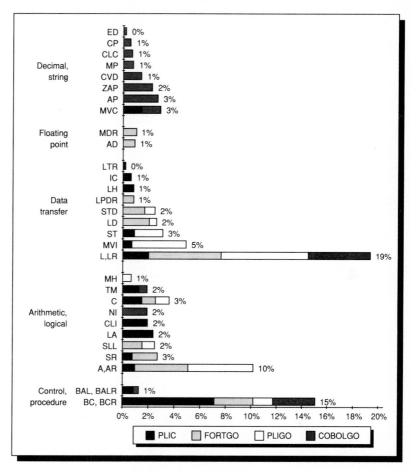

FIGURE 4.28 Combined data for the four programs on the 360. Compare this with Figure 4.24, where the data for the VAX are graphed.

Instruction Mixes

Now let's examine the data for the instruction mixes. Figure 4.28 shows the most heavily used instructions in the four 360 benchmarks. As Figure 4.28 illustrates, variations among the programs are very large. The PL/I compiler has an extraordinarily large number of branches, while the PL/I execution has very few. The use of arithmetic and logical operators is fairly uniform with the exception of the COBOL program, which uses decimal operations instead.

Comparing these programs to the VAX, the much lower frequency of branches—16% on the 360 versus 23% on the VAX—stands out. The number of branches in a program is largely fixed by the program, except for some architectural anomalies and possible compiler optimizations (such as loop unrolling—discussed in Chapter 6—but not used by these compilers). Thus, the percentage of branches is an indirect measure of instruction power or density, since it says how many other instructions are required for each branch. We would expect the VAX with its more powerful addressing modes and multiple memory operands per instruction to have a high instruction density and a higher branch frequency. We see further evidence of greater instruction density of the VAX in the higher frequency of data transfers on the 360—more data is moved explicitly on the 360 rather than used as memory operands, as on the VAX. However, we cannot draw any specific quantitative conclusions about instruction density because the measured programs and compilers are different.

Also very different is the percentage of character and string operations used by the 360 versus the VAX for the two COBOL applications. Finally, the FORTRAN execution uses a much larger number of integer operations on the 360; this may be traceable to differences arising when the VAX uses an addressing mode but the 360 must use explicit instructions for address calculations.

As we have seen, the differences in instruction usage on the 360 and VAX are fairly significant. The next two architectures differ from these first two even more dramatically.

Measurements of 8086 Usage

The data in this section were collected by Adams and Zimmerman [1989] in a study of seven programs running on an IBM PC under MS DOS 3.1. They collected the data by single-stepping the programs and collecting data after every instruction execution, just as was done for the VAX. The three programs used here, a brief description, and the number of instructions executed are shown in Figure 4.29. As with the VAX and 360, we will begin by examining operand access and addressing modes, and then progress to instruction mixes.

Addressing Modes and Instruction Length

Our first measurement on the 8086, shown in Figure 4.30, graphs the origins of operands. Immediates play a small role, while register access slightly dominates memory access. Compared to the VAX, these programs on the 8086 use a higher frequency of memory operands. The limited register set of the 8086 probably

Program	Benchmark class	Instruction count	Program function
Lotus	Business	2,904,931	Lotus 1-2-3 calculating a 128-cell worksheet four times
MASM	General integer	2,365,711	Microsoft Macro Assembler assembling a 500-line program
Turbo C	Compiler	1,806,143	Turbo C compiling Dhrystone

FIGURE 4.29 Three programs used for 8086 measurements. The benchmarks are written in a combination of 8086 Assembler and in C.

plays a role in increasing the memory traffic, which substantially exceeds that of the 360, if we ignore the COBOL program (which must use SS instructions) on the 360.

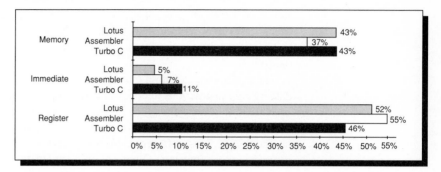

FIGURE 4.30   Three classes of basic operand access on the 8086 and their distribution. The implied use of the accumulator register (AX), which occurs in a number of instructions, is counted as a register access.

In the above programs 41% of the operand references are memory accesses. Figure 4.31 shows the distribution of addressing modes for these memory references.

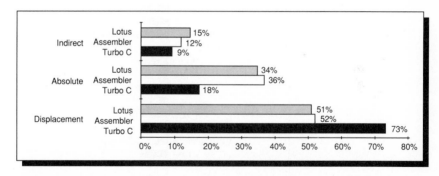

FIGURE 4.31   The 8086 memory addressing modes shown in this graph account for almost all the memory references in the three programs. Memory addressing modes indexed and based have been combined, since their effective address calculations are the same. Register indirect mode is in effect based with a zero offset, equivalent to the VAX register-deferred mode. If register indirect were counted as a based mode with zero offset, about two-thirds of the memory references would be displacement mode. The other two remaining modes are essentially unused in the three programs.

The variable-length instructions, use of implicit registers, and small size of the register specifier combine to yield a fairly short average instruction. For these three programs the average instruction length is approximately 2.5 bytes.

Instruction Mixes on the 8086

The instructions responsible for greater than 1.5% of the executions for the 8086 running the three programs are shown graphically in Figure 4.32. The displayed subset of the instruction set accounts for a higher proportion of all instruction executions (90%) than it does on the VAX or 360. As we might suspect, the architectures with smaller instruction repertoires use a higher percentage of their opcodes.

The major distinguishing characteristic among the programs is the shift from data transfer instructions to control instructions in Lotus. Lotus makes heavy use of the LOOP instruction, which may account for that shift.

The overall frequency of move instructions is much larger on the 8086 than on the VAX. This difference probably arises because the 8086 has fewer general-purpose registers. Other possible explanations include the use of string instructions that generate a sequence of move instructions, and explicit movement of data among segments to ease processing. The total branch frequency is not very different between the 8086 and VAX, though the distribution of different types of control instructions is very different. The percentage of arithmetic operations on the 8086 is much smaller, due at least partially to the larger number of move instructions.

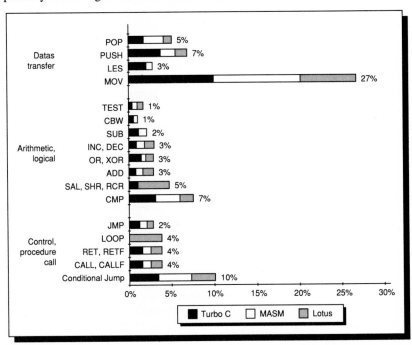

FIGURE 4.32 Distribution of instruction frequencies on the 8086 shown in the same format used for the VAX and 360.

In this and the preceding two sections we saw machines designed in the 1960s (the 360) and the 1970s (the VAX and the 8086). In the next section we will talk about a machine typical of those designed in the 1980s and its usage.

Instruction Set Usage Measurements on DLX

As with the other architectures we have looked at thus far, we start our examination of instruction set usage on DLX with measurements of operand location and move from there to instruction mixes. The DLX data throughout the book was measured using the MIPS R2000/3000 architecture and adjusting the data to reflect the differences between DLX and the MIPS architecture. The MIPS compiler technology with optimization level 2, which does full global optimization with register allocation, was used to compile the programs. A special program called pixie was used to instrument the object module. The instrumented object module produces a monitoring file that is used to produce detailed execution statistics.

Addressing Mode Usage

Operand usage is shown in Figure 4.33. This data is very uniform across the applications on DLX. Compared to the VAX, a much higher percentage of the operand references are to registers: On the VAX, only about half the references are to registers, while roughly three-quarters are on DLX. This probably occurs because of the larger number of registers available on DLX and greater emphasis on register allocation by the DLX compiler.

Since DLX has only a single addressing mode, it makes no sense to ask what the distribution of addressing modes is. However, we noticed earlier that on the VAX and 8086 the deferred addressing mode, which is equivalent to displacement addressing with a zero displacement, was the second or third most popular. Would it be useful to add this mode to DLX?

Example

Using the data on offset values from Figure 3.13 on page 100, determine how often on average deferred mode would be used for the three programs if the case of a zero-offset displacement were made a special mode. In particular, what percentage of the memory references would use it? How much memory bandwidth would be saved if we had a 16-bit instruction for this addressing mode?

Answer

The frequencies of zero-offset displacement values are

GCC: 27%

Spice: 4%

TeX: 17%

The average frequency for a zero-offset value is then $(27\% + 4\% + 17\%)/3 = 16\%$. Thus, the mode would be used by 16% of the loads and stores, which average 32% of the executions. The decrease in instruction bandwidth would be about $\frac{1}{2} * 32\% * 16\%$, or about 3%.

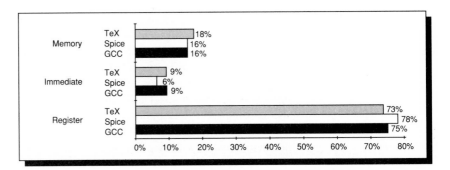

FIGURE 4.33   Distribution of operand accesses for the three benchmarks on DLX. Only accesses for operands—not for effective address calculations—are included. The fact that DLX has only 3-operand register formats probably increases the frequency of register operand access slightly, since some instructions probably have only two unique register operands and use one register as both a source and destination. On a machine like the VAX, such an operation might use a 2-operand instruction and thus be counted as having only 2 register operands. This effect has not been measured.

The other two addressing modes used with some frequency are scaled on the VAX and absolute on the 8086. Scaled addressing mode is synthesized on DLX with a separate add; the presence of this address mode is significantly affected by the compiler technology. Better optimizers use the indexed mode less often because the optimization of induction variable elimination obviates the need for indexed addressing and for scaling (see the discussion in Section 3.7). The direct mode is synthesized by dedicating a register to point to a global area and accessing variables with a displacement from that register. Because only scalar variables (i.e., not structures or arrays) need to be accessed in this way, this works very well for most programs.

Instruction Mixes on DLX

Figure 4.34 shows the instruction mixes for our three programs plus the U.S. Steel COBOL benchmark—the most widely employed COBOL benchmark. The benchmark is a synthetic program of about 1,000 lines in length. It is included here because its behavior is substantially different from FORTRAN and C programs. Measurements on COBOL are also interesting because they reflect what changes in instruction set usage occur when decimal arithmetic is not directly supported by decimal instructions. Let's first look at the differences among the programs before we consider how these mixes compare to the VAX.

The significant differences among these programs are surprising. Both Spice and TeX stand out as having very low branch frequency. The effect of translating the decimal arithmetic of COBOL into binary arithmetic is clearly seen in the large percentage of arithmetic operations in US Steel. Shifts, logical operators, and load immediates, which are all used to do fast decimal-binary conversion, occur in significant frequencies. US Steel's low frequency of data transfer is certainly affected by this increase in arithmetic and logical operations. Interestingly, only the call frequency of US Steel is high enough to account for more than 1% of the instruction executions (the frequency of JAL is about 1% for the other three benchmarks).

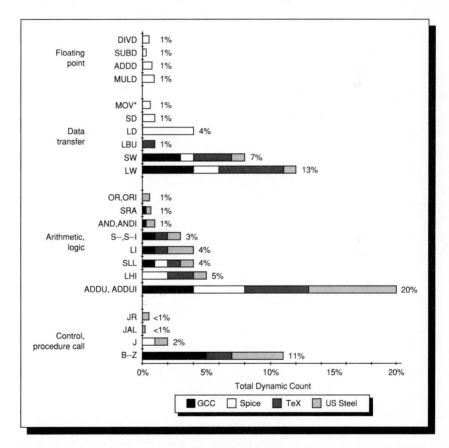

FIGURE 4.34   The DLX instruction mix visible over four programs with breakdown showing each program's contribution. What is remarkable is how a small number of instructions—conditional branch, add, load, and store—dominate across all four programs. The opcode LI is really an ADDUI with R0 as an operand; the high frequency of ADDU and ADDUI is discussed below.

These mixes differ dramatically from the VAX (or other machines in this section). One difference is the very high percentage of `ADDU` and `ADDUI` instructions. These instructions are used for a variety of purposes where the other machines may use a different instruction or a more powerful addressing mode or instruction. Among the most frequent uses for `ADDU` and `ADDUI` are: register–register copies (coded as `ADDU` with R0), synthesizing an address mode such as scaled, and incrementing the stack pointer on a procedure call.

It is interesting to compare the branch frequency between DLX and the VAX, since the absolute branch count should be approximately equal (for reasons discussed earlier), and the ratio of branch frequencies should be about the same as the ratio of overall instruction counts. However, the compilers may affect the type of branch used—conditional branch versus jump—so we need to combine all the branches and jumps, except those used in procedure calls, to make a comparison.

Example

Find the ratio of absolute branches on the VAX versus DLX for the three common benchmarks. The ratio of instruction counts, measured in Section 3.8 is

$$\frac{\text{InstructionsDLX}}{\text{InstructionsVAX}} = 2.0$$

Use the data in Appendix C for exact percentages of branches.

Answer

From Appendix C, we find that the average branch frequency on DLX is $\frac{19\%+2\%+7\%}{3} = 9.3\%$, while the average for the VAX is 17.3%. Thus, the ratio of the branch counts is

$$\frac{\text{Branches}_{DLX}}{\text{Branches}_{VAX}} = \frac{9.3\% * \text{Instructions}_{DLX}}{17.3\% * \text{Instructions}_{VAX}}$$

$$= \frac{9.3 * 2.0 * \text{Instructions}_{VAX}}{17.3 * \text{Instructions}_{VAX}}$$

$$= \frac{18.6}{17.3} = 1.08$$

So DLX does about 8% more branches.

In the arithmetic and logical instructions, GCC and US Steel are the most different between the VAX and DLX. We know US Steel differs because of the absence of decimal instructions—it would be interesting to see what the instruction mix on such a program would look like with the new VAX compilers that avoid the decimal instructions. Another major difference between the two machines is the lower frequency of compare instructions and test instructions on DLX. The use of compare with zero in the branch instruction is responsible for this. Because the set instructions are also used to set logical variables, we cannot know exactly what percentage of conditional branches on DLX do not need a compare, but we can guess that it is between 75% and 80%.

The difference in data transfers has been discussed extensively at the end of Chapter 3 (for a machine very close to DLX) and in the previous subsection. We know that the larger number of registers (at least twice as many) and more ambitious register allocator mean that the load and store frequency is lower on DLX than on the VAX.

We have now seen instruction mixes for four very different machines. In Appendix D we can see how these mixes differ when we look at time distributions rather than frequency of occurrence, and in the next section we will review some of our key observations and point out some additional pitfalls using data we have examined in this and earlier sections.

4.7 | Fallacies and Pitfalls

*Fallacy: There is such a thing as **a** typical program.*

Many people would like to believe that there is a single "typical" program that could be used to design an optimal instruction set. For example, see the synthetic benchmarks discussed in Section 2.2. The data in this chapter clearly show that programs can vary significantly in how they use an instruction set. For example, the frequency of control-flow instructions on DLX varied from 5% to 23%. The variations are even larger on an instruction set that has specific features for supporting a class of applications, such as decimal or floating-point instructions that are unused by other applications. There is a related pitfall.

Pitfall: Designing an architecture on the basis of small benchmarks or large benchmarks from a restricted application domain when the machine is intended to be general purpose.

Many programs exhibit somewhat biased behavior or do not use a particular aspect of an architecture. Obviously, choosing TeX or GCC benchmarks to design the instruction set might result in a machine that wouldn't do well on a program like Spice or COBOLX. A more subtle example arises when choosing a representative, but synthetic, benchmark. For example, Dhrystone (see Section 2.2) does a procedure call approximately every 40 instructions on a machine like DLX—the number of procedure calls is more than half the number of conditional branches! By comparison, in GCC a call occurs about once every 100 instructions, and branches are 15 times more frequent than procedure calls.

Fallacy: An architecture with flaws cannot be successful.

The IBM 360 is often criticized in the literature—the branches are not PC-relative, and the offset is too small in based addressing. Yet, the machine has been an enormous success because it did several new things properly. First, the architecture has a big enough address space. Second, it is byte addressed and handles bytes well. Third, it is a general-purpose register machine. Finally, it is simple enough that it can be efficiently implemented across a wide performance and cost range.

The 8086 provides an even more dramatic example. The 8086 architecture is the only widespread architecture in existence today that is not truly a general-purpose register machine. Furthermore, the segmented address space of the 8086 causes major problems both for programmers and compiler writers. Despite these major difficulties, the 8086 architecture—because of its selection as the microprocessor in the IBM PC—has been enormously successful.

Fallacy: One can design a flawless architecture.

All architecture design involves tradeoffs made in the context of a set of hardware and software technologies. Over time those technologies are likely to change, and decisions that may have been correct at the time they were made look like mistakes. For example, in 1975 the VAX designers overemphasized the importance of code-size efficiency and underestimated how important ease of decoding and pipelining would be ten years later. Almost all architectures eventually succumb to the lack of sufficient address space. However, avoiding this problem in the long run would probably mean compromising the efficiency of the architecture in the short run.

Fallacy: In instruction mixes, time distribution and frequency distribution will be close.

Appendix D shows the time distributions for our benchmark programs and compares the time and frequency distributions. A simple example of where these distributions are very different is in the COBOLGO program on the 360. Figure 4.35 shows the top instructions by frequency and by time. The two highest occurring instructions are responsible for 33% of the instruction executions in COBOLGO, but only 4% of the execution time! Remember that time distributions are dependent on both the architecture and the **implementation** used for the measurement. Hence, time distributions may differ from model to model, while frequency distributions will be the same, provided neither the software nor the program changes. This large difference between time and frequency distributions does not exist for simpler load/store architectures, such as DLX.

Pitfall: Examining only the worst-case or average behavior of an instruction as design input.

The best example of this comes from the use of MVC on an IBM 360. The instruction can move overlapped fields of characters, but this occurs less than 1% of the time, and then usually to clear a field. The average length of a move as measured by Shustek was ten bytes, but more than three-quarters of the moves were either one byte or four bytes in length. Assuming worst-case behavior (overlapping strings) or average length can each lead to suboptimal design decisions.

Top instructions by frequency	Frequency	Top instructions by time distribution	Percentage of time
L, LR	19%	ZAP	16%
BC, BCR	14%	AP	16%
AP	11%	MP	13%
ZAP	9%	MVC	9%
MVC	7%	CVD	5%

FIGURE 4.35   The top five instructions by frequency and by time for the COBOLGO benchmark run on the 360. The actual frequency or percentage of time is also shown. Further data appears in Appendix D.

4.8 | Concluding Remarks

We have seen that instruction sets can vary quite dramatically, both in how they access operands and in the operations that can be performed by a single instruction. The comparison of opcode usage across architectures by instruction frequency is summarized in Figure 4.36. This figure shows that even very different architectures behave similarly in their use of instruction classes. However, this should also remind us that performance may be only distantly related to instruction usage—the execution-time distributions for these architectures in Appendix D look very different indeed.

Dramatic though the variation in instruction usage is across architectures, it is equally dramatic across applications. We have seen that floating-point programs, COBOL programs, and C systems programs differ in how they use a machine. Large segments of the instruction set are unused by some programs. When such application-specific features are not part of the instruction set—for example, the absence of decimal instructions in DLX—the impact is a shift in the use of other parts of the instruction. Even across two programs written in the same language—GCC and TeX, or PLIC and PLIGO—the differences in instruction usage can be significant.

Instruction-usage data are an important input for the architect, but they do not necessarily tell us what are the most time-consuming instructions. The next several chapters will help explain why the difference arises by quantifying the CPI difference among instructions and machines.

Machine	Program	Control	Arithmetic, logical	Data transfer	Floating point	Decimal, string	Totals
VAX	GCC	30%	40%	19%			89%
VAX	Spice	18%	23%	15%	23%		79%
VAX	TeX	30%	33%	28%			91%
VAX	COBOLX	25%	24%	4%		38%	91%
360	PLIC	32%	29%	17%		4%	82%
360	FORTGO	13%	35%	40%	7%		95%
360	PLIGO	5%	29%	56%			90%
360	COBOLGO	16%	9%	20%		40%	85%
8086	Turbo C	21%	23%	49%			93%
8086	MASM	20%	24%	46%			90%
8086	Lotus	32%	26%	30%			88%
DLX	GCC	24%	35%	27%			86%
DLX	Spice	4%	29%	35%	15%		83%
DLX	TeX	10%	41%	33%			84%
DLX	US Steel	23%	49%	10%			82%

FIGURE 4.36 The frequency of instruction distribution for each benchmark broken into five classes of instructions. Because only instructions with frequencies greater than 1.5% have been included in previous figures, the totals are less than 100%.

4.9 | Historical Perspective and References

Although a large number of machines have been developed in the same time frames as the four machines covered in this chapter, the discussion here is confined to these machines and measurements of them.

The IBM 360 was introduced in 1964 with six models and a 25:1 performance ratio. Amdahl, Blaauw, and Brooks [1964] discuss the architecture of the IBM 360 and the concept of permitting multiple object-code–compatible implementations. The notion of an instruction set architecture as we understand it today was the most important aspect of the 360. The architecture also introduced several important innovations, now in wide use:

1. 32-bit architecture

2. Byte-addressable memory with 8-bit bytes

3. 8-, 16-, 32-, and 64-bit data sizes

In 1971, IBM shipped the first System/370 (models 155 and 165), which included a number of significant extensions of the 360, as discussed by Case and Padegs [1978], who also discuss the early history of System/360. The most important addition was virtual memory, though virtual memory 370s did not ship until 1972 when a virtual-memory operating system was ready. By 1978, the high-end 370 was several hundred times faster than the low-end 360s shipped ten years earlier. In 1984, the 24-bit addressing model built into the IBM 360 needed to be abandoned, and the 370-XA (eXtended Architecture) was introduced. While old 24-bit programs could be supported without change, several instructions could not function in the same manner when extended to a 32-bit addressing model (31-bit addresses supported) because they would not produce 31-bit addresses. Converting the operating system, which was written mostly in assembly language, was no doubt the biggest task.

Several studies of the IBM 360 and instruction measurement have been made. Shustek's thesis [1978] is the best known and most complete study of the 360/370 architecture. He made several observations about instruction set complexity that were not fully appreciated until some years later. Another important study of the 360 is the Toronto study by Alexander and Wortman [1975] done on an IBM 360 using 19 XPL programs.

In the mid-1970s, DEC realized that the PDP-11 was running out of address space. The 16-bit space had been extended in several creative ways. However, as Strecker and Bell [1976] observed, the small address space was a problem that could not be overcome, but only postponed.

In 1978, DEC introduced the VAX. Strecker [1978] described the architecture and called the VAX "a Virtual Address eXtension of the PDP-11." One of DEC's primary goals was to keep the installed base of PDP-11 customers. Thus, the customers were to think of the VAX as a 32-bit successor to the PDP-11. A 32-bit PDP-11 was possible—there were three designs—but Strecker reports that they were "overly compromised in terms of efficiency, functionality, programming ease." The chosen solution was to design a new architecture and include a PDP-11 compatibility mode that would run PDP-11 programs without change. This mode also allowed PDP-11 compilers to run and to continue to be used. The VAX-11/780 was made similar to the PDP-11 in many ways. These are among the most important:

1. Data types and formats are mostly equivalent to those on the PDP-11. The F and D floating formats came from the PDP-11. G and H formats were added later. The use of the term "word" to describe a 16-bit quantity was carried from the PDP-11 to the VAX.

2. The assembly language was made similar to the PDP-11's.

3. The same buses were supported (Unibus and Massbus).

4. The operating system, VMS, was "an evolution" of the RSX-11M/IAS OS (as opposed to the DECsystem 10/20 OS, which was a more advanced system).

5. The file system was basically the same.

The VAX-11/780 was the first machine announced in the VAX series. It is one of the most successful and heavily studied machines ever built. The cornerstone of DEC's strategy was a single architecture, VAX, running a single operating system, VMS. This strategy worked well for over ten years. The large number of papers reporting instruction mixes, implementation measurements, and analysis of the VAX make it an ideal case study.

Wiecek [1982] reported on the use of various architectural features in running a workload consisting of six compilers. Emer did a set of measurements (reported by Clark and Levy [1982]) on the instruction set utilization of the VAX when running four very different programs and when running the operating system. A good detailed description of the architecture, including memory management and an examination of several of the VAX implementations, can be found in Levy and Eckhouse [1989].

The first microprocessors were produced late in the first half of the 1970s. The Intel 4004 and 8008 were extremely simple 4-bit and 8-bit accumulator-style machines. Morse et al. [1980] describe the evolution of the 8086 from the 8080 in the late 1970s in an attempt to provide a 16-bit machine with better throughput. At that time almost all programming for microprocessors was done in assembly language—both memory and compilers were in short supply. Intel wanted to keep its base of 8080 users, so the 8086 was designed to be "compatible" with the 8080. The 8086 was **never** object-code compatible with the 8080, but the machines were close enough that translation of assembly language programs could be done automatically.

In early 1980, IBM selected a version of the 8086 with an 8-bit external bus, called the 8088, for use in the IBM PC. (They chose the 8-bit version to reduce the cost of the machine.) This choice, together with the tremendous success of the IBM PC and its clones (made possible because IBM opened the architecture of the PC), has made the 8086 architecture ubiquitous. While the 68000 was chosen for the popular Macintosh, the Macintosh was never as pervasive as the PC (partly because Apple did not allow clones), and the 68000 did not acquire the same software leverage that the 8086 enjoys. The Motorola 68000 may have been more significant **technically** than the 8086, but the impact of the selection by IBM and IBM's open architecture strategy dominated the technical advantages of the 68000 in the market. As discussed in Section 4.4, the 80186, 80286, 80386, and 80486 have extended the architecture and provided a series of performance enhancements.

There are numerous descriptions of the 80x86 architecture that have been published—Wakerly's [1989] is both concise and easy to understand. Crawford and Gelsinger [1988] is a thorough description of the 80386. The work of Adams and Zimmerman [1989] represents the first detailed, published study of the dynamic use of the architecture that we are aware of; the data on the 8086 used in this book come from their study.

The simple load/store machines from which DLX is derived are commonly called RISC *(reduced instruction set computer)* architectures. The roots of RISC architectures go back to machines like the 6600, where Thornton, Cray, and others recognized the importance of instruction set simplicity in building a fast machine. Cray continued his tradition of keeping machines simple in the CRAY-1. However, DLX and its close relatives are built primarily on the work of three research projects: the Berkeley RISC processor, the IBM 801, and the Stanford MIPS processor. These architectures have attracted enormous industrial interest because of claims of a performance advantage of anywhere from two to five times over other machines using the same technology.

Begun in the late 1970s, the IBM project was the first to start but was the last to become public. The IBM machine was designed as an ECL minicomputer, while the university projects were both MOS-based microprocessors. John Cocke is considered to be the father of the 801 design. He received both the Eckert-Mauchly and Turing awards in recognition of his contribution. Radin [1982] describes the highlights of the 801 architecture. The 801 was an experimental project, but was never designed to be a product. In fact, to keep down cost and complexity, the machine was built with only 24-bit registers.

In 1980, Patterson and his colleagues at Berkeley began the project that was to give this architectural approach its name (see Patterson and Ditzel [1980]). They built two machines called RISC-I and RISC-II. Because the IBM project was not widely known or discussed, the role played by the Berkeley group in promoting the RISC approach was critical to the acceptance of the technology. In addition to a simple load/store architecture, this machine introduced register windows—an idea that has been adopted by several commercial RISC machines (this concept is discussed further in Chapter 8). The Berkeley group went on to build RISC machines targeted toward Smalltalk, described by Ungar et al. [1984], and LISP, described by Taylor et al. [1987].

In 1981, Hennessy and his colleagues at Stanford published a description of the Stanford MIPS machine. Efficient pipelining and compiler-assisted scheduling of the pipeline were both key aspects of the original MIPS design.

These three early RISC machines had much in common. Both the university projects were interested in designing a simple machine that could be built in VLSI within the university environment. All three machines—the 801, MIPS, and RISC-II—used a simple load/store architecture, fixed-format 32-bit instructions, and emphasized efficient pipelining. Patterson [1985] describes the three machines and the basic design principles that have come to characterize what a RISC machine is. Hennessy [1984] is another view of the same ideas, as well as other issues in VLSI processor design.

In 1985, Hennessy published an explanation of the RISC performance advantage and traced its roots to a substantially lower CPI—under two for a RISC machine and over ten for a VAX-11/780 (though not with identical workloads). A paper by Emer and Clark [1984] characterizing VAX-11/780 performance was instrumental in helping the RISC researchers understand the source of the performance advantage seen by their machines.

Since the university projects finished up, in the 1983-84 timeframe, the technology has been widely embraced by industry. Many of the early computers (before 1986) laid claim to being RISC machines. However, these claims were often born more of marketing ambition than of engineering reality.

In 1986, the computer industry began to announce processors based on the technology explored by the three RISC research projects. Moussoris et al. [1986]

describe the MIPS R2000 integer processor; while Kane [1987] is a complete description of the architecture. Hewlett-Packard converted their existing minicomputer line to RISC architectures; the HP Precision Architecture is described by Lee [1989]. IBM never directly turned the 801 into a product. Instead, the ideas were adopted for a new, low-end architecture that was incorporated in the IBM RT-PC and is described in a collection of papers [Waters 1986]. In 1990, IBM announced a new RISC architecture (the RS 6000), which is the first super scalar RISC machine (see chapter 6). In 1987, Sun Microsystems began delivering machines based on the SPARC architecture, a derivative of the Berkeley RISC-II machine; SPARC is described in Garner et al. [1988]. Starting in 1987, semiconductor manufacturers began to become suppliers of RISC microprocessors. With its announcement of the AMD 29000, AMD was the first major semiconductor manufacturer to deliver a RISC machine. In 1988, Motorola announced the availability of its RISC machine, the 88000.

Prior to the RISC architecture movement, the major trend had been highly microcoded architectures aimed at reducing the semantic gap. DEC, with the VAX, and Intel, with the iAPX 432, were among the leaders in this approach. In 1989, DEC and Intel both announced RISC products—the DECstation 3100 (based on the MIPS Computer Systems R2000) and the Intel i860, a new RISC microprocessor. With these announcements (and the IBM RS6000), RISC technology has achieved very broad acceptance. In 1990 it is hard to find a computer company without a RISC product.

References

ADAMS, T. AND R. ZIMMERMAN [1989]. "An analysis of 8086 instruction set usage in MS DOS programs," *Proc. Third Symposium on Architectural Support for Programming Languages and Systems* (April) Boston, 152–161.

ALEXANDER, W. G. AND D. B. WORTMAN [1975]. "Static and dynamic characteristics of XPL programs," *Computer* 8:11 (November) 41–46.

AMDAHL, G., G. BLAAUW, AND F. BROOKS [1964]. "Architecture of the IBM System/360," *IBM J. of Research and Development* 8:2 (April) 87–101.

CASE, R. AND A. PADEGS [1978]. "Architecture of the IBM System/370," *Comm. ACM* 21:1 (January) 73–96.

CHOW, F., M. HIMELSTEIN, E. KILLIAN, AND L. WEBER [1986]. "Engineering a RISC compiler system," *Proc. COMPCON* (March), San Francisco, 132–137.

CLARK, D. AND H. LEVY [1982]. "Measurement and analysis of instruction set use in the VAX-11/780," *Proc. Ninth Symposium on Computer Architecture* (April), Austin, Tex., 9–17.

CRAWFORD, J. AND P. GELSINGER [1988]. *Programming the 80386,* Sybex Books, Alameda, Calif.

EMER, J. S. AND D. W. CLARK [1984]. "A characterization of processor performance in the VAX-11/780," *Proc. 11th Symposium on Computer Architecture* (June), Ann Arbor, Mich., 301–310.

GARNER, R., A. AGARWAL, F. BRIGGS, E. BROWN, D. HOUGH, B. JOY, S. KLEIMAN, S. MUNCHNIK, M. NAMJOO, D. PATTERSON, J. PENDLETON, AND R. TUCK [1988]. "Scalable processor architecture (SPARC)," *COMPCON, IEEE* (March), San Francisco, 278–283.

HENNESSY, J. [1984]. "VLSI processor architecture," *IEEE Trans. on Computers* C-33:11 (December) 1221–1246.

HENNESSY, J. [1985]. "VLSI RISC processors," *VLSI Systems Design* VI:10 (October) 22–32.

HENNESSY, J., N. JOUPPI, F. BASKETT, AND J. GILL [1981]. "MIPS: A VLSI processor architecture," *Proc. CMU Conf. on VLSI Systems and Computations* (October), Computer Science Press, Rockville, Md.

KANE, G. [1986]. *MIPS R2000 RISC Architecture,* Prentice Hall, Englewood Cliffs, N.J.

LEE, R. [1989]. "Precision architecture," *Computer* 22:1 (January) 78–91.

LEVY, H. AND R. ECKHOUSE [1989]. *Computer Programming and Architecture: The VAX,* Digital Press, Boston.

MORSE, S., B. RAVENAL, S. MAZOR, AND W. POHLMAN [1980]. "Intel Microprocessors—8008 to 8086," *Computer* 13:10 (October).

MOUSSOURIS, J., L. CRUDELE, D. FREITAS, C. HANSEN, E. HUDSON, S. PRZYBYLSKI, T. RIORDAN, AND C. ROWEN [1986]. "A CMOS RISC processor with integrated system functions," *Proc. COMPCON, IEEE* (March), San Francisco.

PATTERSON, D. [1985]. "Reduced Instruction Set Computers," *Comm. ACM* 28:1 (January) 8–21.

PATTERSON, D. A. AND D. R. DITZEL [1980]. "The case for the reduced instruction set computer," *Computer Architecture News* 8:6 (October), 25–33.

RADIN, G. [1982]. "The 801 minicomputer," *Proc. Symposium Architectural Support for Programming Languages and Operating Systems* (March), Palo Alto, Calif. 39–47.

SHUSTEK, L. J. [1978]. "Analysis and performance of computer instruction sets," Ph.D. Thesis (May), Stanford Univ., Stanford, Calif.

STRECKER, W. [1978]. "VAX-11/780: A virtual address extension to the DEC PDP-11 family," *Proc. AFIPS NCC* 47, 967–980.

STRECKER, W. D. AND C. G. BELL [1976]. "Computer structures: What have we learned from the PDP-11?," *Proc. Third Symposium on Computer Architecture.*

TAYLOR, G., P. HILFINGER, J. LARUS, D. PATTERSON, AND B. ZORN [1986]. "Evaluation of the SPUR LISP architecture," *Proc. 13th Symposium on Computer Architecture (*June), Tokyo.

UNGAR, D., R. BLAU, P. FOLEY, D. SAMPLES, AND D. PATTERSON [1984]. "Architecture of SOAR: Smalltalk on a RISC," *Proc. 11th Symposium on Computer Architecture* (June), Ann Arbor, Mich., 188–197.

WAKERLY, J. [1989]. *Microcomputer Architecture and Programming,* J. Wiley, New York.

WATERS, F., ED. [1986]. *IBM RT Personal Computer Technology,* IBM, Austin, Tex., SA 23-1057.

WIECEK, C. [1982]. "A case study of the VAX 11 instruction set usage for compiler execution," *Proc. Symposium on Architectural Support for Programming Languages and Operating Systems* (March), IEEE/ACM, Palo Alto, Calif., 177–184.

E X E R C I S E S

In these exercises you will often need to know the frequency of individual instructions in a mix. Figures C.1 through C.4 supply the data corresponding to Figures 4.24, 4.28, 4.32, and 4.34. Additionally, some problems involve the execution-time distribution rather than the frequency distribution. The information on instruction-time distribution appears in Appendix D; problems that require data from Appendices C or D include the letter C or D within the brackets, e.g., <C,D>.

In doing these exercises you will need to work with measurements that may not total 100%. In some cases you will need to normalize the data to the actual total. For example, if we were asked to find the frequency of MOV_ instructions in Spice running on the VAX, we would proceed as follows (using data from Figure C.1):

Frequency of measured MOV_ in table = 9% + 6% = 15%

Fraction of all instructions executed included in Figure C.1 for Spice = 79%

We now normalize the 15%. This is equivalent to assuming that the unmeasured 21% of the instruction mix behaves the way as the measured portion. Since there are unmeasured MOV_ instructions this is the most logical approach.

$$\text{Frequency of MOV\_ in Spice on VAX} = \frac{15\%}{79\%} = 19\%$$

If, however, we were asked to find the frequency of MOVL in Spice, we know that it is exactly 9%, since we have a complete measurement for this instruction type.

4.1 [20/20] <4.2,4.6,C> You are being interviewed by Digital Equipment Corporation for a job as lead computer designer of future VAX computers. To see if you know what you are talking about, before they hire you they want to ask you a few questions. They have allowed you to bring your notes, including Section 4.6 and Appendix C.

You remember an example in Chapter 4 where you were told that the average VAX instruction had 1.8 operands. You also recall that opcodes are almost always 1 byte long.

a. [20] They ask you to derive the average size of a VAX instruction for the TeX benchmark. Use the addressing-mode frequency data in 4.22 and 4.23, the information on sizes of displacements in Figure 3.35 (page 133), the information on immediate sizes in Figure 3.15 (page 102), and the length of the VAX addressing modes shown in Figure 4.3. (This should be a more accurate estimate than the example that appears on page 170, but ignore addressing modes that account for less than 5% of the occurences.)

b. [20] They then ask you to evaluate the performance of their new machine with a 100-MHz clock. They tell you that the average CPI for everything except instruction fetch and operand fetch is 3 clocks. They also tell you that

■ each data memory specifier and access takes an additional 2 clocks, and

■ every 4 bytes of instructions fetched by the instruction fetch unit take one clock.

Can you find the effective native MIPS?

4.2 [20/22/22] <4.2,4.3,4.5> Consider the following fragment of C code:

```
for (i=1; i<=100; i++)
     {A[i] = B[i] + C;}
```

Assume that A are B are arrays of 32-bit integers, and C and i are 32-bit integers. Assume that all data values are kept in memory (at addresses 0, 5000, 1500, and 2000 for A, B, C, and i, respectively) except when they are operated on.

a. [20] Write the code for DLX; how many instructions are required dynamically? How many memory data references will be executed? What is the code size?

b. [22] Write the code for the VAX; how many instructions are required dynamically? How many memory data references will be executed? What is the code size?

c. [22] Write the code for the 360; how many instructions are required dynamically? How many memory data references will be executed? What is the code size? For simplicity, you may assume that register R1 contains the address of the first instruction in the loop.

4.3 [20/22/22] <4.2,4.3,4.5> For this question use the code sequence of problem 4.2, but put the scalar data—the value of i and the address of the array variables (but not the actual array)—in registers and keep them there whenever possible.

a. [20] Write the code for DLX; how many instructions are required dynamically? How many memory-data references will be executed? What is the code size?

b. [22] Write the code for the VAX; how many instructions are required dynamically? How many memory data references will be executed? What is the code size?

c. [22] Write the code for the 360; how many instructions are required dynamically? How many memory data references will be executed? What is the code size? Assume R1 is set-up as in Exercise 4.2 part C.

4.4 [15] <4.6> When designing memory systems it becomes useful to know the frequency of memory reads versus writes and also accesses for instructions versus data. Using the average instruction-mix information for DLX in Appendix C, find

■ the percentage of all memory accesses that are for data

■ the percentage of data accesses that are reads

■ the percentage of all memory accesses that are reads

Ignore the size of a datum when counting accesses.

4.5 [15] <4.3,4.6> Due to the lack of a PC-relative branch, a branch on a 360 often requires two instructions. This has been a major criticism of the architecture. Let's figure out what this omission costs, assuming that an extra instruction is always needed for a conditional branch on the 360, but that the extra instruction would not be necessary with PC-relative branches. Using the average data from Figure 4.28 (page 175) for branches, determine how many more instructions the standard 360 executes than a 360 with PC-relative branches. (Remember that the only branches are BC and BCR.)

4.6 [15] <4.2,4.6> We are interested in adding an instruction to the VAX architecture that compares an operand to zero and branches. Assume that

■ only instructions that set the condition code for a conditional branch could be eliminated,

■ 80% of the conditional branches require an instruction whose only purpose is to set the condition, and

■ 90% of all branches that have an instruction that just sets the condition (i.e., the just-mentioned 80%) are based on a compare against 0.

Using the average VAX data from Figure 4.24 (page 172) what percentage more instructions would a standard VAX execute compared to the VAX with the compare-and-branch instruction added?

4.7 [18] <4.5,4.6> Compute the effective CPI for DLX. Suppose we have made the following measurements of average CPI for instructions:

All R–R instructions		1 clock cycle
Loads/stores		1.4 clock cycles
Conditional branches		
	taken	2.0 clock cycles
	not taken	1.5 clock cycles
Jumps		1.2 clock cycles

Assume that 60% of the conditional branches are taken. Average the instruction frequencies of GCC and TeX to obtain the instruction mix.

4.8 [15] <4.2,4.5> Rather than have immediates supported for many instruction types, some architectures, such as the 360, collect immediates in memory (in a literal pool) and access them from there. Suppose the VAX didn't have immediate-mode addressing, but instead put immediates in memory and accessed them using displacement-mode addressing. What would be the increase in the frequency that displacement mode was used? Use the average of the measurements in Figures 4.22 and 4.23 for this problem.

4.9 [20/10] <4.5,4.6> Consider adding a new index addressing mode to DLX. The addressing mode adds two registers and an 11-bit signed offset to get the effective address.

Our compiler will be changed so that code sequences of the form

```
ADD R1, R1, R2
LW  Rd, O(R1)      (or store)
```

will be replaced with a load (or store) using the new addressing mode. Use the overall average instruction frequencies in evaluating this addition.

a. [20] Assume that the addressing mode can be used for 10% of the displacement loads and stores (accounting for both the frequency of this type of address calculation and the shorter offset). What is the ratio of instruction count on the enhanced DLX compared to the original DLX?

b. [10] If the new addressing mode lengthens the clock cycle by 5%, which machine will be faster and by how much?

4.10 [12] <4.2,4.5,D> Assume the average number of instructions involved in a call and return on DLX is 8. The average frequency of a JAL instruction in the benchmarks is 1%. If all instructions on DLX take the same number of cycles, how does the percentage of cycles in calls and returns on DLX compare to the percentage of cycles in CALLS and RET on the VAX?

4.11 [22/22] <4.2,4.3,4.6,D> Some people believe that the most frequent instructions are also the simplest, while others have pointed out that the most time-consuming instructions are often not the most frequent.

a. [22] Using the data in Figure D.1, find the CPI of the five most time-consuming instructions on the VAX that have an average execution frequency of at least 2%. Assume the overall VAX CPI is 10.

b. [22] Find the CPI for the five most time-consuming instructions on the 360 that have at least a 3% average frequency, using the data in Figure D.2. Assume the overall 360 CPI is 4.

4.12 [20/20/10] <4.4, 4.6,D> You have been hired to try to convert the 8086 architecture to be more register–register oriented. To do this, you will need more registers, and hence more encoding space, since the encodings are already tight. Assume that you have determined that eliminating the PUSH and POP instructions can yield the encoding space needed. Suppose that increasing the number of registers reduces the frequency of each of the memory-referencing instructions (PUSH, POP, LES, and MOV) by 25%, but that each remaining PUSH or POP instruction must be replaced by a two-instruction sequence. Use the average data from Figures 4.30–4.32 (pages 177–178), the average CPI of 14.1, and Figure D.5 to answer the following questions about this new machine—the RR8086— versus the 8086.

a. [20] Which machine executes more instructions and by how much?

b. [20] Using the information in Appendix D, determine which machine has a higher CPI and by how much?

c. [10] Assuming the clock rates are identical, which machine is faster and by how much?

4.13 [25/15] <4.2–4.5> Find a C compiler and compile the code shown in Exercise 4.2 for a load/store machine or one of the machines covered in this chapter. Compile the code both optimized and unoptimized.

a. [25] Find the instruction count, dynamic instruction bytes fetched, and data accesses done for both the optimized and unoptimized versions.

b. [15] Try to improve the code by hand, and compute the same measures as in Part a for your hand-optimized version.

4.14 [30] <4.6> If you have access to a VAX, compile the code for Spice and try to determine why it makes much smaller use of immediates than programs like GCC and TeX (see Figure 4.22 on page 169).

4.15 [30] <4.6> If you have access to an 8086-based machine, compile some programs and look at the frequency of MOV instructions. How does it correspond to the frequency in Figure 4.32 (page 178). By examining the code, can you find some reasons why the frequency of MOVs is so high?

4.16 [30/30] <4.6, 4.7> Small synthetic benchmarks can be very misleading when used for measuring instruction mixes. This is particularly true when these benchmarks are optimized. In these exercises we want to explore these differences. These programming exercises can be done with a VAX, any load/store machine, or using the DLX compiler and simulator.

a.   [30] Compile Whetstone with optimization for a VAX, or a load/store machine similar to DLX (e.g., a DECstation or a SPARCstation), or the DLX simulator. Compute the instruction mix for the top twenty instructions. How do the optimized and unoptimized mixes compare? How does the optimized mix compare to the mix for Spice on the same or a similar machine?

b.   [30] Compile Dhrystone with optimization for a VAX, or a load/store machine similar to DLX (e.g., a DECstation or a SPARCstation), or the DLX simulator. Compute the instruction mix for the top twenty instructions. How do the optimized and unoptimized mixes compare? How does the optimized mix compare to the mix for TeX on the same or a similar machine?

4.17 [30] <4.6> Many computer manufacturers now include tools or simulators that allow you to measure the instruction set usage of a user program. Among the methods in use are machine simulation, hardware-supported trapping, and a compiler technique that instruments the object-code module by inserting counters. Find a processor available to you that includes such a tool. Use it to measure the instruction set mix for one of TeX, GCC, or Spice. Compare the results to those shown in this chapter.

4.18 [30] <4.5,4.6> DLX has only three operand formats for its register–register operations. Many operations might use the same destination register as one of the sources. We could introduce a new instruction format into DLX called R_2 that has only two operands and is a total of 24 bits in length. By using this instruction type whenever an operation had only two different register operands, we could reduce the instruction bandwidth required for a program. Modify the DLX simulator to count the frequency of register–register operations with only two different register operands. Using the benchmarks that come with the simulator, determine how much more instruction bandwidth DLX requires than DLX with the R_2 format.

4.19 [35] <D> Devise a method to measure the CPI of a machine—preferably one of the machines discussed in this chapter or a relative of DLX. Using the instruction-mix data, choose the top ten instructions and measure their CPI. How does the frequency ranking compare to the time taken? How do your measurements compare to the numbers shown in Appendix D? Try to explain any differences in both time-versus-frequency ranking and any differences between your measures and those in Appendix D.

4.20 [35] <4.5,4.6> What are the benefits of more powerful addressing modes? Assume that three VAX addressing modes—autoincrement, displacement deferred, and scaled—were added to DLX. Change the C compiler to incorporate the use of these modes. Measure the change in instruction count with these new modes for several benchmark programs. Compare the instruction mixes with those for standard DLX. How do the usage patterns compare to those for the VAX shown in Figure 4.23 (page 170)?

4.21 [35/35/30] <4.5,4.6> How much does the flexibility of memory–memory instructions reduce instruction count compared to a load/store machine? This programming assignment will help you find out.

a.   [35] Assume DLX has an instruction format that allows one of the source operands to be in memory. Modify the C code generator for DLX so that it uses this new instruction type. Use several C programs to measure the effectiveness of your change. How many more instructions does DLX require versus this new machine that appears to be closer to the 360? How often is the register–memory format used? How do the instruction mixes differ from those in Section 4.6?

b.   [35] Assume that DLX has instruction formats that allow any operand (or all three) to be memory references. Modify the C code generator for DLX so that it uses these new instruction formats. Use several programs to measure the usage of these instructions. How many more instructions does DLX require versus this new machine that appears to be closer to the VAX? How do the instruction mixes differ from those in Section 4.6? How many memory operands does the average instruction have?

c.   [30] Design an instruction format for the machines described in Parts a and b; compare the dynamic instruction bandwidth required for these two machines versus DLX.

4.22 [40] <4.6> Some manufacturers have not yet seen the value of measuring instruction set mixes. Maybe you can help them. Pick a machine for which such a tool is not widely available. Construct one for that machine. If the machine has a single-step mode—as in the VAX or 8086—you can use it to create your tool. Otherwise, an object code translation, as used in the MIPS compiler system [Chow 1986] might be more appropriate. If you measure the activity of a machine using the benchmarks in this text (GCC, Spice, and TeX), and are willing to share the results, please contact the publisher.

4.23 [25] <E> How much do the instruction set variations among the RISC machines discussed in Appendix E affect performance. Choose at least three small programs (e.g., a sort), and code these programs in DLX and two other assembly languages. What is the resulting difference in instruction count?

4.24 [40] <E> Choose one of the machines discussed in Appendix E. Modify the DLX code generator and DLX simulator to generate code for and simulate the machine you chose. Using as many benchmarks as practical, measure the instruction count differences seen between DLX and the machine you chose.

*In analyzing the functions of the contemplated device, certain
classificatory distinctions suggest themselves immediately ...
First: Since the device is primarily a computer it will have to
perform the elementary operations of arithmetic most
frequently ... a* central arithmetic *part of the device will
probably have to exist... Second: The logical control of the
device, that is the proper sequencing of its operations, can be
most efficiently carried out by a central control organ.*

John von Neumann, *First Draft of a Report on the EDVAC* (1945)

5 Basic Processor Implementation Techniques

5.1 Introduction

Architecture shapes a building, but carpentry determines the quality of its construction. The carpentry of computing is implementation, which sets two of three performance components: CPI (clock cycles per instruction) and clock cycle time.

In the four decades of constructing computers, much has been learned about implementation—certainly more than can fit in one chapter. Our goal in this chapter will be to lay the foundations of processor implementation, with emphasis on control and interrupts. (Floating point is ignored in this chapter; readers are referred to Appendix A.) While some material is simple, Chapters 6 and 7 build on this foundation and show the road to faster computers. (If this is a review, go quickly over Sections 5.1 to 5.3 and then take a look at the examples in Section 5.7, which compare performance of hardwired versus microprogrammed control for DLX.)

The computer was divided into basic components by von Neumann, and these components still remain today: The CPU, or the *processor,* is the core of the computer and contains everything except the memory, input, and output. The processor is further divided into computation and control.

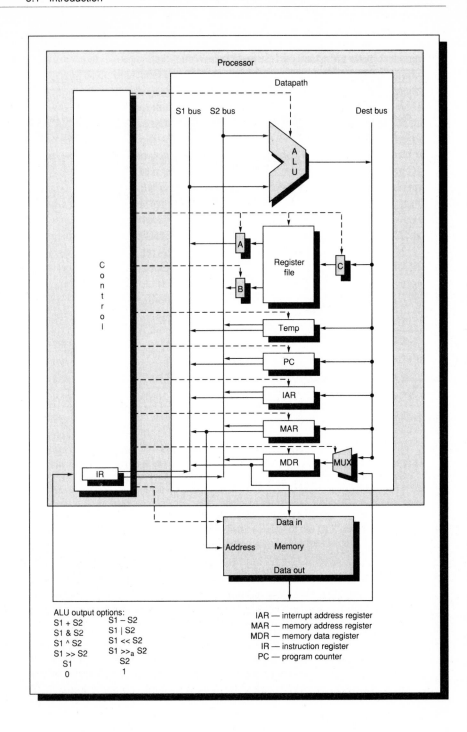

ALU output options:

S1 + S2	S1 − S2
S1 & S2	S1 | S2
S1 ^ S2	S1 << S2
S1 >> S2	S1 >>$_a$ S2
S1	S2
0	1

IAR — interrupt address register
MAR — memory address register
MDR — memory data register
IR — instruction register
PC — program counter

5.2 | Processor Datapath

Today the "arithmetic" organ of von Neumann is called the *datapath*. It consists of execution units, such as arithmetic logic units (ALUs) or shifters, the registers, and the communication paths between them, as Figure 5.1 illustrates. From the programmer's perspective, the datapath contains most of the *state* of the processor—the information that must be saved for a program to be suspended and then restored for execution to continue. In addition to the user-visible general-purpose registers, the state includes the program counter (PC), the interrupt address register (IAR), and the program status register; the latter contains all the status flags for a machine, such as interrupt enable, condition codes, and so forth.

Because an implementation is created for a specific hardware technology, it is the implementation that sets the clock cycle time. The clock cycle time in turn is determined by the slowest circuits that operate during a clock cycle period—within the processor, the datapath frequently has that honor. The datapath will also dominate the cost of the processor, typically requiring half the transistors and half the processor area. While it does all the computation, affects performance, and dominates cost, the datapath is the simplest portion of the processor to design.

Some have held the large quantity of papers on ALU designs and fast-carry schemes responsible for the loss of our rain forests, with papers on circuit designs for registers with multiple read and write ports only slightly less culpable. While this is surely an exaggeration, there are numerous options. (See Appendix A, Section A.8, for a few carry schemes.) Given the resources available and the desired goals of cost and performance, it is the designer's job to select the best style of ALU, the proper number of ports in the register file, and then march onward.

FIGURE 5.1 (See adjoining page.)   A typical processor, divided into control and datapath, plus memory. The paths for control are in dashed lines and the paths for data transfer are in solid lines. The processor uses three buses: S1, S2, and Dest. The fundamental operation of the datapath is reading operands from the register file, operating on them in the ALU, and then storing the result back. Since the register file does not need to be read and written every clock cycle, most designers follow the advice of making the frequent case fast by breaking this sequence into multiple clock cycles and making the clock cycle shorter. Thus, in this datapath there are latches on the two outputs of the register file (called A and B) and a latch on the input (C). The register file contains the 32 general-purpose registers of DLX. (Register 0 of the register file always has the value 0, matching the definition of register 0 in the DLX instruction set.) The program counter (PC) and interrupt address register (IAR) are also part of the state of the machine. There are also registers, not part of the state, used in the execution of instructions: memory address register (MAR), memory data register (MDR), instruction register (IR), and temporary register (Temp). The Temp register is a scratch register that is available for temporary storage for control to perform some DLX instructions. Note that the only path from the S1 and S2 buses to the Dest bus is through the ALU.

5.3 | Basic Steps of Execution

Before discussing control, let's first review the steps of instruction execution. For the DLX instruction set (excluding floating point), all instructions can be broken into five basic steps: fetch, decode, execute, memory-access, and write-result. Each step may take one or several clock cycles in the processor shown in Figure 5.1 (page 200). Here are the five steps (see the page facing the inside back cover for a review of the register transfer language notation):

1. Instruction fetch step:

    $$\text{MAR} \leftarrow \text{PC; IR} \leftarrow \text{M[MAR]}$$

    Operation: Send out the PC and fetch the instruction from memory into the instruction register. PC is transferred to MAR because it has a connection to the memory address in Figure 5.1, but PC doesn't.

2. Instruction decode/register fetch step:

    $$\text{A} \leftarrow \text{Rs1; B} \leftarrow \text{Rs2; PC} \leftarrow \text{PC} + 4$$

    Operation: Decode the instruction and access the register file to read the registers. Also, increment the PC to point to the next instruction.

    Decoding can be done in parallel with reading registers, which means that two registers' values are sent to the A and B latches **before** the instruction is decoded. How this is possible can be seen by glancing at the DLX instruction format (Figure 4.19 on page 166), which shows that the *source registers* are always at the same location in an instruction. Thus, registers can be read because the register specifiers are unambiguous. (This technique is known as *fixed-field decoding*.) Since the immediate portion of an instruction is also identical in every DLX format, the sign-extended immediate is also calculated during this step in case it is needed in the next step.

3. Execution/effective address step:

    The ALU is operating on the operands prepared in the prior step, performing one of three functions depending on the DLX instruction type.

    Memory reference:

    $$\text{MAR} \leftarrow \text{A} + (\text{IR}_{16})^{16}\#\#\text{IR}_{16..31} \text{ ; MDR} \leftarrow \text{Rd}$$

    Operation: The ALU is adding the operands to form the effective address, and the MDR is loaded for a store.

ALU instruction:

$$\text{ALUoutput} \leftarrow \text{A } op \text{ (B or } (\text{IR}_{16})^{16}\#\#\text{IR}_{16..31})$$

Operation: The ALU is performing the operation specified by the opcode on the value in A (Rs1) and on the value in B or the sign-extended immediate.

Branch/Jump:

$$\text{ALUoutput} \leftarrow \text{PC} + (\text{IR}_{16})^{16}\#\#\text{IR}_{16..31}; \text{ cond} \leftarrow (\text{A } op \text{ 0})$$

Operation: The ALU is adding the PC to the sign-extended immediate value (16-bit for branch and 26-bit for jump) to compute the address of the branch target. For conditional branches, a register, which has been read in the prior step, is checked to decide if this address should be inserted into the PC. The comparison operation *op* is the relational operator determined by the opcode; for example, *op* is "==" for the instruction BEQZ.

The load/store architecture of DLX means that effective address and execution steps can be combined into a single step, since no instruction needs to both calculate an address and perform an operation on the data. Other integer instructions not included above are JAL and TRAP. These are similar to jumps, except JAL stores the return address in R31 and TRAP stores it in IAR.

4. Memory access/branch completion step: The only DLX instructions active in this step are loads, stores, branches, and jumps.

Memory reference:

$$\text{MDR} \leftarrow \text{M[MAR] or M[MAR]} \leftarrow \text{MDR}$$

Operation: Access memory if needed. If instruction is a load, data returns from memory; if it is a store, then the data writes into memory. In either case the address used is the one computed during the prior step.

Branch:

$$\text{if (cond) PC} \leftarrow \text{ALUoutput (branch)}$$

Operation: If the instruction branches, the PC is replaced with the branch destination address. For jumps the condition is always true.

5. Write-back step:

$$\text{Rd} \leftarrow \text{ALUoutput or MDR}$$

Operation: Write the result into the register file, whether coming from the memory system or from the ALU.

Now that we have had an overview of the work that must be performed to execute an instruction, we are ready to look at the two main techniques for implementing control.

5.4 | Hardwired Control

If the datapath design is simple, then some part of processor design must be difficult, and that part is control. Specifying control is on the critical path of any computer project; and it is where most errors are found when a new computer is debugged. Control can be simplified—the easiest way is to simplify the instruction set—but that is the subject of Chapters 3 and 4.

Given an instruction set description, such as the description of DLX in Chapter 4, and a datapath design, such as Figure 5.1 (page 200), the next step is defining the control unit. The control unit tells the datapath what to do every clock cycle during the execution of instructions. This is typically specified by a *finite-state diagram*. Every state corresponds to one clock cycle, and the operations to be performed during the clock cycle are written within the state. Each instruction takes several clock cycles to complete; Chapter 6 shows how to overlap execution to reduce the clock cycles per instruction to as low as one.

Figure 5.2 shows a portion of a finite-state diagram for the first two steps of instruction execution in DLX. The first step is spread over all three states: The memory-address register is loaded from PC during the first state, the instruction register is loaded from memory during the second state, and the PC is incremented in the third state. This third state also performs step 2, loading the two register operands, Rs1 and Rs2, into the A and B registers for use in the later states. In Section 5.7 the full finite-state diagram for DLX is shown.

Turning a state diagram into hardware is the next step. The alternatives for doing this depend on the implementation technology. One way to bound the complexity of control is by the product

$$\text{States} * \text{Control inputs} * \text{Control outputs}$$

where

States = the number of states in the finite-state machine controller;

Control inputs = the number of signals examined by the control unit;

Control outputs = the number of control outputs generated for the hardware, including bits to specify the next state.

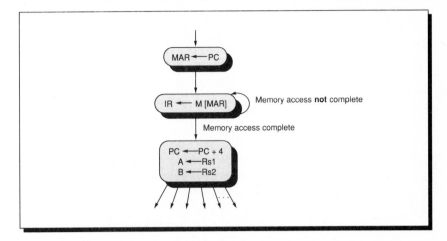

FIGURE 5.2 The top level of the DLX finite-state diagram. The first two steps of instruction execution, instruction fetch and instruction decode/register fetch, are shown. The second state repeats until the instruction is fetched from memory. The last three steps of instruction execution—execution/effective address, memory access, and write back—are found in Section 5.7.

Figure 5.3 shows an organization for control of DLX. Let's say the DLX finite-state diagram contains 50 states, requiring 6 bits to represent the state. Thus, the control inputs must include these 6 bits, some number of bits (say 3) to select conditions from the datapath and memory interface unit, plus instruction bits. Register specifiers and immediates are sent directly to the hardware, so there is no need to send all 32 bits of DLX instructions as control inputs. The DLX opcode is 6 bits, and only 6 bits of the extended opcode (the "func" field) are used, making a total of 12 instruction bits for control inputs. Given those inputs, control can be specified as a big table. Each row of the table contains the values of the control lines to perform the operations required by that state and supplies the next state number. Let's assume there are 40 control lines.

Reducing Hardware Costs of Hardwired Control

The straightforward implementation of a table is with a *read only memory* (ROM). In this example, 2^{21} words, each 40 bits wide (10 MB of ROM!), would be required. It will be a long time before we can afford this much hardware for control. Fortunately, little of this table has unique information, so its size can be reduced by keeping only the rows with unique information—at the cost of more complicated address decoding. Such a hardware construct is called a *programmed logic array* (PLA). This essentially reduces the hardware from 2^{21} words to 50 words while increasing address decoding logic. Computer-aided design programs can reduce the hardware requirements even further by

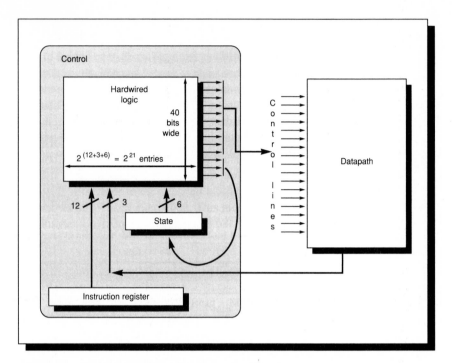

FIGURE 5.3   Control specified as a table for a simple instruction set. The control inputs consist of 6 input lines for the 50 states ($\log_2 50 = 5.6$), 3 inputs from the datapath, and 12 instruction bits (the 6-bit opcode plus 6 bits of the extended opcode). The number of control lines is assumed to be 40.

minimizing the number of "minterms," which is essentially the number of unique rows. In real machines, even a single PLA is sometimes prohibitive because its size grows as the product of the unique rows times the sum of the inputs and outputs. In such a case, a large table is factored into several smaller PLAs, whose outputs are multiplexed to choose the correct control.

Oddly enough, the numbering of the states in the finite-state diagram can make a difference in the size of the PLA. The idea here is to try to assign similar state numbers to states that perform similar operations. Differentiating the bit patterns that represent the state number by only one bit—say 010010 and 010011—make the inputs close for the same output. There are also computer-aided design programs to help with this *state-assignment problem*.

Since the instruction bits are also inputs to the control PLA, they can affect the complexity of the PLA just as numbering of the states does. Thus, care should be taken when selecting opcodes since it may affect the cost of control.

Readers interested in taking this design further are referred to the many excellent texts on logic design.

Performance of Hardwired Control

When designing the detailed control for a machine, we want to minimize the average CPI, the clock cycle, the amount of hardware to specify control, and the time to develop a correct controller. Minimizing CPI means reducing the average number of states along the path of execution of an instruction, since each clock cycle corresponds to a state. This is typically done by making changes to the datapath to combine or eliminate states.

Example

Let's change the hardware so that the PC can be used directly to address memory without going through MAR first. How should the state diagram be changed to take advantage of this improvement, and what would be the change in performance?

Answer

From Figure 5.2 (page 205) we see that the first state copies PC into MAR. This proposed hardware change makes that state unnecessary, and Figure 5.4 shows the appropriately modified state diagram. This change saves one clock cycle from every instruction. Suppose the average number of CPI was originally 7. Provided there was no impact on clock cycle time, this change would make the machine 17% faster.

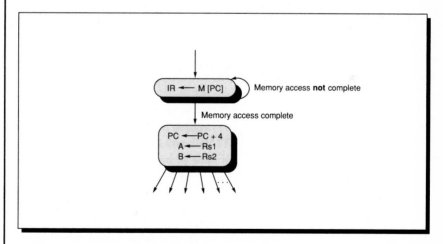

FIGURE 5.4 Figure 5.2 modified to remove the loading of MAR from PC in the first state and to use the PC value directly to address memory.

5.5 | Microprogrammed Control

After constructing the first full-scale, operational, stored-program computer in 1949, Maurice Wilkes reflected on the process. I/O was easy—teletypewriters could just be purchased directly from the telegraph company. Memory and the datapath were highly repetitive, and that made things simpler. But control was neither easy nor repetitive, so Wilkes set out to discover a better way to design control. His solution was to turn the control unit into a miniature computer by having a table to specify control of the datapath and a second table to determine control flow at the micro level. Wilkes called his invention *microprogramming* and attached the prefix "micro" to traditional terms used at the control level: microinstruction, microcode, microprogram, and so on. (To avoid confusion the prefix "macro" is sometimes used to describe the higher level, e.g., macroinstruction and macroprogram.) Microinstructions specify all the control signals for the datapath, plus the ability to conditionally decide which micro-

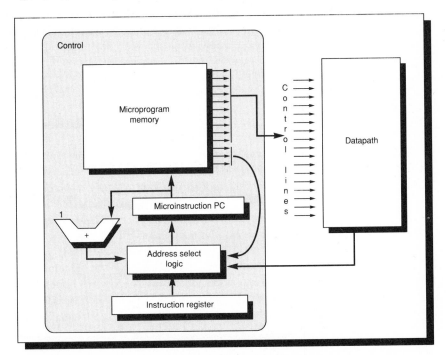

FIGURE 5.5   A basic microcoded engine. Unlike Figure 5.3 (page 206), there is an incrementer and special logic to select the next microinstruction. There are two approaches to specifying the next microinstruction: use a microinstruction program counter, as shown above, or include a next microinstruction address in every microinstruction. Microprogram memory is sometimes called ROM because most early machines use ROM for control stores.

instruction should be executed next. As the name "microprogramming" suggests, once the datapath and memory for the microinstructions are designed, control becomes essentially a programming task; that is, the task of writing an interpreter for the instruction set. The invention of microprogramming enabled the instruction set to be changed by altering the contents of control store without touching the hardware. As we will see in Section 5.10, this ability played an important role in the IBM 360 family—one that was a surprise to its designers.

Figure 5.5 shows an organization for a simple microprogrammed control. The structure of a microprogram is very similar to the state diagram, with a microinstruction for each state in the diagram.

ABCs of Microprogramming

While it doesn't matter to the hardware how the control lines are grouped within a microinstruction, control lines performing related functions are traditionally placed next to each other for ease of understanding. Groups of related control lines are called *fields* and are given names in a microinstruction format. Figure 5.6 shows a microinstruction format with eight fields, each named to reflect its function. Microprogramming can be thought of as supplying the proper bit pattern in each field, much like assembly language programming of "macroinstructions."

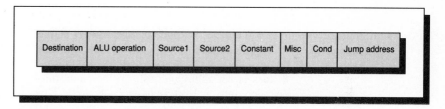

FIGURE 5.6   Example microinstruction with eight fields (used for DLX in Section 5.7).

A program counter can be used to supply the next microinstruction, as shown in Figure 5.5, but some computers dedicate a field in every microinstruction to the address of the next instruction. Some even provide multiple next-address fields to handle conditional branches.

While conditional branches could be used to decode an instruction by testing the opcode one bit at a time, this tedious approach is too slow in practice. The simplest fast instruction decoding scheme is to jam the macroinstruction opcode into the middle of the address of the next microinstruction, similar to an indexed jump instruction in assembly language. A more refined approach is to use the opcode to index a table containing microinstruction addresses that supply the next address, similar to a jump table in assembly code.

The microprogram memory, or *control store*, is the most visible and easily measured hardware in microprogrammed control; hence, it is the focus of techniques to reduce hardware costs. Techniques to trim control-store size include reducing the number of microinstructions, reducing the width of each microinstruction, or both. Just as cost is traditionally measured by control-store size, performance is traditionally measured by CPI. The wise microprogrammer knows the frequency of macroinstructions by using statistics like those in Chapter 4, and hence knows where and how time is best spent—instructions demanding the largest part of execution time are optimized for speed, and the others are optimized for space.

In four decades of microprogramming history there have been a wide variety of terms and techniques for microprogramming. In fact, a workshop has met annually on this subject since 1968. Before looking at a few examples, let us remember that control techniques—whether hardwired or microcoded—are judged by their impact on hardware cost, clock cycle time, CPI, and development time. In the next two sections we will examine how hardware costs can be lowered by reducing control-store size. First we look at two techniques to reduce the width of microinstructions, then one technique to reduce the number of microinstructions.

Reducing Hardware Costs by Encoding Control Lines

The ideal approach to reducing control store is to first write the complete microprogram in a symbolic notation and then measure how control lines are set in each microinstruction. By taking measurements we are able to recognize control bits that can be encoded into a smaller field. If no more than one of, say, 8 lines is set simultaneously in the same microinstruction, then they can be encoded into a 3-bit field ($\log_2 8 = 3$). This change saves 5 bits in every microinstruction and does not hurt CPI, though it does mean the extra hardware cost of a 3-to-8 decoder needed to generate the original 8 control lines. Nevertheless, shaving 5 bits off control-store width will usually overcome the cost of the decoder.

This technique of reducing field width is called *encoding*. To further save space, control lines may be encoded together if they are only occasionally set in the same microinstruction; two microinstructions instead of one are then required when both must be set. As long as this doesn't happen in critical routines, the narrower microinstruction may justify a few extra words of control store.

There are dangers to encoding. For example, if an encoded control line is on the critical timing path, or if the hardware it controls is on the critical path, then the clock cycle time will suffer. A more subtle danger is that a later revision of the microcode might encounter situations where control lines would be set in the same microinstruction, either hurting performance or requiring changes to the hardware that could lengthen the development cycle.

Example

Assume we want to encode the three fields that specify a register on a bus—Destination, Source1, and Source2—in the DLX microinstruction format in Figure 5.6. How many bits of control store can be saved versus unencoded fields?

Answer

Figure 5.7 lists the registers for each source and destination of the datapath in Figure 5.1 (page 200). Note that the destination field must be able to specify that nothing is modified. Without encoding, the 3 fields require 7 + 9 + 9, or 25 bits. Since $\log_2 7 \approx 2.8$ and $\log_2 9 \approx 3.2$, the encoded fields require 3 + 4 + 4, or 11 bits. Thus, encoding these 3 fields saves 14 bits per microinstruction.

Number	Destination	Source1/Source2
0	(None)	A/B
1	C	Temp
2	Temp	PC
3	PC	IAR
4	IAR	MAR
5	MAR	MDR
6	MDR	IR (16-bit imm)
7	---	IR (26-bit imm)
8	---	Constant

FIGURE 5.7   The sources and destinations specified in the three fields of Figure 5.6 from the datapath description in Figure 5.1. A and B are not separate entries because A can only transfer on the S1 bus and B can only transfer on the S2 bus (see Figure 5.1 on pages 200–201). The last entry in the third column, Constant, is used by control to specify a constant needed in an ALU operation (e.g., 4). See Section 5.7 for its use.

Reducing Hardware Costs with Multiple Microinstruction Formats

Microinstructions can be made narrower still if they are broken into different formats and given an opcode or *format field* to distinguish them. The format field gives all the unspecified control lines their default values, so as not to change anything else in the machine, and is similar to the opcode of a macroinstruction.

Reducing hardware costs by using format fields has its own performance cost—namely, executing more microinstructions. Generally, a microprogram using a single microinstruction format can specify any combination of operations in a datapath and will take fewer clock cycles than a microprogram made up of restricted microinstructions. Narrower machines are cheaper because memory chips are also narrow and tall: It takes many fewer chips for a 16K word by 24-bit memory than for a 4K word by 96-bit memory. (When control memory is on the processor chip, this hardware advantage is no longer true.)

This narrow but tall approach is often called *vertical microcode,* while the wide but short approach is called *horizontal microcode.* It should be noted that the terms "vertical miocrocode" and "horizontal microcode" have no universal definition—the designers of the 8086 considered its 21-bit microinstruction to be more horizontal than other single-chip computers of the time. The related terms *maximally encoded* and *minimally encoded* lead to less confusion.

Figure 5.8 plots control-store size against microinstruction width for three families of computers. Notice that for each family the total size is similar, even though the width varies by a factor of 6. As a rule, minimally encoded control stores use more bits, and the narrow but tall aspect of memory chips means that maximally encoded control stores naturally have more entries. Sometimes designers of minimally encoded machines don't have the option of shorter RAM chips, causing wide microinstruction machines to end up with many words of control store. Since the hardware costs are not lower if microcode doesn't use up all the space in control store, machines in this class can end up with much larger control stores than expected from other implementations. The ECL RAMs available to build the VAX 8800, for example, led to 2000 K bits of control store.

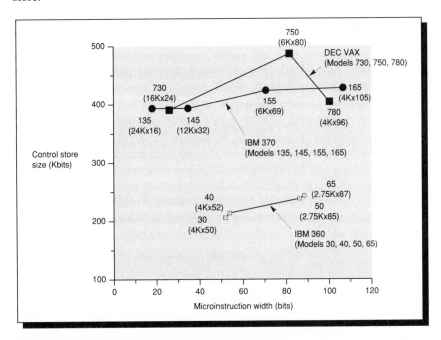

FIGURE 5.8 Size of control store versus width of microinstructions for 11 computer models. Each point is identified by the length and width of control store (not including parity). Models selected from each family are ones that shipped about the same time: IBM 360 models 30, 40, 50, and 65 all shipped in 1965; IBM 370 models 145, 155, and 165 shipped in 1971, with the 135 following in the next year; and the VAX model 780 was shipped in 1978, followed by the 750 in 1980 and the 730 in 1982. The development of the VAX designs all overlapped one another inside DEC.

Reducing Hardware Costs by Adding Hardwired Control to Share Microcode

The other approach to reducing control store is to reduce the number of microinstructions rather than their width. Microsubroutines provide one approach, as well as routines with common "tail" sequences sharing code by jumps.

More sharing can be done with hardwired control assistance. For example, many microarchitectures allow bits of the instruction register to specify the correct register. Another common assist is to use portions of the instruction register to specify the ALU operation. Each of these assists is under microprogrammed control and is invoked with a special value in the appropriate field. The 8086 uses both techniques, giving one 4-line routine responsibility for 32 opcodes. The drawback of adding hardwired control is it may stretch the development cycle because it no longer involves programming, but requires hardware layout for designing and debugging.

This section and the previous two give techniques for reducing cost. The following sections present three techniques for improving performance.

Reducing CPI with Special Case Microcode

As we have noted, the wise microprogrammer knows when to save space and when to spend it. An instance of this is dedicating extra microcode for frequent instructions, thereby reducing CPI. For example, the VAX 8800 uses its large control store for many versions of the CALLS instruction, optimized for register saving depending upon the value in the register-save mask. Candidates for special case microcode can be uncovered by instruction mix measurements, such as those found in Chapter 4 or in Appendix B, or by counting the frequency of use of each microinstruction in an existing implementation (see Emer and Clark [1984]).

Reducing CPI by Adding Hardwired Control

Adding hardwired control can reduce costs as well as improve performance. For example, VAX operands can be in memory or registers, but later machines reduce CPI by having special code for register–register or register–memory moves and adds: ADDL2 Rn, 10(Rm) takes five or more cycles on the 780, but as few as one on the 8600. Another example is in the memory interface, where the straightforward solution is for microcode to continuously test and branch until memory is ready. Because of the delay between the time a condition becomes true and the time the next microinstruction is read, this approach can add one extra clock to each memory access. The importance of the memory interface is underlined by the 780 and 8800 statistics—20% of the 780 clock cycles and 23% of the 8800 are waiting for memory to be ready, these are called stalls. A *stall* is where an instruction must pause one or more clock cycles waiting for some resource to be available. In this chapter stalls occur only when waiting for memory; in the next chapter we'll see other reasons for stalls.

Many machines approach this problem by having the hardware stall a microinstruction that tries to access the memory-data register before the memory operation is completed. (This can be accomplished by freezing the microinstruction address so that the same microinstruction is executed until the condition is met.) The instant the memory reference is ready, the microinstruction that needs the data is allowed to complete, avoiding the extra clock delay to access control memory.

Reducing CPI by Parallelism

Sometimes CPI can be reduced with more operations per microinstruction. This technique, which usually requires a wider microinstruction, increases parallelism with more datapath operations. It is another characteristic of machines labeled horizontal. Examples of this performance gain can be seen in the fact that the fastest models of each family in Figure 5.8 also have the widest microinstructions. Making the microinstruction wider does not guarantee increased performance, however. An example where the potential gain was not realized is found in a microprocessor very similar to the 8086, except that another bus was added to the datapath, requiring six more bits in its microinstruction. This could have reduced the execution phase from three clock cycles to two for many popular 8086 instructions. Unfortunately, these popular macroinstructions were grouped with macroinstructions that couldn't take advantage of this optimization, so they all had to run at the slower rate.

5.6 | Interrupts and Other Entanglements

Control is the hard part of processor design, and the hard part of control is *interrupts*—events other than branches that change the normal flow of instruction execution. Detecting interrupt conditions within an instruction can often be on the critical timing path of a machine, possibly affecting the clock cycle time, and thus performance. Without proper attention to interrupts during design, adding interrupts to a complicated implementation can even foul up the works so as to make the design impracticable.

Invented to detect arithmetic errors and signal real-time events, interrupts have been handed a flock of difficult duties. Here are 11 examples:

I/O device request

Invoking an operating system service from a user program

Tracing instruction execution

Breakpoint (programmer-requested interrupt)

Arithmetic overflow or underflow

Page fault (not in main memory)

Misaligned memory accesses (if alignment is required)

Memory-protection violation

Using an undefined instruction

Hardware malfunctions

Power failure

	IBM 360	VAX	Motorola 680x0	Intel 80x86
I/O device request	Input/output interruption	Device interrupt	Exception (Level 0...7 autovector)	Vectored interrupt
Invoking the operating system service from a user program	Supervisor call interruption	Exception (change mode supervisor trap)	Exception (unimplemented instruction)—on Macintosh	Interrupt (INT instruction)
Tracing instruction execution	NA	Exception (trace fault)	Exception (trace)	Interrupt (single-step trap)
Breakpoint	NA	Exception (breakpoint fault)	Exception (illegal instruction or breakpoint)	Interrupt (breakpoint trap)
Arithmetic overflow or underflow	Program interruption (overflow or underflow exception)	Exception (integer overflow trap or floating underflow fault)	Exception (floating-point coprocessor errors)	Interrupt (overflow trap or math unit exception)
Page fault (not in main memory)	NA (only in 370)	Exception (translation not valid fault)	Exception (memory-management unit errors)	Interrupt (page fault)
Misaligned memory accesses	Program interruption (specification exception)	NA	Exception (address error)	NA
Memory protection violations	Program interruption (protection exception)	Exception (access control violation fault)	Exception (bus error)	Interrupt (protection exception)
Using undefined instructions	Program interruption (operation exception)	Exception (opcode privileged/ reserved fault)	Exception (illegal instruction or break-point/unimplemented instruction)	Interrupt (invalid opcode)
Hardware malfunctions	Machine-check interruption	Exception (machine-check abort)	Exception (bus error)	NA
Power failure	Machine-check interruption	Urgent interrupt	NA	Nonmaskable interrupt

FIGURE 5.9 Names of 11 interrupt classes on four computers. Every event on the IBM 360 and 80x86 is called an *interrupt,* while every event on the 680x0 is called an *exception.* VAX divides events into *interrupts* or *exceptions.* Adjectives *device, software,* and *urgent* are used with VAX interrupts, while VAX exceptions are subdivided into *faults, traps,* and *aborts.*

The enlarged responsibility of interrupts has led to the confusing situation of each computer vendor inventing a different term for the same event, as Figure 5.9 on page 215 illustrates. Intel and IBM still call such events *interrupts,* but Motorola calls them *exceptions;* and, depending on the circumstances, DEC calls them *exceptions, faults, aborts, traps,* or *interrupts.* To give some idea of how often interrupts occur, Figure 5.10 shows the frequency on the VAX 8800.

Event	Time between events
I/O interrupt	2.7 ms
Interval timer interrupt	10.0 ms
Software interrupt	1.5 ms
Any interrupt	0.9 ms
Any hardware interrupt	2.1 ms

FIGURE 5.10   Frequency of different interrupts on the VAX 8800 running a multiuser workload on the VMS timesharing system. Real-time operating systems used in embedded controllers may have a higher interrupt rate than a general-purpose timesharing system. (Collected by Clark, Bannon, and Keller [1988].)

Clearly, there is no consistent convention for naming these events. Rather than imposing one, then, let's review the reasons for the different names. The events can be characterized on five independent axes:

1. Synchronous versus asynchronous. If the event occurs at the same place every time the program is executed with the same data and memory allocation, the event is synchronous. With the exception of hardware malfunctions, asynchronous events are caused by devices external to the processor and memory.

2. User request versus coerced. If the user task directly asks for it, it is a user-request event.

3. User maskable versus user nonmaskable. If it can be masked or disabled by a user task, the event is user maskable.

4. Within versus between instructions. This classification depends on whether the event prevents instruction completion by occurring in the middle of execution—no matter how short—or whether it is recognized between instructions.

5. Resume versus terminate. If the program's execution stops after the interrupt, it is a terminating event.

The difficult task is implementing interrupts occurring within instructions where the instruction must be resumed. Another program must be invoked to collect the state of the program, correct the cause of an interrupt, and then restore the state of the program before an instruction can be tried again.

Figure 5.11 classifies the examples from Figure 5.9 according to these five categories.

	Synchronous vs. asynchronous	User request vs. coerced	User maskable vs. nonmaskable	Within vs. between instructions	Resume vs. terminate
I/O device request	Asynchronous	Coerced	Nonmaskable	Between	Resume
Invoking operating system service	Synchronous	User request	Nonmaskable	Between	Resume
Tracing instruction execution	Synchronous	User request	User maskable	Between	Resume
Breakpoint	Synchronous	User request	User maskable	Between	Resume
Integer arithmetic overflow	Synchronous	Coerced	User maskable	Within	Terminate
Floating-point arithmetic overflow or underflow	Synchronous	Coerced	User maskable	Within	Resume
Page fault	Synchronous	Coerced	Nonmaskable	Within	Resume
Misaligned memory accesses	Synchronous	Coerced	User maskable	Within	Terminate
Memory-protection violations	Synchronous	Coerced	Nonmaskable	Within	Terminate
Using undefined instructions	Synchronous	Coerced	Nonmaskable	Within	Terminate
Hardware malfunctions	Asynchronous	Coerced	Nonmaskable	Within	Terminate
Power failure	Asynchronous	Coerced	Nonmaskable	Within	Terminate

FIGURE 5.11   The events of Figure 5.9 classified using five categories.

How Control Checks for Interrupts

Integrating interrupts with control means modifying the finite-state diagram to check for interrupts. Interrupts that occur between instructions are checked either at the beginning of the finite-state diagram—before an instruction is decoded—or at the end—after the execution of an instruction is completed. Interrupts that can occur within an instruction are generally detected in the state that causes the action or in a state that follows it. For example, Figure 5.12 shows Figure 5.4 (page 207) modified to check for interrupts.

We assume DLX transfers the return address into a new programmer-visible register, the interrupt return-address register. Control then loads PC with the address of the interrupt routine for that interrupt.

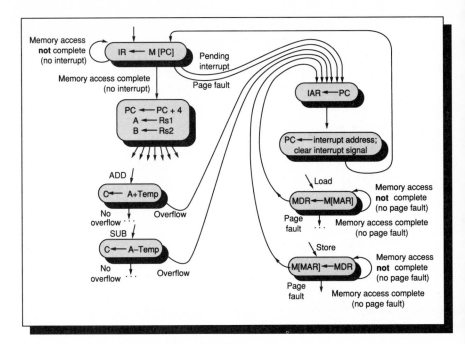

FIGURE 5.12   The top-level view of the DLX finite-state diagram (Figure 5.4 on page 207) modified to check for interrupts. Either a between interrupt or an instruction page fault invokes the control that saves the PC and then loads it with the address of the appropriate interrupt routine. The lower portion of the figure shows interrupts resulting in page faults of data accesses or arithmetic overflow.

What's Hard About Interrupts

The conflicting terminology is confusing, but that is not what makes the hard part of control hard. Even though interrupts are rare, the hardware must be designed so that the full state of the machine can be saved, including an indication of the offending event, and the PC of the instruction to be executed after the interrupt is serviced. This difficulty is exacerbated by events occurring during the middle of execution, for many instructions also require the hardware to restore the machine to the state just before the event occurred—the beginning of the instruction. This last requirement is so difficult that computers are awarded the title *restartable* if they pass that test. That supercomputers and many early microprocessors do not earn that badge of honor illustrates both the difficulty of interrupts and the potential cost in hardware complexity and execution speed.

No engineers deserve more admiration than those who built the first VAX, DEC's first restartable minicomputer. The variable-length instructions mean the computer can fetch 50 bytes of one instruction before discovering that the next byte of the instruction is not in main memory—a situation that requires the saved PC to point 50 bytes earlier. Imagine the difficulties of restarting an instruction with six operands, each of which could be misaligned and thus be partially in memory and partially on disk!

The instructions that are hardest to restart are those that modify some of the machine state before it is known whether interrupts can occur. The VAX autoincrement and autodecrement addressing modes would naturally modify registers during the addressing phase of execution rather than at the writeback phase, and so would be vulnerable to this difficulty. To avoid this problem, recent VAXes keep a history queue of the register specifiers and the operations on the registers, so that the operations can be reversed on an interrupt. Another approach, used on the earlier VAXes, is to record the specifiers and the original values of the registers, restoring the original values on interrupt. (The primary difference is that it only takes a few bits to record how the address was changed due to autoincrement or autodecrement versus the full 32-bit register value.)

It is not just addressing modes that make the VAX difficult to restart; long-running instructions mean that interrupts must be checked in the middle of execution to prevent long interrupt latency. MOVC3, for example, copies up to 2^{16} bytes and can take tens of milliseconds to finish—far too long to wait for an urgent event. On the other hand, even if there were a way to undo copying in the middle of execution so that MOVC3 could be restarted, interrupts would occur so frequently, relative to this long-running instruction (see Figure 5.10 on page 216), that MOVC3 would be restarted repeatedly under those conditions. Such wasted effort from incomplete copies would render MOVC3 worse than useless.

DEC divided the problem to conquer it. First, the operands—source address, length, and destination address—are fetched from memory and placed into general-purpose registers R1, R2, and R3. If an interrupt occurs during this first phase, these registers are restored, and the MOVC3 is restarted from scratch. After this first phase, every time a byte is copied, the length (R2) is decremented and addresses (R1 and R3) are incremented. If an interrupt occurs during this second phase, MOVC3 sets the *first part done* (FPD) bit in the program status word. When the interrupt is serviced and the instruction is reexecuted, it first checks the FPD bit to see if the operands have already been placed in registers. If so, the VAX doesn't fetch the address and length operands, but just continues with the current values in the registers, since that is all that remains to be copied. This permits more rapid response to interrupts while allowing long-running instructions to make progress between interrupts.

IBM had a similar problem. The 360 included the MVC instruction, which copies up to 256 bytes of data. For the early machines without virtual memory, the machine simply waited until the instruction was completed before servicing interrupts. With the inclusion of virtual memory in the 370, the problem could no longer be ignored. Control first tries to access all possible pages, forcing all possible virtual memory miss interrupts to occur before moving any data. If any interrupts occur in this phase, the instruction is restarted. Control then ignores interrupts until the instruction is complete. To allow longer copies, the 370 includes MVCL, which can move up to 2^{24} bytes. The operands are in registers and are updated as a part of execution—like the VAX, except that there is no need for FPD since the operands are always in registers. (Or, to speak historically, the VAX solution is like the IBM 370, which came first.)

5.7 | **Putting It All Together: Control for DLX**

The control for DLX is presented here to tie together the ideas from the previous three sections. We begin with a finite-state diagram to represent hardwired control and end with microprogrammed control. Both versions of DLX control are used to demonstrate tradeoffs to reduce cost or to improve performance. Because the figures are already too large, the checking for data page faults or arithmetic overflow shown in Figure 5.12 (page 218) is not included in this section. (Exercise 5.12 adds them.)

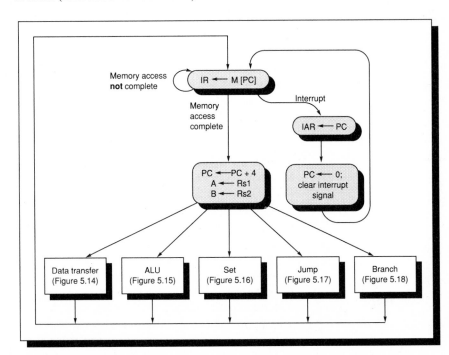

FIGURE 5.13 The top-level view of the DLX finite-state diagram for the non-floating-point instructions. The first two steps of instruction execution—instruction fetch and instruction decode/register fetch—are shown. The first state repeats until the instruction is fetched from memory or an interrupt is detected. If an interrupt is detected, the PC is saved in IAR and PC is set to the address of the interrupt routine. The last three steps of instruction execution—execution/effective address, memory access, and write back—are shown in Figures 5.14 to 5.18 on pages 221–224.

Rather than trying to draw the DLX finite-state machine in a single figure showing all 52 states, Figure 5.13 (see page 220) shows just the top level, containing 4 states plus references to the rest of the states detailed in Figures 5.14 (below) through 5.18 (page 224). Unlike Figure 5.2 (page 205), Figure 5.13 takes advantage of the change to the datapath allowing PC to address memory directly without going through MAR (Figure 5.4 on page 207).

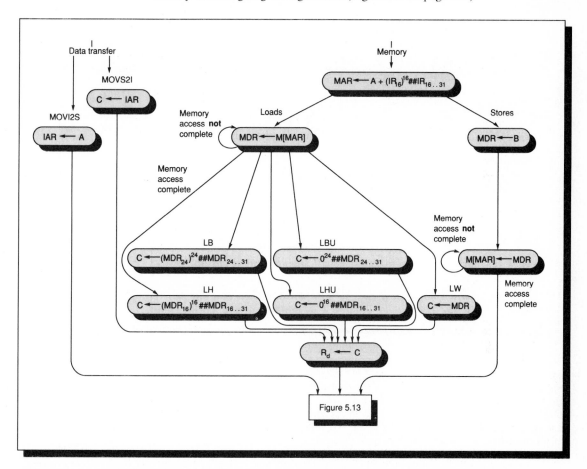

FIGURE 5.14 The effective address calculation, memory-access, and write-back states for the memory-access and data-transfer instructions of DLX. For loads, the second state repeats until the data is fetched from memory. The final state of stores repeats until the write is complete. While the operation of all five loads is shown in the states of this figure, the proper operation of writes depends on the memory system writing bytes and halfwords, without disturbing the rest of the word in memory, and correctly aligning the bytes and halfwords (see Figure 3.10, page 97) over the proper bytes of memory. On completion of execution control transfers to Figure 5.13, found on page 220.

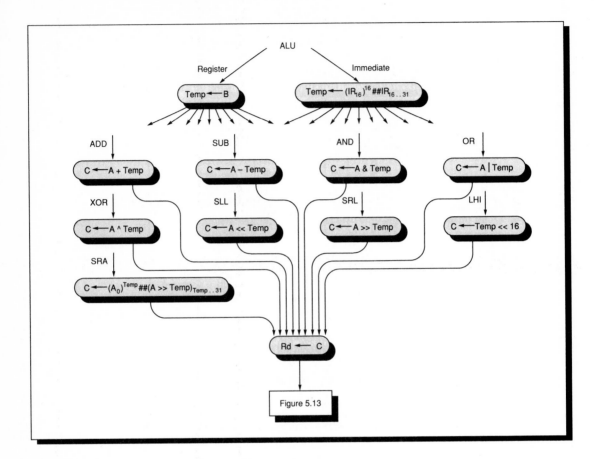

FIGURE 5.15   The execution and write-back states for the ALU instructions of DLX. After putting a register or the sign-extended 16-bit immediate into Temp, 1 of the 9 instructions is executed, and the result (C) is written back into the register file. Only SRA and LHI may not be self-explanatory: The SRA instruction shifts right while it sign extends the operand and LHI loads the upper 16 bits of the register while zeroing the lower 16 bits. (The C operators << and >> shift left and right, respectively; they fill with zeros unless bits are concatenated explicitly using ##, e.g., sign extension). As mentioned above, the check for overflow in ADD and SUB is not included to simplify the figure. On completion of execution control transfers to Figure 5.13 (page 220).

FIGURE 5.16 (See adjoining page.)   The execution and write-back states for the Set instructions of DLX. After putting a register or the sign-extended 16-bit immediate into Temp, 1 of the 6 instructions compares A to Temp and then sets C to 1 or 0, depending on whether the condition is true or false. C is then written back into the register file, and then execution control transfers to Figure 5.13 (page 220). The dashed lines in this figure and Figure 5.18 are used to make it easier to follow intersecting lines.

FIGURE 5.17 (See adjoining page.)   The execution and write-back states for the jump instructions of DLX. With jump and link instructions, the return address is first placed in C before the new value is loaded into PC. Trap saves it in IAR. Note that the immediate in these instructions is 10 bits longer than the 16-bit immediate in all other instructions. Jump and link instructions conclude by writing the return address back into R31. On completion of execution, control transfers to Figure 5.13 (page 220).

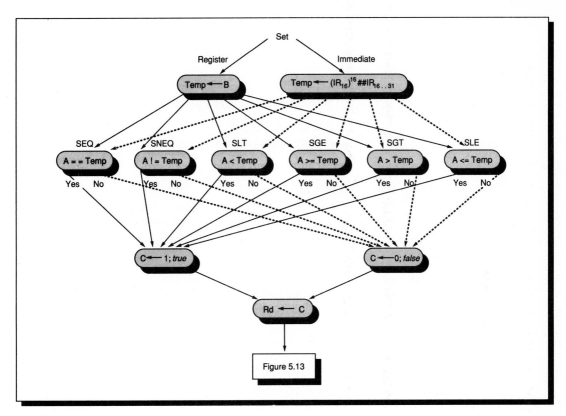

FIGURE 5.16

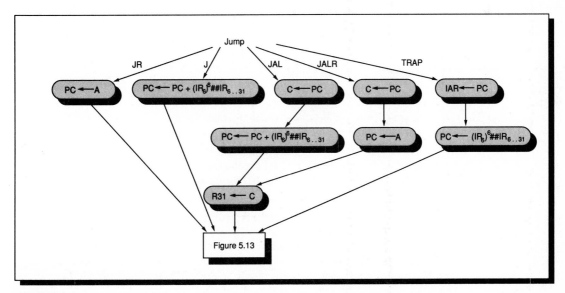

FIGURE 5.17

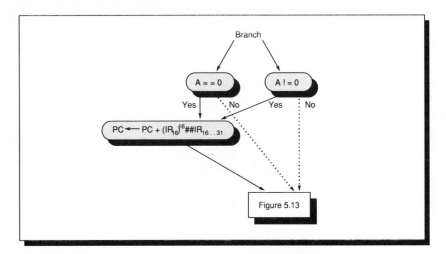

FIGURE 5.18   The execution states for the branch instructions of DLX. The PC is loaded with the sum of the PC and the immediate only if the condition is true. On completion of execution, control transfers to Figure 5.13, found on page 220.

Performance of Hardwired Control for DLX

As stated in Section 5.4, the goal for control designs is to minimize CPI, clock cycle time, amount of control hardware, and development time. CPI is just the average number of states along the execution path of an instruction.

Example

Let's assume that hardwired control directly implements the finite-state diagram in Figures 5.13 to 5.18. What is the CPI for DLX running GCC?

Answer

The number of clock cycles to execute each DLX instruction is determined by simply counting the states of an instruction. Starting at the top, every instruction spends at least two clock cycles in the states in Figure 5.13 (ignoring interrupts). The actual number depends on the average number of times the state accessing memory must repeat because memory is not ready. (These wasted clock cycles are usually called *memory stall cycles* or *wait states*.) In cache-based machines this value is typically 0 (i.e., no repetitions since cache access is 1 cycle) when the data is found in the cache, and 10 or higher when it is not.

The time for the remaining portion of instruction execution comes from the additional figures. Besides two cycles for fetch and decode, loads take four more cycles plus clock cycles waiting for the data access, while stores take just three more clock cycles plus wait states. Three extra clock cycles are also needed by ALU instructions, and set instructions take four. Figure 5.17 shows that jumps take just one extra clock cycle with jump and links taking three. Branches depend on the result: Taken branches use two more clock cycles while

DLX instructions	Minimum clock cycles	Memory accesses	Total clock cycles
Loads	6	2	8
Stores	5	2	7
ALU	5	1	6
Set	6	1	7
Jumps	3	1	4
Jump and links	5	1	6
Branch (taken)	4	1	5
Branch (not taken)	3	1	4

FIGURE 5.19 Clock cycles per instruction for DLX categories using the state diagram in Figures 5.13 through 5.18. Determining the total clock cycles per category requires multiplying the number of memory accesses—including instruction fetches—times the average number of wait states, and adding this product to the minimum number of clock cycles. We assume an average of 1 clock cycle per memory access. For example, loads take eight clock cycles if the average number of wait states is one.

untaken branches need just one. Adding these times to the first portion of instruction execution yields the clock cycles per DLX instruction class shown in Figure 5.19.

From Chapter 2, one way to calculate CPI is

$$\text{CPI} = \sum_{i=1}^{n} \left(\text{CPI}_i * \frac{\text{I}_i}{\text{Instruction count}} \right)$$

Using the DLX instruction mix from Figure C.4 in Appendix C for GCC (normalized to 100%), the percentage of taken branches from Figure 3.22 (page 107), and one for the average number of wait states per memory access, the DLX CPI for this datapath and state diagram is calculated:

Loads	8	* 21%	=	1.68
Stores	7	* 12%	=	0.84
ALU	6	* 37%	=	2.22
Set	7	* 6%	=	0.42
Jumps	4	* 2%	=	0.08
Jump and links	6	* 0%	=	0.00
Branch (taken)	5	* 12%	=	0.60
Branch (not taken)	4	* 11%	=	0.44
		Total CPI:		6.28

Thus, the DLX CPI for GCC is about 6.3.

Improving DLX Performance When Control Is Hardwired

As mentioned above, performance is improved by reducing the number of states an instruction must pass through during execution. Sometimes, performance can be improved by removing intermediate calculations that select one of several options, either by adding hardware that uses information in the opcode to later select the appropriate option, or by simply increasing the number of states.

Example

Let's look at improving the performance of ALU instructions by removing the top two states in Figure 5.15 on page 222, which load either a register or an immediate into Temp. One approach uses a new hardware option. Let's call it "X" (see Figure 5.20). The X option selects either the B register or the 16-bit immediate, depending on the opcode in IR. A second approach is simply to increase the number of execution states so that there are separate states for ALU instructions using immediate versus ALU instructions using registers.

For each option, what would be the change in performance, and how should the state diagram be changed? Also, how many states are needed in each option?

Answer

Either change reduces ALU execution time from five to four clock cycles plus wait states. From Figure C.4, ALU operations are about 37% of the instructions for GCC, lowering CPI from 6.3 to 5.9, and making the machine about 7% faster. Figure 5.20 shows Figure 5.15 modified to use the X option instead of the two states that load Temp, while Figure 5.21 simply has many more states to achieve the same result. The total number of states are 50 and 58, respectively.

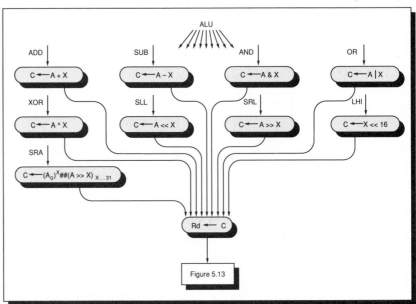

FIGURE 5.20 Figure 5.15 modified to remove the two states loading Temp. The states use the new X option to mean that either B or $(IR_{16})^{16}\#\#IR_{16..31}$ is the operand, depending on the DLX opcode.

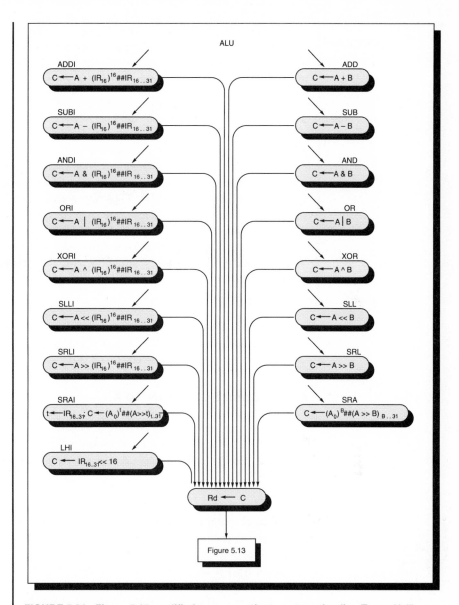

FIGURE 5.21 Figure 5.15 modified to remove the two states loading Temp. Unlike Figure 5.20, this requires no new hardware options in the datapath, but simply more control states.

Control can affect the clock cycle time, either because control itself takes longer than the corresponding operations in the datapath, or because the datapath operations selected by control lengthens the worst-case clock cycle time.

Example   Assume a machine with a 10-ns clock cycle (100-MHz clock rate). Suppose that on closer inspection the designer discovered that all states could be executed in 9 ns, except states that use the shifter. Would it be wise to split those states, taking two 9-ns clock cycles for shift states and one 9-ns clock for everything else?

Answer   Assuming the improvement in the previous example, the average instruction execution time for the 100-MHz machine is 5.9*10 ns or 59 ns. The shifter is only used in the states of four instructions: SLL, SRL, SRA, and LHI (see Figure 5.20). In fact, each of these instructions takes 5 clock cycles (including one wait state for memory access), and only one of the five original clock cycles need be split into two new clock cycles. Thus, the average execution time of these instructions changes from 5*10 ns, or 50 ns, to 6*9 ns, or 54 ns. From Figure C.4 these 4 instructions are about 11% of the instructions executed for GCC (after normalization), making the average instruction execution time 89% * (5.9*9 ns) + 11%*54 ns or 53 ns. Thus, splitting the shift state results in a machine that is about 10% faster—a wise decision. (See Exercise 5.8 for a more sophisticated version of this tradeoff.)

Hardwired control is completed by listing the control signals activated in each state, assigning numbers to the states, and finally generating the PLA. Now let's implement control using microcode in a ROM.

Microcoded Control for DLX

A custom format such as this is a slave to the architecture of the hardware and instruction set which it serves. The format must strike a proper compromise between ROM size, ROM-output decoding circuitry size, and machine execution rate.

Jim McKevit et al. [1977]

Before microprogramming can commence, the microinstruction set must be determined. The first step is to list the possible entries for each field of the DLX microinstruction format from Figure 5.6 on page 209. Figure 5.7 on page 211 lists them for the Destination, Source1, and Source2 fields. Figure 5.22 below shows the values for the remaining fields.

Sequencing of microinstructions requires further explanation. The microprogrammed control includes a microprogram counter to specify the address of the next microinstruction if a branch is not taken, as in Figure 5.5 on page 208. In addition to the branches using the Jump address field, three tables are used to decode the DLX macroinstructions. These tables are indexed with the opcodes of the DLX instruction, and supply a microprogram address depending on the value in the opcode. Their use will become clear as we examine the DLX microprogram.

Value	ALU		Misc		Cond	
0	ADD	+	Instr Read	$IR \leftarrow M[PC]$	- - -	*Go to next sequential microinstruction*
1	SUB	–	Data Read	$MDR \leftarrow M[MAR]$	Uncond	*Always jump*
2	RSUB (reverse sub)	$-_r$	Write	$M[MAR] \leftarrow MDR$	Int?	*Pending (between instruction) interrupt?*
3	AND	&	AB← RF	*Load A&B from Reg. File*	Mem?	*Memory access not complete?*
4	OR	/	Rd←C	*Write Rd*	Zero?	*Is the ALU output zero?*
5	XOR	^	R31←C	*Write R31 (for call)*	Negative?	*Is the ALU output less than zero?*
6	SLL	<<			Load?	*Is the macroinstruction a DLX load?*
7	SRL	>>			Decode1 (Fig. 5.24)	*Address table 1 determines next micro-instruction (uses main opcode)*
8	SRA	$>>_a$			Decode2 (Fig. 5.26)	*Address table 2 determines next micro-instruction (uses "func" opcode)*
9	Pass S1	*S1*			Decode3 (Fig. 5.26)	*Address table 3 determines next micro-instruction (uses main opcode)*
10	Pass S2	*S2*				

FIGURE 5.22   The options for three fields of the DLX microinstruction format in Figure 5.6 on page 209. The possible names are shown on the left of the field name, with an explanation of each field to the right. The real microinstruction would contain a bit pattern corresponding to the number in the first column. Combined with Figure 5.7 (page 211), all the fields are defined except the Constant and Jump address fields, which contain numbers supplied by the microprogrammer. $>>_a$ is an abbreviation for shift right arithmetic and $-_r$ means reverse subtract ($B -_r A = A - B$).

Following the lead of the state diagram, the DLX microprogram is divided into Figures 5.23, 5.25, 5.27, 5.28, and 5.29, with each section of microcode corresponding to one of Figures 5.13 to 5.18 (pages 220–224). The first state in Figure 5.13 becomes the first two microinstructions in Figure 5.23. The first microinstruction (address 0) branches to microinstruction 3 if there is an interrupt pending. Microinstruction 1 fetches an instruction from memory, branching back to itself as long as the memory access is not complete. Microinstruction 2 increments the PC by 4, loads A and B, and then does the first-level decoding. The address of the next microinstruction then depends on which macroinstruction is in the instruction register. The microinstruction addresses for this first-level macroinstruction decode are specified in Figure 5.24. (In reality, the table shown in this figure is specified after the microprogram is written, as both the number of entries and the corresponding locations aren't known until then.)

Loc	Label	Dest	ALU	S1	S2	C	Misc	Cond	Jump label	Comment
0	Ifetch:							Interrupt?	Intrpt	*Check interrupt*
1	Iloop:						Instr Read	Mem?	Iloop	*IR ←M[PC]; wait for memory*
2		PC	ADD	PC	Constant	4	AB←RF	Decode1		
3	Intrpt:	IAR	Pass S1	PC						*Interrupt*
4		PC	Pass S2		Constant	0		Uncond	Ifetch	*PC←0 & go fetch next instruction*

FIGURE 5.23   The first section of the DLX microprogram, corresponding to the states in Figure 5.13 (page 220).
The first column contains the absolute address of the microinstruction, followed by a label. The rest of the fields contain values from Figures 5.7 (page 211) and 5.22 for the microinstruction format in Figure 5.6 (page 209). As an example, microinstruction 2 corresponds to the second state of Figure 5.13. It sends the output from the ALU into PC, tells the ALU to add, puts PC onto the Source1 bus, and a constant from the microinstruction (whose value is 4) onto the Source2 bus. In addition, A and B are loaded from the register file according to the specifiers in IR. Finally, the address of the next microinstruction to be executed comes from decode table 1 (Figure 5.24), which depends on the opcode in the instruction register (IR).

Opcodes (symbolically specified)	Absolute address	Label	Figure
Memory	5	Mem:	5.25
Move to special	20	MovI2S:	5.25
Move from special	21	MovS2I:	5.25
S2 = B	23	Reg:	5.27
S2 = Immediate	24	Imm:	5.27
Branch equal zero	50	Beq:	5.29
Branch not equal zero	52	Bne:	5.29
Jump	54	Jump:	5.29
Jump register	55	JReg:	5.29
Jump and link	56	JAL:	5.29
Jump and link register	58	JALR:	5.29
Trap	60	Trap:	5.29

FIGURE 5.24   Opcodes and corresponding addresses for decode table 1. The opcodes are shown symbolically on the left, followed by the addresses with the absolute microinstruction address, a label, and the figure where the microcode can be found. If this table were implemented with a ROM it would contain 64 entries corresponding to the 6-bit opcode of DLX. As this would clearly result in many redundant or unspecified entries, a PLA could be used to minimize hardware.

Figure 5.25 contains the DLX load and store instructions. Microinstruction 5 calculates the effective address, and branches to microinstruction 9 if the macroinstruction in the IR is a load. If not, microinstruction 6 loads MDR with the value to be stored, and microinstruction 7 jumps to itself until the memory is finished writing the data. Microinstruction 8 then jumps back to microinstruction 0 (Figure 5.23) to begin the execution cycle all over again. If the macroinstruction was a load, microinstruction 9 loops until the data has been read. Microinstruction 10 then uses decode table 2 (specified in Figure 5.26) to specify the address of the next microinstruction. Unlike the first decode table, this table is used by other microinstructions. (There is no conflict in multiple uses since the opcodes for each instance are different.)

Suppose the instruction were load halfword. Figure 5.26 shows that the result of decode 2 would be to jump to microinstruction 15. This microinstruction shifts the contents of MDR to the left 16 bits and stores the result in Temp. The following microinstruction shifts Temp right arithmetically 16 bits and puts the result in C. C now contains the 16 rightmost bits of MDR, with the upper 16 bits containing the extended sign. This microinstruction jumps to location 22, which writes C back into the destination register specifier in IR, and then jumps to fetch the next macroinstruction starting at location 0 (Figure 5.23).

Loc	Label	Dest	ALU	S1	S2	C	Misc	Cond	Jump label	Comment
5	Mem:	MAR	ADD	A	imm16			Load?	Load	*Memory instruct.*
6	Store:	MDR	Pass S2		B					*Store*
7	Dloop:						Data write	Mem?	Dloop	
8								Uncond	Ifetch	*Fetch next instr.*
9	Load:						Data read	Mem?	Load	*Load MDR*
10								Decode2		
11	LB:	Temp	SLL	MDR	Constant	24				*Load byte; shift left to remove upper 24 bits*
12		C	SRA	Temp	Constant	24		Uncond	Write1	*Shift right arithmetic to sign extend*
13	LBU:	Temp	SLL	MDR	Constant	24				*LB unsigned*
14		C	SRL	Temp	Constant	24		Uncond	Write1	*Shift right logical*
15	LH:	Temp	SLL	MDR	Constant	16				*Load half*
16		C	SRA	Temp	Constant	16		Uncond	Write1	*Shift right arithmetic*
17	LHU:	Temp	SLL	MDR	Constant	16				*LH Unsigned*
18		C	SRL	Temp	Constant	16		Uncond	Write1	*Shift right logical*
19	LW:	C	Pass S1	MDR				Uncond	Write1	*Load word*
20	MovI2S:	IAR	Pass S1	A				Uncond	Ifetch	*Move to special*
21	MovS2I:	C	Pass S1	IAR						*Move from spec.*
22	Write1:						Rd←C	Uncond	Ifetch	*Write back & go fetch next instruction*

FIGURE 5.25 The section of the DLX microprogram for loads and stores, corresponding to the states in Figure 5.14 (page 221). The microcode for bytes and halfwords takes an extra microinstruction to align the data (see Figure 3.10, page 97). Note that microinstruction 5 loads A from Rd, just in case the instruction is a store. The label Ifetch is for microinstruction 0 in Figure 5.23 on page 230.

Opcode	Absolute address	Label	Figure
Load byte	11	LB:	5.25
Load byte unsigned	13	LBU:	5.25
Load half	15	LH:	5.25
Load half unsigned	17	LHU:	5.25
Load word	19	LW:	5.25
ADD	25	ADD/I:	5.27
SUB	26	SUB/I:	5.27
AND	27	AND/I:	5.27
OR	28	OR/I:	5.27
XOR	29	XOR/I:	5.27
SLL	30	SLL/I:	5.27
SRL	31	SRL/I:	5.27
SRA	32	SRA/I:	5.27
LHI	33	LHI:	5.27
Set equal	35	SEQ/I:	5.28
Set not equal	37	SNE/I:	5.28
Set less than	39	SLT/I:	5.28
Set greater than or equal	41	SGE/I:	5.28
Set greater than	43	SGT/I:	5.28
Set less than or equal	45	SLE/I:	5.28

FIGURE 5.26 Opcodes and corresponding addresses for decode tables 2 and 3. The opcodes are shown symbolically on the left, followed by the absolute microinstruction address, the corresponding label, and the figure where the microcode can be found. Since the opcodes are shown symbolically, and they go to the same place in both tables, the same information can be used for specifying decode tables 2 and 3. This similarity is attributable to the immediate version and register version of the DLX instructions sharing the same microcode. If a table were implemented with a ROM, it would contain 64 entries corresponding to the 6-bit opcode of DLX. Again, the many redundant or unspecified entries suggest the use of a PLA to minimize hardware cost.

The ALU instructions are found in Figure 5.27. The first two microinstructions correspond to the states at the top of Figure 5.15 (page 222). After loading Temp with either the register or the immediate, each uses a decode table to vector to the microinstruction that executes the ALU instruction. To save microcode space, the same microinstruction is used whether the operand is a register or an immediate. One of the microinstructions between 25 and 33 is executed, storing its result in C. It then jumps to microinstruction 34, which stores C into the register specified in the IR, and in turn jumps to fetch the next macroinstruction.

Loc	Label	Dest	ALU	S1	S2	C	Misc	Cond	Jump label	Comment
23	Reg:	Temp	Pass S2		B			Decode2		*source2 = reg*
24	Imm:	Temp	Pass S2		Imm			Decode3		*source2 = imm.*
25	ADD/I:	C	ADD	A	Temp			Uncond	Write2	*ADD*
26	SUB/I:	C	SUB	A	Temp			Uncond	Write2	*SUB*
27	AND/I:	C	AND	A	Temp			Uncond	Write2	*AND*
28	OR/I:	C	OR	A	Temp			Uncond	Write2	*OR*
29	XOR/I:	C	XOR	A	Temp			Uncond	Write2	*XOR*
30	SLL/I:	C	SLL	A	Temp			Uncond	Write2	*SLL*
31	SRL/I:	C	SRL	A	Temp			Uncond	Write2	*SRL*
32	SRA/I:	C	SRA	A	Temp			Uncond	Write2	*SRA*
33	LHI:	C	SLL	Temp	Constant	16		Uncond	Write2	*LHI*
34	Write2:						Rd←C	Uncond	Ifetch	*Write back & go fetch next instruction*

FIGURE 5.27   Like the first two states in Figure 5.15 (page 222), microinstructions 23 and 24 load Temp with an operand and then vector to the appropriate microinstruction, depending on the opcode in IR. One of the nine following microinstructions is executed, leaving its result in C. C is written back into the register specified in the register destination field of DLX macroinstruction in IR in microinstruction 34.

Loc	Label	Dest	ALU	S1	S2	C	Misc	Cond	Jump label	Comment
35	SEQ/I:		SUB	A	Temp			Zero?	Set1	*Set equal*
36		C	Pass S2		Constant	0		Uncond	Write4	*A≠T (set to false)*
37	SNE/I:		SUB	A	Temp			Zero?	Set0	*Set not equal*
38		C	Pass S2		Constant	1		Uncond	Write4	*A≠T (set to true)*
39	SLT/I:		SUB	A	Temp			Negative?	Set1	*Set less than*
40		C	Pass S2		Constant	0		Uncond	Write4	*A≥T (set to false)*
41	SGE/I:		SUB	A	Temp			Negative?	Set0	*Set GT or equal*
42		C	Pass S2		Constant	1		Uncond	Write4	*A≥T (set to true)*
43	SGT/I:		RSUB	A	Temp			Negative?	Set1	*Set greater than*
44		C	Pass S2		Constant	0		Uncond	Write4	*T≥A (set to false)*
45	SLE/I:		RSUB	A	Temp			Negative?	Set0	*Set LT or equal*
46		C	Pass S2		Constant	1		Uncond	Write4	*T≥A (set to true)*
47	Set0:	C	Pass S2		Constant	0		Uncond	Write4	*Set to 0 = false*
48	Set1:	C	Pass S2		Constant	1				*Set to 1 = true*
49	Write4:						Rd←C	Uncond	Ifetch	*Write back & fetch next instruction*

FIGURE 5.28   Corresponding to Figure 5.16 (pages 222–223), this microcode performs the DLX Set instructions. As in the previous figure, to save space these same microinstructions execute either the version of set using registers or the version using immediates. The tricky microcode is found in microinstructions 43 and 45, where the subtraction Temp – A is unlike the earlier microcode. Remember that A–$_r$ Temp = Temp – A (see Figure 5.22 on page 229).

Figure 5.28 corresponds to the states in Figure 5.16 (pages 222–223), except that the top two states that load Temp are microinstructions 23 and 24 of the previous figure; the decode tables will either jump to locations 25 to 34 in Figure 5.27, or 35 to 45 in Figure 5.28, depending on the opcode. The microinstructions for Set perform relative tests by having the ALU subtract Temp from A and then test the ALU output to see if the result is zero or negative. Depending on the test result, C is set to 1 or 0 and written back in the register file before going to fetch the next macroinstruction. Tests for A = Temp, A ≠ Temp, A < Temp, and A ≥ Temp are straightforward using these conditions on the ALU output A − Temp. A > Temp and A ≤ Temp, on the other hand, are not simple, but can be done using the negative condition with the subtraction reversed:

$$(\text{Temp} - A < 0) \ = \ (\text{Temp} < A) \ = \ (A > \text{Temp})$$

If the result is negative, then A > Temp, otherwise A ≤ Temp. Voila!

Figure 5.29 contains the last of the DLX microcode and corresponds to the states found in Figures 5.17 and 5.18 (pages 222–224). Microinstruction 50, corresponding to the macroinstruction branch on equal zero, tests if A equals zero. If it does, the macroinstruction branch succeeds, and the microinstruction jumps to the microinstruction 53. This microinstruction loads the PC with the PC-relative address and then jumps to the microcode that fetches the new macroinstruction (location 0). If A does not equal zero, the macroinstruction branch fails, so that the next sequential microinstruction (51) executes, jumping to location 0 without changing the PC.

A state usually corresponds to a single microinstruction, although in a few cases above two microinstructions were needed. The jump and link instructions have the reverse case, with two states collapsing into one microinstruction. The actions in the last two states of jump and link in Figure 5.17 are found in microinstruction 57, and similarly for the jump and link register with microinstruction 59. These microinstructions load the PC with the PC-relative branch address **and** save C into R31.

Loc	Label	Dest	ALU	S1	S2	C	Misc	Cond	Jump label	Comment
50	Beq:		SUB	A	Constant	0		0?	Branch	*Instr is branch =0*
51								Uncond	Ifetch	*≠0: not taken*
52	Bne:		SUB	A	Constant	0		0?	Ifetch	*Instr is branch ≠ 0*
53	Branch:	PC	ADD	PC	imm16			Uncond	Ifetch	*≠0: taken*
54	Jump:	PC	ADD	PC	imm26			Uncond	Ifetch	*Jump*
55	JReg:	PC	Pass S1	A				Uncond	Ifetch	*Jump register*
56	JAL:	C	Pass S1	PC						*Jump and link*
57		PC	ADD	PC	imm26		R31←C	Uncond	Ifetch	*Jump & save PC*
58	JALR:	C	Pass S1	PC						*Jump & link reg*
59		PC	Pass S1	A			R31←C	Uncond	Ifetch	*Jump & save PC*
60	Trap:	IAR	Pass S1	PC						*Trap*
61		PC	Pass S2		imm26			Uncond	Ifetch	

FIGURE 5.29   The microcode for branch and jump DLX instructions, corresponding to the states in Figures 5.17 and 5.18 on pages 222–224.

Performance of Microcoded Control for DLX

Before trying to improve performance or reduce costs of control, the existing performance must be assessed. Again, the process is to count the clock cycles for each instruction, but this time there is a larger variety in performance.

All instructions execute microinstructions 0, 1, and 2 in Figure 5.23 (page 230), giving a base of 3 clocks plus wait states, depending on the repetition of microinstruction 1. The clock cycles for the rest of the categories are:

4 for stores, plus wait states

5 for load word, plus wait states

6 for load byte or load half (signed or unsigned), plus wait states

3 for ALU

4 for set

2 for branch equal zero (taken or untaken)

2 for branch not equal zero (taken)

1 for branch not equal zero (untaken)

1 for jumps

2 for jump and links

Using the instruction mix for GCC in Figure C.4, and assuming an average of 1 wait state per memory access, the CPI is 7.68. This is higher than the hardwired control CPI, because the test for interrupt takes another clock cycle at the beginning, loads and stores are slower, and branch equal zero is slower for the untaken case.

Reducing Cost and Improving Performance of DLX When Control Is Microcoded

The size of a completely unencoded version of the DLX microinstruction is calculated from the number of entries in Figures 5.7 (page 211) and 5.22 (page 229) plus the size of the Constant and Jump address fields. The largest constant in the fields is 24, which requires 5 bits, and the largest address is 61, which requires 6. Figure 5.30 shows the microinstruction fields, the unencoded widths, and the encoded widths. Encoding almost halves the size of control store.

	Dest	ALU operation	Source1	Source2	Constant	Misc	Cond	Jump address	Total
Unencoded	7	11	9	9	5	6	10	6	= 63 bits
Encoded	3	4	4	4	5	3	4	6	= 33 bits

FIGURE 5.30 Width of field in bits of unencoded and encoded microinstruction formats. Note that the Constant and Jump address fields are not encoded in this example, placing fewer restrictions on the microprogram using the encoded format.

The microinstruction can be further shrunk by introducing multiple microinstruction formats and by combining independent fields.

Example

Figure 5.31 shows an encoded version of the original DLX microinstruction
format and the version with two formats: one for ALU operations and one for
miscellaneous and branch operations. A bit is added to distinguish the two
formats. The ALU/Jump (A/J) microinstruction performs the ALU operations
specified in the microinstruction; the address of the next microinstruction is
specified in the Jump address. For the Transfer/Misc/Branch (T/M/B) microinstruction, the ALU performs Pass S1, while the Misc and Cond fields specify
the rest of the operations. The primary change in interpretation of the fields in
the new formats is that the ALU condition being tested in the T/M/B format
refers to the ALU output from the *prior* A/J microinstruction since there is no
ALU operation in T/M/B format. In both formats the Constant and Jump fields
are combined into a single field under the assumption they are not used at the
same time. (For the A/J format, the appearance of a constant in a source field
results in fetching the following microinstruction.) The new formats shrink
width from the original 33 bits to 22 bits, but the actual size savings depends on
the number of extra microinstructions needed because of the reduced options.

What is the increase in number of microinstructions, compared to the single
format, for the microcode in Figure 5.23 (page 230)?

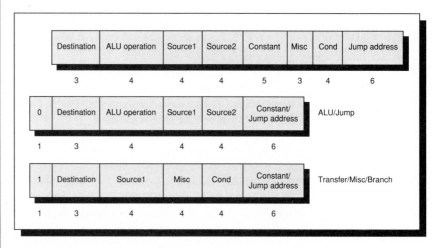

**FIGURE 5.31 The original DLX microinstruction format at the top and the dual-
format version below.** Note that the Misc field is expanded from 3 to 4 bits in the T/M/B to
make the two formats the same length.

Answer

Figure 5.32 shows the increase in the number of microinstructions over Figure
5.23 (page 230) because of the restrictions of each format. The five microinstructions in the original format expand to six in the new format. Microinstruction 2 is the only one that expands to two microinstructions for this example.

Loc	Label	Type	Dest	ALU	S1	S2	Misc	Cond	Const/Jump	Comment
0	Ifetch:	M/T/B		---		---		Interrupt?	Intrpt	*Check interrupt*
1	Iloop:	M/T/B		---		---	Instr Read	Mem?	Iloop	*IR ←M[PC]; wait for memory*
2		A/J	PC	ADD	PC	Constant	---	---	4	*Increment PC*
3		M/T/B		---		---	AB← RF	Decode1		
4	Intrpt:	A/J	IAR	Pass S1	PC		---	---	5	*Interrupt*
5		A/J	PC	SUB	Temp	Temp	---	---	Ifetch	*PC←0 (t minus t=0) & go fetch next instruction*

FIGURE 5.32   Version of Figure 5.23 (page 230) using the dual-format microinstruction in Figure 5.31. Note that ALU/Jump microinstructions check the S1 and S2 fields for a constant specifier to see if the next address is sequential (as in microinstruction 2); otherwise they go to the Jump address (as in microinstructions 4 and 5). The microprogrammer changed the last microinstruction to generate a zero by subtracting a register from itself rather than through straightforward use of constant 0. Using the constant would have required an additional microinstruction since this format goes to the next sequential instruction if a constant is used. (See Figure 5.31.)

Sometimes performance can be improved by finding faster sequences of microcode, but normally it requires changes to the hardware. The branch equal zero instruction takes one extra clock cycle when the branch is not taken with hardwired control, but two with microcoded control; while branch not equal zero has the same performance for hardwired and microcoded control. Why would the former differ in performance? Figure 5.29 shows that microinstruction 52 branches on zero to fetch the next microinstruction, which is correct for the branch on not equal zero macroinstruction. Microinstruction 50 also tests for zero for the branch on zero macroinstruction and branches to the microinstruction that loads the new PC. The not zero case is handled by the following microinstruction (51), which jumps to fetch the next instruction— hence, one clock cycle for untaken branch on not equal zero and two for untaken branch on equal zero. One solution is simply to add "not zero" to the microcode branch conditions in Figure 5.22 (page 229) and change the branch on equal microcode to the version in Figure 5.33. Since there are only ten branch conditions, adding the eleventh would not require more than the four bits needed for an encoded version of that field.

Loc	Label	Dest	ALU	S1	S2	C	Misc	Cond	Jump label	Comment
50	Beq:		SUB	A	Constant	0		not 0?	Ifetch	*Branch =0*
51		PC	ADD	PC	imm16			Uncond	Ifetch	*=0: taken*

FIGURE 5.33   Branch not equal microcode from Figure 5.29 (page 234) rewritten by using a not zero condition in microinstruction 44.

This change drops the CPI from 7.68 to 7.63 for microcoded control, yet this is still higher than the CPI for hardwired control.

Example

Let's improve microcoded control so that the CPI for GCC is closer to the original CPI under hardwired control.

Answer

The main performance culprit is the separate test for interrupts in Figure 5.23. By modifying the hardware, decode1 can kill two birds with one stone: In addition to jumping to the appropriate microinstructions corresponding to the opcode, it also jumps to the interrupt microcode if an interrupt is pending. Figure 5.34 shows the revised microcode. This modification saves one clock cycle from each instruction, reducing the CPI to 6.63.

Loc	Label	Dest	ALU	S1	S2	C	Misc	Cond	Jump label	Comment
0	Ifetch:						Instr Read	Mem?	Ifetch	*IR ←M[PC]; wait for memory*
1		PC	ADD	PC	Constant	4	AB←RF	Decode1		*Also go to interrupt if pending interrupt*
2	Intrpt:	IAR	SUB	PC	Constant	4				*Interrupt: undo PC increment*
3		PC	Pass S2		Constant	0		Uncond	Ifetch	*PC←0 & go fetch next instruction*

FIGURE 5.34   Revised microcode that takes advantage of a change of the hardware to have decode1 go to microinstruction 2 if there is a pending interrupt. This microinstruction must reverse the increment of PC in the prior microinstruction so that the correct value is saved.

5.8 | Fallacies and Pitfalls

Pitfall: Microcode implementing a complex instruction may not be faster than macrocode.

At one time, microcode had the advantage of being fetched from a much faster memory than macrocode. Since caches came into use in 1968, microcode no longer has such a consistent edge in fetch time. Microcode does, however, still have the advantage of using internal temporary registers in the computation, which can be helpful on machines with few general-purpose registers. The disadvantage of microcode is that the algorithms must be selected before the machine is announced and can't be changed until the next model of the architecture; macrocode, on the other hand, can utilize improvements in its algorithms at any time during the life of the machine.

The VAX Index instruction provides an example: The instruction checks to see if the index is between two bounds, one of which is usually zero. The VAX-11/780 microcode uses two compares and two branches to do this, while macrocode can perform the same check in one compare and one branch. The macrocode checks the index against the upper limit using **unsigned** comparisons, rather than two's complement comparisons. This treats a negative index (less than zero and so failing the comparison) as if it were a very large number, thus exceeding the upper limit. (The algorithm can be used with nonzero lower bounds by first subtracting the lower bound from the index.) Replacing the index instruction by this VAX macrocode always improves performance on the VAX-11/780.

Fallacy: If there is space in control store, new instructions are free of cost.

Since the length of control store is usually a power of two, at times there may be unused control store available to expand the instruction set. The analogy here is that of building a house and discovering, near completion, that you have enough land and materials left to add a room. This room wouldn't be free, however, since there would be the costs of labor and maintenance for the life of the home. The temptation to add "free" instructions can only occur when the instruction set is not fixed, as is likely to be the case in the first model of a computer. Because instruction set compatibility is a long-term requirement, all future models of this machine will be forced to include these "free" instructions, even if space is later at a premium. This expansion also ignores the cost of a longer development time to test the added instructions, as well as the possibility of costs of repairing bugs in them after the hardware is shipped.

Fallacy: Users find writable control store helpful.

Bugs in microcode persuaded designers of minicomputers and mainframes that it would be wiser to use RAM than ROM for control store. Doing so would enable microcode bugs to be repaired by shipping customers floppy disks rather than by having the field engineer pull boards and replace chips. Some customers and some manufacturers also decided that users should be allowed to write microcode; this opportunity became known as *writable control store* (WCS). Yet by the time WCS was offered, the world had changed to make WCS less attractive than originally envisioned:

■ The tools for writing microcode were much poorer than those for writing macrocode. (The authors and many others stepped into that breach to provide better microprogramming tools.)

■ At a time when main memory was expanding, WCS was limited to 1–4KB microinstructions. (Few programming tasks are harder than forcing code into too small a memory.)

- Microcoded control became increasingly tailored to the native macroinstruction set, making microprogramming less useful for tasks other than that for which it was intended.

- With the advent of timesharing, programs might run for only milliseconds before switching to other tasks. This meant that WCS would have to be swapped if more than one program needed it, and reloading WCS could easily take longer than a few milliseconds.

- Timesharing also meant that programs had to be protected from each other. Because, at such a low level, microprograms can circumvent all protection barriers, microprograms written by users were notoriously untrustworthy.

- The increasing demand for virtual memory meant that microprograms had to be restartable—any memory access could force the computation to be shelved.

- Finally, companies like DEC that offered WCS provided no customer support for those who wanted to write microcode.

Many customers ordered WCS, but few benefited from it. The death of WCS has been by a thousand small cuts, and WCS is not an option on current computers.

5.9 | Concluding Remarks

In his first paper [1953] Wilkes identified advantages of microprogramming that still hold true today. One of these advantages is that microprogramming helps accommodate change. This can happen late in the development cycle, where simply changing some 0s to 1s in the control store can sometimes save redesigning hardware. A related advantage is that by emulating other instruction sets in microcode, software compatibility is simplified. Microprogramming also reduces the cost of adding more complex instructions to a standard micro-architecture to just the cost of a few more words of control store (although there is the pitfall that once an instruction set is created assuming microprogrammed control, it is difficult to ever build a machine without using it). This flexibility allows hardware construction to begin before the instruction set and microcode have been completely written, because specifying control is just a matter of programming. Finally, microprogramming now has the further advantage of having a large set of tools that have been developed to help write, edit, assemble, and debug microcode.

   The drawback of microcode has always been performance. This is because microprogramming is a slave to memory technology: The clock cycle time is limited by the time to read microinstructions from control store. In the 1950s, microprogramming was impractical since virtually the only technology available for control store was the same one used for main memory. In the late 1960s and early 1970s, semiconductor memory was available for control store, while main memory was constructed from core. The factor of ten in cycle time that differentiated the two technologies opened the door for microcode. The popularity of cache memory in the 1970s once again closed this gap, and machines were again built with the same technology for control store and memory.

For these reasons instruction sets invented since 1985 have not relied on microcode. Though no one likes to predict the future—least of all in writing—it is the authors' opinion that microprogramming is bound to memory technology. If in some future technology ROM becomes much faster than RAM, or if caches are no longer effective, microcode may regain its popularity.

5.10 | Historical Perspective and References

Interrupts go back to computer industry pioneers Eckert and Mauchly. Interrupts were first used to signal arithmetic overflow on the UNIVAC I and later to alert a UNIVAC 1103 to start online data collection for a wind tunnel (see Codd [1962]). After the success of the first commercial computer, the UNIVAC 1101 in 1953, the first commercial computer to have interrupts, the 1103, was brought out. Interrupts were first used for I/O by A.L. Leiner in the National Bureau of Standards DYSEAC [Smotherman 1989].

Maurice Wilkes learned computer design in a summer workshop from Eckert and Mauchly and then went on to build the first full-scale, operational, stored-program computer—the EDSAC. From that experience he realized the difficulty of control. He thought of a more centralized control using a diode matrix and, after visiting the Whirlwind computer in the U.S., wrote:

I found that it did indeed have a centralized control based on the use of a matrix of diodes. It was, however, only capable of producing a fixed sequence of 8 pulses—a different sequence for each instruction, but nevertheless fixed as far as a particular instruction was concerned. It was not, I think, until I got back to Cambridge that I realized that the solution was to turn the control unit into a computer in miniature by adding a second matrix to determine the flow of control at the microlevel and by providing for conditional micro-instructions. [Wilkes 1985, 178]

Wilkes [1953] was ahead of his time in recognizing that problem. Unfortunately, the solution was also ahead of its time: To provide control, microprogramming relies on fast memory that was not available in the 1950s. Thus, Wilkes's ideas remained primarily academic conjecture for a decade, although he did construct the EDSAC 2 using microprogrammed control in 1958 with ROM made from magnetic cores.

IBM brought microprogramming into the spotlight in 1964 with the IBM 360 family. Before this event, IBM saw itself as many small businesses selling different machines with their own price and performance levels, but also with their own instruction sets. (Recall that little programming was done in high-level languages, so that programs written for one IBM machine would not run on another.) Gene Amdahl, one of the chief architects of the IBM 360, said that managers of each subsidiary agreed to the 360 family of computers only because they were convinced that microprogramming made it feasible—if you could take the same hardware and microprogram it with several different instruction sets, they reasoned, then you must also be able to take different hardware and microprogram them to run the same instruction set. To be sure of the viability of microprogramming, the IBM vice president of engineering even visited Wilkes surreptitiously and had a "theoretical" discussion of the pros and cons of microcode. IBM believed the idea was so important to their plans that they pushed the memory technology inside the company to make microprogramming feasible.

Stewart Tucker of IBM was saddled with the responsibility of porting software from the IBM 7090 to the new IBM 360. Thinking about the possibilities of microcode, he suggested expanding the control store to include simulators, or interpreters, for older machines. Tucker [1967] coined the term *emulation* for this, meaning full simulation at the microprogrammed level. Occasionally, emulation on the 360 was actually faster than the original hardware. Emulation became so popular with customers in the early years of the 360 that it was sometimes hard to tell which instruction set ran more programs.

Once the giant of the industry began using microcode, the rest soon followed. A difficulty in adopting microcode was that the necessary memory technology was not widely available, but that was soon solved by semiconductor ROM and later RAM. The microprocessor industry followed the same history, with limited resources of the earliest chips forcing hardwired control. But as the resources increased, the advantages of simpler design and ease of change persuaded many to use microprogramming.

With the increasing popularity of microprogramming came more sophisticated instruction sets, including virtual memory. Microprogramming may well have aided the spread of virtual memory, since microcode made it easier to cope with the difficulties that arose from mapping addresses and restarting instructions. The IBM 370 model 138, for example, implemented virtual memory entirely in microcode without any hardware support.

Over the years, most microarchitectures became more and more dedicated to support the intended instruction set, so that reprogramming for a different instruction set failed to offer satisfactory performance. With the passage of time came much larger control stores, and it became possible to consider a machine as elaborate as the VAX. To offer a single chip VAX in 1984 DEC reduced the instructions interpreted by microcode by trapping some instructions and performing them in software: 20% of VAX instructions are responsible for 60% of the microcode, yet are only executed 0.2% of the time. Figure 5.35 shows the reduction in control store by subsetting the instruction set. (The VAX is so tied to microcode that we venture to predict it will be impossible to build a full-instruction-set VAX without microcode.) The microarchitecture of one of the simpler subsetted VAXes, the MicroVAX-I, is described in Levy and Eckhouse [1989].

	Full instruction set (VLSI VAX)	Subset instruction set (MicroVAX 32)
% instructions implemented	100%	80%
Size of control store (bits)	480 K	64 K
Number of chips in processor	9	2
% performance of VAX-11/780	100%	90%

FIGURE 5.35   By trapping some VAX instructions and addressing modes, control store was reduced almost eight-fold. The second chip of the subset VAX is for floating point.

While this book was being written, a landmark legal precedent concerning microcode was set. The question under litigation in *NEC v. Intel* was whether microcode is like writing, and thereby deserves copyright protection (Intel), or whether it is like hardware, which can be patented but not copyrighted (NEC). The importance of this matter lies in the fact that while it is trivial to get a copyright, getting a patent can take as long as a college education. A program can be copyrighted, so the question then follows: What is and isn't a program? Here is the legislated definition:

A 'computer program' is a set of statements or instructions to be used directly or indirectly in a computer in order to bring about a certain result.

After years of preparation and trial, a judge did declare that a microprogram was a program. The lawyers for the losing side then asked him to rescind his decision on grounds of partiality. They had discovered that through an investment club, the judge owned $80 of stock belonging to the client he ruled for. (The tempting sum really was only $80, highly frustrating to one of the authors who acted as an expert witness on the case!) The case was retried, and the new judge ruled that "microcode ... comes squarely within the definition of a 'computer program'..." [Gray 1989, 4]. Of course, the fact that two judges in two different trials made the same decision doesn't mean that the matter is closed—there are still higher levels of appeal available.

References

CLARK, D. W., P. J. BANNON, AND J. B. KELLER [1988]. "Measuring VAX 8800 performance with a histogram hardware monitor," *Proc. 15th Annual Symposium on Computer Architecture* (May–June), Honolulu, Hawaii, 176–185.

CODD, E. F. [1962]. "Multiprogramming," in F.L. Alt and M. Rubinoff, *Advances in Computers,* vol. 3, Academic Press, New York, 82.

EMER, J. S. AND D. W. CLARK [1984]. "A characterization of processor performance in the VAX-11/780," *Proc. 11th Symposium on Computer Architecture* (June), Ann Arbor, Mich., 301–310.

GRAY, W. P. [1989]. Memorandum of Decision, No. C-84-20799-WPG, U.S. District Court for the Northern District of California (February 7, 1989).

LEVY, H. M. AND R. H. ECKHOUSE, JR. [1989]. *Computer Programming and Architecture: The VAX,* 2nd ed., Digital Press, Bedford, Mass. 358–372

MCKEVITT, J., ET AL. [1977]. *8086 Design Report,* internal memorandum.

PATTERSON, D. A. [1983]. "Microprogramming," *Scientific American* 248:3 (March), 36–43.

REIGEL, E. W., U. FABER, AND D. A. FISCHER, [1972]. "The Interpreter—a microprogrammable building block system," *Proc. AFIPS 1972 Spring Joint Computer Conf.* 40, 705–723.

SMOTHERMAN, M. [1989]. "A sequencing-based taxonomy of I/O systems and review of historical machines," *Computer Architecture News* 17:5 (September), 5–15.

TUCKER, S. G. [1967]. "Microprogram control for the System/360," *IBM Systems Journal* 6:4, 222–241.

WILKES, M. V. [1953]. "The best way to design an automatic calculating machine," in *Manchester University Computer Inaugural Conf.*, 1951, Ferranti, Ltd., London. (Not published until 1953.) Reprinted in "The Genesis of Microprogramming" in *Annals of the History of Computing* 8:116.

WILKES, M. V. [1985]. *Memoirs of a Computer Pioneer,* The MIT Press, Cambridge, Mass.

WILKES, M. V. AND J. B. STRINGER [1953]. "Microprogramming and the design of the control circuits in an electronic digital computer," *Proc. Cambridge Philosophical Society* 49:230–238. Also reprinted in D. P. Siewiorek, C. G. Bell, and A. Newell, *Computer Structures: Principles and Examples* (1982), McGraw-Hill, New York, 158–163, and in "The Genesis of Microprogramming" in *Annals of the History of Computing* 8:116.

E X E R C I S E S

If finite-state diagrams and microprogramming are review topics, you may want to skip over questions 5.5 through 5.14.

5.1 [15/10/15/15] <5.5> One technique that tries to get the best of both the worlds of vertical and horizontal microarchitectures is a *two-level* control store, as illustrated by Figure 5.36. It tries to combine small control-store size with wide instructions. To avoid confusion the bottom level uses the prefix *nano-*, yielding the terms "nanoinstruction," "nanocode," and so forth. This technique was used in the Motorola 68000, 68010, and 68020, but it was originated in the Burroughs D-machine [Reigel, Faber, and Fischer 1972]. The idea is that the first level has many vertical instructions that point to the few unique horizontal instructions in the second level. The Burroughs D-machine was a general-purpose computer offering writable control store. Its microinstructions were 16 bits wide, with 12 of those bits specifying a nanoaddress, and the nanoinstructions were 56 bits wide. One instruction set interpreter used 1124 microinstructions and 123 nanoinstructions.

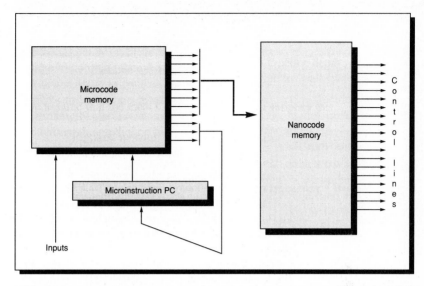

FIGURE 5.36 Two-level microprogrammed implementation showing relationship of microcode and nanocode.

a. [15] <5.5> What is the general formula showing when a two-level control store scheme like Burroughs D-machine uses fewer bits than a single-level control store? Assume there are *M* microinstructions each *a* bits wide and *N* nanoinstructions each *b* bits wide.

b. [10] Was the two-level control store of the D-machine successful in reducing control-store size versus a single-level control store for the interpreter?

c. [15] After the code was optimized to improve CPI by 10%, the resulting code had 940 microinstructions and 161 nanoinstructions. Was the two-level control store of the D-machine successful in reducing control-store size versus a single-level control store for the **optimized** interpreter?

d. [15] Did optimization increase or decrease the total number of bits needed to specify control? Why would the number of microinstructions decrease and the number of nanoinstructions increase?

5.2 [15] <5.5,5.6> One advantage of microcode is that it can handle rare cases without having the overhead of invoking the operating system before executing the trap routine. Suppose a machine with a CPI of 1.5 has an operating system that takes 100 clock cycles on a trap before it can execute the appropriate code. Suppose the trap code takes 10 clock cycles whether it is microcode or macrocode. For an instruction occurring 5% of the time, what percentage of the time must it trap before a microcode implementation is 1% faster overall than a macrocode implementation?

5.3 [20/20/30] <4.2,5.5,5.6> Let's explore the impact of subsetting an architecture as described in Figure 5.35. Suppose the MOVC3 instruction were left out of a VAX.

a. [20] Write the VAX macrocode to replace MOVC3.

b. [20] Assume the operands are placed in registers R0, R1, and R2 after a trap. Using the data for COBOLX in Figure C.1 in Appendix C on instruction usage (assuming all MOVC_ are MOVC3) and assuming the average MOVC3 moves 15 bytes, what would be the percentage change in instruction count if MOVC3 were not interpreted by microcode? (Ignore the cost of traps for this instruction.)

c. [30] If you have access to a VAX, time the speed of MOVC3 versus a macrocode version of the routine from part a. Assuming that the trap overhead is 20 clock cycles, what is the impact on performance of trapping to software for MOVC3?

5.4 [15] <5.6> Assume we have a machine with a clock cycle time of 10 ns and a base CPI of 5. Because of the possibilities of interrupts we must have extra registers containing copies of the values of the registers at the beginning of the instruction. These registers are usually called *shadow registers*. Assume that the average instruction has two register operands that must be restored on an interrupt. The interrupt rate is 100 interrupts per second, and the interrupt cost is 30 cycles plus the time to restore the shadowed registers, each of which takes 10 cycles. What is the effective CPI after accounting for interrupts? What is the performance lost from interrupts?

5.5-5.7 Given the processor design and finite-state diagram for DLX as modified in the end of the hardwired-control portion of Section 5.7, explore the impact of performance of the following changes. In each case show the modified portion of the finite-state machine, describe the changes to the processor (if necessary), the change in the number of states, and calculate the change in CPI using the DLX instruction mix statistics in Figure C.4 for GCC. Show the reasons for the change.

5.5 [12] <5.7> Like the change to the ALU instructions in the second example in Section 5.7 and shown in Figures 5.20 and 5.21, remove the states that load Temp for the Set instructions in Figure 5.16 first by adding the "X" option and then by increasing the number of states.

5.6 [15] <5.7> Suppose that the memory interface was optimized so that it was not necessary to load MAR before a memory access, nor did the data have to be transferred in MDR for a read or write. Instead, any register on the S1 bus could specify the address, any register on the S2 bus could supply the data on a write, and any register on the Dest bus could receive data on a read.

5.7 [22] <5.7> Most computers overlap the fetching of the next instruction with the execution of the current instruction. Propose a scheme that overlaps all instruction fetches except jumps, branches, and stores. You must reorganize the finite-state machine so that the instruction is already fetched, possibly even partially decoded.

5.8 [15] <5.7> The example in Section 5.7 on page 228 assumes everything but the shifter can scale to 9 ns. Alas, the memory system can rarely scale as easily as the CPU. Reperform the analysis in this example, but this time assume that average number of memory wait states is 2 at the 9-ns clock cycle versus 1 at 10 ns in addition to the slowdown for shifts.

5.9-5.14 These questions address use of the microcoded control of DLX as shown in Figures 5.23, 5.25, and 5.27–5.29. In each case show the modified portion of the microcode; describe the changes to the processor (if necessary), the microinstruction fields (if necessary), and the change in the number of microinstructions; and calculate the change in CPI using the DLX instruction-mix statistics in Appendix C for GCC. Show the reasons for the change.

5.9 [15] <5.7> Like the change to the ALU instructions in the second example in Section 5.7, remove the microinstructions that load Temp for the Set instructions in Figure 5.28 (page 233) first by adding the "X" option and then by increasing the number of microinstructions.

5.10 [25] <5.7> Continuing the example in Figure 5.32 (page 237), rewrite the microcode found in Figure 5.29 (page 234) using the dual-format microinstructions of Figure 5.31 (page 236). What is the relative frequency of each type of microinstruction? What is the savings in control-store size versus the original DLX format? What is the change in CPI?

5.11 [20] <3.4, 5.7> Load byte and Load half take a clock cycle longer than Load word because of the alignment of data (see Figure 3.10 on page 97 and Figure 5.25 on page 231). Propose a change that eliminates the extra clock for these instructions. How does this change affect the CPI of GCC? How does it affect the CPI of TeX?

5.12 [20] <5.6, 5.7> Change the microcode to perform the following interrupt tests: page fault, arithmetic overflow or underflow, misaligned memory accesses, and using undefined instructions. Make whatever changes are needed to the microarchitecture and microinstruction format. What is the change in size and performance to perform these tests?

5.13 [20] <5.7> The computer designer must be careful not to tailor her design too closely to a particular, single program. Reevaluate the performance impact of all the example performance improvements in Exercises 5.9 to 5.12 this time using the average instruction mix data in Figure C.4. How do the programs affect the evaluations?

5.14 [20] <5.6, 5.7> Starting with the microcode in Figures 5.27 (page 233) and 5.34 (page 238), revise the microcode so that the next macroinstruction is fetched as early as possible during the ALU instructions. Assume a "perfect" memory system, taking one clock cycle per memory reference. Although technically this improvement speeds up instructions that **follow** ALU instructions, the easiest way to account for higher performance is as faster ALU instructions. How much faster are the ALU instructions? How does it affect overall performance according to GCC statistics?

5.15 [30] <4,5.6> If you have access to a machine that uses one of the instruction sets in Chapter 4, determine the worst-case interrupt latency for that implementation of the architecture. Be sure you are measuring the raw machine latency and **not** the operating system overhead.

5.16 [30] <5.6> Computer architects have sometimes been forced to support instructions that were never published in the original instruction set manual. This situation arises because some programs are created that inadvertently set unused instruction fields to values other than the architect expected, which raises havoc when the architect tries to use those values to extend the instruction set. IBM solved that problem in the System 370 by trapping on every possible undefined field. Try executing instructions with undefined fields on a computer to see what happens. Do your new instructions compute anything useful? If so, would you use these new instructions in programs?

5.17 [35] <5.4, 5.5, 5.7> Take the datapath in Figure 5.1 and build a simulator that can perform any of the operations needed to implement the DLX instruction set. Now implement the DLX instruction set using:

Microprogrammed control, and

Hardwired control.

For hardwired control see if you can find PLA minimization and state-assignment programs to reduce the cost of control. From these two designs, determine the performance of each implementation and the cost in terms of gates or in terms of silicon area.

5.18 [35] <2.2, 5.5, 5.7> The similarities between the microinstructions and the macro-instructions of DLX suggest that performance can be gained by writing a program that translates from DLX macrocode to DLX microcode. (This is the insight that inspired WCS.) Write such a program and benchmark it. What is the resulting expansion of code size?

5.19 [50] <2.2, 4.4, 5.10> Recent attempts have been made to run existing software on hardwired control machines by building hand-tuned simulators for popular machines. Write such a simulator for the 8086 instruction set. Run some existing IBM PC programs, and see how fast your simulator is relative to an 8-MHz 8086.

5.20 [Discussion] <4,5.5,5.10> Hypothesis: If the first implementation of an architecture uses microprogramming, it affects the instruction set architecture. Why might this be true? Looking at examples in Chapter 4 or elsewhere, give supporting or contradicting evidence from real machines. Which machines will always use microcode? Why? Which machines will never use microcode? Why? What control implementation do you think the architect had in mind when designing the instruction set architecture?

5.21 [Discussion] <5.5,5.10> Wilkes invented microprogramming in large to simplify construction of control. Since 1980 there has been an explosion of computer-aided design software whose goal is also to simplify construction of control. Hypothesis: The advances in computer-aided design software have rendered microprogramming unnecessary. Find evidence to support and refute the hypothesis.

5.22 [Discussion] <5.10> The DLX instructions and the DLX microinstructions have many similarities. What would make it difficult for a compiler to produce DLX microcode rather than macrocode? What changes to the microarchitecture would make the DLX microcode more useful for this application?

It is quite a three-pipe problem.

Sir Arthur Conan Doyle, *The Adventures of Sherlock Holmes*

6 Pipelining

6.1 | What Is Pipelining?

Pipelining is an implementation technique whereby multiple instructions are overlapped in execution. Today, pipelining is the key implementation technique used to make fast CPUs.

A pipeline is like an assembly line: Each step in the pipeline completes a part of the instruction. As in a car assembly line, the work to be done in an instruction is broken into smaller pieces, each of which takes a fraction of the time needed to complete the entire instruction. Each of these steps is called a *pipe stage* or a *pipe segment*. The stages are connected one to the next to form a pipe—instructions enter at one end, are processed through the stages, and exit at the other end.

The throughput of the pipeline is determined by how often an instruction exits the pipeline. Because the pipe stages are hooked together, all the stages must be ready to proceed at the same time. The time required between moving an instruction one step down the pipeline is a machine cycle. The length of a machine cycle is determined by the time required for the slowest pipe stage (because all stages proceed at the same time). Often the machine cycle is one clock cycle (sometimes it is two, or rarely more), though the clock may have multiple phases.

The pipeline designer's goal is to balance the length of the pipeline stages. If the stages are perfectly balanced, then the time per instruction on the pipelined machine—assuming ideal conditions (i.e., no stalls)—is equal to

$$\frac{\text{Time per instruction on nonpipelined machine}}{\text{Number of pipe stages}}$$

Under these conditions, the speedup from pipelining equals the number of pipe stages. Usually, however, the stages will not be perfectly balanced; furthermore, pipelining does involve some overhead. Thus, the time per instruction on the pipelined machine will not have its minimum possible value, though it can be close (say within 10%).

Pipelining yields a reduction in the average execution time per instruction. This reduction can be obtained by decreasing the clock cycle time of the pipelined machine or by decreasing the number of clock cycles per instruction, or by both. Typically, the biggest impact is in the number of clock cycles per instruction, though the clock cycle is often shorter in a pipelined machine (especially in pipelined supercomputers). In the advanced pipelining sections of this chapter we will see how deep pipelines can be used to both decrease the clock cycle and maintain a low CPI.

Pipelining is an implementation technique that exploits parallelism among the instructions in a sequential instruction stream. It has the substantial advantage that, unlike some speedup techniques (see Chapters 7 and 10), it is not visible to the programmer. In this chapter we will first cover the concept of pipelining using DLX and a simplified version of its pipeline. We will then look at the problems pipelining introduces and the performance attainable under typical situations. Later in the chapter we will examine advanced techniques that can be used to overcome the difficulties that are encountered in pipelined machines and that may lower the performance attainable from pipelining.

We use DLX largely because its simplicity makes it easy to demonstrate the principles of pipelining. The same principles apply to more complex instruction sets, though the corresponding pipelines are more complex. We will see an example of such a pipeline in the Putting It All Together section.

6.2 | The Basic Pipeline for DLX

Remember that in Chapter 5 (Section 5.3) we discussed how DLX could be implemented with five basic execution steps:

1. IF—instruction fetch

2. ID—instruction decode and register fetch

3. EX—execution and effective address calculation

4. MEM—memory access

5. WB—write back

Instruction	Clock number								
number	1	2	3	4	5	6	7	8	9
Instruction i	IF	ID	EX	MEM	WB				
Instruction $i+1$		IF	ID	EX	MEM	WB			
Instruction $i+2$			IF	ID	EX	MEM	WB		
Instruction $i+3$				IF	ID	EX	MEM	WB	
Instruction $i+4$					IF	ID	EX	MEM	WB

FIGURE 6.1   Simple DLX pipeline. On each clock cycle another instruction is fetched and begins its five-step execution. If an instruction is started every clock cycle, the performance will be five times that of a machine that is not pipelined.

We can pipeline DLX by simply fetching a new instruction **on each clock cycle.** Each of the steps above becomes a *pipe stage*—a step in the pipeline—resulting in the execution pattern shown in Figure 6.1. While each instruction still takes five clock cycles, during each clock cycle the hardware is executing some part of five different instructions.

Pipelining increases the CPU instruction throughput—the number of instructions completed per unit of time—but it does not reduce the execution time of an individual instruction. In fact, it usually slightly increases the execution time of each instruction due to overhead in the control of the pipeline. The increase in instruction throughput means that a program runs faster and has lower total execution time, even though no single instruction runs faster!

The fact that the execution time of each instruction remains unchanged puts limits on the practical depth of a pipeline, as we will see in the next section. Other design considerations limit the clock rate that can be attained by deeper pipelining. The most important consideration is the combined effect of latch delay and clock skew. Latches are required between pipe stages, adding setup time plus the delay through those latches to each clock period. Clock skew also contributes to the lower limit on the clock cycle. Once the clock cycle is as small as the sum of the clock skew and latch overhead, no further pipelining is useful.

Example

Consider a nonpipelined machine with five execution steps of lengths 50 ns, 50 ns, 60 ns, 50 ns, and 50 ns. Suppose that due to clock skew and setup, pipelining the machine adds 5 ns of overhead to each execution stage. Ignoring any latency impact, how much speedup in the instruction execution rate will we gain from a pipeline?

Answer

Figure 6.2 shows the execution pattern on the nonpipelined machine and on the pipelined machine.

The average instruction execution time on the nonpipelined machine is

Average instruction execution time = 50+50+60+50+50 ns = 260 ns

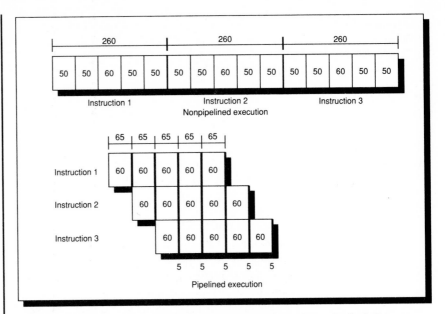

FIGURE 6.2   The execution pattern for three instructions shown for both the non-pipelined and pipelined versions. In the nonpipelined version, the three instructions are executed sequentially. In the pipelined version, the shaded areas represent the overhead of 5 ns per pipestage. The length of the pipestages must all be the same: 60 ns plus the 5-ns overhead. The latency of an instruction increases from 260 ns in the nonpipelined machine to 325 ns in the pipelined machine.

In the pipelined implementation, the clock must run at the speed of the slowest stage plus overhead, which will be 60 + 5 or 65 ns; this is the average instruction execution time. Thus, the speedup from pipelining is

$$\text{Speedup} = \frac{\text{Average instruction time without pipeline}}{\text{Average instruction time with pipeline}}$$

$$= \frac{260}{65} = 4 \text{ times}$$

The 5-ns overhead essentially establishes a limit on the effectiveness of pipelining. If the overhead is not affected by changes in the clock cycle, Amdahl's Law tells us that the overhead limits the speedup.

Because the latches in a pipelined design can have a significant impact on the clock speed, designers have looked for latches that permit the highest possible clock rate. The Earle latch (invented by J. G. Earle [1965]) has three properties that make it especially useful in pipelined machines. First, it is relatively insensitive to clock skew. Second, the delay through the latch is always a constant two-gate delay, avoiding the introduction of skew in the data passing through the latch. Finally, two levels of logic can be done in the latch without increasing the latch delay time. This means that two levels of logic in the pipeline can be overlapped with the latch, so the majority of the overhead from the latch can be hidden. We will not be analyzing the pipeline designs in this chapter at this level of detail. The interested reader should see Kunkel and Smith [1986].

The next two sections will add refinements and address some problems that can occur in this pipeline. In this discussion (up to the last segment of Section 6.5) we will focus on the pipeline for the integer portion of DLX. The complications that arise in the floating-point pipeline will be treated in Section 6.6.

6.3 | Making the Pipeline Work

Your instinct is right if you find it hard to believe that pipelining is as simple as this, because it's not. In this and the following three sections, we will make our DLX pipeline "real" by dealing with problems that pipelining introduces.

To begin with, we have to determine what happens on every clock cycle of the machine and make sure that overlapping instructions doesn't overcommit resources. For example, a single ALU cannot be asked to compute an effective address and perform a subtract operation at the same time. As we will see, the simplicity of the DLX instruction set makes resource evaluation relatively easy.

The operations that occur during instruction execution, which were discussed in Section 5.3 of Chapter 5, are modified to execute in a pipeline as shown in Figure 6.3. The figure lists the major functional units in our DLX implementation, the pipe stages, and what has to happen in each stage of the pipeline. The vertical axis is labeled with the pipeline stages, while the horizontal axis shows major resources. Each intersection shows what happens for that resource in that stage. In Figure 6.4 we will show similar information using the instruction type as the horizontal axis. The combination of instructions that may be in the pipeline at any one time is arbitrary. Thus, the combined needs of all instruction types at any pipe stage determine what resources are needed at that stage.

Every pipe stage is active on every clock cycle. This requires all operations in a pipe stage to complete in one clock and any combination of operations to be able to occur at once. Here are the most important implications for the data path, as specified in Chapter 5:

1. The PC must be incremented on each clock. This must be done in IF rather than ID. This will require an additional incrementer, since the ALU is already busy on every cycle and cannot be used to increment the PC.

2. A new instruction must be fetched on every clock—this is also done in IF.

3. A new data word is needed on every clock cycle—this is done in MEM.

4. There must be a separate MDR for loads (LMDR) and stores (SMDR), since when they are back-to-back, they overlap in time.

5. Three additional latches are needed to hold values that are needed later in the pipeline, but may be modified by a subsequent instruction. The values latched are the instruction, the ALU output, and the next PC.

Stage	PC unit	Memory	Data path
IF	PC← PC+4;	IR←Mem[PC];	
ID	PC1← PC	IR1←IR	A← Rs1; B← Rs2;
EX			DMAR← A + $(IR1_{16})^{16}$##$IR1_{16..31}$; SMDR←B; or ALUoutput← A *op* (B or $(IR1_{16})^{16}$##$IR1_{16..31}$); or ALUoutput←PC1 + $(IR1_{16})^{16}$##$IR1_{16..31}$; cond← (A *op* 0);
MEM	if (cond) PC←ALUoutput	LMDR← Mem[DMAR] or Mem[DMAR]←SMDR	ALUoutput1← ALUoutput
WB			Rd← ALUoutput1 or LMDR

FIGURE 6.3 The table shows the major functional units and what may happen in every pipe stage in each unit. In several of the stages not all of the actions listed can occur, because they apply under different assumptions about the instruction. For example, there are three operations within the ALU during the EX stage. The first occurs only on a load or store; the second on ALU operations (with the input being B or the lower 16 bits of the IR, according to whether the instruction is register–register or register–immediate); the third operation occurs only on branches. For simplicity, we have shown the branch case only—jumps will add a 26-bit offset to the PC. The variables ALUouput1, PC1, and IR1 save values for use in later stages of the pipeline. Designing the memory system to support a data load or store on every clock cycle is challenging; see Chapter 8 for an in-depth discussion. This type of table and that in Figure 6.4 are loosely based on Davidson's [1971] pipeline reservation tables.

Stage	ALU instruction	Load or store instruction	Branch instruction
IF	IR←Mem[PC]; PC←PC+4;	IR←Mem[PC]; PC←PC+4;	IR←Mem[PC]; PC←PC+4;
ID	A←Rs1; B←Rs2; PC1←PC IR1←IR	A←Rs1; B←Rs2; PC1←PC IR1←IR	A←Rs1; B←Rs2; PC1←PC IR1←IR
EX	ALUoutput←A *op* B; or ALUoutput←A *op* $((IR1_{16})^{16}$##$IR1_{16..31})$;	DMAR← A+ $((IR1_{16})^{16}$##$IR1_{16..31})$; SMDR← B;	ALUoutput←PC1 + $((IR1_{16})^{16}$##$IR1_{16..31})$; cond←(A *op* 0);
MEM	ALUoutput1← ALUoutput	LMDR←Mem[DMAR]; or Mem[DMAR]←SMDR;	if (cond) PC←ALUoutput;
WB	Rd←ALUoutput1;	Rd←LMDR;	

FIGURE 6.4 Events on every pipe stage of the DLX pipeline. Because the instruction is not yet decoded, the first two pipe stages are always identical. Note that it was critical to be able to fetch the registers before decoding the instruction; otherwise another pipeline stage would be required. Due to the fixed instruction format, both register fields are always decoded and the registers accessed (though they are sometimes not needed); the PC and immediate fields can be sent to the ALU as well. At the beginning of the ALU operation the correct inputs are multiplexed in, based on the opcode. With this organization all instruction-dependent operations occur in the EX stage or later. As in Figure 6.3, we include the case for branches, but not jumps, which will have a 26-bit offset rather than a 16-bit offset. Jumps are essentially like branches.

Probably the biggest impact of pipelining on the machine resources is in the memory system. Although the memory-access time has not changed, the peak memory bandwidth must be increased by five times over the nonpipelined machine because two memory accesses are required on every clock in the pipelined machine versus two accesses every five clock cycles in a nonpipelined machine with the same number of steps per instruction. To provide two memory accesses every clock, most machines will use separate instruction and data caches (see Chapter 8, Section 8.3).

During the EX stage, the ALU can be used for three different functions: an effective data-address calculation, a branch-address calculation, or an ALU instruction. Fortunately, the DLX instructions are simple; an instruction in EX does at most one of these, so no conflict arises.

The pipeline we now have for DLX would function just fine if every instruction were independent of every other instruction in the pipeline. In reality, instructions in the pipeline can be dependent on one another; this is the topic of the next section.

6.4 | The Major Hurdle of Pipelining— Pipeline Hazards

There are situations, called *hazards*, that prevent the next instruction in the instruction stream from executing during its designated clock cycle. Hazards reduce the performance from the ideal speedup gained by pipelining. There are three classes of hazards:

1. *Structural hazards* arise from resource conflicts when the hardware cannot support all possible combinations of instructions in simultaneous overlapped execution.

2. *Data hazards* arise when an instruction depends on the results of a previous instruction in a way that is exposed by the overlapping of instructions in the pipeline.

3. *Control hazards* arise from the pipelining of branches and other instructions that change the PC.

Hazards in pipelines can make it necessary to stall the pipeline. The major difference between stalls in a pipelined machine and stalls in a nonpipelined machine (such as those we saw in DLX in Chapter 5) occurs because there are multiple instructions under execution at once. A stall in a pipelined machine often requires that some instructions be allowed to proceed, while others are delayed. Typically, when an instruction is stalled, all instructions later in the pipeline than the stalled instruction are also stalled. Instructions earlier than the stalled instruction can continue, but no new instructions are fetched during the stall. We will see several examples of how stalls operate in this section—don't worry, they aren't as complex as they might sound!

A stall causes the pipeline performance to degrade from the ideal performance. Let's look at a simple equation for finding the actual speedup from pipelining, starting with the formula from the previous section.

$$\text{Pipeline speedup} = \frac{\text{Average instruction time without pipeline}}{\text{Average instruction time with pipeline}}$$

$$= \frac{\text{CPI without pipelining} * \text{Clock cycle without pipelining}}{\text{CPI with pipelining} * \text{Clock cycle with pipelining}}$$

$$= \frac{\text{Clock cycle without pipelining}}{\text{Clock cycle with pipelining}} * \frac{\text{CPI without pipelining}}{\text{CPI with pipelining}}$$

Remember that pipelining can be thought of as decreasing the CPI or the clock cycle time; let's treat it as decreasing the CPI. The ideal CPI on a pipelined machine is usually

$$\text{Ideal CPI} = \frac{\text{CPI without pipelining}}{\text{Pipeline depth}}$$

Rearranging this and substituting into the speedup equation yields:

$$\text{Speedup} = \frac{\text{Clock cycle without pipelining}}{\text{Clock cycle with pipelining}} * \frac{\text{Ideal CPI} * \text{Pipeline depth}}{\text{CPI with pipelining}}$$

If we confine ourselves to pipeline stalls,

CPI with pipelining = Ideal CPI + Pipeline stall clock cycles per instruction

We can substitute and obtain:

$$\text{Speedup} = \frac{\text{Clock cycle without pipelining}}{\text{Clock cycle with pipelining}} * \frac{\text{Ideal CPI} * \text{Pipeline depth}}{\text{Ideal CPI} + \text{Pipeline stall cycles}}$$

While this gives a general formula for pipeline speedup (ignoring stalls other than from the pipeline), in most instances a simpler equation can be used. Often, we choose to ignore the potential increase in the clock cycle due to pipelining overhead. This makes the clock rates equal and allows us to drop the first term. A simpler formula can now be used:

$$\text{Pipeline speedup} = \frac{\text{Ideal CPI} * \text{Pipeline depth}}{\text{Ideal CPI} + \text{Pipeline stall cycles}}$$

While we will use this simpler form for evaluating the DLX pipeline, a designer must be careful not to discount the potential impact on clock rate in evaluating pipelining strategies.

Structural Hazards

When a machine is pipelined, the overlapped execution of instructions requires pipelining of functional units and duplication of resources to allow all possible combinations of instructions in the pipeline. If some combination of instructions cannot be accommodated due to resource conflicts, the machine is said to have a *structural hazard*. The most common instances of structural hazards arise when some functional unit is not fully pipelined. Then a sequence of instructions that all use that functional unit cannot be sequentially initiated in the pipeline. Another common way that structural hazards appear is when some resource has not been duplicated enough to allow all combinations of instructions in the pipeline to execute. For example, a machine may have only one register-file write port, but under certain circumstances, the pipeline might want to perform two writes in a clock cycle. This will generate a structural hazard. When a sequence of instructions encounters this hazard, the pipeline will stall one of the instructions until the required unit is available.

Many pipelined machines share a single memory pipeline for data and instructions. As a result, when an instruction contains a data-memory reference, the pipeline must stall for one clock cycle; the machine cannot fetch the next instruction because the data reference is using the memory port. Figure 6.5 shows what a one-memory-port pipeline looks like when it stalls during a load. We will see another type of stall when we talk about data hazards.

Instruction	Clock cycle number								
	1	**2**	**3**	**4**	**5**	**6**	**7**	**8**	**9**
Load instruction	IF	ID	EX	MEM	WB				
Instruction $i+1$		IF	ID	EX	MEM	WB			
Instruction $i+2$			IF	ID	EX	MEM	WB		
Instruction $i+3$				stall	IF	ID	EX	MEM	WB
Instruction $i+4$						IF	ID	EX	MEM

FIGURE 6.5 A pipeline stalled for a structural hazard—a load with one memory port. With only one memory port, the pipeline cannot initiate a data fetch and instruction fetch in the same cycle. A load instruction effectively steals an instruction-fetch cycle, causing the pipeline to stall—no instruction is initiated on clock cycle 4 (which normally would be instruction $i+3$). Because the instruction being fetched is stalled, all other instructions in the pipeline can proceed normally. The stall cycle will continue to pass through the pipeline.

Example

Suppose that data references constitute 30% of the mix and that the ideal CPI of the pipelined machine, ignoring the structural hazard, is 1.2. Disregarding any other performance losses, how much faster is the ideal machine without the memory structural hazard, versus the machine with the hazard?

Answer

The ideal machine will be faster by the ratio of the speedup of the ideal machine over the real machine. Since the clock rates are unaffected, we can use the following for speedup:

$$\text{Pipeline speedup} = \frac{\text{Ideal CPI} * \text{Pipeline depth}}{\text{Ideal CPI} + \text{Pipeline stall cycles}}$$

Since the ideal machine has no stalls, its speedup is simply $\dfrac{1.2*\text{Pipeline depth}}{1.2}$.

The speedup of the real machine is $\dfrac{1.2*\text{Pipeline depth}}{1.2 + 0.3*1} = \dfrac{1.2*\text{Pipeline depth}}{1.5}$.

$$\frac{\text{Speedup}_{\text{ideal}}}{\text{Speedup}_{\text{real}}} = \frac{\left(\dfrac{1.2*\text{Pipeline depth}}{1.2}\right)}{\left(\dfrac{1.2*\text{Pipeline depth}}{1.5}\right)} = \frac{1.5}{1.2} = 1.25$$

Thus, the machine without the structural hazard is 25% faster.

If all other factors are equal, a machine without structural hazards will always have a lower CPI. Why, then, would a designer allow structural hazards? There are two reasons: to reduce cost and to reduce the latency of the unit. Pipelining all the functional units may be too costly. Machines that support one-clock-cycle memory references require twice as much total memory bandwidth and often have higher bandwidth at the pins. Likewise, fully pipelining a floating-point multiplier consumes lots of gates. If the structural hazard would not occur often, it may not be worth the cost to avoid it. It is also usually possible to design a nonpipelined unit, or one that isn't fully pipelined, with a shorter total delay than a fully pipelined unit. For example, both the CDC 7600 and the MIPS R2010 floating-point unit choose shorter latency (fewer clocks per operation) versus full pipelining. As we will see shortly, reducing latency has other performance benefits and can frequently overcome the disadvantage of the structural hazard.

Example

Many recent machines do not have fully pipelined floating-point units. For example, suppose we had an implementation of DLX with a 5-clock-cycle latency for floating-point multiply, but no pipelining. Will this structural hazard have a large or small performance impact on Spice running on DLX? For simplicity, assume that the floating-point multiplies are uniformly distributed.

Answer

The data in Figure C.4 show that floating-point multiply has a frequency of 6% in Spice. Our proposed pipeline can handle up to a 20% frequency of floating-point multiplies—one every five clock cycles. This means that the performance benefit of fully pipelining the floating-point multiply is likely to be low, as long as the floating-point multiplies are not clustered but are distributed uniformly. If they were clustered, the impact could be much larger.

Data Hazards

A major effect of pipelining is to change the relative timing of instructions by overlapping their execution. This introduces data and control hazards. Data hazards occur when the order of access to operands is changed by the pipeline versus the normal order encountered by sequentially executing instructions. Consider the pipelined execution of these instructions:

```
ADD    R1,R2,R3
SUB    R4,R1,R5
```

The SUB instruction has a source, R1, that is the destination of the ADD instruction. As shown in Figure 6.6, the ADD instruction writes the value of R1 in the WB pipe stage, but the SUB instruction reads the value during its ID stage. This problem is called a *data hazard*. Unless precautions are taken to prevent it, the SUB instruction will read the wrong value and try to use it. In fact, the value used by the SUB instruction is not even deterministic: Though we might think it logical to assume that SUB would always use the value of R1 that was assigned by an instruction prior to ADD, this is not always the case. If an interrupt should occur between the ADD and SUB instructions, the WB stage of the ADD will complete, and the value of R1 at that point **will** be the result of the ADD. This unpredictable behavior is obviously unacceptable.

Instruction	Clock cycle					
	1	2	3	4	5	6
ADD instruction	IF	ID	EX	MEM	WB—data written here	
SUB instruction		IF	ID—data read here	EX	MEM	WB

FIGURE 6.6   The ADD instruction writes a register that is a source operand for the SUB instruction. But the ADD doesn't **finish** writing the data into the register file until three clock cycles after SUB **begins** reading it!

The problem posed in this example can be solved with a simple hardware technique called *forwarding* (also called *bypassing* and sometimes *short-circuiting*). This technique works as follows: The ALU result is always fed back to the ALU input latches. If the forwarding hardware detects that the previous ALU operation has written the register corresponding to a source for the current ALU operation, control logic selects the forwarded result as the ALU input rather than the value read from the register file. Notice that with forwarding, if the SUB is stalled, the ADD will be completed, and the bypass will not be activated, causing the value from the register to be used. This is also true for the case of an interrupt between the two instructions.

In our DLX pipeline, we must pass results to not only the instruction that immediately follows, but also to the instruction after that. By the third instruction down the line, the ID and WB stages overlap; however, as the write is not finished until the end of WB, we must continue to forward the result. Figure 6.7 shows a set of instructions in the pipeline and the forwarding operations that can occur.

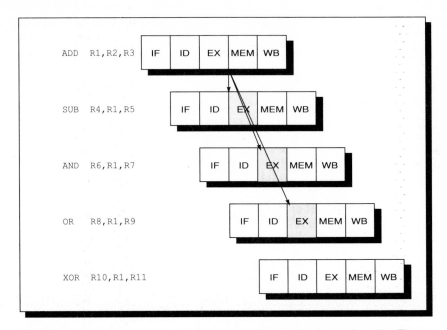

FIGURE 6.7 A set of instructions in the pipeline that need to forward results. The ADD instruction sets R1, and the next four instructions use it. The value of R1 must be bypassed to the SUB, AND, and OR instructions. By the time the XOR instruction goes to read R1 in the ID phase, the ADD instruction has completed WB, and the value is available.

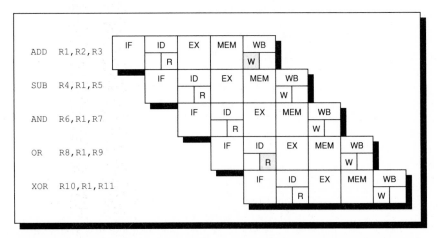

FIGURE 6.8 The same instruction sequence as shown in Figure 6.7, with register reads and writes occurring in opposite halves of the ID and WB stages. The SUB and AND instructions will still require the value of R1 to be bypassed to them, and this will happen as they enter their EX stage. However, by the time of the OR instruction, which also uses R1, the write of R1 has completed, and no forwarding is required. The XOR depends on the ADD, but the value of R1 from the ADD is always written back the cycle before XOR reaches its ID stage and reads it.

It is desirable to cut down the number of instructions that must be bypassed, since each level requires special hardware. Remembering that the register file is accessed twice in a clock cycle, it is possible to do the register writes in the first half of WB and the reads in the second half of ID. This eliminates the need to bypass to a third instruction, as shown in Figure 6.8.

Each level of bypass requires a latch and a pair of comparators to examine whether the adjacent instructions share a destination and a source. Figure 6.9 shows the structure of the ALU and its bypass unit as well as what values are in the bypass registers for the instruction sequence in Figure 6.7. Two ALU result buffers are needed to hold ALU results to be stored into the destination register in the next two WB stages. For ALU operations, the result is always forwarded when the instruction using the result as a source enters its EX stage. (The instruction that computed the value to be forwarded may be in its MEM or WB stages.) The results in the buffers can be inputs into either port on the ALU, via a pair of multiplexers. Multiplexer control can be done by either the control unit (which must then track the destinations and sources of all operations in the pipeline) or locally by logic associated with the bypass (in which case the bypass buffers will contain tags giving the register numbers the values are destined for). In either event, the logic must test if either of the two previous instructions wrote a register that is the input to the current instruction. If so, then the multiplexer select is set to choose from the appropriate result register rather than from the bus. Because the ALU operates in a single pipeline stage, there is no need for a pipeline stall with any combination of ALU instructions once the bypasses have been implemented.

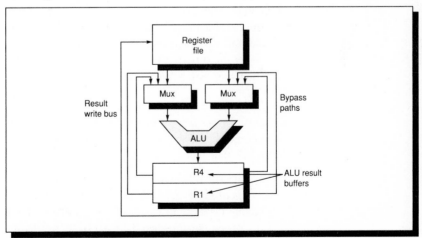

FIGURE 6.9 The ALU with its bypass unit. The contents of the buffer are shown at the point where the AND instruction of the code sequence in Figure 6.8 is about to begin the EX stage. The ADD instruction that computed R1 (in the second buffer) is in its WB stage, and the left input multiplexer is set to pass the just-computed value of R1 (not the value read from the register file) as the first operand to the AND instruction. The result of the subtract, R4, is in the first buffer. These buffers correspond to the variables ALUoutput and ALUoutput1 in Figures 6.3 and 6.4.

A hazard is created whenever there is a dependence between instructions, and they are close enough that the overlap caused by pipelining would change the order of access to an operand. Our example hazards have all been with register operands, but it is also possible for a pair of instructions to create a dependence by writing and reading the same memory location. In our DLX pipeline, however, memory references are always kept in order, preventing this type of hazard from arising. Cache misses could cause the memory references to get out of order if we allowed the processor to continue working on later instructions while an earlier instruction that missed the cache was accessing memory. For DLX's pipeline we just stall the entire pipeline, effectively making the instruction that contained the miss run for multiple clock cycles. In an advanced section of this chapter, Section 6.7, we will discuss machines that allow loads and stores to be executed in an order different from that in the program. All the data hazards discussed in this section, however, involve registers within the CPU.

Forwarding can be generalized to include passing a result directly to the functional unit that requires it: A result is forwarded from the output of one unit to the input of another, rather than just from the result of a unit to the input of the same unit. Take, for example, the following sequence:

```
ADD    R1,R2,R3
SW     25(R1),R1
```

To prevent a stall in this sequence, we would need to forward the value of R1 from the ALU both to the ALU, so that it can be used in the effective address calculation, and to the MDR (memory data register), so that it can be stored without any stall cycles.

Data hazards may be classified as one of three types, depending on the order of read and write accesses in the instructions. By convention, the hazards are named by the ordering in the program that must be preserved by the pipeline. Consider two instructions i and j, with i occurring before j. The possible data hazards are:

- RAW *(read after write)* — j tries to read a source before i writes it, so j incorrectly gets the old value. This is the most common type of hazard and the one that appears in Figures 6.6 and 6.7.

- WAR *(write after read)* — j tries to write a destination before it is read by i, so i incorrectly gets the new value. This cannot happen in our example pipeline because all reads are early (in ID) and all writes are late (in WB). This hazard occurs when there are some instructions that write results early in the instruction pipeline, and other instructions that read a source after a write of an instruction later in the pipeline. For example, autoincrement addressing can create a WAR hazard.

- WAW *(write after write)* — j tries to write an operand before it is written by i. The writes end up being performed in the wrong order, leaving the value written by i rather than the value written by j in the destination. This hazard is present only in pipelines that write in more than one pipe stage (or allow an instruction to proceed even when a previous instruction is stalled). The DLX pipeline writes a register only in WB and avoids this class of hazards.

Note that the RAR *(read after read)* case is not a hazard.

Not all data hazards can be handled without a performance effect. Consider the following sequence of instructions:

```
LW   R1,32(R6)
ADD R4,R1,R7
SUB R5,R1,R8
AND R6,R1,R7
```

This case is different from the situation with back-to-back ALU operations. The `LW` instruction does not have the data until the end of the MEM cycle, while the `ADD` instruction needs to have the data by the beginning of that clock cycle. Thus, the data hazard from using the result of a load instruction cannot be completely eliminated with simple hardware. We **can** forward the result immediately to the ALU from the MDR, and for the `SUB` instruction— which begins two clock cycles after the load—the result arrives in time, as shown in Figure 6.10. However, for the `ADD` instruction, the forwarded result arrives too late—at the end of a clock cycle, though it is needed at the beginning.

LW R1,32(R6)	IF	ID	EX	**MEM**	WB
ADD R4,R1,R7		IF	ID	**EX**	MEM
SUB R5,R1,R8			IF	ID	**EX**
AND R6,R1,R7				IF	**ID**

FIGURE 6.10 Pipeline hazard occurring when the result of a load instruction is used by the next instruction as a source operand and is forwarded. The value is available when it returns from memory at the end of the load instruction's MEM cycle. However, it is needed at the beginning of that clock cycle for the `ADD` (the EX stage of the add). The load value can be forwarded to the `SUB` instruction and will arrive in time for that instruction (EX). The `AND` can simply read the value during ID since it reads the registers in the second half of the cycle and the value is written in the first half.

The load instruction has a delay or latency that cannot be eliminated by forwarding alone—to do so would require the data-access time to be zero. The most common solution to this problem is a hardware addition called a *pipeline interlock*. In general, a *pipeline interlock* detects a hazard and stalls the pipeline until the hazard is cleared. In this case, the interlock stalls the pipeline beginning with the instruction that wants to use the data until the sourcing instruction produces it. This delay cycle, called a *pipeline stall* or *bubble*, allows the load data to arrive from memory; it can now be forwarded by the hardware. The CPI for the stalled instruction increases by the length of the stall (one clock cycle in this case). The stalled pipeline is shown in Figure 6.11.

Any instruction	IF	ID	EX	MEM	WB				
LW R1,32(R6)		IF	ID	EX	**MEM**	WB			
ADD R4,R1,R7			IF	ID	*stall*	**EX**	MEM	WB	
SUB R5,R1,R8				IF	*stall*	**ID**	EX	MEM	WB
AND R6,R1,R7					*stall*	IF	ID	EX	MEM	WB

FIGURE 6.11   The effect of the stall on the pipeline. All instructions starting with the instruction that has the dependence are delayed. With the delay, the value of the load that returns in MEM can now be forwarded to the EX cycle of the ADD instruction. Because of the stall, the SUB instruction will now read the value from the registers during its ID cycle rather than having it forwarded from the MDR.

The process of letting an instruction move from the instruction decode stage (ID) into the execution stage (EX) of this pipeline is usually called *instruction issue*; and an instruction that has made this step is said to have *issued*. For the DLX integer pipeline, all the data hazards can be checked during the ID phase of the pipeline. If a data hazard exists, the instruction is stalled before it is issued. Later in this chapter, we will look at situations where instruction issue is much more complex. Detecting interlocks early in the pipeline reduces the hardware complexity because the hardware never has to suspend an instruction that has updated the state of the machine, unless the entire machine is stalled.

Example

Suppose that 20% of the instructions are loads, and half the time the instruction following a load instruction depends on the result of the load. If this hazard creates a single-cycle delay, how much faster is the ideal pipelined machine (with a CPI of 1) that does not delay the pipeline, compared to a more realistic pipeline? Ignore any stalls other than pipeline stalls.

Answer

The ideal machine will be faster by the ratio of the CPIs. The CPI for an instruction following a load is 1.5, since they stall half the time. Since loads are 20% of the mix, the effective CPI is $(0.8*1 + 0.2*1.5) = 1.1$. This yields a performance ratio of $\frac{1.1}{1}$. Hence, the ideal machine is 10% faster.

Many types of stalls are quite frequent. The typical code-generation pattern for a statement such as A=B+C produces a stall for a load of the second data value. Figure 6.12 shows that the store need not result in another stall, since the result of the addition can be forwarded to the MDR. Machines where the operands may come from memory for arithmetic operations will need to stall the pipeline in the middle of the instruction to wait for memory to complete its access.

LW R1,B	IF	ID	EX	MEM	WB				
LW R2,C		IF	ID	EX	MEM	WB			
ADD R3,R1,R2			IF	ID	stall	EX	MEM	WB	
SW A,R3				IF	stall	ID	EX	MEM	WB

FIGURE 6.12 The DLX code sequence for A=B+C. The ADD instruction must be stalled to allow the load of C to complete. The SW need not be delayed further because the forwarding hardware passes the result from the ALU directly to the MDR for storing.

Rather than just allow the pipeline to stall, the compiler could try to schedule the pipeline to avoid these stalls, by rearranging the code sequence to eliminate the hazard. For example, the compiler would try to avoid generating code with a load followed by an immediate use of the load destination register. This technique, called *pipeline scheduling* or *instruction scheduling,* was first used in the 1960s, and became an area of major interest in the 1980s as pipelined machines became more widespread.

Example

Generate DLX code that avoids pipeline stalls for the following sequence:

$$a = b + c;$$
$$d = e - f;$$

Assume loads have a latency of one clock cycle.

Answer

Here is the scheduled code:

```
     LW   Rb,b
     LW   Rc,c
     LW   Re,e         ; swapped with next instruction to avoid stall
     ADD  Ra,Rb,Rc
     LW   Rf,f
     SW   a,Ra         ; store/load interchanged to avoid stall in SUB
     SUB  Rd,Re,Rf
     SW   d,Rd
```

Both load interlocks (LW Rc,c/ADD Ra,Rb,Rc and LW Rf,f/SUB Rd,Re,Rf) have been eliminated. There is a dependence between the ALU instruction and the store, but the pipeline structure allows the result to be forwarded. Notice that the use of different registers for the first and second statements was critical for this schedule to be legal. In particular, if the variable e were loaded into the same register as b or c, this schedule would not be legal. In general, pipeline scheduling can increase the register count required. In Section 6.8, we will see that this increase can be substantial for machines that can issue multiple instructions in one clock.

This technique works sufficiently well that some machines rely on software to avoid this type of hazard. A load requiring that the following instruction not use its result is called a *delayed load*. The pipeline slot after a load is often called the *load delay* or *delay slot*. When the compiler cannot schedule the interlock, a no-op instruction may be inserted. This does not affect running time, but only increases the code space versus a machine with the interlock. Whether or not the hardware detects this interlock and stalls the pipeline, performance will be enhanced if the compiler schedules instructions. If the stall occurs, the performance impact will be the same, whether the machine executes an idle cycle or executes a no-op. Figure 6.13 shows that scheduling can eliminate the majority of these delays. It is clear from this figure that load delays in GCC are significantly harder to schedule than in Spice or TeX.

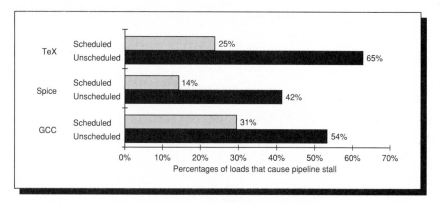

FIGURE 6.13 Percentage of the loads that result in a stall with the DLX pipeline. The black bars show the amount without compiler scheduling; the gray bars show the effect of a good, but simple, scheduling algorithm. These data show scheduling effectiveness after global optimization (see Chapter 3, Section 3.7). Global optimization actually makes scheduling relatively harder because there are fewer candidates available for scheduling into delay slots. For example, on GCC and TeX, when the programs are scheduled but not globally optimized, the percentage of load delays that result in a stall drops to 22% and 19%, respectively.

Implementing Data Hazard Detection in Simple Pipelines

How pipeline interlocks are implemented depends quite heavily on the length and complexity of the pipeline. For a complex machine with long-running instructions and multicycle interdependences, a central table that keeps track of the availability of operands and the outstanding writes may be needed (see Section 6.7). For the DLX integer pipeline, the only interlock we need to enforce is load followed by immediate use. This can be done with a simple comparator that looks for this pattern of load destination and source. The hardware required to detect and control the load data hazard and to forward the load result is as follows:

- Additional multiplexers on the inputs to the ALU (just as was required for the bypass hardware for register–register instructions)

- Extra paths from the MDR to both multiplexer inputs to the ALU

- A buffer to save the destination-register numbers from the prior two instructions (the same as for register–register forwarding)

- Four comparators to compare the two possible source register fields with the destination fields of the prior instructions and look for a match

The comparators check for a load interlock at the beginning of the EX cycle. The four possibilities and the required actions are shown in Figure 6.14.

For DLX, the hazard detection and forwarding hardware is reasonably simple; we will see that things become much more complicated when the pipelines are very deep (Section 6.6). But before we do that, let's see what happens with branches in our DLX pipeline.

Situation	Example code sequence	Action

No dependence	LW **R1**, 45 (R2)
	ADD R5,R6,R7
	SUB R8,R6,R7
	OR R9,R6,R7
		No hazard possible because no dependence exists on R1 in the immediately following three instructions.

Dependence requiring stall	LW **R1**, 45 (R2)
	ADD R5,**R1**,R7
	SUB R8,R6,R7
	OR R9,R6,R7
		Comparators detect the use of R1 in the ADD and stall the ADD (and SUB and OR) before the ADD begins EX.

Dependence overcome by forwarding	LW **R1**, 45 (R2)
	ADD R5,R6,R7
	SUB R8,**R1**,R7
	OR R9,R6,R7
		Comparators detect use of R1 in SUB and forward result of load to ALU in time for SUB to begin EX.

Dependence with accesses in order	LW **R1**, 45 (R2)
	ADD R5,R6,R7
	SUB R8,R6,R7
	OR R9,**R1**,R7
		No action required because the read of R1 by OR occurs in the second half of the ID phase, while the write of the loaded data occurred in the first half. See Figure 6.8 (page 262).

FIGURE 6.14 Situations that the pipeline hazard detection hardware can see by comparing the destination and sources of adjacent instructions. This table indicates that the only compare needed is between the destination and the sources on the two instructions following the instruction that wrote the destination. In the case of a stall, the pipeline dependences will look like the third case, once execution continues.

Control Hazards

Control hazards can cause a greater performance loss for our DLX pipeline than do data hazards. When a branch is executed, it may or may not change the PC to something other than its current value plus 4. (Recall that if a branch changes the PC to its target address, it is a *taken* branch; if it falls through, it is *not taken,* or *untaken.*) If instruction *i* is a taken branch, then the PC is normally not changed until the end of MEM, after the completion of the address calculation and comparison, as shown in Figure 6.4 (page 256). This means stalling for three clock cycles, at the end of which the new PC is known and the proper instruction can be fetched. This effect is called a *control* or *branch hazard.* Figure 6.15 shows a three-cycle stall for a control hazard.

Branch instruction	IF	ID	EX	MEM	WB					
Instruction *i*+1		*stall*	*stall*	*stall*	IF	ID	EX	MEM	WB	
Instruction *i*+2			*stall*	*stall*	*stall*	IF	ID	EX	MEM	WB
Instruction *i*+3				*stall*	*stall*	*stall*	IF	ID	EX	MEM
Instruction *i*+4					*stall*	*stall*	*stall*	IF	ID	EX
Instruction *i*+5						*stall*	*stall*	*stall*	IF	ID
Instruction *i*+6							*stall*	*stall*	*stall*	IF

FIGURE 6.15   Ideal DLX pipeline stalling after a control hazard. The instruction labeled instruction *i+k* represents the *k*th instruction executed after the branch. There is a difficulty in that the branch instruction is not decoded until after instruction *i* +1 has been fetched. This figure shows the conceptual difficulty, while Figure 6.16 shows what really happens.

Branch instruction	IF	ID	EX	MEM	WB					
Instruction *i*+1		IF	*stall*	*stall*	IF	ID	EX	MEM	WB	
Instruction *i*+2			*stall*	*stall*	*stall*	IF	ID	EX	MEM	WB
Instruction *i*+3				*stall*	*stall*	*stall*	IF	ID	EX	MEM
Instruction *i*+4					*stall*	*stall*	*stall*	IF	ID	EX
Instruction *i*+5						*stall*	*stall*	*stall*	IF	ID
Instruction *i*+6							*stall*	*stall*	*stall*	IF

FIGURE 6.16   What might really happen in the DLX pipeline. Instruction *i* +1 is fetched, but the instruction is ignored and the fetch is restarted once the branch target is known. It is probably obvious that if the branch is not taken, the second IF for instruction *i* +1 is redundant. This will be addressed shortly.

The pipeline in Figure 6.15 is not possible because we don't know that the instruction is a branch until after the fetch of the next instruction. Figure 6.16 fixes this by simply redoing the fetch once the target is known.

Three clock cycles wasted for every branch is a significant loss. With a 30% branch frequency and an ideal CPI of 1, the machine with branch stalls achieves only about half the ideal speedup from pipelining. Thus, reducing the branch penalty becomes critical. The number of clock cycles in a branch stall can be reduced in two steps:

1. Find out whether the branch is taken or not earlier in the pipeline.

2. Compute the taken PC (address of the branch target) earlier.

To optimize the branch behavior, **both** of these must be done—it doesn't help to know the target of the branch without knowing whether the next instruction to execute is the target or the instruction at PC+4. Both steps should be taken as early in the pipeline as possible.

In DLX, the branches (BEQZ and BNEZ) require testing only equality to zero. Thus, it is possible to complete this decision by the end of the ID cycle using special logic devoted to this test. To take advantage of an early decision on whether the branch is taken, both PCs (taken and not taken) must be computed early. Computing the branch target address requires a separate adder, which can add during ID. With the separate adder and a branch decision made during ID, there is only a one-clock-cycle stall on branches. Figure 6.17 shows the branch portion of the revised resource allocation table from Figure 6.4 (page 256).

In some machines, branch hazards are even more expensive in clock cycles than in our example, since the time to evaluate the branch condition and compute the destination can be even longer. For example, a machine with separate

Pipe stage	Branch instruction
IF	`IR←Mem[PC];` `PC←PC+4;`

ID	`A← Rs1;  B← Rs2;  PC1← PC;   IR1← IR;`
	`BTA←PC+((IR`$_{16}$`)`^{16}`## IR`$_{16..31}$`)`
	`if (Rs1 `*op*` 0) PC←BTA`

EX	
MEM	
WB	

FIGURE 6.17 Revised pipeline structure (see Figure 6.4, page 256) showing the use of a separate adder to compute the branch target address. The operations that are new or have changed are in bold. Because the branch target address (BTA) addition happens during ID, it will happen for all instructions; the branch condition (Rs1 *op* 0) will also be done for all instructions. The last operation in ID is to replace the PC. We must know that the instruction is a branch before we perform this step. This requires decoding the instruction before the end of ID, or doing this operation at the very beginning of EX when the PC is sent out. Because the branch is done by the end of ID, the EX, MEM, and WB stages are unused for branches. An additional complication arises for jumps that have a longer offset than branches. We can resolve this by using an additional adder that sums the PC and lower 26 bits of the IR. Alternatively, we could attempt a clever scheme that does a 16-bit add in the first half of the cycle and determines whether to add in 10 bits from IR in the second half of the cycle, by decoding the jump opcodes early.

decode and register fetch stages will probably have a *branch delay*—the length of the control hazard—that is at least one clock cycle longer. The branch delay, unless it is dealt with, turns into a branch penalty. Many VAXes have branch delays of four clock cycles or more, and large, deeply pipelined machines often have branch penalties of six or seven. In general, the deeper the pipeline, the worse the branch penalty in clock cycles. Of course, the relative performance effect of a longer branch penalty depends on the overall CPI of the machine. A high CPI machine can afford to have more expensive branches because the percentage of the machine's performance that will be lost from branches is less.

Before talking about methods for reducing the pipeline penalties that can arise from branches, let's take a brief look at the dynamic behavior of branches.

Branch Behavior in Programs

Since branches can dramatically affect pipeline performance, we should look at their behavior so as to get some ideas about how the penalties of branches and jumps might be reduced. We already know the branch frequencies for our programs from Chapter 4. Figure 6.18 reviews the overall frequency of control-flow operations for three of the machines and gives the breakdown between branches and jumps.

All of the machines show a conditional branch frequency of 11%–17%, while the frequency of unconditional branches varies between 2% and 8%. An obvious

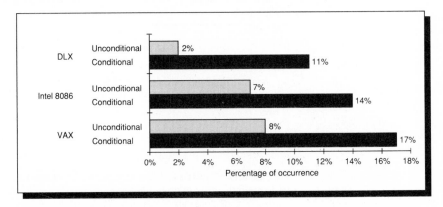

FIGURE 6.18   The frequency of instructions (branches, jumps, calls, and returns) that may change the PC. These data represent the average over the programs measured in Chapter 4. Instructions are divided into two classes: branches, which are conditional (including loop branches), and those that are unconditional (jumps, calls, and returns). The 360 is omitted because the ordinary unconditional branches are not separated from the conditional branches. Emer and Clark [1984] reported that 38% of the instructions executed in their measurements of the VAX were instructions that could change the PC. They measured that 67% of these instructions actually cause a branch in control flow. Their data were taken on a timesharing workload and reflect many uses; their measurement of branch frequency is much higher than the one in this chart.

question is, how many of the branches are taken? Knowing the breakdown between taken and untaken branches is important because this will affect strategies for reducing the branch penalties. For the VAX, Clark and Levy [1984] measured simple conditional branches to be taken with a frequency of just about 50%. Other branches, which occur much less often, have different ratios. Most bit-testing branches are not taken, and loop branches are taken with about 90% probability.

For DLX, we measured the branch behavior in Chapter 3 and summarized it in Figure 3.22 (page 107). That data showed 53% of the conditional branches are taken. Finally, 75% of the branches executed are forward-going branches. With this data in mind, let's look at ways to reduce branch penalties.

Reducing Pipeline Branch Penalties

There are several methods for dealing with the pipeline stalls due to branch delay, and four simple compile-time schemes are discussed in this section. In these schemes the predictions are static—they are fixed for each branch during the entire execution, and the predictions are compile-time guesses. More ambitious schemes using hardware to predict branches dynamically are discussed in Section 6.7.

The easiest scheme is to freeze the pipeline, holding any instructions after the branch until the branch destination is known. The attractiveness of this solution lies primarily in its simplicity. It is the solution used earlier in the pipeline shown in Figures 6.15 and 6.16.

A better and only slightly more complex scheme is to predict the branch as not taken, simply allowing the hardware to continue as if the branch were not

Untaken branch instruction	IF	**ID**	EX	MEM	WB				
Instruction i+1		**IF**	ID	EX	MEM	WB			
Instruction i+2			IF	ID	EX	MEM	WB		
Instruction i+3				IF	ID	EX	MEM	WB	
Instruction i+4					IF	ID	EX	MEM	WB

Taken branch instruction	IF	**ID**	EX	MEM	WB				
Instruction i+1		**IF**	**IF**	ID	EX	MEM	WB		
Instruction i+2			*stall*	IF	ID	EX	MEM	WB	
Instruction i+3				*stall*	IF	ID	EX	MEM	WB
Instruction i+4					*stall*	IF	ID	EX	MEM

FIGURE 6.19 The predict-not-taken scheme and the pipeline sequence when the branch is untaken (on the top) and taken (on the bottom). When the branch is untaken, determined during ID, we have fetched the fall through and just continue. If the branch is taken during ID, we restart the fetch at the branch target. This causes all instructions following the branch to stall one clock cycle.

executed. Here, care must be taken not to change the machine state until the branch outcome is definitely known. The complexity that arises from this—that is, knowing when the state might be changed by an instruction and how to "back out" a change—might cause us to reconsider the simpler solution of flushing the pipeline. In the DLX pipeline, this *predict-not-taken* scheme is implemented by continuing to fetch instructions as if the branch were a normal instruction. The pipeline looks as if nothing out of the ordinary is happening. If the branch is taken, however, we need to stop the pipeline and restart the fetch. Figure 6.19 shows both situations.

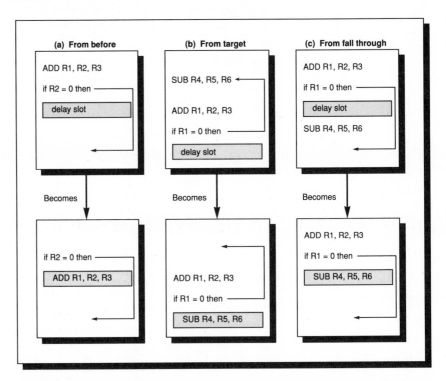

FIGURE 6.20   Scheduling the branch-delay slot. The top picture in each pair shows the code before scheduling, and the bottom picture shows the scheduled code. In (a) the delay slot is scheduled with an independent instruction from before the branch. This is the best choice. Strategies (b) and (c) are used when (a) is not possible. In the code sequences for (b) and (c), the use of R1 in the branch condition prevents the ADD instruction (whose destination is R1) from being moved after the branch. In (b) the branch-delay slot is scheduled from the target of the branch; usually the target instruction will need to be copied because it can be reached by another path. Strategy (b) is preferred when the branch is taken with high probability, such as a loop branch. Finally, the branch may be scheduled from the not-taken fall through, as in (c). To make this optimization legal for (b) or (c), it must be "OK" to execute the SUB instruction when the branch goes in the unexpected direction. By "OK" we mean that the work is wasted, but the program will still execute correctly. This is the case, for example, if R4 were a temporary register unused when the branch goes in the unexpected direction.

An alternative scheme is to predict the branch as taken. As soon as the branch is decoded and the target address is computed, we assume the branch to be taken and begin fetching and executing at the target. Since in our DLX pipeline we don't know the target address any earlier than we know the branch outcome, there is no advantage in this approach. However, in some machines—especially those with condition codes or more powerful (and hence slower) branch conditions—the branch target is known before the branch outcome, and this scheme makes sense.

Some machines have used another technique called delayed branch, which has been used in many microprogrammed control units. In a *delayed branch*, the execution cycle with a branch delay of length n is:

```
branch instruction
sequential successor₁
sequential successor₂
........
sequential successorₙ
branch target if taken
```

The sequential successors are in the *branch-delay slots*. As with load-delay slots, the job of the software is to make the successor instructions valid and useful. A number of optimizations are used. Figure 6.20 shows the three ways in which the branch delay can be scheduled. Figure 6.21 shows the different constraints for each of these branch-scheduling schemes, as well as situations in which they win.

The primary limitations on delayed-branch scheduling arise from the restrictions on the instructions that are scheduled into the delay slots and from our ability to predict at compile time whether a branch is likely to be taken or not. Figure 6.22 shows the effectiveness of the branch scheduling in DLX with a single branch-delay slot using a simple branch-scheduling algorithm. It shows that

Scheduling strategy	Requirements	Improves performance when?
(a) From before branch	Branch must not depend on the rescheduled instructions.	Always.
(b) From target	Must be OK to execute rescheduled instructions if branch is not taken. May need to duplicate instructions.	When branch is taken. May enlarge program if instructions are duplicated.
(c) From fall through	Must be OK to execute instructions if branch is taken.	When branch is not taken.

FIGURE 6.21 Delayed-branch–scheduling schemes and their requirements. The origin of the instruction being scheduled into the delay slot determines the scheduling strategy. The compiler must enforce the requirements when looking for instructions to schedule the delay slot. When the slots cannot be scheduled, they are filled with no-op instructions. In strategy (b), if the branch target is also accessible from another point in the program—as it would be if it were the head of a loop—the target instructions must be copied and not just moved.

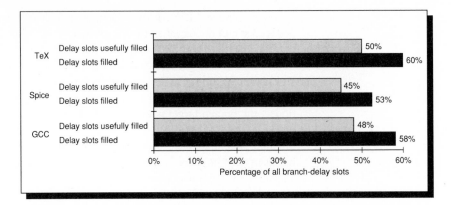

FIGURE 6.22   Frequency with which a single branch-delay slot is filled and how often the instruction is useful to the computation. The solid bar shows the percentage of the branch-delay slots occupied by some instruction other than a no-op. The difference between 100% and the dark column represents those branches that are followed by a no-op. The shaded bar shows how often those instructions do useful work. The difference between the shaded and solid bars is the percentage of instructions executed in a branch delay but not contributing to the computation. These instructions occur because optimization (b) is only useful when the branch is taken. If optimization (c) were used it would also contribute to this difference, since it is only useful when the branch is not taken.

slightly more than half the branch-delay slots are filled, and most of the filled slots do useful work. On average about 80% of the filled delay slots contribute to the computation. This number seems surprising, since branches are only taken about 53% of the time. The success rate is high because about one-half of the branch delays are being filled with an instruction from before the branch (strategy (a)), which is useful independent of whether the branch is taken.

When the scheduler in Figure 6.22 cannot use strategy (a)—moving an instruction from before the branch to fill the branch-delay slot—it uses only strategy (b)—moving it from the target. (For simplicity reasons, the schedule does not use strategy (c).) In total, nearly half the branch-delay slots are dynamically useful, eliminating one-half the branch stalls. Looking at Figure 6.22 we see that the primary limitation is the number of empty slots—those filled with no-ops. It is unlikely that the ratio of useful slots to filled slots, about 80%, can be improved, since this would require much better accuracy in predicting branches. In the Exercises we consider an extension of the delayed-branch idea that tries to fill more slots.

There is a small additional hardware cost for delayed branches. Because of the delayed effect of branches, multiple PCs (one plus the length of the delay) are needed to correctly restore the state when an interrupt occurs. Consider when the interrupt occurs after a taken-branch instruction is completed, but before all the instructions in the delay slots and the branch target are completed. In this case, the PC's of the delay slots and the PC of the branch target must be saved, since they are not sequential.

What is the effective performance of each of these schemes? The effective pipeline speedup with branch penalties is

$$\text{Pipeline speedup} = \frac{\text{Ideal CPI} * \text{Pipeline depth}}{\text{Ideal CPI} + \text{Pipeline stall cycle}}$$

If we assume that the ideal CPI is 1, then we can simplify this:

$$\text{Pipeline speedup} = \frac{\text{Pipeline depth}}{1 + \text{Pipeline stall cycles from branches}}$$

Since

Pipeline stall cycles from branches = Branch frequency * Branch penalty

we obtain:

$$\text{Pipeline speedup} = \frac{\text{Pipeline depth}}{(1 + \text{Branch frequency} * \text{Branch penalty})}$$

Using the DLX measurements in this section, Figure 6.23 shows several hardware options for dealing with branches, along with their performances (assuming a base CPI of 1).

Scheduling scheme	Branch penalty	Effective CPI	Pipeline speedup over nonpipelined machine	Pipeline speedup over stall pipeline on branch
Stall pipeline	3	1.42	3.52	1.00
Predict taken	1	1.14	4.39	1.25
Predict not taken	1	1.09	4.59	1.30
Delayed branch	0.5	1.07	4.67	1.33

FIGURE 6.23 Overall costs of a variety of branch schemes with the DLX pipeline. These data are for our DLX pipeline using the measured control-instruction frequency of 14% and the measurements of delay-slot filling from Figure 6.22. In addition, we know that 65% of the control instructions actually change the PC (taken branches plus unconditional changes). Shown are both the resultant CPI and the speedup over a nonpipelined machine, which we assume would have a CPI of 5 without any branch penalties. The last column of the table gives the speedup over a scheme that always stalls on branches.

Remember that the numbers in this section are **dramatically** affected by the length of the pipeline delay and the base CPI. A longer pipeline delay will cause an increase in the penalty and a larger percentage of wasted time. A delay of only one clock cycle is small—many machines have minimum delays of five or more. With a low CPI, the delay must be kept small, while a higher base CPI would reduce the relative penalty from branches.

Summary: Performance of the DLX Integer Pipeline

We close this section on hazard detection and elimination by showing the total distribution of idle clock cycles for our benchmarks when run on the DLX integer pipeline with software for pipeline scheduling. Figure 6.24 shows the distribution of clock cycles lost to load delays and branch delays in our three programs, by combining the separate measurements shown in Figures 6.13 (page 268) and 6.22.

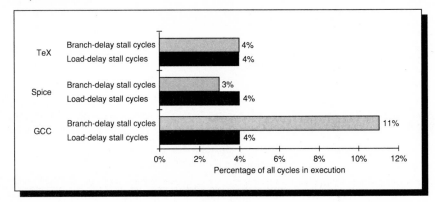

FIGURE 6.24 Percentage of the clock cycles spent on delays versus executing instructions. This assumes a perfect memory system; the clock-cycle count and instruction count would be identical if there were no integer pipeline stalls. This graph says that from 7% to 15% of the clock cycles are stalls; the remaining 85% to 93% are clock cycles that issue instructions. The Spice clock cycles do not include stalls in the FP pipeline, which will be shown at the end of Section 6.6. The pipeline scheduler fills load delays before branch delays and this affects the distribution of delay cycles.

For the GCC and TeX programs, the effective CPI (ignoring any stalls except those from pipeline hazards) on this pipelined version of DLX is 1.1. Compare this to the CPI for the complete nonpipelined, hardwired version of DLX described in Chapter 5 (Section 5.7), which is 5.8. Ignoring all other sources of stalls and assuming that the clock rates will be the same, the performance improvement from pipelining is 5.3 times.

6.5 | What Makes Pipelining Hard to Implement

Now that we understand how to detect and resolve hazards, we can deal with some complications that we have avoided so far. In Chapter 5 we saw that interrupts are among the most difficult aspects of implementing a machine; pipelining increases that difficulty. In the second part of this section, we discuss some of the challenges raised by different instruction sets.

Dealing with Interrupts

Interrupts are harder to handle in a pipelined machine because the overlapping of instructions makes it more difficult to know whether an instruction can safely change the state of the machine. In a pipelined machine, an instruction is executed piece by piece and is not completed for several clock cycles. Yet in the process of executing it may need to update the machine state. Meanwhile, an interrupt can force the machine to abort the instruction's execution before it is completed.

As in nonpipelined implementations, the most difficult interrupts have two properties: (1) they occur within instructions, and (2) they must be restartable. In our DLX pipeline, for example, a virtual memory page fault resulting from a data fetch cannot occur until sometime in the MEM cycle of the instruction. By the time that fault is seen, several other instructions will be in execution. Since a page fault must be restartable and requires the intervention of another process, such as the operating system, the pipeline must be safely shut down and the state saved so that the instruction can be restarted in the correct state. This is usually implemented by saving the PC of the instruction (during IF) to restart it. If the restarted instruction is not a branch then we will continue to fetch the sequential successors and begin their execution in the normal fashion. If the restarted instruction is a branch, then we will evaluate the branch condition and begin fetching from either the target or the fall through. When an interrupt occurs, we can take the following steps to save the pipeline state safely:

1. Force a trap instruction into the pipeline on the next IF.

2. Until the trap is taken, turn off all writes for the faulting instruction and for all instructions that follow in the pipeline. This prevents any state changes for instructions that will not be completed before the interrupt is handled.

3. After the interrupt-handling routine in the operating system receives control, it immediately saves the PC of the faulting instruction. This value will be used to return from the interrupt later.

When we use delayed branches it is no longer possible to re-create the state of the machine with the single PC of the interrupted instruction, because the instructions in the pipeline may not be sequentially related. In particular, when the instruction that causes the interrupt is a branch-delay slot, and the branch was taken, then the instructions to restart are those in the slot plus the instruction at the branch target. The branch itself has completed execution and is not restarted. The addresses of the instructions in the branch-delay slot and the target are not sequential. So we need to save and restore a number of PCs that is one more than the length of the branch delay. This is done in the third step above.

After the interrupt has been handled, special instructions return the machine from the interrupt by reloading the PCs and restarting the instruction stream (using RFE in DLX). If the pipeline can be stopped so that the instructions just before the faulting instruction are completed and those after it can be restarted from scratch, the pipeline is said to have *precise interrupts*. Ideally, the faulting instruction would not have changed the state, and correctly handling some interrupts requires that the faulting instruction have no effects. For other interrupts, such as floating-point exceptions, the faulting instruction on some machines writes its result before the interrupt can be handled. In such cases, the hardware must be prepared to retrieve the source operands, even if the destination is identical to one of the source operands.

Supporting precise interrupts is a requirement in many systems, while in others it is valuable because it simplifies the operating system interface. At a minimum, any machine with demand paging or IEEE arithmetic trap handlers must make its interrupts precise, either in the hardware or with some software support.

Precise interrupts are challenging because of the same problems that make instructions difficult to restart. As we saw in the last chapter, restarting is complicated by the fact that instructions can change the state of the machine before they are **guaranteed** to complete (sometimes called *committed* instructions). Because instructions in the pipeline may have dependences, not updating the machine state is impractical if the pipeline is to keep going. Thus, as a machine is more heavily pipelined, it becomes necessary to be able to back out of any state changes made before the instruction is committed (as discussed in Chapter 5). Fortunately, DLX has no such instructions, given the pipeline we have used.

Figure 6.25 (page 281) shows the DLX pipeline stages and which "problem" interrupts might occur in each stage. Because in pipelining there are multiple instructions in execution, multiple interrupts may occur on the same clock cycle. For example, consider this instruction sequence:

LW	IF	ID	EX	MEM	WB	
ADD		IF	ID	EX	MEM	WB

This pair of instructions can cause a data page fault and an arithmetic interrupt at the same time, since the LW is in MEM while the ADD is in EX. This case can be handled by dealing with only the data page fault and then restarting the execution. The second interrupt will reoccur (but not the first, if the software is correct), and when it does it can be handled independently.

In reality, the situation is not all this straightforward. Interrupts may occur out of order; that is, an instruction may cause an interrupt before an earlier instruction causes one. Consider again the above sequence of instructions LW; ADD. The LW can get a data page fault, seen when the instruction is in MEM, and the ADD can get an instruction page fault, seen when the ADD instruction is in IF. The instruction page fault will actually occur first, even though it is caused by a later instruction! This situation can be resolved in two ways. To explain them, let's call the instruction in the position of the LW "instruction *i*" and the instruction in the position of the ADD "instruction *i*+1."

Pipeline stage	Problem interrupts occurring
IF	Page fault on instruction fetch; misaligned memory access; memory-protection violation
ID	Undefined or illegal opcode
EX	Arithmetic interrupt
MEM	Page fault on data fetch; misaligned memory access; memory-protection violation
WB	None

FIGURE 6.25 Interrupts from Chapter 5 that cause stop and restart of the DLX pipeline in a transparent fashion. The pipeline stage where these interrupts occur is also shown. Interrupts raised from instruction or data-memory access account for six out of seven cases. These interrupts and their corresponding names in other processors are in Figures 5.9 and 5.11.

The first approach is completely precise and is the simplest to understand for the user of the architecture. The hardware posts each interrupt in a status vector carried along with each instruction as it goes down the pipeline. When an instruction enters WB (or is about to leave MEM), the interrupt status vector is checked. If any interrupts are posted, they are handled in the order in which they would occur in time—the interrupt corresponding to the earliest instruction is handled first. This guarantees that all interrupts will be seen on instruction i before any are seen on $i+1$. Of course, any action taken on behalf of instruction i may be invalid, but because no state is changed until WB, this is not a problem in the DLX pipeline. Nevertheless, pipeline control may want to disable any actions on behalf of an instruction i (and its successors) as soon as the interrupt is recognized. For pipelines that could update state earlier than WB, this disabling is required.

The second approach is to handle an interrupt as soon as it appears. This could be regarded as slightly less precise because interrupts occur in an order different from the order they would occur in if there were no pipelining. Figure 6.26 shows two interrupts occurring in the DLX pipeline. Because the interrupt at instruction $i+1$ is handled when it appears, the pipeline must be stopped immediately without completing any instructions that have yet to change state. For the DLX pipeline, this will be $i-2$, $i-1$, i, and $i+1$, assuming the interrupt is recognized at the end of the IF stage of the ADD instruction. The pipeline is then restarted with instruction $i-2$. Since the instruction causing the interrupt can be any of $i-2$, ..., $i+1$, the operating system must determine which instruction faulted. This is easy to figure out if the type of interrupt and its corresponding pipe stage are known. For example, only $i+1$ (the ADD instruction) could get an instruction page fault at this point, and only $i-2$ could get a data page fault. After handling the fault for $i+1$ and restarting at $i-2$, the data page fault will be encountered on instruction i, which will cause i, ..., $i+3$ to be interrupted. The data page fault can then be handled.

Instruction $i-3$	IF	ID	EX	MEM	WB				
Instruction $i-2$		IF	ID	EX	MEM	*WB*			
Instruction $i-1$			IF	ID	EX	*MEM*	*WB*		
Instruction i (LW)				IF	ID	*EX*	*MEM*	*WB*	
Instruction $i+1$ (ADD)					**IF**	*ID*	*EX*	*MEM*	*WB*
Instruction $i+2$						*IF*	*ID*	*EX*	*MEM*	*WB*

Instruction $i-3$	IF	ID	EX	MEM	WB				
Instruction $i-2$		IF	ID	EX	MEM	WB			
Instruction $i-1$			IF	ID	EX	MEM	WB		
Instruction i (LW)				IF	ID	EX	**MEM**	*WB*	
Instruction $i+1$ (ADD)					IF	ID	*EX*	*MEM*	*WB*
Instruction $i+2$						IF	*ID*	*EX*	*MEM*	*WB*
Instruction $i+3$							*IF*	*ID*	*EX*	*MEM*
Instruction $i+4$								IF	ID	EX

FIGURE 6.26 The actions taken for interrupts occurring at different points in the pipeline and handled immediately. This shows the instructions interrupted when an instruction page fault occurs in instruction $i+1$ (in the top diagram), and a data page fault in instruction i in the bottom diagram. The pipe stages in bold are the cycles during which the interrupt is recognized. The pipe stages in italics are the instructions that will not be completed due to the interrupt, and will need to be restarted. Because the earliest effect of the interrupt is on the pipe stage after it occurs, instructions that are in the WB stage when the interrupt occurs will complete, while those that have not yet reached WB will be stopped and restarted.

Instruction Set Complications

Another set of difficulties arises from odd bits of state that may create additional pipeline hazards or may require extra hardware to save and restore. Condition codes are a good example of this. Many machines set the condition codes implicitly as part of the instruction. At first glance, this looks like a good idea, since condition codes decouple the evaluation of the condition from the actual branch. However, implicitly set condition codes can cause difficulties in making branches fast. They limit the effectiveness of branch scheduling because most operations will modify the condition code, making it hard to schedule instructions between the setting of the condition code and the branch. Furthermore, in machines with condition codes, the processor must decide when the branch condition is fixed. This involves finding out when the condition code has been set for the last time prior to the branch. On the VAX, most instructions set the condition code, so that an implementation will have to stall if it tries to determine the branch condition early. Alternatively, the branch condition can be evaluated by the branch late in the pipeline, but this still leads to a long branch delay. On the 360/370 many, but not all, instructions set the condition codes. Figure 6.27 shows how the situation differs on the DLX, the VAX, and the 360 for the following C code sequence, assuming that b and d are initially in registers R2 and R3 (and should not be destroyed):

$$a = b + d;$$
$$if\ (b==0)\ \ldots$$

DLX	VAX	IBM 360
ADD R1,R2,R3	ADDL3 a,R2,R3	LR R1,R2
...	...	AR R1,R3
SW a,R1	CL R2,0	ST a,R1
...	BEQL label	...
BEQZ R2,label		LTR R2,R2
		BZ label

FIGURE 6.27 **Code sequence for the above two statements.** Because the ADD computes the sum of b and d, and the branch condition depends only on b, an explicit compare (on R2) is needed on the VAX and 360. On DLX, the branch depends only on R2 and can be arbitrarily far away from it. (In addition the SW could be moved into the branch-delay slot.) On the VAX all ALU operations and moves set the condition codes, so that a compare must be right before the branch. On the 360, for this example the instruction load and test register (LTR) is used to set the condition code. However, most loads on the 360 do not set the condition codes; thus, a load (or a store) could be moved between the LTR and the branch.

Provided there is lots of hardware to spare, **all** instructions before the branch in the pipeline can be examined to decide when the branch is determined. Of course, architectures with explicitly set condition codes avoid this difficulty. However, pipeline control must still track the last instruction that sets the condition code to know when the branch condition is decided. In effect, the condition code must be treated as an operand requiring hazard detection for RAW hazards on branches, just as DLX must do on the registers.

A final thorny area in pipelining is multicycle operations. Imagine trying to pipeline a sequence of VAX instructions such as this:

```
MOVL R1,R2
ADDL3 42(R1),56(R1)+,@(R1)
SUBL2 R2,R3
MOVC3 @(R1)[R2],74(R2),R3
```

These instructions differ radically in the number of clock cycles they will require, from as low as one up to hundreds of clock cycles. They also require different numbers of data memory accesses, from zero to possibly hundreds. Data hazards are very complex and occur both between and within instructions.

The simple solution of making all instructions execute for the same number of clock cycles is unacceptable because it introduces an enormous number of hazards and bypass conditions, and makes an immensely long pipeline. Pipelining the VAX at the instruction level is difficult (as we will see in Section 6.9), but a clever solution was found by the VAX 8800 designers. They pipeline the microinstruction execution; because the microinstructions are simple (they look a lot like DLX), the pipeline control is much easier. While it is not clear that this approach can achieve quite as low a CPI as an instruction-level pipeline for the VAX, it is much simpler, possibly leading to a shorter clock cycle time.

Load/store machines that have simple operations with similar amounts of work pipeline more easily. If architects realize the relationship between instruction set design and pipelining, they can design architectures for more efficient pipelining. In the next section we will see how the DLX pipeline deals with long-running instructions.

6.6 | Extending the DLX Pipeline to Handle Multicycle Operations

We now want to explore how our DLX pipeline can be extended to handle floating-point operations. This section concentrates on the basic approach and the design alternatives, and closes with some performance measurements of a DLX floating-point pipeline.

It is impractical to require that all DLX floating-point operations complete in one clock cycle, or even in two. Doing so would mean either accepting a slow clock or using enormous amounts of logic in the floating-point units, or both. Instead, the floating-point pipeline will allow for a longer latency for operations. This is easier to grasp if we imagine the floating-point instructions as having the same pipeline as the integer instructions, with two important changes. First, the EX cycle may be repeated as many times as needed to complete the operation; the number of repetitions can vary for different operations. Second, there may be multiple floating-point functional units. A stall will occur if the instruction to be issued will either cause a structural hazard for the functional unit it uses or cause a data hazard.

For this section let's assume that there are four separate functional units in our DLX implementation:

1. The main integer unit

2. FP and integer multiplier

3. FP adder

4. FP and integer divider

The integer unit handles all loads and stores to either register set, all the integer operations (except multiply and divide), and branches. For now we will also assume that the execution stages of the other functional units are not pipelined, so that no other instruction using the functional unit may issue until the previous instruction leaves EX. Moreover, if an instruction cannot proceed to the EX stage, the entire pipeline behind that instruction will be stalled. Figure 6.28 shows the resulting pipeline structure. In the next section we will deal with schemes that allow the pipeline to progress when there are more functional units or when the functional units are pipelined.

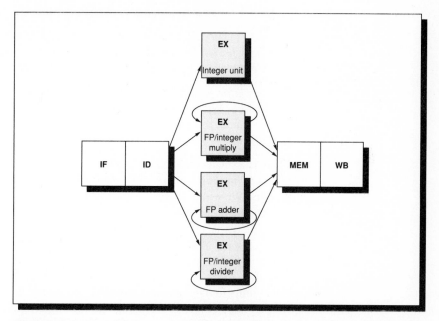

FIGURE 6.28   The DLX pipeline with three additional nonpipelined, floating-point, functional units. Because only one instruction issues on every clock cycle, all instructions go through the standard pipeline for integer operations. The floating-point operations simply loop when they reach the EX stage. After they have finished the EX stage, they proceed to MEM and WB to complete execution.

Since the EX stage may be repeated many times—30 to 50 repetitions for a floating-point divide would not be unreasonable—we must find a way to track long potential dependences and resolve hazards that last over tens of clock cycles, rather than just one or two. There is also the overlap between integer and floating-point instructions to deal with. However, overlapped integer and FP instructions do not complicate hazard detection, except on floating-point memory references and moves between the register sets. This is because, except for these memory references and moves, the FP and integer registers are distinct, and all integer instructions operate on the integer registers while the floating-point operations operate only on their own registers. This simplification of pipeline control is a major advantage of having separate register files for integer and floating-point data.

For now, let's assume that all floating-point operations take the same number of clock cycles—say 20 in the EX stage. What kind of hazard-detection circuitry will we need? Because all operations take the same amount of time, and register reads and writes always occur in the same stage, only RAW hazards are possible; no WAR or WAW hazards can occur. Thus, all we need to track is the destination register of each active functional unit. When we want to issue a new floating-point instruction, we take the following steps:

1. *Check for structural hazard*—Wait until the required functional unit is not busy.

2. *Check for a RAW data hazard*—Wait until the source registers are not listed as destinations by any of the EX stages in the functional units.

3. *Check for forwarding*—Test if the destination register of an instruction in MEM or WB is one of the source registers of the floating-point instruction; if so, enable the input multiplexer to use that result, rather than the register contents.

There is a small complication arising from conflicts between floating-point loads and floating-point operations when they both reach the WB stage simultaneously. We will deal presently with this situation in a more general fashion.

The above discussion assumes that the FP-functional-unit execution times were all the same. However, this does not hold up under practical scrutiny: Floating-point adds can typically be done in less than 5 clock cycles, multiplies in less than 10, and divides in about 20 or more. What we want is to allow the execution times of the functional units to differ, while still allowing the functional units to overlap execution. This would not change the basic structure of the pipeline in Figure 6.28, though it may cause the number of iterations around the loops to vary. Overlapping the execution of instructions whose running times differ, however, creates three complications: contention for register access at the end of the pipeline, the possibility of WAR and WAW hazards, and greater difficulty in providing precise interrupts.

We have already seen that FP loads and FP operations can contend for the floating-point register file on writes. When floating-point operations vary in execution time, they can also collide when trying to write results. This problem can be resolved by establishing a static priority for use of the WB stage. If multiple instructions wish to enter the MEM stage simultaneously, all instructions except the one with the highest priority are stalled in their EX stage. A simple, though sometimes suboptimal, heuristic is to give priority to the unit with the longest latency, since that is the one most likely to be the cause of the bottleneck. Although this scheme is reasonably simple to implement, this change to the DLX pipeline is quite significant. In the integer pipeline, all hazards were checked before the instruction issued to the EX stage. With this scheme for determining access to the result write port, instructions can stall after they issue.

Overlapping instructions with different execution times could introduce WAR and WAW hazards into our DLX pipeline, because the time at which instructions write is no longer fixed. If all instructions still read their registers at the same time, no WAR hazards will be introduced.

WAW hazards are introduced because instructions can write their results in a different order than they appear. For example, consider the following code sequence:

```
DIVF    F0,F2,F4
SUBF    F0,F8,F10
```

A WAW hazard occurs between the divide and the subtract operations: The subtract will complete first, writing its result before the divide writes its result. Note that this hazard only occurs when the result of the divide will be overwritten **without** any instruction ever using it! If there were a use of F0 between the DIVF and the SUBF, the pipeline would stall because of a data dependence, and the SUBF would not issue until the DIVF was completed. We could argue that, for our pipeline, WAW hazards only occur when a useless instruction is executed, but we must still detect them and make sure that the result of the SUBF appears in F0 when we are done. (As we will see in Section 6.10, such sequences sometimes do occur in reasonable code.)

There are two possible ways to handle this WAW hazard. The first approach is to delay the issue of the subtract instruction until the DIVF enters MEM. The second approach is to stamp out the result of the divide by detecting the hazard and telling the divide unit not to write its result. Then, the SUBF can issue right away. Because this hazard is rare, either scheme will work fine—you can pick whatever is simpler to implement. As a pipeline gets more complex, however, we will need to devote increasing resources to determining when an instruction can issue.

Another problem caused by these long-running instructions can be illustrated with a very similar sequence of code:

```
DIVF    F0,F2,F4
ADDF    F10,F10,F8
SUBF    F12,F12,F14
```

This code sequence looks straightforward; there are no dependences. The problem with which we are concerned arises because an instruction issued early may complete after an instruction issued later. In this example, we can expect ADDF and SUBF to complete **before** the DIVF completes. This is called *out-of-order completion* and is common in pipelines with long-running operations. Since hazard detection will prevent any dependence among instructions from being violated, why is out-of-order completion a problem? Suppose that the SUBF causes a floating-point–arithmetic interrupt at a point where the ADDF has completed but the DIVF has not. The result will be an imprecise interrupt, something we are trying to avoid. It may appear that this could be handled by letting the floating-point pipeline drain, as we do for the integer pipeline. But the interrupt may be in a position where this is not possible. For example, if the

DIVF decided to take a floating-point–arithmetic interrupt after the add completed, we could not have a precise interrupt at the hardware level. In fact, since the ADDF destroys one of its operands, we could not restore the state to what it was before the DIVF, even with software help.

This problem is being created because instructions are completing in a different order from the order in which they were issued. There are four possible approaches to dealing with out-of-order completion. The first is to ignore the problem and settle for imprecise interrupts. This approach was used in the 1960s and early 1970s. It is still used in some supercomputers, where certain classes of interrupts are not allowed or are handled by the hardware without stopping the pipeline. But it is difficult to use this approach in most machines built today, due to features such as virtual memory and the IEEE floating-point standard, which essentially require precise interrupts, through a combination of hardware and software.

A second approach is to queue the results of an operation until all the operations that were issued earlier are complete. Some machines actually use this solution, but it becomes expensive when the difference in running times among operations is long, since the number of results to queue can become large. Furthermore, results from the queue must be bypassed so as to continue issuing instructions while waiting for the longer instruction. This requires a large number of comparators and a very large multiplexer. There are two viable variations on this basic approach. The first is a *history file*, used in the CYBER 180/990. The history file keeps track of the original values of registers. When an interrupt occurs and the state must be rolled back earlier than some instruction that completed out of order, the original value of the register can be restored from the history file. A similar technique is used for autoincrement and autodecrement addressing on machines like VAXes. Another approach, the *future file*, proposed by J. Smith and Plezkun [1988], keeps the newer value of a register; when all earlier instructions have completed, the main register file is updated from the future file. On an interrupt, the main register file has the precise values for the interrupted state.

A third technique in use is to allow the interrupts to become somewhat imprecise, but keep enough information so that the trap-handling routines can create a precise sequence for the interrupt. This means knowing what operations were in the pipeline and their PCs. Then, after handling a trap, the software finishes any instructions that precede the latest instruction completed, and the sequence can restart. Consider the following worst-case code sequence:

Instruction$_1$—a long-running instruction that eventually interrupts execution

Instruction$_2$, ... , instruction$_{n-1}$—a series of instructions that are not completed

Instruction$_n$—an instruction that is finished

Given the PCs of all the instructions in the pipeline and the interrupt return PC, the software can find the state of instruction$_1$ and instruction$_n$. Since instruction$_n$ has completed, we will want to restart execution at instruction$_{n+1}$. After handling the interrupt, the software must simulate the execution of $instruction_1$, ... , $instruction_{n-1}$. Then we can return from the interrupt and restart at $instruction_{n+1}$. The complexity of executing these instructions properly by the handler is the major difficulty of this scheme. There is an important simplification: If $instruction_2$, ... , $instruction_n$ are all integer instructions, then we know that if $instruction_n$ has completed, all of $instruction_2$, ... , $instruction_{n-1}$ have also completed. Thus, only floating-point operations need to be handled. To make this scheme tractable the number of floating-point instructions that can be overlapped in execution can be limited. For example, if we only overlap two instructions, then only the interrupting instruction need be completed by software. This restriction may reduce the potential throughput if the FP pipelines are deep or if there is a significant number of FP functional units. This approach is used in the SPARC architecture to allow overlap of floating-point and integer operations.

The final technique is a hybrid scheme that allows the instruction issue to continue only if it is certain that all the instructions before the issuing instruction will complete without causing an interrupt. This guarantees that when an interrupt occurs, no instructions after the interrupting one will be completed, and all of the instructions before the interrupting one can be completed. This sometimes means stalling the machine to maintain precise interrupts. To make this scheme work, the floating-point functional units must determine if an interrupt is possible early in the EX stage (in the first three clock cycles in the DLX pipeline), so as to prevent further instructions from completing. This scheme is used in the MIPS R2000/3000 architecture and is discussed further in Appendix A, Section A.7.

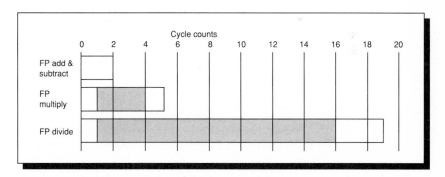

FIGURE 6.29   Total clock cycle count and permissible overlap among double-precision, floating-point operations on the MIPS R2010/3010 FP unit. The overall length of the bar shows the total number of EX cycles required to complete the operation. For example, after five clock cycles a multiply result is available. The shaded regions are times during which FP operations can be overlapped. As is common in most FP units, some of the FP logic is shared—the rounding logic, for example, is often shared. This means that FP operations with different running times cannot overlap arbitrarily. Also note that multiply and divide are not pipelined in this FP unit, so only one multiply or divide can be outstanding. The motivation for this pipeline design is discussed further in Appendix A (page A-31).

Performance of a DLX FP Pipeline

To look at the FP pipeline performance of DLX, we need to specify the latency and issue restrictions for the FP operations. We have chosen to use the pipeline structure of the MIPS R2010/3010 FP unit. While this unit has some structural hazards, it tends to have low-latency FP operations compared to most other FP units. The latencies and issue restrictions for DP floating-point operations are depicted in Figure 6.29 (page 289).

Figure 6.30 gives the breakdown of integer and floating-point stalls for Spice. There are four classes of stalls: load delays, branch delays, floating-point structural delays, and floating-point data hazards. The compiler tries to schedule both load and FP delays before it schedules branch delays. Interestingly, about 27% of the time in Spice is spent waiting for a floating-point result. Since the structural hazards are small, further pipelining of the floating-point unit would not gain much. In fact, the impact might easily be negative if the floating-point pipeline latency became longer.

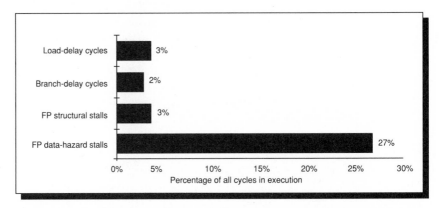

FIGURE 6.30   Percentage of clock cycles in Spice that are pipeline stalls. This again assumes a perfect memory system with no memory-system stalls. In total, 35% of the clock cycles in Spice are stalls, and without any stalls Spice would run about 50% faster. The percentage of stalls differs from Figure 6.24 (page 278) because this cycle count includes all the FP stalls, while the previous graph includes only the integer stalls.

6.7 | Advanced Pipelining— Dynamic Scheduling in Pipelines

So far we have assumed that our pipeline fetches an instruction and issues it, unless there is a data dependence between an instruction already in the pipeline and the fetched instruction. If there is a data dependence, then we stall the instruction and cease fetching and issuing until the dependence is cleared. Software is responsible for scheduling the instructions to minimize these stalls. This approach, which is called *static scheduling*, while first used in the 1960s, has become popular more recently. Many of the earlier, heavily pipelined machines used *dynamic scheduling*, whereby the hardware rearranges the instruction execution to reduce the stalls.

Dynamic scheduling offers a couple of advantages: It enables handling some cases when dependences are unknown at compile time, and it simplifies the compiler. It also allows code that was compiled with one pipeline in mind to run efficiently on a different pipeline. As we will see, these advantages are gained at a significant increase in hardware complexity. The first two parts of this section deal with reducing the cost of data dependences, especially in deeply pipelined machines. Corresponding to the dynamic hardware techniques for scheduling around data dependences are dynamic techniques for handling branches. These techniques are used for two purposes: to predict whether a branch will be taken, and to find the target more quickly. *Hardware branch prediction*, the name for these techniques, is the topic of the third part of this advanced section.

Dynamic Scheduling Around Hazards with a Scoreboard

The major limitation of the pipelining techniques we have used so far is that they all use in-order instruction issue. If an instruction is stalled in the pipeline, no later instructions can proceed. If there are multiple functional units, these units could lie idle. So, if instruction *j* depends on a long-running instruction *i*, currently in execution in the pipeline, then all instructions after *j* must be stalled until *i* is finished and *j* can execute. For example, consider this code:

```
DIVF    F0,F2,F4
ADDF    F10,F0,F8
SUBF    F6,F6,F14
```

The SUBF instruction cannot execute because the dependence of ADDF on DIVF causes the pipeline to stall; yet SUBF does not depend on anything in the pipeline. This is a performance limitation that can be eliminated by not requiring instructions to execute in order.

In the DLX pipeline, both structural and data hazards were checked at ID: When an instruction could execute properly, it was issued from ID. To allow us to begin executing the SUBF in the above example, we must separate the issue process into two parts: checking the structural hazards, and waiting for the absence of a data hazard. We can still check for structural hazards when we issue the instruction; thus, we still use in-order instruction issue. However, we want the instructions to begin execution as soon as their data operands are available. Thus, the pipeline will do *out-of-order execution*, which obviously implies *out-of-order completion*.

In introducing out-of-order execution, we have essentially split two pipe stages of DLX into three pipe stages. The two stages in DLX were:

1. ID—decode instruction, check for all hazards, and fetch operands

2. EX—execute instruction

In the DLX pipeline all instructions passed through issue stage in order, and a stalled instruction in ID caused a stall for all instructions behind it. The three stages we will need to allow out-of-order execution are:

1. Issue—decode instructions, check for structural hazards

2. Read operands—wait until no data hazards, then read operands

3. Execute

These three stages replace the ID and EX stages in the simple DLX pipeline.

While all instructions pass through the issue stage in order (in-order issue), they can be stalled or bypass each other in the second stage (read operands), and thus enter execution out of order. *Scoreboarding* is a technique for allowing instructions to execute out of order when there are sufficient resources and no data

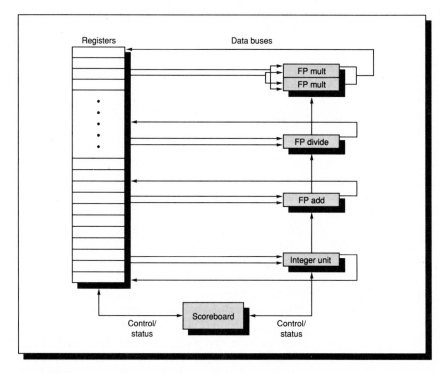

FIGURE 6.31 This shows the basic structure of a DLX machine with a scoreboard.
The scoreboard's function is to control instruction execution (vertical control lines). All data flows between the register file and the functional units over the buses (the horizontal lines, called trunks in the CDC 6600). There are two FP multipliers, an FP divider, an FP adder, and an integer unit. One set of buses (two inputs and one output) serves a group of functional units. The details of the scoreboard are shown in Figures 6.32–6.35.

dependences; it is named after the CDC 6600 scoreboard, which developed this capability.

Before we see how scoreboarding could be used in the DLX pipeline, it is important to observe that WAR hazards, which did not exist in the DLX floating-point or integer pipelines, may exist when instructions are executed out of order. Assume our earlier example has changed so that the SUBF destination is F8. If ADDF and SUBF use two different functional units, then it is possible to execute the SUBF before the ADDF, but it will yield an incorrect result if ADDF has not read F8 before SUBF writes its result. The hazard for this case can be avoided by two rules: (1) read registers only during Read Operands, and (2) queue both the ADDF operation **and** copies of its operands. Of course, WAW hazards must still be detected, such as would occur if the destination of the SUBF were F10. This WAW hazard can be eliminated by stalling the issue of the SUBF instruction.

The goal of a scoreboard is to maintain an execution rate of one instruction per clock cycle (when there are no structural hazards) by executing an instruction as early as possible. Thus, when the instruction at the front of the queue is stalled, other instructions can be issued and executed if they do not depend on any active or stalled instruction. The scoreboard takes full responsibility for instruction issue and execution, including all hazard detection. Taking advantage of out-of-order execution requires multiple instructions to be in their EX stage simultaneously. This can be achieved with either multiple functional units or with pipelined functional units. Since these two capabilities—pipelined functional units and multiple functional units—are essentially equivalent for the purposes of pipeline control, we will assume the machine has multiple functional units.

The CDC 6600 had 16 separate functional units, including 4 floating-point units, 5 units for memory references, and 7 units for integer operations. On DLX, scoreboards make sense only on the floating-point unit. Let's assume that there are two multipliers, one adder, one divide unit, and a single integer unit for all memory references, branches, and integer operations. Although this example is much smaller than the CDC 6600, it is sufficiently powerful to demonstrate the principles. Because both DLX and the CDC 6600 are load/store, the techniques are nearly identical for the two machines. Figure 6.31 shows what the machine looks like.

Every instruction goes through the scoreboard, where a picture of the data dependences is constructed; this step corresponds to instruction issue and replaces part of the ID step in the DLX pipeline. This picture then determines when the instruction can read its operands and begin execution. If the scoreboard decides the instruction cannot execute immediately, it monitors every change in the hardware and decides when the instruction can execute. The scoreboard also controls when an instruction can write its result into the destination register. Thus, all hazard detection and resolution is centralized in the scoreboard. We will see a picture of the scoreboard later (Figure 6.32 on page 296), but first we need to understand the steps in the issue and execution segment of the pipeline.

Each instruction undergoes four steps in executing. (Since we are concentrating on the FP operations, we will not consider a step for memory access.) Let's first examine the steps informally and then look in detail at how the scoreboard keeps the necessary information that determines when to progress from one step to the next. The four steps, which replace the ID, EX, and WB steps in the standard DLX pipeline, are as follows:

1. Issue—If a functional unit for the instruction is free and no other active instruction has the same destination register, the scoreboard issues the instruction to the functional unit and updates its internal data structure. By ensuring that no other active functional unit wants to write its result into the destination register, we guarantee that WAW hazards cannot be present. If a structural or WAW hazard exists, then the instruction issue stalls, and no further instructions will issue until these hazards are cleared. This step replaces a portion of the ID step in the DLX pipeline.

2. Read operands—The scoreboard monitors the availability of the source operands. A source operand is available if no active instruction is going to write it, or if the register containing the operand is being written by a currently active functional unit. When the source operands are available, the scoreboard tells the functional unit to proceed to read the operands from the registers and begin execution. The scoreboard resolves RAW hazards dynamically in this step, and instructions may be sent into execution out of order. This step, together with Issue, completes the function of the ID step in the simple DLX pipeline.

3. Execution—The functional unit begins execution upon receiving operands. When the result is ready, it notifies the scoreboard that it has completed execution. This step replaces the EX step in the DLX pipeline and takes multiple cycles in the DLX FP pipeline.

4. Write result—Once the scoreboard is aware that the functional unit has completed execution, the scoreboard checks for WAR hazards. A WAR hazard exists if there is a code sequence like the following:

```
DIVF   F0,F2,F4
ADDF   F10,F0,F8
SUBF   F8,F8,F14
```

ADDF has a source operand F8, which is the same register as the destination of SUBF. But ADDF actually depends on an earlier instruction. The scoreboard will still stall the SUBF until ADDF reads its operands. In general, then, a completing instruction cannot be allowed to write its results when

- there is an instruction that has not read its operands,

- one of the operands is the same register as the result of the completing instruction, and

- the other operand was the result of an earlier instruction.

If this WAR hazard does not exist, or when it clears, the scoreboard tells the functional unit to store its result to the destination register. This step replaces the WB step in the simple DLX pipeline.

Based on its own data structure, the scoreboard controls the instruction progression from one step to the next by communicating with the functional units. But there is a small complication: There is only a limited number of source operands and result buses to the register file. The scoreboard must guarantee that the number of functional units allowed to proceed into steps 2 and 4 do not exceed the number of buses available. We will not go into further detail on this, other than to mention that the CDC 6600 solved this problem by grouping the 16 functional units together into four groups and supplying a set of buses, called *data trunks*, for each group. Only one unit in a group could read its operands or write its result during a clock.

Now let's look at the detailed data structure maintained by a DLX scoreboard with five functional units. Figure 6.32 (page 296) shows what the scoreboard's information looks like for a simple sequence of instructions:

```
LF      F6,34(R2)
LF      F2,45(R3)
MULTF   F0,F2,F4
SUBF    F8,F6,F2
DIVF    F10,F0,F6
ADDF    F6,F8,F2
```

There are three parts to the scoreboard:

1. Instruction status—Indicates which of the four steps the instruction is in.

2. Functional unit status—Indicates the state of the functional unit (FU). There are nine fields for each functional unit:

   Busy—Indicates whether the unit is busy or not

   Op—Operation to perform in the unit (e.g., add or subtract)

   Fi—Destination register

   Fj,Fk—Source-register numbers

   Qj,Qk—Number of the units producing source registers Fj, Fk

   Rj,Rk—Flags indicating when Fj, Fk are ready; fields are reset when new values are read so that the scoreboard knows that the source operand has been read (this is required to handle WAR hazards)

3. Register result status—Indicates which functional unit will write a register, if an active instruction has the register as its destination.

Instruction status				
Instruction	**Issue**	**Read operands**	**Execution complete**	**Write result**
LF F6,34(R2)	√	√	√	√
LF F2,45(R3)	√	√	√	
MULTF F0,F2,F4	√			
SUBF F8,F6,F2	√			
DIVF F10,F0,F6	√			
ADDF F6,F8,F2				

Functional unit status										
FU no.	**Name**	**Busy**	**Op**	**Fi**	**Fj**	**Fk**	**Qj**	**Qk**	**Rj**	**Rk**
1	Integer	Yes	Load	F2	R3				No	No
2	Mult1	Yes	Mult	F0	F2	F4	1		No	Yes
3	Mult2	No								
4	Add	Yes	Sub	F8	F6	F2		1	Yes	No
5	Divide	Yes	Div	F10	F0	F6	2		No	Yes

Register result status									
	F0	**F2**	**F4**	**F6**	**F8**	**F10**	**F12**	**...**	**F30**
FU no.	2	1			4	5			

FIGURE 6.32 Components of the scoreboard. Each instruction that has issued or is pending issue has an entry in the instruction-status table. There is one entry in the functional-unit–status table for each functional unit. Once an instruction issues, the record of its operands is kept in the functional-unit–status table. Finally, the register-result table indicates which unit will produce each pending result; the number of entries is equal to the number of registers. The instruction-status register says that (1) the first LF has completed and written its result, and (2) the second LF has completed execution but has not yet written its result. The MULTF, SUBF, and DIVF have all issued but are stalled, waiting for their operands. The functional-unit status says that the first multiply unit is waiting for the integer unit, the add unit is waiting for the integer unit, and the divide unit is waiting for the first multiply unit. The ADDF instruction is stalled due to a structural hazard; it will clear when the SUBF completes. If an entry in one of these scoreboard tables is not being used, it is left blank. For example, the Rk field is not used on a load, and the Mult2 unit is unused, hence its fields have no meaning. Also, once an operand has been read, the Rj and Rk fields are set to No. These are left blank to minimize the complexity of the tables.

Now let's look at how the code sequence begun in Figure 6.32 continues execution. After that, we will be able to examine in detail the conditions that the scoreboard uses to control execution.

Example	Assume the following EX cycle latencies for the floating-point functional units: Add is 2 clock cycles, multiply is 10 clock cycles, and divide is 40 clock cycles. Using the code segment in Figure 6.32, and beginning with the point indicated by the instruction status in Figure 6.32, show what the status tables look like when MULTF and DIVF are each ready to go to the write-result state.
Answer	There are RAW data hazards from the second LF to MULTF and SUBF, from MULTF to DIVF, and from SUBF to ADDF. There is a WAR data hazard between DIVF and ADDF. Finally, there is a structural hazard on the add functional unit for ADDF. What the tables look like when MULTF and DIVF are ready to go to write result are shown in Figures 6.33 and 6.34, respectively.

Instruction status				
Instruction	**Issue**	**Read operands**	**Execution complete**	**Write result**
LF F6,34(R2)	√	√	√	√
LF F2,45(R3)	√	√	√	√
MULTF F0,F2,F4	√	√	√	
SUBF F8,F6,F2	√	√	√	√
DIVF F10,F0,F6	√			
ADDF F6,F8,F2	√	√	√	

Functional unit status										
FU no.	**Name**	**Busy**	**Op**	**Fi**	**Fj**	**Fk**	**Qj**	**Qk**	**Rj**	**Rk**
1	Integer	No								
2	Mult1	Yes	Mult	F0	F2	F4			No	No
3	Mult2	No								
4	Add	Yes	Add	F6	F8	F2			No	No
5	Divide	Yes	Div	F10	F0	F6	2		No	Yes

Register result status									
	F0	**F2**	**F4**	**F6**	**F8**	**F10**	**F12**	**...**	**F30**
FU no.	2			4		5			

FIGURE 6.33 Scoreboard tables just before the MULTF goes to write result. The DIVF has not yet read its operands, since it has a dependence on the result of the multiply. The ADDF has read its operands and is in execution, although it was forced to wait until the SUBF finished to get the functional unit. ADDF cannot proceed to write result because of the WAR hazard on F6, which is used by the DIVF.

Instruction status				
Instruction	**Issue**	**Read operands**	**Execution complete**	**Write result**
LF F6,34(R2)	√	√	√	√
LF F2,45(R3)	√	√	√	√
MULTF F0,F2,F4	√	√	√	√
SUBF F8,F6,F2	√	√	√	√
DIVF F10,F0,F6	√	√	√	
ADDF F6,F8,F2	√	√	√	√

FU no.	Name	Busy	Op	Fi	Fj	Fk	Qj	Qk	Rj	Rk
							Functional unit status			
1	Integer	No								
2	Mult1	No								
3	Mult2	No								
4	Add	No								
5	Divide	Yes	Div	F10	F0	F6			No	No

Register Result status									
	F0	**F2**	**F4**	**F6**	**F8**	**F10**	**F12**	**...**	**F30**
FU no.						5			

FIGURE 6.34 Scoreboard tables just before the DIVF goes to write result. ADDF was able to complete as soon as DIVF passed through read operands and got a copy of F6. Only the DIVF remains to finish.

Instruction status	Wait until	Bookkeeping
Issue	Not busy (FU) and not result(D)	Busy(FU)← yes; Result(D)←FU; Op(FU)←*op*; Fi(FU)←D; Fj(FU)←S1; Fk(FU)←S2; Qj←Result(S1); Qk←Result(S2); Rj← not Qj; Rk← not Qk
Read operands	Rj and Rk	Rj←No; Rk←No
Execution complete	Functional unit done	
Write result	∀*f*((Fj(*f*)≠Fi(FU) or Rj(*f*)=No) & (Fk(*f*) ≠Fi(FU) or Rk(*f*)=No))	∀*f*(if Qj(*f*)=FU then Rj(*f*)←Yes); ∀*f*(if Qk(*f*)=FU then Rk(*f*)←Yes); Result(Fi(FU))←Clear; Busy(FU)←No

FIGURE 6.35 Required checks and bookkeeping actions for each step in instruction execution. FU stands for the functional unit used by the instruction, D is the destination register, S1 and S2 are the source registers, and *op* is the operation to be done. To access the scoreboard entry named F_j for functional unit FU we use the notation F_j(FU). Result(D) is the value of the result register field for register D. The test on the write-result case prevents the write when there is a WAR hazard. For simplicity we assume that all of the bookkeeping operations are done in one clock cycle.

Now we can see how the scoreboard works in detail by looking at what has to happen for the scoreboard to allow each instruction to proceed. Figure 6.35 shows what the scoreboard requires for each instruction to advance and the bookkeeping action necessary when the instruction does advance.

The costs and benefits of scoreboarding are an interesting question. The CDC 6600 designers measured a performance improvement of 1.7 for FORTRAN programs and 2.5 for hand-coded assembly language. However, this was measured in the days before software pipeline scheduling, semiconductor main memory, and caches (which lower memory-access time). The scoreboard on the CDC 6600 had about as much logic as one of the functional units, which is surprisingly low. The main cost was in the large number of buses—about four times as many as would be required if the machine only executed instructions in order (or if it only initiated one instruction per Execute cycle).

The scoreboard does not handle a few situations as well as it might. For example, when an instruction writes its result, a dependent instruction in the pipeline must wait for access to the register file because all results are written through the register file and never forwarded. This increases the latency and limits the ability of multiple instructions waiting for a result to initiate. WAW hazards would be very infrequent, so the stalls they cause are probably not a significant concern in the CDC 6600. However, in the next section we will see that dynamic scheduling offers the possibility of overlapping the execution of multiple iterations of a loop. To do this effectively requires a scheme for handling WAW hazards, which are likely to increase in frequency when multiple iterations are overlapped.

Another Dynamic Scheduling Approach— The Tomasulo Algorithm

Another approach to parallel execution around hazards was used by the IBM 360/91 floating-point unit. This scheme was credited to R. Tomasulo and is named after him. The IBM 360/91 was completed about three years after the CDC 6600, before caches appeared in commercial machines. IBM's goal was to achieve high floating-point performance from an instruction set and from compilers designed for the entire 360 computer family, rather than for only floating-point–intensive applications. Remember that the 360 architecture has only four double-precision floating-point registers, which limits the effectiveness of compiler scheduling; this fact was another motivation for the Tomasulo approach. Lastly, the IBM 360/91 had long memory accesses and long floating-point delays, which the Tomasulo algorithm was designed to overcome. At the end of the section, we will see that Tomasulo's algorithm can also support the overlapped execution of multiple iterations of a loop.

We will explain the algorithm, which focuses on the floating-point unit, in the context of a pipelined, floating-point unit for DLX. The primary difference between DLX and the 360 is the presence of register–memory instructions in the latter machine. Because Tomasulo's algorithm uses a load functional unit, no significant changes are needed to add register–memory addressing modes; the primary addition is another bus. The IBM 360/91 also had pipelined functional units, rather than multiple functional units. The only difference between these is that a pipelined unit can start at most one operation per clock cycle. Since there are really no fundamental differences, we describe the algorithm as if there were multiple functional units. The IBM 360/91 could accommodate three operations for the floating-point adder and two for the floating-point multiplier. In addition, up to six floating-point loads, or memory references, and up to three floating-point stores could be outstanding. Load data buffers and store data buffers are used for this function. Although we will not discuss the load and store units, we do need to include the buffers for operands.

Tomasulo's scheme shares many ideas with the CDC 6600 scoreboard, so we assume the reader has understood the scoreboard thoroughly. There are, however, two significant differences. First, hazard detection and execution control are distributed—*reservation stations* at each functional unit control when an instruction can begin execution at that unit. This function is centralized in the scoreboard on the CDC 6600. Second, results are passed directly to functional units rather than going through the registers. The IBM 360/91 has a common result bus (called the *common data bus,* or CDB) that allows all units waiting for an operand to be loaded simultaneously. The CDC 6600 writes results into registers, where waiting functional units may have to contend for them. Also, the CDC 6600 has multiple completion buses (two in the floating-point unit), while the IBM 360/91 has only one.

Figure 6.36 shows the basic structure of a Tomasulo-based floating-point unit for DLX; none of the execution control tables are shown. The reservation stations hold instructions that have been issued and are awaiting execution at a functional unit, as well as the information needed to control the instruction once it has begun execution to the unit. The load buffers and store buffers hold data coming from and going to memory. The floating-point registers are connected by a pair of buses to the functional units and by a single bus to the store buffers. All results from the functional units and from memory are sent on the common data bus, which goes everywhere except to the load buffer. All the buffers and reservation stations have tag fields, employed by hazard control.

Before we describe the details of the reservation stations and the algorithm, let's look at the steps an instruction goes through—just as we did for the scoreboard. Since operands are transmitted differently than in a scoreboard, there are only three steps:

1. Issue—Get an instruction from the floating-point operation queue. If the operation is a floating-point operation, issue it if there is an empty reservation station, and send the operands to the reservation station if they are in the registers. If the operation is a load or store, it can issue if there is an available buffer. If there is not an empty reservation station or an empty buffer, then there is a structural hazard and the instruction stalls until a station or buffer is freed.

2. Execute—If one or more of the operands is not yet available, monitor the CDB while waiting for the register to be computed. This step checks for RAW hazards. When both operands are available, execute the operation.

3. Write result—When the result is available, write it on the CDB and from there into the registers and any functional units waiting for this result.

Although these steps are fundamentally similar to those in the scoreboard, there are three important differences. First, there is no checking for WAW and WAR hazards—these are eliminated as a byproduct of the algorithm, as we will see shortly. Second, the CDB is used to broadcast results rather than waiting on the registers. Third, the loads and stores are treated as basic functional units.

The data structures used to detect and eliminate hazards are attached to the reservation stations, the register file, and the load and store buffers. Although different information is attached to different objects, everything except the load

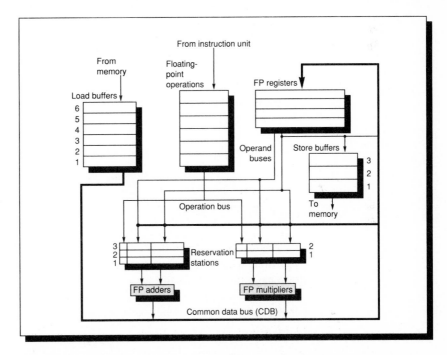

FIGURE 6.36 The basic structure of a DLX FP unit using Tomasulo's algorithm.
Floating-point operations are sent from the instruction unit into a queue (called the FLOS, or floating-point operation stack, in the IBM 360/91) when they are issued. The reservation stations include the operation and the actual operands, as well as information used for detecting and resolving hazards. There are load buffers to hold the results of outstanding loads and store buffers to hold the addresses of outstanding stores waiting for their operands. All results from either the FP units or the load unit are put on the common data bus (CDB), which goes to the FP register file as well as the reservation stations and store buffers. The FP adders implement addition and subtraction, while the FP multipliers do multiplication and division.

buffers contains a tag field per entry. The tag field is a four-bit quantity that denotes one of the five reservation stations or one of the six load buffers. The tag field is used to describe which functional unit will produce a result needed as a source operand. Unused values, such as zero, indicate that the operand is already available. In describing the information, the scoreboard names are used wherever this will not lead to confusion. The names used by the IBM 360/91 are also shown. It is important to remember that the tags in the Tomasulo scheme refer to the buffer or unit that will produce a result; the register number is discarded when an instruction issues to a reservation station.

Each reservation station has six fields:

Op—The operation to perform on source operands S1 and S2.

Qj,Qk—The reservation stations that will produce the corresponding source operand; a value of zero indicates that the source operand is already available in Vi or Vj, or is unnecessary. The IBM 360/91 calls these SINKunit and SOURCEunit.

Vj,Vk—The value of the source operands. These are called SINK and SOURCE on the IBM 360/91. Note that only one of the V field or the Q field is valid for each operand.

Busy—Indicates that this reservation station and its accompanying functional unit are occupied.

The register file and store buffer each have a field, Qi:

Qi—The number of the functional unit that will produce a value to be stored into this register or into memory. If the value of Qi is zero, no currently active instruction is computing a result destined for this register or buffer. For a register, this means the value is given by the register contents.

The load and store buffers each require a busy field, indicating when a buffer is available due to completion of a load or store assigned there. The store buffer also has a field V, the value to be stored.

Before we examine the algorithm in detail, let's see what the system of tables looks like for the following code sequence:

```
1.  LF      F6,34(R2)
2.  LF      F2,45(R3)
3.  MULTF   F0,F2,F4
4.  SUBF    F8,F6,F2
5.  DIVF    F10,F0,F6
6.  ADDF    F6,F8,F2
```

We saw what the scoreboard looked like for this program when only the first load had written its result. Figure 6.37 depicts the reservation stations, load and store buffers, and the register tags. The numbers appended to the names add, mult, and load stand for the tag for that reservation station—Add1 is the tag for the result from the first add unit. In addition we have included a central table called "Instruction status." This table is included only to help the reader understand the algorithm; it is **not** actually a part of the hardware. Instead, the state of each operation that has issued is kept in a reservation station.

There are two important differences from scoreboards that are observable in these tables. First, the value of an operand is stored in the reservation station in one of the V fields as soon as it is available; it is not read from the register file once the instruction has issued. Second, the ADDF instruction has issued. This was blocked in the scoreboard by a structural hazard.

Instruction status			
Instruction	**Issue**	**Execute**	**Write result**
LF F6,34(R2)	√	√	√
LF F2,45(R3)	√	√	
MULTF F0,F2,F4	√		
SUBF F8,F6,F2	√		
DIVF F10,F0,F6	√		
ADDF F6,F8,F2	√		

Reservation stations						
Name	**Busy**	**Op**	**Vj**	**Vk**	**Qj**	**Qk**
Add1	Yes	SUB	(Load1)			Load2
Add2	Yes	ADD			Add1	Load2
Add3	No					
Mult1	Yes	MULT		(F4)	Load2	
Mult2	Yes	DIV		(Load1)	Mult1	

Register status									
Field	**F0**	**F2**	**F4**	**F6**	**F8**	**F10**	**F12**	**...**	**F30**
Qi	Mult1	Load2		Add2	Add1	Mult2			
Busy	Yes	Yes	No	Yes	Yes	Yes	No	...	No

FIGURE 6.37 Reservation stations and register tags. All of the instructions have issued, but only the first load instruction has completed and written its result to the CDB. The instruction-status table is not actually present, but the equivalent information is distributed throughout the hardware. The notation (X), where X is either a register number or a functional unit, indicates that this field contains the result of the functional unit X or the contents of register X at the time of issue. The other instructions are all at reservation stations or, as in the case of instruction 2, completing a memory reference. The load and store buffers are not shown. Load buffer 2 is the only busy load buffer and it is performing on behalf of instruction 2 in the sequence—loading from memory address R3 + 45. There are no stores, so the store buffer is not shown. Remember that an operand is specified by either the Q field or the V field at any time.

The big advantages of the Tomasulo scheme are (1) the distribution of the hazard detection logic, and (2) the elimination of stalls for WAW and WAR hazards. The first advantage arises from the distributed reservation stations and the use of the CDB. If multiple instructions are waiting on a single result, and each instruction already has its other operand, then the instructions can be released simultaneously by the broadcast on the CDB. In the scoreboard the waiting instructions must all read their results from the registers when register buses are available.

WAW and WAR hazards are eliminated by renaming registers using the reservation stations. For example, in our code sequence in Figure 6.37 we have issued both the DIVF and the ADDF, even though there is a WAR hazard involving F6. The hazard is eliminated in one of two ways. If the instruction providing the value for the DIVF has completed, then Vk will store the result, allowing DIVF to execute independent of the ADDF (this is the case shown). On the other hand, if the LF had not completed, then Qk would point to the Load1 and the DIVF instruction would be independent of the ADDF. Thus, in either case, the ADDF can issue and begin executing. Any uses of the result of the MULTF would point to the reservation station, allowing the ADDF to complete and store its value into the registers without affecting the DIVF. We'll see an example of the elimination of a WAW hazard shortly. But let's first look at how our earlier example continues execution.

Example

Assume the same latencies for the floating-point functional units as we did for Figure 6.34: Add is 2 clock cycles, multiply is 10 clock cycles, and divide is 40 clock cycles. With the same code segment, show what the status tables look like when the MULTF is ready to go to write result.

Answer

The result is shown in the three tables in Figure 6.38. Unlike the example with the scoreboard, ADDF has completed since the operands of DIVF are copied, thereby overcoming the WAR hazard.

Instruction status			
Instruction	**Issue**	**Execute**	**Write result**
LF F6,34(R2)	√	√	√
LF F2,45(R3)	√	√	√
MULTF F0,F2,F4	√	√	
SUBF F8,F6,F2	√	√	√
DIVF F10,F0,F6	√		
ADDF F6,F8,F2	√	√	√

Reservation stations						
Name	**Busy**	**Op**	**Vj**	**Vk**	**Qj**	**Qk**
Add1	No					
Add2	No					
Add3	No					
Mult1	Yes	MULT	(Load2)	(F4)		
Mult2	Yes	DIV		(Load1)	Mult1	

Register status									
Field	**F0**	**F2**	**F4**	**F6**	**F8**	**F10**	**F12**	**...**	**F30**
Qi	Mult1					Mult2			
Busy	Yes	No	No	No	No	Yes	No	...	No

FIGURE 6.38 Multiply and divide are the only instructions not finished. This is different from the scoreboard case, because the elimination of WAR hazards allowed the ADDF to finish right after the SUBF on which it depended.

Figure 6.39 gives the steps for each instruction to go through. Load and stores are only slightly special. A load can be executed as soon as it is available. When execution is completed and the CDB is available, a load puts its result on the CDB like any functional unit. Stores receive their values from the CDB or from the register file and execute autonomously; when they are done they turn the busy field off to indicate availability, just like a load buffer or reservation station.

Instruction status	Wait until	Action or bookkeeping

Issue	Station or buffer empty	```if (Register[S1].Qi ≠0)```
		    ```{RS[r].Qj← Register[S1].Qi}```
		```else {RS[r].Vj← S1; RS[r].Qj← 0};```
		```if (Register[S2].Qi≠0)```
		```{RS[r].Qk← Register[S2].Qi};```
		```else {RS[r].Vk← S2; RS[r].Qk← 0}```
		```RS[r].Busy←yes;```
		```Register[D].Qi=r;```

Execute	(RS[r].Qj=0) and (RS[r].Qk=0)	None—operands are in Vj and Vk

Write result	Execution completed at r and CDB available	$\forall x$(if ```(Register[x].Qi=r)``` ```{Fx← result;```
		    ```Register[x].Qi← 0});```
		$\forall x$(if ```(RS[x].Qj=r) {RS[x].Vj← result;```
		    ```RS[x].Qj ← 0});```
		$\forall x$(if ```(RS[x].Qk=r) {RS[x].Vk← result;```
		    ```RS[x].Qk ← 0});```
		$\forall x$(if ```(Store[x].Qi=r) {Store[x].V← result;```
		    ```Store[x].Qi ← 0});```
		```RS[r].Busy←No```

FIGURE 6.39 Steps in the algorithm and what is required for each step. For the issuing instruction, D is the destination, S1 and S2 are the sources, and r is the reservation station or buffer that D is assigned to. RS is the reservation-station data structure. The value returned by a reservation station or by the load unit is called the "result." Register is the register data structure, while Store is the store-buffer data structure. When an instruction is issued, the destination register has its Qi field set to the number of the buffer or reservation station to which the instruction is issued. If the operands are available in the registers, they are stored in the V fields. Otherwise, the Q fields are set to indicate the reservation station that will produce the values needed as source operands. The instruction waits at the reservation station until both its operands are available, indicated by zero in the Q fields. The Q fields are set to zero either when this instruction is issued, or when an instruction on which this instruction depends completes and does its write back. When an instruction has finished execution and the CDB is available, it can do its write back. All the buffers, registers, and reservation stations whose value of Qj or Qk is the same as the completing reservation station update their values from the CDB and mark the Q fields to indicate that values have been received. Thus, the CDB can broadcast its result to many destinations in a single clock cycle, and if the waiting instructions have their operands, they can all begin execution on the next clock cycle. For simplicity we assume that all bookkeeping actions are done in a single cycle.

To understand the full power of eliminating WAW and WAR hazards through dynamic renaming of registers, we must look at a loop. Consider the following simple sequence for multiplying the elements of a vector by a scalar in F2:

```
Loop:   LD     F0,0(R1)
        MULTD  F4,F0,F2
        SD     0(R1),F4
        SUB    R1,R1,#8
        BNEZ   R1,Loop   ; branches if R1≠0
```

With a branch-taken strategy, using reservation stations will allow multiple executions of this loop to proceed at once. This advantage is gained without unrolling the loop—in effect, the loop is unrolled dynamically by the hardware. In the 360 architecture, the presence of only 4 FP registers would severely limit the use of unrolling. (We will see shortly, when we unroll a loop and schedule it to avoid interlocks, many more registers are required.) Tomasulo's algorithm supports the overlapped execution of multiple copies of the same loop with only a small number of registers used by the program.

Let's assume we have issued all the instructions in two successive iterations of the loop, but none of the floating-point loads/stores or operations has completed. The reservation stations, register-status tables, and load and store buffers at this point are shown in Figure 6.40. (The integer ALU operation is ignored, and it is assumed the branch was predicted as taken.) Once the system reaches this state, two copies of the loop could be sustained with a CPI close to one provided the multiplies could complete in four clock cycles. We will see how compiler techniques can achieve a similar result in Section 6.8.

An additional element that is critical to making Tomasulo's algorithm work is shown in this example. The load instruction from the second loop iteration could easily complete before the store from the first iteration, although the normal sequential order is different. The load and store can safely be done in a different order, provided the load and store access different addresses. This is checked by examining the addresses in the store buffer whenever a load is issued. If the load address matches the store-buffer address, we must stop and wait until the store buffer gets a value; we can then access it or get the value from memory.

This scheme can yield very high performance, provided the cost of branches can be kept small—this is a problem we will look at later in this section. There are also limitations imposed by the complexity of the Tomasulo scheme, which requires a large amount of hardware. In particular, there are many associative stores that must run at high speed, as well as complex control logic. Lastly, the performance gain is limited by the single completion bus (CDB). While additional CDBs can be added, each CDB must interact with all the pipeline hardware, including the reservation stations. In particular, the associative tag-matching hardware would need to be duplicated at all stations for each CDB.

While Tomasulo's scheme may be appealing if the designer is forced to pipeline an architecture that is difficult to schedule code for or has a shortage of registers, the authors believe that the advantages of the Tomasulo approach are limited for architectures that can be efficiently pipelined and statically scheduled with software. However, as available gate counts grow and the limits of software scheduling are reached, we may see dynamic scheduling employed. One possible direction is a hybrid organization that uses dynamic scheduling for loads and stores, while statically scheduling register–register operations.

Reducing Branch Penalties with Dynamic Hardware Prediction

The previous section describes techniques for overcoming data hazards. If control hazards are not addressed, Amdahl's Law predicts, they will limit pipelined-execution performance. Earlier, we looked at simple hardware schemes for

Instruction status				
Instruction	**From iteration**	**Issue**	**Execute**	**Write result**
LD F0,0(R1)	1	√	√	
MULTD F4,F0,F2	1	√		
SD 0(R1),F4	1	√		
LD F0,0(R1)	2	√	√	
MULTD F4,F0,F2	2	√		
SD 0(R1),F4	2	√		

Reservation stations						
Name	**Busy**	**Fm**	**Vj**	**Vk**	**Qj**	**Qk**
Add1	No					
Add2	No					
Add3	No					
Mult1	Yes	MULT		(F2)	Load1	
Mult2	Yes	MULT		(F2)	Load2	

Register status									
Field	**F0**	**F2**	**F4**	**F6**	**F8**	**F10**	**F12**	**...**	**F30**
Qi	Load2		Mult2						
Busy	yes	no	yes	no	no	no			

Store buffers			
Field	**Store 1**	**Store 2**	**Store 3**
Qi	Mult1	Mult2	
Busy	Yes	Yes	No
Address	(R1)	(R1)–8	

Load buffers			
Field	**Load 1**	**Load 2**	**Load 3**
Address	(R1)	(R1)–8	
Busy	Yes	Yes	No

FIGURE 6.40 Two active iterations of the loop with no instruction having yet completed. Load and store buffers are included, with addresses to be loaded from and stored to. The loads are in the load buffer; entries in the multiplier reservation stations indicate that the outstanding loads are the sources. The store buffers indicate that the multiply destination is their value to store.

dealing with branches (assume taken or not taken) and software-oriented approaches (delayed branches). This section focuses on using hardware to dynamically predict the outcome of a branch—the prediction will change if the branch changes its behavior while the program is running.

The simplest dynamic branch-prediction scheme is a *branch-prediction buffer*. A branch-prediction buffer is a small memory indexed by the lower portion of the branch instruction address. The memory contains a bit that says whether the branch was recently taken or not. This is the simplest sort of buffer; it has no tags and is useful only to reduce the branch delay when it is longer than the time to compute the possible target PCs. We don't know, in fact, if the prediction is correct—it may have been put there by another branch that has the same low-order address bits. But this doesn't matter. It is assumed to be correct, and fetching begins in the predicted direction. If the branch prediction turns out to be wrong, the prediction bit is inverted.

This simple one-bit prediction scheme has a performance shortcoming: If a branch is almost always taken, then when it is not taken, we will predict incorrectly twice, rather than once. Consider a loop branch whose behavior is taken nine times sequentially, then not taken once. If the next time around it is predicted not taken, the prediction will be wrong. Thus, the prediction accuracy will only be 80%, even on branches that are 90% taken. To remedy this, two-bit prediction schemes are often used. In a two-bit scheme, a prediction must miss twice in a row before it is changed. Figure 6.41 shows the finite-state machine for the two-bit prediction scheme.

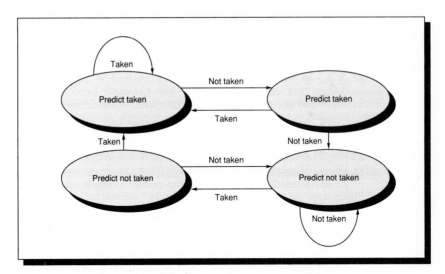

FIGURE 6.41 This shows the states in a two-bit prediction scheme. By using two bits rather than one, a branch that strongly favors taken or not taken—as many branches do—will be mispredicted only once. The two bits are used to encode the four states in the system.

The branch-prediction buffer can be implemented as a small, special cache accessed with the instruction address during the IF pipe stage, or as a pair of bits attached to each block in the instruction cache and fetched with the instruction (see Section 8.3 in Chapter 8). If the instruction is predicted as a branch and if the branch is predicted as taken, fetching begins from the target as soon as the

PC is known. Otherwise, fetching and sequential executing continue. If the prediction turns out to be wrong, the prediction bits are changed as shown in Figure 6.41. While this scheme is useful for most pipelines, the DLX pipeline finds out both whether the branch is taken and what the target of the branch is at the same time. Thus, this scheme does not help for the simple DLX pipeline; we will explore a scheme that can work for DLX a little later. First, let's see how well a prediction buffer works with a longer pipeline.

The accuracy of a two-bit prediction scheme is affected by how often the prediction for each branch is correct and by how often the entry in the prediction buffer matches the branch being executed. When the entry does not match, the prediction bit is used anyway because no better information is available. Even if the entry was for another branch, the guess could be a lucky one. In fact, there is about a 50% probability of being correct, even if the prediction is for some other branch. Studies of branch-prediction schemes have found that two-bit prediction has an accuracy of about 90% when the entry in the buffer is the branch entry. A buffer of between 500 and 1000 entries has a hit rate of 90%. The overall prediction accuracy is given by

Accuracy = (% predicted correctly ∗ % that prediction is for this instruction) +

(% lucky guess) ∗ (1–% that prediction is for this instruction)

Accuracy = (90% ∗ 90%) + (50% ∗ 10%) = 86%

This number is higher than our success rate for filling delayed branches and would be useful in a pipeline with a longer branch delay. Now let's look at a dynamic prediction scheme that is useable for DLX and see how it compares to our branch-delay scheme.

To reduce the branch penalty on DLX, we need to know from what address to fetch by the end of IF. This means we must know whether the as yet undecoded instruction is a branch and, if it is a branch, what the next PC should be. If the instruction is a branch and we know what the next PC should be, we can have a branch penalty of zero. A branch-prediction cache that stores the predicted address for the next instruction after a branch is called a *branch-target buffer*. Because we are predicting the next instruction address and will send it out **before** decoding the instruction, we **must** know whether the fetched instruction is predicted as a taken branch. We also want to know whether the address in the target buffer is for a taken or not-taken prediction, so that we can reduce the time to find a mispredicted branch. Figure 6.42 shows what the branch-target buffer looks like. If the PC of the fetched instruction matches a PC in the buffer, then the corresponding predicted PC is used as the next PC. In Chapter 8 we will discuss caches in much more detail; we will see that the hardware for this branch-target buffer is similar to the hardware for a cache.

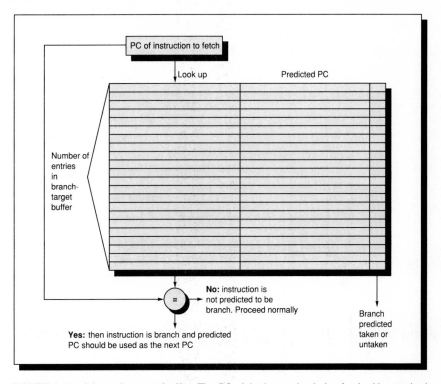

FIGURE 6.42   A branch-target buffer. The PC of the instruction being fetched is matched against a set of instruction addresses stored in the first column; these represent the addresses of known branches. If the PC matches one of these entries, then the instruction being fetched is a branch. If it is a branch, then the second field, predicted PC, contains the prediction for the next PC after the branch. Fetching begins immediately at that address. The third field just tracks whether the branch was predicted taken or untaken and helps keep the misprediction penalty small.

If a matching entry is found in the branch-target buffer, fetching begins immediately at the predicted PC. Note that (unlike a branch-prediction buffer) the entry must be for this instruction, because the predicted PC will be sent out before it is known whether this instruction is even a branch. If we did not check whether the entry matched this PC, then the wrong PC would be sent out for instructions that were not branches, resulting in a slower machine. Figure 6.43 shows the steps followed when using a branch-target buffer and when these steps occur in the pipeline. From this we can see that there will be no branch delay if a branch-prediction entry is found in the buffer and is correct. Otherwise, there will be a penalty of at least one clock cycle. In practice, there could be a penalty of two clock cycles because the branch-target buffer must be updated. We could assume that the instruction following a branch or at the branch target is not a branch, and do the update during that instruction time. However, this does complicate the control. Instead, we will take a two-clock-cycle penalty when the branch is not correctly predicted.

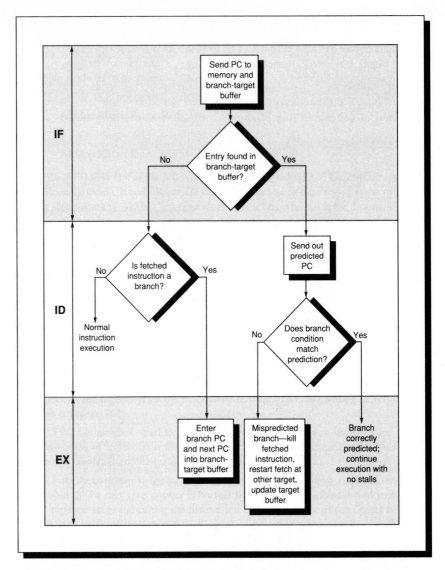

FIGURE 6.43 The steps involved in handling an instruction with a branch-target buffer. If the PC of an instruction is found in the buffer, then the instruction must be a branch, and fetching immediately begins from the predicted PC in ID. If the entry is not found and it subsequently turns out to be a branch, it is entered in the buffer along with the target, which is known at the end of ID. If the instruction is a branch, is found, and is correctly predicted, then execution proceeds with no delays. If the prediction is incorrect, we suffer a one-clock-cycle delay fetching the wrong instruction and restart the fetch one clock cycle later. If the branch is not found in the buffer and the instruction turns out to be a branch, we will have proceeded as if the instruction were a branch and can turn this into an assume-not-taken strategy; the penalty will differ depending on whether the branch is actually taken or not.

To evaluate how well a branch-target buffer works, we first must determine what the penalties are in all possible cases. Figure 6.44 contains this information.

Instruction in buffer	Prediction	Actual branch	Penalty cycles
Yes	Taken	Taken	0
Yes	Taken	Not taken	2
Yes	Not taken	Not taken	0
Yes	Not taken	Taken	2
No		Taken	2
No		Not taken	1

FIGURE 6.44 Penalties for all possible combinations of whether the branch is in the buffer, how it is predicted, and what it actually does. There is no branch penalty if everything is correctly predicted and the branch is found in the target buffer. If the branch is not correctly predicted, the penalty is equal to one clock cycle to update the buffer with the correct information (during which an instruction cannot be fetched) and one clock cycle, if needed, to restart fetching the next correct instruction for the branch. If the branch is not found and not taken, the penalty is only one clock cycle because the pipeline assumes not taken when it is not aware that the instruction is a branch. Other mismatches cost two clock cycles, since we must restart the fetch and update the buffer.

Using the same probabilities as for a branch-prediction buffer—90% probability of finding the entry and 90% probability of correct prediction—and the taken/not taken percentage taken from earlier in this chapter, we can find the total branch penalty:

Branch penalty = % branches found in buffer * % incorrect predictions * 2 +
(1–% branches found in buffer) * % taken branches * 2 +
(1–% branches found in buffer) * % untaken branches * 1

Branch penalty = 90% * 10% * 2 + 10% * 60% * 2 + 10% * 40% * 1

Branch penalty = 0.34 clock cycles

This compares with a branch penalty for delayed branches of about 0.5 clock cycles per branch. Remember, though, that the improvement from dynamic branch prediction will grow as the branch delay grows.

Branch-prediction schemes are limited both by prediction accuracy and by the penalty for misprediction. It is unlikely that we can improve the effective branch-prediction success much above 80% to 90%. Instead, we can try to reduce the penalty for misprediction. This is done by fetching from both the predicted and unpredicted direction. This requires that the memory system be dual ported or have an interleaved cache. While this adds cost to the system, it may be the only way to reduce branch penalties below a certain point.

We have seen a variety of software-based static schemes and hardware-based dynamic schemes for trying to boost the performance of our pipelined machine. Pipelining tries to exploit the potential for parallelism among sequential instructions. In the ideal case all the instructions would be independent, and our DLX pipeline would exploit parallelism among the five instructions simultaneously in the pipeline. Both the static scheduling techniques of the last section and the dynamic techniques of this section focus on maintaining the throughput of the pipeline at one instruction per clock. In the next section we will look at techniques that attempt to exploit overlap more than by the factor of 5, to which we are restricted with the simple DLX pipeline.

6.8 | Advanced Pipelining—Taking Advantage of More Instruction-Level Parallelism

To improve performance further we would like to decrease the CPI to less than one. But the CPI cannot be reduced below one if we issue only one instruction every clock cycle. The goal of the techniques discussed in this section is to allow multiple instructions to issue in a clock cycle.

As we know from earlier sections, to keep a pipeline full, parallelism among instructions must be exploited by finding sequences of unrelated instructions that can be overlapped in the pipeline. Two related instructions must be separated by a distance equal to the pipeline latency of the first of the instructions. Throughout this section we will assume the latencies shown in Figure 6.45. Branches still have a one-clock-cycle delay. We assume that the functional units are fully pipelined or replicated, and that an operation can be issued on every clock cycle.

As we try to execute more instructions on every clock cycle and try to overlap more instructions, we will need to find and exploit more instruction-level parallelism. Thus, before looking at pipeline organizations that require more parallelism among instructions, let's look at a simple compiler technique that will help create additional parallelism.

Instruction producing result	Destination instruction	Latency in clocks
FP ALU op	Another FP ALU op	3
FP ALU op	Store double	2
Load double	FP ALU op	1
Load double	Store double	0

FIGURE 6.45   Latencies of operations used in this section. The first column shows the originating instruction type. The second column is the type of the consuming instruction. The last column is the separation in clock cycles to avoid a stall. These numbers are similar to the average latencies we would see on an FP unit, like the one we described for DLX in Figure 6.29 (page 289).

Increasing Instruction-Level Parallelism with Loop Unrolling

To compare the approaches discussed in this section, we will use a simple loop that adds a scalar value to a vector in memory. The DLX code, not accounting for the pipeline, looks like this:

```
Loop:  LD    F0,0(R1)     ; load the vector element
       ADDD  F4,F0,F2     ; add the scalar in F2
       SD    0(R1),F4     ; store the vector element
       SUB   R1,R1,#8     ; decrement the pointer by
                          ; 8 bytes (per DW)
       BNEZ  R1,LOOP      ; branch when it's zero
```

For simplicity, we assume the array starts at location 0. If it were located elsewhere, the loop would require one additional integer instruction.

Let's start by seeing how well this loop will run when it is scheduled on a simple pipeline for DLX with the latencies discussed above.

Example

Show how the vector add loop would look on DLX, both scheduled and unscheduled, including any stalls or idle clock cycles.

Answer

Without any scheduling the loop will execute as follows:

```
                               Clock cycle issued
Loop:  LD    F0,0(R1)                 1
       stall                          2
       ADDD  F4,F0,F2                 3
       stall                          4
       stall                          5
       SD    0(R1),F4                 6
       SUB   R1,R1,#8                 7
       BNEZ  R1,LOOP                  8
       stall                          9
```

This requires 9 clock cycles per iteration. We can schedule the loop to obtain

```
Loop:  LD    F0,0(R1)
       stall
       ADDD  F4,F0,F2
       SUB   R1,R1,#8
       BNEZ  R1,LOOP      ; delayed branch
       SD    8(R1),F4     ; changed because interchanged with SUB
```

Execution time has been reduced from 9 clock cycles to 6.

Notice that to create this schedule, the compiler had to determine that it could swap the SUB and SD by changing the address the SD stored to: The address was 0(R1) and is now 8(R1). This is not trivial, since most compilers would see that the SD instruction depends on the SUB and would refuse to interchange them. A smarter compiler could figure out the relationship and perform the interchange. The dependence among the LD, ADDD, and SD determines the clock cycle count for this loop.

In the above example, we complete one loop iteration and finish one vector element every 6 clock cycles, but the actual work of operating on the vector element takes just 3 of those 6 clock cycles. The remaining 3 clock cycles consist of loop overhead—the SUB and BNEZ—and a stall. To eliminate these 3 clock cycles we need to get more operations within the loop. A simple scheme for increasing the number of instructions between executions of the loop branch is *loop unrolling*. This is done by simply replicating the loop body multiple times, adjusting the loop termination code, and then scheduling the unrolled loop. To allow effective scheduling of the loop, we will want to use different registers for each iteration, thus increasing the register count.

Example

Show what our loop looks like unrolled three times (yielding four copies of the loop body), assuming R1 is initially a multiple of 4. Eliminate any obviously redundant computations, and do not reuse any of the registers.

Answer

Here is the result after dropping the unnecessary SUB and BNEZ operations duplicated during unrolling.

```
Loop:   LD      F0,0(R1)
        ADDD    F4,F0,F2
        SD      0(R1),F4  ;drop SUB & BNEZ
        LD      F6,-8(R1)
        ADDD    F8,F6,F2
        SD      -8(R1),F8  ;drop SUB & BNEZ
        LD      F10,-16(R1)
        ADDD    F12,F10,F2
        SD      -16(R1),F12  ;drop SUB & BNEZ
        LD      F14,-24(R1)
        ADDD    F16,F14,F2
        SD      -24(R1),F16
        SUB     R1,R1,#32
        BNEZ    R1,LOOP
```

We have eliminated three branches and three decrements of R1. The addresses on the loads and stores have been compensated for. Without scheduling, every operation is followed by a dependent operation, and thus will cause a stall. This loop will run in 27 clock cycles—each LD takes 2 clock cycles, each ADDD 3, the branch 2, and all other instructions 1—or 6.8 clock cycles for each of the four elements.

Although this unrolled version is currently slower than the scheduled version of the original loop, this will change when we schedule the unrolled loop. Loop unrolling is normally done early in the compilation process, so that redundant computations can be exposed and eliminated by the optimizer.

In real programs we do not normally know the upper bound on the loop. Suppose it is n, and we would like to unroll the loop k times. Instead of a single unrolled loop, we generate a pair of loops. The first executes (n mod k) times and has a body that is the original loop. The unrolled version of the loop is surrounded by an outer loop that iterates (n div k) times. In the above example, unrolling improves the performance of this loop by eliminating overhead instructions, though it increases code size substantially. What will happen to the performance increase when the loop is scheduled on DLX?

Example

Show the unrolled loop in the previous example after it has been scheduled on DLX.

Answer

```
Loop:   LD      F0,0(R1)
        LD      F6,-8(R1)
        LD      F10,-16(R1)
        LD      F14,-24(R1)
        ADDD    F4,F0,F2
        ADDD    F8,F6,F2
        ADDD    F12,F10,F2
        ADDD    F16,F14,F2
        SD      0(R1),F4
        SD      -8(R1),F8
        SD      -16(R1),F12
        SUB     R1,R1,#32    ;branch dependence
        BNEZ    R1,LOOP
        SD      -24(R1),F16 ; 8-32 = -24
```

The execution time of the unrolled loop has dropped to a total of 14 clock cycles, or 3.5 clock cycles per element, compared to 6.8 per element before scheduling.

The gain from scheduling on the unrolled loop is even larger than on the original loop. This is because unrolling the loop exposes more computation that can be scheduled. Scheduling the loop in this fashion necessitates realizing that the loads and stores are independent and can be interchanged.

Loop unrolling is a simple but useful method for increasing the size of straightline code fragments that can be scheduled effectively. This compile-time transformation is similar to what Tomasulo's algorithm does with register renaming and out-of-order execution. As we will see, this is very important in attempts to lower the CPI by issuing instructions at a high rate.

A Superscalar Version of DLX

One method of decreasing the CPI of DLX is to **issue** more than one instruction per clock cycle. This would allow the instruction-execution rate to exceed the clock rate. Machines that issue multiple independent instructions per clock cycle when they are properly scheduled by the compiler have been called *superscalar machines*. In a superscalar machine, the hardware can issue a small number (say 2 to 4) of independent instructions in a single clock. However, if the instructions in the instruction stream are dependent or don't meet certain criteria, only the first instruction in sequence will be issued. A machine where the compiler has complete responsibility for creating a package of instructions that can be simultaneously issued, and the hardware does not dynamically make any decisions about multiple issue, should probably be regarded as a type of VLIW (very long instruction word), which we discuss in the next section.

What would the DLX machine look like as a superscalar? Let's assume two instructions issued per clock cycle. One of the instructions could be a load, store, branch, or integer ALU operation, and the other could be any floating-point operation. As we will see, issue of an integer operation in parallel with a floating-point operation is much simpler and less demanding than arbitrary dual issue.

Issuing two instructions per cycle will require fetching and decoding 64 bits of instructions. To keep the decoding simple, we could require that the instructions be paired and aligned on a 64-bit boundary, with the integer portion appearing first. Figure 6.46 shows how the instructions look as they go into the pipeline in pairs. This table does not address how the floating-point operations extend the EX cycle, but it is no different in the superscalar case than it was for the ordinary DLX pipeline; the concepts of Section 6.6 apply directly. With this pipeline, we have substantially boosted the rate at which we can issue floating-point instructions. To make this worthwhile, however, we need either pipelined floating-point units or multiple independent units. Otherwise, floating-point instructions can only be fetched, and not issued, since all the floating units will be busy.

Instruction type	Pipe	Stages							
Integer instruction	IF	ID	EX	MEM	WB				
FP instruction	IF	ID	EX	MEM	WB				
Integer instruction		IF	ID	EX	MEM	WB			
FP instruction		IF	ID	EX	MEM	WB			
Integer instruction			IF	ID	EX	MEM	WB		
FP instruction			IF	ID	EX	MEM	WB		
Integer instruction				IF	ID	EX	MEM	WB	
FP instruction				IF	ID	EX	MEM	WB	

FIGURE 6.46 Superscalar pipeline in operation. The integer and floating-point instructions are issued at the same time, and each executes at its own pace through the pipeline. This scheme will only improve the performance of programs with a fair amount of floating point.

By issuing an integer and a floating-point operation in parallel, the need for additional hardware is minimized—integer and floating-point operations use different register sets and different functional units. The only conflict arises when the integer instruction is a floating-point load, store, or move. This creates contention for the floating-point register ports and may also create a hazard if the floating-point operation uses the result of a floating-point load issued at the same time. Both problems could be solved by detecting this contention as a structural hazard and delaying the issue of the floating-point instruction. The contention could also be eliminated by providing two additional ports, a read and a write, on the floating-point register file. We would also need to add several additional bypass paths to avoid performance loss.

There is another difficulty that may limit the effectiveness of a superscalar pipeline. In our simple DLX pipeline, loads had a latency of one clock cycle; this prevented one instruction from using the result without stalling. In the superscalar pipeline, the result of a load instruction cannot be used on the same clock cycle or on the next clock cycle. This means that the next three instructions cannot use the load result without stalling; without extra ports, moves between the register sets are similarly affected. The branch delay also becomes three instructions. To effectively exploit the parallelism available in a superscalar machine, more ambitious compiler-scheduling techniques, as well as more complex instruction decoding, will need to be implemented. Loop unrolling helps generate larger straightline fragments for scheduling; more powerful compiler techniques are discussed near the end of this section.

Let's see how well loop unrolling and scheduling work on a superscalar version of DLX with the same delays in clock cycles.

Example

How would the unrolled loop on page 317 be scheduled on a superscalar pipeline for DLX? To schedule it without any delays, we will need to unroll it to make five copies of the body.

Answer

The resulting code is shown in Figure 6.47.

	Integer instruction	FP instruction	Clock cycle
Loop:	LD F0,0(R1)		1
	LD F6,-8(R1)		2
	LD F10,-16(R1)	ADDD F4,F0,F2	3
	LD F14,-24(R1)	ADDD F8,F6,F2	4
	LD F18,-32(R1)	ADDD F12,F10,F2	5
	SD 0(R1),F4	ADDD F16,F14,F2	6
	SD -8(R1),F8	ADDD F20,F18,F2	7
	SD -16(R1),F12		8
	SD -24(R1),F16		9
	SUB R1,R1,#40		10
	BNEZ R1,LOOP		11
	SD 8(R1),F20		12

FIGURE 6.47 The unrolled and scheduled code as it would look on a superscalar DLX.

This unrolled superscalar loop now runs in 12 clock cycles per iteration, or 2.4 clock cycles per element, versus 3.5 for the scheduled and unrolled loop on the ordinary DLX pipeline. In this example, the performance of the superscalar DLX is limited by the balance between integer and floating-point computation. Every floating-point instruction is issued together with an integer instruction, but there are not enough floating-point instructions to keep the floating-point pipeline full. When scheduled, the original loop ran in 6 clock cycles per iteration. We have improved on that by a factor of 2.5, more than half of which came from loop unrolling, which took us from 6 to 3.5, with the rest coming from issuing more than one instruction per clock cycle.

Ideally, our superscalar machine will pick up two instructions and issue them both if the first is an integer and the second is a floating-point instruction. If they do not fit this pattern, which can be quickly detected, then they are issued sequentially. This points to one of the major advantages of a general superscalar machine: There is little impact on code density, and even unscheduled programs can be run. The number of issues and classes of instructions that can be issued together are the major factors that differentiate superscalar processors.

Multiple Instruction Issue with Dynamic Scheduling

Multiple instruction issue can also be applied to dynamically scheduled machines. We could start with either the scoreboard scheme or Tomasulo's algorithm. Let's assume we want to extend Tomasulo's algorithm to support issuing two instructions per clock cycle, one integer and one floating point. We do not want to issue instructions in the queue out of order, since this makes the bookkeeping in the register file impossible. Rather, by employing data structures for the integer and floating-point registers, both types of instructions can be issued to their respective reservation stations, as long as the two instructions at the head of the instruction queue do not access the same register set. Unfortunately, this approach bars issuing two instructions with a dependence in the same clock cycle. This is, of course, true in the superscalar case, where it is clearly the compiler's problem. There are three approaches that can be used to achieve dual issue. First, we could use software scheduling to ensure that dependent instructions do not appear adjacent. However, this would require pipeline-scheduling software, thereby defeating one of the advantages of dynamically scheduled pipelines.

A second approach is to pipeline the instruction-issue stage so that it runs twice as fast as the basic clock rate. This permits updating the tables before processing the next instruction; then the two instructions can begin execution at once.

The third approach is based on the observation that if multiple instructions are not being issued to the same functional unit, then it will only be loads and stores that will create dependences among instructions that we wish to issue together. The need for reservation tables for loads and stores can be eliminated by using queues for the result of a load and for the source operand of a store. Since dynamic scheduling is most effective for loads and stores, while static scheduling is highly effective in register–register code sequences, we could use static scheduling to eliminate reservation stations completely and rely only on the queues for loads and stores. This style of machine organization has been called a *decoupled architecture*.

For simplicity, let us assume that we have pipelined the instruction issue logic so that we can issue two operations that are dependent but use different functional units. Let's see how this would work with our example.

Example

Consider the execution of our simple loop on a DLX pipeline extended with Tomasulo's algorithm and with multiple issue. Assume that both a floating-point and an integer operation can be issued on every clock cycle, even if they are related. The number of cycles of latency per instruction is the same. Assume that issue and write results take one cycle each, and that there is dynamic branch-prediction hardware. Create a table showing when each instruction issues, begins execution, and writes its result, for the first two iterations of the loop. Here is the original loop:

```
Loop:    LD    F0,0(R1)
         ADDD  F4,F0,F2
         SD    0(R1),F4
         SUB   R1,R1,#8
         BNEZ  R1,LOOP
```

Answer   The loop will be dynamically unwound and, whenever possible, instructions will be issued in pairs. The result is shown in Figure 6.48. The loop runs in $4 + \dfrac{7}{n}$ clock cycles per result for n iterations. For large n this approaches 4 clock cycles per result.

Iteration number	Instructions		Issues at clock-cycle number	Executes at clock-cycle number	Writes result at clock-cycle number
1	LD	F0,0(R1)	1	2	4
1	ADDD	F4,F0,F2	1	5	8
1	SD	0(R1),F4	2	9	
1	SUB	R1,R1,#8	3	4	5
1	BNEZ	R1,LOOP	4	5	
2	LD	F0,0(R1)	5	6	8
2	ADDD	F4,F0,F2	5	9	12
2	SD	0(R1),F4	6	13	
2	SUB	R1,R1,#8	7	8	9
2	BNEZ	R1,LOOP	8	9	

FIGURE 6.48 The time of issue, execution, and writing result for a dual-issue version of our Tomasulo pipeline. The write-result stage does not apply to either stores or branches, since they do not write any registers.

The number of dual issues is small because there is only one floating-point operation per iteration. The relative number of dual-issued instructions would be helped by the compiler partially unwinding the loop to reduce the instruction count by eliminating loop overhead. With that transformation, the loop would run as fast as on a superscalar machine. We will return to this transformation in Exercises 6.16 and 6.17.

The VLIW Approach

Our superscalar DLX machine can issue two instructions per clock cycle. That could perhaps be extended to three or at most four, but it becomes difficult to determine whether three or four instructions can all issue simultaneously without knowing what order the instructions could be in when fetched and what dependencies might exist among them. An alternative is an LIW (*Long Instruction Word*) or VLIW (*Very Long Instruction Word*) architecture. VLIWs use multiple, independent functional units. Rather than attempting to issue multiple, independent instructions to the units, a VLIW packages the multiple operations into one very long instruction, hence the name. A VLIW instruction might include two integer operations, two floating-point operations, two memory references, and a branch. An instruction would have a set of fields for each functional unit—perhaps 16 to 24 bits per unit, yielding an instruction length of between 112 and 168 bits. To keep the functional units busy there must be enough work in a straightline code sequence to keep the instructions scheduled. This is accomplished by unrolling loops and scheduling code across basic blocks using a technique called *trace scheduling*. In addition to eliminating branches by unrolling loops, trace scheduling provides a method to move instructions across branch points. We will discuss trace scheduling more in the next section. For now, let's assume we have a technique to generate long, straightline code sequences for building up VLIW instructions.

Example

Suppose we have a VLIW that could issue two memory references, two FP operations, and one integer operation or branch in every clock cycle. Show an unrolled version of the vector sum loop for such a machine. Unroll as many times as necessary to eliminate any stalls. Ignore the branch-delay slot.

Answer

The code is shown in Figure 6.49. The loop has been unrolled 6 times, which eliminates stalls, and runs in 9 cycles. This yields a running rate of 7 results in 9 cycles, or 1.28 cycles per result.

Memory reference 1	Memory reference 2	FP operation 1	FP operation 2	Integer operation / branch
LD F0,0(R1)	LD F6,-8(R1)			
LD F10,-16(R1)	LD F14,-24(R1)			
LD F18,-32(R1)	LD F22,-40(R1)	ADDD F4,F0,F2	ADDD F8,F6,F2	
LD F26,-48(R1)		ADDD F12,F10,F2	ADDD F16,F14,F2	
		ADDD F20,F18,F2	ADDD F24,F22,F2	
SD 0(R1),F4	SD -8(R1),F8	ADDD F28,F26,F2		
SD -16(R1),F12	SD -24(R1),F16			
SD -32(R1),F20	SD -40(R1),F24			SUB R1,R1,#48
SD -0(R1),F28				BNEZ R1,LOOP

FIGURE 6.49 VLIW instructions that occupy the inner loop and replace the unrolled sequence. This code takes nine cycles assuming no branch delay; normally the branch would also be scheduled. The issue rate is 23 operations in 9 clock cycles, or 2.5 operations per cycle. The efficiency, the percentage of available slots that contained an operation, is about 60%. To achieve this issue rate requires a much larger number of registers than DLX would normally use in this loop.

What are the limitations and costs of a VLIW approach? If we can issue 5 operations per clock cycle, why not 50? Three different limitations are encountered: limited parallelism, limited hardware resources, and code size explosion. The first is the simplest: There is a limited amount of parallelism available in instruction sequences. Unless loops are unrolled very large numbers of times, there may not be enough operations to fill the instructions. At first glance, it might appear that 5 instructions that could be executed in parallel would be sufficient to keep our VLIW completely busy. This, however, is not the case. Several of these functional units—the memory, the branch, and the floating-point units—will be pipelined, requiring a much larger number of operations that can be executed in parallel. For example, if the floating-point pipeline has 8 steps, the 2 operations being issued on a clock cycle cannot depend on any of the 14 operations already in the floating-point pipeline. Thus, we need to find a number of independent operations roughly equal to the average pipeline depth times the number of functional units. This means about 15 to 20 operations would be needed to keep a VLIW with 5 functional units busy.

The second cost, the hardware resources for a VLIW, seem quite straightforward; duplicating the floating-point and integer functional units is easy and cost scales linearly. However, there is a large increase in the memory- and register-file bandwidth. Even with a split floating-point and integer register file, our VLIW will require 5 read ports and 2 write ports on the integer register file and 4 read ports and 2 write ports on the floating-point register file. This bandwidth cannot be supported without some substantial cost in the size of the register file and possible degradation of clock speed. Our 5-unit VLIW also has 2 data memory ports. Furthermore, if we wanted to expand it, we would need to continue adding memory ports. Adding only arithmetic units would not help, since the machine would be starved for memory bandwidth. As the number of data memory ports grows, so does the complexity of the memory system. To allow multiple memory accesses in parallel, the memory must be broken into banks containing different addresses with the hope that the operations in a single instruction do not have conflicting accesses. A conflict will cause the entire machine to stall, since all the functional units must be kept synchronized. This same factor makes it extremely difficult to use data caches in a VLIW.

Finally, there is the problem of code size. There are two different elements that combine to increase code size substantially. First, generating enough operations in a straightline code fragment requires ambitiously unrolling loops, which increases code size. Second, whenever instructions are not full, the unused functional units translate to wasted bits in the instruction encoding. In Figure 6.49, we saw that only about 60% of the functional units were used; almost half of each instruction was empty. To combat this problem, clever encodings are sometimes used. For example, there may be only one large immediate field for use by any functional unit. Another technique is to compress the instructions in main memory and expand them when they are read into the cache or are decoded.

The major challenge for these machines is to try to exploit large amounts of instruction-level parallelism. When the parallelism comes from unrolling simple loops, the original loop probably could have been run efficiently on a vector machine (see the next chapter). It is not clear that a VLIW is preferred over a vector machine for such applications; the costs are similar, and the vector machine is typically the same speed or faster. The open question in 1990 is whether there are large classes of applications that are not suitable for vector machines, but still offer enough parallelism to justify the VLIW approach rather than a simpler one, such as a superscalar machine.

Increasing Instruction-Level Parallelism with Software Pipelining and Trace Scheduling

We have already seen that one compiler technique, loop unrolling, is used to help exploit parallelism among instructions. Loop unrolling creates longer sequences of straightline code, which can be used to exploit more instruction-level parallelism. There are two other more general techniques that have been developed for this purpose: software pipelining and trace scheduling.

Software pipelining is a technique for reorganizing loops such that each iteration in the software-pipelined code is made from instruction sequences chosen from different iterations in the original code segment. This is most easily understood by looking at the scheduled code for the superscalar version of DLX. The scheduler essentially interleaves instructions from different loop iterations, putting together all the loads, then all the adds, then all the stores. A software-pipelined loop interleaves instructions from different iterations without unrolling the loop. This technique is the software counterpart to what Tomasulo's algorithm does in hardware. The software-pipelined loop would contain one load, one add, and one store, each from a different iteration. There is also some startup code that is needed before the loop begins as well as code to finish up after the loop is completed. We will ignore these in this discussion.

Example

Show a software-pipelined version of this loop:

```
Loop:   LD     F0,0(R1)
        ADDD   F4,F0,F2
        SD     0(R1),F4
        SUB    R1,R1,#8
        BNEZ   R1,LOOP
```

You may omit the start-up and clean-up code.

Answer

Given the vector M in memory, and ignoring the start-up and finishing code, we have:

```
Loop:     SD   0(R1),F4    ;stores into M[i]
          ADDD F4,F0,F2     ;adds to M[i-1]
          LD   F0,-16(R1)  ;loads M[i-2]
          BNEZ R1,LOOP
          SUB  R1,R1,#8    ;subtract in delay slot
```

This loop can be run at a rate of 5 cycles per result, ignoring the start-up and clean-up portions. Because the load fetches two array elements beyond the element count, the loop should run for two fewer iterations. This would be accomplished by decrementing R1 by 16 prior to the loop.

Software pipelining can be thought of as symbolic loop unrolling. Indeed, some of the algorithms for software pipelining use loop unrolling to figure out how to software pipeline the loop. The major advantage of software pipelining over straight loop unrolling is that software pipelining consumes less code space. Software pipelining and loop unrolling, in addition to yielding a better scheduled inner loop, each reduce a different type of overhead. Loop unrolling reduces the overhead of the loop—the branch and counter-update code. Software pipelining reduces the time when the loop is not running at peak speed to once per loop at the beginning and end. If we unroll a loop that does 100 iterations a constant number of times, say 4, we pay the overhead 100/4 = 25 times—every time the inner unrolled loop is reinitiated. Figure 6.50 shows this behavior graphically. Because these techniques attack two different types of overhead, the best performance comes from doing both.

The other technique used to generate additional parallelism is *trace scheduling*. This is particularly useful for VLIWs, for which the technique was originally developed. Trace scheduling is a combination of two separate processes. The first process, called *trace selection* tries to find the most likely sequence of operations to put together into a small number of instructions; this sequence is called a *trace*. Loop unrolling is used to generate long traces, since loop branches are taken with high probability. Once a trace is selected, the second process, called *trace compaction*, tries to squeeze the trace into a small number of wide instructions. Trace compaction attempts to move operations as early as it can in a sequence (trace), packing the operations into as few wide instructions as possible.

There are two different considerations in compacting a trace: data dependences, which force a partial order on operations, and branch points, which create places across which code cannot be easily moved. In essence, the code wants to be compacted into the shortest possible sequence that preserves the data dependences; branches are the main impediment to this process. The major advantage of trace scheduling over simpler pipeline-scheduling techniques is that it includes a method to move code across branches. Figure 6.51 shows a code fragment, which may be thought of as an iteration of an unrolled loop, and the trace selected.

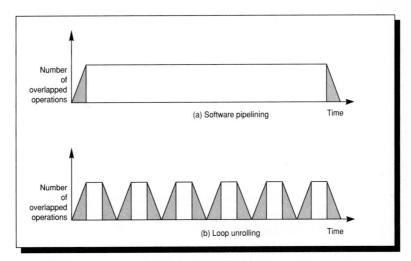

FIGURE 6.50 This shows the execution pattern for (a) a software-pipelined loop and (b) an unrolled loop. The shaded areas are the times when the loop is not running with maximum overlap or parallelism among instructions. This occurs once at loop beginning and once at the end for the software-pipelined loop. For the unrolled loop it occurs $\frac{m}{n}$ times if the loop has a total of m executions and is unrolled n times. Each block represents an unroll of n iterations. Increasing the number of unrolls will reduce the start-up and clean-up overhead.

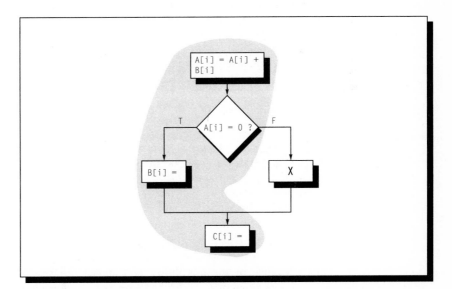

FIGURE 6.51 A code fragment and the trace selected shaded with gray. This trace would be selected first, if the probability of the true branch being taken were much higher than the probability of the false branch being taken. The branch from the decision (A[i]=0) to X is a branch **out** of the trace, and the branch from X to the assignment to C is a branch **into** the trace. These branches are what make compacting the trace difficult.

Once the trace is selected as shown in Figure 6.51, it must be compacted so as to fill the wide instruction word. Compacting the trace involves moving the assignments to variables B and C up to the block before the branch decision. Let's first consider the problem of moving the assignment to B. If the assignment to B is moved above the branch (and thus out of the trace), the code in X would be affected if it used B, since moving the assignment would change the value of B. Thus, to move the assignment to B, B must not be read in X. One could imagine more clever schemes if B were read in X—for example, making a shadow copy and updating B later. Such schemes are generally not used, both because they are complex to implement and because they will slow down the program if the trace selected is not optimal and the operations end up requiring additional instructions. Also, because the assignment to B is moved before the if test, for this schedule to be valid either X also assigns to B or B is not read after the if statement.

Moving the assignment to C up to before the first branch requires first moving it over the branch from X into the trace. To do this, a copy is made of the assignment to C on the branch into the trace. A check must still be done, as was done for B, to make sure that the assignment can be moved over the branch out of the trace. If C is successfully moved to before the first branch and the "false" direction of the branch—the branch off the trace—is taken, the assignment to C will have been done twice. This may be slower than the original code, depending on whether this operation or other moved operations create additional work in the main trace. Ironically, the more successful the trace-scheduling algorithm is in moving code across the branch, the higher the penalty for misprediction.

Loop unrolling, trace scheduling, and software pipelining all aim at trying to increase the amount of local instruction parallelism that can be exploited by a machine issuing more than one instruction on every clock cycle. The effectiveness of each of these techniques and their suitability for various architectural approaches are among the most significant open research areas in pipelined-processor design.

6.9 | Putting It All Together: A Pipelined VAX

In this section we will examine the pipeline of the VAX 8600, a macropipelined VAX. This machine is described in detail by DeRosa et al. [1985] and Troiani et al. [1985]. The 8600 pipeline is a more dynamic structure than the DLX integer pipeline. This is because the processing steps may take multiple cycles in one stage of the pipeline. Additionally, the hazard detection is more complicated because of the possibility that stages progress independently and because instructions may modify registers before they complete. Techniques similar to those used in the DLX FP pipeline to handle variable-length instructions are used in the 8600 pipeline.

The 8600 is macropipelined—the pipeline understands the structure of VAX instructions and overlaps their execution, checking the hazards on the instruction operands. By comparison, the VAX 8800 is micropipelined—microinstructions are overlapped and hazard detection occurs in the microprogram unit. A different issue of the Digital Technical Journal [Digital 1987] describes this machine, and Clark [1987] describes the pipeline and its performance. The designs are interesting to compare.

Figure 6.52 shows the 8600 partitioned into four major structural components. The MBox is responsible for address translation and memory access (see Chapter 8). The IBox is the heart of the 8600 pipeline; it is responsible for instruction fetch and decode, operand address calculation, and operand fetch. The EBox and FBox are responsible for execution of integer and floating-point operations, and their primary function is to implement the opcode portion of an instruction. (Because the FBox is optional, the EBox also contains microcode to do the floating point, albeit at much lower performance. The optional presence of the FBox further complicates the operand processing in the EBox.) Since the EBox and FBox are not pipelined, we will focus our attention primarily on the IBox. In explaining the IBox function we will refer to the EBox occasionally; usually the same comments apply to the FBox.

Figure 6.53 breaks the execution of a VAX instruction into four overlapped steps. The number of clock cycles per step may vary widely, though each step in the pipeline takes at least one clock.

A VAX instruction may take many clock cycles in a given step. For example, with multiple memory operands, the instruction will take multiple clock cycles in the Opfetch step. Because of this, an instruction that takes many cycles at a

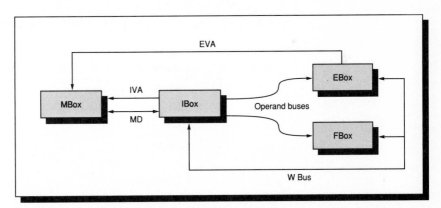

FIGURE 6.52 The basic structure of the 8600 consists of an MBox (responsible for memory access), IBox (handles instruction and operand processing), EBox (all opcode interpretation except floating point), and FBox (performs floating-point operations). These four units are connected by six major buses. The IVA and EVA carry the address for a memory access to the MBox from the IBox and EBox. The MD bus carries memory data to or from the MBox; all such data flows through the IBox. The EBox initiates memory access directly with the MBox only under unusual conditions (e.g., misaligned references). The operand buses carry operands from the IBox (where they are fetched from memory or registers) to the EBox and FBox. Finally, the W Bus carries results to be written from the EBox and FBox to the GPRs and to memory, via the IBox.

Step	Function	Located in
1. Ifetch	Prefetch instruction bytes and decode them	IBox
2. Opfetch	Operand address calculation and fetch	IBox
3. Execution	Execute opcode and write result	EBox, FBox
4. Result store	Write result to memory or registers	EBox, IBox

FIGURE 6.53   The basic structure of the 8600 pipeline has four stages, each taking from 1 to a large number of clock cycles. Up to four VAX instructions are being processed at once.

stage may cause a back up in the pipeline; this back up may eventually reach the Ifetch step, where it will cause the pipeline to simply stop fetching instructions. Additionally, several resources (e.g., the W Bus and GPR ports) are contended for by multiple stages in the pipeline. In general, these problems are resolved on the fly using a fixed-priority scheme.

Operand Decode and Fetch

Much of the work in interpreting a VAX instruction is in the operand specifier and decode process, and this is the heart of the IBox. Substantial effort is devoted to decoding and fetching operands as fast as possible to keep instructions flowing through the pipeline. Figure 6.54 shows the number of cycles spent in Opfetch under ideal conditions (no cache misses or other stalls from the memory hierarchy) for each operand specifier. If the result is a register, the EBox stores

Specifier	Cycles
Literal or immediate	1
Register	1
Deferred	1
Displacement	1
PC-relative and absolute	1
Autodecrement	1
Autoincrement	2
Autoincrement deferred	5
Displacement deferred	4
PC-relative deferred	4

FIGURE 6.54   The minimum number of cycles spent in Opfetch by operand specifier. This shows the data for an operand of type byte, word, or longword that is read. Modified and written operands take an additional cycle, except for register mode and immediate or literal, where writes are not allowed. Quadword and octaword operands may take much longer. If any stalls are encountered, the cycle count will increase.

the result. If the result is a memory operand, Opfetch calculates the address and waits for the EBox to signal ready, then the IBox stores the result during the Result store step. If an instruction result is to be stored in memory, the EBox signals to the IBox when it enters the last cycle of execution for the instruction. This allows Opfetch to overlap the first cycle of a two-cycle memory write with the last cycle of execution (even if the operation only takes one cycle).

To maximize the performance of the machine, there are three copies of the GPRs—in the IBox, EBox, and FBox. A write is broadcast from the FBox, EBox, or IBox (in the case of autoincrement or autodecrement addressing) to the other two units, so that their copies of the registers can be updated.

Handling Data Dependences

Register hazards are tracked in Opfetch by maintaining a small table of registers that will be written. Whenever an instruction passes through Opfetch, its result register is marked as busy. If an instruction that uses that register arrives in Opfetch and sees the busy flag set, it stalls until the flag is cleared. This prevents RAW hazards. The busy flag is cleared when the register is written. Because there are only two stages after Opfetch (execute and write memory result), the busy flag can be implemented as a two-entry associative memory. Writes are maintained in order and always at the end of the pipeline, and all reads are done in Opfetch. This eliminates all explicit WAW and WAR hazards. The only possible remaining hazards are those that can occur on implicit operands, such as the registers written by a MOVC3. Hazards on implicit operands are prevented by explicit control in the microcode.

Opfetch optimizes the case when the last operand specifier is a register by processing the register operand specifier at the same time as the next-to-last specifier. In addition, when the result register of an instruction is the source operand of the next instruction, rather than stall the dependent instruction, Opfetch merely signals this relationship to the EBox, allowing execution to proceed without a stall. This is like the bypassing in our DLX pipeline.

Memory hazards between reads and writes are easily resolved because there is a single memory port, and the IBox decodes all operand addresses.

Handling Control Dependences

There are two aspects to handling branches in a VAX: synchronizing on the condition code and dealing with the branch hazard. Most of the branch processing is handled by the IBox. A predict-taken strategy is used; the following steps are taken when the IBox sees a branch:

1. Compute the branch target address, send it to the MBox, and initiate a fetch from the target address. Wait for the EBox to issue CCSYNC, which indicates that the condition codes will be available in the next clock cycle.

2. Evaluate the condition codes from the EBox to check the prediction. If the prediction was incorrect, the access initiated in the MBox is aborted. The current PC points at the next instruction or its first operand specifier.

3. Assuming the branch was taken, the IBox flushes the prefetch and decode stages and begins loading the instruction register and processing the new target stream. If the branch was not taken, the access to the potential target has already been killed and the pipeline can continue just using what is in the prefetch and decode stages.

Simple conditional branches (BEQL, BNEQ), the unconditional branches (BRB, BRW), and the computed branches (e.g., AOBLEQ) are handled by the IBox. The EBox handles more complex branches and also the instructions used for calls and returns.

An Example

To really understand how this pipeline works, let's look at how a code sequence executes. This example is somewhat simplified, but is sufficient to demonstrate the major pipeline interactions. The code sequence we will consider is as follows (remember that for consistency the result of the ADDL3 is given first):

```
        ADDL3     R1,R2,56(R3)
        CMPL      45(R1),@54(R2)
        BEQL      target
        MOVL      ...
target: SUBL3     ...
```

Figure 6.55 shows an annotated pipeline diagram of how these instructions would progress through the 8600 pipeline.

Dealing with Interrupts

The 8600 maintains three program counters so that instruction interruption and restart are possible. These program counters and what they designate are:

- Current Program Counter—points to the next byte to be processed and consumed in Opfetch.

- IBox Starting Address—points to the instruction currently in Opfetch.

- EBox Starting Address—points to the instruction executing in the EBox or FBox.

In addition, the prefetch unit keeps an address to prefetch from (the VIBA, Virtual Instruction Buffer Address), but this does not affect interrupt handling. When an exception is caused by a prefetch operation, the byte in the instruction buffer is marked. When Opfetch eventually asks for the byte, it will see the exception, and the Current Program Counter will have the address of the byte that caused the exception.

	Clock Cycle								
Instr.	1	2	3	4	5	6	7	8	9
ADDL3	**IF**: Fetch `ADDL`.	**IF**: Continue prefetch if space and MBox available.	**IF**: Decode `R1`.	**IF**: Decode `R2`. **OP**: Fetch `R1`.	**IF**: Decode `56(R3)`. **OP**: Fetch `R2`.	**OP**: Compute `56+(R3)`. **EX**: get first operand.	**OP**: Start write. **EX**: Add.	**WR**: Store.	
CMPL						**IF**: Decode `45(R1)`.		**IF**: Decode `@54(R2)`. **OP**: Fetch `45(R1)`.	**OP**: Fetch `54(R2)`.
BEQL								**IF**: Decode `BEQL` displace.	
SUBL									

	Clock Cycle								
Instr.	10	11	12	13	14	15	16	17	18
ADDL3									
CMPL	**OP**: stall. **EX**: get first operand.	**OP**: get indirect address.	**OP**: Fetch `@54(R2)`.		**EX**: compare and set CC.				
BEQL				**OP**: Load VA.	**OP**: Fetch branch target.	**OP**: Fetch target +4; load VIBA; flush IBuffer.			
SUBL						**IF**: Decode `SUBL3`.	**OP**: Fetch first operand.	**OP**: Fetch second operand.	

FIGURE 6.55   The VAX 8600 executing a code sequence. The top portion shows the events on clock ticks 1–9, while the bottom portion shows the events on clock ticks 10–18. The pipeline stages are abbreviated as IF (Instruction Fetch), OP (Opfetch), EX (Execution), and WR (Write Result) and are shown in bold. Each instruction passes through the 8600 pipeline as soon as the pipe stage is empty and the required data is available. Note that an instruction can be in both the IF and OP stages at the same time. This figure assumes that at the beginning of cycle 1, the prefetch buffer is empty. The prefetch in the IF stage continues to fetch instructions as long as there is room in the prefetch buffer and an available MBox cycle. It is omitted from the diagram for simplicity. The action "stall" indicates a stall for a memory operand during Opfetch. In total, the three VAX instructions executed take 15 cycles, assuming no stalls from the memory system. This sequence was chosen to demonstrate the functioning of the pipeline—it is not necessarily typical.

These PCs are updated when an instruction enters the corresponding pipeline stage. Hence, if an interrupt occurs in a given stage, the PC can be set back to the beginning of that instruction. These PCs are needed because the length of VAX instructions is variable and can only be determined by finding the opcode byte.

In addition to restoring the starting address of the instruction that caused the interrupt, we must unwind any register updates done by addressing modes processed in Opfetch for instructions that are after the instruction that interrupts the processor. The IBox maintains a log of updates to the register file done on behalf of multiple instructions, as we did in Section 5.6. The effects of any changes are undone and the PC is restored. This allows the operating system to have a clean machine state to work from.

Final Remarks

The 8600 uses a four-step pipeline. The theoretical peak performance with the 80-ns clock is 12.5 million VAX instructions per second. Some simple sequences of instructions can actually attain this peak performance with a CPI of 1. Typically, the performance on integer code is about 1.75 million VAX instructions per second for a CPI of about 7. This yields about 3.5 times the performance of a VAX-11/780.

6.10 | Fallacies and Pitfalls

Fallacy: Instruction set design has little impact on pipelining.

This is perhaps the most prominent misconception about pipelining and one that was widely held until recently. Many of the difficulties of pipelining arise because of instruction set complications. Here are some examples, many of which are mentioned in the chapter:

- Variable instruction lengths and running times can lead to imbalance among pipeline stages causing other stages to back up. They also severely complicate hazard detection and the maintenance of precise interrupts. Of course, there are exceptions to every rule. For example, caches cause instruction running times to vary when they miss; however, the performance advantages of caches make the added complexity acceptable. To minimize the complexity, most machines freeze the pipeline on a cache miss. Other machines try to continue running parts of the pipeline; though this is very complex, it may overcome some of the performance losses from cache misses.

- Sophisticated addressing modes can lead to different sorts of problems. Addressing modes that update registers, such as post autoincrement, complicate hazard detection. They also slightly increase the complexity of instruction restart. Other addressing modes that require multiple memory accesses substantially complicate pipeline control and make it difficult to keep the pipeline flowing smoothly.

- Architectures that allow writes into the instruction space (self-modifying code) can cause trouble for pipelining (as well as for cache designs). For example, if an instruction in the pipeline can modify another instruction, we must constantly check if the address being written to by an instruction corresponds to the address of an instruction further on in the pipeline. If so, the pipeline must be flushed or the instruction in the pipeline somehow updated.

- Implicitly set condition codes increase the difficulty of finding when a branch has been decided and the difficulty of scheduling branch delays. The former problem occurs when the condition-code setting is not uniform, making it difficult to decide which instruction sets the condition code last. The latter problem occurs when the setting of the condition code is not under program control. This makes it hard to find instructions that can be scheduled between the condition evaluation and the branch. Many newer architectures avoid condition codes or set them explicitly under program control to eliminate the pipelining difficulties.

As a simple example, suppose the DLX instruction format were more complex, so that a separate, decode pipe stage were required before register fetch. This would increase the branch delay to two clock cycles. At best, the second branch-delay slot would be wasted at least as often as the first. Gross [1983] found that a second delay slot was only used half as often as the first. This would lead to a performance penalty for the second delay slot of more than 0.1 clock cycles per instruction.

Pitfall: Unexpected execution sequences may cause unexpected hazards.

At first glance, WAW hazards look like they should never occur because no compiler would ever generate two writes to the same register without an intervening read. But they can occur when the sequence was unexpected. For example, the first write might be in the delay slot of a taken branch when the scheduler thought the branch would not be taken. Here is the code sequence that could cause this:

```
        BNEZ    R1,foo
        DIVD    F0,F2,F4    ; moved into delay slot
                           ; from fall through

        .....

        .....
foo:    LD      F0,qrs
```

If the branch is taken, then before the DIVD can complete the LD will reach WB, causing a WAW hazard. The hardware must detect this and may stall the issue of the LD. Another way this can happen is if the second write is in a trap routine. This occurs when an instruction that traps and is writing results continues and completes after an instruction that writes the same register in the trap handler. The hardware must detect and prevent this as well.

Fallacy: Increasing the depth of pipelining always increases performance.

Two factors combine to limit the performance improvement gained by pipelining. Data dependences in the code mean that increasing the pipeline depth will increase the CPI, since a larger percentage of the cycles will become stalls. Second, clock skew and latch overhead combine to limit the decrease in clock period obtained by further pipelining. Figure 6.56 shows the tradeoff between pipeline depth and performance for the first 14 of the Livermore Loops (see Chapter 2, page 43). The performance flattens out when the pipeline depth reaches 4 and actually drops when the execution portion is pipelined 16 deep.

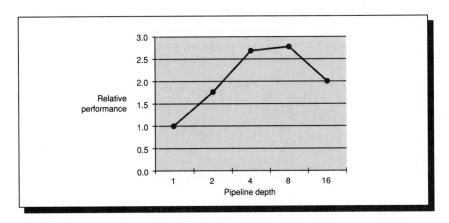

FIGURE 6.56 The depth of pipelining versus the speedup obtained. This data is based on Table 2 in Kunkel and Smith [1986]. The x axis shows the number of stages in the EX portion of the floating-point pipeline. A single-stage pipeline corresponds to 32 levels of logic, which might be appropriate for a single FP operation.

Pitfall: Evaluating a scheduler on the basis of unoptimized code.

Unoptimized code—containing redundant loads, stores, and other operations that might be eliminated by an optimizer—is much easier to schedule than "tight" optimized code. In GCC running on a DECstation 3100, the frequency of idle clock cycles increases by 18% from the unoptimized and scheduled code to the optimized and scheduled code. TeX shows a 20% increase for the same measurement. To fairly evaluate a scheduler you must use optimized code, since in the real system you will derive a good performance from other optimizations in addition to scheduling.

Pitfall: Extensive pipelining can impact other aspects of a design, leading to overall lower cost/performance.

The best example of this phenomenon comes from two implementations of the VAX, the 8600 and the 8700. We discussed the instruction pipeline of the 8600 in Section 6.9. When the 8600 was initially delivered, it had a cycle time of 80 ns. Subsequently, a redesigned version, called the 8650, with a 55-ns clock was introduced. The 8700 has a much simpler pipeline that operates at the microinstruction level. The 8700 CPU is much smaller and has a faster clock rate, 45 ns. The overall outcome is that the 8650 has a CPI advantage of about 20%, but the 8700 has a clock rate that is about 20% faster. Thus, the 8700 achieves the same performance with much less hardware.

6.11 | Concluding Remarks

Figure 6.57 shows how the various pipelining approaches affect both clock speed and CPI. This figure does not account for instruction-count differences. Since performance is clock speed divided by CPI (ignoring instruction-count differences), machines in the top left corner will be slowest, and machines in the bottom right corner will be fastest. However, the machines that move towards the lower right corner will probably achieve their maximum performance on the narrowest range of applications.

Machines that are *underpipelined* lump multiple DLX pipestages into one. The clock cannot be run as fast, and the CPI will be only marginally lower. The DLX pipeline achieves a CPI very close to 1 (ignoring memory-system stalls) at a reasonable clock speed. Architectural simplicity and efficient pipelining are two of the most important attributes of the RISC (Reduced Instruction Set Computer) machines. DLX constitutes an example of such a machine. We have chosen to use the term load/store architecture because the ideas apply to a broad range of machines, and not just to the machines that identify themselves as RISCs. Much of the discussion in the first part of this chapter centered around the key ideas developed by the RISC projects.

Machines with higher clock rates and deeper pipelines have been called *superpipelined*. Superpipelined machines are characterized by pipelining all functional units. A superpipelined version of DLX might have a 10-stage pipeline, rather than the 5-stage pipeline described earlier. Other than increasing the complexity of pipeline scheduling and pipeline control, superpipelined machines are not fundamentally different from the machines we have already examined in this chapter. Due to limited instruction-level parallelism, a super-pipelined machine will have a slightly higher CPI than a DLX-style pipeline, but its advantage in clock cycle time should be larger than the disadvantage in CPI.

Superscalar processors can have clock cycle times very close to that of a DLX pipeline and maintain a smaller CPI. The VLIW machines can have a substantially lower CPI, but tend to have a significantly higher clock cycle time for the reasons discussed in this chapter. The vector machines effectively use both techniques. They are usually superpipelined and have powerful vector operations that can be considered equivalent to issuing multiple independent operations on a machine like DLX. We will explore vector machines in detail in the next chapter.

Going out from the top left corner on either axis in Figure 6.57, the requirement to exploit more instruction-level parallelism increases; at the same time, of course, fewer programs will run at maximum speed.

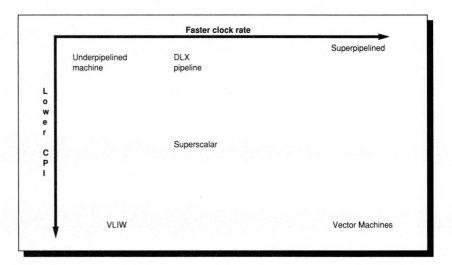

FIGURE 6.57   Increasing the instruction-issue rate lowers the CPI, while a deeper pipeline increases the clock rate. Various machines combine these techniques.

6.12 | Historical Perspective and References

This section describes some of the major advances in pipelining and ends with some of the recent literature on high-performance pipelining.

The first general-purpose pipelined machine is considered to be Stretch, the IBM 7030. Stretch followed on the IBM 704 and had a goal of being 100 times faster than the 704. The goals were a stretch from the state of the art at that time—hence the nickname. The plan was to obtain a factor of 1.6 from overlapping fetch, decode, and execute, using a 4-stage pipeline. Bloch [1959] and Bucholtz [1962] describe the design and engineering tradeoffs, including the use of ALU bypasses.

In 1964 CDC delivered the first CDC 6600. The CDC 6600 was unique in many ways. In addition to introducing scoreboarding, the CDC 6600 was the first machine to make extensive use of multiple functional units. It also had peripheral processors that used a timeshared pipeline. The interaction between pipelining and instruction set design was understood, and the instruction set was kept simple to promote pipelining. The CDC 6600 also used an advanced packaging technology. Thornton [1964] describes the pipeline and I/O processor architecture, including the concept of out-of-order instruction execution. Thornton's book [1970] provides an excellent description of the entire machine, from technology to architecture, and includes a foreword by Cray. (Unfortunately, this book is currently out of print.) The CDC 6600 also has an instruction scheduler for the FORTRAN compilers, described by Thorlin [1967].

The IBM 360/91 introduced many new concepts, including tagging of data, register renaming, dynamic detection of memory hazards, and generalized forwarding. Tomasulo's algorithm is described in his 1967 paper. Anderson, Sparacio, and Tomasulo [1967] describe other aspects of the machine, including the use of branch prediction. Patt and his colleagues have described an approach, called HPSm, that is an extension of Tomasulo's algorithm [Hwu and Patt 1986].

A series of general pipelining descriptions that appeared in the late 1970s and early 1980s provided most of the terminology and described most of the basic techniques used in simple pipelines. These surveys include Keller [1975], Ramamoorthy and Li [1977], Chen [1980], and Kogge's book [1981], devoted entirely to pipelining. Davidson and his colleagues [1971, 1975] developed the concept of pipeline reservation tables as a design methodology for multicycle pipelines with feedback (also described in Kogge [1981]). Many designers use a variation of these concepts, as we did in Figures 6.3 and 6.4.

The RISC machines refined the notion of compiler-scheduled pipelines in the early 1980s. The concepts of delayed branches and delayed loads—common in microprogramming—were extended into the high-level architecture. The Stanford MIPS architecture made the pipeline structure purposely visible to the compiler and allowed multiple operations per instruction. Schemes for scheduling the pipeline in the compiler were described by Sites [1979] for the Cray, by Hennessy and Gross [1983], (and in Gross's thesis [1983]) and by Gibbons and Muchnik [1986]. Rymarczyk [1982] describes the interlock conditions that pro–grammers should be aware of for a 360-like machine; this paper also shows the complex interaction between pipelining and an instruction set not designed to be pipelined.

J. E. Smith and his colleagues have written a number of papers examining instruction issue, interrupt handling, and pipeline depth for high-speed scalar machines. Kunkel and Smith [1986] evaluate the impact of pipeline overhead and dependences on the choice of optimal pipeline depth; they also have an excellent discussion of latch design and its impact on pipelining. Smith and Plezkun [1988] evaluate a variety of techniques for preserving precise interrupts, including the future file concept mentioned in Section 6.6. Weiss and Smith [1984] evaluate a variety of hardware pipeline scheduling and instruction-issue techniques.

Dynamic hardware branch-prediction schemes are described by J. E. Smith [1981] and by A. Smith and Lee [1984]. Ditzel [1987] describes a novel branch-target buffer for CRISP. McFarling and Hennessy [1986] is a quantitative comparison of a variety of compile-time and run-time branch-prediction schemes.

A series of early papers, including Tjaden and Flynn [1970] and Foster and Riseman [1972], concluded that only small amounts of parallelism could be available at the instruction level without investing an enormous amount of hardware. These papers dampened the appeal of multiple instruction issue for more than ten years. Nicolau and Fisher [1984] published a paper asserting the presence of large amounts of potential instruction-level parallelism.

Charlesworth [1981] reports on the Floating Point Systems AP-120B, one of the first wide-instruction machines containing multiple operations per instruction. Floating Point Systems applied the concept of software pipelining—albeit by hand, rather than with a compiler—by writing assembly language libraries to use the machine efficiently. Weiss and J. E. Smith [1987] compare software pipelining versus loop unrolling as techniques for scheduling code on a pipelined machine. Lam [1988] presents algorithms for software pipelining and evaluates their use on Warp, a wide-instruction-word machine. Along with his colleagues at Yale, Fisher [1983] proposed creating a machine with a very wide instruction (512 bits), and named this type of machine a VLIW. Code was generated for the machine using trace scheduling, which Fisher [1981] had developed originally for generating horizontal microcode. The implementation of trace scheduling for the Yale machine is described by Fisher, et. al. [1984] and by Ellis [1986]. The Multiflow machine (see Colwell et. al. [1987]) commercialized the concepts developed at Yale.

Several researchers proposed techniques for multiple instruction issue. Agerwala and Cocke [1987] proposed this approach as an extension of the RISC ideas, and coined the name "superscalar." IBM described a machine based on these ideas in late 1989 (see Bakoglu et al. [1989]). In 1990, the IBM was announced as the RS/6000. The implementation can issue up to four instructions per clock. A good description of the machine, its background, and software appears in IBM [1990]. The Apollo DN 10000 and the Intel i860 both offer multiple instruction issue, though the requirements for multiple issue are rather rigid. The Intel i860 should probably be considered a LIW machine because the program must explicitly indicate whether instruction pairs should be dual issued. Although the pairs are ordinary instructions, there are substantial limitations on what can appear as a member of a dual-issued pair. The Intel 960CA and Tandem Cyclone are examples of superscalar machines with complex instruction sets.

J. E. Smith and his colleagues at Wisconsin [1984] proposed the decoupled approach that included multiple issue with dynamic pipeline scheduling. The Astronautics ZS-1 described by Smith et al. [1987] embodies this approach and uses queues to connect the load/store unit and the operation units. J. E. Smith [1989] also describes the advantages of dynamic scheduling and compares that approach to static scheduling. Dehnert, Hsu, and Bratt [1989] explain the architecture and performance of the Cydrome Cydra 5, a machine with a wide instruction word that provides dynamic register renaming. The Cydra 5 is a unique blend of hardware and software aimed at extracting instruction-level parallelism.

Recently there have been a number of papers exploring the tradeoffs among alternative pipelining approaches. Jouppi and Wall [1989] examine the performance differences between superpipelined and superscalar systems, concluding that their performance is similar, but that superpipelined machines may require less hardware to achieve the same performance. Sohi and Vajapeyam [1989] give measurements of available parallelism for wide-instruction-word machines. Smith, Johnson, and Horowitz [1989] recount studies of available instruction-level parallelism in nonscientific code using an ambitious hardware scheme that allows multiple-instruction execution.

References

AGERWALA, T. AND J. COCKE [1987]. "High performance reduced instruction set processors," IBM Tech. Rep. (March).

ANDERSON, D. W., F. J. SPARACIO, AND R. M. TOMASULO [1967]. "The IBM 360 Model 91: Machine philosophy and instruction handling," *IBM J. of Research and Development* 11:1 (January) 8–24.

BAKOGLU, H. B., G. F. GROHOSKI, L. E. THATCHER, J. A. KAHLE, C. R. MOORE, D. P. TUTTLE, W. E. MAULE, W. R. HARDELL, D. A. HICKS, M. NGUYEN PHU, R. K. MONTOYE, W. T. GLOVER , AND S. DHAWAN [1989]. "IBM second-generation RISC machine organization," Proc. Int'l Conf. on Computer Design, IEEE (October) Rye, N.Y., 138–142.

BLOCH, E. [1959]. "The engineering design of the Stretch computer," *Proc. Fall Joint Computer Conf.,* 48–59.

BUCHOLTZ, W. [1962]. *Planning a Computer System: Project Stretch,* McGraw-Hill, New York.

CHARLESWORTH, A. E. [1981]. "An approach to scientific array processing: The architecture design of the AP-120B/FPS-164 family," *Computer* 14:12 (December) 12–30.

CHEN, T. C. [1980]. "Overlap and parallel processing" in *Introduction to Computer Architecture,* H. Stone, ed., Science Research Associates, Chicago, 427–486.

CLARK, D. W. [1987]. "Pipelining and performance in the VAX 8800 processor," *Proc. Second Conf. on Architectural Support for Programming Languages and Operating Systems,* IEEE/ACM (March), Palo Alto, Calif., 173–177.

COLWELL, R. P., R. P. NIX, J. J. O'DONNELL, D. B. PAPWORTH, AND B. K. RODMAN [1987]. "A VLIW architecture for a trace scheduling compiler," *Proc. Second Conf. on Architectural Support for Programming Languages and Operating Systems,* IEEE/ACM (March), Palo Alto, Calif., 180–192.

DAVIDSON, E. S. [1971]. "The design and control of pipelined function generators," *Proc. Conf. on Systems, Networks, and Computers,* IEEE (January), Oaxtepec, Mexico, 19–21.

DAVIDSON, E. S., A. T. THOMAS, L. E. SHAR, AND J. H. PATEL [1975]. "Effective control for pipelined processors," *COMPCON, IEEE* (March), San Francisco, 181–184.

DEHNERT, J. C., P. Y.-T. HSU, AND J. P. BRATT [1989]. "Overlapped loop support on the Cydra 5," *Proc. Third Conf. on Architectural Support for Programming Languages and Operating Systems* (April), IEEE/ACM, Boston, 26–39.

DEROSA, J., R. GLACKEMEYER, AND T. KNIGHT [1985]. "Design and implementation of the VAX 8600 pipeline," *Computer* 18:5 (May) 38–48.

DIGITAL EQUIPMENT CORPORATION [1987]. *Digital Technical J.* 4 (March), Hudson, Mass. (This entire issue is devoted to the VAX 8800 processor.)

DITZEL, D. R. AND H. R. MCLELLAN [1987]. "Branch folding in the CRISP microprocessor: Reducing the branch delay to zero," *Proc. 14th Symposium on Computer Architecture* (June), Pittsburgh, 2–7.

EARLE, J. G. [1965]. "Latched carry-save adder," *IBM Technical Disclosure Bull.* 7 (March) 909–910.

ELLIS, J. R., [1986]. *Bulldog: A Compiler for VLIW Architectures*, The MIT Press,1986.

EMER, J. S. AND D. W CLARK [1984]. "A characterization of processor performance in the VAX-11/780," *Proc. 11th Symposium on Computer Architecture* (June), Ann Arbor, Mich., 301–310.

FISHER, J. A. [1981]. "Trace Scheduling: A Technique for Global Microcode Compaction," *IEEE Trans. on Computers* 30:7 (July), 478-490.

FISHER, J. A. [1983]. "Very long instruction word architectures and ELI-512," *Proc. Tenth Symposium on Computer Architecture* (June), Stockholm, Sweden., 140-150.

FISHER J. A., J. R. ELLIS, J. C. RUTTENBERG, AND A. NICOLAU [1984]. "Parallel processing: A smart compiler and a dumb machine," *Proc. SIGPLAN Conf. on Compiler Construction* (June), Palo Alto, CA, 11-16.

FOSTER, C. C. AND E. M. RISEMAN [1972]. "Percolation of code to enhance parallel dispatching and execution," *IEEE Trans. on Computers* C-21:12 (December) 1411–1415.

GIBBONS, P. B. AND S. S. MUCHNIK [1986]. "Efficient Instruction Scheduling for a Pipelined Processor," *SIGPLAN '86 Symposium on Compiler Construction, ACM* (June), Palo Alto, CA, 11-16.

GROSS, T. R. [1983]. *Code Optimization of Pipeline Constraints,* Ph.D. Thesis (December), Computer Systems Lab., Stanford Univ.

HENNESSY, J. L. AND T. R. GROSS [1983]. "Postpass code optimization of pipeline constraints," *ACM Trans. on Programming Languages and Systems* 5:3 (July) 422-448

HWU, W.-M. AND Y. PATT [1986]. "HPSm, a high performance restricted data flow architecture having minimum functionality," *Proc. 13th Symposium on Computer Architecture* (June), Tokyo, 297–307.

IBM [1990]. "The IBM RISC System/6000 processor," collection of papers, *IBM Jour. of Research and Development* 34:1, (January), 119 pages.

JOUPPI N. P. AND D. W. WALL [1989]. "Available instruction-level parallelism for superscalar and superpipelined machines," *Proc. Third Conf. on Architectural Support for Programming Languages and Operating Systems,* IEEE/ACM (April), Boston, 272–282.

KELLER R. M. [1975]. "Look-ahead processors," *ACM Computing Surveys* 7:4 (December) 177–195.

KOGGE, P. M. [1981]. *The Architecture of Pipelined Computers,* McGraw-Hill, New York.

KUNKEL, S. R. AND J. E. SMITH [1986]. "Optimal pipelining in supercomputers," *Proc. 13th Symposium on Computer Architecture* (June), Tokyo, 404–414.

LAM, M. [1988]. "Software pipelining: An effective scheduling technique for VLIW machines," *SIGPLAN Conf. on Programming Language Design and Implementation,* ACM (June), Atlanta, Ga., 318–328.

MCFARLING, S. AND J. HENNESSY [1986]. "Reducing the cost of branches," *Proc. 13th Symposium on Computer Architecture* (June), Tokyo, 396–403.

NICOLAU, A. AND J. A. FISHER [1984]. "Measuring the parallelism available for very long instruction work architectures," *IEEE Trans. on Computers* C-33:11 (November) 968–976.

RAMAMOORTHY, C. V. AND H. F. LI [1977]. "Pipeline architecture," *ACM Computing Surveys* 9:1 (March) 61–102.

RYMARCZYK, J. [1982]. "Coding guidelines for pipelined processors," *Proc. Symposium on Architectural Support for Programming Languages and Operating Systems,* IEEE/ACM (March), Palo Alto, Calif., 12–19.

SITES, R. [1979]. *Instruction Ordering for the CRAY-1 Computer,* Tech. Rep. 78-CS-023 (July), Dept. of Computer Science, Univ. of Calif., San Diego.

SMITH, A. AND J. LEE [1984]. "Branch prediction strategies and branch target buffer design," *Computer* 17:1 (January) 6–22.

SMITH, J. E. [1981]. "A study of branch prediction strategies," *Proc. Eighth Symposium on Computer Architecture* (May), Minneapolis, 135–148.

SMITH, J. E. [1984]. "Decoupled access/execute computer architectures," *ACM Trans. on Computer Systems* 2:4 (November), 289–308.

SMITH, J. E. [1989]. "Dynamic instruction scheduling and the Astronautics ZS-1," *Computer* 22:7 (July) 21–35.

SMITH, J. E. AND A. R. PLEZKUN [1988]. "Implementing precise interrupts in pipelined processors," *IEEE Trans. on Computers* 37:5 (May) 562–573.

SMITH, J. E., G. E. DERMER, B. D. VANDERWARN, S. D. KLINGER, C. M. ROZEWSKI, D. L. FOWLER, K. R. SCIDMORE, J. P. LAUDON [1987]. "The ZS-1 central processor," *Proc. Second Conf. on Architectural Support for Programming Languages and Operating Systems,* IEEE/ACM (March), Palo Alto, Calif., 199–204.

SMITH, M. D., M. JOHNSON, AND M. A. HOROWITZ [1989]. "Limits on multiple instruction issue," *Proc. Third Conf. on Architectural Support for Programming Languages and Operating Systems,* IEEE/ACM (April), Boston, Mass., 290–302.

SOHI , G. S., AND S. VAJAPEYAM [1989]. "Tradeoffs in instruction format design for horizontal architectures," *Proc. Third Conf. on Architectural Support for Programming Languages and Operating Systems,* IEEE/ACM (April), Boston, Mass. 15–25.

THORLIN, J. F. [1967]. "Code generation for PIE (parallel instruction execution) computers," *Spring Joint Computer Conf.* (April), Atlantic City, N.J.

THORNTON, J. E. [1964]. "Parallel operation in the Control Data 6600," *Proc. Fall Joint Computer Conf.* 26, 33–40.

THORNTON, J. E. [1970]. *Design of a Computer, the Control Data 6600,* Scott, Foresman, Glenview, Ill.

TJADEN, G. S. AND M. J. FLYNN [1970]. "Detection and parallel execution of independent instructions," *IEEE Trans. on Computers* C-19:10 (October) 889–895.

TOMASULO, R. M. [1967]. "An efficient algorithm for exploiting multiple arithmetic units," *IBM J. of Research and Development* 11:1 (January) 25–33.

TROIANI, M., S. S. CHING, N. N. QUAYNOR, J. E. BLOEM, AND F. C. COLON OSORIO [1985]. "The VAX 8600 I Box, a pipelined implementation of the VAX architecture," *Digital Technical J.* 1 (August) 4–19.

WEISS, S. AND J. E. SMITH [1984]. "Instruction issue logic for pipelined supercomputers," *Proc. 11th Symposium on Computer Architecture* (June), Ann Arbor, Mich., 110–118.

WEISS, S. AND J. E. SMITH [1987]. "A study of scalar compilation techniques for pipelined supercomputers," *Proc. Second Conf. on Architectural Support for Programming Languages and Operating Systems* (March), IEEE/ACM, Palo Alto, Calif., 105–109.

E X E R C I S E S

6.1 [12/12/15/20/15/15] <6.2–6.4> Consider an architecture with two instruction formats: a register–register format and a register–memory format. There is a single memory addressing mode (offset + base register).

There is a set of ALU operations with format:

$$\text{ALUop Rdest, Rsrc}_1, \text{Rsrc}_2$$

or

$$\text{ALUop Rdest, Rsrc}_1, \text{MEM}$$

Where the ALUop is one of the following: Add, Subtract, And, Or, Load (Rsrc_1 ignored), Store (Rdest ignored). Rsrc or Rdest are registers. MEM is a base register and offset pair and is a source for any ALUop, except a store instruction where it is the destination.

Branches use a full compare of two registers and are PC-relative. Assume that this machine is pipelined so that a new instruction is started every clock cycle. The following pipeline structure—similar to that used in the VAX 8800 micropipeline—is used:

```
IF    RF    ALU1  MEM   ALU2  WB
      IF    RF    ALU1  MEM   ALU2  WB
            IF    RF    ALU1  MEM   ALU2  WB
                  IF    RF    ALU1  MEM   ALU2  WB
                        IF    RF    ALU1  MEM   ALU2  WB
                              IF    RF    ALU1  MEM   ALU2  WB
```

The first ALU stage is used for effective address calculation for memory references and branches. The second ALU cycle is used for operations and branch comparison. RF is both a decode and register-fetch cycle. Assume reading in RF and writing in WB occur as in Figure 6.8 (page 262).

a. [12] Find the number of adders needed, counting any adder or incrementer; show a combination of instructions and pipe stages that justify this answer. You need only give one combination that maximizes the adder count.

b. [12] Find the number of register read and write ports and memory read and write ports required. Show that your answer is correct by showing a combination of instructions and pipeline stage indicating the instruction and the number of read ports and write ports required for that instruction.

c. [15] Determine any *data forwarding* between the two separate ALUs used for the ALU1 and ALU2 pipe stages. Put in all forwarding of ALU to ALU needed to avoid or reduce stalls. Show the relationship between the two instructions involved in forwarding.

d. [20] Show any other data-forwarding requirements for the units listed below by giving an example of the source instruction and destination instruction of the forwarding. Each example should show the maximum separation of the two instructions. How many instructions can each example forward across? You need only consider the following units: MDR_{in} (memory data in register), MDR_{out} (memory-data register for outgoing data), ALU_1, and ALU_2. Include any forwarding that is required to prevent or reduce stalls.

e. [15] Give an example of all remaining hazards after all forwarding of parts C and D above has been implemented. What is the maximum number of stalls for each hazard?

f. [15] Show all control hazard types by example and state the length of the stall. The control hazards should be resolved as early as possible (but not using a delayed branch).

6.2 [12] <6.1–6.4> A machine is called "underpipelined" if additional levels of pipelining can be added without changing the pipeline-stall behavior appreciably. Suppose that the DLX pipeline was changed to four stages by merging ID and EX and lengthening the clock cycle by 50%. How much faster would the conventional DLX pipeline be versus the underpipelined DLX on integer code only? Make sure you include the effect of any change in pipeline stalls using the data in Figure 6.24 (page 278).

6.3 [15] <6.2–6.4> We know that a four-deep pipelined implementation has the following hazard frequencies and stall requirements between an instruction i and its successors:

$i + 1$ (and not on $i + 2$)	20%	2 cycle stall
$i + 2$	5%	1 cycle stall

Assume that the clock rate of the pipelined machine is four times the clock rate of the nonpipelined implementation. What is the effective performance increase from pipelining if we ignore the effect of hazards? What is the effective performance increase from pipelining if we account for the effect of pipelining hazards?

6.4 [15] <6.3> Suppose the branch frequencies (as percentages of all instructions) are as follows:

Conditional branches	20%
Jumps and calls	5%
Conditional branches	60% are taken

We are examining a four-deep pipeline where the branch is resolved at the end of the second cycle for unconditional branches, and at the end of the third cycle for conditional branches. Assuming that only the first pipe stage can always be done independent of whether the branch goes and ignoring other pipeline stalls, how much faster would the machine be without any branch hazards?

6.5 [20] <6.4> Several designers have proposed the concept of canceling branches (also called squashing or nullifying), as a way to improve the performance of delayed branches. (Several of the machines discussed in Appendix E have this capability.) The idea is to allow the branch to indicate that the instruction in the delay slot should be aborted if the branch is mispredicted. The advantage of canceling branches is that the delay slot can **always** be filled, since the branch can abort the contents of the delay slot if mispredicted. The compiler need not worry about whether the instruction is OK to execute when the branch is mispredicted.

A simple version of canceling branches cancels if the branch is not taken; assume this type of canceling branch. Use the data in Figure 6.18 (page 272) for branch frequency. Assume that 27% of the branch-delay slots are filled using strategy (a) of Figure 6.20 (page 274) with standard delayed branches, and that the rest of the slots are filled using canceling branches and strategy (b). Using the taken/not taken data for Spice from Figure 3.22 on page 107, show the effectiveness of this scheme with canceling branches for Spice using the same format as the graph in Figure 6.22 (page 276). How much faster on Spice would a machine with canceling branches run, assuming there is no clock-speed penalty compared to a machine with only delayed branches? Assume CPI without branch stalls is 1.

6.6 [20/15/20] <6.2–6.4> Suppose that we have the following pipeline layout:

Stage	Function
1	Instruction fetch
2	Operand decode
3	Execution or memory access (branch resolution)

All data dependences are between the register written in Stage 3 of instruction *i* and a register read in Stage 2 of instruction *i* + *1*, before instruction *i* has completed. The probability of such an interlock occurring is $1/p$.

We are considering a change in the machine organization that would write back the result of an instruction during an effective 4th pipe stage. This would decrease the length of the clock cycle by *d* (i.e., if the length of the clock cycle was T, it is now T–*d*). The probability of a dependence between instruction *i* and instruction *i* +2 is p^{-2}. (Assume that the value of p^{-1} excludes instructions that would interlock on *i* +2.) The branch would also be resolved during the fourth stage.

a. [20] Considering only the data hazard, find the lower bound on *d* that makes this a profitable change. Assume that each result has exactly one use and that the basic clock cycle has length T.

b. [15] Suppose that the probability of an interlock between *i* and *i+n* were $0.3 - 0.1n$ for $1 \leq n \leq 3$. What increase in the clock rate is needed so that this change improves performance?

c. [20] Now assume that we have used forwarding to eliminate the extra hazard introduced by the change. That is, for all *data* hazards the pipeline length is *effectively* 3. This design may still not be worthwhile because of the impact of control hazards coming from a four-stage versus a three-stage pipeline. Assume that only Stage 1 of the pipeline can be safely executed before we decide whether a branch goes or not and that all branches are conditional. We want to know what the impact of branch hazards can be before this longer pipeline does not yield high performance. Find an upper bound on the percent of conditional branches in programs in terms of the ratio of *d* to the original clock-cycle time, so that the longer pipeline has better performance. What if *d* is a 10% reduction, what is the maximum percentage of conditional branches, before we lose with this longer pipeline? Assume the taken-branch frequency for conditional branches is 60%.

6.7 [12] <6.7> A shortcoming of the scoreboard approach occurs when multiple functional units that share input buses are waiting for a single result. The units cannot start simultaneously, but must serialize. This is not true in Tomasulo's algorithm. Give a code sequence that uses no more than 10 instructions and shows this problem. Use the FP latencies from Figure 6.29 (page 289) and the same functional units in both examples. Indicate where the Tomasulo approach can continue, but the scoreboard approach must stall.

6.8 [15] <6.7> Tomasulo's algorithm also has a disadvantage versus the scoreboard: only one result can complete per clock, due to the CDB. Using the FP latencies from Figure 6.29 (page 289) and the same functional units in both cases, find a code sequence of no more than 10 instructions where scoreboard does not stall, but Tomasulo's algorithm must. Indicate where this occurs in your sequence.

6.9 [15] <6.7> Suppose we have a deeply pipelined machine, for which we implement a branch-target buffer for the conditional branches only. Assume that the misprediction penalty is always 4 cycles and the buffer miss penalty is always 3 cycles. Assume 90% hit rate and 90% accuracy, and the branch statistics in Figure 6.18 (page 272). How much faster is the machine with the branch-target buffer versus a machine that has a fixed 2-cycle branch penalty? Assume a base CPI without branch stalls of 1.

6.10 [15] <6.7> Some designers have proposed using branch-target buffers to obtain a zero-delay unconditional branch (see Ditzel and McLellan [1987]). The buffer simply caches the target instruction rather than the target PC. On an unconditional branch that hits in the branch-target buffer, the target instruction is fetched and sent to the pipeline in place of the unconditional branch. Assuming a 90% hit rate, a base CPI of 1, and the data in Figure 6.18 (page 272), how much improvement is gained by this enhancement versus a machine whose effective CPI is 1.1.

6.11–6.19 For these problems we will look at how a common vector loop runs on a variety of pipelined versions of DLX. The loop is the so-called SAXPY loop (discussed extensively in Chapter 7). The loop implements the vector operation Y = a*X+Y for a vector of length 100. Here is the DLX code for the loop:

```
foo:    LD       F2,0(R1)     ;load X(i)

        MULTD    F4,F2,F0     ;multiply a*X(i)

        LD       F6,0(R2)     ;load Y(i)

        ADDD     F6,F4,F6     ;add aX(i) + Y(i)

        SD       0(R2),F6     ;store Y(i)

        ADDI     R1,R1,8      ;increment X index

        ADDI     R2,R2,8      ;increment Y index

        SGTI     R3,R1,done ;test if done

        BEQZ     R3,foo       ; loop if not done
```

For these problems, assume that the integer operations issue and complete in one clock cycle and that their results are fully bypassed. Ignore the branch delay. You will use the FP latencies shown in Figure 6.29 (page 289) unless stated otherwise. Assume the FP units are not pipelined unless the problem states otherwise.

6.11 [20] <6.2–6.6> For this problem use the pipeline constraints shown in Figure 6.29 (page 289). Show the number of stall cycles for each instruction and what clock cycle the instruction begins execution (i.e., enters its first EX cycle) on the first iteration of the loop. How many clock cycles does each loop iteration take?

6.12 [22] <6.7> Using the DLX code for SAXPY above, show the state of the scoreboard tables (as in Figure 6.32) when the SGTI instruction reaches Write result. Assume that issue and read operands each take a cycle. Assume that there are three integer functional units and they take only a single execution cycle (including loads and stores). Assume the functional unit count described in Section 6.7 with the FP latencies of Figure 6.29. The branch should not be included in the scoreboard.

6.13 [22] <6.7> Use the DLX code for SAXPY above and the latencies of Figure 6.29. Assuming Tomasulo's algorithm for the hardware with the functional units described in Section 6.7, show the state of the reservation stations and register-status tables (as in

Figure 6.37) when the `SGTI` writes its result on the CDB. Make the same assumptions about latencies and functional units as Exercise 6.12.

6.14 [22] <6.7> Using the DLX code for SAXPY above, assume a scoreboard with the functional units described in the algorithm for the hardware, plus three integer functional units (also used for load/store). Assume the following latencies in clock cycles:

FP multiply	10
FP add	6
FP load/store	2
All integer operations	1

Show the state of the scoreboard (as in Figure 6.32) when the branch issues for the second time. Assume the branch was correctly predicted taken and took one cycle. How many clock cycles does each loop iteration take? You may ignore any register port/bus conflicts.

6.15 [25] <6.7> Use the DLX code for SAXPY above. Assume Tomasulo's algorithm for the hardware using the functional-unit count shown in Section 6.7. Assume the following latencies in clock cycles:

FP multiply	10
FP add	6
FP load/store	2
All integer operations	1

Show the state of the reservation stations and register status tables (as in Figure 6.37) when the branch is executed for the second time. Assume the branch was correctly predicted as taken. How many clock cycles does each loop iteration take?

6.16 [22] <6.8> Unwind the DLX code for SAXPY three times and schedule it for the standard DLX pipeline. Assume the FP latencies of Figure 6.29. When unwinding, you should optimize the code as in Section 6.8. Significant reordering of the code will be needed to maximize performance. What is the speedup over the original loop?

6.17 [25] <6.8> Assume a superscalar architecture that can issue any two independent operations in a clock cycle (including two integer operations). Unwind the DLX code for SAXPY three times and schedule it assuming the FP latencies of Figure 6.29. Assume one fully-pipelined copy of each functional unit (e.g., FP adder, FP multiplier). How many clock cycles will each iteration on the original code take? When unwinding, you should optimize the code as in Section 6.8. What is the speedup versus the original code?

6.18 [25] <6.8> In a superpipelined machine, rather than have multiple functional units, we would fully pipeline all the units. Suppose we designed a superpipelined DLX that had twice the clock rate of our standard DLX pipeline and could issue any two unrelated operations in the same time that the normal DLX pipeline issued one operation. Unroll the DLX SAXPY code three times and schedule it for this superpipelined machine assuming the FP latencies of Figure 6.29. How many clock cycles does each loop iteration take? Remember that these clock cycles are half as long as those on a standard DLX pipeline or a superscalar DLX.

6.19 [20] <6.8> Start with the SAXPY code and the machine used in Figure 6.49. Unroll the SAXPY loop three times, performing simple optimizations (as on page 315). Fill in a table like Figure 6.49 for the unrolled loop. How many clock cycles does each loop iteration take?

6.20 [35] <6.1–6.4> Change the DLX instruction simulator to be pipelined. Measure the frequency of empty branch-delay slots, the frequency of load delays, and the frequency of FP stalls for a variety of integer and FP programs. Also, measure the frequency of forwarding operations. Determine what the performance impact of eliminating forwarding and stalling would be.

6.21 [35] <6.6> Using a DLX simulator, create a DLX pipeline simulator. Explore the impact of lengthening the FP pipelines, assuming both fully pipelined and nonpipelined FP units. How does clustering of FP operations affect the results? Which FP units are most susceptible to changes in the FP pipeline length?

6.22 [40] <6.4–6.6> Write an instruction scheduler for DLX that works on DLX assembly language. Evaluate your scheduler using either profiles of programs or with a pipeline simulator. If the DLX C compiler does optimization, evaluate your scheduler's performance both with and without optimization.

6.23 [35] <6.4–6.6> Write a DLX pipeline simulator that uses Tomasulo's algorithm with the functional units described. Evaluate the performance of this machine compared to the straightforward DLX pipeline.

6.24 [Discussion] <6.7> Dynamic instruction scheduling requires a considerable investment in hardware. In return, this capability allows the hardware to run programs that could not be run at full speed with only compile-time, static scheduling. What tradeoffs should be taken into account in trying to decide between a dynamically and a statically scheduled scheme? What sort of situations in both hardware technology and program characteristics are likely to favor one approach or the other?

6.25 [Discussion] <6.7> There is a subtle problem that must be considered when implementing Tomasulo's algorithm. It might be called the "two ships passing in the night problem." What happens if an instruction is being passed to a reservation station during the same clock period as one of its operands is going onto the common data bus? Before an instruction is in a reservation station, the operands are fetched from the register file; but once it is in the station, the operands are always obtained from the CDB. Since the instruction and its operand tag are in transit to the reservation station, the tag cannot be matched against the tag on the CDB. So there is a possibility that the instruction will then sit in the reservation station forever waiting for its operand, which it just missed. How might this problem be solved? You might consider subdividing one of the steps in the algorithm into multiple parts. (This intriguing problem is courtesy of J. E. Smith.)

6.26 [Discussion] <6.8> Discuss the advantages and disadvantages of a superscalar implementation, a superpipelined implementation, and a VLIW approach in the context of DLX. What levels of instruction-level parallelism favor each approach? What other concerns would you consider in choosing which type of machine to build?

I'm certainly not inventing vector machines. There are three kinds that I know of existing today. They are represented by the Illiac-IV, the (CDC) Star machine, and the TI (ASC) machine. Those three were all pioneering machines. . . . One of the problems of being a pioneer is you always make mistakes and I never, never want to be a pioneer. It's always best to come second when you can look at the mistakes the pioneers made.

Seymour Cray, Public Lecture at Lawrence Livermore Laboratories on the
Introduction of the CRAY-1 (1976)

7 Vector Processors

7.1 Why Vector Machines?

In the last chapter we looked at pipelining in detail and saw that pipeline scheduling, issuing multiple instructions per clock cycle, and more deeply pipelining a processor could as much as double the performance of a machine. Yet there are limits on the performance improvement that pipelining can achieve. These limits are set by two primary factors:

- Clock cycle time—The clock cycle time can be decreased by making the pipelines deeper, but a deeper pipeline will increase the pipeline dependences and result in a higher CPI. At some point, each increase in pipeline depth has a corresponding increase in CPI. As we saw in Section 6.10, very deep pipelining can slow down a processor.

- Instruction fetch and decode rate—This limitation, sometimes called the *Flynn bottleneck* (based on Flynn [1966]), prevents fetching and issuing of more than a few instructions per clock cycle. We saw that for most pipelined machines the average number of instruction issues per clock was less than one.

The dual limitations imposed by deeper pipelines and issuing multiple instructions can be viewed from the standpoint of either clock rate or CPI: It is just as difficult to schedule a pipeline that is n times deeper as it is to schedule a machine that issues n instructions per clock cycle.

High-speed, pipelined machines are particularly useful for large scientific and engineering applications. A high-speed pipelined machine will usually use a cache to avoid forcing memory reference instructions to have very long latency. However, big, long-running, scientific programs often have very large active data sets that are often accessed with low locality, yielding poor performance from the memory hierarchy. The resulting impact is a decrease in cache performance. This problem could be overcome by not caching these structures if it were possible to determine the memory-access patterns and pipeline the accesses efficiently. Compiler assistance may help address this problem in the future (see Section 10.7).

Vector machines provide high-level operations that work on *vectors*—linear arrays of numbers. A typical vector operation might add two 64-entry, floating-point vectors to obtain a single 64-entry vector result. The vector instruction is equivalent to an entire loop, with each iteration computing one of the 64 elements of the result, updating the indices, and branching back to the beginning.

Vector operations have several important properties that solve most of the problems mentioned above:

- The computation of each result is independent of the computation of previous results, allowing a very deep pipeline *without* generating any data hazards. Essentially, the absence of data hazards was determined by the compiler or programmer when they decided that a vector instruction could be used.

- A single vector instruction specifies a great deal of work—it is equivalent to executing an entire loop. Thus, the instruction bandwidth requirement is reduced, and the Flynn bottleneck is considerably mitigated.

- Vector instructions that access memory have a known access pattern. If the vector's elements are all adjacent, then fetching the vector from a set of heavily interleaved memory banks works very well. The high latency of initiating a main memory access versus accessing a cache is amortized because a single access is initiated for the entire vector rather than to a single word. Thus, the cost of the latency to main memory is seen only once for the entire vector, rather than once for each word of the vector.

- Because an entire loop is replaced by a vector instruction whose behavior is predetermined, control hazards that would normally arise from the loop branch are nonexistent.

For these reasons, vector operations can be made faster than a sequence of scalar operations on the same number of data items, and designers are motivated to include vector units if the applications domain can use them frequently.

As mentioned above, vector machines pipeline the operations on the individual elements of a vector. The pipeline includes not only the arithmetic operations (multiplication, addition, and so on), but also memory accesses and effective address calculations. In addition, most high-end vector machines allow multiple vector operations to be done at the same time, creating parallelism among the operations on different elements. In this chapter, we focus on vector machines that gain performance by pipelining and instruction overlap. In Chapter 10, we discuss parallel machines that operate on many elements in parallel rather than in pipelined fashion.

7.2 | Basic Vector Architecture

A vector machine typically consists of an ordinary pipelined scalar unit plus a vector unit. All functional units within the vector unit have a latency of several clock cycles. This allows a shorter clock cycle time and is compatible with long-running, vector operations that can be deeply pipelined without generating hazards. Most vector machines allow the vectors to be dealt with as floating-point numbers (FP), as integers, or as logical data, though we will focus on floating point. The scalar unit is basically no different from the type of pipelined CPU discussed in Chapter 6.

There are two primary types of vector architectures: vector-register machines and memory–memory vector machines. In a *vector-register machine*, all vector operations—except load and store—are among the vector registers. These machines are the vector counterpart of a load/store architecture. All major vector machines being shipped in 1990 use a vector-register architecture; these include the Cray Research machines (CRAY-1, CRAY-2, X-MP, and Y-MP), the Japanese supercomputers (NEC SX/2, Fujitsu VP200, and the Hitachi S820), and the mini-supercomputers (Convex C-1 and C-2). In a *memory–memory vector machine* all vector operations are memory to memory. The first vector machines were of this type, as were CDC's machines. From this point on we will focus on vector-register architectures only; we will briefly return to memory–memory vector architectures at the end of the chapter (Section 7.8) to discuss why they have not been as successful as vector-register architectures.

We begin with a vector-register machine consisting of the primary components shown in Figure 7.1 (page 354). This machine, which is loosely based on the CRAY-1, is the foundation for discussion throughout most of this chapter. We will call it DLXV; its integer portion is DLX, and its vector portion is the logical vector extension of DLX. The rest of this section examines how the basic architecture of DLXV relates to other machines.

The primary components of the instruction set architecture of DLXV are:

- Vector registers—Each vector register is a fixed-length bank holding a single vector. DLXV has eight vector registers, and each vector register holds 64 doublewords. Each vector register must have at least two read ports and one write port in DLXV. This will allow a high degree of overlap among vector operations to different vector registers. (The CRAY-1 manages to implement the register file with only a single port per register using some clever implementation techniques.)

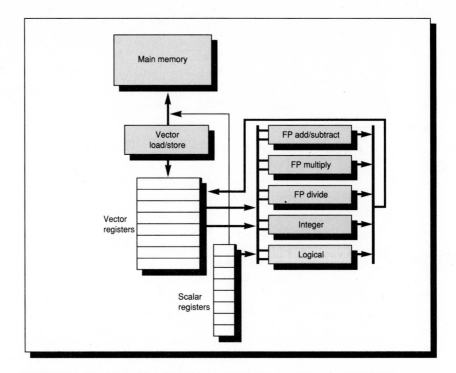

FIGURE 7.1 The basic structure of a vector-register architecture, DLXV. This machine has a scalar architecture just like DLX. There are also eight 64-element vector registers, and all the functional units are vector functional units. Special vector operations and vector loads and stores are defined. We show vector units for logical and integer operations. These are included so that DLXV looks like a standard vector machine, which usually includes these units. However, we will not be discussing these units except in the Exercises. In Section 7.6 we add chaining, which will require additional interconnect capability.

- Vector functional units—Each unit is fully pipelined and can start a new operation on every clock cycle. A control unit is needed to detect hazards, both on conflicts for the functional units (structural hazards) and on conflicts for register accesses (data hazards). DLXV has five functional units, as shown in Figure 7.1. For simplicity, we will focus exclusively on the floating-point functional units.

- Vector load/store unit—A vector memory unit that loads or stores a vector to or from memory. The DLXV vector loads and stores are fully pipelined, so that words can be moved between the vector registers and memory with a bandwidth of one word per clock cycle, after an initial latency.

- A set of scalar registers—These can also provide data as input to the vector functional units, as well as compute addresses to pass to the vector load/store unit. These are the normal 32 general-purpose registers and 32 floating-point registers of DLX.

Figure 7.2 shows the characteristics of some typical vector machines, including the size and count of the registers, the number and types of functional units, and the number of load/store units.

In DLXV, the vector operation has the same name as the DLX name with the letter "V" appended. These are double-precision, floating-point, vector operations. (We have omitted single-precision FP operations and integer and logical operations for simplicity.) Thus, ADDV is an add of two double-precision vectors. The vector operations take as their input either a pair of vector registers (ADDV) or a vector register and a scalar register designated by appending "SV" (ADDSV). In the latter case, the value in the scalar register is used as the input for all operations—the operation ADDSV will add the contents of a scalar register to each element in a vector register. Vector operations always have a vector destination register. The names LV and SV denote vector load and vector store, and load or store an entire vector of double-precision data. One operand is

Machine	Year announced	Vector registers	Elements per vector register (64-bit elements)	Vector functional units	Vector load / store units
CRAY-1	1976	8	64	6: add, multiply, reciprocal, integer add, logical, shift	1
CRAY X-MP CRAY Y-MP	1983 1988	8	64	8: FP add, FP multiply, FP reciprocal, integer add, 2 logical, shift, population count/parity	2 loads 1 store
CRAY-2	1985	8	64	5: FP add, FP multiply, FP reciprocal/sqrt, integer (add shift, population count), logical	1
Fujitsu VP100/200	1982	8–256	32–1024	3: FP or integer add/logical, multiply, divide	2
Hitachi S810/820	1983	32	256	4: 2 integer add/logical, 1 multiply-add and 1 multiply/divide–add unit	4
Convex C-1	1985	8	128	4: multiply, add, divide, integer/logical	1
NEC SX/2	1984	8 + 8192	256 variable	16: 4 integer add/logical, 4 FP multiply/divide, 4 FP add, 4 shift	8
DLXV	1990	8	64	5: multiply, divide, add, integer add, logical	1

FIGURE 7.2   Characteristics of several vector-register architectures. The vector functional units include all operation units used by the vector instructions. The functional units are floating point unless stated otherwise. If the machine is a multiprocessor, the entries correspond to the characteristics of one processor. Each vector load/store unit represents the ability to do an independent, overlapped transfer to or from the vector registers. The Fujitsu VP200's vector registers are configurable: The size and count of the 8K 64-bit entries may be varied inversely to one another (e.g., 8 registers each 1K elements long, or 128 registers each 64 elements long). The NEC SX/2 has 8 fixed registers of length 256, plus 8K of configurable 64-bit registers. The reciprocal unit on the CRAY machines is used to do division (and square root on the CRAY-2). Add pipelines perform floating-point add and subtract. The multiply/divide–add unit on the Hitachi S810/200 performs an FP multiply or divide followed by an add or subtract (while the multiply-add unit performs a multiply followed by an add or subtract). Note that most machines use the vector FP multiply and divide units for vector integer multiply and divide, just like DLX, and several of the machines use the same units for FP scalar and FP vector operations.

the vector register to be loaded or stored; the other operand, which is a DLX general-purpose register, is the starting address of the vector in memory. Figure 7.3 lists the DLXV vector instructions. In addition to the vector registers, we need two additional special-purpose registers: the vector-length and vector-mask registers. We will discuss these registers and their purpose in Sections 7.3 and 7.6, respectively.

Vector instruction	Operands	Function
ADDV	V1,V2,V3	Add elements of V2 and V3, then put each result in V1.
ADDSV	V1,F0,V2	Add F0 to each element of V2, then put each result in V1.
SUBV	V1,V2,V3	Subtract elements of V3 from V2, then put each result in V1.
SUBVS	V1,V2,F0	Subtract F0 from elements of V2, then put each result in V1.
SUBSV	V1,F0,V2	Subtract elements of V2 from F0, then put each result in V1.
MULTV	V1,V2,V3	Multiply elements of V2 and V3, then put each result in V1.
MULTSV	V1,F0,V2	Multiply F0 by each element of V2, then put each result in V1.
DIVV	V1,V2,V3	Divide elements of V2 by V3, then put each result in V1.
DIVVS	V1,V2,F0	Divide elements of V2 by F0, then put each result in V1.
DIVSV	V1,F0,V2	Divide F0 by elements of V2, then put each result in V1.
LV	V1,R1	Load vector register V1 from memory starting at address R1.
SV	R1,V1	Store vector register V1 into memory starting at address R1.
LVWS	V1,(R1,R2)	Load V1 from address at R1 with stride in R2, i.e., R1+i*R2.
SVWS	(R1,R2),V1	Store V1 from address at R1 with stride in R2, i.e., R1+i*R2.
LVI	V1,(R1+V2)	Load V1 with vector whose elements are at R1+V2(i), i.e., V2 is an index.
SVI	(R1+V2),V1	Store V1 with vector whose elements are at R1+V2(i), i.e., V2 is an index.
CVI	V1,R1	Create an index vector by storing the values 0,1*R1,2*R1,...,63*R1 into V1.
S__V	V1,V2	Compare (EQ, NE, GT, LT, GE, LE) the elements in V1 and V2. If condition is
S__SV	F0,V1	true put a 1 in the corresponding bit vector; otherwise put 0. Put resulting bit vector in vector-mask register (VM). The instruction S__SV performs the same compare but using a scalar value as one operand.
POP	R1,VM	Count the 1s in the vector-mask register and store count in R1.
CVM		Set the vector-mask register to all 1s.
MOVI2S	VLR,R1	Move contents of R1 to the vector-length register.
MOVS2I	R1,VLR	Move the contents of the vector-length register to R1.
MOVF2S	VM,F0	Move contents of F0 to the vector-mask register.
MOVS2F	F0,VM	Move contents of vector-mask register to F0.

FIGURE 7.3 The DLXV vector instructions. Only the double-precision FP operations are shown. In addition to the vector registers there are two special registers VLR (discussed in Section 7.3) and VM (discussed in Section 7.6). The operations with stride are explained in Section 7.3, and the use of the index creation and indexed load/store operations are explained in Section 7.6.

A vector machine is best understood by looking at a vector loop on DLXV. Let's take a typical vector problem, which will be used throughout this chapter:

$$Y = a * X + Y$$

X and Y are vectors, initially resident in memory, and a is a scalar. This is the so-called SAXPY or DAXPY (Single-precision or Double-precision A*X Plus Y) loop that forms the inner loop of the Linpack benchmark. Linpack is a collection of linear algrebra routines; the Gaussian elimination portion of Linpack is the segment used as a benchmark. SAXPY represents a small piece of the program, though it takes most of the time in the benchmark.

For now, let us assume that the number of elements, or length, of a vector register (64) matches the length of the vector operation we are interested in. (This restriction will be lifted shortly.)

Example

Show the code for DLX and DLXV for the DAXPY loop. Assume that the starting addresses of X and Y are in Rx and Ry, respectively.

Answer

Here is the DLX code.

```
        LD      F0,a
        ADDI    R4,Rx,#512   ;last address to load
loop:
        LD      F2,0(Rx)     ;load X(i)
        MULTD   F2,F0,F2     ;a*X(i)
        LD      F4,0(Ry)     ;load Y(i)
        ADDD    F4,F2,F4     ;a*X(i) + Y(i)
        SD      F4,0(Ry)     ;store into Y(i)
        ADDI    Rx,Rx,#8     ;increment index to X
        ADDI    Ry,Ry,#8     ;increment index to Y
        SUB     R20,R4,Rx    ;compute bound
        BNZ     R20,loop     ;check if done
```

Here is the code for DLXV for DAXPY.

```
        LD      F0,a         ;load scalar a
        LV      V1,Rx        ;load vector X
        MULTSV  V2,F0,V1     ;vector-scalar multiply
        LV      V3,Ry        ;load vector Y
        ADDV    V4,V2,V3     ;add
        SV      Ry,V4        ;store the result
```

There are some interesting comparisons between the two code segments in the example above. The most dramatic is that the vector machine greatly reduces the dynamic instruction bandwidth, executing only 6 instructions versus almost 600 for DLX. This reduction occurs both because the vector operations work on

64 elements, and because the overhead instructions that constitute nearly half the loop on DLX are not present in the DLXV code.

Another important difference is the frequency of pipeline interlocks. In the straightforward DLX code every `ADDD` must wait for a `MULTD`, and every `SD` must wait for the `ADDD`. On the vector machine, each vector instruction operates on all the vector elements independently. Thus, pipeline stalls are required only once per vector operation, rather than once per vector element. In this example, the pipeline-stall frequency on DLX will be about 64 times higher than it is on DLXV. The pipeline stalls can be eliminated on DLX by using software pipelining or loop unrolling (as we saw in Chapter 6, Section 6.8). However, the large difference in instruction bandwidth cannot be reduced.

Vector Start-up Time and Initiation Rate

Let's investigate the running time of this vector code on DLXV. The running time of each vector operation in the loop has two components—the *start-up time* and the *initiation rate*. The start-up time comes from the pipelining latency of the vector operation and is principally determined by how deep the pipeline is for the functional unit used. For example, a latency of 10 clock cycles means both that the operation takes 10 clock cycles and that the pipeline is 10 deep. (In discussions of the performance of vector operations, clock cycles are customarily used as the metric.) The initiation rate is the time per result once a vector instruction is running; this rate is usually one per clock cycle for individual operations, though some supercomputers have vector operations that can produce 2 or more results per clock, and others have units that may not be fully pipelined. The *completion rate* must at least equal the initiation rate—otherwise there is no place to put results. Hence, the time to complete a single vector operation of length n is:

$$\text{Start-up time} + n * \text{Initiation rate}$$

Example   Suppose the start-up time for a vector multiply is 10 clock cycles. After start-up the initiation rate is one per clock cycle. What is the number of clock cycles per result (i.e., one element of the vector) for a 64-element vector?

Answer $$\text{Clock cycles per result} = \frac{\text{Total time}}{\text{Vector length}}$$

$$= \frac{\text{Start-up time} + 64 * \text{Initiation rate}}{64}$$

$$= \frac{10 + 64}{64} = 1.16 \text{ clock cycles.}$$

Figure 7.4 shows the effect of start-up time and initiation rate on vector performance. The effect of increasing start-up time on a slow-running vector is small, while the same increase in start-up time on a system with an initiation rate of one per clock decreases performance by a factor of nearly two.

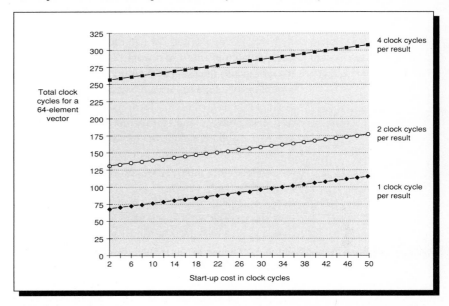

FIGURE 7.4   Total running time increases with start-up cost from 2 to 50 clock cycles per operation on the x axis. The impact of start-up time is much greater for fast-running than for slow-running vectors. The operation running at one clock cycle per result increases its run time by 75%, while the operation running at four clock cycles per result increases by less than 20%.

What determines the start-up and initiation rates? Let's first consider the operations that do not involve a memory access. For register–register operations the start-up time (in clock cycles) is equal to the depth of the functional unit pipeline, since this is the time to get the first result. In the earlier example, the depth of 10 gave a start-up time of 10 clock cycles. In the next few sections, we will see that there are other costs involved that increase the start-up time. The initiation rate is determined by how often the corresponding vector functional unit can accept an operand. If it is fully pipelined, then it can start an operation on new operands every clock cycle, yielding an initiation rate of one per clock (as in the earlier example).

Start-up time for an operation comprises the total latency for the functional unit implementing that operation. If the initiation rate is to be kept at 1 clock per result, then

$$\text{Pipeline depth} = \left\lceil \frac{\text{Total functional unit time}}{\text{Clock cycle time}} \right\rceil$$

For example, if an operation takes 10 clock cycles, it must be pipelined 10 deep to achieve an initiation rate of one per clock. Pipeline depth, then, is determined by the complexity of the operation and the clock cycle time of the machine. The pipeline depths of functional units vary widely—from 2 to 20 stages is not uncommon—though the most heavily used units have start-up times of 4 to 8 clocks.

For DLXV, we will choose the same pipeline depths as the CRAY-1. All functional units are fully pipelined. Pipeline depths are six clock cycles for floating-point add and seven clock cycles for floating-point multiply. If a vector computation depends on an uncompleted computation and will need to be stalled, it adds an extra 4-clock-cycle start-up penalty. This penalty is typical on vector machines and arises due to the lack of bypassing: the penalty is the time to write and then read the operands and is only seen when there is a dependence. Thus, back-to-back dependent vector operations will see the full latency of a vector operation. On DLXV, as on most vector machines, independent vector operations using different functional units can issue without any penalty or delay. Independent vector operations may also be fully overlapped, and each instruction issue only takes one clock. Thus, when the operations are independent and different, DLXV can overlap vector operations, just as DLX can overlap integer and floating-point operations.

Because DLXV is fully pipelined, the initiation rate for a vector instruction is always 1. However, a sequence of vector operations will not be able to run at that rate, due to start-up costs. The term *sustained rate* is applied to this situation and refers to the time per element for a collection of related vector operations. Here an element is not the result of a single vector operation, but one result of a series of vector operations. The time per element, then, is the time required for each operation to produce an element. For example, in the SAXPY loop, the sustained rate will be the time to compute and store one element of the result vector Y.

Example   For a vector length of 64 on DLXV and the following two vector instructions, what is the sustained rate for the sequence, and the effective number of floating-point operations per clock for the sequence?

```
MULTV V1,V2,V3
ADDV  V4,V5,V6
```

Answer   Let's look at the start and completion times of these independent operations (remember that the start-up times are 7 cycles for multiply and 6 cycles for add):

Operation	Start	Complete
MULTV	0	7 + 64 = 71
ADDV	1	1 + 6 + 64 = 71

The sustained rate is one element per clock—remember that sustained rate requires all vector operations to produce a result. The sequence executes 128

FLOPs (FLoating-point OPerations) in 71 clock cycles, for a rate of 1.8 FLOPs per clock. A vector machine can sustain a throughput of more than one operation per clock cycle by issuing independent vector operations to different vector functional units.

The behavior of the load/store vector unit is significantly more complicated. The start-up time for a load is the time to get the first word from memory into a register. If the rest of the vector can be supplied without stalling, then the vector initiation rate is equal to the rate at which new words are fetched or stored. Typically, penalties for start-ups on load/store units are higher than for functional units—up to 50 clock cycles on some machines. For DLXV we will assume a low start-up time of 12 clock cycles, since the CRAY-1 and CRAY X-MP have load/store start-up times of between 9 and 17 clock cycles. For stores, we will not usually care about the start-up time, since stores do not directly produce results. However, when an instruction must wait for a store to complete (as a load might have to with only one memory pipeline), the load may see part or all of the 12-cycle latency of a store. Figure 7.5 summarizes the start-up penalties for DLXV vector operations.

Operation	Start-up penalty
Vector add	6
Vector multiply	7
Vector divide	20
Vector load	12

FIGURE 7.5 Start-up penalties on DLXV. These are the start-up penalties in clock cycles for DLXV vector operations. When a vector instruction depends on another vector instruction that has not completed at the time the second vector instruction issues, the start-up penalty is increased by 4 clock cycles.

To maintain an initiation rate of one word fetched or stored per clock, the memory system must be capable of producing or accepting this much data. This is usually done by creating multiple *memory banks*. Each memory bank is like a small, separate memory that can access different addresses in parallel with other banks. The words are then transferred from the memory at the maximum rate (one per clock in DLXV).

There are two possible implementation techniques for memory banks. One approach is to synchronize all the banks and to access them in parallel, latching the result in each bank. Once the result is latched, the next access can begin while the words are transferred. An alternative implementation technique uses independent bank phasing. On the first access, all the banks are accessed in parallel, and then the words are transferred one at a time from the banks. Once a bank has transmitted or stored its data, it begins the next access immediately. The first approach (synchronized accesses) requires more latches, but has simpler control than an approach that uses independent bank phasing. The concept of memory banks is similar to but not identical to interleaving, as we will see in Figure 7.6. We discuss interleaving extensively in Chapter 8, Section 8.4.

Assuming each bank is one double-precision-word wide, if an initiation rate of one per clock is to be maintained, the following must hold:

Number of memory banks ≥ Memory-bank access time in clock cycles

To see why this relationship exists, think about a vector load of 64 double-precision words. Let the addresses of the vector elements be given by k_i, where

k_i = Starting address of the vector + (i-1) * Distance between vector elements.

For double-precision vector elements that are adjacent, the distance between elements will be 8 bytes. The addresses of the vector elements to be accessed by a bank will be the values of k_i such that

k_i mod number of banks = Bank number

Let's look at the first access by each bank. After a time equal to the memory-access time, all the memory banks will have fetched a double-precision word, and the words can begin returning to the vector registers. (This requires, of course, that the accesses be aligned on doubleword boundaries.) Words are sent serially from the banks, starting with the bank fetching from the lowest address. If the banks are synchronized, the next accesses start immediately; if the banks are phased, then the next access begins after an element is transmitted from the bank. In either case, a bank begins its next access at a byte address that is (8 * number of banks) higher than the last byte address. Because the memory-access time in clock cycles is less than the number of memory banks and because the words are transferred from the banks in round-robin order at a rate of one transfer per clock cycle, a bank will complete the next access before its turn to transmit data comes again. To simplify addressing, the number of memory banks is usually made a power of two. As we will see shortly, designers will probably want to have more than the minimum number of required banks so as to minimize memory stalls.

Example   Suppose we want to fetch a vector of 64 elements starting at byte address of 136, and a memory access takes 6 clocks. How many memory banks must we have? With what addresses are the banks accessed? When will the various elements arrive at the CPU?

Answer   Six clocks per access require at least 6 banks, but because we want the number of banks to be a power of two, we choose to have 8 banks. Figure 7.6 shows what byte addresses each bank accesses within each time period. Remember that a bank begins a new access as soon as it has completed the old access.

Beginning at clock no.	Bank							
	0	**1**	**2**	**3**	**4**	**5**	**6**	**7**
0	192	136	144	152	160	168	176	184
6	256	200	208	216	224	232	240	248
14	320	264	272	280	288	296	304	312
22	384	328	336	344	352	360	368	376

FIGURE 7.6 Memory addresses (in bytes) by bank number and time slot at which access begins. The exact time when a bank transmits its data is given by the address it accesses minus the starting address divided by 8 plus the memory latency (6 clocks). It is important to observe that Bank 0 accesses a word in the next block (i.e., it accesses 192 rather than 128 and then 256 rather than 192, and so on). If Bank 0 were to start at the lower address we would require an extra cycle to transmit the data, and we would transmit one value unnecessarily. While this problem is not severe for this example, if we had 64 banks, up to 63 unnecessary clock cycles and transfers could occur. The fact that Bank 0 does not access a word in the same block of 8 distinguishes this type of memory system from interleaved memory. Normally, interleaved memory systems combine the bank address and the base starting address by concatenation rather than addition. Also, interleaved memories are almost always implemented with synchronized access. Memory banks require address latches for each bank, which are not normally needed in a system with only interleaving.

Figure 7.7 shows the timing for the first few sets of accesses for an 8–bank system with a 6–clock-cycle access latency. Two important observations about these two figures are these: First, notice that the exact address fetched by a bank is largely determined by the lower-order bits in the bank number; however, the initial access to a bank is always within 8 doublewords of the initial address. Second, notice that once the initial latency is overcome (6 clocks in this case), the pattern is to access a bank every n clock cycles, where n is the total number of banks ($n=8$ in this case).

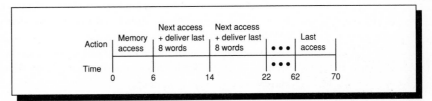

FIGURE 7.7 Access timing for the first 64 double-precision words of the load. After the 6–clock-cycle initial latency, 8 double-precision words are returned every 8 clock cycles.

The number of banks in the memory system and the pipeline depth in the functional units are essentially counterparts, since they determine the initiation rates for operations using these units. The processor cannot access memory faster than the memory cycle time. Thus, if memory is built from DRAM, where cycle time is about twice the access time, the processor will usually need twice as many banks as the computations above would give. This characteristic of DRAM is discussed further in Chapter 8, Section 8.4.

7.3 | Two Real–World Issues: Vector Length and Stride

This section deals with two issues that transpire in real programs. These are what to do when the vector length in a program is not exactly 64, and how to deal with nonadjacent elements in vectors when a matrix is laid out in memory. First, let's deal with the issue of vector length.

Vector-Length Control

A vector-register machine has a natural vector length determined by the number of elements in each vector register. This length, which is 64 for DLXV, is unlikely to match the real vector length in a program. Moreover, in a real program the length of a particular vector operation is often unknown at compile time. In fact, a single piece of code may require different vector lengths. For example, consider this code:

```
        do 10 i = 1,n
10          Y(i) = a * X(i) + Y(i)
```

The size of all the vector operations depends on n, which may not even be known until run-time! The value of n might also be a parameter to the procedure and therefore be subject to change during execution.

The solution to these problems is to create a *vector-length register* (VLR). The VLR controls the length of any vector operation, including a vector load or store. The value in the VLR, however, cannot be any greater than the length of the vector registers. This solves our problem as long as the real length is less than the *maximum vector length* (MVL) defined by the machine.

What if the value of n is not known at compile time, and thus may be greater than MVL? To tackle this problem, a technique called *strip mining* is used. Strip mining is the generation of code such that each vector operation is done for a size less than or equal to the MVL. The strip-mined version of the SAXPY loop written in FORTRAN, the major language used for scientific applications, is shown with C-style comments:

```
low = 1
VL = (n mod MVL)  /*find the odd size piece*/
do 1 j = 0,(n / MVL)  /*outer loop*/
    do 10 i = low,low+VL-1  /*runs for length VL*/
        Y(i) = a*X(i) + Y(i)  /*main operation*/
10  continue
    low = low+VL /*start of next vector*/
    VL = MVL /*reset the length to max*/
1  continue
```

The term n / MVL represents truncating integer division (which is what FORTRAN does) and is used throughout this section. The effect of this loop is to block the vector into segments which are then processed by the inner loop. The length of the first segment is (n mod MVL) and all subsequent segments are of length MVL. This is depicted in Figure 7.8.

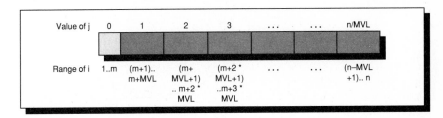

FIGURE 7.8 A vector of arbitrary length processed with strip mining. All blocks but the first are of length MVL, utilizing the full power of the vector machine. In this figure, the variable *m* is used for the expression (n mod MVL).

The inner loop of the code above is vectorizable with length VL, which is equal to either (n mod MVL) or MVL. The VLR register must be set twice—once at each place where the variable VL in the code is assigned. With multiple vector operations executing in parallel, the hardware must copy the value of VLR when a vector operation issues, in case VLR is changed for a subsequent vector operation.

In the previous section, start-up overhead could be computed independently for each vector operation. With strip mining, a significant percentage of the start-up cost will be the strip-mining overhead itself; and, therefore, computing the start-up overhead will be more complex.

Let's see how significant these added overheads are. Consider a simple loop:

```
        do 10 i  =  1,n
  10      A(i)  =  B(i)
```

The compiler will generate two nested loops for this code, just as our earlier example does. The inner loop contains a sequence of two vector operations, LV (load vector) followed by SV (store vector). Each loop iteration of the original vector operation would require two clocks if there were no start-up penalties of any kind. The start-up penalties consist of two types: vector start-up overhead and strip-mining overhead. For DLXV the vector start-up overhead is 12 clock cycles for the vector load plus a 4-clock-cycle delay because the store depends on the load, for a total of 16 clock cycles. We can ignore the store latency, since nothing depends on it. Figure 7.9 (page 366) shows the impact of the vector start-up cost alone as the vector grows from length 1 to length 64. This start-up cost can decrease the throughput rate by a factor of as much as 9, depending on the vector length.

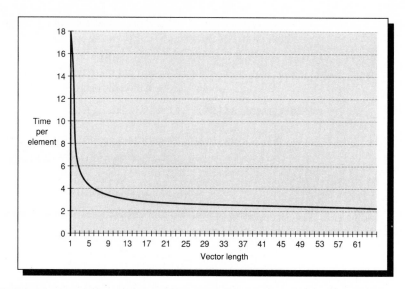

FIGURE 7.9   The impact of just the vector start-up cost on a loop consisting of a vector assignment. For short vectors, the impact of the 16-cycle start-up cost is enormous, decreasing performance by up to nine times. The strip-mining overhead has not been included.

In Section 7.4, we will see a unified performance model that incorporates all the start-up and overhead costs. First, let's examine how to implement vectors with nonsequential memory accesses.

Vector Stride

The second problem this section addresses is that the position in memory of adjacent elements in a vector may not be sequential. Consider the straight-forward code for matrix multiply:

```
do 10 i = 1,100
    do 10 j = 1,100
        A(i,j) = 0.0
        do 10 k = 1,100
10              A(i,j) = A(i,j)+B(i,k)*C(k,j)
```

At the statement labeled 10 we could vectorize the multiplication of each row of B with each column of C and strip-mine the inner loop with k as the index variable. To do so, we must consider how adjacent elements in B and adjacent elements in C are addressed. When an array is allocated memory it is linearized and must be laid out in either *row-major* or *column-major* order. Row-major order, used by most languages except FORTRAN, lays out the rows first, making elements B(i,j) and B(i,j+1) adjacent. Column-major order, used by FORTRAN, makes B(i,j) and B(i+1,j) adjacent. Figure 7.10 illustrates these two alternatives. Let's look at the accesses to B and C in the inner loop of the matrix multiply. In FORTRAN, the accesses to the elements of B will be nonadjacent in memory, and each iteration will access an element that is separated by an entire row of the array. In this case, the elements of B that are accessed by iterations in the inner loop are separated by the row size times 8 (the number of bytes per entry) for a total of 800 bytes.

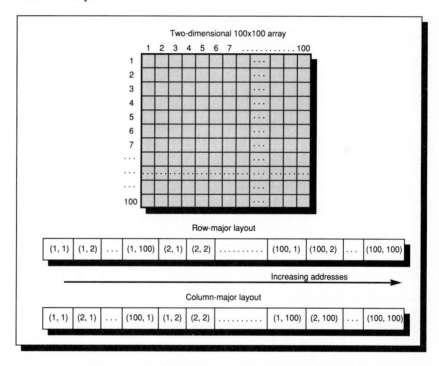

FIGURE 7.10 Matrix for a two-dimensional array and corresponding layouts in one-dimensional storage. In row-major order, successive row elements are adjacent in storage, while in column-major order, successive column elements are adjacent. It is easy to imagine extending this to arrays with more dimensions.

This distance separating elements that are to be merged into a single vector is called the *stride*. In the current example, using column-major layout for the matrices means that matrix C has a stride of 1, or 1 doubleword (8 bytes), separating successive elements, and matrix B has a stride of 100, or 100 doublewords (800 bytes).

Once a vector is loaded into a vector register it acts as if it had logically adjacent elements. This enables a vector-register machine to handle strides greater than one, called *nonunit strides*, by making more general vector-load and vector-store operations. For example, if we could load a row of B into a vector register, we could then treat the row as logically adjacent.

Thus, it is desirable for the vector load and store operations to specify a stride in addition to a starting address. On a DLXV, where the addressable unit is a byte, the stride for our example would be 800. The value must be computed dynamically, since the size of the matrix may not be known at compile time, or—just like vector length—may change for different executions of the same statement. The vector stride, like the vector starting address, can be put in a general-purpose register, where it is used for the life of the vector operation. Then the DLXV instruction LVWS (Load Vector With Stride) can be used to fetch the vector into a vector register. Likewise, when a nonunit stride vector is being stored, SVWS (Store Vector With Stride) can be used. In some vector machines the loads and stores always have a stride value stored in a register, so there is only a single instruction.

Memory-unit complications can occur from supporting strides greater than one. Earlier, we saw that a vector-memory operation could proceed at full speed if the number of memory banks was at least as large as the memory-access time in clock cycles. However, once nonunit strides are introduced it becomes possible to request accesses from the same bank at a higher rate than the memory-access time. This situation is called *memory-bank conflict* and results in each load seeing a larger portion of the memory-access time. A memory-bank conflict occurs whenever the same bank is asked to do an access before it has completed another. Thus, a bank conflict, and hence a stall, will occur if:

$$\frac{\text{Least common multiple (Stride,Number of banks)}}{\text{Stride}} < \text{Memory-access latency}$$

Example

Suppose we have 16 memory banks with an access time of 12 clocks. How long will it take to complete a 64-element vector load with a stride of 1? With a stride of 32?

Answer

Since the number of banks is larger than the load latency, for a stride of 1, the load will take $12 + 64 = 76$ clock cycles, or 1.2 clocks per element. The worst possible stride is a value that is a multiple of the number of memory banks, as in this case with a stride of 32 and 16 memory banks. Every access to memory will collide with the previous one. This leads to an access time of 12 clock cycles per element and a total time for the vector load of 768 clock cycles.

Memory bank conflicts will not occur if the stride and number of banks are relatively prime with respect to each other and there are enough banks to avoid conflicts in the unit-stride case. Increasing the number of memory banks to a number greater than the minimum to prevent stalls with a stride of length 1 will decrease the stall frequency for some other strides. For example, with 64 banks, a stride of 32 will stall on every other access, rather than every access. If we originally had a stride of 8 and 16 banks, every other access would stall; while with 64 banks, a stride of 8 will stall on every eighth access. If we have multiple memory pipelines, we will also need more banks to prevent conflicts. In the

1990s, most vector supercomputers have at least 64 banks, and some have as many as 512.

7.4 | A Simple Model for Vector Performance

This section presents a model for understanding the performance of a vectorized loop. There are three key components of the running time of a strip-mined loop whose body is a sequence of vector instructions:

1. The time for each vector operation in the loop to process one element, ignoring the start-up costs, which we call $T_{element}$. The vector sequence often has a single result, in which case $T_{element}$ is the time to produce an element in that result. If the vector sequence produces multiple results, $T_{element}$ is the time to produce one element in each result. This time depends only on the execution of vector instructions. We will see an example shortly.

2. The overhead for each strip-mined block of vector instructions. This overhead consists of the cost of executing the scalar code for strip mining of each block, T_{loop}, plus the vector start-up cost for each block, T_{start}.

3. The overhead from computing the starting addresses and setting up the vector control. This occurs once for the entire vector operation. This time, T_{base}, consists solely of scalar overhead instructions.

These components can be used to state the total running time for a vector sequence operating on a vector of length n, which we will call T_n:

$$T_n = T_{base} + \left\lceil \frac{n}{MVL} \right\rceil * (T_{loop} + T_{start}) + n * T_{element}$$

The values of T_{start} and T_{loop} are both compiler and machine dependent, while the value of $T_{element}$ depends mainly on the hardware. The exact vector sequence affects all three values; the effect on $T_{element}$ is probably the most pronounced, with T_{start} and T_{loop} less affected.

For simplicity, we will use constant values for T_{base} and for T_{loop} on DLXV. Based on a variety of measurements of CRAY-1 vector execution, the values chosen are 10 for T_{base} and 15 for T_{loop}. At first glance, you might think that these values, especially T_{loop}, are too small. The overhead in each loop requires: setting up the vector starting addresses and the strides, incrementing counters, and executing a loop branch. However, these scalar instructions can be overlapped with the vector instructions, minimizing the time spent on these overhead functions. The values of T_{base} and T_{loop} of course depend on the loop structure, but the dependence is slight compared to the connection between the vector code and the values of $T_{element}$ and T_{start}.

Example

What is the execution time for the vector operation A = B * s, where s is a scalar and the length of the vectors A and B is 200?

Answer

Here is the strip-mined DLXV code, assuming the addresses of A and B are initially in Ra and Rb, and s is in Fs:

```
        ADDI    R2,R0,#1600  ;no. bytes in vector
        ADD     R2,R2,Ra     ;end of A vector
        ADDI    R1,R0,#8     ;strip-mined length
        MOVI2S  VLR,R1       ;load vector length
        ADDI    R1,R0,#64    ;length in bytes
        ADDI    R3,R0,#64    ;vector length of other pieces
loop:   LV      V1,Rb        ;load B
        MULTSV  V2,Fs,V1     ;vector * scalar
        SV      Ra,V2        ;store A
        ADD     Ra,Ra,R1     ;next segment of A
        ADD     Rb,Rb,R1     ;next segment of B
        ADDI    R1,R0,#512   ;full vector length (bytes)
        MOVI2S  VLR,R3       ;set length to 64
        SUB     R4,R2,Ra     ;at the end of A?
        BNZ     R4,LOOP      ;if not, go back
```

From this code, we can see that: $T_{element} = 3$, for the load, multiply and store of each value of the vector. Furthermore, our assumptions for DLXV are $T_{loop} = 15$ and $T_{base} = 10$. Let's use our basic formula:

$$T_n = T_{base} + \left\lceil \frac{n}{MVL} \right\rceil * (T_{loop} + T_{start}) + n * T_{element}$$

$$T_{200} = 10 + (4) * (15 + T_{start}) + 200 * 3$$

$$T_{200} = 10 + 4 * (15 + T_{start}) + 600 = 670 + 4 * T_{start}$$

The value of T_{start} is the sum of

- The vector load start-up of 12 clock cycles,
- The 4–clock-cycle stall due to the dependence between the load and multiply,
- A 7–clock-cycle start-up for the multiply, plus
- A 4–clock-cycle stall due to the dependence between the multiply and store.

Thus, the value of T_{start} is given by:

$$T_{start} = 12 + 4 + 7 + 4 = 27$$

So, the overall value becomes

$$T_{200} = 670 + 4 * 27 = 778$$

The execution time per element with all start-up costs is then $\frac{778}{200} = 3.9$, compared with an ideal case of 3.

Figure 7.11 shows the overhead and effective rates per element for the above example (A = B*s) with various vector lengths. Compared to the simpler model of start-up, illustrated in Figure 7.9 on page 366, we see that the overhead accounting for all sources is higher. In this example, the vector start-up cost, which is what is plotted in Figure 7.9, accounts for only about half the total overhead per element.

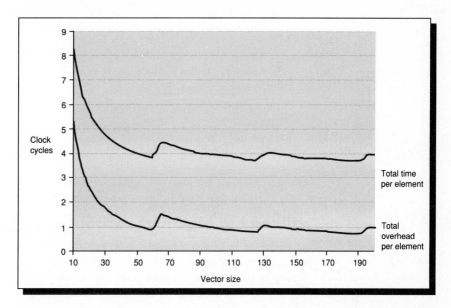

FIGURE 7.11   This shows the total execution time per element and the total overhead time per element, versus the vector length for the example on page 370. For short vectors the total start-up time is more than one-half of the total time, while for long vectors it reduces to about one-third of the total time. The sudden jumps occur when the vector length crosses a multiple of 64, forcing another iteration of the strip-mining code and execution of a set of vector instructions. These operations increase T_n by $T_{loop} + T_{start}$.

7.5 Compiler Technology for Vector Machines

To make effective use of a vector machine a compiler must be able to recognize that a loop (or part of a loop) is vectorizable and generate the appropriate vector code. This involves determining what dependences exist among the operands in the loop. For now, we will consider only dependences that occur when an operand is written at one point and read at a later point. These correspond to RAW (read after write—see page 264) hazards. Consider a loop like this one:

```
        do 10 i=1,100
1           A(i+1) = A(i) + B(i)
2           B(i+1) = B(i) + A(i+1)
10      continue
```

Call the numbered statements 1 and 2 in the loop body S1 and S2, respectively. The possible different types of dependences are

1. S1 uses a value computed by S1 in an earlier iteration. This is true for S1 since iteration i+1 uses the value A(i) that was computed in iteration i as A(i+1). The same is true of S2 for B(i) and B(i+1).

2. S1 uses a value computed by S2 in an earlier iteration. This is true since S1 uses the value of B(i+1) in iteration i+1 that is computed by S2 in iteration i.

3. S2 uses a value computed by S1 in the same iteration. This is true for the value A(i+1).

Because the vector operations are pipelined and the latency may be quite long, an early iteration may not complete before a later iteration begins: Thus, the values that will be written by the early iteration may not have been written before the later iteration begins. Consequently, if situation 1 or 2 exists, vectorizing the loop will introduce a RAW hazard—a hazard that a vector machine does not check for. This means that if any of the three dependences in situation 1 and 2 exist, the loop is not vectorizable, and the compiler will not generate vector instructions for this code. In situation 3, the normal hazard-detection hardware could handle the situation. A loop containing only dependences like those in situation 3 can therefore be vectorized, as we will see soon. The dependences in the first two situations, which involve the use of values computed on earlier loop iterations, are called *loop-carried dependences.*

The first task of the compiler is to determine whether there are any loop-carried dependences within the loop body. The compiler accomplishes this with a dependence-analysis algorithm. Because the statements in the loop body involve arrays, dependence analysis is complex. (If there weren't arrays, there would be nothing to vectorize.) The simplest case occurs when an array name appears only on one side of an assignment statement. Take, for example, this variation of our earlier loop:

```
    do   10 i=1,100
         A(i) = B(i) + C(i)
         D(i) = A(i) * E(i)
10       continue
```

If the arrays A, B, C, D, and E are different, then no loop-carried dependence can exist. There is a dependence between the two statements for the vector A. If the compiler realized that there were two accesses to A, it might try not to reload A the second statement, instead doing the vector multiply using the result register from the vector add. In this case, the processor would see the potential RAW hazard and stall the issue of the vector multiply. If the compiler stored A and reloaded it, then the loads and stores would occur in order, yielding correct execution.

Often the same name appears as both a source and destination within a loop, as it did in the SAXPY loop. There, Y appears on both sides of the assignment:

```
do 10 i=1,100
    Y(i) = a*X(i) + Y(i)
10 continue
```

In this case there is still no loop-carried dependence because the assignment to Y does not depend on a value of Y computed in an earlier iteration. However, the following loop, which is called a *recurrence*, does contain a loop-carried dependence:

```
do 10 i=2,100
    Y(i) = Y(i-1) + Y(i)
10 continue
```

The dependence can be seen by unwinding the loop: In iteration j the value of $Y(j-1)$ is used, but that element is stored in iteration $j-1$, creating a loop-carried dependence.

How does the compiler detect dependences in general? Suppose we have written to an array element with index value $a * i + b$ and accessed with index value $c * i + d$, where i is the for-loop index variable that runs from m to n. A dependence exists if two conditions hold:

1. There are two iteration indices, j and k, both within the limits of the for loop.

2. The loop stores into an array element indexed by $a*j+b$ and later fetches from that **same** array element when it is indexed by $c*k+d$. That is, $a*j+b = c*k+d$.

In general, we may not be able to determine whether a dependence exists at compile time. For example, the values of $a, b, c,$ and d may not be known, making it impossible to tell if a dependence exists. In other cases, the dependence testing may be very expensive but decidable at compile time. For example, the accesses may depend on the iteration indices of multiply nested loops. Many programs do not contain these complex structures, but instead contain simple indices where $a, b, c,$ and d are all constants. For these cases, it is possible to devise reasonable tests for dependence.

A simple and sufficient test used to detect dependences is the *greatest common divisor*, or GCD. It is based on the observation that if a loop-carried dependence exists, then GCD (c,a) must **divide** $(d-b)$. (Remember that an integer, x, *divides* another integer, y, if there is no remainder when we do the division $\frac{y}{x}$ and get an integer result.) The GCD test is sufficient to guarantee that no dependence exists (see Exercise 7.10); however, there are cases where the GCD test succeeds, but no dependence exists. For example, this can arise because the GCD test does not take the loop bounds into account. A more complex test is the Banerjee test, named after U. Banerjee [1979], that accounts for loop bounds, but is still not exact. An exact test can always be done by solving equations for integer values, but this can be expensive for complex loop structures.

Example

Use the GCD test to determine whether dependences exist in the following loop:

$$\textbf{do } 10 \ \ i=1,100$$
$$10 \quad \ \ X(2*i+3) \ = \ X(2*i) \ * \ 5.0$$

Answer

Given the values $a=2$, $b=3$, $c=2$, and $d=0$, then $GCD(a,c) = 2$, and $d-b = -3$. Since 2 does not divide -3, no dependence is possible.

A *true data dependence* arises from a RAW hazard and will prevent vectorization of the loop as a single vector sequence. There are cases where the loop can be vectorized as two separate vector sequences (see Exercise 7.11). There are also dependences corresponding to a WAR (write after read) hazard, called an *antidependence*, and to a WAW (write after write) hazard, called an *output dependence*. Antidependences and output dependences are not true data dependences. They are name conflicts and can be eliminated by renaming of registers in the compiler in a method similar to how Tomasulo's algorithm renames registers at run time (see Section 6.7 in Chapter 6). Vectorizing compilers often use compile-time renaming to eliminate antidependences and output dependences.

Example

The following loop has an antidependence (WAR) and an output dependence (WAW). Find all the true dependences, output dependences, and antidependences, and eliminate the output dependences and antidependences by renaming.

```
          do 10 i=1,100
1                 Y(i) = X(i) / s
2                 X(i) = X(i) + s
3                 Z(i) = Y(i) + s
4                 Y(i) = s - Y(i)
10       continue
```

Answer

There are true dependences from statement 1 to statement 3 and from statement 1 to statement 4 because of Y(i). These are not loop carried, so they will not prevent vectorization. However, the dependences will force statements 3 and 4 to wait for statement 1 to complete, even though statements 3 and 4 use a different functional unit than statement 1. In the next section we will see a technique for eliminating this serialization.

There is an antidependence from statement 1 to statement 2, and an output dependence from statement 1 to statement 4. The following version of the loop eliminates these false (or pseudo) dependences.

```
        do 10 i=1,100
C       Y renamed to T to remove output dependence
1           T(i) = X(i) / s
C       X renamed to X1 to remove antidependence
2           X1(i) = X(i) + s
3           Z(i) = T(i) + s
4           Y(i) = s - T(i)
10      continue
```

After the loop the variable X has been renamed X1. In code that follows the loop, the compiler can simply replace the name X by X1. Renaming does not require an actual copy operation; it can be done by substituting names or by register allocation.

Besides deciding which loops are vectorizable, the compiler must generate strip-mining code and allocate vector registers. Most vectorization transformations are done at the source level, although some optimizations involve coordinating high-level source transformations with lower-level, machine-dependent transformations. Efficient allocation of vector registers is such an optimization and is perhaps the most difficult optimization—one that many vectorizing compilers do not attempt.

Effectiveness of Vectorization Techniques

Two factors affect the success with which a program can be run in vector mode. The first factor is the structure of the program itself: do the loops have true data dependences, or can they be restructured so as not to have such dependences? This factor is influenced by the algorithms chosen and, to some extent, how they are coded. The second factor is the capability of the compiler. While no compiler can vectorize a loop where no parallelism among the loop iterations exists, there is tremendous variation in the ability of compilers to determine whether a loop can be vectorized.

As an indication of the level of vectorization that can be achieved in scientific programs, let's look at the vectorization levels observed for the Perfect Club benchmarks, discussed in Section 2.7 of Chapter 2. These benchmarks are large, real scientific applications. Figure 7.12 (page 376) shows the percentage of floating-point operations in each benchmark and the percentage executed in vector mode on the CRAY X-MP. The wide variation in level of vectorization has been observed by several studies of the performance of applications on vector machines. While better compilers might improve the level of vectorization in some of these programs, most will require rewriting to achieve significant increases in vectorization. For example, let's look at our version of the Spice benchmark in detail. In Spice with the input chosen we found that only 3.7% of the floating-point operations are executed in vector mode on the CRAY X-MP, and the vector version runs only 0.5% faster than the scalar version. Clearly, a new program or a significant rewrite will be needed to obtain the benefits of a vector machine on Spice.

Benchmark name	FP operations	FP operations executed in vector mode
ADM	23%	68%
DYFESM	26%	95%
FLO52	41%	100%
MDG	28%	27%
MG3D	31%	86%
OCEAN	28%	58%
QCD	14%	1%
SPICE	16%	7%
TRACK	9%	23%
TRFD	22%	10%

FIGURE 7.12   Level of vectorization among the Perfect Club benchmarks when executed on the CRAY X-MP. The first column contains the percentage of operations that are floating point, while the second contains the percentage of FP operations executed in vector instructions. Note that this run of Spice with different inputs shows a higher vectorization ratio.

There is also tremendous variation in how well compilers do in vectorizing programs. As a summary of the state of vectorizing compilers, consider the data in Figure 7.13, which shows the extent of vectorization for different machines using a test suite of 100 hand-written FORTRAN kernels. The kernels were designed to test vectorization capability and can all be vectorized by hand; we will see several examples of these loops in the Exercises.

Machine	Compiler	Completely vectorized	Partially vectorized	Not vectorized
Ardent Titan-1	FORTRAN V1.0	62	6	32
CDC CYBER-205	VAST-2 V2.21	62	5	33
Convex C-series	FC5.0	69	5	26
CRAY X-MP	CFT77 V3.0	69	3	28
CRAY X-MP	CFT V1.15	50	1	49
CRAY-2	CFT2 V3.1a	27	1	72
ETA-10	FTN 77 V1.0	62	7	31
Hitachi S810/820	FORT77/HAP V20-2B	67	4	29
IBM 3090/VF	VS FORTRAN V2.4	52	4	44
NEC SX/2	FORTRAN77 / SX V.040	66	5	29
Stellar GS 1000	F77 prerelease	48	11	41

FIGURE 7.13   Result of applying vectorizing compilers to the 100 FORTRAN test kernels. For each machine we indicate how many loops were completely vectorized, partially vectorized, and unvectorized. These loops were collected by Callahan, Dongarra, and Levine [1988]. The machines shown are those mentioned at some point in this chapter. Two different compilers for the CRAY X-MP show the large dependence on compiler technology.

7.6 | Enhancing Vector Performance

Three techniques for improving the performance of vector machines are discussed in this section. The first deals with making a sequence of dependent vector operations run faster. The other two deal with expanding the class of loops that can be run in vector mode. The first technique, chaining, originated in the CRAY-1, but is now supported on many vector machines. The techniques discussed in the second and third parts of this section are taken from a variety of machines and are, in general, more extensive than the capabilities provided on the CRAY-1 or CRAY X-MP architectures.

Chaining—The Concept of Forwarding Extended to Vector Registers

Consider the simple vector sequence

```
MULTV       V1,V2,V3
ADDV        V4,V1,V5
```

In DLXV as it currently stands these two instructions run in time equal to

$$T_{element} * \text{Vector length} + \text{Start-up time}_{ADDV} + \text{stall time} + \text{Start-up time}_{MULTV}$$

$$= 2 * \text{Vector length} + 6 + 4 + 7$$

$$= 2 * \text{Vector length} + 17$$

Because of the dependence, the MULTV must complete before the ADDV can begin. However, if the vector register, V1 in this case, is treated not as a single entity but as a group of individual registers, then the pipelining concept of forwarding can be extended to work on individual elements of a vector. This idea, which will allow the ADDV to start earlier in this example, is called *chaining*. Chaining allows a vector operation to start as soon as the individual elements of its vector source operand become available: The results from the first functional unit in the chain are forwarded to the second functional unit. (Of course, they must be different units to avoid using the same unit twice per clock!) In a chained sequence the initiation rate is equal to one per clock cycle if the functional units in the chained operations are all fully pipelined. Even though the operations depend on one another, chaining allows the operations to proceed in parallel on separate elements of the vector. A sustained rate (ignoring start-up) of two floating-point operations per clock cycle can be achieved, even though the operations are dependent!

The total running time for the above sequence becomes

$$\text{Vector length} + \text{Start-up time}_{ADDV} + \text{Start-up time}_{MULTV}$$

Figure 7.14 shows the timing of a chained and an unchained version of the above pair of vector instructions with a vector length of 64. In Figure 7.14, the total time for chained operation is 77 clock cycles. With 128 floating-point operations done in that time, 1.7 FLOPs per clock cycle are obtained, versus a total time of 145 clock cycles or 0.9 FLOPs per clock cycle for the unchained version.

We will see in Section 7.7 that chaining plays a major role in boosting vector performance.

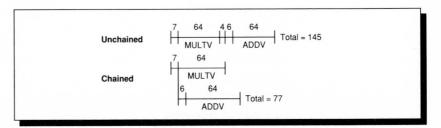

FIGURE 7.14 Timings for a sequence of dependent vector operations ADDV and MULTV, both unchained and chained. The 4–clock-cycle delay comes from a stall for dependence, described earlier; the 6– and 7–clock-cycle delays are the latency of the adder and multiplier.

Conditionally Executed Statements and Sparse Matrices

In the last section, we saw that many programs only achieved low to moderate levels of vectorization. Because of Amdahl's Law, the speedup on such programs will be very limited. Two reasons why higher levels of vectorization are not achieved are the presence of conditionals (if statements) inside loops and the use of sparse matrices. Programs that contain if statements in loops cannot be run in vector mode using the techniques we have discussed so far because the if statements introduce control flow into a loop. Likewise, sparse matrices cannot be efficiently implemented using any of the capabilities we have seen so far; this is a major factor in the lack of vectorization for Spice. This section discusses techniques that allow programs with these structures to execute in vector mode. Let's start with conditional execution.

Consider the following loop:

```
do 100 i = 1, 64
    if (A(i) .ne. 0) then
        A(i) = A(i) - B(i)
    endif
100 continue
```

This loop cannot normally be vectorized because of the conditional execution of the body. However, if the inner loop could be run for the iterations for which $A(i) \neq 0$, then the subtraction could be vectorized.

Vector-mask control helps us do this. The *vector-mask control* takes a Boolean vector of length MVL. When the *vector-mask register* is loaded with the result of a vector test, any vector instructions to be executed operate only on the vector elements whose corresponding entries in the vector-mask register are 1. The entries in the destination vector register that correspond to a 0 in the mask register are unaffected by the vector operation. Clearing the vector-mask register sets it to all 1s, making subsequent vector instructions operate on all vector elements. The following code can now be used for the above loop, assuming that the starting addresses of A and B are in Ra and Rb respectively:

```
LV    V1,Ra      ;load vector A into V1
LV    V2,Rb      ;load vector B
LD    F0,#0      ;load FP zero into F0
SNESV F0,V1      ;sets the VM to 1 if V1(i)≠F0
SUBV  V1,V1,V2   ;subtract under vector mask
CVM              ;set the vector mask to all 1s
SV    Ra,V1      ;store the result in A
```

Most modern vector machines provide vector-mask control. The vector-mask capability described here is available on some machines, but others allow the use of the vector mask with only a small number of instructions.

Using a vector-mask register does, however, have disadvantages. First, execution time is not decreased, even though some elements in the vector are not operated on. Second, in some vector machines the vector mask serves only to disable the storing of the result into the destination register, and the actual operation still occurs. Thus, if the operation in the above example were a divide rather than a subtract and the test was on B rather than A, false floating-point exceptions might result since the operation was actually done. Machines that mask the operation as well as the result store avoid this problem.

Now, let's turn to sparse matrices; later we will show another method for handling conditional execution. We have dealt with vectors in which the elements are separated by a constant stride. If an application called for a sparse matrix, we might see code that looks like:

```
        do    100 i = 1,n
100           A(K(i)) = A(K(i)) + C(M(i))
```

This code implements a sparse vector sum on the arrays A and C, using index vectors K and M to designate to the nonzero elements of A and C. (A and C must have the same number of nonzero elements—n of them.) Another common representation for sparse matrices uses a bit vector to say which elements exist, and often both representations exist in the same program. Sparse matrices are found in many codes, and there are many ways to implement them, depending on the data structure used in the program.

The primary mechanism for supporting sparse matrices is scatter-gather operations using index vectors. A *gather* operation takes an *index vector*, and fetches the vector whose elements are at the addresses given by adding a base address to the offsets given in the index vector. The result is a nonsparse vector in a vector register. After these elements are operated on in dense form, the sparse vector can be stored in expanded form by a *scatter* store, using the same index vector. Hardware support for such operations is called *scatter-gather* and appeared on the CDC STAR-100. The instructions LVI (Load Vector Indexed) and SVI (Store Vector Indexed) provide these operations in DLXV. For example, assuming that Ra, Rc, Rk, and Rm contain the starting addresses of the vectors in the above sequence, the inner loop of the sequence can be coded with vector instructions such as:

```
LV   Vk,Rk          ;load K
LVI  Va,(Ra+Vk)     ;load A(K(I))
LV   Vm,Rm          ;load M
LVI  Vc,(Rc+Vm)     ;load C(M(I))
ADDV Va,Va,Vc       ;add them
SVI  (Ra+Vk),Va     ;store A(K(I))
```

This technique allows code with sparse matrices to be run in vector mode. The source code above would **never** be automatically vectorized by a compiler because the compiler cannot know that the elements of K are distinct values, and thus that no dependences exist. Instead, a programmer directive would tell the compiler that it could run the loop in vector mode.

A scatter/gather capability is included on many of the newest super-computers. Such operations rarely run at one element per clock, but they are still much faster than the alternative, which may be a scalar loop. If the sparsity properties of a matrix change, a new index vector must be computed. Many machines provide support for computing the index vector quickly. The CVI (Create Vector Index) instruction in DLXV creates an index vector given a stride (m), where the values in the index vector are $0,m,2*m,...,63*m$. Some machines provide an instruction to create a compressed index vector whose entries correspond to the positions with a 1 in the mask register. Other vector architectures provide a method to compress a vector. In DLXV, we define the CVI instruction to always create a compressed index vector using the vector mask. When the vector mask is all ones a standard index vector will be created.

The indexed loads/stores and the CVI instruction provide an alternative method to support conditional execution. Here is a vector sequence that implements the loop we saw on page 379:

```
LV      V1,Ra         ;load vector A into V1
LD      F0,#0         ;load FP zero into F0
SNESV   F0,V1         ;sets the VM to 1 if V1(i)≠F0
ADDI    Rc,#8
CVI     V2,Rc         ;generates indices in V2
POP     R1,VM         ;find the number of 1's in VM
MOVI2S  VLR,R1        ;load vector length register
CVM
LVI     V3,(Ra+V2)    ;load the nonzero A elements
LVI     V4,(Rb+V2)    ;load corresponding B elements
SUBV    V3,V3,V4      ;do the subtract
SVI     (Ra+V2),V3    ;store A back
```

Whether the implementation using scatter/gather is better than the conditionally executed version depends on the frequency with which the condition holds and the cost of the operations. Ignoring chaining, the running time of the first version (on page 379) is $5n + c_1$. The running time of the second version using indexed loads and stores with a running time of one element per clock is $4n + 4*f*n + c_2$, where f is the fraction of elements for which the condition is true (i.e., $A \neq 0$). If we assume that the values of c_1 and c_2 are comparable, or that they are much smaller than n, we can find when this second technique is better.

$$\text{Time}_1 = 5n$$

$$\text{Time}_2 = 4n + 4*f*n$$

We want Time$_1 \geq$ Time$_2$, so

$$5n \geq 4n + 4*f*n$$

$$\frac{1}{4} \geq f$$

That is, the second method is faster if less than one-quarter of the elements are nonzero. In many cases the frequency of execution is much lower. If the index vector can be reused, or if the number of vector statements within the if statement grows, the advantage of the scatter/gather approach will increase sharply.

Vector Reduction

As we saw in Section 7.5, some loop structures are not easily vectorized. One common structure is a *reduction*—a loop that reduces an array to a single value by repeated application of an operation. This is a special case of a recurrence. A common example occurs in dot product:

```
dot = 0.0
do 10 i=1,64
10        dot = dot + A(i) * B(i)
```

This loop has an obvious loop-carried dependence (on dot) and cannot be vectorized in a straightforward fashion. The first thing a good vectorizing compiler would do is split the loop to separate out the vectorizable portion and the recurrence and perhaps rewrite the loop as:

```
do 10 i=1,64
10        dot(i) = A(i) * B(i)

do 20 i=2,64
20        dot(1) = dot(1) + dot(i)
```

The variable dot has been expanded into a vector; this transformation is called *scalar expansion*.

One simple scheme for compiling the loop with the recurrence is to add sequences of progressively shorter vectors—two 32-element vectors, then two 16-element vectors, and so on. This technique has been called *recursive doubling*. It is faster than doing all the operations in scalar mode. Many vector machines provide hardware assist for doing reductions, as we will see next.

Example   Show how the FORTRAN code would look for execution of the second loop in the code fragment above using recursive doubling.

Answer | Here is the code:

```
            len = 32
            do 100 j=1,6
                  do 10 i=1,len
    10                     dot(i) = dot(i) + dot(i+len)
                  len = len / 2
    100   continue
```

When the loop is done, the sum is in dot(1).

In some vector machines, the vector registers are addressable, and another technique, sometimes called partial sums, can be used. This is discussed in Exercise 7.12. There is an important caveat in the use of vector techniques for reduction. To make reduction work, we are relying on the associativity of the operator being used for the reduction. Because of rounding and finite range, however, floating-point arithmetic is not strictly associative. For this reason, most compilers require the programmer to indicate whether associativity can be used to more efficiently compile reductions.

7.7 | Putting It All Together: Evaluating the Performance of Vector Processors

In this section we look at different measures of performance for vector machines and what they tell us about the machine. To determine the performance of a machine on a vector problem we must look at the start-up cost and the sustained rate. The simplest and best way to report the performance of a vector machine on a loop is to give the execution time of the vector loop. For vector loops people often give the MFLOPS (Millions FLoating point Operations Per Second) rating rather than execution time. We use the notation R_n for the MFLOPS rating on a vector of length n. Using the measurements T_n (time) or R_n (rate) is equivalent if the number of FLOPs is agreed upon (see Chapter 2, Section 2.2, page 35 for an extensive discussion on MFLOPS). In any event, either measurement should include the overhead.

In this section we examine the performance of DLXV on our SAXPY loop by looking at performance from different viewpoints. We will continue to compute the execution time of a vector loop using the equation developed in Section 7.4. At the same time, we will look at different ways to measure performance using the computed time. The constant values for T_{loop} and T_{base} used in this section introduce some small amount of error, which will be ignored.

Measures of Vector Performance

Because vector length is so important in establishing the performance of a machine, length-related measures are often applied in addition to time and MFLOPs. These length-related measures tend to vary dramatically across different machines and are interesting to compare. (Remember, though, that **time** is always the measure of interest when comparing the relative speed of two machines.) Three of the most important length-related measures are:

R_∞—The MFLOPS rate on an infinite-length vector. Although this measure may be of interest when estimating peak performance, real problems do not have unlimited vector lengths, and the overhead penalties encountered in real problems will be larger. (R_n is the MFLOPS rate for a vector of length n.)

$N_{1/2}$—The vector length needed to reach one-half of R_∞. This is a good measure of the impact of overhead.

N_v—The vector length needed to make vector mode faster than scalar mode. This measures both overhead and the speed of scalars relative to vectors.

Let's look at these measures for our SAXPY problem running on DLXV. When chained, the inner loop of the SAXPY code looks like this (assuming that Rx and Ry hold starting addresses):

```
LV      V1,Rx       ;load the vector X
MULTSV  V2,S1,V1    ;vector*scalar-chained to LV X
LV      V3,Ry       ;vector load Y
ADDV    V4,V2,V3    ;sum aX + Y, chained to LV Y
SV      Ry,V4       ;store the vector Y
```

Recall our performance equation for the execution time of a vector loop with n elements, T_n:

$$T_n = T_{base} + \left\lceil \frac{n}{MVL} \right\rceil * (T_{loop} + T_{start}) + n * T_{element}$$

Since there are three memory references and only one memory pipeline, the value of $T_{element}$ must be at least 3, and chaining allows it to be exactly 3. If $T_{element}$ were a complete indication of performance, the loop would run at a MFLOPS rate of $\frac{2}{3}$ * clock rate (since there are 2 FLOPS per iteration). Thus, based only on the $T_{element}$ time, an 80-MHz DLXV would run this loop at 53 MFLOPS. But the Linpack benchmark, whose core is this computation, runs at only 13 MFLOPS (without some sophisticated compiler optimization we discuss in the Exercises) on an 80-MHz CRAY-1, DLXV's cousin! Let's see what accounts for the difference.

The Peak Performance of DLXV on SAXPY

First, we should determine what the peak performance, R_∞, really is, since we know it differs from the ideal 53-MFLOPS rate. Figure 7.15 shows the timing within each block of strip-mined code.

Operation		Starts at clock number	Completes at clock number	Comment
LV	V1,Rx	0	$12 + 64 = 76$	Simple latency
MULTV	a,V1	$12 + 1 = 13$	$13 + 7 + 64 = 84$	Chained to LV
LV	V2,Ry	$76 + 1 = 77$	$77 + 12 + 64 = 153$	Starts after first LV done (memory contention)
ADDV	V3,V1,V2	$77 + 1 + 12 = 90$	$90 + 6 + 64 = 160$	Chained to MULTV and LV
SV	Ry,V3	$160 + 1 + 4 = 165$	$165 + 12 + 64 = 241$	Must wait on ADDV; not chained (memory contention)

FIGURE 7.15   The SAXPY loop when chained in DLXV. There are three distinct types of delays: 4–clock-cycle delays when a nonchained dependence occurs, latency delays that occur when waiting for a result for the pipeline (6 for add, 7 for multiply, and 12 for memory access), and delays due to contention for the memory pipeline. The last cause is what makes the time per element at least 3 clocks.

From the data in Figure 7.15 and the value of $T_{element}$, we know that

$$T_{start} = 241 - 64 * T_{element} = 241 - 192 = 49$$

This value is equal to the sum of the latencies of the functional units: $12 + 7 + 12 + 6 + 12 = 49$.

Using MVL = 64, $T_{loop} = 15$, $T_{base} = 10$, and $T_{element} = 3$ in the performance equation, the time for an n-element operation is

$$T_n = 10 + \left\lceil \frac{n}{64} \right\rceil * (15 + 49) + 3n$$

$$T_n = 10 + n + 64 + 3n = 4n + 74$$

The sustained rate is actually over 4 clock cycles per iteration, rather than the theoretical rate of 3 clocks per iteration, which ignores overhead. The major part of the difference is the cost of the overhead for each block of 64 elements. The basic start-up overhead, T_{base}, adds only $\dfrac{10}{n}$ to the time for each element. This overhead disappears with long vectors.

We can now compute R_∞ for an 80-MHz clock as

$$R_\infty = \lim_{n \to \infty} \left(\frac{\text{Operations per iteration} * \text{Clock rate}}{\text{Clock cycles per iteration}} \right)$$

The numerator is independent of n, hence

$$R_\infty = \frac{\text{Operations per iteration} * \text{Clock rate}}{\lim_{n \to \infty} (\text{Clock cycles per iteration})}$$

$$\lim_{n \to \infty} (\text{Clock cycles per iteration}) = \lim_{n \to \infty} \left(\frac{T_n}{n}\right) = \lim_{n \to \infty} \left(\frac{4n + 74}{n}\right) = 4$$

$$R_\infty = \frac{2 * 80 \text{ MHz}}{4} = 40 \text{ MFLOPS}$$

Sustained Performance of Linpack on DLXV

The Linpack benchmark is a Gaussian elimination on a 100x100 matrix. Thus, the vector element lengths range from 99 down to 1. A vector of length k is used k times. Thus, the average vector length is given by:

$$\frac{\sum_{i=1}^{99} i^2}{\sum_{i=1}^{99} i} = 66.3$$

Now we can obtain an accurate estimate of the performance of SAXPY using a vector length of 66.

$$T_{66} = 10 + 2 * (15 + 49) + 66 * 3 = 10 + 128 + 198 = 336$$

$$R_{66} = \frac{2 * 66 * 80}{336} \text{MFLOPS} = 31.4 \text{ MFLOPS}$$

In reality, Linpack does not spend all its time in the inner loop. The benchmark's actual performance can be found by taking the weighted harmonic mean of the MFLOPS ratings inside the inner loop (31.4 MFLOPS) and outside that loop (about 0.5 MFLOPS). We can compute the weighting factors by knowing the percentage of the time inside the inner loop after vectorization.

The percentage in the inner loop after vectorization can be obtained using Amdahl's Law if we know the percentage in scalar and the speedup from vectorization. In scalar mode, about 75% of the execution time is spent in the inner loop, and the speedup from vectorization is about 5 times. With this information the percentage of time in the inner loop after vectorization can be computed:

$$\text{Total relative time after vectorization} = \frac{0.75}{5} + 0.25$$

$$= 0.15 + 0.25 = 0.40$$

Percentage of time in inner loop after vectorization $\;=\dfrac{0.15}{0.40}=37.5\%$

The remaining 62.5% of the time is spent outside the main loop. Thus, the overall MFLOPS rating is

$$\text{Percentage}_{\text{inner}} * \text{MFLOPS}_{\text{inner}} + \text{Percentage}_{\text{other}} * \text{MFLOPS}_{\text{other}}$$

$$= 37.5\% * 31.4 + 62.5\% * 0.5 = 12.1 \text{ MFLOPS}$$

This is comparable to the rate at which the CRAY-1 runs this benchmark.

Example   What is $N_{1/2}$ for just the inner loop of SAXPY for DLXV with an 80-MHz clock?

Answer   Using R_{∞} as the peak rate, we want to know the vector length that will achieve about 20 MFLOPS. So,

$$\dfrac{\dfrac{\text{Clock cycles}}{\text{Iteration}}}{} = \dfrac{\dfrac{\text{FLOPS}}{\text{Iteration}} * \dfrac{\text{Clocks}}{\text{Second}}}{\dfrac{\text{FLOPS}}{\text{Second}}}$$

$$= \dfrac{2 * 80 \text{ MHz}}{20 \text{ MFLOPS}} = 8$$

Hence, a rate of 20 MFLOPS means that a loop iteration completes every 8 clock cycles on average, or that $\dfrac{T_n}{n}=8$. Using our equation and assuming that $n \le 64$,

$$T_n = 10 + 1 * 64 + 3 * n$$

Substituting for T_n in the first equation, we obtain

$$8\,n \;=\; 74 + 3 * n$$

$$5n \;=\; 74$$

$$n \;=\; 14.8$$

So $N_{1/2} = 15$; that is, a vector of length 15 gives approximately one-half the peak performance for the SAXPY loop on DLXV.

Example   What is the vector length, N_v, such that the vector operation runs faster than the scalar?

Answer

Again, we know that $N_v < 64$. The time to do one iteration in scalar mode can be estimated as $10 + 12 + 12 + 7 + 6 = 47$ clocks, where 10 is the estimate of the loop overhead, known to be somewhat less than the strip-mining loop overhead. In the last problem, we showed that this vector loop runs in vector mode in time $T_n = 74 + 3*n$ clock cycles for a vector of length ≤ 64. Therefore,

$$74 + 3n = 47n$$

$$n = \frac{74}{44}$$

$$N_v = 2$$

For the SAXPY loop, vector mode is faster than scalar as long as the vector has at least two elements. This number is surprisingly small, as we will see in the next section (Fallacies and Pitfalls).

SAXPY Performance on an Enhanced DLXV

SAXPY, like many vector problems, is memory limited. Consequently, performance could be improved by adding more memory-access pipelines. This is the major architectural difference between the CRAY X-MP and the CRAY-1. The CRAY X-MP has three memory pipelines, compared to the CRAY-1's single memory pipeline, and the X-MP has more flexible chaining. How does this affect performance?

Example

What would be the value of T_{66} for SAXPY on DLXV if we added two more memory pipelines?

Answer

Figure 7.16 is a version of Figure 7.15 (page 385), adjusted for multiple memory pipelines.

Operation	Starts at clock number	Completes at clock number	Comment
LV V1,Rx	0	12 + 64 = 76	Simple latency
MULTV a,V1	12 + 1 = 13	13 + 7 + 64 = 84	Chained to LV
LV V2,Ry	2	2 + 12 + 64 = 78	Starts immediately
ADDV V3,V1,V2	13 + 1 + 7 = 21	21 + 6 + 64 = 91	Chained to MULTV and LV
SV Ry,V3	21 + 1 + 6 = 28	28 + 12 + 64 = 104	Chained to ADDV

FIGURE 7.16 The SAXPY loop when chained in DLXV with three memory pipelines. The only delays are latency delays that occur when waiting for a result for the pipeline (6 for add, 7 for multiply, and 12 for each memory access).

With three memory pipelines, the performance is greatly improved. Here's our standard performance equation:

$$T_n = T_{base} + \left\lceil \frac{n}{MVL} \right\rceil * (T_{loop} + T_{start}) + n * T_{element}$$

With three memory pipelines the value of $T_{element}$ becomes 1, so that

$$T_{start} = 104 - 64 * T_{element} = 104 - 64 = 40$$

The reduction in stalls reduces the start-up penalty for each sequence. The values of T_{loop} and T_{base}, 15 and 10, remain the same. Therefore, for an average vector length of 66, we have:

$$T_{66} = T_{base} + \left\lceil \frac{66}{64} \right\rceil * (T_{loop} + T_{start}) + 66 * T_{element}$$

$$T_{66} = 10 + 2 * (15 + 40) + 66 * 1 = 186$$

With three memory pipelines, we have reduced the clock-cycle count for sustained performance from 336 to 186, a factor of 1.8. Note the effect of Amdahl's Law: We improved the theoretical peak rate, as measured by $T_{element}$, by a factor of 3, but only achieved an overall improvement of a factor of 1.8 in sustained performance. Because the speedup outside the inner loop is likely to be less than 1.8, the overall improvement in run time for the benchmark will also be less.

Another improvement could come from allowing the start-up of one loop iteration before another completes. This requires that one vector operation be allowed to begin using a functional unit, before another operation has completed. This complicates the instruction issue logic substantially, but has the advantage that the start-up overhead will only occur once, independent of the vector length. On a long vector the overhead per block ($T_{loop} + T_{start}$) can be completely amortized. In this way a machine with vector registers can have both low start-up overhead for short vectors and high peak performance for very long vectors.

Example

What would be the values of R_{∞} and T_{66} for SAXPY on DLXV if we added two more memory pipelines and allowed the strip-mining and start-up overhead to be fully overlapped?

Answer

$$R_{\infty} = \lim_{n \to \infty} \left(\frac{\text{Operations per iteration} * \text{Clock rate}}{\text{Clock cycles per iteration}} \right)$$

$$\lim_{n \to \infty} (\text{Clock cycles per iteration}) = \lim_{n \to \infty} \left(\frac{T_n}{n} \right)$$

Since $T_n = n + 40 + 10 + 15 = n + 65$,

$$\lim_{n \to \infty} \left(\frac{T_n}{n} \right) = \lim_{n \to \infty} \left(\frac{n + 65}{n} \right) = 1$$

$$R_\infty = \frac{2 * 80 \text{ MHz}}{1} = 160 \text{ MFLOPS}$$

Thus, adding the extra memory pipelines and more flexible issue logic yields an improvement in peak performance of a factor of 4. However, $T_{66} = 131$, so for shorter vectors, the sustained performance improvement is about 40%.

In summary, we have examined several measures of vector performance. Theoretical peak performance can be calculated based purely on the value of $T_{element}$ as

$$\frac{\text{Number of FLOPS per iteration} * \text{Clock rate}}{T_{element}}$$

By including the loop overhead, we can calculate values for peak performance for an infinite-length vector (R_∞), and also for sustained performance R_n for a vector of length n, which is computed as:

$$R_n = \frac{\text{Number of FLOPS per iteration} * n * \text{Clock rate}}{T_n}$$

Using these measures we also can find $N_{1/2}$ and N_v, which give us another way of looking at the start-up overhead for vectors and the ratio of vector to scalar speed. A wide variety of measures of performance of vector machines are useful in understanding the wide range of performance that applications may see on a vector machine.

7.8 | Fallacies and Pitfalls

Pitfall: Concentrating on peak performance and ignoring start-up overhead.

Early vector machines such as the TI ASC and the CDC STAR-100 had long start-up times. For some vector problems, N_v could be greater than 100! Today, the Japanese supercomputers often have higher sustained rates than the Cray Research machines. But with start-up overheads that are 50–100% higher, the faster sustained rates often provide no real advantage. On the CYBER-205 the start-up overhead for SAXPY is 158 clock cycles, substantially increasing the break-even point. With a single vector unit, which contains 2 memory pipelines, the CYBER-205 can sustain a rate of 2 clocks per iteration. The time for SAXPY for a vector of length n is therefore roughly $158 + 2n$. If the clock rates of the CRAY-1 and the CYBER-205 were identical, the CRAY-1 would be faster until $n > 64$. Because the CRAY-1 clock is also faster (even though the 205 is newer), the crossover point is over 100. Comparing a four-vector-pipeline CYBER-205 (the maximum-size machine) to the CRAY X-MP that was delivered shortly after the 205, the 205 completes two results per clock cycle—twice as fast as the X-MP. However, vectors must be longer than about 200 for the CYBER-205 to be faster. The problem of start-up overhead has been the major difficulty for the memory–memory vector architectures.

Pitfall: Increasing vector performance, without comparable increases in scalar performance.

This is another area where Seymour Cray rewrote the rules. Many of the early vector machines had comparatively slow scalar units (as well as large start-up overheads). Even today, machines with higher peak vector performance, can be outperformed by a machine with lower vector performance but better scalar performance. Good scalar performance keeps down overhead costs (strip mining, for example) and reduces the impact of Amdahl's Law. A good example of this comes from comparing a fast scalar machine and a vector machine with lower scalar performance. The Livermore FORTRAN kernels are a collection of 24 scientific kernels with varying degrees of vectorization (see Chapter 2; Section 2.2). Figure 7.17 shows the performance of two different machines on this benchmark. Despite the vector machine's higher peak performance, its low scalar performance makes it slower than a fast scalar machine. The next fallacy is closely related.

Machine	Minimum rate for any loop	Maximum rate for any loop	Harmonic mean of all 24 loops
MIPS M/120-5	0.80 MFLOPS	3.89 MFLOPS	1.85 MFLOPS
Stardent-1500	0.41 MFLOPS	10.08 MFLOPS	1.72 MFLOPS

FIGURE 7.17 Performance measurements for the Livermore FORTRAN kernels on two different machines. Both the MIPS M/120-5 and the Stardent-1500 (formerly the Ardent Titan-1) use a 16.7-MHz MIPS R2000 chip for the main CPU. The Stardent-1500 uses its vector unit for scalar FP and has about half the scalar performance (as measured by the minimum rate) of the MIPS M/120, which uses the MIPS R2010 FP chip. The vector machine is more than a factor of 2.5 times faster for a highly vectorizable loop (maximum rate). However, the lower scalar performance of the Stardent-1500 negates the higher vector performance when total performance is measured by the harmonic mean on all 24 loops.

*Fallacy: The scalar performance of the **best** supercomputers is low.*

The supercomputers from Cray Research have always had good scalar performance. Measurements of the CRAY Y-MP running (the nonvectorizable) Spice benchmark show this. When our Spice benchmark is run on the CRAY Y-MP in scalar mode it executes 665 million instructions, with a CPI of 4.1. By comparison, the DECstation 3100 executes 738 million instructions with a CPI of 2.1.

Although the DECstation uses fewer cycles, the Y-MP uses fewer instructions and is much faster overall, since it has a clock cycle one-tenth as long.

Fallacy: You can get vector performance without providing memory bandwidth.

As we saw with the SAXPY loop, memory bandwidth is quite important. SAXPY requires 1.5 memory references per floating-point operation, and this ratio is typical of many scientific codes. Even if the floating-point operations took no time, a CRAY-1 could not increase the performance of the vector sequence used, since it is memory limited. Recently, the CRAY-1 performance on Linpack has jumped because the compiler used clever transformations to change the computation so that values could be kept in the vector registers. This lowered the number of memory references per FLOP and improved the performance by nearly a factor of 2! Thus, the memory bandwidth on the CRAY-1 became sufficient for a loop that formerly required more bandwidth.

7.9 | Concluding Remarks

In the late 1980s rapid performance increases in efficiently pipelined scalar machines lead to a dramatic closing of the gap between vector supercomputers, costing millions of dollars, and fast, pipelined, VLSI microprocessors costing less than $100,000. The basic reason for this was the rapidly decreasing CPI of the scalar machines.

For scientific programs, an interesting counterpart to CPI is clock cycles per FLOP, or CPF. We saw in this chapter that for vector machines this number was typically in the range of 2 (for a CRAY X-MP style machine) to 4 (for a CRAY-1 style machine). In the last chapter, we saw that the pipelined machine varied from about 6 (for DLX) down to about 2.5 (for a superscalar DLX with no memory system losses running a SAXPY-type loop).

Recent trends in vector machine design have focused on high peak-vector performance and multiprocessing. Meanwhile, high-speed scalar machines concentrate on keeping the ratio of peak to sustained performance near one. Thus, if the peak rates advance comparably, the sustained rates of the scalar machines will advance more quickly, and the scalar machines will continue to close the CPF gap. These multiple-issue scalar machines can rival or exceed the performance of vector machines with comparable clock speeds, especially for levels of vectorization below 70%. Furthermore, the differences in clock rate are largely technology driven—the low-end, microprocessor-based vector machines have clock rates comparable to the pipelined machines using microprocessor technology. (In fact, they often use the same microprocessors!) In the future, we can expect high-speed pipelined scalar machines to be built with clock rates that will rival those of the current vector supercomputers. However, the vector machines should retain a performance advantage for problems with very long vectors that can use multiple memory pipelines and achieve performance close to the peak.

The 1990s will be interesting as the pipelined scalar machines that exploit more instruction-level parallelism and are usually much cheaper (because their peak performance and hence total hardware is much less) begin to offer performance levels for many applications that are difficult to distinguish from those of vector machines.

7.10 | Historical Perspective and References

The first vector machines were the CDC STAR-100 (see Hintz and Tate [1972]) and the TI ASC (see Watson [1972]), both announced in 1972. Both were memory–memory vector machines. They had relatively slow scalar units—the STAR used the same units for scalars and vectors—making the scalar pipeline extremely deep. Both machines had high start-up overhead and worked on vectors of several hundred to several thousand elements. The crossover between scalar and vector could be over 50 elements. It appears that not enough attention was paid to the role of Amdahl's Law on these two machines.

Cray, who worked on the 6600 and the 7600 at CDC, founded Cray Research and introduced the CRAY-1 in 1976 (see Russell [1978]). The CRAY-1 used a vector-register architecture to significantly lower start-up overhead. He also had efficient support for nonunit stride and invented chaining. Most importantly, the CRAY-1 was also the fastest scalar machine in the world at that time. This matching of good scalar and vector performance was probably the most significant factor in making the CRAY-1 a success. Some customers bought the machine primarily for its outstanding scalar performance. Many subsequent vector machines are based on the architecture of this first commercially successful vector machine. Baskett and Keller [1977] is a good evaluation of the CRAY-1.

In 1981, CDC started shipping the CYBER-205 (see Lincoln [1982]). The 205 had the same basic architecture as the STAR, but offered improved performance all around as well as expansibility of the vector unit with up to four vector pipelines, each with multiple functional units and a wide load/store pipe that provided multiple words per clock. The peak performance of the CYBER-205 greatly exceeded the performance of the CRAY-1. However, on real programs, the performance difference was much smaller.

The CDC STAR machine and its descendant, the CYBER-205, were memory–memory vector machines. To keep the hardware simple and support the high bandwidth requirements (up to 3 memory references per FLOP), these machines did not efficiently handle nonunit stride. While most loops have unit stride, a nonunit stride loop had poor performance on these machines because memory-to-memory data movements were required to gather together (and scatter back) the nonadjacent vector elements.

Schneck [1987] described several of the early pipelined machines (e.g., Stretch) through the first vector machines including the 205 and CRAY-1. Dongarra [1986] did another good survey, focusing on more recent machines.

In 1983, Cray shipped the first CRAY X-MP (see Chen [1983]). With an improved clock rate (9.5 ns versus 12.5 on the CRAY-1), better chaining support, and multiple memory pipelines, this machine maintained the Cray Research lead in supercomputers. The CRAY-2, a completely new design configurable with up to four processors, was introduced later. It has a much faster clock than the X-MP, but also much deeper pipelines. The CRAY-2 lacks chaining, has an enormous memory latency, and has only one memory pipe per processor. In general, it is only faster than the CRAY X-MP on problems that require its very large main memory.

In 1983, the Japanese computer vendors entered the supercomputer marketplace, starting with the Fujitsu VP100 and VP200 (Miura and Uchida [1983]), and later expanding to include the Hitachi S810, and the NEC SX/2 (see Watanabe [1987]). These machines have proved to be close to the CRAY X-MP in performance. In general, these three machines have much higher peak performance than the CRAY X-MP, though because of large start-up overhead, their typical performance is often lower than the CRAY X-MP (see Figure 2.24 in Chapter 2). The CRAY X-MP favored a multiple-processor approach, first offering a two-processor version and later a four-processor machine. In contrast, the three Japanese machines had expandable vector capabilities. In 1988, Cray Research introduced the CRAY Y-MP—a bigger and faster version of the X-MP. The Y-MP allows up to 8 processors and lowers the cycle time to 6 ns. With a full complement of 8 processors, the Y-MP is generally the fastest supercomputer, though the single-processor Japanese supercomputers may be faster than a one-processor Y-MP. In late 1989 Cray Research was split into two companies, both aimed at building high-end machines available in the early 1990s. Seymour Cray continues to head the spin-off, which is now called Cray Computer Corporation.

In the early 1980s, CDC spun out a group, called ETA, to build a new supercomputer, the ETA-10, capable of 10 GigaFLOPs. The ETA machine delivered in the late 1980s (see Fazio [1987]) used low-temperature CMOS in a configuration with up to 10 processors. Each processor retained the memory–memory architecture based on the CYBER-205. Although the ETA-10 achieved enormous peak performance, its scalar speed was not comparable. In 1989 CDC, the first supercomputer vendor, closed ETA and left the supercomputer design business.

In 1986, IBM introduced the System/370 vector architecture (see Moore et al. [1987]) and its first implementation in the 3090 Vector Facility. The architecture extends the System/370 architecture with 171 vector instructions. The 3090/VF is integrated into the 3090 CPU. Unlike most other vector machines, the 3090/VF routes its vectors through the cache.

The 1980s also saw the arrival of smaller-scale vector machines, called minisupercomputers. Priced at roughly one-tenth the cost of a supercomputer ($0.5 to

$1 million versus $5 to $10 million), these machines caught on quickly. Although many companies joined the market, the two companies that have been most successful are Convex and Alliant. Convex started with a uniprocessor vector machine (C-1) and now offers a small multiprocessor (C-2); they emphasize Cray software capability. Alliant [1987] has concentrated more on the multiprocessor aspects; they build an eight-processor machine, with each processor offering vector capability.

The basis for modern vectorizing compiler technology and the notion of data dependence was developed by Kuck and his colleagues [1974] at the University of Illinois. Banerjee [1979] developed the test named after him. Padua and Wolf [1986] gave a good overview of vectorizing compiler technology.

Benchmark studies of various supercomputers including attempts to understand the performance differences have been undertaken by Lubeck, Moore and Mendez [1985], Bucher [1983], and Jordan [1987]. In Chapter 2, we discussed several benchmark suites aimed at scientific usage and often employed for supercomputer benchmarking, including Linpack, the Lawrence Livermore Laboratories FORTRAN kernels, and the Perfect Club suite.

In the late 1980s, graphics supercomputers arrived on the market from Stellar [Sporer, Moss, and Mathais 1988] and Ardent [Miranker, Rubenstein, and Sanguinetti 1988]. The Stellar machine used a timeshared pipeline to allow high-speed vector processing and efficient multitasking. This approach was used earlier in a machine designed by B. J. Smith [1981] called the HEP and built by Denelcor in the mid-1980s. This approach does not yield high-speed scalar performance, as evident in the scalar benchmarks of the Stellar machine. The Ardent machine combines a RISC processor (the MIPS R2000) with a custom vector unit. These vector machines, which cost about $100K, brought vector capabilities to a new potential market. In late 1989, Stellar and Ardent were merged to form Stardent, and the Ardent architecture is being shipped from the combined company.

From this overview we can see the progress vector machines have made. In less than 20 years they have gone from unproven, new architectures to playing a significant role in the goal to provide engineers and scientists with ever larger amounts of computing power.

References

ALLIANT COMPUTER SYSTEMS CORP. [1987]. *Alliant FX/Series: Product Summary* (June), Acton, Mass.

BANERJEE, U. [1979]. *Speedup of Ordinary Programs*, Ph.D. Thesis, Dept. of Computer Science, Univ. of Illinois at Urbana-Champaign (October).

BASKETT, F. AND T. W. KELLER [1977]. "An Evaluation of the CRAY-1 Computer," in *High Speed Computer and Algorithm Organization*, Kuck, D. J., Lawrie, D. H. and A. H. Sameh, eds., Academic Press, 71-84.

BUCHER, I. Y. [1983]. "The computational speed of supercomputers," *Proc. SIGMETRICS Conf. on Measuring and Modeling of Computer Systems,* ACM (August) 151–165.

CALLAHAN, D., J. DONGARRA, AND D. LEVINE [1988]. "Vectorizing compilers: A test suite and results," *Supercomputing '88,* ACM/IEEE (November), Orlando, Fla., 98–105.

CHEN, S. [1983]. "Large-scale and high-speed multiprocessor system for scientific applications," *Proc. NATO Advanced Research Work on High Speed Computing* (June); also in K. Hwang, ed., "Supercomputers: Design and applications," *IEEE* (August) 1984.

DONGARRA, J. J. [1986]. "A survey of high performance computers," *COMPCON, IEEE* (March) 8–11.

FAZIO, D. [1987]. "It's really much more fun building a supercomputer than it is simply inventing one," *COMPCON, IEEE* (February) 102-105.

FLYNN, M. J. [1966]. "Very high-speed computing systems," *Proc. IEEE* 54:12 (December) 1901–1909.

HINTZ, R. G. AND D. P. TATE [1972]. "Control data STAR-100 processor design," *COMPCON, IEEE* (September) 1–4.

JORDAN, K. E. [1987]. "Performance comparison of large-scale scientific computers: Scalar mainframes, mainframes with vector facilities, and supercomputers," *Computer* 20:3 (March) 10–23.

KUCK, D., P. P. BUDNIK, S.-C. CHEN, D. H. LAWRIE, R. A. TOWLE, R. E. STREBENDT, E. W. DAVIS, JR., J. HAN, P. W. KRASKA, Y. MURAOKA [1974]. "Measurements of parallelism in ordinary FORTRAN programs," *Computer* 7:1 (January) 37–46.

LINCOLN, N. R. [1982]. "Technology and design trade offs in the creation of a modern supercomputer," *IEEE Trans. on Computers* C-31:5 (May) 363–376.

LUBECK, O., J. MOORE, AND R. MENDEZ [1985]. "A benchmark comparison of three supercomputers: Fujitsu VP-200, Hitachi S810/20, and CRAY X-MP/2," *Computer* 18:1 (January) 10–29.

MIRANKER, G. S., J. RUBENSTEIN, AND J. SANGUINETTI [1988]. "Squeezing a Cray-class supercomputer into a single-user package," *COMPCON, IEEE* (March) 452–456.

MIURA, K. AND K. UCHIDA [1983]. "FACOM vector processing system: VP100/200," *Proc. NATO Advanced Research Work on High Speed Computing* (June); also in K. Hwang, ed., "Supercomputers: Design and applications," *IEEE* (August 1984) 59–73.

MOORE, B., A. PADEGS, R. SMITH, AND W. BUCHOLZ [1987]. "Concepts of the System/370 vector architecture," *Proc. 14th Symposium on Computer Architecture* (June), ACM/IEEE, Pittsburgh, Pa., 282–292.

PADUA, D. AND M. WOLFE [1986]. "Advanced compiler optimizations for supercomputers," *Comm. ACM* 29:12 (December) 1184–1201.

RUSSELL, R. M. [1978]. "The CRAY-1 computer system," *Comm. of the ACM* 21:1 (January) 63–72.

SCHNECK, P. B. [1987]. *Supercomputer Architecture,* Kluwer Academic Publishers, Norwell, Mass.

SMITH, B. J. [1981]. "Architecture and applications of the HEP multiprocessor system," *Real-Time Signal Processing IV* 298 (August) 241–248.

SPORER, M., F. H. MOSS AND C. J. MATHAIS [1988]. "An introduction to the architecture of the Stellar Graphics supercomputer," *COMPCON, IEEE* (March) 464–467.

WATANABE, T. [1987]. "Architecture and performance of the NEC supercomputer SX system," *Parallel Computing* 5, 247–255.

WATSON, W. J. [1972]. "The TI ASC–A highly modular and flexible super computer architecture," *Proc. AFIPS Fall Joint Computer Conf.,* 221–228.

EXERCISES

In these Exercises assume DLXV has a clock rate of 80 MHz and that $T_{base} = 10$ and $T_{loop} = 15$. Also assume that the store latency is always included in the running time.

7.1 [10] <7.1–7.2> Write a DLXV vector sequence that achieves the peak MFLOPS performance of the machine (use the functional unit and instruction description in Section 7.2). Assuming an 80-MHz clock rate, what is the peak MFLOPS?

7.2 [20/15/15] <7.1–7.6> Consider the following vector code run on an 80-MHz version of DLXV for a fixed vector length of 64:

```
LV      V1,Ra
MULTV   V2,V1,V3
ADDV    V4,V1,V3
SV      Rb,V2
SV      Rc,V4
```

Ignore all strip-mining overhead, but assume that the store latency must be included in the time to perform the loop. The entire sequence produces 64 results.

a. [20] Assuming no chaining and a single memory pipeline, how many clock cycles per result (including both stores as one result) does this vector sequence require?

b. [15] If the vector sequence is chained, how many clock cycles per result does this sequence require?

c. [15] Suppose DLXV had three memory pipelines and chaining. If there were no bank conflicts in the accesses for the above loop, how many clock cycles are required per result for this sequence?

7.3 [20/20/15/15/20/20/20] <7.2–7.7> Consider the following FORTRAN code:

```
do 10 i=1,n
    A(i) = A(i) + B(i)
    B(i) = x * B(i)
10  continue
```

Use the techniques of Section 7.7 to estimate performance throughout this exercise assuming an 80-MHz version of DLXV.

a. [20] Write the best DLXV vector code for the inner portion of the loop. Assume x is in F0 and the addresses of A and B are in Ra and Rb, respectively.

b. [20] Find the total time for this loop on DLXV (T_{100}). What is the MFLOP rating for the loop (R_{100})?

c. [15] Find R_∞ for this loop.

d. [15] Find $N_{1/2}$ for this loop.

e. [20] Find N_v for this loop. Assume the scalar code has been pipeline scheduled so that each memory reference takes six cycles and each FP operation takes 3 cycles. Assume the scalar overhead is also T_{loop}.

f. [20] Assume DLXV has two memory pipelines. Write vector code that takes advantage of the second memory pipeline.

g. [20] Compute T_{100} and R_{100} for DLX with two memory pipelines.

7.4 [20/10] <7.3> Suppose we have a version of DLXV with eight memory banks (each a doubleword wide) and a memory-access time of eight cycles.

a. [20] If a load vector of length 64 is executed with a stride of 20 doublewords, how many cycles will the load take to complete?

b. [10] What percentage of the memory bandwidth do you achieve on a 64-element load at stride 20 versus stride 1?

7.5 [12/12/20] <7.4–7.7> Consider the following loop:

```
        C = 0.0
        do 10 i=1,64
            A(i) = A(i) + B(i)
            C = C + A(i)
10      continue
```

a. [12] Split the loop into two loops: one with no dependence and one with a dependence. Write these loops in FORTRAN—as a source-to-source transformation. This optimization is called *loop fission*.

b. [12] Write the DLXV vector code for the loop without a dependence.

c. [20] Write the DLXV code to evaluate the dependent loop using recursive doubling.

7.6 [20/15/20/20] <7.5–7.7> The compiled Linpack performance of the CRAY-1 (designed in 1976) was almost doubled by a better compiler in 1989. Let's look at a simple example of how this might occur. Consider the "SAXPY–like" loop (where k is a parameter to the procedure containing the loop):

```
        do 10 i=1,64
            do 10 j=1,64
                Y(k,j) = a*X(i,j) + Y(k,j)
10      continue
```

a. [20] Write the **straightforward** code sequence for just the inner loop in DLXV vector instructions.

b. [15] Using the techniques of Section 7.7, estimate the performance of this code on DLXV by finding T_{64} in clock cycles. You may assume that T_{base} applies once and T_{loop} of overhead is incurred for each iteration of the outer loop. What limits the performance?

c. [20] Rewrite the DLXV code to reduce the performance limitation; show the resulting inner loop in DLXV vector instructions. (Hint: think about what establishes $T_{element}$; can you affect it?) Find the total time for the resulting sequence.

d. [20] Estimate the performance of your new version using the techniques of Section 7.7 and finding T_{64}.

7.7 [15/15/25] <7.6> Consider the following code.

```
        do 10 i=1,64
            if (B(i) .ne. 0) then
                A(i) = A(i) / B(i)
            endif
   10   continue
```

Assume that the addresses of A and B are in Ra and Rb, respectively, and that F0 contains 0.

a. [15] Write the DLXV code for this loop using the vector-mask capability.

b. [15] Write the DLXV code for this loop using scatter/gather.

c. [25] Estimate the performance (T_{100} in clock cycles) of these two vector loops assuming a divide latency of 20 cycles. Assume that all vector instructions run at one result per clock, independent of the setting of the vector-mask register. Assume that 50% of the entries of B are 0. Considering hardware costs, which would you build if the above loop **was** typical?

7.8 [15/20/15/15] <7.1–7.7> In Figure 2.24 of Chapter 2 (page 75), we saw that the difference between peak and sustained performance could be large: For one problem, a Hitachi S810 had a peak speed twice as high as the CRAY X-MP, while for another more realistic problem the CRAY X-MP was twice as fast as the Hitachi machine. Let's examine why this might occur using two versions of DLXV and the following code sequences:

```
    C       Code sequence 1
            do 10 i=1,10000
                A(i) = x * A(i) + y * A(i)
   10       continue


    C       Code sequence 2
            do 10 i=1,100
                A(i) = x * A(i)
   10       continue
```

Assume there is a version of DLXV (call it DLXVII) that has two copies of every floating-point functional unit with full chaining among them. Assume that both DLXV and DLXVII have two load/store units. Because of the extra functional units and the increased complexity of assigning operations to units, all the overheads (T_{base}, T_{loop}, and the start-up overheads per vector operation) are doubled.

a. [15] Find the number of clock cycles for code sequence 1 on DLXV.

b. [20] Find the number of clock cycles on code sequence 1 for DLXVII. How does this compare to DLXV?

c. [15] Find the number of clock cycles on code sequence 2 for DLXV.

d. [15] Find the number of clock cycles on code sequence 2 for DLXVII. How does this compare to DLXV?

7.9 [15/15/20] <7.5> In this problem we will examine some of the vector loop tests discussed in Section 7.5 and summarized in Figure 7.13 (page 377).

a. [15] Here is a simple code fragment:

```
do 400 i = 2,100,2
   a(i-1) = a(50*i+1)
400   continue
```

To use the GCD test this loop must first be "normalized"—written so that the index starts at 1 and increments by 1 on every iteration. Write a normalized version of the loop (change the indices as needed), then use the GCD test to see if it vectorizes.

b. [15] Here is another loop:

```
do 400 i = 2,100,2
   a(i) = a(i-1)
400   continue
```

Normalize the loop and use the GCD test to detect a dependence. Is there a real dependence in this loop?

c. [20] Here is a tricky piece of code with two-dimensional arrays. Can it be vectorized? If so, how? Rewrite the **source** code so that it is clear that the loop can be vectorized, if possible.

```
do 290 j = 2,n
   do 290 i = 2,j
      aa(i,j)=aa(i-1,j)*aa(i-1,j)+bb(i,j)
290   continue
```

7.10 [25] <7.5> Show that if for two array elements $A(a*i+b)$ and $A(c*i+d)$ there is a true dependence, then $GCD(c,a)$ divides $(d-b)$.

7.11 [12/15] <7.5> Consider the following loop:

```
do 10 i = 2,n
   A(i) = B
10   C(i) = A(i-1)
```

a. [12] Show there is a loop-carried dependence in this code fragment.

b.   [15] Rewrite the code in Fortran so that it can be vectorized as two separate vector sequences.

7.12 [25] <7.6> Because the difference between vector and scalar modes is so large on a supercomputer and the machines often cost tens of millions of dollars, programmers are frequently willing to go to extraordinary effort to achieve good performance. This often includes tricky assembly language programming. An interesting problem is to write a vectorizable sort for floating-point numbers—a task sometimes required in scientific code. Choose a sorting algorithm and write a version for DLXV that uses vector operations as much as possible. (Hint: One good choice is quicksort where the vector compares and compress/expand capability can be used.)

7.13 [25] <7.6> In some vector machines, the vector registers are addressable, and the operands to a vector operation may be two different parts of the same vector register. This allows another solution for the reduction shown on page 382. The key idea in partial sums is to reduce the vector to m sums where m is the total latency through the vector functional unit including the operand read and write times. Assume that the DLXV vector registers are addressable (e.g., you can initiate a vector operation with the operand V1(16), indicating that the input operand began with element 16). Also, assume that the total latency for adds including operand read and write is eight cycles. Write a DLXV code sequence that reduces the contents of V1 to eight partial sums. It can be done with one vector operation.

7.14 [40] <7.2–7.6> Extend the DLX simulator to be a DLXV simulator including the ability to count clock cycles. Write some short benchmark programs in DLX and DLXV assembly language. Measure the speedup on DLXV, the percentage of vectorization, and usage of the functional units.

7.15 [50] <7.5> Modify the DLX compiler to include a dependence checker. Run some scientific code and loops through it and measure what percentage of the statements could be vectorized.

7.16 [Discussion] Some proponents of vector machines might argue that the vector processors have provided the best path to ever-increasing amounts of computer power by focusing their attention on boosting peak vector performance. Others would argue that the emphasis on peak performance is misplaced because an increasing percentage of the programs are dominated by nonvector performance. (Remember Amdahl's Law?) The proponents would respond that programmers should work to make their programs vectorizable. What do you think about this argument?

7.17 [Discussion] Consider the points raised in the Concluding Remarks (Section 7.9). This topic—the relative advantages of pipelined scalar machines versus FP vector machines—is the source of much debate in the early 1990s. What advantages do you see for each side? What would you do in this situation?

Ideally one would desire an indefinitely large memory capacity such that any particular . . . word would be immediately available. . . . We are . . . forced to recognize the possibility of constructing a hierarchy of memories, each of which has greater capacity than the preceding but which is less quickly accessible.

A. W. Burks, H. H. Goldstine, and J. von Neumann,
*Preliminary Discussion of the Logical Design
of an Electronic Computing Instrument* (1946)

8 Memory-Hierarchy Design

8.1 Introduction: Principle of Locality

Computer pioneers correctly predicted that programmers would want unlimited amounts of fast memory. As the 90/10 rule in the first chapter predicts, most programs fortunately do not access all code or data uniformly (see Section 1.3, pages 8–12). The 90/10 rule can be restated as the *principle of locality*. This hypothesis, which holds that all programs favor a portion of their address space at any instant of time, has two dimensions:

- *Temporal locality* (locality in time)—If an item is referenced, it will tend to be referenced again soon.

- *Spatial locality* (locality in space)—If an item is referenced, nearby items will tend to be referenced soon.

A memory hierarchy is a natural reaction to locality and technology. The principle of locality and the guideline that smaller hardware is faster yield the concept of a hierarchy based on different speeds and sizes. Since slower memory is cheaper, a memory hierarchy is organized into several levels—each smaller, faster, and more expensive per byte than the level below. The levels of the hierarchy subset one another; all data in one level is also found in the level below, and all data in that lower level is found in the one below it, and so on until we reach the bottom of the hierarchy.

This chapter includes a half-dozen examples that demonstrate how taking advantage of the principle of locality can improve performance. All these strategies map addresses from a larger memory to a smaller but faster memory. As part of address mapping, the memory hierarchy is usually given the responsibility of address checking; protection schemes used for doing this are covered in this chapter. Later we will explore advanced memory hierarchy topics and trace a memory access through three levels of memory on the VAX-11/780.

8.2 | General Principles of Memory Hierarchy

Before proceeding with examples of the memory hierarchy, let's define some general terms applicable to all memory hierarchies. A memory hierarchy normally consists of many levels, but it is managed between two adjacent levels at a time. The *upper* level—the one closer to the processor—is smaller and faster than the *lower* level (see Figure 8.1). The minimum unit of information that can be either present or not present in the two-level hierarchy is called a *block*. The size of a block may be either fixed or variable. If it is fixed, the memory size is a multiple of that block size. Most of this chapter will be concerned with fixed block sizes, although a variable block design is discussed in Section 8.6.

Success or failure of an access to the upper level is designated as a hit or a miss: A *hit* is a memory access found in the upper level, while a *miss* means it is not found in that level. *Hit rate*, or hit ratio—like a batting average—is the fraction of memory accesses found in the upper level. This is sometimes represented as a percentage. *Miss rate* (1.0 – hit rate) is the fraction of memory accesses not found in the upper level.

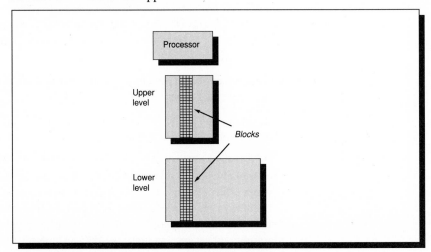

FIGURE 8.1   Every pair of levels in the memory hierarchy can be thought of as having an upper and lower level. Within each level the unit of information that is present or not is called a *block*.

Since performance is the major reason for having a memory hierarchy, the speed of hits and misses is important. *Hit time* is the time to access the upper level of the memory hierarchy, which includes the time to determine whether the access is a hit or a miss. *Miss penalty* is the time to replace a block in the upper level with the corresponding block from the lower level, plus the time to deliver this block to the requesting device (normally the CPU). The miss penalty is further divided into two components: *access time*—the time to access the first word of a block on a miss; and *transfer time*—the additional time to transfer the remaining words in the block. Access time is related to the latency of the lower-level memory, while transfer time is related to the bandwidth between the lower-level and upper-level memories. (Sometimes *access latency* is used to mean access time.)

The memory address is divided into pieces that access each part of the hierarchy. The *block-frame address* is the higher-order piece of the address that identifies a block at that level of the hierarchy (see Figure 8.2). The *block-offset address* is the lower-order piece of the address and identifies an item within a block. The size of the block-offset address is $\log_2$ (size of block); the size of the block-frame address is then the size of the full address at this level less the size of the block-offset address.

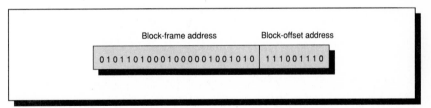

FIGURE 8.2 Example of the frame address and offset address portions of a 32-bit lower-level memory address. In this case the block size is 512, making the size of the offset address 9 bits and the size of the block-frame address 23 bits.

Evaluating Performance of a Memory Hierarchy

Because instruction count is independent of the hardware, it is tempting to evaluate CPU performance using that number. As we saw in Chapters 2 and 4, however, such indirect performance measures have waylaid many a computer designer. The corresponding temptation for evaluating memory-hierarchy performance is to concentrate on miss rate, for it, too, is independent of the speed of the hardware. As we shall see, miss rate can be just as misleading as instruction count. A better measure of memory-hierarchy performance is the average time to access memory:

Average memory-access time = Hit time + Miss rate * Miss penalty

The components of average access time can be measured either in absolute time—say, 10 nanoseconds on a hit—or in the number of clock cycles that the

CPU waits for the memory—such as a miss penalty of 12 clock cycles. Remember that average memory-access time is still an indirect measure of performance; so while it is a better measure than miss rate, it is not a substitute for execution time.

The relationship of block size to miss penalty and miss rate is shown abstractly in Figure 8.3. These representations assume that the size of the upper-level memory does not change. The access-time portion of the miss penalty is not affected by block size, but the transfer time does increase with block size. If access time is large, initially there will be little additional miss penalty relative to access time as block size increases. However, increasing block size means fewer blocks in the upper-level memory. Increasing block size lowers the miss rate until the reduced misses of larger blocks (spatial locality) are outweighed by the increased misses as the number of blocks shrinks (temporal locality).

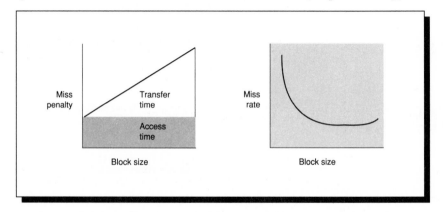

FIGURE 8.3 Block size versus miss penalty and miss rate. The transfer-time portion of the miss penalty obviously grows with increasing block size. For a fixed-size upper-level memory, miss rates fall with increasing block size until so much of the block is not used that it displaces useful information in the upper level, and miss rates begin to rise. The point on the curve on the right where miss rates begin to rise with increasing block size is sometimes called the *pollution point*.

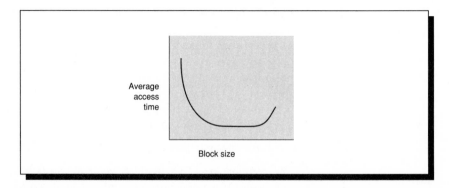

FIGURE 8.4 The relationship between average memory-access time and block size.

The goal of a memory hierarchy is to reduce execution time, not misses. Hence, computer designers favor a block size with the lowest average access time rather than the lowest miss rate. This is related to the product of miss rate and miss penalty, as Figure 8.4 shows abstractly. Of course, overall CPU performance is the ultimate performance test, so care must be taken when reducing average memory-access time to be sure that changes to clock cycle time and CPI improve overall performance as well as average memory-access time.

Implications of a Memory Hierarchy to the CPU

Processors designed without a memory hierarchy are simpler because memory accesses always take the same amount of time. Misses in a memory hierarchy mean that the CPU must be able to handle variable memory-access times. If the miss penalty is on the order of tens of clock cycles, the processor normally waits for the memory transfer to complete. On the other hand, if the miss penalty is thousands of processor clock cycles, it is too wasteful to let the CPU sit idle; in this case, the CPU is interrupted and used for another process during the miss handling. Thus, avoiding the overhead of a long miss penalty means any memory access can result in a CPU interrupt. This also means the CPU must be able to recover any memory address that can cause such an interrupt, so that the system can know what to transfer to satisfy the miss (see Section 5.6). When the memory transfer is complete, the original process is restored, and the instruction that missed is retried.

The processor must also have some mechanism to determine whether or not information is in the top level of the memory hierarchy. This check happens on every memory access and affects hit time; maintaining acceptable performance usually requires the check to be implemented in hardware. The final implication of a memory hierarchy is that the computer must have a mechanism to transfer blocks between upper- and lower-level memory. If the block transfer is tens of clock cycles, it is controlled by hardware; if it is thousands of clock cycles, it can be controlled by software.

Four Questions for Classifying Memory Hierarchies

The fundamental principles that drive all memory hierarchies allow us to use terms that transcend the levels we are talking about. These same principles allow us to pose four questions about any level of the hierarchy:

Q1: Where can a block be placed in the upper level? (*Block placement*)

Q2: How is a block found if it is in the upper level? (*Block identification*)

Q3: Which block should be replaced on a miss? (*Block replacement*)

Q4: What happens on a write? (*Write strategy*)

These questions will help us gain an understanding of the different tradeoffs demanded by the relationships of memories at different levels of a hierarchy.

8.3 | Caches

Cache: a safe place for hiding or storing things.

Webster's New World Dictionary of the American Language,
Second College Edition (1976)

Cache is the name first chosen to represent the level of the memory hierarchy between the CPU and main memory, and that is the dominant use of the term. While the concept of caches is younger than the IBM 360 architecture, caches appear today in every class of computer and in some computers more than once. In fact, the word has become so popular that it has replaced "buffer" in many computer-science circles.

The general terms defined in the prior section can be used for caches, although the word *line* is often used instead of block. Figure 8.5 shows the typical range of memory-hierarchy parameters for caches.

Block (line) size	4 – 128 bytes
Hit time	1 – 4 clock cycles (normally 1)
Miss penalty	8 – 32 clock cycles
(Access time)	(6 – 10 clock cycles)
(Transfer time)	(2 – 22 clock cycles)
Miss rate	1% – 20%
Cache size	1 KB – 256 KB

FIGURE 8.5   Typical values of key memory-hierarchy parameters for caches in 1990 workstations and minicomputers.

Now let's examine caches in more detail by answering the four memory-hierarchy questions.

Q1: Where Can a Block Be Placed in a Cache?

Restrictions on where a block is placed create three categories of cache organization:

■ If each block has only one place it can appear in the cache, the cache is said to be *direct mapped*. The mapping is usually (block-frame address) modulo (number of blocks in cache).

■ If a block can be placed anywhere in the cache, the cache is said to be *fully associative*.

- If a block can be placed in a restricted set of places in the cache, the cache is said to be *set associative*. A *set* is a group of two or more blocks in the cache. A block is first mapped onto a set, and then the block can be placed anywhere within the set. The set is usually chosen by bit selection; that is, (block-frame address) modulo (number of **sets** in cache). If there are *n* blocks in a set, the cache placement is called *n-way set associative*.

The range of caches from direct mapped to fully associative is really a continuum of levels of set associativity: Direct mapped is simply one-way set associative and a fully associative cache with *m* blocks could be called *m*-way set associative. Figure 8.6 shows where block 12 can be placed in a cache according to the block-placement policy.

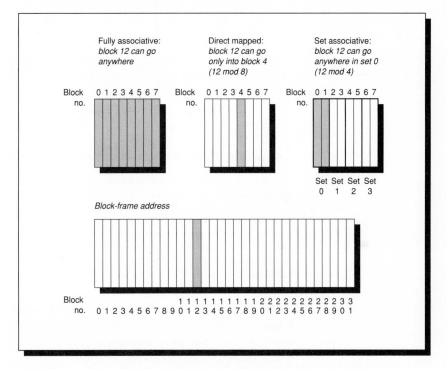

FIGURE 8.6   The cache has 8 blocks, while memory has 32 blocks. The set-associative organization has 4 sets with 2 blocks per set, called two-way set associative. (Real caches contain hundreds of blocks and real memories contain hundreds of thousands of blocks.) Assume that there is nothing in the cache and that the block-frame address in question identifies lower-level block 12. The three options for caches are shown left to right. In fully associative, block 12 from the lower level can go into any of the 8 blocks of the cache. With direct mapped, block 12 can only be placed into block 4 (12 modulo 8). Set associative, which has some of both features, allows the block to be placed anywhere in set 0 (12 modulo 4). With two blocks per set, this means block 12 can be placed either in block 0 or block 1 of the cache.

Q2: How Is a Block Found If It Is in the Cache?

Caches include an address tag on each block that gives the block-frame address. The tag of every cache block that might contain the desired information is checked to see if it matches the block-frame address from the CPU. Figure 8.7 gives an example. Because speed is of the essence, all possible tags are searched in parallel; serial search would make set associativity counterproductive.

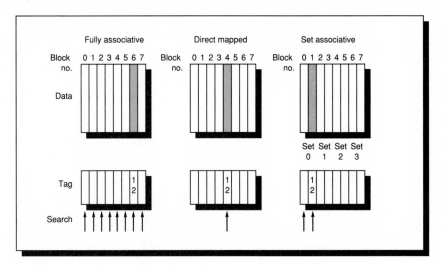

FIGURE 8.7 In fully associative placement, the block for block-frame address 12 can appear in any of the 8 blocks; thus, all 8 tags must be searched. The desired data is found in cache block 6 in this example. In direct-mapped placement there is only one cache block where memory block 12 can be found. In set-associative placement, with 4 sets, memory block 12 must be in set 0 (12 mod 4); thus, the tags of cache blocks 0 and 1 are checked. In this case the data is found in cache block 1. Speed of cache access dictates that searching must be performed in parallel for fully associative and set-associative mappings.

There must be a way to know that a cache block does not have valid information. The most common procedure is to add a *valid bit* to the tag to say whether or not this entry contains a valid address. If the bit is not set, there cannot be a match on this address.

A common omission in finding the cost of caches is to forget the cost of the tag memory. One tag is required for each block. An advantage of increasing block sizes is that the tag overhead per cache entry becomes a smaller fraction of the total cost of the cache.

Before proceeding to the next question, let's explore the relationship of a CPU address to the cache. Figure 8.8 shows how an address is divided into three fields to find data in a set-associative cache: the *block-offset* field used to select the desired data from the block, the *index* field used to select the set, and the *tag* field used for the comparison. While the comparison could be made on more of the address than the tag, there is no need:

- Checking the index would be redundant, since it was used to select the set to be checked (an address stored in set 0, for example, must have 0 in the index field or it couldn't be stored in set 0).

- The offset is unnecessary in the comparison because all block offsets match and the entire block is present or not.

If the total size is kept the same, increasing associativity increases the number of blocks per set, thereby decreasing the size of the index and increasing the size of the tag. That is, the tag/index boundary in Figure 8.8 moves to the right with increasing associativity.

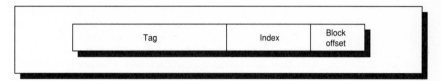

FIGURE 8.8   The 3 portions of an address in a set-associative or direct-mapped cache. The tag is used to check all the blocks in the set and the index is used to select the set. The block offset is the address of the desired data within the block.

Q3: Which Block Should Be Replaced on a Cache Miss?

If the choice were between a block that has valid data and a block that doesn't, then it would be easy to select which block to replace. Alas, the high hit rate of caches means that the overwhelming decision is between blocks that have valid data.

A benefit of direct-mapped placement is that hardware decisions are simplified. In fact, so simple that there is no choice: Only one block is checked for a hit, and only that block can be replaced. With fully associative or set-associative placement, there are several blocks to choose from on a miss. There are two primary strategies employed for selecting which block to replace:

- *Random*—To spread allocation uniformly, candidate blocks are randomly selected. Some systems use a scheme for spreading data across a set of blocks in a pseudorandomized manner to get reproducible behavior, which is particularly useful during hardware debugging.

- *Least-recently used* (LRU)—To reduce the chance of throwing out information that will be needed soon, accesses to blocks are recorded. The block replaced is the one that has been unused for the longest time. This makes use of a corollary of temporal locality: If recently used blocks are likely to be used again, then the best candidate for disposal is the least recently used. Figure 8.9 (page 412) shows which block is the least-recently used for a sequence of block-frame addresses in a fully associative memory hierarchy.

A virtue of random is that it is simple to build in hardware. As the number of blocks to keep track of increases, LRU becomes increasingly expensive and is frequently only approximated. Figure 8.10 shows the difference in miss rates between LRU and random replacement. Replacement policy plays a greater role in smaller caches than in larger caches where there are more choices of what to replace.

Block-frame addresses		3	2	1	0	0	2	3	1	3	0
LRU block number	0	0	0	0	0	3	3	3	1	0	0	2

FIGURE 8.9   Least-recently used blocks for a sequence of block-frame addresses in a fully associative memory hierarchy. This assumes that there are 4 blocks and that in the beginning the LRU block is number 0. The LRU block number is shown below each new block reference. Another policy, *First-in–first-out* (FIFO), simply discards the block that was used N unique accesses before, independent of its reference pattern in the last N – 1 references. Random replacement generally outperforms FIFO and it is easier to implement.

Associativity: Size	2-way		4-way		8-way	
	LRU	**Random**	**LRU**	**Random**	**LRU**	**Random**
16 KB	5.18%	5.69%	4.67%	5.29%	4.39%	4.96%
64 KB	1.88%	2.01%	1.54%	1.66%	1.39%	1.53%
256 KB	1.15%	1.17%	1.13%	1.13%	1.12%	1.12%

FIGURE 8.10   Miss rates comparing least-recently used versus random replacement for several sizes and associativities. This data was collected for a block size of 16 bytes using one of the VAX traces containing user and operating system code (SAVE0). This trace is included in the software supplement for course use. There is little difference between LRU and random for larger size caches in this trace.

Q4: What Happens on a Write?

Reads dominate cache accesses. All instruction accesses are reads, and most instructions don't write to memory. Figure 4.34 (page 181) suggests a mix of 9% stores and 17% loads for four DLX programs, making writes less than 10% of the memory traffic. Making the common case fast means optimizing caches for reads, but Amdahl's Law reminds us that high-performance designs cannot neglect the speed of writes.

Fortunately, the common case is also the easy case to make fast. The block can be read at the same time that the tag is read and compared, so the block read begins as soon as the block-frame address is available. If the read is a hit, the block is passed on to the CPU immediately. If it is a miss, there is no benefit— but also no harm.

Such is not the case for writes. The processor specifies the size of the write, usually between 1 and 8 bytes; only that portion of a block can be changed. In general this means a read-modify-write sequence of operations on the block: read the original block, modify one portion, and write the new block value. Moreover, modifying a block cannot begin until the tag is checked to see if it is a hit. Because tag checking cannot occur in parallel, then, writes normally take longer than reads.

Thus, it is the write policies that distinguish many cache designs. There are two basic options when writing to the cache:

- *Write through* (or *store through*)—The information is written to both the block in the cache **and** to the block in the lower-level memory.

- *Write back* (also called *copy back* or *store in*)—The information is written only to the block in the cache. The modified cache block is written to main memory only when it is replaced.

Write-back cache blocks are called *clean* or *dirty*, depending on whether the information in the cache differs from that in lower-level memory. To reduce the frequency of writing back blocks on replacement, a feature called the *dirty bit* is commonly used. This status bit indicates whether or not the block was modified while in the cache. If it wasn't, the block is not written, since the lower level has the same information as the cache.

Both write back and write through have their advantages. With write back, writes occur at the speed of the cache memory, and multiple writes within a block require only one write to the lower-level memory. Since every write doesn't go to memory, write back uses less memory bandwidth, making write back attractive in multiprocessors. With write through, read misses don't result in writes to the lower level, and write through is easier to implement than write back. Write through also has the advantage that main memory has the most current copy of the data. This is important in multiprocessors and for I/O, which we shall examine in Section 8.8. Hence, multiprocessors want write back to reduce the memory traffic per processor and write through to keep the cache and memory consistent.

When the CPU must wait for writes to complete during write throughs, the CPU is said to *write stall*. A common optimization to reduce write stalls is a *write buffer*, which allows the processor to continue while the memory is updated. As we shall see in Section 8.8, write stalls can occur even with write buffers.

There are two options on a write miss:

- *Write allocate* (also called *fetch on write*)—The block is loaded, followed by the write-hit actions above. This is similar to a read miss.

- *No write allocate* (also called *write around*)—The block is modified in the lower level and not loaded into the cache.

While either write-miss policy could be used with write through or write back, generally write-back caches use write allocate (hoping that subsequent writes to that block will be captured by the cache) and write-through caches often use no write allocate (since subsequent writes to that block will still have to go to memory).

An Example Cache: The VAX-11/780 Cache

To give substance to these ideas, Figure 8.11 shows the organization of the cache on the VAX-11/780. The cache contains 8192 bytes of data in 8-byte blocks with two-way–set-associative placement, random replacement, write through with a one-word write buffer, and no write allocate on a write miss.

Let's trace a cache hit through the steps of a hit as labeled in Figure 8.11. (The five steps are shown as circled numbers.) The address coming into the cache is divided into two fields: the 29-bit block-frame address and 3-bit block offset. The block-frame address is further divided into an address tag and cache index. Step 1 shows this division.

The cache index selects the set to be tested to see if the block is in the cache. (A set is one block from each bank in Figure 8.11.) The size of the index depends on cache size, block size, and set associativity. In this case, a 9-bit index results:

$$\frac{\text{Blocks}}{\text{Bank}} = \frac{\text{Cache size}}{\text{Block size} * \text{Set associativity}} = \frac{8192}{8 * 2} = 512 = 2^9$$

In a two-way–set-associative cache, the index is sent to both banks. This is step 2.

After reading an address tag from each bank, the tag portion of the block-frame address is compared to the tags. This is step 3 in the figure. To be sure the tag contains valid information, the valid bit must be set, or the results of the comparison are ignored.

Assuming one of the tags does match, a 2:1 multiplexer (step 4) is set to select the block from the matching set. Why can't both tags match? It is the job of the replacement algorithm to make sure that an address appears in only one block. To reduce the hit time, the data is read at the same time as the address tags; thus, by the time the block multiplexer is ready, the data is also ready.

This step is needed in set-associative caches, but it can be omitted from direct-mapped caches since there is no selection to be made. The multiplexer used in this step can be on the critical timing path, endangering the clock cycle time of the CPU. (The example on pages 418–419 and the fallacy on page 481 explore the trade-off of lower miss rates and higher clock cycle time.)

In the final step the word is sent to the CPU. All five steps occur within a single CPU clock cycle.

What happens on a miss? The cache sends a stall signal to the CPU telling it to wait, and two words (eight bytes) are read from memory. That takes 6 clock cycles on the VAX-11/780 (ignoring bus interference). When the data arrives, the cache must pick a block to replace; the VAX-11/780 selects one of the two blocks at random. Replacing a block means updating the data, the address tag, and the valid bit. Once this is done, the cache goes through a regular hit cycle and returns the data to the CPU.

Writes are more complicated in the VAX-11/780, as they are in any cache. If the word to be written is in the cache, the first four steps are the same. The next step is to write the data in the block, then write the changed-data portion into the

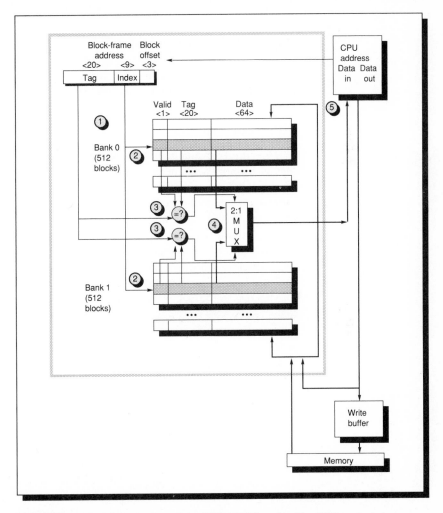

FIGURE 8.11 The organization of the VAX-11/780 cache. The 8-KB cache is two-way set associative with 8-byte blocks. It has 512 sets with two blocks per set; the set is selected by the 9-bit index. The five steps of a read hit, shown as circled numbers in order of occurrence, label this organization. The line from memory to the cache is used on a miss to load the cache. Multiplexing as found in step 4 is not needed in a direct-mapped cache. Note that the offset is connected to chip select of the data SRAMs to allow the proper words to be sent to the 2:1 multiplexer.

cache. The VAX-11/780 uses no write allocate. Consequently, on a write miss the CPU writes "around" the cache to lower-level memory and does not affect the cache.

Since this is a write-through cache, the process isn't yet over. The word is also sent to a one-word write buffer. If the write buffer is empty, the word and full address are written in the buffer, and we are finished. The CPU continues working while the write buffer writes the word to memory. If the buffer is full, the cache (and CPU) must wait until the buffer is empty.

Cache Performance

CPU time can be divided into the clock cycles the CPU spends executing the program and the clock cycles the CPU spends waiting for the memory system. Thus,

$$\text{CPU time} = (\text{CPU-execution clock cycles} + \text{Memory-stall clock cycles}) * \text{Clock cycle time}$$

To simplify evaluation of cache alternatives, sometimes designers assume that all memory stalls are due to the cache. This is true for many machines; on machines where this is not true, the cache still dominates stalls that are not exclusively due to the cache. We use this simplifying assumption here, but it is important to account for **all** memory stalls when calculating final performance!

The formula above raises the question whether the clock cycles for a cache access should be considered part of CPU-execution clock cycles or part of memory-stall clock cycles. While either convention is defensible, the most widely accepted is to include hit clock cycles in CPU-execution clock cycles.

Memory-stall clock cycles can then be defined in terms of the number of memory accesses per program, miss penalty (in clock cycles), and miss rate for reads and writes:

$$\text{Memory-stall clock cycles} = \frac{\text{Reads}}{\text{Program}} * \text{Read miss rate} * \text{Read miss penalty}$$

$$+ \frac{\text{Writes}}{\text{Program}} * \text{Write miss rate} * \text{Write miss penalty}$$

We simplify the complete formula by combining the reads and writes together:

$$\text{Memory-stall clock cycles} = \frac{\text{Memory accessess}}{\text{Program}} * \text{Miss rate} * \text{Miss penalty}$$

Factoring instruction count (IC) from execution time and memory stall cycles, we now get a CPU-time formula that includes memory accesses per instruction, miss rate, and miss penalty:

$$\text{CPU time} = \text{IC} * \left(\text{CPI}_{\text{Execution}} + \frac{\text{Memory accesses}}{\text{Instruction}} * \text{Miss rate} * \text{Miss penalty} \right) * \text{Clock cycle time}$$

Some designers prefer measuring miss rate as *misses per instruction* rather than misses per memory reference:

$$\frac{\text{Misses}}{\text{Instruction}} = \frac{\text{Memory accesses}}{\text{Instruction}} * \text{Miss rate}$$

The advantage of this measure is that it is independent of the hardware implementation. For example, the VAX-11/780 instruction unit can make repeated references to a single byte (see Section 8.7), which can artificially reduce the miss rate if measured as misses per memory reference rather than per instruction executed. The drawback is that this measure is architecture dependent, thus it is most popular with architects working with a single computer family. They then use this version of the CPU-time formula:

$$\text{CPU time} = \text{IC} * \left(\text{CPI}_{\text{Execution}} + \frac{\text{Misses}}{\text{Instruction}} * \text{Miss penalty} \right) * \text{Clock cycle time}$$

We can now explore the consequences of caches on performance.

Example Let's use the VAX-11/780 as a first example. The cache miss penalty is 6 clock cycles, and all instructions normally take 8.5 clock cycles (ignoring memory stalls). Assume the miss rate is 11%, and there is an average of 3.0 memory references per instruction. What is the impact on performance when behavior of the cache is included?

Answer $$\text{CPU time} = \text{IC} * \left(\text{CPI}_{\text{Execution}} + \frac{\text{Memory-stall clock cycles}}{\text{Instruction}} \right) * \text{Clock cycle time}$$

The performance, including cache misses, is

$$\text{CPU time}_{\text{with cache}} = \text{IC} * (8.5 + 3.0 * 11\% * 6) * \text{Clock cycle time}$$

$$= \text{Instruction count} * 10.5 * \text{Clock cycle time}$$

The clock cycle time and instruction count are the same, with or without a cache, so CPU time increases with CPI from 8.5 to 10.5. Hence, the impact of the memory hierarchy is to stretch the CPU time by 24%.

Example Let's now calculate the impact on performance when behavior of the cache is included on a machine with a lower CPI. Assume that the cache miss penalty is 10 clock cycles and, on average, instructions take 1.5 clock cycles; the miss rate is 11%, and there is an average of 1.4 memory references per instruction.

Answer $$\text{CPU time} = \text{IC} * \left(\text{CPI}_{\text{Execution}} + \frac{\text{Memory-stall clock cycles}}{\text{Instruction}} \right) * \text{Clock cycle time}$$

Making the same assumptions as in the previous example on cache hits, the performance, including cache misses, is

$$\text{CPU time}_{\text{with cache}} = \text{IC} * (1.5 + 1.4*11\%*10) * \text{Clock cycle time}$$

$$= \text{Instruction count}*3.0*\text{Clock cycle time}$$

The clock cycle time and instruction count are the same, with or without a cache, so CPU time increases with CPI from 1.5 to 3.0. Including cache behavior doubles execution time.

As these examples illustrate, cache-behavior penalties range from significant to enormous. Furthermore, cache misses have a double-barreled impact on a CPU with a low CPI and a fast clock:

1. The lower the CPI, the more pronounced the impact is.

2. Independent of the CPU, main memories have similar memory-access times, since they are built from the same memory chips. When calculating CPI, the cache miss penalty is measured in **CPU** clock cycles needed for a miss. Therefore, a higher CPU clock rate leads to a larger miss penalty, even if main memories are the same speed.

The importance of the cache for CPUs with low CPI and high clock rates is thus greater; and, consequently, greater is the danger of neglecting cache behavior in assessing performance of such machines.

While minimizing average memory-access time is a reasonable goal and we will use it in much of this chapter, keep in mind that the final goal is to reduce CPU execution time.

Example

What is the impact of two different cache organizations on the performance of a CPU? Assume that the CPI is normally 1.5 with a clock cycle time of 20 ns, that there are 1.3 memory references per instruction, and that the size of both caches is 64 KB. One cache is direct mapped and the other is two-way set associative. Since the speed of the CPU is tied directly to the speed of the caches, assume the CPU clock cycle time must be stretched 8.5% to accommodate the selection multiplexer of the set-associative cache (step 4 in Figure 8.11 on page 415.) To the first approximation, the cache miss penalty is 200 ns for either cache organization. (In practice it must be rounded up or down to an integer number of clock cycles.) First, calculate the average memory-access time, and then CPU performance.

Answer

Figure 8.12 on page 421 shows that the miss rate of a direct-mapped 64-KB cache is 3.9% and the miss rate for a two-way–set-associative cache of the same size is 3.0%. Average memory-access time is

Average memory-access time = Hit time + Miss rate * Miss penalty

Thus, the time for each organization is

$$\text{Average memory-access time}_{1\text{-way}} = 20 + .039*200 = 27.8 \text{ ns}$$

$$\text{Average memory-access time}_{2\text{-way}} = 20*1.085 + .030*200 = 27.7 \text{ ns}$$

The average memory-access time is better for the two-way–set-associative cache.

CPU performance is

$$\text{CPU time} = \text{IC} * \left(\text{CPI}_{\text{Execution}} + \frac{\text{Misses}}{\text{Instruction}} * \text{Miss penalty} \right) * \text{Clock cycle time}$$

$$= \text{IC} * \left(\text{CPI}_{\text{Execution}} * \text{Clock cycle time} + \right.$$

$$\left. \frac{\text{Memory accesses}}{\text{Instruction}} * \text{Miss rate} * \text{Miss penalty} * \text{Clock cycle time} \right)$$

Substituting 200ns for (Miss penalty * Clock cycle time), the performance of each cache organization is

$$\text{CPU time}_{1\text{-way}} = \text{IC}*(1.5*20 + 1.3*0.039*200) = 40.1*\text{IC}$$

$$\text{CPU time}_{2\text{-way}} = \text{IC}*(1.5*20*1.085 + 1.3*0.030*200) = 40.4*\text{IC}$$

and relative performance is

$$\frac{\text{CPU time}_{2\text{-way}}}{\text{CPU time}_{1\text{-way}}} = \frac{40.4 * \text{Instruction count}}{40.1 * \text{Instruction count}}$$

In contrast to the results of average access-time comparison, the direct-mapped cache leads to slightly better performance. Since CPU time is our bottom-line evaluation (and direct mapped is simpler to build), the preferred cache is direct mapped in this example. (See the fallacy on page 481 for more on this kind of trade-off.)

The Three Sources of Cache Misses: Compulsory, Capacity, and Conflicts

An intuitive model of cache behavior attributes all misses to one of three sources:

- *Compulsory*—The first access to a block is not in the cache, so the block must be brought into the cache. These are also called *cold start misses* or *first reference misses*.

- *Capacity*—If the cache cannot contain all the blocks needed during execution of a program, capacity misses will occur due to blocks being discarded and later retrieved.

■ *Conflict*—If the block-placement strategy is set associative or direct mapped, conflict misses (in addition to compulsory and capacity misses) will occur because a block can be discarded and later retrieved if too many blocks map to its set. These are also called *collision misses*.

Figure 8.12 shows the relative frequency of cache misses, broken down by the "three Cs." To show the benefit of associativity, conflict misses are divided into misses caused by each decrease in associativity. The categories are labeled *n*-way, meaning the misses caused by going to the lower level of associativity from the next one above. Here are the four categories:

8-way: from fully associative (no conflicts) to 8-way associative

4-way: from 8-way associative to 4-way associative

2-way: from 4-way associative to 2-way associative

1-way: from 2-way associative to 1-way associative (direct mapped)

Figure 8.13 (page 422) presents the same data graphically. The top graph shows absolute miss rates; the bottom graph plots percentage of all the misses by cache size.

Having identified the three Cs, what can a computer designer do about them? Conceptually, conflicts are the easiest: Fully associative placement avoids all conflict misses. Associativity is expensive in hardware, however, and may slow access time (see the example above or the second fallacy in Section 8.10), leading to lower overall performance. There is little to be done about capacity except to buy larger memory chips. If the upper-level memory is much smaller than what is needed for a program, and a significant percentage of the time is spent moving data between two levels in the hierarchy, the memory hierarchy is said to *thrash*. Because so many replacements are required, thrashing means the machine runs close to the speed of the lower-level memory, or maybe even slower due to the miss overhead. Making blocks larger reduces the number of compulsory misses, but it can increase conflict misses.

The three C's give insight into the cause of misses, but this simple model has its limits. For example, increasing cache size reduces conflict misses as well as capacity misses, since a larger cache spreads out references. Thus, a miss might move from one category to the other as parameters change. Three C's ignore replacement policy, since it is difficult to model and since, in general, it is of less significance. In specific circumstances the replacement policy can actually lead to anomalous behavior, such as poorer miss rates for larger associativity, which is directly contradictory to the three C's model.

Cache size	Degree associative	Total miss rate	Miss-rate components (relative percent) *(Sum = 100% of total miss rate)*					
			Compulsory		Capacity		Conflict	
1 KB	1-way	0.191	0.009	5%	0.141	73%	0.042	22%
1 KB	2-way	0.161	0.009	6%	0.141	87%	0.012	7%
1 KB	4-way	0.152	0.009	6%	0.141	92%	0.003	2%
1 KB	8-way	0.149	0.009	6%	0.141	94%	0.000	0%
2 KB	1-way	0.148	0.009	6%	0.103	70%	0.036	24%
2 KB	2-way	0.122	0.009	7%	0.103	84%	0.010	8%
2 KB	4-way	0.115	0.009	8%	0.103	90%	0.003	2%
2 KB	8-way	0.113	0.009	8%	0.103	91%	0.001	1%
4 KB	1-way	0.109	0.009	8%	0.073	67%	0.027	25%
4 KB	2-way	0.095	0.009	9%	0.073	77%	0.013	14%
4 KB	4-way	0.087	0.009	10%	0.073	84%	0.005	6%
4 KB	8-way	0.084	0.009	11%	0.073	87%	0.002	3%
8 KB	1-way	0.087	0.009	10%	0.052	60%	0.026	30%
8 KB	2-way	0.069	0.009	13%	0.052	75%	0.008	12%
8 KB	4-way	0.065	0.009	14%	0.052	80%	0.004	6%
8 KB	8-way	0.063	0.009	14%	0.052	83%	0.002	3%
16 KB	1-way	0.066	0.009	14%	0.038	57%	0.019	29%
16 KB	2-way	0.054	0.009	17%	0.038	70%	0.007	13%
16 KB	4-way	0.049	0.009	18%	0.038	76%	0.003	6%
16 KB	8-way	0.048	0.009	19%	0.038	78%	0.001	3%
32 KB	1-way	0.050	0.009	18%	0.028	55%	0.013	27%
32 KB	2-way	0.041	0.009	22%	0.028	68%	0.004	11%
32 KB	4-way	0.038	0.009	23%	0.028	73%	0.001	4%
32 KB	8-way	0.038	0.009	24%	0.028	74%	0.001	2%
64 KB	1-way	0.039	0.009	23%	0.019	50%	0.011	27%
64 KB	2-way	0.030	0.009	30%	0.019	65%	0.002	5%
64 KB	4-way	0.028	0.009	32%	0.019	68%	0.000	0%
64 KB	8-way	0.028	0.009	32%	0.019	68%	0.000	0%
128 KB	1-way	0.026	0.009	34%	0.004	16%	0.013	50%
128 KB	2-way	0.020	0.009	46%	0.004	21%	0.006	33%
128 KB	4-way	0.016	0.009	55%	0.004	25%	0.003	20%
128 KB	8-way	0.015	0.009	59%	0.004	27%	0.002	14%

FIGURE 8.12   Total miss rate for each size cache and percentage of each according to the "three Cs." Compulsory misses are independent of cache size, while capacity misses decrease as capacity increases. Hill [1987] measured this trace using 32-byte blocks and LRU replacement. It was generated on a VAX-11 running Ultrix by mixing three systems' traces, using a multiprogramming workload and three user traces. The total length was just over a million addresses; the largest piece of data referenced during the trace was 221 KB. Figure 8.13 (page 422) shows the same information graphically. Note that the 2:1 cache rule of thumb (inside front cover) is supported by the statistics in this table: a direct-mapped cache of size N has about the same miss rate as a 2-way–set-associative cache of size N/2.

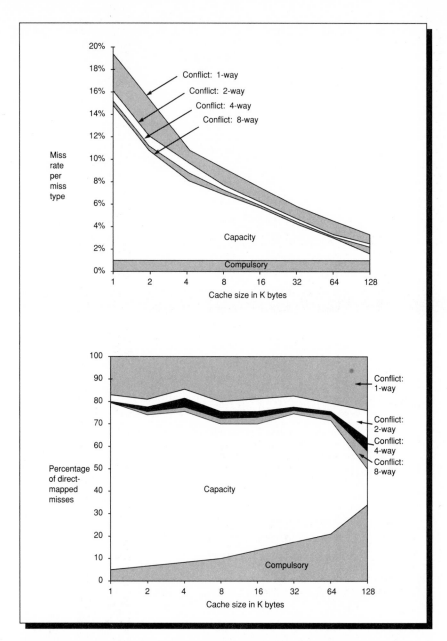

FIGURE 8.13 Total miss rate (top) and distribution of miss rate (bottom) for each size cache according to three Cs for the data in Figure 8.12 (page 421). The top diagram is the actual miss rates, while the bottom diagram is scaled to the direct-mapped miss ratio.

Choices for Block Sizes in Caches

Figures 8.3 and 8.4 (page 406) showed the abstract tradeoff of block size versus miss rate and memory-access time. Figures 8.14 and 8.15 (page 424) show the specific numbers for a set of programs and cache sizes. Larger block sizes reduce compulsory misses, as the principle of spatial locality suggests. At the same time, larger blocks also reduce the number of blocks in the cache, increasing conflict misses.

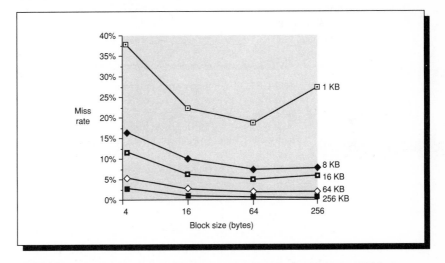

FIGURE 8.14   Miss rate versus block size. Note that for a 1-KB cache, 256-byte blocks have a higher miss rate than either 16- or 64-byte blocks. (The smallest block is 4 bytes.) In this particular example, the cache would have to be 256 KB in order for increasing block size to always result in decreased misses. This data was collected for a direct-mapped cache using one of the VAX traces containing user and operating system code, which is distributed with this book (SAVE0).

Instruction-Only or Data-Only Caches Versus Unified Caches

Unlike other levels of the memory hierarchy, caches are sometimes divided into instruction-only and data-only caches. Caches that can contain either instructions or data are *unified* caches, or *mixed* caches. The CPU knows whether it is issuing an instruction address or a data address, so there can be separate ports for both, thereby doubling the bandwidth between the cache and the CPU. (Section 6.4 in Chapter 6 shows the advantages of dual memory ports for pipelined execution.) Separate caches also offers the opportunity of optimizing each cache separately: different capacities, block sizes, and associativities may lead to better performance. Splitting thus affects the cost and performance far beyond what is indicated by the change in miss rates. We limit our discussion to that point now simply to show how miss rates for instructions differ from miss rates for data.

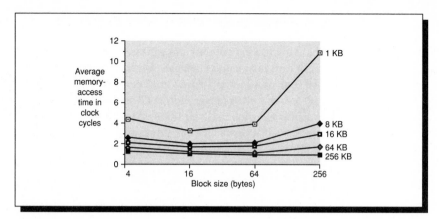

FIGURE 8.15 Average access time versus block size using the miss rates in Figure 8.14. This assumes an 8–clock-cycle latency and that the memory and bus can transfer 4 bytes per clock cycle. On a miss all the blocks are loaded into the cache before the requested word is sent to the CPU. The lowest average memory-access time is either for 16-byte or 64-byte blocks, and 256-byte blocks are better than 4-byte blocks only for the largest cache.

Figure 8.16 shows that instruction-only caches have lower miss rates than data-only caches. Separating instructions and data removes misses due to conflicts between instruction blocks and data blocks, but the split also fixes the cache space devoted to each type. A fair comparison of separate instruction and data caches to unified caches requires the total cache size to be the same. Therefore, a separate 1-KB instruction cache and 1-KB data cache should be compared to a unified 2-KB cache. Calculating the average miss rate with separate instruction-only and data-only caches necessitates knowing the percentage of memory references to each cache.

Size	Instruction only	Data only	Unified
0.25 KB	22.2%	26.8%	28.6%
0.50 KB	17.9%	20.9%	23.9%
1 KB	14.3%	16.0%	19.0%
2 KB	11.6%	11.8%	14.9%
4 KB	8.6%	8.7%	11.2%
8 KB	5.8%	6.8%	8.3%
16 KB	3.6%	5.3%	5.9%
32 KB	2.2%	4.0%	4.3%
64 KB	1.4%	2.8%	2.9%
128 KB	1.0%	2.1%	1.9%
256 KB	0.9%	1.9%	1.6%

FIGURE 8.16 Miss rates for instruction-only, data-only, and unified caches of different sizes. The data are for a 2-way–associative cache using LRU replacement with 16-byte blocks for an average of user/system traces on the VAX-11 and system traces on the IBM 370 [Hill 1987]. The percentage of instruction references in these traces is about 53%.

Example	Which has the lower miss rate: a 16-KB instruction cache with a 16-KB data cache or a 32-KB unified cache? Assume 53% of the references are instructions.
Answer	As stated in the legend of Figure 8.16, 53% of the memory accesses are instruction references. Thus, the overall miss rate for the split caches is

$$53\% * 3.6\% + 47\% * 5.3\% = 4.4\%$$

A 32-KB unified cache has a slightly lower miss rate of 4.3%.

8.4 | Main Memory

… the one single development that put computers on their feet was the invention of a reliable form of memory, namely, the core memory. … Its cost was reasonable, it was reliable and, because it was reliable, it could in due course be made large.

Maurice Wilkes, *Memoirs of a Computer Pioneer* (1985, p. 209)

Provided there is only one level of cache, main memory is the next level down in the hierarchy. Main memory satisfies the demands of caches and vector units, and serves as the I/O interface as it is the destination of input as well as the source for output. Unlike caches, performance measures of main memory emphasize both latency and bandwidth. Generally, main memory latency (which affects the cache miss penalty) is the primary concern of the cache, while main-memory bandwidth is the primary concern of I/O and vector units. As cache blocks grow from 4-8 bytes to 64–256 bytes, main memory bandwidth becomes important to caches as well. The relationship of main memory and I/O is discussed in Chapter 9.

Memory latency is traditionally quoted using two measures—access time and cycle time. *Access time* is the time between when a read is requested and when the desired word arrives, while *cycle time* is the minimum time between requests to memory. In the 1970s, as DRAMs grew in capacity the cost of a package with all the necessary address lines became an issue. The solution was to multiplex the address lines, thereby cutting the number of address pins in half. The top half of the address comes first, during the *row-access strobe*, or RAS. This is followed by the second half of the address during the *column-access strobe*, or CAS. These names come from the internal chip organization, for the memory is organized as a rectangular matrix addressed by rows and columns.

An additional requirement of DRAMs derives from the property signified by its first letter, D, for dynamic. Every DRAM must have every row accessed within a certain time window, such as 2 milliseconds, or the information in the DRAM can be lost. This requirement means that the memory system is occasionally unavailable because it is sending a signal telling every chip to refresh. The cost of a refresh is typically a full memory access (RAS and CAS) for each row of the DRAM. Since the memory matrix in a DRAM is likely to be square, the number of steps in a refresh is usually the square root of the DRAM capacity.

In contrast to DRAMs are SRAMs—the first letter standing for "static." The dynamic nature of the circuits for DRAM require data to be written back after being read, hence the difference between the access time and the cycle time and also the need to refresh. SRAMs use more circuits per bit to prevent the information from being disturbed when read. Thus, unlike DRAMs, there is no difference between access time and cycle time and there is no need to refresh SRAM. In DRAM designs the emphasis is on capacity, while SRAM designs are concerned with both capacity **and** speed. (Because of this concern, SRAM address lines are not multiplexed.) For memories designed in comparable technologies, the capacity of DRAMs is roughly 16 times that of SRAMs, and the cycle time of SRAMs is 8 to 16 times faster than DRAMs.

The main memory of virtually every computer sold in the last decade is composed of semiconductor DRAMs (and virtually all caches use SRAM). Amdahl suggested a rule of thumb that memory capacity should grow linearly with CPU speed to keep a balanced system (see Section 1.4), and CPU designers rely on DRAMs to supply that demand: they expect a four-fold improvement in capacity every three years. Unfortunately, the performance of DRAMs is growing at a much slower rate. Figure 8.17 shows a performance improvement in row-access time of about 22% per generation, or 7% per year. As noted in Chapter 1, CPU performance improved 18% to 35% per year prior to 1985, and since that time has jumped to 50% to 100% per year. Figure 8.18 plots these optimistic and pessimistic CPU performance projections against the steady 7% performance improvement in DRAM speeds.

| Year of introduction | Chip size | Row access (RAS) | | Column access (CAS) | Cycle time |
		Slowest DRAM	Fastest DRAM		
1980	64 Kbit	180 ns	150 ns	75 ns	250 ns
1983	256 Kbit	150 ns	120 ns	50 ns	220 ns
1986	1 Mbit	120 ns	100 ns	25 ns	190 ns
1989	4 Mbit	100 ns	80 ns	20 ns	165 ns
1992?	16 Mbit	≈85 ns	≈65 ns	≈15 ns	≈140 ns

FIGURE 8.17   Times of fast and slow DRAMs with each generation. The improvement by a factor of two in column access accompanied the switch from NMOS DRAMs to CMOS DRAMs. With three years per generation, the performance improvement of row access time is about 7% per year. Data in the last row represent predicted performance for 16-Mbit DRAMs, which are not yet available.

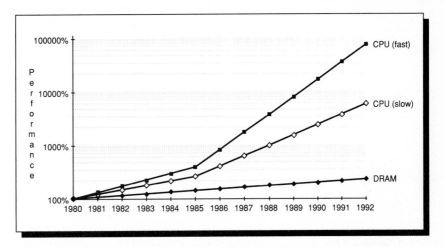

FIGURE 8.18 Starting with 1980 performance as a baseline, the performance of DRAMs and CPUs are plotted over time. The DRAM baseline is 64 KB in 1980, with three years to the next generation. The slow CPU line assumes a 19% improvement per year until 1985 and a 50% improvement thereafter. The fast CPU line assumes a 26% performance improvement between 1980 and 1985 and 100% per year thereafter. Note that the vertical axis must be on a logarithmic scale to record the size of the CPU–DRAM performance gap.

The CPU–DRAM performance gap is clearly a problem on the horizon—Amdahl's Law warns us what will happen if we ignore one portion of the computation while trying to speed up the rest. Section 8.8 will describe what can be done with cache organization to reduce this performance gap, but simply making caches larger cannot eliminate it. Innovative organizations of main memory are needed as well. In the rest of this section we will examine techniques for organizing memory to improve performance, including techniques especially for DRAMs.

Organizations for Improving Main Memory Performance

While it is generally easier to improve memory bandwidth with new organizations than it is to reduce latency, a bandwidth improvement does allow cache-block size to increase without a corresponding increase in the miss penalty.

Let's illustrate these organizations with the case of satisfying a cache miss. Assume the performance of the basic memory organization is

1 clock cycle to send the address

6 clock cycles for the access time per word

1 clock cycle to send a word of data

Given a cache block of four words, the miss penalty is 32 clock cycles, with a memory bandwidth of one-half byte per clock cycle.

Figure 8.19 shows some of the options to faster memory systems. The simplest approach to increasing memory bandwidth, then, is to make the memory wider.

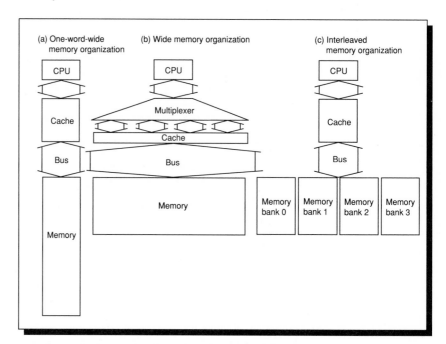

FIGURE 8.19 Three examples of bus width, memory width, and memory interleaving to achieve higher memory bandwidth. (a) is the simplest design, with everything the width of one word; (b) shows a wider memory, bus, and cache; while (c) shows a narrow bus and cache with an interleaved memory.

Wider Main Memory

Caches are often organized with a width of one word because most CPU accesses are that size. Main memory, in turn, is one word wide to match the width of the cache. Doubling or quadrupling the width of the memory will therefore double or quadruple the memory bandwidth. With a main memory width of two words the miss penalty in our example would drop from 4∗8 or 32 clock cycles to 2∗8 or 16 clock cycles. At four words wide the miss penalty is just 1∗8 clock cycles. The bandwidth is then one byte per clock cycle at two words wide and two bytes per clock cycle when the memory is four words wide.

There is cost in the wider bus. The CPU will still access the cache a word at a time, so there now needs to be a multiplexer between the cache and the CPU— and that multiplexer may be on the critical timing path. (If the cache is faster than the bus, however, the multiplexer can be placed between the cache and the bus.) Another drawback is that since main memory is traditionally expansible by the customer, the minimum increment is doubled or quadrupled. Finally, memories with error correction have difficulties with writes to a portion of the protected block (e.g., a write of a byte); the rest of the data must be read so that the new error correction code can be calculated and stored when the data is written. If the error correction is done over the full width, the wider memory will increase the frequency of such "read-modify-write" sequences because more writes become partial block writes. Many designs of wider memory have separate error correction every 32 bits since most writes are that size. One example of wider main memory was a computer whose cache, bus, and memory were all 512 bits wide.

Interleaved Memory

Memory chips can be organized in banks to read or write multiple words at a time rather than a single word. The banks are one word wide so that the width of the bus and the cache need not change, but sending addresses to several banks permits them all to read simultaneously. For example, sending an address to four banks (with access times shown on page 427) yields a miss penalty of 1+6+4*1 or 11 clock cycles, giving a bandwidth of about 1.5 bytes per clock cycle. Banks are also valuable on writes. While back-to-back writes would normally have to wait for earlier writes to finish, banks allow one clock cycle for each write, provided the writes are not destined to the same bank.

The mapping of addresses to banks affects the behavior of the memory system. The example above assumes the addresses of the four banks are interleaved at the word level—bank 0 has all words whose address modulo 4 is 0, bank 1 has all words whose address modulo 4 is 1, and so on. This mapping is referred to as the *interleaving factor*; *interleaved memory* normally means banks of memory that are word interleaved. This optimizes sequential memory accesses. A cache-read miss is an ideal match to word-interleaved memory, as the words in a block are read sequentially. Write-back caches make writes as well as reads sequential, getting even more efficiency from interleaved memory.

Example   What can interleaving and a wide memory buy? Consider the following description of a machine and its cache performance:

Block size = 1 word

Memory bus width = 1 word

Miss rate = 15%

Memory accesses per instruction = 1.2

Cache miss penalty = 8 cycles (as above)

Average cycles per instruction (ignoring cache misses) = 2

If we change the block size to two words, the miss rate falls to 10%, and a four-word block has a miss rate of 5%. What is the improvement in performance of interleaving two ways and four ways versus doubling the width of memory and the bus, assuming the access times on page 427.

Answer

The CPI for the base machine using one-word blocks is

$$2 + (1.2*15\%*8) = 3.44$$

Since the clock cycle time and instruction count won't change in this example, we can calculate performance improvement by just comparing CPI.

Increasing the block size to two words gives the following options:

32-bit bus and memory, no interleaving $= 2 + (1.2*10\%*2*8)$ $= 3.92$

32-bit bus and memory, interleaving $= 2 + (1.2*10\%*(1+6+2))$ $= 3.08$

64-bit bus and memory, no interleaving $= 2 + (1.2*10\%*1*8)$ $= 2.96$

Thus, doubling the block size slows down the straightforward implementation (3.92 versus 3.44), while interleaving or wider memory is 12% or 16% faster, respectively. If we increase the block size to four, the following is obtained:

32-bit bus and memory, no interleaving $= 2 + (1.2*5\%*4*8)$ $= 3.92$

32-bit bus and memory, interleaving $= 2 + (1.2*5\%*(1+6+4))$ $= 2.66$

64-bit bus and memory, no interleaving $= 2 + (1.2*5\%*2*8)$ $= 2.96$

Again, the larger block hurts performance for the simple case, although the interleaved 32-bit memory is now fastest—29% versus 16% for the wider memory and bus.

The original motivation for memory banks was interleaving sequential accesses. A further reason is to allow multiple independent accesses. Multiple memory controllers allow banks (or sets of word-interleaved banks) to operate independently. For example, an input device may use one controller and its memory, the cache may use another, and a vector unit may use a third. To reduce the chances of conflicts many banks are needed; the NEC SX/3, for instance, has up to 128 banks.

As capacity per memory chip increases, there are fewer chips in the same-sized memory system, making multiple banks much more expensive. For example, a 16-MB main memory takes 512 memory chips of 256 K (262,144) x 1 bits, easily organized into 16 banks of 32 memory chips. But it takes only 32 4-M (4,194,304) x 1-bit memory chips for 16 MB, making one bank the limit. This is the main disadvantage of interleaved memory banks. Even though the

Amdahl/Case rule of thumb for balanced computer systems recommends increasing memory capacity with increasing CPU performance, the 60% growth in DRAM capacity exceeded the rate of increase in CPU performance in the past (page 17 of Chapter 1). If the rate of increase of CPU speeds seen in the late 1980s can be maintained (Figure 8.18, page 427) and these systems follow the Amdahl/Case rule of thumb, then the number of chips may not be reduced.

A second disadvantage of interleaving is again the difficulty of main memory expansion. Since memory-control hardware will likely need equal-sized banks, doubling the main memory will probably be the minimum increment.

DRAM-Specific Interleaving for Improving Main Memory Performance

DRAM access times are divided into row access and column access. DRAMs buffer a row of bits inside the DRAM for the column access. This row is usually the square root of the DRAM size—1024 bits for 1 Mbit, 2048 for 4 Mbits, and so on. All DRAMs come with optional timing signals that allow repeated accesses to the buffer without a row-access time. There are three versions for this optimization:

- *Nibble mode*—The DRAM can supply three extra bits from sequential locations for every row access.

- *Page mode*—The buffer acts like a SRAM; by changing column address, random bits can be accessed in the buffer until the next row access or refresh time.

- *Static column*—Very similar to page mode, except that it's not necessary to hit the column-access strobe line every time the column address changes; this option has been nicknamed SCRAM, for static column DRAM.

Starting with the 1-Mbit DRAMs, most dies can perform any of the three options, with the optimization selected at the time the die is packaged by choosing which pads to wire up. These operations change the definition of cycle time for DRAMs. Figure 8.20 (page 432) shows the traditional cycle time plus the fastest speed between accesses in the optimized mode.

The advantage of these optimizations is that they use the circuitry already on the DRAMs, adding little cost to the system while achieving almost a fourfold improvement in bandwidth. For example, nibble mode was designed to take advantage of the same program behavior as interleaved memory. The chip reads four bits at a time internally, supplying four bits externally in the time of four optimized cycles. Unless the bus transfer time is faster than the optimized cycle time, the cost of four-way interleaved memory is only more complicated timing control. Page mode and static column could also be used to get even higher interleaving with slightly more complex control. DRAMs also tend to have weak tristate buffers, implying traditional interleaving with more memory chips must include buffer chips for each memory bank.

Chip size	Row access Slowest DRAM	Fastest DRAM	Column access	Cycle time	Optimized time nibble, page, static column
64 Kbits	180 ns	150 ns	75 ns	250 ns	150 ns
256 Kbits	150 ns	120 ns	50 ns	220 ns	100 ns
1 Mbits	120 ns	100 ns	25 ns	190 ns	50 ns
4 Mbits	100 ns	80 ns	20 ns	165 ns	40 ns
16 Mbits	$\approx$85 ns	$\approx$65 ns	$\approx$15 ns	$\approx$140 ns	$\approx$30 ns

FIGURE 8.20   DRAM cycle time for the optimized accesses. This is Figure 8.17 (page 426) with a column added to show the optimized cycle time for the three modes. Starting with the 1-Mbit DRAM, optimized cycle time is about four times faster than unoptimized cycle time. It is so much faster that page mode was renamed *fast page mode*. The optimized cycle time is the same no matter which of the 3 optimized modes is selected.

Thus, the authors expect that most main memory systems in the future will use such techniques to reduce the CPU–DRAM performance gap. Unlike traditional interleaved memories, there are no disadvantages using these DRAM modes as DRAMs scale upward in capacity, nor is there the problem of the minimum expansion increment in main memory.

One possibility that recently arrived is DRAMs that do not multiplex the address lines. At the cost of a larger package, a full random access falls between a row-access time and a column-access time in Figure 8.20. If unencoded DRAMs can stay close to the price per bit of the high volume encoded DRAMs, the computer architect will have another option in his bag of tricks for memory design.

8.5 | Virtual Memory

... a system has been devised to make the core drum combination appear to the programmer as a single level store, the requisite transfers taking place automatically.

Kilburn et al. [1962]

At any instant in time computers are running multiple processes, each with its own address space. (Processes are described in the next section.) It would be too expensive to dedicate a full-address-space worth of memory for each process, especially since many processes use only a small part of their address space. Hence, there must be a means of sharing a smaller amount of physical memory between many processes. One way to do this, *virtual memory*, divides physical memory into blocks and allocates them to different processes. Inherent in such an approach must be a *protection* scheme that restricts a process to the blocks belonging just to that process. Most forms of virtual memory also reduce the time to start a program, since not all code and data need be in physical memory before a program can begin.

While virtual memory is essential for current computers, sharing is not the reason virtual memory was invented. In former days if a program became too large for physical memory, it was up to the programmer to make it fit. Programmers divided programs into pieces and then identified the pieces that were mutually exclusive. These *overlays* were loaded or unloaded under user program control during execution, with the programmer ensuring that the program never tried to access more physical main memory in the machine. As one can well imagine, this responsibility eroded programmer productivity. Virtual memory, invented to relieve programmers of this burden, automatically managed the two levels of the memory hierarchy represented by main memory and secondary storage.

In addition to sharing protected memory space and automatically managing the memory hierarchy, virtual memory also simplifies loading the program for execution. Called *relocation*, this procedure allows the same program to run in any location in physical memory. (Prior to the popularity of virtual memory, machines would include a relocation register just for that purpose.) An alternative to a hardware solution would be software that changed all addresses in a program each time it was run.

Several general memory-hierarchy terms from Section 8.3 apply to virtual memory, while some other terms are different. *Page* or *segment* is used for block, and *page fault*, or *address fault*, is used for miss. With virtual memory, the CPU produces *virtual addresses* that are translated by a combination of hardware and software to *physical addresses*, which can be used to access main memory. This process is called *memory mapping* or *address translation*. Today, the two memory hierarchy levels controlled by virtual memory are DRAMs and magnetic disks. Figure 8.21 shows a typical range of memory hierarchy parameters for virtual memory.

Block (page) size	512 – 8192 bytes
Hit time	1–10 clock cycles
Miss penalty	100,000 – 600,000 clock cycles
(Access time)	(100,000–500,000 clock cycles)
(Transfer time)	(10,000–100,000 clock cycles)
Miss rate	0.00001%–0.001%
Main memory size	4 MB – 2048 MB

FIGURE 8.21 Typical ranges of parameters for virtual memory. These figures, contrasted with the values for caches in Figure 8.5 (page 408), represent increases of 10 to 100,000 times.

There are further differences between caches and virtual memory beyond those quantitative ones seen by comparing Figure 8.21 (page 433) to Figure 8.5 (page 408):

- Replacement on cache misses is primarily controlled by hardware, while virtual memory replacement is primarily controlled by the operating system; the longer miss penalty means the operating system can afford to get involved and spend more time deciding what to replace.

- The size of the processor address determines the size of virtual memory, but the cache size is normally independent of the processor address.

- In addition to acting as the lower-level memory for main memory in the hierarchy, secondary storage is also used for the file system that is not normally part of the address space; most of secondary storage is in fact taken up by the file system.

Virtual memory encompasses several related techniques. Virtual memory systems can be categorized into two classes: those with fixed-size blocks, called *pages*, and those with variable size blocks, called *segments*. Pages are typically fixed at 512 to 8192 bytes, while segment size varies. The largest segment supported on any machine ranges from 2^{16} bytes up to 2^{32} bytes; the smallest segment is one byte.

The decision to use paged virtual memory versus segmented virtual memory affects the CPU. Paged addressing has a single, fixed-size address divided into page number and offset within a page, analogous to cache addressing. A single address does not work for segmented addresses; the variable size of segments requires one word for a segment number and one word for an offset within a segment, for a total of two words. An unsegmented address space is simpler for the compiler.

The pros and cons of these two approaches have been well documented in operating systems textbooks; these are summarized in Figure 8.22. Because of the replacement problem (the third line of the figure), few machines today use pure segmentation. Some machines use a hybrid approach, called *paged segments*, in which a segment is an integral number of pages. This simplifies replacement because memory need not be contiguous, and the full segments need not be in main memory.

We are now ready to answer the four memory-hierarchy questions for virtual memory.

Q1: Where Can a Block Be Placed in Main Memory?

The miss penalty for virtual memory involves access to a rotating magnetic storage device and is therefore quite high. Given the choice of lower miss rates or a simpler placement algorithm, operating systems designers always pick lower miss rates because of the horrendous cost of a miss. Thus, operating systems allow blocks to be placed anywhere in main memory. According to the terminology in Figure 8.6 (page 409), this strategy would be labeled fully associative.

Q2: How Is a Block Found If It Is in Main Memory?

Both paging and segmentation rely on a data structure that is indexed by the page or segment number. This data structure contains the physical address of the block. For paging, the offset is simply concatenated to this physical page address (see Figure 8.23, page 436). For segmentation, the offset is added to the segment's physical address to obtain the final virtual address.

	Page	**Segment**
Words per address	One	Two (segment and offset)
Programmer visible?	Invisible to application programmer	May be visible to application programmer
Replacing a block	Trivial (all blocks are the same size)	Hard (must find contiguous, variable-size, unused portion of main memory)
Memory use inefficiency	Internal fragmentation (unused portion of page)	*External fragmentation* (unused pieces of main memory)
Efficient disk traffic	Yes (adjust page size to balance access time and transfer time)	Not always (small segments may transfer just a few bytes)

FIGURE 8.22 Paging versus segmentation. Both can waste memory, depending on the block size and how well the segments fit together in main memory. Programming languages with unrestricted pointers require both the segment and the address to be passed. A hybrid approach, called *paged segments*, shoots for the best of both worlds: segments are composed of pages, so replacing a block is easy, yet a segment may be treated as a logical unit.

This data structure containing the physical page addresses usually takes the form of a *page table*. Indexed by the virtual page number, the size of the table is the number of pages in the virtual-address space. Given a 28-bit virtual address, 4 KB pages, and 4 bytes per page-table entry, the size of the page table would be 256 KB. To reduce the size of this data structure, some machines apply a hashing function to the virtual address so that the data structure need only be the size of the number of **physical** pages in main memory; this number would be much smaller than the number of virtual pages. Such a structure is called an *inverted page table*. Using the example above, a 64-MB physical memory would only need 64 KB (4*64 MB/4 KB) for an inverted page table.

To reduce address translation time, computers use a cache dedicated to these address translations, called a translation-lookaside buffer, or simply translation buffer. They are described in more detail shortly.

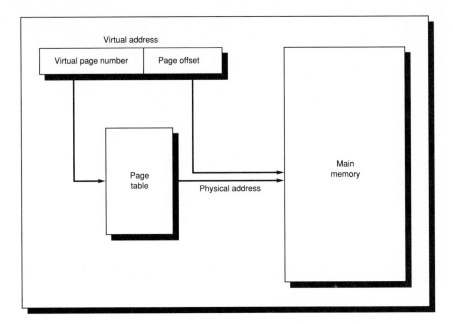

FIGURE 8.23   The mapping of a virtual address to a physical address via a page table.

Q3: Which Block Should Be Replaced on a Virtual Memory Miss?

As mentioned above, the overriding operating system guideline is minimizing page faults. Consistent with this, almost all operating systems try to replace the least-recently used (LRU) block, because that is the one least likely to be needed. To help the operating system estimate LRU, many machines provide a *use bit* or *reference bit*, which is set whenever a page is accessed. The operating system periodically clears the use bits and later records them so it can determine which pages were touched during a particular time period. By keeping track in this way, the operating system can select a page that is among the least-recently referenced.

Q4: What Happens on a Write?

The level below main memory contains rotating magnetic disks that take hundreds of thousands of clock cycles to access. Because of the great discrepancy in access time, no one has yet built a virtual memory operating system that can write through main memory straight to disk on every store by the CPU. (This remark should not be interpreted as an opportunity to become famous by being the first to build one!) Thus, the write strategy is always write back. Since the cost of an unnecessary access to the next-lower level is so high, virtual memory systems include a dirty bit so that the only blocks written to disk are those that have been altered since they were loaded from the disk.

Selecting a Page Size

The most obvious architectural parameter is the page size. Choosing the page is a question of balancing forces that favor a larger page size versus those favoring a smaller size. The following favor a larger size:

- The size of the page table is inversely proportional to the page size; memory (or other resources used for the memory map) can therefore be saved by making the pages bigger.

- Transferring larger pages to or from secondary storage, possibly over a network, is more efficient than transferring smaller pages.

(The larger page size may also help in address translation of cache addresses; see Section 8.8.)

The main motivation for a smaller page size is conserving storage. A small page size will result in less wasted storage when a contiguous region of virtual memory is not equal in size to a multiple of the page size. The term for this unused memory in a page is *internal fragmentation*. Assuming that each process has three primary segments (text, heap, and stack), the average wasted storage per process will be 1.5 times the page size. This is negligible for machines with megabytes of memory and page sizes in the range of 2 KB to 8 KB. Of course, when the page sizes become very large (more than 32 KB), lots of storage (both main and secondary) may be wasted, as well as I/O bandwidth. A final concern is process start-up time; many processes are small, so larger page sizes would lengthen the time to invoke a process.

Techniques for Fast Address Translation

Page tables are usually so large that they are stored in main memory and often paged themselves. This means that every memory access takes at least twice as long, with one memory access to obtain the physical address and a second access to get the data. This cost is far too dear.

One remedy is to remember the last translation, so that the mapping process is skipped if the current address refers to the same page as the last one. A more general solution is to again rely on the principle of locality; if the references have locality, then the address translations for the references must also have locality. By keeping these address translations in a special cache, a memory access rarely requires a second access to translate the data. This special address translation cache is referred to as a *translation-lookaside buffer* or TLB, also called a "translation buffer," or TB. A TLB entry is like a cache entry where the tag holds portions of the virtual address and the data portion holds a physical page-frame number, protection field, use bit, and dirty bit. To change the physical page-frame number or protection of an entry in the page table the operating system must make sure the old entry is not in the TLB; otherwise, the

system won't behave properly. Note that this dirty bit means the corresponding
page is dirty, not that the address translation in the TLB is dirty nor that a
particular block in the data cache is dirty. Figure 8.24 shows typical parameters
for TLBs.

Block size	4 – 8 bytes (1 page-table entry)
Hit time	1 clock cycle
Miss penalty	10 – 30 clock cycles
Miss rate	0.1% – 2%
TLB size	32 – 8192 bytes

FIGURE 8.24 Typical values of key memory-hierarchy parameters for TLBs. TLBs
are simply caches for the virtual-to-physical address translations found in the page tables.

One architectural challenge stems from the difficulty of combining caches
with virtual memory. The virtual address must first go through the TLB **before**
the physical address can access the cache, meaning that the cache hit time must
be stretched to allow for address translation (or the pipeline could be stretched as
in Chapter 6). One way to reduce hit time is to access the cache with the page
offset, the portion of the virtual address that does not need to be translated.
While the cache address tags are being read, the virtual portion of the address
(the page-frame address) is sent to the TLB to be translated. The address
comparison is then between the physical address from the TLB and the cache
tag. Since the TLB is usually smaller and faster than the cache-address-tag
memory, simultaneous TLB reading need not slow down cache hit times. The
drawback with this scheme is that a direct-mapped cache can be no bigger than a
page. Another option, virtually addressed caches, is discussed in Section 8.8.

8.6 | Protection and Examples of Virtual Memory

The invention of multiprogramming led to new demands for protection and
sharing between programs. These are closely tied to virtual memory in
computers today, and so we cover the topic here along with two examples of
virtual memory.

Multiprogramming lead to the concept of a *process*. Metaphorically, a
process is a program's breathing air and living space; that is, a running program
plus any state needed to continue running the program. Timesharing means
sharing the CPU and memory with several users at the same time to give the
appearance that every user has his own machine. Thus, at any instant it must be
possible to switch from one process to another. This is called a *process switch* or
context switch. Figure 8.25 shows the frequency of these switches on the VAX
8700.

Instructions between process switches	19,353
Clock cycles between process switches	170,113
Time between process switches	7.7 ms

FIGURE 8.25 Frequency of process switches on VAX 8700 for timesharing workload. Most switching occurs on interrupts caused by I/O events or by the interval timer (see Figure 5.10, page 216). Since neither the latency of the I/O device nor the timer is affected by the speed of the CPU clock, faster machines generally execute more clock cycles and instructions between process switches.

A process must operate correctly whether it executes continuously from start to finish or is interrupted repeatedly and switched with other processes. The responsibility for maintaining correct process behavior is shared by the computer designer, who must ensure that the CPU portion of the process state can be saved and restored, and the operating system designer, who must guarantee that processes do not interfere with each others' computations. The safest way to protect the state of one process from another would be to copy the current information to disk. But a process switch would then take seconds—far too long for a timesharing environment. The problem is solved by operating systems partitioning main memory so that several different processes have their state in memory at the same time. This means that the operating system designer needs help from the computer designer to provide protection so that one process cannot modify another. Besides protection, the computers also provide for sharing of code and data between processes, to allow communication between processes or to save memory by reducing the number of copies of identical information.

Protecting Processes

The simplest protection mechanism is a pair of registers that checks every address to be sure that it falls between the two limits traditionally called *base* and *bound*. An address is valid if

$$\text{Base} \leq \text{Address} \leq \text{Bound}$$

In some systems the address is considered an unsigned number that is always added to the base, so the valid test is just

$$(\text{Base} + \text{Address}) \leq \text{Bound}$$

For user processes to be protected from each other, they can't change the base and bounds registers, yet the operating system must be able to change the registers so that it can switch processes. Hence, the computer designer has three more responsibilities in helping the operating system designer protect processes from each other:

1. Provide at least two modes indicating whether the running process is a user process or an operating system process, sometimes called a *kernel* process, a *supervisor* process or an *executive* process.

2. Provide a portion of the CPU state that a user process can use but not write. This includes the base/bound registers, a user/supervisor mode bit(s), and the interrupt enable/disable bit. Users are prevented from writing this state because the operating system cannot control user processes if users can change the address-range checks, disable interrupts, or give themselves supervisor privileges.

3. Provide mechanisms whereby the CPU can go from user mode to supervisor mode and vice versa. The first direction is typically accomplished by a *system call*, implemented as a special instruction that transfers control to a dedicated location in supervisor code space. The PC from the point of the system call is saved, and the CPU is placed in supervisor mode. The return to user mode is like a subroutine return that restores the previous user/supervisor mode.

Base and bound constitute the minimum protection system. Virtual memory provides an alternative to this simple model. As we have seen, the CPU address must go through a mapping from virtual to physical address. This provides the opportunity for the hardware to check further for errors in the program or to protect processes from each other. The simplest way of doing this is to add access permission flags to each page or segment. For example, since few programs today intentionally modify their own code, an operating system can detect accidental writes to code by offering read-only protection to pages. This can be extended by adding a user/kernel bit to prevent a user program from trying to access pages that belong to the kernel. As long as the CPU provides a read/write signal and a user/kernel signal, it is easy for the address translation hardware to detect stray memory accesses before they can do damage. As seen in Section 5.6 of Chapter 5, such reckless behavior interrupts the CPU. Obviously, user programs cannot be allowed to modify the page table.

Protection can be escalated, depending on the apprehension of the computer designer or the purchaser. Rings added to the CPU-protection structure expand memory-access protection from two levels (user and kernel) to many more. Like a military classification system of top secret, secret, classified, and unclassified, concentric *rings* of security levels allow the most trusted to access anything, the second most trusted to access everything except the innermost level, and so on down to "civilian" programs which are the least trusted and, hence, have the most limited range of accesses. There may also be restrictions on the entrance point between the levels. The 80286 protection structure, which uses rings, is described later in this section. It is not clear today whether rings are an improvement on the simple system of user and kernel modes.

As the designer's apprehension escalates to trepidation, these simple rings may not suffice. The fact that a program in the inner sanctum can access anything calls for a new classification system. Instead of a military model, the analogy of this next model is to keys and locks: A program can't unlock access to the data unless it has the key. For these keys, or *capabilities*, to be useful, the hardware and operating system must be able to explicitly pass them from one program to another without allowing a program itself to forge them. Such checking requires a great deal of hardware support.

A Paged Virtual Memory Example:
VAX-11 Memory Management and the VAX-11/780 TLB

The VAX architecture uses a combination of segmentation and paging. This combination provides protection while minimizing page-table size. The address space is first divided into two segments: process (bit 31 = 0) and system (bit 31=1). Every process has its own private space and shares system space with every other process. The process address space is further subdivided into two regions called P0 and P1, using bit 30 to distinguish them. Area P0 (bit 30 = 0) grows from address 0 upward while P1 (bit 30 = 1) grows downward to 0. Figure 8.26 shows the layout of P0 and P1. The two segments can grow until one exceeds its 2^{30} address-space size and its virtual memory is exhausted. Many systems today use some such combination of predivided segments and paging. The approach provides many advantages: Segmentation divides system and process address space and conserves page-table space, while paging provides virtual memory, relocation, and protection.

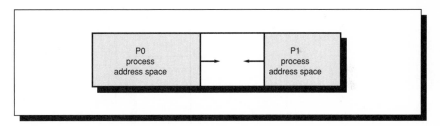

FIGURE 8.26   The organization of P0 and P1 in the VAX. This is the process half of the address space, selected with a 0 in bit 31 of a virtual address. Bit 30 of the address divides P0 and P1. Operating systems put the text and heap areas into P0 and a downward growing stack into P1.

To conserve page-table space, each of the three regions—P0 process, P1 process, and system—is provided with a pair of base-bound registers that indicate the start and limit of the page table for each region. The alternative would be to have a single page table that covers the full address space, independent of the program's actual size. The small size of the VAX pages—512 bytes, yielding large page tables—makes such conservation especially important.

Figure 8.27 (page 442) shows the mapping of a VAX address. The two most-significant bits of an address select which segment or base-bound–register pair to use in selecting a page table and checking the reference. A one in the first bit selects the system page table, whose base and length are found respectively in the system base register and in the system length register. A zero in the first bit of an address (as in the figure) selects page table P0 or P1, found by the P0 or P1 base registers and checked by the P0 or P1 limit (bound) registers. The P0 and P1 page tables are in the system-space virtual memory, while the system page table is in physical memory.

This offers an interesting way to conserve physical memory. Since the P0 and P1 page tables are also in virtual memory, this means the page tables can be paged. Just as some code and data can remain on disk during program execution, the page-table translation entries for that code and data can remain on disk until they are used. This is especially important for programs whose memory size varies dynamically during execution, as page tables can be increased as P0 or P1 space grows. In the worst case, then, a process page fault can result in a second page fault bringing in the missing piece of the process page table needed to complete the address translation. What prevents all pages tables from being

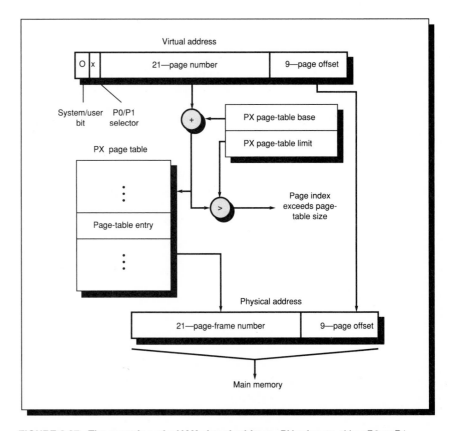

FIGURE 8.27   The mapping of a VAX virtual address. PX refers to either P0 or P1.

migrated to secondary storage? Some system page tables are loaded into physical memory when the operating system is booted and are prevented from migrating to disk. Thus, eventually a series of faults must cross an address stored in the system page table that is "frozen" into main memory.

While this explains translation of legal addresses, what prevents the user from creating illegal address translations and getting into mischief? The page tables themselves are protected from being written to by user programs. Thus, the user can try any virtual address, but by controlling the page-table entries the operating system controls what physical memory is accessed. Sharing of memory between processes is accomplished by having a page-table entry in each address space point to the same physical-memory page.

A *page-table entry* (PTE) on the VAX is straightforward. Other than the physical page-frame number these are the only architecture-defined fields:

M—the *modify bit* indicating the page is dirty

V—the *valid bit* indicating this PTE has a valid address

PROT—four protection bits

Note that there is no reference or use bit. Hence, a page-replacement algorithm such as LRU must rely on the modify bit or some software technique to measure usage. Rather than simply a kernel/user protection structure, the VAX uses a four-level structure consisting of kernel, executive, supervisor, and user. The four protection bits in the PTE contain 16 encodings of selected combinations of no access, read-only access, and read-write access, with the four security levels. For example, 1001 means read-write access for kernel and executive-level processes, read access for supervisor-level processes, and no access for user-level processes. To further isolate these four levels, each has its own stack and its own copy of the stack pointer (R15).

The first implementation of this architecture was the VAX-11/780, which employs a TLB to reduce address-translation time. Figure 8.28 shows the key parameters of this TLB.

Block size	1 PTE (4 bytes)
Hit time	1 clock cycle
Miss penalty (average)	22 clock cycles
Miss rate	$1\% - 2\%$
Cache size	128 PTEs (512 bytes)
Block selection	Random
Write strategy	(Not applicable)
Block placement	2-way set associative

FIGURE 8.28   Memory hierarchy parameters of the VAX-11/780 TLB.

Figure 8.29 shows the VAX-11/780 TLB organization, with each step of a translation labeled. The TLB uses two-way–set-associative placement; thus, the translation begins (steps 1 and 2) by sending a portion of the virtual address ("index") to both sets to select the two tags that are to be compared. Of course, the tag must be marked valid to allow a match. At the same time, the type of memory access is checked for a violation (also in step 2) against protection information in the TLB.

For reasons similar to those in the cache case, there is no need to include the 9 bits of the VAX page offset in the TLB; nor is there reason to include the 6 address bits to index the TLB. The remaining bits are used in the comparison (step 3). The matching address tag sends the corresponding physical address through the multiplexer (step 4). The page offset is then combined with the physical page frame to form a full physical address (step 5).

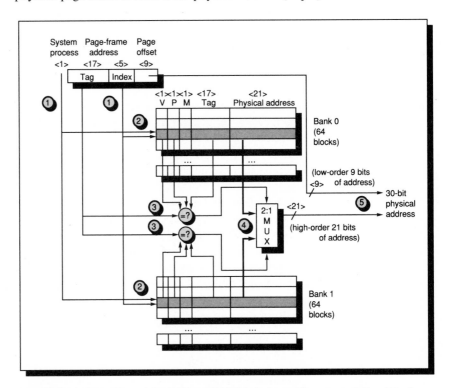

FIGURE 8.29   Operation of the VAX-11/780 TLB during address translation. The five steps of a TLB hit are shown as circled numbers.

There is one unusual feature of the VAX-11/780 TLB: The TLB is further subdivided to make sure the process portion of the address occupies no more than 50% of the TLB entries. The top 32 entries of each bank are reserved for system space, and the bottom 32 are reserved for process space. The most significant bit of the address is used to select the appropriate half of the TLB (step 1). Since the system portion of the address space is the same for all processes, a process switch invalidates only the lower 32 entries of each bank for the VAX-11/780 TLB. This restriction had two goals. The first was to reduce the process-switch time by reducing the number of TLB entries that had to be invalidated; the second was to improve performance by preventing the system or user process from throwing out the other's translations when process switches were frequent. Splitting the TLB will usually lead to higher overall TLB miss rate, but may reduce the peak TLB miss rate in heavily process-switching environments.

A Segmented Virtual Memory Example: Protection in the Intel 80286/80386

The second system is the most dangerous system a man ever designs. . . . The general tendency is to over-design the second system, using all the ideas and frills that were cautiously sidetracked on the first one.

F. P. Brooks, Jr., *The Mythical Man-Month* (1975)

The original 8086 used segments for addressing, yet it provided nothing for virtual memory or for protection. Segments had base registers but no bound registers and no access checks; and before a segment register could be loaded the corresponding segment had to be in physical memory. Intel's dedication to virtual memory and protection is evident in subsequent models, with a few fields extended to support larger addresses.

Like the VAX, the 80286 has four levels of protection. The innermost level (0) corresponds to VAX kernel mode, and the outermost level (3) corresponds to VAX user mode. The 80286 also follows the VAX by having separate stacks for each level to avoid security breaches between the levels. There are also data structures analogous to VAX page tables that contain the physical addresses for segments, as well as a list of checks to be made on translated addresses.

The Intel designers did not stop there. The 80286 divides the address space, allowing both the operating system and the user access to the full space. The 80286 user can call an operating system routine in this space and even pass parameters to it retaining full protection. This is not a trivial action, since the stack for the operating system is different from the user's stack. Moreover, the 80286 allows the operating system to maintain the protection level of the called routine for the parameters that are passed to it. This potential loophole in protection is prevented by not allowing the user to ask the operating system to access something indirectly that he would not have been able to access himself. Such security loopholes are called *Trojan horses*.

The 80286 designers were guided by the principle of trusting the operating system as little as possible, while supporting sharing and protection. As an example of the use of such protected sharing, suppose a payroll program writes checks and also updates the year-to-date information on total salary and benefits payments. Thus, we want to give the program the ability to read the salary and year-to-date information and modify the year-to-date information but not the salary. We shall see the mechanism to support such features shortly. In the rest of this section we will look at the big picture of the 80286 protection and examine its motivation. Readers interested in the detailed picture can find it in a comprehensive book by Crawford and Gelsinger [1987].

Adding Bounds Checking and Memory Mapping

The first step in enhancing the 80286 was getting the segmented addressing to check bounds as well as supply a base. Rather than a base address, as in the 8086, segment registers in the 80286 contain an index to a virtual memory data structure called a *descriptor table*. Descriptor tables play the role of page tables in the VAX. On the 80286 the equivalent of a page-table entry is a *segment descriptor*. It contains fields found in PTEs:

A *present bit*—equivalent to the PTE valid bit, used to indicate this is a valid translation

A *base field*—equivalent to a page-frame address, containing the physical address of the first byte of the segment

An *access bit*—like the reference bit or use bit in some architectures that is helpful for replacement algorithms

An *attributes field*—like the protection field in the VAX PTE, which specifies the valid operations and protection levels for operations that use this segment

There is also a *limit field*, not found in paged systems, which establishes the upper bound of valid offsets for this segment. Figure 8.30 shows examples of 80286 segment descriptors.

Adding Sharing and Protection

The Intel designers' next step was to provide for protected sharing. Like the VAX, half of the address space is shared by all processes and half is unique to each process, called *global address space* and *local address space*, respectively. Each half is given a descriptor table with the appropriate name. A descriptor pointing to a shared segment is placed in the global-descriptor table, while a descriptor for a private segment is placed in the local-descriptor table.

A program loads an 80286 segment register with an index to the table **and** a bit saying which table it desires. The operation is checked according to the attributes in the descriptor, the physical address being formed by adding the offset in the CPU to the base in the descriptor, provided the offset is less than the limit field. Unlike the encoding of operations and levels in the VAX PTE, every segment descriptor has a separate two-bit field to give the legal access level of this segment. A violation occurs only if the program tries to use a segment with a lower protection level in the segment descriptor.

We can now show how to invoke the payroll program to update the year-to-date information without allowing it to update salaries. The program could be given a descriptor to the information that has the writable field clear, meaning it can read but not write the data. A trusted program can then be supplied that will only write the year-to-date information and is given a descriptor with the writable field set (Figure 8.30). The payroll program invokes the trusted code using a code-segment descriptor with the conforming field set (Figure 8.30). This means the called program takes on the privilege level of the code being called rather than the privilege level of the caller. Hence, the payroll program can read the salaries and call a trusted program to update the year-to-date totals, yet the payroll program cannot modify the salaries. If a Trojan horse exists in this system, to be effective it must be located in the trusted code whose only job is to update the year-to-date information. The argument for this style of protection is that limiting the scope of the vulnerability enhances security.

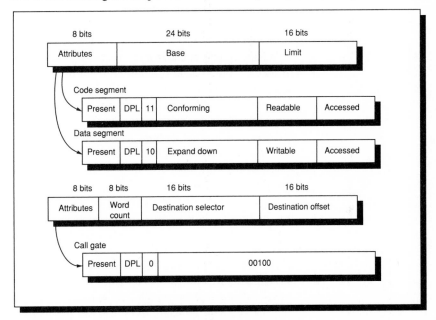

FIGURE 8.30 The 80286 segment descriptors are all 48 bits long and are distinguished by bits in the attributes field. *Base, limit, present, readable,* and *writable* are all self-explanatory. DPL means *descriptor privilege level*—this is checked against the code privilege level to see if the access will be allowed. *Conforming* says the code takes on the privilege level of the code being called rather than the privilege level of the caller; it is used for library routines. The *expand-down field* flips the check to let the base field be the high-water mark and the limit field be the low-water mark. As one might expect, this is used for stack segments that grow down. *Word count* controls the number of words copied from the current stack to the new stack on a call gate. The other two fields of the call-gate descriptor, *destination selector* and *destination offset*, select the descriptor of the destination of the call and the offset into it. There are many more than these three segment descriptors in the 80286. The principal change in the 80386 was to lengthen the base by eight bits and the limit by four bits.

Adding Safe Calls from User to OS Gates and Inheriting Protection Level for Parameters

Allowing the user to jump into the operating system is a bold step. How, then, can a hardware designer increase the chances of a safe system without trusting the operating system or any other piece of code? The 80286 approach is to restrict where the user can enter a piece of code, to safely place parameters on the proper stack, and to make sure the user parameters don't get the protection level of the called code.

To restrict entry into others' code, the 80286 provides a special segment descriptor, or *call gate*, identified by a bit in the attributes field. Unlike other descriptors, call gates are full physical addresses of an object in memory; the offset supplied by the CPU is ignored. As stated above, their purpose is to prevent the user from randomly jumping anywhere into a protected or more- privileged code segment. In our programming example, this means the only place the payroll program can invoke the trusted code is at the proper boundary. This is needed to make conforming segments work as intended.

What happens if caller and callee are "mutually suspicious," so that neither trusts each other? The solution is found in the word-count field in the bottom descriptor in Figure 8.30 (page 447). When a call instruction invokes a call-gate descriptor, the descriptor will copy the number of words specified in the descriptor from the local stack onto the stack corresponding to the level of this segment. This allows the user to pass parameters by first pushing them onto the local stack. The hardware then safely transfers them onto the correct stack. A return from a call gate will pop the parameters off both stacks and copy any return values to the proper stack.

This still leaves open the potential loophole of having the operating system use the user's address, passed as parameters, with the operating system's security level, instead of with the user's level. The 80286 solves this problem by dedicating two bits in every CPU segment register to the *requested protection level*. When an operating system routine is invoked, it can execute an instruction that sets this two-bit field in all address parameters with the protection level of the user that called the routine. Thus, when these address parameters are loaded into the segment registers, they will set the requested protection level to the proper value. The 80286 hardware then uses the requested protection level to prevent any foolishness: No segment can be accessed from the system routine using those parameters if it has a more-privileged protection level than requested.

Summary: Protection on the VAX Versus the 80286

If the 80286 protection model looks harder to build than the VAX model, that's because it is. This effort must be especially frustrating for the 80286 engineers, since most customers just use the 80286 as a fast 8086 and don't exploit the elaborate protection mechanism. Also, the fact that the protection model is a mismatch for the simple paging protection of UNIX means it will be used only by someone writing an operating system specially for this computer. OS/2 from Microsoft is the best candidate, but only time will tell whether the performance cost of such protection is justified for a personal-computer operating system. Two questions remain: Will the considerable protection-engineering effort, which must be borne by each generation of the 80x86 family, be put to good use, and will it prove any safer in practice than a paging system?

8.7 | More Optimizations Based on Program Behavior

Making the frequent case fast is the inspiration for almost all inventions aimed at improving performance. In this section are two more examples of hardware optimized to program behavior. The first fetches instructions before they are needed, and the second avoids saving registers to memory on procedure calls.

Instruction-Prefetch Buffers

Many machines use an *instruction-prefetch buffer* to take advantage of the normal sequential execution of instructions. Typically, an instruction buffer contains two to eight sequential instructions; as each instruction is consumed by the CPU, a subsequent instruction word is prefetched. Prefetching only makes sense if the memory system can deliver instructions much faster than the CPU can consume them; otherwise the buffer cannot get ahead of the CPU. This can be accomplished by having a wider path that fetches more than one instruction at a time, or by simply having a faster memory system than the CPU. The drawback to instruction buffers is that they increase memory traffic by requesting words of instructions that may never be needed by the CPU, as is the case when a branch is taken. Instruction-prefetch buffers are also useful for aligning variable-sized instructions.

The 8-byte instruction-prefetch buffer (IB) of the VAX-11/780, shown in Figure 8.31 (page 450), will serve as an example. The opcode of the current instruction is in the high-order byte of the IB; as pieces of the instruction are consumed, the whole buffer is shifted to the left by the appropriate amount. The left-most byte can correspond to any byte address, while the rest of the bytes in the IB must be sequential. The Vs in the figure represent a valid bit per byte of the instruction buffer and indicate the sequential bytes that contain valid instructions.

The IB tries to stay ahead of the PC. Whenever at least one byte is free in the IB, a read is requested for an aligned 32-bit word that contains that byte; only 32-bit words are prefetched from the memory. When the 32-bit prefetched word arrives, the IB loads as much of it as it has space for. A 32-bit instruction word therefore takes between one and four fetches from memory, depending on luck.

When the PC changes due to a branch or interrupt, the IB may have prefetched one or two unneeded instructions. The PC change causes all the valid bits to be turned off, and the IB is reloaded. Section 8.9 examines the performance impact of the IB.

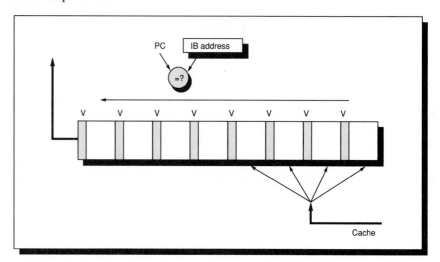

FIGURE 8.31   The VAX-11/780 instruction-prefetch buffer. Every byte has a valid bit to determine the number of consecutive bytes that have valid instructions. The instruction decoder can read the top four bytes of the buffer in a single clock cycle.

Registers and Register Windows

Figures 3.28 and 3.29 (pages 117–118) in Chapter 3 show that saving registers on procedure calls and restoring them on returns can account for 5% to 40% of the data memory references. As an alternative, several banks of registers can be used, with a new one allocated on each call. Although this could limit the depth of procedure calls, the limitation is avoided by operating the banks as a circular buffer, providing unlimited depth. This technique has been termed *register windows*.

Figure 8.32 shows the essence of the idea. On the x axis is time, measured in procedure calls or returns; on the y axis is the depth or nesting of procedure calls. Each call moves down the y axis, and each return moves up. The boxes show memory being accessed to save some of the buffer, either when it is full and is followed by a call (*window overflow*) or when it is empty and is followed by a return (*window underflow*). The figure shows eight window overflows and two window underflows during this section of program execution. Over the life of the program the number of overflows and underflows will equalize.

One might well ask what the trade-off is between buffer size and overflows or underflows. Figure 8.33 shows the shape of the curve for several programs written in several programming languages. The knee of the curve seems to be six to eight banks. While this holds for most programs, the optimization is based on

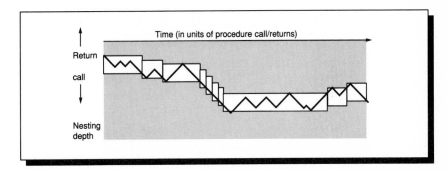

FIGURE 8.32 Change in procedure nesting depth over time. The boxes show procedure calls and returns inside the buffer before a window overflow or underflow. The program starts with three calls, a return, a call, a return, three calls, and then a window overflow.

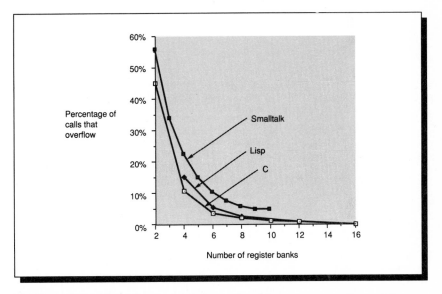

FIGURE 8.33 Number of banks or windows of registers versus overflow rate for several programs in C, LISP, and Smalltalk. The programs measured for C include a C compiler, a Pascal interpreter, troff, a sort program, and a few UNIX utilities [Halbert and Kessler 1980].The LISP measurements include a circuit simulator, a theorem prover, and several small LISP benchmarks [Taylor et al. 1986]. The Smalltalk programs come from the Smalltalk macro benchmarks [McCall 1983] which include a compiler, browser, and decompiler [Blakken 1983 and Ungar 1987].

program-specific patterns of calls and returns that might be quite different in some other programs. The worst case for register windows would be hundreds of calls followed by hundreds of returns. This would make Figure 8.32 look like seismograph output during an earthquake, and the performance impact would be just as devastating!

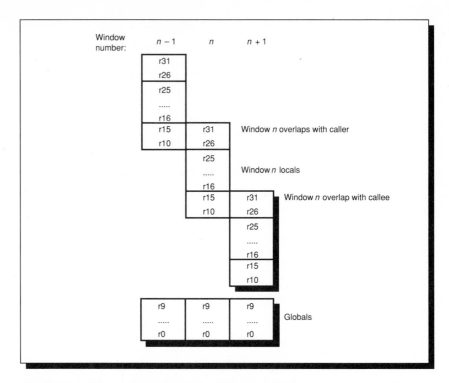

FIGURE 8.34   Parameters can be passed in registers if there are common registers between two banks or windows. This scheme divides registers into globals, which don't change on a procedure call, and locals, which do change. By having an overlap between locals for adjacent procedure calls and renumbering the registers on a call, the outgoing parameters of the caller become the incoming parameters of the callee. For example, a value placed in register 15 before a call is in register 31 after the call.

The difficulty of passing parameters in registers presents a drawback: If each procedure has its own unique set of registers, then nothing is common. This can be overcome by overlapping the register banks or windows such that there is a common area in which to pass parameters. Figure 8.34 shows one such design. Six registers overlap each window, with R15 to R10 of the caller's registers becoming R31 to R26 after the call. Ten registers are not included in the windows, so there are 16 (32 − 10 − 6) registers per window even though each procedure sees 32 registers at a time.

From Figure 8.33 we can estimate the percentage of calls that overflow the windows or returns that underflow them, but to understand the impact on performance we must know the cost an overflow or underflow. With an overlapping register design, like the one on SPARC, the cost is saving 16 registers on an overflow (or restoring 16 registers on an underflow) plus the cost of interrupt. On the Sun 4 today it takes about 60 clock cycles for an overflow or underflow.

The Pros and Cons of Register Windows

Depending on the application, programming language, and user practices, the compiler can close the gap between machines with and without register windows. Most machines, for example, have separate floating-point registers, which means that floating-point-intensive programs will be unaffected by register windows. Also, many data references are to objects that cannot be allocated in registers, like arrays or structures (see Figures 3.28 and 3.29 on pages 117–118 of Chapter 3).

An optimization called *interprocedural register allocation* allows more intelligent allocation of registers across procedure boundaries. Unfortunately, interprocedural register allocation works best when procedures are compiled or linked at the same time. Long compilation and link time do not match the emphasis on a rapid debug-edit-compile cycle in current dynamic languages like LISP and Smalltalk. Interprocedural register allocation is not generally applicable to object-oriented languages like Objective C and Smalltalk because in the dynamic equivalent of a procedure call the compiler doesn't know which procedure will be invoked on such calls. Register windows also simplify some compiler decisions, since there is no extra cost in using a register that will not be saved or restored separately.

	GCC	TeX
Percentage of DLX instructions call or return	1.8%	3.6%
Registers stored per call	2.3	3.2
Loads DLX	3,928,710	2,811,545
Loads SPARC	3,313,317	2,736,979
Ratio loads DLX / SPARC	1.20	1.03
Stores DLX	2,037,226	1,974,078
Stores SPARC	1,246,538	1,401,186
Ratio stores DLX / SPARC	1.60	1.41

FIGURE 8.35 Benefits of register windows on loads and stores for non–floating-point programs. The first row shows the percentage of DLX instructions executed that are calls or returns. The second row shows the average number of register saves and restores per call on the DLX architecture with optimization level O2. The following rows show the total number of loads and stores for each optimization and for the SPARC architecture, which has register windows. The data below includes the loads and stores due to window overflow and window underflow. GCC executes about 20% more loads and 60% more stores on DLX than on a machine with register windows, while TeX executes about 3% more loads and 41% more stores. These savings correspond to about 7% of the instruction count for GCC and 5% for TeX. How this translates into memory-system performance depends on the details of the rest of the memory hierarchy. Interprocedural register allocation closes this gap. For example, using O3 optimization on TeX reduces the number of DLX loads by 5% to 2,671,631 and the number of stores by 10% to 1,791,831. Note that the inputs for these programs were not the same as those used in Chapters 2 or 4. (Spice was not included because register windows offer no benefit for floating-point programs.)

The danger of register windows is that the larger number of registers could slow down the clock rate. So far, this has not been the case for commercial machines. The SPARC architecture (with register windows) and the MIPS R2000 architecture (without) are contemporary machines built in several technologies. The SPARC clock rate has not been slower than MIPS for implementations in similar technologies, probably because cache-access times dominate register-access times in implementations to date of either architecture. A second concern is the impact of register windows on process-switch time. Sun Microsystems has found that UNIX operating system vagaries dominate process-switch time, and less than 20% of the process-switch time is spent on saving or restoring registers. Figure 8.35 (page 453) compares some measures of the benefits of register windows on our benchmark programs.

8.8 | Advanced Topics—Improving Cache-Memory Performance

This section covers advanced topics in cache memories, going through new ideas at a much quicker pace than previous sections. The central points of this chapter are not lost if this section is skipped; in fact, the Putting It All Together section that follows is independent of this material.

The increasing gap between CPU and main memory speeds has attracted the attention of many architects. After making some easy decisions in the beginning, the architect faces a threefold dilemma when attempting to further reduce average access time:

- Increasing block size doesn't improve average access time; the lower miss rate doesn't offset the higher miss penalty.

- Making the cache bigger would make it slower, jeopardizing the CPU clock rate.

- Making the cache more associative would also make it slower, again jeopardizing the CPU clock rate.

Moreover, the miss rate calculated from user programs paints too rosy a picture. Figure 8.36 shows the real cache miss rate for a running program, including the operating system code invoked by the programs. This reveals the average access time to be worse than expected.

This section covers a plethora of techniques for improving cache performance: subblock placement, write buffers, out-of-order fetching, virtually addressed caches, two-level caches, and issues relating to cache coherency. The cache-coherency sections include an example of the stale-data problem, a survey of coherency alternatives, an example cache protocol, a synchronization algorithm used in cache coherent multiprocessors, a timeline showing multiprocessor synchronization, and comments about the impact of memory consistency on parallel processors.

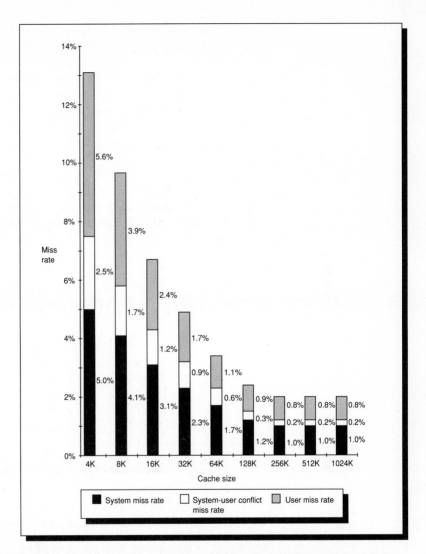

FIGURE 8.36 The miss rate of a program, including the operating system code it invokes, versus cache size. The top category is what would be measured from a user trace; the bottom category is the miss rate for the operating system code; and the middle category is the miss rate due to conflicts between the user code and system code. Agarwal [1987] collected these statistics for the Ultrix operating system running on a VAX, assuming direct-mapped caches with a block size of 16 bytes.

Reducing Hit Times—Making Writes Faster

As mentioned before, writes usually take more than one clock cycle because the tag must be checked before writing the data. There are two ways to do faster writes.

The first, used on the VAX 8800, pipelines the writes for a write-through cache. Tags and data are split so that they can be addressed independently. As usual, the cache compares the tag with the current write address. The difference is that the memory access during this comparison uses the address and data from the **previous** write. Therefore, writes can be performed back to back at one per clock cycle because the CPU does not have to wait for the write to the cache if the first stage is a hit. The 8800 pipeline does not affect read hits—the second stage of the write occurs during the first stage of the next write or during a cache miss.

Another way of reducing writes to one clock cycle involves caches that must be direct mapped, using a technique known as *subblock placement*. Like the VAX-11/780 instruction buffer, there is a valid bit on units smaller than the full block, called *subblocks*. The valid bits specify some parts of the block as valid and some parts as invalid. A match of the tag doesn't mean the word is necessarily in the cache, as the valid bits for that word must also be on. Figure 8.37 gives an example. Note that for caches with subblock placement a block can no longer be defined as the minimum unit transferred between cache and memory. For such caches a block is defined as the unit of information associated with an address tag.

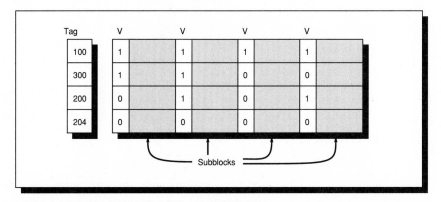

FIGURE 8.37 In this example there are four subblocks per block. In the first block (top) all the valid bits are on, equivalent to the valid bit being on for a block in a normal cache. In the last block (bottom), the opposite is true; no valid bits are on. In the second block, locations 300 and 301 are valid and will be hits, while locations 302 and 303 will be misses. For the third block, locations 201 and 203 are hits. If, instead of this organization, there were 16 blocks the size of the subblock, 16 tags would be needed instead of 4.

Subblock placement was invented to reduce the long miss penalty of large blocks (since only a part of a large block need be read) and to reduce the tag storage for small caches. It can also help write hits by **always** writing the word (no matter what happens with the tag match), turning the valid bit on, and then sending the word to memory. Let's look at the cases to see why this trick works:

- *Tag match and valid bit already set.* Writing the block was the proper action, and nothing was lost by setting the valid bit on again.

- *Tag match and valid bit not set.* The tag match means that this is the proper block; writing the data into the block makes it appropriate to turn the valid bit on.

- *Tag mismatch.* This is a miss and will modify the data portion of the block. However, as this is a write-through cache, no harm was done; memory still has an up-to-date copy of the old value. Only the tag to the address of the write need be changed because the valid bit has already been set. If the block size is one word and the store instruction is writing one word, then the write is complete. When the block is larger than a word or if the instruction is a byte or halfword store, then either the rest of the valid bits are turned off (allocating the subblock without fetching the rest of the block) or memory is requested to send the missing part of the block (write allocate).

This trick isn't possible with a write-back cache because the only valid copy of the data may be in the block, and it could be overwritten before checking the tag.

Reducing Miss Penalty—Making Write Misses Faster

Now that we have seen how to make write hits faster, let's look at write misses. With a write-through cache the most important improvement is a write buffer (page 416) of the proper size (see the fallacy on page 482 in Section 8.10). Write buffers, however, do complicate things in that they might have the updated value of a location needed on a read miss.

Example

Look at this code sequence:

```
SW   512(R0),R3   ; M[512] ← R3  (cache index 0)
LW   R1,1024(R0)  ; R1 ← M[1024]  (cache index 0)
LW   R2,512(R0)   ; R2 ← M[512]  (cache index 0)
```

Assume a direct-mapped cache that maps 512 and 1024 to the same block, and a four-word write buffer. Will R3 always equal R2?

Answer

Let's follow the cache to see the danger. The data in R3 is placed into the write buffer after the store. The following load uses the same cache index and is therefore a miss. We then try to load the data from location 512 into register R2; this also results in a miss. If the write buffer hasn't completed writing to location 512 in memory, the read of location 512 will put the old, wrong value into the cache block, and then into R2. Without proper precautions, R3 would not be equal to R2!

The simplest way out of this dilemma is for the read miss to wait until the write buffer is empty. However, a write buffer of a few words in a write-through cache will almost always have data in the buffer on a miss, thereby increasing the read miss penalty. The designers of the MIPS M/1000 estimated that waiting for a four-word buffer to empty would have increased the average read miss penalty by 50%. The alternative is to check the contents of the write buffer on a read miss, and if there are no conflicts and the memory system is available, let the read miss continue.

The cost of writes in a write-back cache can also be reduced. By just adding a full block buffer to store a dirty block, the read can happen first. After the new data is loaded into the block, the CPU continues execution. The buffer then writes in parallel with the CPU. Similar to the situation above, if a read miss occurs the CPU can stall until the buffer is empty.

Reducing Miss Penalty—Making Read Misses Faster

Making writes faster is helpful, but it is reads that dominate cache accesses. The strategy to making read misses faster is to be impatient: Don't wait for the full block to be loaded before sending the requested word to the CPU. Here are two specific strategies:

- *Early restart*—As soon as the requested word of the block arrives, send it to the CPU and let the CPU continue execution.

- *Out-of-order fetch*—Request the missed word first from memory and send it to the CPU as soon as it arrives; let the CPU continue execution while filling the rest of the words in the block. Out-of-order fetch is also called *wrapped* fetch.

Alas, these read tricks are not as important as they sound. Spatial locality—the reason for big blocks in the first place—dictates that the next cache request is likely to be to the same block. Also, handling another request while trying to fill the rest of a block quickly gets complicated.

A more subtle reason why out-of-order fetch will not be as rewarding as one might think is that not all the words of a block have an equal likelihood of being accessed first. With a 16-word block in an instruction cache, for example, the average block entry point is 2.8 words from the left-most byte. If entries were evenly distributed, the average would be 8 words. The high-order word is the most likely one, due to sequential accesses from prior blocks on instruction fetches and sequentially stepping through arrays for data caches.

For pipelined machines that allow out-of-order completion using a scoreboard or Tomasulo-style control (Section 6.7 of Chapter 6), the CPU need not stall on a cache miss, offering another way to reduce memory stalls. Spatial locality suggests this optimization (called a *lock-up free cache*) may be limited in practice, since again the next reference is likely to be to the same block.

Making Cache Hits Faster—Virtually Addressed Caches

Miss penalty is an important part of average access time, but hit time affects both the average access time and the clock rate of the CPU. Helping the hit time may therefore help everything. A solution mentioned earlier is to use the physical part of the address to index the cache while sending the virtual address through the TLB. The limitation is that a direct-mapped cache can be no bigger than the page size. To allow large cache sizes with the 4-KB pages in the System/370, IBM uses high associativity so that they can still access the cache with a physical index. The IBM 3033, for example, is 16-way set associative, even though studies show there is little benefit to miss rates above 4-way set associativity.

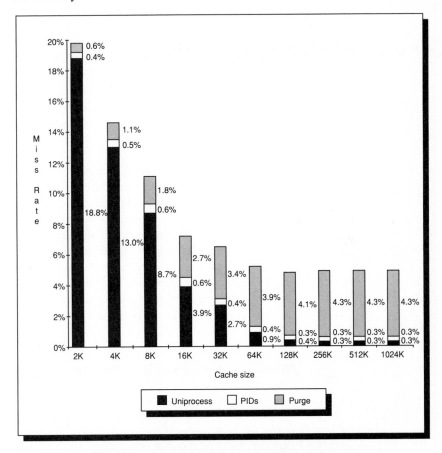

FIGURE 8.38 Miss rate versus cache size of a program measured three ways: without process switches (uniprocess), with process switches using a process-identifier tag (PIDs), and with process switches but without PIDs (purge). PIDs increase the uniprocess absolute miss rate by 0.3 to 0.6 and save 0.6 to 4.3 over purging. Agarwal [1987] collected these statistics for the Ultrix operating system running on a VAX, assuming direct-mapped caches with a block size of 16 bytes.

One scheme for fast cache hits without this size restriction is go to a more heavily pipelined memory access where the TLB is just one step of the pipeline. The TLB is a distinct unit that is smaller than the cache, and thus easily pipelined. This scheme doesn't change memory latency, but relies on the efficiency of the CPU pipeline to achieve higher memory bandwidth.

Another alternative is to match on virtual addresses directly. Such caches are termed *virtual caches*. This eliminates the TLB translation time from a cache hit. Why doesn't everyone build virtually addressed caches? One reason is that every time a process is switched, the virtual addresses refer to different physical addresses, requiring the cache to be flushed. Figure 8.38 (page 459) shows the impact on miss rates of this flushing. One solution is to increase the width of the cache-address tag with a *process-identifier tag* (PID). If the operating system assigns these tags to processes, it only need flush the cache when a PID is recycled (the PID provides protection). Figure 8.38 shows that improvement.

Another reason why virtual caches are not more universally adopted has to do with operating systems and user programs that use two different virtual addresses for the same physical address. These duplicate addresses, called *synonyms* or *aliases*, could result in two copies of the same data in a virtual cache; if one is modified, the other will have the wrong value. With a physical cache this wouldn't happen, since the accesses would first be translated to the same physical cache block. There are hardware schemes, called *anti-aliasing*, that can guarantee every cache block a unique physical address, but software can make this much easier by forcing aliases to share some address bits. The version of UNIX from Sun Microsystems, for example, requires all aliases to be identical in the last 18 bits of their addresses. Thus, a direct-mapped cache that is 2^{18} (256K) bytes or smaller can never have duplicate physical addresses for blocks. This requirement also simplifies anti-aliasing hardware for larger caches or for set-associative caches. (Of course, the best software solution from the hardware designers perspective is to do away with aliases!)

The final area of concern with virtual addresses is I/O. I/O typically uses physical addresses and thus would require mapping to virtual addresses to interact with a virtual cache. (The impact of I/O on caches is further discussed below.)

Reducing Miss Penalty—Two-Level Caches

Let's return our attention to miss penalty. CPUs are getting faster and main memories are getting larger, but slower relative to the faster CPUs. The question facing the architect is: Should I make the cache faster to keep pace with the speed of CPUs, or make the cache larger to overcome the widening gap between the CPU and main memory? One answer is: Both. By adding another level of cache between the original cache and memory, the first-level cache can be small enough to match the clock cycle time of the CPU while the second-level cache can be large enough to capture many accesses that would go to main memory.

Definitions for a second level of cache are not always straightforward. Let's start with the definition of *average memory-access time* for a two-level cache. Using the subscripts L1 and L2 to refer respectively to a first-level and a second-level cache, the original formula is

$$\text{Average memory-access time} = \text{Hit time}_{L1} + \text{Miss rate}_{L1} * \text{Miss penalty}_{L1}$$

and

$$\text{Miss penalty}_{L1} = \text{Hit time}_{L2} + \text{Miss rate}_{L2} * \text{Miss penalty}_{L2}$$

so

$$\text{Average memory-access time} = \text{Hit time}_{L1} + \text{Miss rate}_{L1} *$$
$$(\text{Hit time}_{L2} + \text{Miss rate}_{L2} * \text{Miss penalty}_{L2})$$

In this formula, the success of the second-level miss rate is measured on the left-overs from the first-level cache. To avoid ambiguity, these terms are adopted here for a two-level cache system:

- *Local miss rate*—The number of misses in the cache divided by the total number of memory accesses to this cache; this is miss rate$_{L2}$ above.

- *Global miss rate*—The number of misses in the cache divided by the total number of memory accesses generated by the CPU; using the terms above, this is miss rate$_{L1}$ * miss rate$_{L2}$.

Example

Suppose that in 1000 memory references there are 40 misses in the first-level cache and 20 misses in the second-level cache. What are the various miss rates?

Answer

The miss rate for the first-level cache is 40/1000 or 4%. The local miss rate for the second-level cache is 20/40 or 50%. The global miss rate of the second-level cache is 20/1000 or 2%.

Figure 8.39 (page 462) and Figure 8.40 (page 463) show how miss rates and relative execution time change with the size of a second-level cache. Figure 8.41 (page 463) shows typical parameters of second-level caches.

With these definitions in place, we can consider the parameters of second-level caches. The foremost difference between the two levels is that the speed of the first-level cache affects the clock rate of the CPU, while the speed of the second-level cache only affects the miss penalty of the first-level cache. Thus, we can consider many alternatives in the second-level cache that would be ill chosen for the first-level cache. There is but one consideration for the design of the second-level cache: Will it lower the average memory-access–time portion of the CPI?

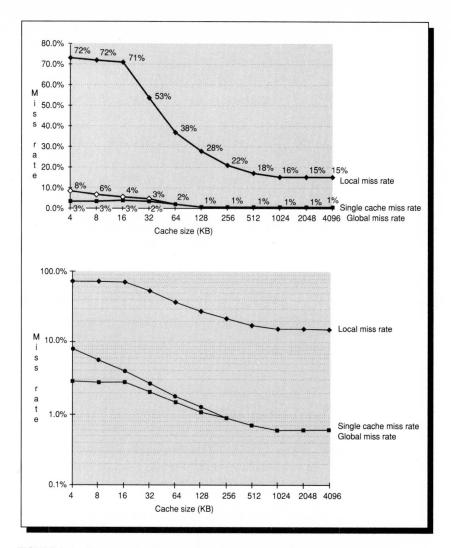

FIGURE 8.39 Miss rates versus cache size. The top graph shows the results plotted on a linear scale as we have done with earlier figures, while the bottom graph shows the results plotted on a log scale. As miss rates shrink the log scale makes the differences easier to follow. The miss rate of a single-level cache versus size is plotted against the local miss rate and global miss rate of a second-level cache using a 32-KB first-level cache. Second-level caches **smaller** than the 32-KB first level have high miss rates (at least for similar block sizes), as this figure illustrates. After 256 KB the single cache and global miss rates are virtually identical. Przybylski [1990] collected these data using traces available with this book: four traces from the VAX system and user programs and four user programs from the MIPS R2000 that were randomly interleaved to duplicate the effect of process switches.

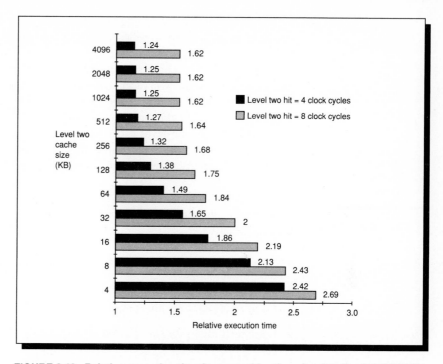

FIGURE 8.40 Relative execution time by second-level–cache size. Przybylski [1990] collected these data using a 32-KB, first-level, write-back cache, varying the size of the second-level cache. The two bars are for different clock cycles for a level two cache hit. The reference execution time of 1.00 is for a 4096-KB, second-level cache with a one–clock-cycle latency on a second-level hit. He used four traces from the VAX system and user programs (available with this book) and four user programs from the MIPS R2000 that were randomly interleaved to duplicate the effect of process switches.

Block (line) size	32 – 256 bytes
Hit time	4 – 10 clock cycles
Miss penalty	30 – 80 clock cycles
(Access time)	(14 – 18 clock cycles)
(Transfer time)	(16 – 64 clock cycles)
Local miss rate	15% – 30%
Cache size	256 KB – 4 MB

FIGURE 8.41 Typical values of key memory-hierarchy parameters for second-level caches.

The initial choice for second-level caches is size. Since everything in the first-level cache is likely to be in the second-level cache, the second-level cache should be bigger. If second-level caches are just a little bigger, the local miss rate will be high. This observation inspires design of huge second-level caches— the size of main memory in recent computers! If the second-level cache is much larger than the first-level cache, then the global miss rate is about the same as a single-level cache of the same size (see Figure 8.39, page 462). Large size means that the second-level cache may have practically no capacity misses, leaving compulsory and a few conflict misses for our attention. One question is whether set associativity makes more sense for second-level caches.

Example

Given the data below, what is the impact of second-level–cache associativity on the miss penalty?

- Two-way set associativity increases hit time by 10% of a CPU clock cycle
- Hit time$_{L2}$ for direct mapped = 4 clock cycles
- Local miss rate$_{L2}$ for direct mapped = 25%
- Local miss rate$_{L2}$ for two-way set associative = 20%
- Miss penalty$_{L2}$ = 30 clock cycles

Answer

For a direct-mapped, second-level cache, the first-level–cache miss penalty is

$$\text{Miss penalty}_{L1} = 4 + 25\% * 30 = 11.5 \text{ clock cycles}$$

Adding the cost of associativity increases the hit cost only 0.1 clock cycles, making the new first-level–cache miss penalty

$$\text{Miss penalty}_{L1} = 4.1 + 20\% * 30 = 10.1 \text{ clock cycles}$$

In reality, second-level caches are almost always synchronized with the first-level cache and CPU. Accordingly, the second-level hit time must be an integral number of clock cycles. If we are lucky, we can shave the second-level hit time to four cycles; if not, we can round up to five cycles. Either choice is an improvement over the direct-mapped, second-level cache:

$$\text{Miss penalty}_{L1} = 4 + 20\% * 30 = 10.0 \text{ clock cycles}$$
$$\text{Miss penalty}_{L1} = 5 + 20\% * 30 = 11.0 \text{ clock cycles}$$

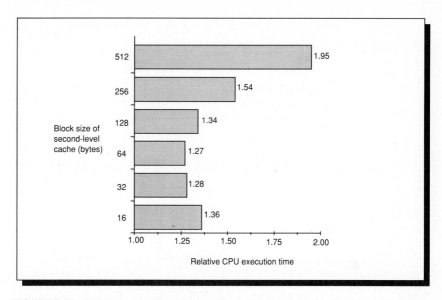

FIGURE 8.42   Relative execution time by block size for a two-level cache. Przybylski [1990] collected these data using a 512-KB second-level cache. He used four traces from the VAX system and user programs (available with this book) and four user programs from the MIPS R2000 that were randomly interleaved to duplicate the effect of process switches.

Higher associativity is worth considering because it has small impact on the second-level hit time and because so much of the average access time is due to misses. However, for these very large caches the benefits of associativity diminish because larger size has eliminated many conflict misses.

As long as spatial locality holds there may be a benefit in increasing block size. Increasing block size can increase conflict misses with small caches since there may not be enough places to put data, therefore increasing miss rate. Because this is not an issue in large, second-level caches, and because memory-access time is relatively longer, larger block sizes are popular. Figure 8.42 shows the variation in execution time as the second-level block size changes.

One final consideration concerns whether all data in the first-level cache is always in the second-level cache. If so, the second-level cache is said to have the *multilevel inclusion property*. Inclusion is desirable because consistency between I/O and caches (or between caches in a multiprocessor) can be determined just by checking the second-level cache.

The drawback to this natural inclusion is that the lower average memory-access times can suggest smaller blocks for the smaller first-level cache and larger blocks for the larger second-level cache. Inclusion can still be maintained in this case with a little extra work on a second-level miss: The second-level cache must invalidate all first-level blocks that map onto the second-level block to be replaced, causing a slightly higher first-level miss rate.

Reducing Miss Rate by Reducing Cache Flushes—I/O

Although there is little more that can improve CPU execution time, there are issues in cache design to improve system performance, particularly for input/output. Because of caches, data can be found in memory or in the cache. As long as the CPU is the sole device changing or reading the data and the cache stands between the CPU and memory, there is little danger in the CPU seeing the old or *stale* copy. I/O means the opportunity exists for other devices to cause copies to be inconsistent or for other devices to read the stale copies. Figure 8.43 illustrates the problem. This is generally referred to as the *cache-coherency* problem.

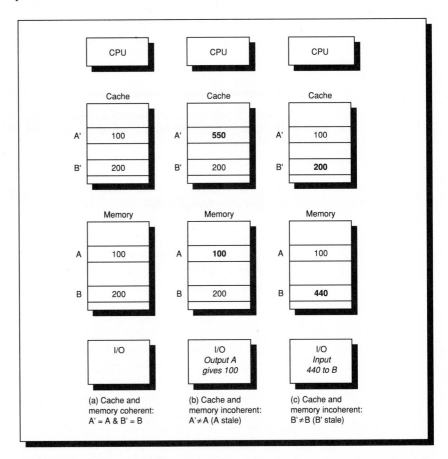

FIGURE 8.43   The cache-coherency problem. A' and B' refer to the cached copies of A and B in memory. (a) shows cache and main memory in a coherent state. In (b) we assume a write-back cache when the CPU writes 550 into A. Now A' has the value but the value in memory has the old, stale value of 100. If an output used the value of A from memory, it would get the stale data. In (c) the I/O system inputs 440 into the memory copy of B, so now B' in the cache has the old, stale data.

The question is this: Where does the I/O occur in the computer—between the I/O device and the cache or between the I/O device and main memory? If input puts data into the cache and output reads data from the cache, both I/O and the CPU see the same data, and the problem is solved. The difficulty in this approach is that it interferes with the CPU. I/O competing with the CPU for cache access will cause the CPU to stall for I/O. Input will also interfere with the cache by displacing some information with the new data that is unlikely to be accessed by the CPU soon. For example, on a page fault the CPU may need to access a few words in a page, but a program is not likely to access every word of the page if it were loaded into the cache.

The goal for the I/O system in a computer with a cache is to prevent the stale-data problem while interfering with the CPU as little as possible. Many systems, therefore, prefer that I/O occur directly to main memory, acting as an I/O buffer. If a write-through cache is used, then memory has an up-to-date copy of the information, and there is no stale-data issue for output. (This is the reason many machines use write through.) Input requires some extra work. The software solution is to guarantee that no blocks of the I/O buffer designated for input are in the cache. In one approach, a buffer page is marked as noncacheable; the operating system always inputs to such a page. In another approach, the operating system flushes the buffer addresses from the cache after the input occurs. A hardware solution is to check the I/O addresses on input to see if they are in the cache. If so, the cache entries are invalidated to avoid stale data. All these approaches can also be used for output with write-back caches. More about this is found in the next chapter.

Reducing Bus Traffic—Multiprocessor Cache Coherency

The cache-coherency problem applies to multiprocessors as well as I/O. Unlike I/O, where multiple data copies is a rare event—one to be avoided whenever possible—a program running on multiple processors will want to have copies of the same data in several caches. Performance of a multiprocessor program depends on the performance of the system when sharing data. The protocols to maintain coherency for multiple processors are called *cache-coherency protocols*. There are two classes of protocols followed to maintain cache coherency:

- *Directory based*—The information about one block of physical memory is kept in just one location.

- *Snooping*—Every cache that has a copy of the data from a block of physical memory also has a copy of the information about it. These caches are usually on a shared-memory bus, and all cache controllers monitor or *snoop* on the bus to determine whether or not they have a copy of the shared block.

In directory-based protocols there is logically a single directory that keeps the state of every block in main memory. Information in the directory can include which caches have copies of the block, whether it is dirty, and so on. Of course directory entries can be distributed so that different requests can go to different memories, thereby reducing contention. However, they retain the characteristic that the sharing status of a block is always in a single known location.

Snooping protocols became popular with multiprocessors using microprocessors and caches on a shared memory because they can use a preexisting physical connection: the bus to memory. Snooping has an edge over directory protocols in that the coherency information is proportional to the number of blocks in a cache rather than the number of blocks in main memory. Directories, on the other hand, do not require a single bus going to all caches and, hence, may scale to more processors.

The coherency problem is for a processor to have exclusive access to write an object and to have the most recent copy when reading an object. Thus, both directory-based and snooping protocols must locate all the caches that share the object to be written. The consequence of a write to shared data is either to invalidate all other copies or to broadcast the write to the shared copies. Because of write-back caches, coherency protocols must also help read misses determine who has the most up-to-date value.

For the remainder of this section we concentrate on snooping caches; the same ideas apply to directory-based caches except the state of the caches is tracked differently, and caches are involved only if the directory says they have a copy of a block whose status must change.

Sharing information is added to the status bits already in a cache block for snooping protocols, and that information is used in monitoring bus activities. On a read miss all caches check to see if they have a copy of the requested block and take the appropriate action, such as supplying the data to the cache that missed. Similarly, on a write all caches check to see if they have a copy and then act, perhaps invalidating their copy or changing their copy to the new value.

Since every bus transaction checks cache-address tags, one might assume that it interferes with the CPU. It would, were it not for duplicating the address-tag portion of the cache (not the whole cache) to get an extra read port for snooping. This way, snooping interferes with the CPU's access to the cache only when there is a coherency problem (although on a miss with snooping the CPU must arbitrate with the bus to change the snoop tags as well as the normal tags). When a coherency operation occurs in the cache the CPU will likely stall, since the cache is unavailable. In multilevel caches, if the coherency check can be limited to the lower cache because of multilevel inclusion, duplicating the address tags will probably not be necessary.

Snooping protocols are of two types, depending on what happens on a write:

■ *Write invalidate*—The writing processor causes all copies in other caches to be invalidated before changing its local copy; it is then free to update the data until another processor asks for it. The writing processor issues an invalidation signal over the bus, and all caches check to see if they have a copy; if so, they must invalidate the block containing the word. Thus, this scheme allows multiple readers but only a single writer.

- *Write broadcast*—Rather than invalidate every block that is shared, the writing processor broadcasts the new data over the bus; all copies are then updated with the new value. This scheme continuously broadcasts writes to shared data while write invalidate deletes all other copies so that there is only one local copy for subsequent writes. Write-broadcast protocols usually allow blocks to be tagged as shared (broadcast) or private (local). One way to think of this protocol is it acts like a write-through cache for shared data (broadcasting to other caches) and a write-back cache for private data (the modified data leaves the cache only on a miss).

Most cache-based multiprocessors use write back caches because it reduces bus traffic and thereby allows more processors on a single bus. Write-back caches use either invalidation or broadcast, and numerous variations exist for both alternatives (see the next section). So far, there is no consensus on which is the superior scheme. Some programs have less coherency overhead with write invalidate, and some with write broadcast. A later section shows how synchronization can be implemented in coherency-based multiprocessors; the accesses for synchronization seem to favor write broadcast.

One early insight has been that block size plays an important role in cache coherency. Take, for example, the case of snooping on a second-level cache with a block size of eight words, and a single word is alternatively written and read by two processors. Whether write invalidation or write broadcast is used, the protocol that only broadcasts or sends a word has an advantage over a scheme that transfers the full block. Another concern of large blocks is called *false sharing*: two different shared variables are located in the same cache block, causing the block to be exchanged between processors even though the processors are accessing different variables. Compiler research is working to reduce cache miss rates by allocating data with high processor locality to the same blocks. Success in this field could increase the desirability of large blocks for multiprocessors.

Measurements to date indicate that shared data has lower spatial and temporal locality than observed for other types of data, independent of the coherency policy.

An Example Protocol

To illustrate the complexities of a cache-coherency protocol, Figure 8.44 (page 470) shows a finite-state transition diagram for a write-invalidation protocol based on write- back policy. The three states of the protocol are duplicated to represent transitions based on CPU actions, as opposed to transitions based on bus operations. This is done only for purposes of this figure; there is only one finite-state machine per cache, with stimuli coming either from the attached CPU or from the bus.

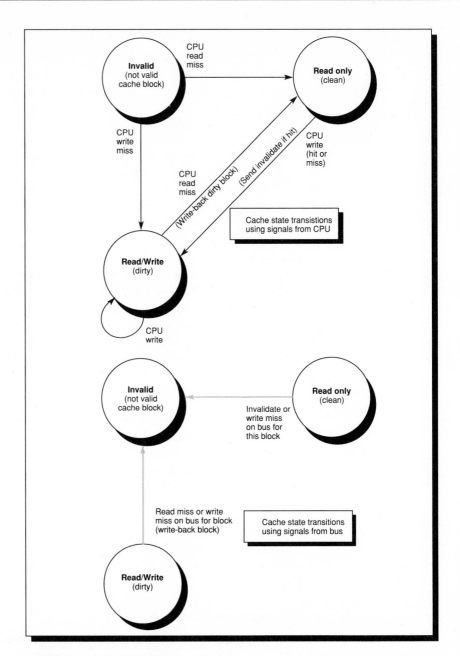

FIGURE 8.44 A write-invalidate, cache-coherency protocol. The upper part of the diagram shows state transitions based on actions of the CPU associated with this cache; the lower part shows transitions based on operations on the bus. There is only one state machine in a cache, although there are two represented here to clarify when a transition occurs. The black arrows and states would be in a normal cache, with the gray arrows added to get cache coherency. In contrast to what is shown here, some protocols call writes to clean data a "write miss," so that there is no separate signal for invalidation.

Transitions happen on read misses, write misses, or write hits; read hits do not change cache state. When the CPU has a read miss, it will change the state of that block to Read only and write back the old block if it was in the Read/Write state (dirty). All the caches snoop on the read miss to see if this block is in their cache. If one has a copy and it is in the Read/Write state, then the block is written to memory and that block is changed to the invalid state. (An optimization not shown in the figure would be to change the state of that block to Read only.) When a CPU writes into a block, that block goes to the Read/Write state. If the write was a hit, an invalidate signal goes out over the bus. Because caches monitor the bus, all check to see if they have a copy of that block; if they do, they invalidate it. If the write was a miss, all caches with copies go to the invalid state.

As you might imagine, there are many variations on cache coherency that are much more complicated than this simple model. The variations include whether or not the other caches try to supply the block if they have a copy, whether or not the block must be invalidated on a read miss, as well as write invalidate versus write broadcast as discussed above. Figure 8.45 summarizes several snooping cache-coherency protocols.

Name	Category	Memory-write policy	Unique feature
Write Once	Write invalidate	Write back after first write	
Synapse N+1	Write invalidate	Write back	Explicit memory ownership
Berkeley	Write invalidate	Write back	Owned shared state
Illinois	Write invalidate	Write back	Clean private state; can supply data from any cache with a clean copy
Firefly	Write broadcast	Write back for private, Write through for shared	Memory updated on broadcast
Dragon	Write broadcast	Write back for private, Write through for shared	Memory not updated on broadcast

FIGURE 8.45 Six snooping protocols summarized. Archibald and Baer [1986] use these names to describe the six protocols, and Eggers [1989] summarizes the similarities and differences as shown above. Figure 8.44 (page 470) is simpler than any of these protocols.

Synchronization Using Coherency

One of the major requirements of a shared-memory multiprocessor is being able to coordinate processes that are working on a common task. Typically, a programmer will use *lock variables* to synchronize the processes.

The difficulty for the architect of a multiprocessor is to provide a mechanism to decide which processor gets the lock and to provide the operation that locks a variable. Arbitration is easy for shared-bus multiprocessors, since the bus is the only path to memory: The processor that gets the bus locks out all other processors from memory. If the CPU and bus provide an atomic swap operation, programmers can create locks with the proper semantics. The adjective *atomic* is key, for it means that a processor can both read a location **and** set it to the locked value in the same bus operation, preventing any other processor from reading or writing memory.

Figure 8.46 shows a typical procedure for locking a variable using an atomic swap instruction. Assume that 0 means unlocked and 1 means locked. A processor first reads the lock variable to test its state. A processor keeps reading and testing until the value indicates that the lock is unlocked. The processor then races against all other processes that were similarly "spin waiting" to see who

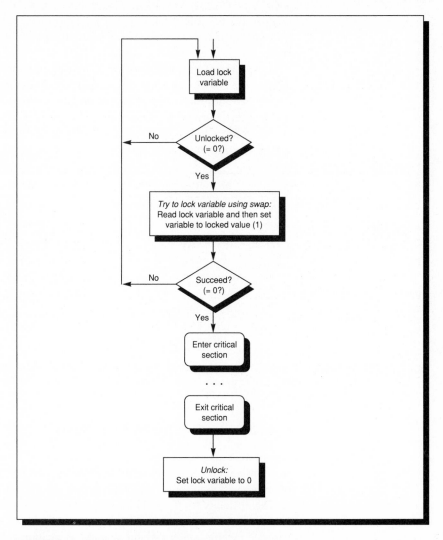

FIGURE 8.46 Steps to acquire a lock to synchronize processes and then to release the lock on exit from the key section of code.

Step	Processor P0	Processor P1	Processor P2	Bus activity
1	Has lock	Spins, testing if lock = 0	Spins, testing if lock = 0	None
2	Set lock to 0 and 0 sent over bus			Write invalidate of lock variable from P0
3		Cache miss	Cache miss	Bus decides to service P2 cache miss
4		(Waits while bus busy)	Lock = 0	Cache miss for P2 satisfied
5		Lock = 0	Swap: read lock and set to 1	Cache miss for P1 satisfied
6		Swap: read lock and set to 1	Value from swap = 0 and 1 sent over bus	Write invalidate of lock variable from P2
7		Value from swap = 1 and 1 sent over bus	Enter critical section	Write invalidate of lock variable from P1
8		Spins, testing if lock = 0		None

FIGURE 8.47   Cache-coherency steps and bus traffic for three processors, P0, P1, and P2. This figure assumes write-invalidate coherency. P0 starts with the lock (step 1). P0 exits and unlocks the lock (step 2). P1 and P2 race to see which reads the unlocked value during the swap (steps 3-5). P2 wins and enters the critical section (steps 6 and 7), while P1 spins and waits (steps 7 and 8).

can lock the variable first. All processes use a swap instruction that reads the old value and stores a 1 into the lock variable. The single winner will see the 0, and the losers will see a 1 that was placed there by the winner. (The losers will continue to set the variable to the locked value, but that doesn't matter.) The winning processor executes the code after the lock and then stores a 0 into the lock variable when it exits, starting the race all over again. Testing the old value and then setting to a new value is why the atomic swap instruction is called *test and set* in some instruction sets.

Let's examine how the "spin lock" scheme of Figure 8.46 works with bus-based cache coherency. One advantage of this algorithm is that it allows processors to spin wait on a local copy of the lock in their caches. This reduces the amount of bus traffic versus lock algorithms that loop trying to perform a test and set. (Figure 8.47 shows the bus and cache operations for multiple processes trying to lock a variable.) Once the processor with the lock stores a 0 into the lock, all other caches see that store and invalidate their copy of the lock variable. They then get the new value for the lock of 0. (With write-broadcast cache coherency as on page 469, the caches would update their copy rather than first invalidate and then load from memory.) This new value starts the race to see who can set the lock first. The winner gets the bus and stores a 1 into the lock; the other caches replace their copy of the lock variable containing 0 with a 1. They read that the variable is already locked and must return to testing and spinning. This scheme has difficulty scaling up to many processors because of the communication traffic generated when the lock is released.

Models of Memory Consistency

When we introduce cache coherency to maintain the consistency of multiple copies of an object, we raise a new question: How consistent must the values seen by two processors be kept? The problem is best understood with an example: Here are two code segments from processes P1 and P2 shown side by side:

```
P1:     A = 0;              P2:     B = 0;
        .....                       .....
        A = 1;                      B = 1;
L1:     if (B == 0) ...   L2:     if (A == 0) ...
```

Assume the processes are running on different processors, and that locations A and B are originally cached by both processors with the initial value of 0. If memory is always consistent, it will be impossible for **both** if statements (labeled L1 and L2) to evaluate their conditions as true (either A=1 or B=1). But suppose write invalidates have a delay, and the processor is allowed to continue during this delay, then it is possible that both P1 and P2 have not seen the invalidations for B and A (respectively) **before** they attempt to read the values. The question that is raised by this example is: How consistent a picture of memory must different processors see?

One approach, called sequential consistency, requires that the result of any execution is the same as if the accesses of each processor were kept in order and the accesses among different processors were arbitrarily interleaved. In this case, the apparent anomaly in the above example cannot occur. Implementing sequential consistency usually requires a processor to delay any memory access until all the invalidations caused by all previous writes are completed. Although this model presents a simple programming paradigm, it reduces potential performance, especially in a machine with a large number of processors, or long interconnect delays.

Alternative models provide a weaker model of memory consistency. For example, the programmer may be required to use synchronization instructions to order memory accesses to the same variable. Now, instead of delaying all accesses until invalidations complete, only synchronization accesses need to be delayed.

Whether programmers expect sequential consistency or some weaker form of consistency is still an open issue in 1990. The example above would work "correctly" with sequential consistency, but not with a weaker model. For weak consistency to produce the same results as sequential consistency, the program would have to be modified to include synchronization operations that order the accesses to variables A and B. It is natural to expect synchronization if you want processes to see the latest data independent of execution rates. Some machines choose to implement sequential consistency as the programming model, while others opt for a weaker consistency. In the future, as attempts are made to build larger multiprocessors, the issue of memory consistency will become increasingly performance critical.

8.9 | Putting It All Together: The VAX-11/780 Memory Hierarchy

The challenge for the memory-hierarchy designer is in choosing parameters that work well together, not in inventing new techniques or simulating a cache in a well-understood configuration. A full example using the VAX-11/780 memory hierarchy is presented here in detail to illuminate the interactions. Although VAX-11/780 is not a very recent machine, measurements and design documentation are available on all aspects of its memory hierarchy. Figure 8.48 gives the overall picture.

Let's start with an instruction fetch just after a branch, when the instruction prefetch buffer is empty. The virtual address in the PC is first sent to the TLB. The most significant bit and the lower five bits of the page-frame address index an entry in each bank of the TLB. Including the most-significant bit, used to distinguish system space from process space, guarantees that half of each bank contains system translations and half contains process translations. The addresses in the tags are compared to see if the entry is a match to the page address requested by the TLB. If the valid bit of the entry is not set then there is no match no matter what the tag comparison says, and a miss is indicated.

If there is a match, the physical address is formed by concatenating the physical page-frame address of the TLB page-table entry with the page-offset portion of the address. To save time, the portion of the TLB containing the PTE is read at the same time as the tags, and a 2:1 multiplexer controlled by the tag-matching logic picks the proper PTE. While the address is being formed, the protection bits of the PTE are checked. Since this is an instruction fetch, there is no problem as long as the page can be read by a process at this level. If there are no protection violations, this physical address is sent to the cache.

At the same time the physical address is sent to the cache, two registers in the CPU instruction-prefetch buffer get the new values. The *virtual-instruction-buffer address* register (VIBA) is given the virtual page frame of the PC, and the *physical-instruction-buffer address* register (PIBA) is given the corresponding physical address. This trick, which was originally used in the first machine with virtual memory, avoids the instruction-prefetch buffer's accessing the TLB as long as the instructions are from the same page. The PIBA is actually given the PC address plus 4, so that it can begin prefetching the next instruction. It continues trying to prefetch ahead of the PC until a jump (a frequent occurrence in the VAX) or until the PIBA tries to cross a page boundary; in either case the VIBA and PIBA are no longer used for translating instruction addresses.

Meanwhile, the cache has just received the physical address of the instruction. With 8-byte blocks, a two-way–set-associative cache, and 512 blocks per set, nine bits of the address are needed to index both banks simultaneously. The partial addresses in the tags are compared with the corresponding bits of the physical PC address to see if there is a match. Of course, there are valid bits in each tag that must be turned on, or there can be no match.

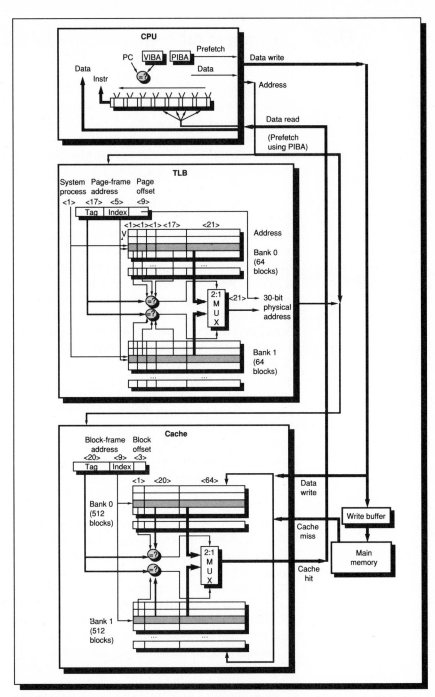

FIGURE 8.48 The overall picture of the VAX-11/780 memory hierarchy. Individual components can be seen in greater detail in Figures 8.11 (page 415), 8.29 (page 444), and 8.31 (page 450).

If there is a match, the lower bits of the physical PC address select the word from the cache block to be sent to the instruction-prefetch unit. Once again, reading data and tags together obviates any additional time delay.

When the word arrives at the prefetch unit, it is placed in the high-order four bytes of the buffer, and those bytes are marked valid. The PIBA immediately begins accessing the cache with the PC address plus 4 to prefetch the next word. As mentioned above, as long as the page-frame address in the PC matches the VIBA, the PIBA bypasses the TLB and goes directly to the cache.

Let's assume this instruction writes a register into memory. The first step will be to send the effective memory address to the TLB for translation. Since this is a write, the modify bit of the matching PTE must also be turned on; this results in a microcode-level trap of the instruction storing the register if the modify bit isn't set already, taking another clock cycle to write the new value in the TLB. The physical address is then sent to the cache. We then go through the same process as before (excluding the read), except that this time it takes an extra clock cycle to modify the portion of the block selected by the write and to write it back into the cache.

In a write-through cache the data must be written to main memory. To avoid the seven-cycle delay of main memory on every write, the VAX-11/780 uses a one-word write buffer. If the buffer is empty, the word is written and the CPU is given the signal to continue. If it is full, the CPU stalls until the buffer is empty.

How well does the 780 work? The bottom line in this evaluation is the percentage of time lost while the CPU is waiting for the memory hierarchy. In one timesharing workload the average number of clock cycles per 780 instruction is 10.6 clock cycles. The breakdown by category is

Compute: 7.3 clock cycles

Read: 0.8 clock cycles

Read stall: 1.0 clock cycles

Write: 0.4 clock cycles

Write stall: 0.4 clock cycles

Instruction-prefetch–buffer stall: 0.7 clock cycles

About 20% of the time the VAX-11/780 stalls while waiting for memory. When the base CPI is 8.5 (compute + read + write), 2.1 clock cycles for the memory hierarchy (read stall + write stall + prefetch stall) may be satisfactory, but it would devastate the performance of a machine with a CPI of 1 to 2.

Let's analyze each unit of the 780 memory hierarchy. An instruction-prefetch–buffer stall means that the buffer is empty, waiting for the cache to supply instructions because of a cache miss, a branch, too many data accesses (they have priority), not enough bytes to decode the instruction, or some combination of the above. The PIBA loadings due to branches versus page crossings vary with the benchmark, but branching is the cause 64% to 91% of the time (median = 76%). The prefetch unit references the cache 2.2 times on average per VAX instruction. The average instruction size is 3.8 bytes, making the effective size of the average prefetch just 1.7 bytes.

Example   Figure 3.33 in Chapter 3 (page 123) shows that the VAX executes many fewer bytes of instructions than DLX. This ignores the instruction-prefetch buffer. How much should we increase the instruction bytes fetched from the cache to include the effect of prefetching?

Answer   We can answer this in a couple of ways. Every prefetch access to the cache actually returns 4 bytes, and the average VAX instruction size is 3.8 bytes; the increase could therefore be

$$\frac{2.2 * 4}{3.8} = 2.32$$

since the prefetch unit references the cache 2.2 times per instruction. This suggests that the bytes fetched from the cache should be increased by 132%. Because the same code may be fetched multiple times by the prefetcher, however, the bandwidth between the cache and memory may not change since the prefetcher cannot cause cache misses.

The question can also be answered in terms of the number of bytes discarded because of a taken branch. About 25% of instructions change the PC on the VAX, and there could be from zero to eight bytes in the prefetch unit when a branch is taken. Assuming an optimistic two bytes, we get a 13% increase:

$$\frac{3.8 + (25\% * 2)}{3.8} = 1.13$$

Assuming six bytes, we get a 39% increase:

$$\frac{3.8 + (25\% * 6)}{3.8} = 1.39$$

While the variable size of VAX instructions does improve the bytes fetched in comparison to DLX, a fairer evaluation of the VAX would increase the bytes fetched from the cache by at least 13% to 39%.

With the instruction-prefetch buffer performing many translations via the PIBA and VIBA, how should TLB misses be measured? The TLB instruction and data-stream miss rates provide one definition:

$$\text{TLB instruction-stream miss rate} = \frac{\text{Misses caused by IB}}{\text{Reloadings of PIBA}}$$

$$\text{TLB data-stream miss rate} = \frac{\text{Misses}}{\text{Requests for 32-bit words of data}}$$

The data-stream definition means references to data objects larger than four bytes count as multiple accesses, as do accesses to unaligned data. Figure 8.49 shows the TLB miss rates.

TLB miss rates	Instruction stream	Data stream	Total
Process	0.7 %	0.6 %	0.7 %
System	15.4 %	5.4 %	7.2 %
Total	3.5 %	1.6 %	1.9 %

FIGURE 8.49 Miss rates for the VAX-11/780 TLB, ignoring the impact of instructions not translated by the TLB. This data was measured on a different timesharing workload than earlier VAX measurements [Clark and Emer 1985].

Overall references to the TLB after filtering by the PIBA are divided into 20% user instruction stream, 62% user data stream, 3% system instruction stream, and 15% system data stream. To account for the filtering of addresses by the PIBA optimization, TLB misses can also be counted as a rate per instruction executed, as in Figure 8.50.

TLB misses per 100 instructions	Instruction stream	Data stream	Total
Process	0.18	0.50	0.68
System	0.62	1.03	1.65
Total	0.80	1.53	2.33

FIGURE 8.50 Misses per hundred instructions for the VAX-11/780 TLB. Unlike Figure 8.49, this overall TLB evaluation accounts for the effect of the PIBA.

The VAX TLB spends on average 21.6 clock cycles on a miss (including 3.5 clock cycles for cache misses for some page-table entries), adding a total of 0.7 clock cycles per instruction for TLB misses to the average instruction. Thus, about a third of the memory-system stalls are due to TLB misses.

The same study by Emer and Clark [1984] showed a significant variation on cache miss rates:

- Data-stream, cache miss rates varied over the day from 12% to 25%, with a mean of 17%.

- Instruction-buffer–stream, cache miss rates varied from 4% to 13%, with a mean of 8%.

- The distribution of accesses to the cache from the CPU was instruction-prefetch–buffer–stream reads, 68%, data-stream reads, 20%, and data-stream writes, 12%. Calculated per instruction, there are about 2.2 references from the instruction-prefetch buffer, 0.8 data reads per instruction, and 0.4 data writes per instruction.

Example   According to the VAX-11/780 Architecture Handbook, for the workload measured in 1978 the TLB miss rate was about 3%. What do the measurements say for the timesharing workload measured in 1984?

Answer   Assuming just one memory reference to get the average VAX instruction of 3.8 bytes, the miss rate is 1%:

$$\frac{\dfrac{2.3 \text{ TLB misses}}{100 \text{ instructions}}}{\dfrac{1+0.8+0.4 \text{ references}}{\text{Instruction}}} = \frac{2.3}{100*2.2} = 0.01$$

Including the VIBA-PIBA, Figure 8.49 on page 479 shows a 1.9% miss rate.

Example   According to the VAX-11/780 Architecture Handbook, for the workload measured in 1978 the cache miss rate was about 5%. What do the measurements say for the timesharing workload measured in 1984?

Answer   The cache miss rate varies. The mean miss rate is

$$68\%*8\% + 20\%*17\% + 12\%*17\% = 11\%$$

In the best case, the answer is

$$68\%*4\% + 20\%*12\% + 12\%*12\% = 7\%$$

In the worst case,

$$68\%*13\% + 20\%*25\% + 12\%*25\% = 17\%$$

8.10 | Fallacies and Pitfalls

As the most naturally quantitative of the computer architecture disciplines, memory hierarchy would seem to be less vulnerable to fallacies and pitfalls. Yet the authors were limited here not by lack of warnings, but by space.

Pitfall: Too small an address space.

Just five years after DEC and Carnegie-Mellon University collaborated to design the new PDP-11 computer family, it was apparent that their creation had a fatal flaw. An architecture announced by IBM six years **before** the PDP-11 is still thriving, with minor modifications, 25 years later. And the DEC VAX, criticized for including unnecessary functions, has sold 100,000 units since the PDP-11 went out of production. Why?

The fatal flaw of the PDP-11 was the size of its addresses as compared to the IBM 360 and the VAX. Address size limits the program length, since the size of a program and the amount of data needed by the program must be less than $2^{address\ size}$. The reason the address size is so hard to change is that it determines the minimum width of anything that can contain an address: PC, register, memory word, and effective-address arithmetic. If there is no plan to expand the address from the start, then the chances of successfully changing address size are so slim that it normally means the end of that computer family. Bell and Strecker [1976] put it like this:

There is only one mistake that can be made in computer design that is difficult to recover from—not having enough address bits for memory addressing and memory management. The PDP-11 followed the unbroken tradition of nearly every known computer. [p. 2]

A partial list of successful machines that eventually starved to death for lack of address bits includes the PDP-8, PDP-10, PDP-11, Intel 8080, Intel 8086, Intel 80186, Intel 80286, AMI 6502, Zilog Z80, CRAY-1, and CRAY X-MP.

Fallacy: Given the hardware resources, the computer designer who selects a set-associative cache over a direct-mapped cache of the same size will get a faster computer.

The question here is whether the extra logic of the set-associative cache affects the hit time, and therefore possibly the CPU clock rate. (See Figure 8.11.) If it does affect hit time, then the question is whether the advantage in lower miss rate offsets the slower hit time. In the mid-1980s many recognized this danger and selected direct-mapped placement; for example, the MIPS M/500, Sun 3/260, and VAX 8800. Hill [1988] makes an eloquent case for direct-mapped caches, including lower costs, faster hit times, and therefore smaller average access times for large, direct-mapped caches. Direct-mapped caches also allow the data read to be sent to the CPU and used even before hit/miss is determined, particularly useful with a pipelined CPU. Hill found about a 10% difference in hit times for TTL or ECL board-level caches and 2% difference for custom CMOS caches, with an absolute change in the miss rates of less than 1% for large caches. Since a direct-mapped cache hit can be accessed faster and hit time typically sets the clock cycle time of the processor, a CPU with a direct-mapped cache can be as fast as or faster than a CPU with a two-way–set-associative cache of the same size. Przybylski, Horowitz, and Hennessy [1988] show several examples of such tradeoffs.

Fallacy: A memory system can be designed using traces from a different architecture.

Figure 8.51 (page 482) shows instruction and data cache miss rates for the same programs on two different architectures. This data is from the first portion of execution of Spice on DLX and the VAX. The shift from data accesses in the

VAX to instruction accesses on DLX seen in Figure 3.33 (page 123) of Chapter 3 is reflected here: 61% of the VAX references and 52% of the misses are to data. Note that while DLX has only three-quarters of the absolute number of data misses, its data miss **rate** is three times higher.

	VAX	DLX
Instruction references	576,169	918,537
Instruction misses	2,033	3,188
Instruction miss rate	0.4%	0.3%
Data references	923,831	264,453
Data misses	2,200	1,595
Data miss rate	0.2%	0.6%
Total references	1,500,000	1,182,990
Percentage of instructions of total references	38%	78%
Total misses	4,233	4,782
Percentage of instruction misses of total misses	48%	67%
Average miss rate	0.3%	0.4%

FIGURE 8.51   Miss rates for VAX and DLX for an initial phase of Spice. The simulation assumes separate instruction and data caches. Each cache is direct mapped, uses 16-byte blocks, and contains 64 KB. Both use write through with write allocate. (Note that unlike Chapter 2, this data was collected using the F77 compiler and was for a portion of the Spice program).

Pitfall: Basing the size of the write buffer on the speed of memory and the average mix of writes.

This seems like a reasonable approach:

$$\text{Write-buffer size} = \frac{\text{Memory references}}{\text{Clock cycle}} * \text{Write percentage} * \text{Clock cycles to write memory}$$

If there is one memory reference per clock cycle, 10% of the memory references are writes, and writing a word of memory takes 10 cycles, then a one-word buffer is added (1*10%*10=1). Calculating for the VAX-11/780 using data from the last section,

$$\frac{3.4 \text{ memory references}}{10.6 \text{ clock cycles}} * \frac{0.4 \text{ writes}}{3.4 \text{ memory references}} * \frac{6 \text{ clock cycles}}{\text{Write}} = 0.22$$

Thus, a one-word buffer seems sufficient.

The pitfall is that when writes come close together, the CPU must stall until the prior write is completed. The single-word write buffer of the VAX-11/780 is the major reason for its write stalling (about 20% of all stalls). The proper question to ask is how large a buffer is needed to keep CPU write stalls to a small amount. The impact of write-buffer size can be established by simulation or estimated with a queuing model.

Pitfall: Extending an address space by adding segments on top of a flat address space.

During the 1970s, many programs grew to the point they couldn't address all of the code and data with just a 16-bit address. Machines were then revised to offer 32-bit addresses, either through a flat 32-bit address space or by adding 16 bits of segment to the existing 16-bit address. From the point of view of marketing, adding segments solves the addressing problem. Unfortunately, there is trouble any time a programming language wants an address that is larger than one segment, such as indices for large arrays, unrestricted pointers, or reference parameters. Moreover, adding segments can turn every address into two words—one for the segment number and one for the segment offset—causing problems in the use of addresses in registers. In the 1990s, 32-bit addresses will be exhausted, and it will be interesting to see if history will repeat itself on the consequences of going to larger flat addresses versus adding segments.

Fallacy: Caches are as fast as registers.

This fallacy is important, because if caches were as fast as registers, there would be no need for registers. Without registers there would be no need for a register allocator, and so compilers could be simpler. The fallacy is difficult to prove quantitatively, yet example after example can be cited. Lampson [1982] summarized this experience:

A register bank is faster than a cache, both because it is smaller, and because the address mechanism is much simpler. Designers of high performance machines have typically found it is possible to read one register and write another in a single cycle, while two cycles [latency] are needed for a cache access. ... Also, since there are not too many registers it is feasible to duplicate or triplicate them, so that several registers can be read out simultaneously. [p. 74]

As mentioned in Chapter 3, the short addresses of registers allow more compact instruction encoding. It seems to the authors that the deterministic access of multiported register banks will always offer lower latency or higher bandwidth, or both, when compared to the nondeterministic access of caches.

8.11 | Concluding Remarks

The difficulty of building a memory system to keep pace with faster CPUs is underscored by the fact that the raw material for main memory is the same as that found in the cheapest computer. It is the principle of locality that saves us here—its soundness is demonstrated at all levels of the memory hierarchy in current computers, from disks to instruction buffers.

	Register windows	Instruction-prefetch buffer	TLB	First-level cache	Second-level cache	Virtual memory
Block size	64 bytes	1 byte	4 – 8 (1 PTE)	4 – 128 bytes	32 – 256 bytes	512 – 8192 bytes
Hit time	1 clock cycle	1 clock cycle	1 clock cycle	1 – 4 clock cycles	4 – 10 clock cycles	1 – 10 clock cycles
Miss penalty	32 – 64 clock cycles	2 – 6 clock cycles	10 – 30 clock cycles	8 – 32 clock cycles	30 – 80 clock cycles	100,000 – 600,000 clock cycles
Miss rate (local)	1% – 3%	10% – 25%	0.1% – 2%	1% – 20%	15% – 30%	0.00001% – 0.001%
Size	512 bytes	6 – 12 bytes	32 – 8192 (8 – 1024 PTEs)	1 KB – 256 KB	256 KB – 4 MB	4 MB – 2048 MB
Backing store	First-level cache	First-level cache	First-level cache	Second-level cache	Static-column DRAM	Disks
Q1: block placement	Circular buffer	N.A. (Queue)	Set associative	Direct mapped	Set associative	Fully associative
Q2: block identification	2 registers: high and low	Valid bits + 1 register	Tag/ block	Tag/ block	Tag/ block	Table
Q3: block replacement	First in– first out	N.A. (Queue)	Random	N.A. (Direct mapped)	Random	LRU
Q4: write strategy	Write back	Flush on write to instruction buffer (if possible)	Flush on write to page table	Write through or write back	Write through or write back	Write back

FIGURE 8.52   Summary of the memory-hierarchy examples in this chapter.

Misses in every level can be categorized by three causes—compulsory, capacity, and conflict—and different techniques work for each case. Figure 8.52 summarizes the attributes of the memory-hierarchy examples described in this chapter.

There tends to be a knee in the curve of memory-hierarchy cost/performance: Above that knee is wasted performance and below that knee is wasted hardware. Architects find that knee by simulation and quantitative analysis.

8.12 | Historical Perspective and References

While the pioneers of computing knew of the need for a memory hierarchy and coined the term, the automatic management of two levels was first proposed by Kilburn, et al. [1962] and demonstrated with the Atlas computer at the University of Manchester. This was the year **before** the IBM 360 was announced. While IBM planned for its introduction with the next generation (System/370), the operating system wasn't up to the challenge in 1970. Virtual memory was announced for the 370 family in 1972, and it was for this machine that the term "translation-lookaside buffer" was coined (see Case and Padegs [1978]). The only computers today without virtual memory are a few supercomputers and personal computers.

Both the Atlas and the IBM 360 provided protection on pages, and over time machines evolved more elaborate mechanisms. The most elaborate mechanism was capabilities, which reached its highest interest in the late 1970s and early 1980s [Fabry 1974 and Wulf, Levin, and Harbison 1981]. Wilkes [1982], one of the early workers on capabilities, had this to say about capabilities:

Anyone who has been concerned with an implementation of the type just described [capability system], or has tried to explain one to others, is likely to feel that complexity has got out of hand. It is particularly disappointing that the attractive idea of capabilities being tickets that can be freely handed around has become lost ….

Compared with a conventional computer system, there will inevitably be a cost to be met in providing a system in which the domains of protection are small and frequently changed. This cost will manifest itself in terms of additional hardware, decreased runtime speed, and increased memory occupancy. It is at present an open question whether, by adoption of the capability approach, the cost can be reduced to reasonable proportions.

Today there is little interest in capabilities either from the operating systems or the computer architecture communities, although there is growing interest in protection and security.

Bell and Strecker [1976] reflected on the PDP-11 and identified a small address space as the only architectural mistake that is difficult to recover from. At the time of the creation of PDP-11, core memories were increasing at a very slow rate, and the competition from 100 other minicomputer companies meant that DEC might not have a cost-competitive product if every address had to go through the 16-bit datapath twice. Hence, the decision to add just 4 more address bits than the predecessor of the PDP-11. The architects of the IBM 360 were aware of the importance of address size and planned for the architecture to extend to 32 bits of address. Only 24 bits were used in the IBM 360, however, because the low-end 360 models would have been even slower with the larger addresses. Unfortunately, the architects didn't reveal their plans to the software people, and the expansion effort was foiled by programmers who stored extra information in the upper eight "unused" address bits.

A few years after the Atlas paper, Wilkes published the first paper describing the concept of a cache [1965]:

The use is discussed of a fast core memory of, say, 32,000 words as slave to a slower core memory of, say, one million words in such a way that in practical cases the effective access time is nearer that of the fast memory than that of the slow memory. [p. 270]

This two-page paper describes a direct-mapped cache. While this is the first publication on caches, the first implementation was probably a direct-mapped instruction cache built at the University of Cambridge. It was based on tunnel diode memory, the fastest form of memory available at the time. Wilkes states that G. Scarott suggested the idea of a cache memory.

Subsequent to that publication, IBM started a project that led to the first commercial machine with a cache, the IBM 360/85 [Liptay 1968]. Gibson [1967] describes how to measure program behavior as memory traffic as well as miss rate and shows how the miss rate varies between programs. Using a sample of 20 programs (each with 3,000,000 references!), Gibson also relied on average memory-access time to compare systems with and without caches. This was over 20 years ago, and yet many used miss rates until recently.

Conti, Gibson, and Pitkowsky [1968] describe the resulting performance of the 360/85. The 360/91 outperforms the 360/85 on only 3 of the 11 programs in the paper, even though the 360/85 has a slower clock cycle time (80 ns versus 60 ns), smaller memory interleaving (4 versus 16), and a slower main memory (1.04 μsec versus 0.75 μsec). This is the first paper to use the term "cache." Strecker [1976] published the first comparative cache-design paper examining caches for the PDP-11. Smith [1982] later published a thorough survey paper, using the terms "spatial locality" and "temporal locality"; this paper has served as a reference for many computer designers. While most studies have relied on simulations, Clark [1983] used a hardware monitor to record cache misses of the VAX-11/780 over several days. Section 8.9 reports these findings, along with the work Clark did with Emer on TLBs [1984, 1985]. A similar study was performed on the VAX 8800 [Clark et al. 1988]. Agarwal, Sites, and Horowitz [1986] changed the microcode of a VAX to make traces of system and user code. These traces are used in this book (and are available through the publisher). Hill [1987] proposed the three Cs used in Section 8.4 to explain cache misses. Caches remain an active area of research, as Smith [1986] has recorded in his extensive bibliography.

Many of the ideas in the advanced cache section have only been tried recently. The inclusion of caches on microprocessors such as the Motorola 68020 gave rise to two-level cache machines; the Sun 3/260 in 1986 was perhaps the first. In 1988, the Silicon Graphics 4D/240 had two levels of caches for data and instructions, with the second level added primarily for cache coherency to allow four-way multiprocessing. The MIPS RC 6280 is probably the first machine to go to two-level caches for the reasons given on page 465 [Roberts, Taylor, and Layman 1990]. Goodman and Chiang [1984] were the first to publish an investigation of static-column DRAM in a memory hierarchy, while Kelly [1988] refined the idea by using virtual addresses. Goodman [1987] showed that aliases can be handled at cache-miss time, and Wang, Baer, and Levy [1989] show that the extra control for this does not look too bad for two levels of cache.

In comparison to the other ideas in the advanced section, cache-coherency research is much older. Tang [1976] published the first cache-coherency protocol using directories, and this approach was implemented in the IBM 3081. Censier and Feautrier [1978] describe a technique with status tags in memory. The first machine to use snooping caches was the Synapse N+1 [Frank 1984]; the first publication on snooping caches was by Goodman [1983]. Archibald and Baer [1986] survey the wide variety of schemes for cache coherency. References on the protocols mentioned in their paper and in Figure 8.45 are Frank [1984] for Synapse; Goodman [1983] for Write Once; Katz et al. [1985] for Berkeley; McCreight [1984] for Dragon; Papamarcos and Patel [1984] for Illinois; and Thacker and Stewart [1987] for Firefly. Baer and Wang [1988] discuss multilevel inclusion. Eggers's [1989] nomenclature for categorizing snooping caches is adopted in this text. Chapter 10, Section 10.7 mentions the use of prefetching to improve cache performance, and Kroft [1981] describes the design of a cache that allows the cache to service subsequent requests while the requested data is prefetched. Przybylski [1990] and the dissertations by Agarwal [1987], Eggers [1989], and Hill [1987] investigate many aspects of the advanced cache topics in more depth.

Papers on another use of locality, register windows or stack caches, are by Patterson and Sequin [1981], Ditzel and McClellan [1982], and Lampson [1982]. Sites wrote an earlier paper [1979] suggesting one way to use the expanding resources of VLSI was to get higher performance by using a lot of registers, and these schemes are one interpretation of that recommendation.

References

AGARWAL, A. [1987]. *Analysis of Cache Performance for Operating Systems and Multiprogramming*, Ph.D. Thesis, Stanford Univ., Tech. Rep. No. CSL-TR-87-332 (May).

AGARWAL, A., R. L. SITES, AND M. HOROWITZ [1986]. "ATUM: A new technique for capturing address traces using microcode," *Proc. 13th Annual Symposium on Computer Architecture* (June 2–5), Tokyo, Japan, 119–127.

ARCHIBALD, J. AND J.-L. BAER [1986]. "Cache coherence protocols: Evaluation using a multiprocessor simulation model," *ACM Trans. on Computer Systems* 4:4 (November) 273–298.

BAER, J.-L. AND W.-H. WANG [1988]. "On the inclusion property for multi-level cache hierarchies," *Proc. 15th Annual Symposium on Computer Architecture* (May–June), Honolulu, 73–80.

BELL , C. G. AND W. D. STRECKER [1976]. "Computer structures: What have we learned from the PDP-11?," *Proc. Third Annual Symposium on Computer Architecture* (January), Pittsburgh, Penn., 1–14.

BLAKKEN, J. [1983]. "Register windows for SOAR," in *Smalltalk On A RISC: Architectural Investigations,* Proc. of CS 292R (April) 126–140, University of California.

CASE, R.P. AND A. PADEGS [1978]. "The architecture of the IBM System/370," *Communications of the ACM* 21:1, 73–96. Also appears in D. P. Siewiorek, C. G. Bell, and A. Newell, *Computer Structures: Principles and Examples* (1982), McGraw-Hill, New York, 830–855.

CENSIER, L. M. AND P. FEAUTRIER [1978]. "A new solution to the coherence problem in multicache systems," *IEEE Trans. on Computers* C-27:12 (December) 1112–1118.

CLARK, D. W. [1983]. "Cache performance of the VAX-11/780," *ACM Trans. on Computer Systems* 1:1, 24–37.

CLARK, D. W. AND J. S. EMER [1985]. "Performance of the VAX-11/780 translation buffer: Simulation and measurement," *ACM Trans. on Computer Systems* 3:1, 31–62.

CLARK, D. W, P. J. BANNON, AND J. B. KELLER [1988]. "Measuring VAX 8800 Performance with a Histogram hardware monitor," *Proc. 15th Annual Symposium on Computer Architecture* (May–June), Honolulu, Hawaii, 176–185.

CONTI, C., D. H. GIBSON, AND S. H. PITOWSKY [1968]. "Structural aspects of the System/360 Model 85, part I: General organization," *IBM Systems J.* 7:1, 2–14.

CRAWFORD, J. H AND P. P. GELSINGER [1987]. *Programming the 80386,* Sybex, Alameda, Calif.

DITZEL, D. R., AND H.R. MCCLELLAN [1982]. "Register allocation for free: The C machine stack cache" *Symposium on Architectural Support for Programming Languages and Operating Systems* (March 1–3), Palo Alto, Calif., 48–56.

EGGERS, S. [1989]. *Simulation Analysis of Data Sharing in Shared Memory Multiprocessors ,* Ph. D. Thesis, Univ. of California, Berkeley, Computer Science Division Tech. Rep. UCB/CSD 89/501 (April).

EMER, J. S. AND D. W. CLARK [1984]. "A characterization of processor performance of the VAX-11/780," *Proc. 11th Annual Symposium on Computer Architecture* (June), Ann Arbor, Mich., 301–310.

FABRY, R. S. [1974]. "Capability based addressing," *Comm. ACM* 17:7 (July) 403–412.

FRANK, S. J. [1984]. "Tightly coupled multiprocessor systems speed memory access times," *Electronics* 57:1 (January) 164–169.

GIBSON, D. H. [1967]. "Considerations in block–oriented systems design," *AFIPS Conf. Proc.* 30, SJCC, 75–80.

GOODMAN, J. R. [1983]. "Using cache memory to reduce processor memory traffic," *Proc. Tenth Annual Symposium on Computer Architecture* (June 5–7), Stockholm, Sweden, 124–131.

GOODMAN, J. R. and M.-C. Chiang [1984]. "The use of static column RAM as a memory hierarchy," *Proc. 11th Annual Symposium on Computer Architecture* (June 5–7), Ann Arbor, Mich., 167–174.

GOODMAN, J. R. [1987]. "Coherency for multiprocessor virtual address caches," *Proc. Second Int'l Conf. on Architectural Support for Programming Languages and Operating Systems*, Palo Alto, Calif., 71–81.

HALBERT, D. C. AND P. B. KESSLER [1980]. "Windows of overlapping register frames," *CS 292R Final Reports* (June) 82–100.

HILL, M. D. [1987]. *Aspects of Cache Memory and Instruction Buffer Performance*, Ph. D. Thesis, Univ. of California at Berkeley Computer Science Division, Tech. Rep. UCB/CSD 87/381 (November).

HILL, M. D. [1988]. "A case for direct mapped caches," *Computer* 21:12 (December) 25–40.

HUGUET, M. AND T. LANG [1985]. "A reduced register file for RISC architectures," *Computer Architecture News* 13:4 (September) 22–31.

KATZ, R., S. EGGERS, D. A. WOOD, C. PERKINS, AND R. G. SHELDON [1985]. "Implementing a cache consistency protocol," *Proc. 12th Annual Symposium on Computer Architecture*, 276–283.

KELLY, E. [1988]. "'SCRAM Cache' in Sun-4/110 beats traditional caches," *Sun Technology* 1:3 (Summer) 19–21.

KILBURN, T., D. B. G. EDWARDS, M. J. LANIGAN, F. H. SUMNER [1962]. "One-level storage system," *IRE Transactions on Electronic Computers* EC-11 (April) 223–235. Also appears in D. P. Siewiorek, C. G. Bell, and A. Newell, *Computer Structures: Principles and Examples* (1982), McGraw-Hill, New York, 135–148.

KROFT, D. [1981]. "Lockup-free instruction fetch/prefetch cache organization," *Proc. Eighth Annual Symposium on Computer Architecture* (May 12–14), Minneapolis, Minn., 81–87.

LAMPSON, B. W. [1982]. "Fast procedure calls," *Symposium on Architectural Support for Programming Languages and Operating Systems* (March 1–3), Palo Alto, Calif., 66–75.

LIPTAY, J. S. [1968]. "Structural aspects of the System/360 Model 85, part II: The cache," *IBM Systems J.* 7:1, 15–21.

MCCALL, K. [1983]. "The Smalltalk-80 benchmarks," *Smalltalk 80: Bits of History, Words of Advice,* G. Krasner, ed., Addison-Wesley, Reading, Mass., 153–174.

MCCREIGHT, E. [1984]. "The Dragon computer system: An early overview," Tech. Rep. Xerox Corp. (September).

MCFARLING, S. [1989]. "Program optimization for instruction caches," *Proc. Third International Conf. on Architectural Support for Programming Languages and Operating Systems* (April 3–6), Boston, Mass., 183–191.

PAPAMARCOS, M. AND J. PATEL [1984]. "A low coherence solution for multiprocessors with private cache memories," *Proc. of the 11th Annual Symposium on Computer Architecture* (June), Ann Arbor, Mich., 348–354.

PRZYBYLSKI, S. A. [1990]. *Cache Design: A Performance-Directed Approach,* Morgan Kaufmann Publishers, San Mateo, Calif.

PRZYBYLSKI, S. A., M. HOROWITZ, AND J. L. HENNESSY [1988]. "Performance tradeoffs in cache design," *Proc. 15th Annual Symposium on Computer Architecture* (May–June), Honolulu, Hawaii, 290–298.

ROBERTS, D., G. TAYLOR, AND T. LAYMAN [1990]. "An ECL RISC microprocessor designed for two-level cache," *IEEE Compcon* (February).

SAMPLES, A. D. AND P. N. HILFINGER [1988]. "Code reorganization for instruction caches," Tech. Rep. UCB/CSD 88/447 (October), Univ. of Calif., Berkeley.

SITES, R. L., [1979]. "How to use 1000 registers," *Caltech Conf. on VLSI* (January).

SMITH, A. J. [1982]. "Cache memories," *Computing Surveys* 14:3 (September) 473–530.

SMITH, A. J. [1986]. "Bibliography and readings on CPU cache memories and related topics," *Computer Architecture News* (January) 22–42.

SMITH, J. E. AND J. R. GOODMAN [1983]. "A study of instruction cache organizations and replacement policies," *Proc. Tenth Annual Symposium on Computer Architecture* (June 5–7), Stockholm, Sweden,, 132–137.

STRECKER, W. D. [1976]. "Cache memories for the PDP-11?," *Proc. Third Annual Symposium on Computer Architecture* (January), Pittsburgh, Penn., 155–158.

TANG, C. K. [1976]. "Cache system design in the tightly coupled multiprocessor system," *Proc. 1976 AFIPS National Computer Conf.*, 749–753.

TAYLOR, G. S., P. N. HILFINGER, J. R. LARUS, D. A. PATTERSON, AND B. G. ZORN [1986]. "Evaluation of the SPUR Lisp architecture," *Proc. 13th Annual Symposium on Computer Architecture* (June 2–5), Tokyo, Japan, 444–452.

THACKER, C. P. AND L. C. STEWART [1987]. "Firefly: a multiprocessor workstation," *Proc. Second Int'l Conf. on Architectural Support for Programming Languages and Operating Systems*, Palo Alto, Calif., 164–172.

UNGAR, D. M. [1987]. *The Design of a High Performance Smalltalk System*, The MIT Press Distinguished Dissertation Series, Cambridge, Mass.

WANG, W.-H., J.-L. BAER, AND H. M. LEVY [1989]. "Organization and performance of a two-level virtual-real cache hierarchy," *Proc. 16th Annual Symposium on Computer Architecture* (May 28–June 1), Jerusalem, Israel , 140–148.

WILKES, M. [1965]. "Slave memories and dynamic storage allocation," *IEEE Trans. Electronic Computers* EC-14:2 (April) 270–271.

WILKES, M. V. [1982]. "Hardware support for memory protection: Capability implementations," *Proc. Symposium on Architectural Support for Programming Languages and Operating Systems* (March 1–3), Palo Alto, Calif., 107–116.

WULF, W. A., R. LEVIN AND S. P. HARBISON [1981]. *Hydra/C.mmp: An Experimental Computer System,* McGraw-Hill, New York.

E X E R C I S E S

8.1 [15/15/12/12] <2.2,8.4> Let's try to show how you can make *unfair* benchmarks. Here are two machines with the same processor and main memory but different cache organizations. Assume the miss time is 10 times a cache-hit time for both machines. Assume writing a 32-bit word takes 5 times as long as a cache hit (for the write-through cache), and that writing a whole 16-byte block takes 10 times as long as a cache-read hit. (for the write-back cache). The caches are unified; that is, they contain both instructions and data.

Cache A: 64 sets, 2 elements per set, each block is 16 bytes, and it uses write through.

Cache B: 128 sets, 1 element per set, each block is 16 bytes, and it uses write back.

a.   [15] Describe a program that makes machine A run as much faster as possible than machine B. (Be sure to state any further assumptions you need, if any.)

b.   [15] Describe a program that makes machine B run as much faster as possible than machine A. (Be sure to state any further assumptions you need, if any.)

c.   [12] Approximately how much faster is the program in Part a on machine A than machine B?

d.   [12] Approximately how much faster is the program in Part b on machine B than machine A?

8.2   [20] <2.2,6.4,8.4> To simplify pipelined execution, some machines insert NOP instructions rather than interlock the pipeline (see pages 273–275 in Chapter 6). Ignoring cache misses, assume that the Spice code takes 2,000,000 clocks in either case (since the version without NOPS still interlocks, which takes an extra clock each time.) Figure 8.53

shows data collected for a portion of Spice execution with a 64-KB, direct-mapped, instruction-only cache with one-word blocks.

	With NOPS	Without NOPS	Ratio with/without
Total references	1,500,000	1,180,000	1.27
Cache misses	34,153	24,908	1.37
Miss rate	2.28	2.10	1.09

FIGURE 8.53 Spice miss rates with and without NOPs.

The conclusion of a study based on Figure 8.53 was that a 9% increase in the miss rate of the program with NOPS will have a small but measurable impact on performance. What is the actual impact on performance assuming a 10-clock miss penalty?

8.3 [15/15] <8.4> You purchased an Acme computer with the following features:

1. 90% of all memory accesses are found in the cache;

2. Each cache block is two words, and the whole block is read on any miss;

3. The processor sends references to its cache at the rate of 10^7 words per second;

4. 25% of the references of (3) are writes;

5. Assume that the bus can support 10^7 words per second, reads or writes;

6. The bus reads or writes a single word at a time (the bus cannot read or write two words at once);

7. Assume at any one time, 30% of the blocks in the cache have been modified;

8. The cache uses write allocate on a write miss.

You are considering adding a peripheral to the bus, and you want to know how much of the bus bandwidth is already used. Calculate the percentage of bus bandwidth used on the average in the two cases below. The percentage is called the *traffic ratio* in the literature. Be sure to state your assumptions.

a. [15] The cache is write through.

b. [15] The cache is write back.

8.4 [20] <8.4> One drawback to the write-back scheme is that writes will probably take two cycles. During the first cycle, we detect whether a hit will occur, and during the second (assuming a hit) we actually write the data. Let's assume that 50% of the blocks are dirty for a write-back cache. Using statistics for loads and stores from DLX in Figure C.4 in Appendix C, estimate the performance of a write-through cache with a one-cycle write versus a write-back cache with a two-cycle write for each of the programs. For this question, assume that the write buffer for write through will never stall the CPU (no penalty). Assume a cache hit takes 1 clock cycle, the cache miss penalty is 10 clock cycles, and a block write from the cache to main memory takes 10 clock cycles. Finally, assume the instruction-cache miss rate is 2% and the data-cache miss rate is 4%.

8.5 [15/20/10] <8.4> To save development time, the Sun 3/280 and the Sun 4/280 used identical memory systems, even though the CPUs were quite different. Assume the same case exists for a new machine, one board using a VAX CPU and the other a DLX CPU. For now assume the miss-rate information in Figure 8.12 and 8.16 (pages 421 and 424) apply to both architectures. Use the average column in Figure C.4 in Appendix C as needed for DLX instruction mix, and the caption of Figure 8.16 (page 424) for VAX instruction/data mix. Assume the following:

Miss penalty is 12 clock cycles.

A perfect write buffer that never stalls the CPU.

The base CPI assuming a perfect memory system is 6.0 for the VAX and 1.5 for DLX.

A unified cache adds 1 extra clock cycle to each load and store of DLX (since there is a single memory port) but not for the VAX.

You are considering three options:

1. A 4-way–set-associative unified cache of 64 KB.

2. Two 2-way–set-associative caches of 32 KB each, one for instructions and one for data.

3. A direct-mapped unified cache of 128 KB. Assume that clock rate is 10% faster in this case since the mapping is direct and the CPU address does not need to drive two caches, nor does the data bus need to be multiplexed. This faster clock rate increases the miss penalty to 13 clock cycles.

a. [15] What is the average memory-access time in clock cycles for each organization?

b. [20] What is the CPI for each machine and cache organization?

c. [10] What cache organization gives the best average performance for the two CPUs?

8.6 [25/15] <2.3,8.4,8.8> Some microprocessors have custom single-chip caches as companions to the CPU. For example, the Motorola 88100 CPU can have up to 8 of the 88200 cache chips. These chips tend to be more expensive than off-the-shelf static RAM chips. The MIPS R3000 includes a comparator on the CPU chip so that cache tags and data can be built from off-the-shelf static RAMs.

a. [25] Using the program that analyzes cache miss rates how many 16K-by-4 cache RAMs must the R3000 use to get the same performance as two 88200 chips? Both designs use separate instruction and data caches. The MIPS design assumes a block size of 16 bytes with subblock placement for each word. The cache is write through with a 4-word write buffer. The Motorola 88200 is 4-way set associative with 16 KB per chip and a 16-byte block using LRU replacement.

b. [15] Here is the data on the price of each chip (quantity 1 as of 8/1/89):

Motorola 88100: $697

Motorola 88200: $875

MIPS R3000 (25 MHz): $300

MIPS R3010 FPU (25 MHz): $350

16K by 4 SRAM (for 25 MHz R3000): $21

Which system will be cheaper and by how much?

8.7 [15/25/15/15] <2.3,8.4> The Intel i860 has its caches on chip and its die size is 1.2 cm∗1.2 cm. It has a 2-way–set-associative, 4-KB instruction cache and a 2-way–set-associative, 8-KB data cache using write through or write back. Both caches use 32-byte blocks. There are no write buffers or process identifiers to reduce cache flushing. The i860 also includes a 64-entry, 4-way–set-associative TLB to map its 4-KB pages. Address translation occurs before the caches are accessed. The Cypress 7C601 CPU chip size is 0.8 cm by 0.7 cm and has no on-board cache—a cache controller chip (7C604) and two 16K ∗ 16 cache chips (7C157) are offered to form a 64-KB unified cache. The controller includes a TLB with 64 entries managed fully associatively with 4096 process identifiers to reduce flushing. It supports 32-byte blocks with direct-mapped placement, and either write through or write back. There is a one-block write buffer for write back and a four-word write buffer for write through. The chip sizes are 1.0 cm by 0.9 cm for the 7C604 and 0.8 cm by 0.7 cm. for the 7C157.

a. [15] Using the cost model of Chapter 2, what is the cost of the Cypress chip set versus the Intel chip? (Use Figure 2.11 on page 62 to determine chip costs by finding the closest die size in that table to the Intel and Cypress die area.)

b. [25] Use the DLX cache traces and cache simulator to determine the average memory-access time for each cache organization. Assume a miss takes 6 clocks latency plus 1 clock for each 32-bit word. Assume both systems run at the same clock rate and use write allocate.

c. [15] What is the comparative cost/performance of these chips using average memory-access time as the measure?

d. [15] What is the percent increase in cost of a color workstation that uses the more expensive chips?

8.8 [25/10/15] <8.4> The CRAY X-MP instruction buffers can be thought of as an instruction-only cache. The total size is 1 KB, broken into 4 blocks of 256 bytes per block. The cache is fully associative and uses a first-in/first-out replacement policy. The access time on a miss is 10 clock cycles, with the transfer time of 64 bytes every clock cycle. The X-MP takes 1 clock cycle on a hit. Use the cache simulator and the DLX traces to determine:

a. [25] Instruction miss rate

b. [10] Average instruction memory-access time measured in clock cycles

c. [15] What does the CPI of the CRAY X-MP have to be for the portion due to instruction cache misses to be 10% or less?

8.9 [25] <8.4> Traces from a single process give too-high estimates for caches used in a multiprocess environment. Write a program that merges the uniprocess DLX traces into a single reference stream. Use the process-switch statistics in Figure 8.25 (page 439) as the average process-switch rate with an exponential distribution about that mean. (Use number of clock cycles rather than instructions, and assume the CPI of DLX is 1.5.) Use the cache simulator on the original traces and the merged trace. What is the miss rate for each assuming a 64-KB direct-mapped cache with 16-byte blocks? (There is a process-identified tag in the cache tag so that the cache doesn't have to be flushed on each switch.)

8.10 [25] <8.4> One approach to reducing misses is to prefetch the next block. A simple but effective strategy is when block i is referenced to make sure block $i+1$ is in the cache, and if not, to prefetch it. Do you think prefetching is more or less effective with increasing block size? Why? Is it more or less effective with increasing cache size? Why? Use statistics from the cache simulator and the traces to support your conclusion.

8.11 [20/25] <8.4> Smith and Goodman [1983] found that for a **small-instruction–only** cache, a cache using direct mapping could consistently outperform one using fully associative with LRU replacement.

a. [20] Explain why this would be possible. (Hint: you can't explain this with the 3C model because it ignores replacement policy.)

b. [25] Use the cache simulator to see if their results hold for the traces.

8.12 [Discussion] <8.4> If you look at conflict misses for a given associativity in Figure 8.12, as capacity increases the conflict misses go up and down. For example, for 2-way–set-associative mapping the miss rate for 2-KB cache is .010, a 4-KB cache is .013, and an 8-KB cache is .008. Why in the world would this happen?

8.13 [30] <8.5> Use the cache simulator and traces to calculate the effectiveness of a 4-bank versus 8-bank interleaved memory. Assume each word transfer takes one clock on the bus and a random access is 8 clocks. Measure the bank conflicts and memory bandwidth for these cases:

a. No cache and no write buffer.

b. A 64-KB, direct-mapped, write-though cache with four-word blocks.

c. A 64-KB, direct-mapped, write-back cache with four-word blocks.

d. A 64-KB, direct-mapped, write-though cache with four-word blocks but the "interleaving" comes from a page-mode DRAM.

e. A 64-KB, direct-mapped, write-back cache with four-word blocks but the "interleaving" comes from a page mode DRAM.

8.14 [20] <8.6> If the base CPI with a perfect memory system is 1.5, what is the CPI for these cache organizations? Use Figure 8.12 (page 421):

a. Direct-mapped, 16-KB unified cache using write back.

b. Two-way–set-associative, 16-KB unified cache using write back.

c. Direct-mapped, 32-KB unified cache using write back.

Assume the memory latency is 6 clocks, the transfer rate is 4 bytes per clock cycle and that 50% of the transfers are dirty. There are 16 bytes per block and 20% of the instructions are data-transfer instructions. The caches fetch words of the block in address order and the CPUs stall until all words of the block arrive. There is no write buffer. Add to the assumptions above a TLB that takes 20 clock cycles on a TLB miss. A TLB does not slow down a cache hit. For the TLB, make the simplifying assumption that 1% of all references aren't found in TLB, either when addresses come directly from the CPU or when addresses come from cache misses. What is the impact on performance of the TLB if the cache above is physical or virtual?

8.15 [30] <3.8,8.9> The example in Section 8.9 (page 478) refines the instructions fetched into the CPU from the cache due to the instruction-prefetch buffer. How does this increase of 13% to 39% in instruction words fetched affect the difference in the instruction words fetched from DLX versus VAX? The extra instruction fetches of the VAX hurt only when they bring something into the cache that is not used before it is displaced, while DLX would seem to need a larger cache for its larger program. Write a simulator emulating the instruction-prefetch buffer to measure the increase in cache misses using the VAX address traces and see if prefetching is a significant increase in cache misses.

8.16 [25–40] <8.7> Study the impact of adding register windows to DLX. This study can range from simply estimating the register-traffic savings to modifying the DLX compiler and simulator to measure costs and benefits directly.

8.17 [10] <8.8> Data General described the design of a three-level cache for an ECL implementation of the 88000 architecture. What is the formula for average access time for a three-level cache?

8.18 [20] <8.8> What is the performance loss for a four-way multiprocessor with I/O devices? Suppose 1% of all data references to the cache cause invalidation to the other data caches and that all CPUs stall four clocks on an invalidation. Assume a 64-KB, direct-mapped cache for data and a 64-KB, direct-mapped cache for instructions with a block size of 32 bytes yields a 1% miss rate for instructions and a 2% miss rate for data, with 20% of all CPU memory references being for data. The CPI of the CPU is 1.5 with a perfect memory system and it takes 10 clocks on a cache miss whether the data is dirty or clean.

8.19 [25] <8.8> Use the traces to calculate the effectiveness of early restart and out-of-order fetch. What is the distribution of first accesses to a block as block size increases from 2 words to 64 words by factors of two for:

a. A 64-KB, instruction-only cache?

b. A 64-KB, data-only cache?

c. A 128-KB unified cache?

Assume direct-mapped placement.

8.20 [30] <8.8> Use the cache simulator and traces with a program you write yourself to compare the effectiveness schemes for fast writes:

a. 1-word buffer and the CPU stalls on a data-read cache miss with a write-through cache.

b. 4-word buffer and the CPU stalls on a data-read cache miss with a write-through cache.

c. 4-word buffer and the CPU stalls on a data-read cache miss only if there is a potential conflict in the addresses with a write-through cache.

d. A write-back cache that writes dirty data first and then loads the missed block.

e. A write-back cache with a one-block write buffer that loads the miss data first and then stalls the CPU on a clean miss if the write buffer is not empty.

f. A write-back cache with a one-block write buffer that loads the miss data first and then stalls the CPU on a clean miss only if the write buffer is not empty and there is a potential conflict in the addresses.

Assume a 64-KB, direct-mapped cache for data and a 64-KB, direct-mapped cache for instructions with a block size of 32 bytes. The CPI of the CPU is 1.5 with a perfect memory system and it takes 14 clocks on a cache miss and 7 clocks to write a single word to memory.

8.21 [30] <8.8> Use the cache simulator and traces with a program you write yourself to create a two-level cache simulator. Use this program to see at what cache size is the global miss rate of a second-level cache approximately the same as a single-level cache of the same capacity.

8.22 [Discussion] <8.6> Some people have argued that with increasing capacity of memory storage per chip, virtual memory is an idea whose time has passed, and they expect to see it dropped from future computers. Find reasons for and against this argument.

8.23 [Discussion] <8.6> So far, few computer systems take advantage of the extra security available with gates and rings found in a machine like the Intel 80286. Construct some scenario whereby the computer industry would switch over to this model of protection.

8.24 [Discussion] <8.4> Recent research has tried to use compilers to improve cache performance (see McFarling [1989] and Samples and Hilfinger [1988]):

a. Which of the 3C's are compilers trying to improve and which are they not? Why?

b. Which mapping is best for compiler improvement? Why?

8.25 [Discussion] <8.3> Many times a new technology has been invented that is expected to make a major change to the memory hierarchy. For the sake of this question, let's suppose that biological computer technology becomes a reality. Suppose biological memory technology has an unusual characteristic: It is as fast as the fastest semiconductor DRAMs, and it can be randomly accessed; but it only costs as much as magnetic-disk memory. It has the further advantage of not being any slower no matter how big it is. The only drawback is that you can only Write it Once, but you can Read it Many times. Thus it is called a "WORM" memory. Because of the way it is manufactured, the WORM- memory module can be easily replaced. See if you can come up with several new ideas to take advantage of WORMs to build better computers using "bio-technology."

I/O certainly has been lagging in the last decade.

Seymour Cray, Public Lecture (1976)

Also, I/O needs a lot of work.

David Kuck, Keynote Address,
15th Annual Symposium on Computer Architecture (1988)

9 | Input/Output

9.1 | Introduction

Input/output has been the orphan of computer architecture. Historically neglected by CPU enthusiasts, the prejudice against I/O is institutionalized in the most widely used performance measure, CPU time (page 35). Whether a computer has the best or the worst I/O system in the world cannot be measured by CPU time, which by definition ignores I/O. The second class citizenship of I/O is even apparent in the label "peripheral" applied to I/O devices.

This attitude is contradicted by common sense. A computer without I/O devices is like a car without wheels—you can't get very far without them. And while CPU time is interesting, response time—the time between when the user types a command and when she gets results—is surely a better measure of performance. The customer who pays for a computer cares about response time, even if the CPU designer doesn't. Finally, as rapid improvements in CPU performance compress traditional classes of computers together, it is I/O that serves to distinguish them:

- The difference between a mainframe computer and a minicomputer is that a mainframe can support many more terminals and disks.

- The difference between a minicomputer and a workstation is that a workstation has a screen, a keyboard, and a mouse.

- The difference between a file server and a workstation is that a file server has disks and tape units but no screen, keyboard, or mouse.

- The difference between a workstation and a personal computer is that workstations are always connected together on a network.

It may come to pass that computers from high-end workstations to low-end supercomputers will use the same "super-microprocessors." Differences in cost and performance would be determined only by the memory and I/O systems (and the number of processors).

I/O's revenge is at hand. Suppose we have a difference between CPU time and response time of 10%, and we speed up the CPU by a factor of 10, while neglecting I/O. Amdahl's Law tells us that we will get a speedup of only 5 times, with half the potential of the CPU wasted. Similarly, making the CPU 100 times faster without improving the I/O would obtain a speedup of only 10 times, squandering 90% of the potential. If, as predicted in Chapter 1, performance of CPUs improves at 50% to 100% per year, and I/O does not improve, every task will become I/O bound. There would be no reason to buy faster CPUs—and no jobs for CPU designers.

While this single chapter cannot fully vindicate I/O, it may at least atone for some of the sins of the past and restore some balance.

Are CPUs Ever Idle?

Some suggest that the prejudice is well founded. I/O speed doesn't matter, they argue, since there is always another process to run while one process waits for a peripheral.

There are several points to make in reply. First, this is an argument that performance is measured as throughput—more tasks per hour—rather than as response time. Plainly, if users didn't care about response time, interactive software never would have been invented, and there would be no workstations today. (The next section gives experimental evidence on the importance of response time.) It may also be expensive to rely on processes while waiting for I/O, since main memory must be larger or else the paging traffic from process switching would actually increase I/O. Furthermore, with desktop computing there is only one person per CPU, and thus fewer processes than in timesharing; many times the only waiting process is the human being! And some applications, such as transaction processing (Section 9.3), place strict limits on response time as part of the performance analysis.

But let's accept the argument at face value and explore it further. Suppose the difference between response time and CPU time today is 10%, and a CPU that is ten times faster can be achieved without changing I/O performance. A process will then spend 50% of its time waiting for I/O, and two processes will have to be perfectly aligned to avoid CPU stalls while waiting for I/O. Any further CPU improvement will only increase CPU idle time.

Thus, I/O throughput can limit system throughput, just as I/O response time limits system response time. Let's see how to predict performance for the whole system.

9.2 | Predicting System Performance

System performance is limited by the slowest part of the path between CPU and I/O devices. The performance of a system can be limited by the speed of any of these pieces of the path, shown in Figure 9.1:

- The CPU

- The cache memory

- The main memory

- The memory–I/O bus

- The I/O controller or I/O channel

- The I/O device

- The speed of the I/O software

- The efficiency of the software's use of the I/O device

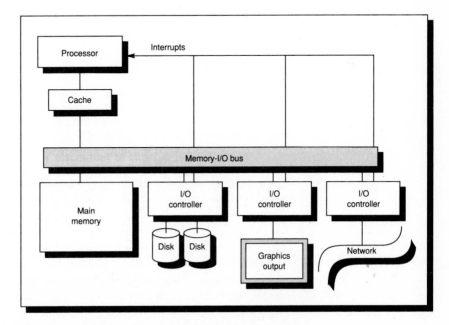

FIGURE 9.1 Typical collection of I/O devices on a computer.

If the system is not balanced, the high performance of some components may be lost due to the low performance of one link in the chain. The art of I/O design is to configure a system such that the speeds of all components are matched.

In earlier chapters we have assumed that the fastest CPU is the single object of our desire, but CPU performance is not the same as system performance. For example, suppose we have two workloads, A and B. Both workloads take 10 seconds to run. Workload A does so little I/O that it is not worth mentioning. Workload B keeps I/O devices busy four seconds, and this time is completely overlapped with CPU activities. Suppose the CPU is replaced by a newer model with five times the performance. Intuitively, we realize that workload A takes two seconds—fully five times faster—but workload B is I/O bound and cannot take less than four seconds. Figure 9.2 illustrates our intuition.

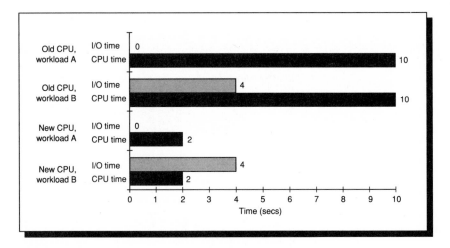

FIGURE 9.2 The overlapped execution of the two workloads with the original CPU and then a CPU with five times the performance. We can see that the elapsed time for workload A is indeed 1/5 of the time with the new CPU, but it is limited to four seconds in workload B because I/O speed is not improved.

Determining the performance of such cases requires a new formula. The elapsed execution time of a workload can be broken into three pieces

$$\text{Time}_{\text{workload}} = \text{Time}_{\text{CPU}} + \text{Time}_{\text{I/O}} - \text{Time}_{\text{overlap}}$$

where Time_{CPU} means the time the CPU is busy, $\text{Time}_{\text{I/O}}$ means the time the I/O system is busy, and $\text{Time}_{\text{overlap}}$ means the time both the CPU and the I/O system are busy. Using workload B with the old CPU in Figure 9.2 as an example, the times in seconds are:

10 for $\text{Time}_{\text{workload}}$,

10 for Time_{CPU},

4 for $\text{Time}_{I/O}$, and

4 for $\text{Time}_{\text{overlap}}$.

Assuming we speed up only the CPU, one way to calculate the time to execute the workload is:

$$\text{Time}_{\text{workload}} = \frac{\text{Time}_{\text{CPU}}}{\text{Speedup}_{\text{CPU}}} + \text{Time}_{I/O} - \frac{\text{Time}_{\text{overlap}}}{\text{Speedup}_{\text{CPU}}}$$

Since the CPU time is shrunk, it stands to reason that the overlap time is also shrunk. The system speedup when we want to improve I/O is equivalent:

$$\text{Time}_{\text{workload}} = \text{Time}_{\text{CPU}} + \frac{\text{Time}_{I/O}}{\text{Speedup}_{I/O}} - \frac{\text{Time}_{\text{overlap}}}{\text{Speedup}_{I/O}}$$

Let's try an example before explaining a limitation of these formulas.

Example   One workload takes 50 seconds to run, with the CPU being busy 30 seconds and the I/O being busy 30 seconds. How much time will the workload take if we replace the CPU with one that has four times the performance?

Answer   The total elapsed time is 50 seconds, yet the sum of CPU time and I/O time is 60 seconds. Thus the overlap time must be 10 seconds. Plugging into the formula:

$$\text{Time}_{\text{workload}} = \frac{\text{Time}_{\text{CPU}}}{\text{Speedup}_{\text{CPU}}} + \text{Time}_{I/O} - \frac{\text{Time}_{\text{overlap}}}{\text{Speedup}_{\text{CPU}}} = \frac{30}{4} + 30 - \frac{10}{4} = 35$$

This example uncovers a complication with this formula: How much of the time that the workload is busy on the faster CPU is overlapped with I/O? Figure 9.3 (page 504) shows three options. Depending on the resulting overlap after speedup, the time for the workload varies from 30 to 37.5 seconds.

In reality we can't know which is correct without measuring the workload on the faster CPU to see what overlap occurs. The formulas above assume option (c) in Figure 9.3; the overlap scales by the same speedup as the CPU, so we will call it $\text{Time}_{\text{scaled}}$ (rather than $\text{Time}_{\text{workload}}$). Maximum overlap assumes that as much of the overlap as possible is maintained, but that the new overlap cannot be larger than the original overlap or the CPU time after speedup. Minimum overlap assumes that as much of the overlap as possible is eliminated, but that the overlap time will not shrink by more than the time removed from the CPU or I/O time. If we introduce the abbreviations $\text{New}_{\text{CPU}} = \text{Time}_{\text{CPU}} / \text{Speedup}_{\text{CPU}}$ and $\text{New}_{I/O} = \text{Time}_{I/O} / \text{Speedup}_{I/O}$, the time of the workload for maximum overlap ($\text{Time}_{\text{best}}$) and minimum overlap ($\text{Time}_{\text{worst}}$) can be written as:

$$\text{Time}_{\text{best}} = \text{New}_{\text{CPU}} + \text{Time}_{I/O} - \text{Minimum}\,(\text{Time}_{\text{overlap}}, \text{New}_{\text{CPU}})$$

$$\text{Time}_{\text{worst}} = \text{New}_{\text{CPU}} + \text{Time}_{I/O} - \text{Maximum}\,(0, \text{Time}_{\text{overlap}} - (\text{Time}_{\text{CPU}} - \text{New}_{\text{CPU}}))$$

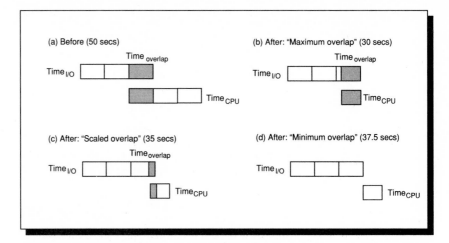

FIGURE 9.3 The original overlap in the example above (a) and three interpretations of overlap after speedup. Each block represents 10 seconds, except that the block for the new CPU time is 7.5 seconds. The overlapped portions of Time$_{CPU}$ and Time$_{I/O}$ are shaded. (b) shows the new Time$_{CPU}$ overlapping completely with I/O, giving a time of the workload of 30 seconds. (c) shows the overlap of the Time$_{CPU}$ is scaled with Speedup$_{CPU}$, giving a total of 35 seconds, with 2.5 seconds of overlapped execution. (d) shows no overlap with I/O, so the total is 37.5 seconds.

Example

Answer

Calculate the three time predictions for workload B in Figure 9.2

$$\text{Time}_{\text{best}} = \frac{10}{5} + 4 - \text{Minimum}\left(\frac{10}{5}, 4\right) = 2 + 4 - 2 = 4$$

$$\text{Time}_{\text{scaled}} = \frac{10}{5} + 4 - \frac{4}{5} = 2 + 4 - 0.8 = 5.2$$

$$\text{Time}_{\text{worst}} = \frac{10}{5} + 4 - \text{Maximum}\left(0, 4 - (10 - \frac{10}{5})\right) = 2 + 4 - 0 = 6$$

Sometimes changes will be made to both the CPU and the I/O system. The formulas become:

$$\text{Time}_{\text{scaled}} = \text{New}_{\text{CPU}} + \text{New}_{\text{I/O}} - \frac{\text{Time}_{\text{overlap}}}{\text{Maximum}(\text{Speedup}_{\text{CPU}}, \text{Speedup}_{\text{I/O}})}$$

$$\text{Time}_{\text{best}} = \text{New}_{\text{CPU}} + \text{New}_{\text{I/O}} - \text{Minimum}(\text{Time}_{\text{overlap}}, \text{New}_{\text{CPU}}, \text{New}_{\text{I/O}})$$

$$\text{Time}_{\text{worst}} = \text{New}_{\text{CPU}} + \text{New}_{\text{I/O}} - \text{Max}(0, \text{Time}_{\text{overlap}} - \text{Max}(\text{Time}_{\text{CPU}} - \text{New}_{\text{CPU}}, \text{Time}_{\text{I/O}} - \text{New}_{\text{I/O}}))$$

The formula for scaled overlap says that the overlap period is reduced by the larger of the two speedups. The formula for maximum overlap ($\text{Time}_{\text{best}}$) says that as much overlap as possible is retained, but the new overlap cannot be larger than the original overlap or the CPU or I/O time after speedup. Finally, the formula for minimum overlap ($\text{Time}_{\text{worst}}$) says that the overlap is reduced by the larger of the time removed from the CPU time and the time removed from the I/O time (but that the overlap time cannot be less than 0). Figure 9.4 shows the three examples of speedup where both the I/O and CPU are improved.

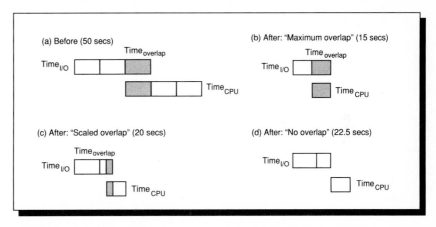

FIGURE 9.4 **Time for workload in Figure 9.3(a) with Speedup$_{\text{CPU}}$ = 4 and Speedup$_{\text{I/O}}$ = 2.**

Let's look at a detailed example showing speedup of both the CPU and I/O.

Example

Suppose a workload on the current systems takes 64 seconds. The CPU is busy the whole time, and the channels connecting the I/O devices to the CPU are busy 36 seconds. The computer manager is considering two upgrade options: either a single CPU that has twice the performance, or two CPUs that have twice the throughput and twice as many channels. The time of the actual I/O devices is so small it can be ignored. For the dual CPU option assume that the workload can be evenly spread between the CPUs and channels. What is the performance improvement for each option?

Answer

Since there is no change to the I/O system with the single faster CPU, time for the workload assuming scaled overlap is then simply

$$\text{Time}_{\text{scaled}} = \frac{\text{Time}_{\text{CPU}}}{\text{Speedup}_{\text{CPU}}} + \text{Time}_{\text{I/O}} - \frac{\text{Time}_{\text{overlap}}}{\text{Speedup}_{\text{CPU}}}$$

$$= \frac{64}{2} + 36 - \frac{36}{2} = 32 + 36 - 18 = 50$$

For the dual CPU with more channels,

$$\text{Time}_{\text{scaled}} = $$

$$\frac{\text{Time}_{\text{CPU}}}{\text{Speedup}_{\text{CPU}}} + \frac{\text{Time}_{\text{I/O}}}{\text{Speedup}_{\text{I/O}}} - \frac{\text{Time}_{\text{overlap}}}{\text{Maximum}(\text{Speedup}_{\text{CPU}}, \text{Speedup}_{\text{I/O}})}$$

$$= \frac{64}{2} + \frac{36}{2} - \frac{36}{\text{Maximum}(2, 2)} = 32 + 18 - 18 = 32$$

Assuming scaled overlap, the dual CPU is more than 50% faster. Using best-case scaling, the dual CPU is 13% faster, while worst-case scaling suggests it is 39% faster.

As these examples demonstrate, we need improvement in I/O performance to match the improvement in CPU performance if we are to achieve faster computer systems. We can now examine metrics of I/O devices to understand how to improve their performance and thus the whole system.

9.3 | I/O Performance Measures

I/O performance has measures that have no counterparts in CPU design. One of these is diversity: Which I/O devices can connect to the computer system? Another is capacity: How many I/O devices can connect to a computer system?

In addition to these unique measures, the traditional measures of performance, response time and throughput also apply to I/O. (I/O throughput is sometimes called "I/O bandwidth" and response time is sometimes called "latency.") The next two figures offer insight into how response time and throughput trade off against each other. Figure 9.5 shows the simple producer-server model. The producer creates tasks to be performed and places them in the queue; the server takes tasks from the queue and performs them.

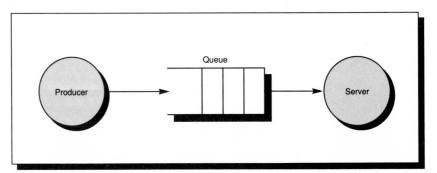

FIGURE 9.5 The traditional producer-server model of response time and throughput.
Response time begins when a task is placed in the queue and ends when it is completed by the server. Throughput is the number of tasks completed by the server in unit time.

Response time is defined as the time a task takes from the moment it is placed in the queue until the server finishes the task. Throughput is simply the average number of tasks completed by the server over a time period. To get the highest possible throughput, the server should never be idle, and thus the queue should never be empty. Response time, on the other hand, counts time spent in the queue and is therefore minimized by the queue being empty.

Another measure of I/O performance is the interference of I/O with CPU execution. Transferring data may interfere with the execution of another process. There is also overhead due to handling I/O interrupts. Our concern here is how many more clock cycles a process will take because of I/O for another process.

Throughput Versus Response Time

Figure 9.6 shows throughput versus response time (or latency), for a typical I/O system. The knee of the curve is the area where a little more throughput results in much longer response time or, conversely, a little shorter response time results in much lower throughput.

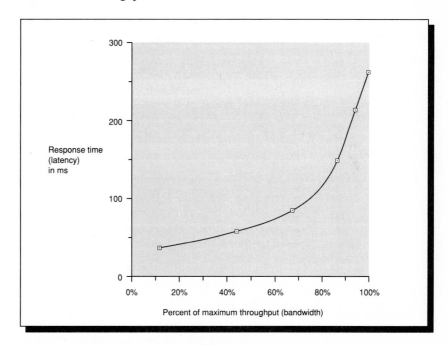

FIGURE 9.6 Throughput versus response time. Latency is normally reported as response time. Note that absolute minimum response time achieves only 11% of the throughput while the response time for 100% throughput takes seven times the minimum response time. Chen [1989] collected these data for an array of magnetic disks.

Life would be simpler if improving performance always meant improvements in both response time and throughput. Adding more servers, as in Figure 9.7, increases throughput: By spreading data across two disks instead of one, tasks may be serviced in parallel. Alas, this does not help response time, unless the workload is held constant and the time in the queues is reduced because of more resources.

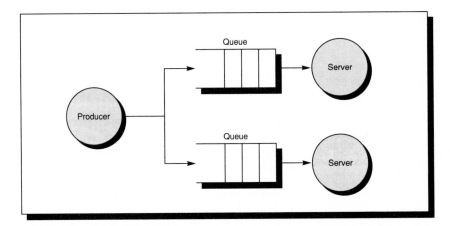

FIGURE 9.7   The single-producer, single-server model of Figure 9.5 is extended with another server and queue. This increases I/O system throughput and takes less time to service producer tasks. Increasing the number of servers is a common technique in I/O systems. There is a potential imbalance problem with two queues; unless data is placed perfectly in the queues, sometimes one server will be idle with an empty queue while the other server is busy with many tasks in its queue.

How does the architect balance these conflicting demands? If the computer is interacting with human beings, Figure 9.8 suggests an answer. This figure presents the results of two studies of interactive environments, one keyboard oriented and one graphical. An interaction or *transaction* with a computer is divided into three parts:

1. *Entry time*: The time for the user to enter the command. In the graphics system in Figure 9.8 it took 0.25 seconds on average to enter the command versus 4.0 seconds for the conventional system.

2. *System response time*: The time between when the user enters the command and the complete response is displayed.

3. *Think time*: The time from the reception of the response until the user begins to enter the next command.

The sum of these three parts is called the *transaction time*. Several studies report that user productivity is inversely proportional to transaction time; transactions per hour measures the work completed per hour by the user.

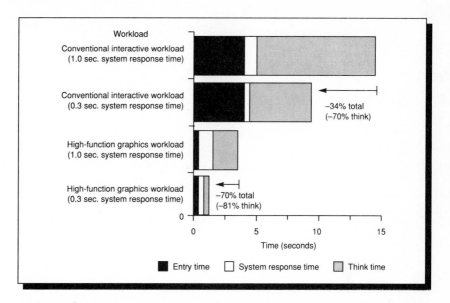

FIGURE 9.8   A user transaction with an interactive computer divided into entry time, system response time, and user think time for a conventional system and graphics system. The entry times are the same independent of system response time. The entry time was 4 seconds for the conventional system and 0.25 seconds for the graphics system. (From Brady [1986].)

The results in Figure 9.8 show that reduction in response time actually decreases transaction time by more than just the response time reduction: Cutting system response time by 0.7 seconds saves 4.9 seconds (34%) from the conventional transaction and 2.0 seconds (70%) from the graphics transaction. This implausible result is explained by human nature; people need less time to think when given a faster response.

Whether these results are explained as a better match to the human attention span or getting people "on a roll," several studies report this behavior. In fact, as computer responses drop below a second, productivity seems to make a more than linear jump. Figure 9.9 (page 510) compares transactions per hour (the inverse of transaction time) of a novice, an average engineer, and an expert performing physical design tasks at graphics displays. System response time magnified talent: a novice with subsecond response time was as productive as an experienced professional with slower response, and the experienced engineer in turn could outperform the expert with a similar advantage in response time. In all cases the number of transactions per hour jumps more than linearly with subsecond response time.

Since humans may be able to get much more work done per day with better response time, it is possible to attach an economic benefit to the customer of lowering response time into the subsecond range [IBM 1982], thereby helping the architect decide how to tip the balance between response time and throughput.

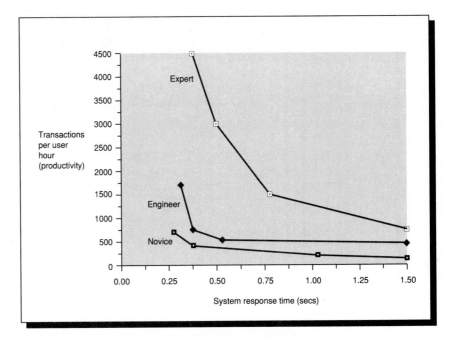

FIGURE 9.9 Transactions per hour versus computer response time for a novice, experienced engineer, and expert doing physical design on a graphics system. Transactions per hour is a measure of productivity. (From IBM [1982].)

Examples of Measurements of I/O Performance— Magnetic Disks

Benchmarks are needed to evaluate I/O performance, just as they are needed to evaluate CPU performance. We begin with benchmarks for magnetic disks. Three traditional applications of disks are with large-scale scientific problems, transaction processing, and file systems.

Supercomputer I/O Benchmarks

Supercomputer I/O is dominated by accesses to large files on magnetic disks. For example, Bucher and Hayes [1980] benchmarked supercomputer I/O using 8-MB sequential file transfers. Many supercomputer installations run batch jobs, each of which may last for hours. In these situations, I/O consists of one large read followed by writes to snapshot the state of the computation should the computer crash. As a result, supercomputer I/O in many cases consists of more output than input. Some models of Cray Research computers have such limited main memory that programmers must break their programs into overlays and swap them to disk (see Section 8.5 of Chapter 8), which also causes large sequential transfers. Thus, the overriding supercomputer I/O measure is data throughput: number of bytes per second that can be transferred between supercomputer main memory and disks during large transfers.

Transaction Processing I/O Benchmarks

In contrast, *transaction processing* (TP) is chiefly concerned with *I/O rate*: the number of disk accesses per second, as opposed to *data rate*, measured as bytes of data per second. TP generally involves changes to a large body of shared information from many terminals, with the TP system guaranteeing proper behavior on a failure. If, for example, a bank's computer fails when a customer withdraws money, the TP system would guarantee that the account is debited if the customer received the money and that the account is unchanged if the money was not received. Airline reservations systems as well as banks are traditional customers for TP.

Two dozen members of the TP community conspired to form a benchmark for the industry and, to avoid the wrath of their legal departments, published the report anonymously [1985]. This benchmark, called DebitCredit, simulates bank tellers and has as its bottom line the number of debit/credit transactions per second (TPS); in 1990, the TPS for high-end machines is about 300. The DebitCredit performs the operation of a customer depositing or withdrawing money. The performance measurement is the peak TPS, with 95% of the transactions having less than a one-second response time. The DebitCredit computes the cost per TPS, based on the five-year cost of the computer-system hardware and software. Disk I/O for DebitCredit is random reads and writes of 100-byte records along with occasional sequential writes.

Depending on how cleverly the transaction-processing system is designed, each transaction results in between two and ten disk I/Os and takes between 5,000 and 20,000 CPU instructions per disk I/O. The variation largely depends on the efficiency of the transaction processing software, although in part it depends on the extent to which disk accesses can be avoided by keeping information in main memory. The benchmark requires that for TPS to increase, the number of tellers and the size of the account file must also increase. Figure 9.10 shows this unusual relationship in which more TPS requires more users.

TPS	Number of ATMs	Account-file size
10	1,000	0.1 GB
100	10,000	1.0 GB
1,000	100,000	10.0 GB
10,000	1,000,000	100.0 GB

FIGURE 9.10 Relationship among TPS, tellers, and account-file size. The DebitCredit benchmark requires that the computer system handle more tellers and larger account files before it can claim a higher transaction-per-second milestone. The benchmark is supposed to include "terminal handling" overhead, but this metric is sometimes ignored.

This is to ensure that the benchmark really measures disk I/O; otherwise a large main memory dedicated to a database cache with a small number of accounts would unfairly yield a very high TPS. (Another perspective is the number of accounts must grow since a person is not likely to use the bank more frequently just because the bank has a faster computer!)

File System I/O Benchmarks

File systems, for which disks are mainly used in timesharing systems, have a different access pattern. Ousterhout et al. [1985] measured a UNIX file system and found that 80% of accesses to files of less than 10 KB and 90% of **all** file accesses were sequential. The distribution by type of file access was 67% reads, 27% writes, and 6% read-write accesses. In 1988, Howard et al. [1988] proposed a file-system benchmark that is becoming popular. Their paper describes five phases of the benchmark, using 70 files with a total size of 200 KB:

MakeDir—Constructs a target subtree that is identical in structure to the source subtree.

Copy—Copies every file from the source subtree to the target subtree.

ScanDir—Recursively traverses the target subtree and examines the status of every file in it. It does not actually read the contents of any file.

ReadAll—Scans every byte of every file in the target subtree once.

Make—Compiles and links all the files in the target subtree. [p. 55]

The file-system measurements of Howard et al. [1988], like those of Ousterhout et al. [1985], found the ratio of disk reads to writes to be about 2:1. This benchmark reflects that measure.

9.4 | Types of I/O Devices

Now that we have covered measurements of I/O performance, let's describe the devices themselves. While the computing model has changed little since 1950, I/O devices have become rich and diverse. Three characteristics are useful in organizing this disparate conglomeration:

- *Behavior*—input (read once), output (write only, cannot be read), or storage (can be reread and usually rewritten)

- *Partner*—either a human or a machine is at the other end of the I/O device, either feeding data on input or reading data on output

- *Data rate*—the peak rate at which data can be transferred between the I/O device and the main memory or CPU

Using these characteristics, a keyboard is an input device used by a human with a peak data rate of about 10 bytes per second. Figure 9.11 shows some of the I/O devices connected to computers.

The advantage of designing I/O devices for humans is that the performance target is fixed. Figure 9.12 shows the I/O performance of people.

Device	Behavior	Partner	Data rate (KB/sec)
Keyboard	Input	Human	0.01
Mouse	Input	Human	0.02
Voice input	Input	Human	0.02
Scanner	Input	Human	200.00
Voice output	Output	Human	0.60
Line printer	Output	Human	1.00
Laser printer	Output	Human	100.00
Graphics display	Output	Human	30,000.00
(CPU to frame buffer)	Output	Human	200.00
Network-terminal	Input or output	Machine	0.05
Network-LAN	Input or output	Machine	200.00
Optical disk	Storage	Machine	500.00
Magnetic tape	Storage	Machine	2,000.00
Magnetic disk	Storage	Machine	2,000.00

FIGURE 9.11 Examples of I/O devices categorized by behavior, partner, and data rate. This is the raw data rate of the device rather than the rate an application would see. Storage devices can be further distinguished by whether they support sequential access (e.g., tapes) or random access (e.g., disks). Note that networks can act either as input or output devices but, unlike storage, cannot reread the same information.

Human organ	I/O rate (KB/sec)	I/O latency (ms)
Ear	8.000–60.000	10
Eye—reading text	0.030–0.375	10
Eye—pattern recognition	125.000	10
Hand—typing	0.010–0.020	100
Voice	0.003–0.015	100

FIGURE 9.12 Peak I/O rates for people. Input via seeing patterns is our highest I/O rate; hence the popularity of graphic output devices. Maberly [1966] says the average reading speed is 28 bytes per second and the maximum is 375 bytes per second. The telephone company sets a 170-ms limit to the time between when an operator pushes a button to accept a call until a voice path must be established. The phone company transmits voice at 8 KB per second. (None of these parameters are expected to change, unless anabolic steroids become a breakfast supplement!)

To put the data rates of each device into perspective, Figure 9.13 shows the relative peak memory bandwidth needed to support each device, assuming a computer had exactly one of each device transferring at its peak rate.

Rather than discuss the characteristics of all I/O devices, we will concentrate on the three devices with the highest data rates: magnetic disks, graphics displays, and local area networks. These are also the devices that have the highest leverage on user productivity. In this chapter we are not talking about floppy disks, but the original "hard" disks. These magnetic disks are what IBM calls *DASD*s, for *Direct-Access Storage Devices*.

Magnetic Disks

I think Silicon Valley was misnamed. If you look back at the dollars shipped in products in the last decade there has been more revenue from magnetic disks than from silicon. They ought to rename the place Iron Oxide Valley.

Al Hoagland, one of the pioneers of magnetic disks (1982)

In spite of repeated attacks by new technologies, magnetic disks have dominated secondary storage since 1965. Magnetic disks play two roles in computer systems:

- Long-term, nonvolatile storage for files, even when no programs are running

- A level of the memory hierarchy below main memory used for virtual memory during program execution (see Section 8.5 in Chapter 8)

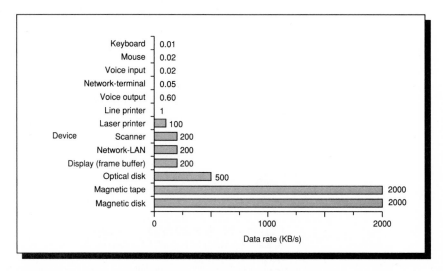

FIGURE 9.13   I/O devices sorted from lowest data rate to highest. The data rate for the graphics display is from the CPU to the frame buffer because the CPU isn't involved in the transfer from the frame buffer to the display (see Graphics Displays subsection below).

As descriptions of magnetic disks can be found in countless books, we will only list the key characteristics with the terms illustrated in Figure 9.14. A magnetic disk consists of a collection of platters (1 to 20), rotating on a spindle at about 3600 revolutions per minute (RPM). These platters are metal disks covered with magnetic recording material on both sides. Disk diameters vary by a factor of five, from 14 to 2.5 inches. Traditionally, the widest disks have the highest performance, and the smallest disks have the lowest cost per disk drive.

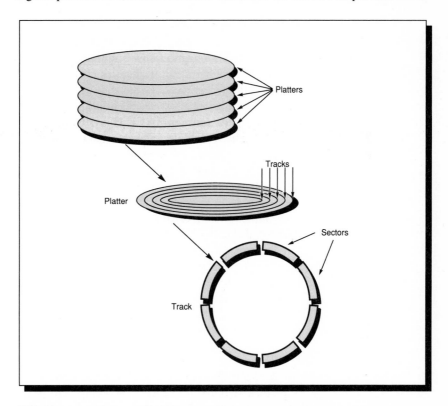

FIGURE 9.14 Disks are organized into platters, tracks, and sectors. Both sides of a platter are coated so that information can be stored on both surfaces.

Each disk surface is divided into concentric circles, designated *tracks*. There are typically 500 to 2000 tracks per surface. Each track in turn is divided into *sectors* that contain the information; each track might have 32 sectors. The sector is the smallest unit that can be read or written. The sequence recorded on the magnetic media is a sector number, a gap, the information for that sector including error correction code, a gap, the sector number of the next sector, and so on. Traditionally all tracks have the same number of sectors; the outer tracks, which are longer, record information at a lower density than the inner tracks. Recording more sectors on the outer tracks than on the inner tracks, called *constant bit density*, is becoming more widespread with the advent of intelligent interface standards such as SCSI (see Section 9.5). IBM mainframe disks allow users to select the size of the sectors, while almost all other systems fix the size of the sector.

To read and write information into a sector, a movable *arm* containing a *read/write head* is located over each surface. Bits are recorded using a run-length limited code, which improves the recording density of the magnetic media. The arms for each surface are connected together and move in conjunction, so that every arm is over the same track of every surface. The term *cylinder* is used to refer to all the tracks under the arms at a given point on all surfaces.

To read or write a sector, the disk controller sends a command to move the arm over the proper track. This operation is called a *seek*, and the time to move the arm to the desired track is called *seek time*. Average seek time is the subject of considerable misunderstanding. Disk manufacturers report minimum seek time, maximum seek time, and average seek time in the manuals. The first two are easy to measure, but average was open to wide interpretation. The industry decided to calculate average seek time as the sum of the time for all possible seeks divided by the number of possible seeks. Average seek times are advertised to be 12 ms to 20 ms, but depending on the application and operating system the actual average seek time may be only 25% to 33% of the advertised number, due to locality of disk references. Section 9.10 has a detailed example.

The time for the requested sector to rotate under the head is the *rotation latency* or *rotational delay*. Most disks rotate at 3600 RPM, and an average latency to the desired information is halfway around the disk; the average rotation time for most disks is therefore

$$\text{Average rotation time} = \frac{0.5}{3600 \text{ RPM}} = 0.0083 \text{ sec} = 8.3 \text{ ms}$$

The next component of a disk access, *transfer time,* is the time to transfer a block of bits, typically a sector, under the read-write head. This is a function of the block size, rotation speed, recording density of a track, and speed of the electronics connecting disk to computer. Transfer rates in 1990 are typically 1 to 4 MB per second.

In addition to the disk drive, there is usually also a device called a *disk controller*. Between the disk controller and main memory is a hierarchy of controllers and data paths, whose complexity varies with the cost of the computer (see Section 9.9). Since the transfer time is often a small portion of a full disk access, the controller in higher performance systems disconnects the data paths from the disks while they are seeking so that other disks can transfer their data to memory.

Thus, the final component of disk-access time is *controller time*, which is the overhead the controller imposes in performing an I/O access. When referring to performance of a disk in a computer system, the time spent waiting for a disk to become free (*queueing delay*) is added to this time.

Example

What is the average time to read or write a 512-byte sector for a typical disk today? The advertised average seek time is 20 ms, the transfer rate is 1MB/sec, and the controller overhead is 2 ms. Assume the disk is idle so that there is no queuing delay.

Answer

Average disk access is equal to average seek time + average rotational delay + transfer time + controller overhead. Using the calculated, average seek time, the answer is

$$20 \text{ ms} + 8.3 \text{ ms} + \frac{0.5 \text{ KB}}{1.0 \text{ MB/sec}} + 2 \text{ ms} = 20 + 8.3 + 0.5 + 2 = 30.8 \text{ ms}$$

Assuming the measured, average seek time is 25% of the calculated number, the answer is

$$5 \text{ ms} + 8.3 \text{ ms} + 0.5 \text{ ms} + 2 \text{ ms} = 15.8 \text{ ms}$$

Figure 9.15 shows characteristics of magnetic disks for four manufacturers. Large-diameter drives have many more megabytes to amortize the cost of electronics, so the traditional wisdom was that they had the lowest cost per megabyte. But this advantage is offset for the small drives by the much higher sales volume, which lowers manufacturing costs: 1990 OEM prices are $2 to $3

Characteristics	IBM 3380	Fujitsu M2361A	Imprimis Wren IV	Conner CP3100
Disk diameter (inches)	14	10.5	5.25	3.5
Formatted data capacity (MB)	7500	600	344	100
MTTF (hours)	52,000	20,000	40,000	30,000
Number of arms/box	4	1	1	1
Maximum I/Os/second/arm	50	40	35	30
Typical I/Os/second/arm	30	24	28	20
Maximum I/Os/second/box	200	40	35	30
Typical I/Os/second/box	120	24	28	20
Transfer rate (MB/sec)	3	2.5	1.5	1
Power/box (W)	1,650	640	35	10
MB/W	1.1	0.9	9.8	10.0
Volume (cu. ft.)	24	3.4	0.1	.03
MB/cu. ft.	310	180	3440	3330

FIGURE 9.15 Characteristics of magnetic disks from four manufacturers. Comparison of IBM 3380 disk model AK4 for mainframe computers, Fujitsu M2361A "Super Eagle" disk for minicomputers, Imprimis Wren IV disk for workstations, and Conner Peripherals CP3100 disk for personal computers. Maximum I/Os/second signifies maximum number of average seeks and average rotates for a single sector access. (Table from Katz, Patterson, and Gibson [1990].)

per megabyte, almost independent of width. The small drives also have advantages in power and volume. The price of a megabyte of disk storage in 1990 is 10 to 30 times cheaper than the price of a megabyte of DRAM in a system.

The Future of Magnetic Disks

The disk industry has concentrated on improving the capacity of disks. Improvement in capacity is customarily expressed as *areal density*, measured in bits per square inch:

$$\text{Areal density} = \frac{\text{Tracks}}{\text{Inch}} \text{ on a disk surface} * \frac{\text{Bits}}{\text{Inch}} \text{ on a track}$$

Areal density can be predicted according to the *maximum areal density* (MAD) formula:

$$\text{MAD} = 10^{(\text{year}-1971)/10} \text{ million bits per square inch}$$

Thus, storage density improves by a factor of 10 every decade, doubling density every three years.

Cost per megabyte has dropped consistently at 20% to 25% per year, with smaller drives playing the larger role in this improvement. Because it is easier to

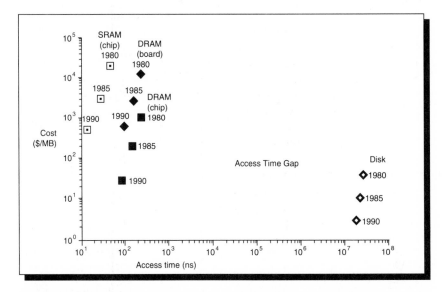

FIGURE 9.16   Cost versus access time for SRAM, DRAM, and magnetic disk in 1980, 1985, and 1990. (Note the difference in cost between a DRAM chip and DRAM chips packaged on a board and ready to plug into a computer.) The two-order-of-magnitude gap in cost and five-order-of-magnitude gap in access times between semiconductor memory and rotating magnetic disk has inspired a host of competing technologies to try to fill it. So far, such attempts have been made obsolete before production by improvements in magnetic disks, DRAMs, or both.

spin the smaller mass, smaller diameter disks save power as well as volume. Smaller drives also have fewer cylinders so the seek distances are shorter. In 1990, 5.25-inch or 3.5-inch drives are probably the leading technology, while the future may see even smaller drives. We can expect significant savings in volume and power, but little in speed. Increasing density (bits per inch on a track) has improved transfer times, and there has been some small improvement in seek speed. Rotation speeds have been steady at 3600 RPM for a decade, but some manufacturers plan to go to 5400 RPM in the early 1990s.

As mentioned earlier, magnetic disks have been challenged many times for supremacy of secondary storage. One reason has been the fabled *Access Time Gap* as shown in Figure 9.16. Many a scientist has tried to invent a technology to fill that gap. Let's look at some of the recent attempts.

Using DRAMs as Disks

A current challenger to disks for dominance of secondary storage is *solid state disks* (SSDs), built from DRAMs with a battery to make the system nonvolatile; and *expanded storage* (ES), a large memory that allows only block transfers to or from main memory. ES acts like a software-controlled cache (the CPU stalls during the block transfer) while SSD involves the operating system just like a transfer from magnetic disks. The advantages of SSD and ES are trivial seek times, higher potential transfer rate, and possibly higher reliability. Unlike just a larger main memory, SSDs and ESs are autonomous: They require special commands to access their storage, and thus are "safe" from some software errors that write over main memory. The block-access nature of SSD and ES allows error correction to be spread over more words, which means lower cost or greater error recovery. For example, IBM's ES uses the greater error recovery to allow it to be constructed from less reliable (and less expensive) DRAMs without sacrificing product availability. SSDs, unlike main memory and ES, may be shared by multiple CPUs because they function as separate units. Placing DRAMs in an I/O device rather than memory is also one way to get around the address-space limits of the current 32-bit computers. The disadvantage of SSD and ES is cost, which is at least ten times per megabyte the cost of magnetic disks.

Optical Disks

Another challenger to magnetic disks is *optical compact disks* or CDs. The *CD/ROM* is removable and inexpensive to manufacture, but it is a read-only media. The newer CD/writable is also removable, but has a high cost per megabyte and low performance. A common misperception about *write-once optical disks* is that once they are written, the information cannot be destroyed; in fact, write once means one reliable write and then a "fuzzy" bitwise ORing of the previous and new data.

So far, magnetic disk challengers have never had a product to market at the right time. By the time a new product ships, disks have made advances as predicted by MAD formula, and costs have dropped accordingly. Optical disks, however, may have the potential to compete with new tape technologies for archival storage.

Disk Arrays

One other future candidate for optimizing storage is not a new technology, but a new organization of disk storage—arrays of small and inexpensive disks. The argument for arrays is that since price per megabyte is independent of disk size, potential throughput can be increased by having many disk drives and, hence, many disk arms. Simply spreading data over multiple disks automatically forces accesses to several disks. (While arrays improve throughput, latency is not necessarily improved.) The drawback to arrays is that with more devices, reliability drops: N devices generally have $1/N$ the reliability of a single device.

Reliability and Availability

This brings us to two terms that are often confused—reliability and availability. The term reliability is commonly used incorrectly to mean availability; if something breaks, but the user can still use the system, it seems as if the system still "works," and hence it seems more reliable. Here is the proper distinction:

Reliability—is anything broken?

Availability—is the system still available to the user?

Adding hardware can therefore improve availability (for example, ECC on memory), but it cannot improve reliability (the DRAM is still broken). Reliability can only be improved by bettering environmental conditions, by building from more reliable components, or by building with fewer components. Another term, *data integrity*, refers to always reporting when information is lost when a failure occurs; this is very important to some applications.

So, while a disk array can never be more reliable than a smaller number of larger disks when each disk has the same failure rate, availability can be improved by adding redundant disks. That is, if a single disk fails, the lost information can be reconstructed from redundant information. The only danger is in getting another disk failure between the time a disk fails and the time it is replaced (termed *mean time to repair* or MTTR). Since the *mean time to failure* (MTTF) of disks is three to five years, and the MTTR is measured in hours, redundancy can make the availability of 100 disks much higher than that of a single disk.

Since disk failures are self-identifying, information can be reconstructed from just parity: The good disks plus the parity disk can be used to calculate the information that is on the failed disk. Hence, the cost of higher availability is

$1/N$, where N is the number of disks protected by parity. Just as direct-mapped associative placement in caches can be considered a special case of set-associative placement (see Section 8.4), the *mirroring* or *shadowing* of disks can be considered the special case of one data disk and one parity disk (N=1). Parity can be accomplished by duplicating the data, so mirrored disks have the advantage of simplifying parity calculation. Duplicating data also means that the controller can improve read performance by reading from the disk of the pair that has the shortest seek distance, although this optimization is at the cost of write performance because the arms of the pair of disks are no longer always over the same track. Of course, the redundancy of $N = 1$ has the highest overhead for increasing disk availability.

The higher throughput, measured either as megabytes per second or as I/Os per second, and the ability to recover from failures make disk arrays attractive. When combined with the advantages of smaller volume and lower power of small-diameter drives, redundant arrays of small or inexpensive drives may play a larger role in future disk systems. The current drawback is the added complexity of a controller for disk arrays.

Graphics Displays

Through computer displays I have landed an airplane on the deck of a moving carrier, observed a nuclear particle hit a potential well, flown in a rocket at nearly the speed of light and watched a computer reveal its innermost workings.

Ivan Sutherland (the "father" of computer graphics), quoted in
"Computer Software for Graphics," *Scientific American* (1984)

While magnetic disks may dominate throughput and cost of I/O devices, the most fascinating I/O device is the graphics display. Based on television technology, a *raster cathode ray tube* (CRT) *display* scans an image out one line at a time, 30 to 60 times per second. At this *refresh rate* the human eye doesn't notice a "flicker" on the screen. The image is composed of a matrix of picture elements, or *pixels*, which can be represented as a matrix of bits, called a *bit map*. Depending on size of screen and resolution, the display matrix consists of 340*512 to 1560*1280 pixels. For black and white displays, often 0 is black and 1 is white. For displays that support over 100 different shades of black and white, sometimes called *gray-scale* displays, 8 bits per pixel are required. A color display might use 8 bits for each of the three primary colors (red, blue, and green), for 24 bits per pixel.

The hardware support for graphics consists mainly of a *raster refresh buffer*, or *frame buffer*, to store the bit map. The image to be represented on screen is stored into the frame buffer, and the bit pattern per pixel is read out to the graphics display at the refresh rate. Figure 9.17 (page 522) shows a frame buffer with four bits per pixel and Figure 9.18 (page 522) shows how the buffer is connected to the bus.

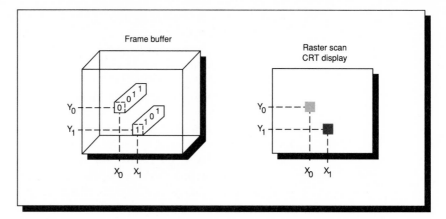

FIGURE 9.17 Each coordinate in the frame buffer on the left determines the shade of the corresponding coordinate for the raster scan CRT display on the right. Pixel (x_0, y_0) contains the bit pattern 0011, which is a lighter shade of gray on the screen than the bit pattern 1101 in pixel (x_1, y_1).

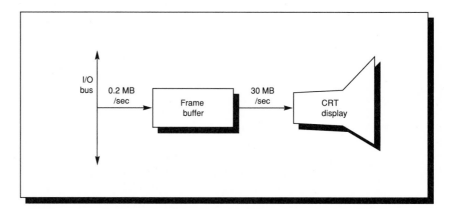

FIGURE 9.18 The frame buffer is connected to both the I/O bus and the display. Because of the high data rate from the buffer to the display, the frame buffer is frequently dual ported.

The goal of the bit map is to faithfully represent what is on the screen. As the computer switches from one image to another, the screen may look "splotchy" during the change. Here are two ways of dealing with this:

■ Change the frame buffer only during the "vertical blanking interval." This is the time the gun in the raster CRT display takes to go back to the upper-left-hand corner before starting to paint the pixels of the next image. This takes 1 to 2 ms of every 16 ms at the 60-Hz refresh rate each time the screen is painted.

- If the vertical blanking interval is not long enough, the frame buffer can be double buffered, so that one is read while the other is being written. This way, images in sequence (as in animation) are drawn in alternate frame buffers. Double buffering, of course, doubles the cost of the memory in the frame buffer.

From the point of view of the CPU, graphics is logically output only. But the frame buffer is capable of being read as well as written, permitting operations to be performed directly on the screen images. These operations are called *bit blts*, for bit block transfer. Bit blts are commonly used for operations such as moving a window or changing the shape of the cursor. A current debate in graphics architecture is whether reading the frame buffer is limited to the operating system or should user programs be able to read it as well.

Cost of Computer Graphics

The CRT monitor itself is based on television technology and is sensitive to consumer demand. Today prices vary from $100 for a black-and-white monitor to $15,000 for a large studio color monitor, not including memory. The amount of memory in a frame buffer depends directly on the size of the screen and the bits per pixel:

$$340*512*1 \text{ bits} = 21.5 \text{ KB}$$

$$1280*1024*24 \text{ bits} = 3840 \text{ KB}$$

(By the way, this bottom dimension is the proposed size for high-definition television.) Note that the memory cost is doubled if double buffering is used.

To reduce costs of a color frame buffer, many systems use a two-level representation that takes advantage of the fact that few pictures need the full pallet of possible colors (see Figure 9.19 on page 524).

The intermediate level contains the full color width of, say, 24 bits and a large collection of the possible colors that can appear on the screen—256 different colors, for example. While this collection is large, it is still much smaller than 2^{24}. This intermediary table has been variously named a *color map*, *color table*, or *video look-up table*. Each pixel need have only enough bits to indicate a color in the color map. As a simple example, Figure 9.19 uses a 4-word color map, which means the frame buffer needs only 2 bits per pixel. The savings for a full-sized color display with a 256-color map is

$$1280*1024*24 - (1280*1024*8 + 256*24)$$

$$= 3,840 \text{ KB} - (1280 \text{ KB} + .75 \text{ KB}) \approx 2560 \text{ KB}$$

This amounts to a threefold reduction in memory size. In 1990 a 256- by 24-bit color map and an analog interface to a color CRT fit in a single chip.

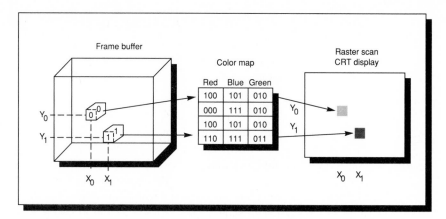

FIGURE 9.19   An example of a color map to reduce the cost of the frame buffer.
Suppose only nine bits per color are needed. Rather than store the full nine bits per pixel in the frame buffer, just enough bits per pixel are stored to index the table containing the unique colors in a picture. Only the color map has the nine bits for the colors in the display. Near photographic color pictures can be produced with about 125 colors using the right shades of the color spectrum; but at least 24 bits are needed to get the right shades! The color map is loaded by the application program, offering each picture its own palette of colors to chose from.

Performance Demands of Graphics Displays

The performance of graphics is determined by the frequency an application needs new images and by the quality of those images. The amount of information transferred from memory to the frame buffer depends on complexity of image, with a full color display requiring almost four megabytes. The transfer rate depends on the speed with which the image should be changed as well as the amount of information. Animation requires at least 15 changes per second for movement to appear smooth on a screen. For interactive graphics, the time to update the frame buffer measures the effectiveness of the application; for people to feel comfortable the total reaction time must be less than a second (see Figure 9.9, page 510). With a drawing system, the portion of the screen one is working on must change almost immediately, as human visual perception is on the order of 0.02 seconds. Figure 9.20 shows some sample graphics tasks and their performance requirements. Note that the frame buffer must have enough bandwidth to refresh the display **and** to allow the CPU to change the image being refreshed.

The high data rate—and the large market of graphics displays—has made a dual-ported DRAM chip popular. This chip has a serial I/O port and internal shift register that is connected to the display in a graphics application in addition to the traditional randomly addressed data port. This chip is so widely used in frame buffers that it is called a *video DRAM*.

Graphics tasks	Bandwidth requirements
Text editor—Scrolling text in window means moving all bits in half the frame buffer about 10 times per second.	0.8 MB/sec
VLSI design—Moving a portion of the design means moving all bits in half of a color frame buffer in less than 0.1 second.	6.3 MB/sec
Television commercial—Showing movie-quality images means changing 24 times per second.	90.0 MB/sec
Visualization of scientific data—About the same as a television commercial.	90.0 MB/sec

FIGURE 9.20   Graphics tasks and their performance requirements. VLSI design uses 8 bits of color while the television commercial and visualization use 24 bits. Bandwidth is measured at the frame buffer.

Future Directions in Graphics Displays

It is safe to predict that people will want better pictures in the future. They will want, for example, more lines on a screen and more bits per inch on a line to make sharper images, more bits per color to make more colorful images, and more bandwidth to allow animation.

To simplify the display of three-dimensional images, a z dimension per pixel can be added to the x and y coordinates. It says where the pixel is located from the viewer along a z axis (e.g., into the CRT). A 3D image starts with z set to the furthest possible location from the viewer and the color set to the background color. To get a proper 3D perspective, the z coordinate stored with the pixel in the frame buffer is checked before placing a color in a pixel. If the new color is closer, the old color is replaced and the z coordinate is updated; if it is further away, the new color is discarded. This scheme is called a *z buffer* approach to *hidden surface elimination*. It adds at least 8 bits per pixel, plus the performance cost of reading and comparing before writing a pixel. The Silicon Graphics 4D series of graphics workstations uses 16 bits for the z dimension in its pixels, meaning objects are assigned a 16-bit number to show how close they are to the viewer.

The increasing number of bits per DRAM chip reduces the number of chips needed in the frame buffer, as well as the number of chips that can simultaneously transfer bits to the screen. This is why video DRAMS are so popular. As capacity increases, the serial ports of video DRAMs will have to become faster and wider to match the demands of future graphics systems.

Networks

There is an old network saying: Bandwidth problems can be cured with money. Latency problems are harder because the speed of light is fixed—you can't bribe God.

David Clark, M.I.T.

Networks are the backbone of current computer systems; a new machine without an optional network interface would be ridiculed. By connecting computers electronically, networked computers have these advantages:

- *Communication*—Information is exchanged between computers at high speeds.

- *Resource sharing*—Rather than each machine having its own I/O devices, devices can be shared by computers on the network.

- *Nonlocal access*—By connecting I/O devices over long distances, users need not be near the computer they are using.

Figure 9.21 shows the characteristics of networks. These characteristics are illustrated below with three examples.

Distance	0.01 to 10,000 kilometers
Speed	0.001 MB/sec to 100 MB/sec
Topology	Bus, ring, star, tree
Shared lines	None (point-to-point) or shared (multidrop)

FIGURE 9.21   Range of network characteristics.

The RS232 standard provides a 0.3- to 19.2-Kbits-per-second *terminal network*. A central computer connects to many terminals over slow but cheap dedicated wires. These point-to-point connections form a star from the central computer, with each terminal ranging from 10 to 100 meters in distance from the computer.

The *local area network*, or LAN, is what is commonly meant today when people mention a network, and *Ethernet* is what most people mean when they mention a LAN. (Ethernet has in fact become such a common term that it is often used as a generic term for LAN.) The Ethernet is essentially a 10,000 Kbits-per-second bus that has no central control. Messages or *packets* are sent over the Ethernet in blocks that vary from 128 bytes to 1530 bytes and take 0.1 ms and 1.5 ms to send, respectively. Since there is no central control, all nodes "listen" to see if there is a message for that node. Without a central arbiter to decide who gets the bus, a computer first listens to make sure it doesn't send a message while another message is on the network. If the network is idle the node tries to send. Of course, some other node may decide to send at the same instant. Luckily, the computer can detect any resulting collisions by listening to what is sent. (Mixed messages will sound like garbage.) To avoid repeated head-on collisions, each node whose packet was trashed backs off a random time before resending. If Ethernets do not have high utilization, this simple approach to arbitration works well. Many LANs become overloaded through poor capacity planning, and response time and throughput can degrade rapidly at higher utilization.

The success of LANs has led to multiples of them at a single site. Connecting computers to separate Ethernets becomes necessary at a certain point because there is a limit to the number of nodes that can be active on a bus if effective communication speeds are to be achieved; one limit is 1024 nodes per Ethernet. There is also a physical limit to the distance of an Ethernet, usually about 1 kilometer. To allow Ethernets to work together, two kinds of devices have been created:

- A *bridge* connects two Ethernets. There are still two independent buses that can simultaneously send messages, but the bridge acts as a filter, allowing only those messages from nodes on one bus to nodes on the other bus to cross over the bridge.

- A *gateway* typically connects several Ethernets. It receives a message, looks up the destination address in a table, and then routes the message over the appropriate network to the proper node. This *routing table* can be changed during execution to reflect the state of the networks. Some use the term *router* instead of gateway since it is closer to the function performed.

When Ethernets are connected together with gateways they form an *Internet*.

Long-haul networks cover distances of 10 to 10,000 kilometers. The first and most famous long-haul network was the ARPANET (named after its funding agency, the Advanced Research Projects Agency of the U.S. government). It transferred at 50 Kbits per second and used point-to-point dedicated lines leased from telephone companies. The host computer talked to an *interface message processor* (IMP), which communicated over the telephone lines. The IMP took information and broke it into 1-Kbit packets. At each hop the packet was stored and then forwarded to the proper IMP according to the address in the packet. The destination IMP reassembled the packets into a message and then gave it to the host. *Fragmentation and reassembly*, as it was called, was done to reduce the latency due to the *store and forward delay*. Most networks today use this *packet switched* approach, where packets are individually routed from source to destination. Figure 9.22 (page 528) summarizes the performance, distance, and costs of these various networks.

While these networks have been presented here as alternatives, a computer system is really a hierarchy of networks, as Figure 9.23 (page 528) shows. To deal with this hierarchy of networks connecting machines that communicate differently, there must be a standard software interface to handle messages. These are called *protocols*, and are typically layered to interface with different levels of software in computer systems. The overhead of these protocols can eat up a significant portion of the network bandwidth.

Just as with disks in Figure 9.6 (page 507), there is a tradeoff of latency and throughput in networks. Small messages give the lowest latency in most networks, but they also result in lower network bandwidth; similarly, a network can achieve higher bandwidth at the cost of longer latency.

Network	Performance (Kbits / sec)	Distance (km)	Cable cost	Connect to network cost	Connector to computer cost
RS232	19	0.1	$0.25 /foot	$1–$5 /connector	$5 /serial port chip
Ethernet	10,000	1	$1–$5 /foot	$100 /transceiver	$50 /Ethernet interface chip
ARPANET	50	10,000	$10,000 /month	$50,000– $100,000/ IMP	$5,000–$10,000 /IMP connection

FIGURE 9.22   The performance, maximum distance, and costs of three example networks. An Internet is simply multiple Ethernets and a bridge, which costs about $2,000 to $5,000, or a gateway, which costs about $20,000 to $50,000.

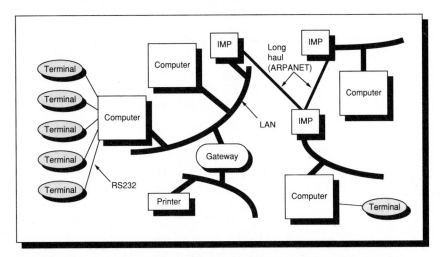

FIGURE 9.23   A computer system today participates in a hierarchy of networks. Ideally, the user is not aware of what network is being used in performing tasks. The gateway routes packets to a particular network, a network routes packets to a particular host computer, and the host computer routes packets to a particular process.

9.5 | Buses—Connecting I/O Devices to CPU/Memory

In a computer system, the various subsystems must have interfaces to one another; for instance, the memory and CPU need to communicate, as well as the CPU and I/O devices. This is commonly done with a *bus*. The bus serves as a shared communication link between the subsystems. The two major advantages of the bus organization are low cost and versatility. By defining a single interconnection scheme, new devices can easily be added, and peripherals may even be ported between computer systems that use a common bus. The cost is low, since a single set of wires is shared multiple ways.

The major disadvantage of a bus is that it creates a communication bottleneck, possibly limiting the maximum I/O throughput. When I/O must pass through a central bus this bandwidth limitation is as real as—and sometimes more severe than—memory bandwidth. In commercial systems, where I/O is very frequent, and in supercomputers, where the necessary I/O rates are very high because the CPU performance is high, designing a bus system capable of meeting the demands of the processor is a major challenge.

One reason bus design is so difficult is that the maximum bus speed is largely limited by physical factors: the length of the bus and the number of devices (and, hence, bus loading). These physical limits prevent arbitrary bus speedup. The desire for high I/O rates (low latency) and high I/O throughput can also lead to conflicting design requirements.

Buses are traditionally classified as *CPU–memory buses* or *I/O buses*. I/O buses may be lengthy, may have many types of devices connected to them, have a wide range in the data bandwidth of the devices connected to them (see Figure 9.1 on page 501), and normally follow a bus standard. CPU–memory buses, on the other hand, are short, generally high speed, and matched to the memory system to maximize memory–CPU bandwidth. During the design phase, the designer of a CPU–memory bus knows all the types of devices that must connect together, while the I/O bus designer must accept devices varying in latency and bandwidth capabilities. To lower costs, some computers have a single bus for both memory and I/O devices.

Let's consider a typical bus transaction. A *bus transaction* includes two parts: sending the address and receiving or sending the data. Bus transactions are usually defined by what they do to memory: A *read* transaction transfers data *from* memory (to either the CPU or an I/O device), and a *write* transaction writes data to the memory. In a read transaction, the address is first sent down the bus to the memory, together with the appropriate control signals indicating a read. The memory responds by returning the data on the bus with the appropriate control signals. A write transaction requires that the CPU or I/O device send both address and data and requires no return of data. Usually the CPU must wait between sending the address and receiving the data on a read, but the CPU often does not wait on writes.

The design of a bus presents several options, as Figure 9.24 (page 530) shows. Like the rest of the computer system, decisions will depend on cost and performance goals. The first three options in the figure are clear choices—separate address and data lines, wider data lines, and multiple-word transfers all give higher performance at more cost.

The next item in the table concerns the number of *bus masters*. These are devices that can initiate a read or write transaction; the CPU, for instance, is always a bus master. A bus has multiple masters when there are multiple CPUs or when I/O devices can initiate a bus transaction. If there are multiple masters, an arbitration scheme is required among the masters to decide who gets the bus next. Arbitration is often a fixed priority, as is the case with daisy-chained devices or an approximately fair scheme that randomly chooses which master gets the bus.

With multiple masters a bus can offer higher bandwidth by going to packets, as opposed to holding the bus for the full transaction. This technique is designated *split transactions*. (Some systems call this ability *connect/disconnect* or a *pipelined bus*.) The read transaction is broken into a read-request transaction that contains the address, and a memory-reply transaction that contains the data. Each transaction must now be tagged so that the CPU and memory can tell what is what. Split transactions make the bus available for other masters while the memory reads the words from the requested address. It also normally means that the CPU must arbitrate for the bus to send the data and the memory must arbitrate for the bus to return the data. Thus, a split-transaction bus has higher bandwidth, but it usually has higher latency than a bus that is held during the complete transaction.

The final item, clocking, concerns whether a bus is synchronous or asynchronous. If a bus is *synchronous* it includes a clock in the control lines and a fixed protocol for address and data relative to the clock. Since little or no logic is needed to decide what to do next, these buses can be both fast and inexpensive. However, they have two major disadvantages. Everything on the bus must run at the same clock rate, and because of clock-skew problems, synchronous buses cannot be long. CPU–memory buses are typically synchronous.

An *asynchronous* bus, on the other hand, is not clocked. Instead, self-timed, handshaking protocols are used between bus sender and receiver. This scheme makes it much easier to accommodate a wide variety of devices and to lengthen the bus without worrying about clock skew or synchronization problems. If a synchronous bus can be used, it is usually faster than an asynchronous bus because of the overhead of synchronizing the bus for each transaction. The choice of synchronous versus asynchronous bus has implications not only for data bandwidth but also for an I/O system's capacity in terms of physical

Option	High performance	Low cost
Bus width	Separate address and data lines	Multiplex address and data lines
Data width	Wider is faster (e.g., 32 bits)	Narrower is cheaper (e.g., 8 bits)
Transfer size	Multiple words has less bus overhead	Single-word transfer is simpler
Bus masters	Multiple (requires arbitration)	Single master (no arbitration)
Split transaction?	Yes—separate Request and Reply packets gets higher bandwidth (needs multiple masters)	No—continuous connection is cheaper and has lower latency
Clocking	Synchronous	Asynchronous

FIGURE 9.24   The main options for a bus. The advantage of separate address and data buses is primarily on writes.

distance and number of devices that can be connected to the bus; asynchronous buses scale better with technological changes. I/O buses are typically asynchronous. Figure 9.25 suggests the relationship of when to use one over the other.

Bus Standards

The number and variety of I/O devices are not fixed on most computer systems, permitting customers to tailor computers to their needs. As the interface to which devices are connected, the I/O bus can also be considered an expansion bus for adding I/O devices over time. Standards that let the computer designer and I/O-device designer work independently, therefore, play a large role in determining the choice of buses. As long as both the computer-system designer and the I/O-device designer meet the requirements, any I/O device can connect to any computer. In fact, an I/O bus standard is the document that defines how to connect them.

Machines sometimes grow to be so popular that their I/O buses become de facto standards; examples are the PDP-11 Unibus and the IBM PC-AT Bus. Once many I/O devices have been built for the popular machine, other computer designers will build their I/O interface so that those devices can plug into their machines as well. Sometimes standards also come from an explicit standards effort on the part of I/O device makers. The *intelligent peripheral interface* (IPI)

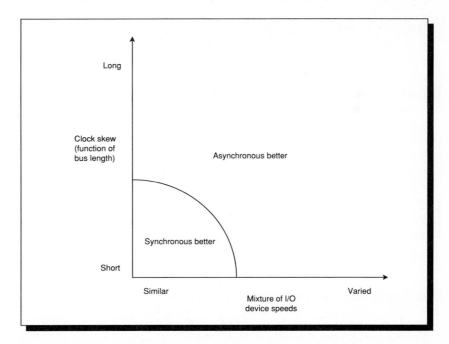

FIGURE 9.25 Preferred bus type as a function of length/clock skew and variation in I/O device speed. Synchronous is best when the distance is short and the I/O devices on the bus all transfer at similar speeds.

and Ethernet are examples of standards from cooperation of manufacturers. If standards are successful, they are eventually blessed by a sanctioning body like ANSI or IEEE. Occasionally, a bus standard comes top-down directly from a standards committee—the FutureBus is one example.

Figure 9.26 summarizes characteristics of several bus standards. Note that the bandwidth entries in the figure are not listed as single numbers for the CPU–memory buses (VME, FutureBus, and Multibus II). Because of the bus overhead, the size of the transfer affects bandwidth significantly. Since the bus usually transfers to or from memory, the speed of the memory also affects the bandwidth. For example, with infinite transfer size and infinitely fast (0 ns) memory, FutureBus is 240% faster than VME, but FutureBus is only about 20% faster than VME for single-word transfers from a 150-ns memory.

	VME bus	FutureBus	Multibus II	IPI	SCSI
Bus width (signals)	128	96	96	16	8
Address/data multiplexed?	Not multi-plexed	Multiplexed	Multiplexed	N/A	N/A
Data width (primary)	16 to 32 bits	32 bits	32 bits	16 bits	8 bits
Transfer size	Single or multiple	Single or multiple	Single or multiple	Single or multiple	Single or multiple
Number of bus masters	Multiple	Multiple	Multiple	Single	Multiple
Split transaction?	No	Optional	Optional	Optional	Optional
Clocking	Asynchronous	Asynchronous	Synchronous	Asynchronous	Either
Bandwidth, 0-ns access memory, single word	25.0 MB/sec	37.0 MB/sec	20.0 MB/sec	25.0 MB/sec	5.0 MB/sec or 1.5 MB/sec
Bandwidth, 150-ns access memory, single word	12.9 MB/sec	15.5 MB/sec	10.0 MB/sec	25.0 MB/sec	5.0 MB/sec or 1.5 MB/sec
Bandwidth, 0-ns access memory, multiple words (infinite block length)	27.9 MB/sec	95.2 MB/sec	40.0 MB/sec	25.0 MB/sec	5.0 MB/sec or 1.5 MB/sec
Bandwidth, 150-ns access memory, multiple words (infinite block length)	13.6 MB/sec	20.8 MB/sec	13.3 MB/sec	25.0 MB/sec	5.0 MB/sec or 1.5 MB/sec
Maximum number of devices	21	20	21	8	7
Maximum bus length	0.5 meter	0.5 meter	0.5 meter	50 meters	25 meters
Standard	IEEE 1014	IEEE 896.1	ANSI/IEEE 1296	ANSI X3.129	ANSI X3.131

FIGURE 9.26 Information on five bus standards. The first three were defined originally as CPU–memory buses and the last two as I/O buses. For the CPU–memory buses the bandwidth calculations assume a fully loaded bus and are given for both single-word transfers and block transfers of unlimited length; measurements are shown both ignoring memory latency and assuming 150-ns access time. Bandwidth assumes the average distance of a transfer is one-third of the backplane length. (Data in the first three columns is from Borrill [1986].) The bandwidth for the I/O buses is given as their maximum data-transfer rate. The SCSI standard offers either asynchronous or synchronous I/O; the asynchronous version transfers at 1.5 MB/sec and the synchronous at 5 MB/sec.

9.6 | Interfacing to the CPU

Having described I/O devices and looked at some of the issues of the connecting bus, we are ready to discuss the CPU end of the interface. The first question is how the physical connection of the I/O bus should be made. The two choices are connecting it to memory or to the cache. In the following section we will discuss the pros and cons of connecting an I/O bus directly to the cache; in this section we examine the more usual case in which the I/O bus is connected to the main memory bus. Figure 9.27 shows a typical organization. In low-cost systems, the I/O bus **is** the memory bus; this means an I/O command on the bus could interfere with a CPU instruction fetch, for example.

Once the physical interface is chosen, the question becomes how does the CPU address an I/O device that it needs to send or receive data. The most common practice is called *memory-mapped* I/O. In this scheme, portions of the address space are assigned to I/O devices. Reads and writes to those addresses may cause data to be transferred; some portion of the I/O space may also be set aside for device control, so commands to the device are just accesses to those memory-mapped addresses. The alternative practice is to use dedicated I/O opcodes in the CPU. In this case, the CPU sends a signal that this address is for I/O devices. Examples of computers with I/O instructions are the Intel 80x86 and the IBM 370 computers. No matter which addressing scheme is selected, each I/O device has registers to provide status and control information. Either

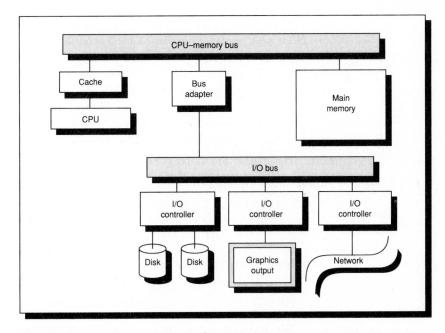

FIGURE 9.27 A typical interface of I/O devices and an I/O bus to the CPU–memory bus.

through loads and stores in memory-mapped I/O or through special instructions, the CPU sets flags to determine the operation the I/O device will perform.

I/O is rarely a single operation. For example, the DEC LP11 line printer has two I/O device registers: one for status information and one for data to be printed. The status register contains a *done bit*, set by the printer when it has printed a character, and an *error bit*, indicating that the printer is jammed or out of paper. Each byte of data to be printed is put into the data register; the CPU must then wait until the printer sets the done bit before it can place another character in the buffer.

This simple interface, in which the CPU periodically checks status bits to see if it is time for the next I/O operation, is called *polling*. As one might expect, the fact that CPUs are so much faster than I/O devices means polling may waste a lot of CPU time. This was recognized long ago, leading to the invention of interrupts to notify the CPU when it is time to do something for the I/O device. *Interrupt-driven* I/O, used by most systems for at least some devices, allows the CPU to work on some other process while waiting on the I/O device. For example, the LP11 has a mode that allows it to interrupt the CPU whenever the done bit or error bit is set. In general-purpose applications, interrupt driven I/O is the key to multitasking operating systems and good response times.

The drawback to interrupts is the operating system overhead on each event. In real-time applications with hundreds of I/O events per second, this overhead can be intolerable. One hybrid solution for real-time systems is to use a clock to periodically interrupt the CPU, at which time the CPU polls all I/O devices.

Delegating I/O Responsibility from the CPU

Interrupt-driven I/O relieves the CPU from waiting for every I/O event, but there are still many CPU cycles spent in transferring data. Transferring a disk block of 2048 words, for instance, would require at least 2048 loads and 2048 stores, as well as the overhead for the interrupt. Since I/O events so often involve block transfers, *direct memory access* (DMA) hardware is added to many computer systems to allow transfers of numbers of words without intervention by the CPU.

DMA is a specialized processor that transfers data between memory and an I/O device, while the CPU goes on with other tasks. Thus, it is external to the CPU and must act as a master on the bus. The CPU first sets up the DMA registers, which contain a memory address and number of bytes to be transferred. Once the DMA transfer is complete, the controller interrupts the CPU. There may be multiple DMA devices in a computer system; for example, DMA is frequently part of the controller for an I/O device.

Increasing the intelligence of the DMA device can further unburden the CPU. Devices called *I/O processors*, (or *I/O controllers*, or *channel controllers*) operate from either fixed programs or from programs downloaded by the operating system. The operating system typically sets up a queue of *I/O control blocks* that contain information such as data location (source and destination) and data size. The I/O processor then takes items from the queue, doing everything requested and sending a single interrupt when the task specified in the I/O control blocks is complete. Whereas the LP11 line printer would cause 4800 interrupts to print a 60-line by 80-character page, an I/O processor could save 4799 of those interrupts.

I/O processors can be compared to multiprocessors in that they facilitate several processes executing simultaneously in the computer system. I/O processors are less general than CPUs, however, since they have dedicated tasks, and thus parallelism is also much more limited. Also, an I/O processor doesn't normally change information, as a CPU does, but just moves information from one place to another.

9.7 | Interfacing to an Operating System

In a manner analogous to the way compilers use an instruction set (see Section 3.7 of Chapter 3), operating systems control what I/O techniques implemented by the hardware will actually be used. For example, many I/O controllers used in early UNIX systems were 16-bit microprocessors. To avoid problems with 16-bit addresses in controllers, UNIX was changed to limit the maximum I/O transfer to 63 KB or less; at the time of this book's publication, that limit is still in effect. Thus, a new I/O controller designed to efficiently transfer 1-MB files would never see more than 63 KB at a time under UNIX, no matter how large the files.

Caches Cause Problems for Operating Systems— Stale Data

The prevalence of caches in computer systems has added to the responsibilities of the operating system. Caches imply the possibility of two copies of the data— one each for cache and main memory—while virtual memory can result in three copies—for cache, memory and disk. This brings up the possibility of *stale data*: the CPU or I/O system could modify one copy without updating the other copies (see Section 8.8 in Chapter 8). Either the operating system or the hardware must make sure that the CPU reads the most recently input data and that I/O outputs the correct data, in the presence of caches and virtual memory. Whether the stale-data problem arises depends in part on where the I/O is connected to the computer. If it is connected to the CPU cache, as shown in Figure 9.28 (page 536), there is no stale-data problem; all I/O devices and the CPU see the most accurate version in the cache, and existing mechanisms in the memory hierarchy ensure that other copies of the data will be updated. The side effect is lost CPU performance, since I/O will replace blocks in the cache with data that are unlikely to be needed by the process running in the CPU at the time of the transfer. In other words, all I/O data goes through the cache but little of it is referenced. This arrangement also requires arbitration between CPU and I/O to decide who accesses the cache. If I/O is connected to memory, as in Figure 9.27 (page 533), then it doesn't interfere with CPU, provided the CPU has a cache. In this situation, however, the stale-data problem occurs. Alternatively, I/O can just invalidate data—either all data that might match (no tag check) or only data that matches.

There are two parts to the stale-data problem:

1. The I/O system sees stale data on output because memory is not up to date.

2 The CPU sees stale data in the cache on input after the I/O system has updated memory.

The first dilemma is how to output correct data if there is a cache and I/O is connected to memory. A write-through cache solves this by ensuring that memory will have the same data as the cache. A write-back cache requires the operating system to flush output addresses to make sure they are not in the cache. This takes time, even if the data is not in the cache, since address checks are sequential. Alternatively, the hardware can check cache tags during output to see if they are in a write-back cache, and only interact with the cache if the output tries to read data that is in the cache.

The second problem is ensuring that the cache won't have stale data after input. The operating system can guarantee that the input data area can't possibly

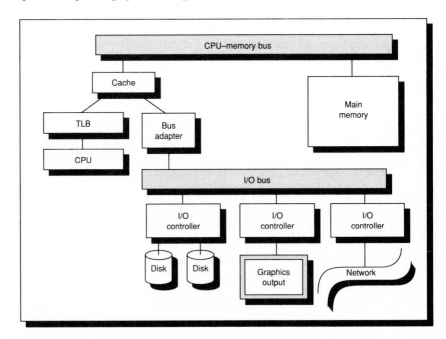

FIGURE 9.28   Example of I/O connected directly to the cache.

be in the cache. If it can't guarantee this, the operating system flushes input addresses to make sure they are not in the cache. Again, this takes time, whether or not the input addresses are in the cache. As before, extra hardware can be added to check tags during an input and invalidate the data if there is a conflict. These problems are basically the same as cache coherency in a multiprocessor, discussed in Section 8.8 of Chapter 8; I/O can be thought of as a second dedicated processor in a multiprocessor.

DMA and Virtual Memory

Given the use of virtual memory, there is the matter of whether DMA should transfer using virtual addresses or physical addresses. Here are some problems with DMA using physically mapped I/O:

- Transferring a buffer that is larger than one page will cause problems, since the pages in the buffer will not usually be mapped to sequential pages in physical memory.

- Suppose DMA is ongoing between memory and a frame buffer, and the operating system removes some of the pages from memory (or relocates them). The DMA would then be transferring data to or from the wrong page of memory.

One answer to these questions is *virtual DMA*. It allows the DMA to use virtual addresses that are mapped to physical addresses during the DMA. Thus, a buffer must be sequential in virtual memory but the pages can be scattered in physical memory. The operating system could update the address tables of a DMA if a process is moved using virtual DMA, or the operating system could "lock" the pages in memory until the DMA is complete. Figure 9.29 (page 538) shows address-translation registers added to the DMA device.

Caches Helping Operating Systems— File or Disk Caches

While the invention of caches made the life of the operating systems designer more difficult, operating systems designers' concern for performance led them to cache-like optimizations, using main memory as a "cache" for disk traffic to improve I/O performance. The impact of using main memory as a buffer or cache for file or disk accesses is demonstrated in Figure 9.30 (page 538). It shows the change in disk I/Os for a cacheless system measured as miss rate (see Section 8.2 in Chapter 8). File caches or disk caches change the number of disk I/Os and the mix of reads and writes; depending on cache size and write policy, between 50% to 70% of all disk accesses could become writes with such caches. Without file or disk caches, between 15% and 33% of all accesses are writes, depending on the environment.

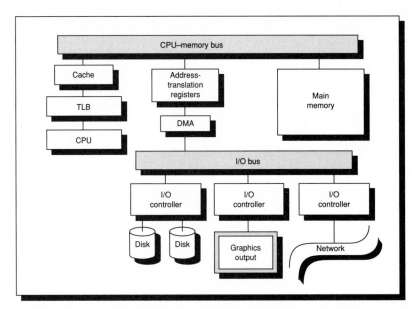

FIGURE 9.29   Virtual DMA requires a register for each page to be transferred in the DMA controller, showing the protection bits and the physical page corresponding to each virtual page.

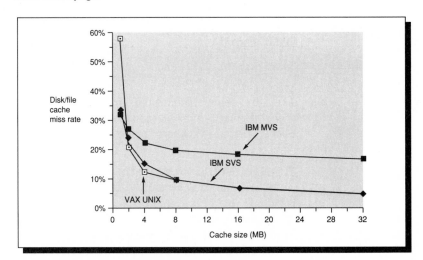

FIGURE 9.30   The effectiveness of a file cache or disk cache on reducing disk I/Os versus cache size. Ousterhout et al. [1985] collected the VAX UNIX data on VAX-11/785s with 8 MB to 16 MB of main memory, running 4.2 BSD UNIX using a 16-KB block size. Smith [1985] collected the IBM SVS and IBM MVS traces on IBM 370/168 using a one-track block size (which varied from 7294 bytes to 19254 bytes, depending on the disk). The difference between a file cache and a disk cache is that the file cache uses logical block numbers while a disk cache uses addresses that have been mapped to the physical sector and track on a disk. This difference is similar to the difference between a virtually addressed and a physically addressed cache (see Section 8.8 in Chapter 8).

9.8 | Designing an I/O System

The art of I/O is finding a design that meets goals for cost and variety of devices while avoiding bottlenecks to I/O performance. This means that components must be balanced between main memory and the I/O device because performance—and hence effective cost/performance—can only be as good as the weakest link in the I/O chain. The architect must also plan for expansion so that customers can tailor the I/O to their applications. This expansibility, both in numbers and types of I/O devices, has its costs in longer backplanes, larger power supplies to support I/O devices, and larger cabinets.

In designing an I/O system, analyze performance, cost, and capacity using varying I/O connection schemes and different numbers of I/O devices of each type. Here is a series of six steps to follow in designing an I/O system. The answers in each step may be dictated by market requirements or simply by cost/performance goals.

1. List the different types of I/O devices to be connected to the machine, or a list of standard buses that the machine will support.

2. List the physical requirements for each I/O device. This includes volume, power, connectors, bus slots, expansion cabinets, and so on.

3. List the cost of each I/O device, including the portion of cost of any controller needed for this device.

4. Record the CPU resource demands of each I/O device. This should include:

   Clock cycles for instructions used to initiate an I/O, to support operation of an I/O device (such as handling interrupts), and complete I/O

   CPU clock stalls due to waiting for I/O to finish using the memory, bus, or cache

   CPU clock cycles to recover from an I/O activity, such as a cache flush

5. List the memory and I/O bus resource demands of each I/O device. Even when the CPU is not using memory, the bandwidth of main memory and the I/O bus are limited.

6. The final step is establishing performance of the different ways to organize these I/O devices. Performance can only be properly evaluated with simulation, though it may be estimated using queuing theory.

You then select the best organization, given your performance and cost goals.

Cost and performance goals affect the selection of the I/O scheme and physical design. Performance can be measured either as megabytes per second or I/Os per second, depending on the needs of the application. For high performance, the only limits should be speed of I/O devices, number of I/O devices, and speed of memory and CPU. For low cost, the only expenses should be those for the I/O devices themselves and for cabling to the CPU. Cost/performance design, of course, tries for the best of both worlds.

To make these ideas clearer, let's go through several examples.

Example

First, let's look at the impact on the CPU of reading a disk page directly into the cache. Make the following assumptions:

Each page is 8 KB and the cache-block size is 16 bytes.

The addresses corresponding to the new page are **not** in the cache.

The CPU will not access any of the data in the new page.

90% of the blocks that were displaced from the cache will be read in again, and each will cause a miss.

The cache uses write back, and 50% of the blocks are dirty on average.

The I/O system buffers a full cache block before writing to the cache (this is called a *speed-matching buffer*, matching transfer bandwidth of the I/O system and memory).

The accesses and misses are spread uniformly to all cache blocks.

There is no other interference between the CPU and I/O for the cache slots.

There are 15,000 misses every one million clock cycles when there is **no** I/O.

The miss penalty is 15 clock cycles, plus 15 more cycles to write the block if it was dirty.

Assuming one page is brought in every one million clock cycles, what is the impact on performance?

Answer

Each page fills 8192/16 or 512 blocks. I/O transfers do not cause cache misses on their own because entire cache blocks are transferred. However, they do displace blocks already in the cache. If half of the displaced blocks are dirty it takes 256*15 clock cycles to write them back to memory. There are also misses from 90% of the blocks displaced in the cache because they are referenced later, adding another 90%*512, or 461 misses. Since this data was placed into the cache from the I/O system, all these blocks are dirty and will need to be written back when replaced. Thus, the total is 256*15 + 461*30 more clock cycles than the original 1,000,000 + 15,000*15. This turns into a 1% decrease in performance:

$$\frac{256*15 + 461*30}{1000000+15000*15} = \frac{17670}{1225000} = 0.014$$

Now let's look at the cost/performance of different I/O organizations. A simple way to perform this analysis is to look at maximum throughput assuming that resources can be used at 100% of their maximum rate without side effects from interference. A later example takes a more realistic view.

Example

Given the following performance and cost information:

a 50-MIPS CPU costing $50,000

an 8-byte-wide memory with a 200-ns cycle time

80 MB/sec I/O bus with room for 20 SCSI buses and controllers

SCSI buses that can transfer 4 MB/sec and support up to 7 disks per bus (these are also called SCSI *strings*)

a $2500 SCSI controller that adds 2 milliseconds (ms) of overhead to perform a disk I/O

an operating system that uses 10,000 CPU instructions for a disk I/O

a choice of a large disk containing 4 GB or a small disk containing 1 GB, each costing $3 per MB

both disks rotate at 3600 RPM, have a 12-ms average seek time, and can transfer 2MB/sec

the storage capacity must be 100 GB, and

the average I/O size is 8 KB

Evaluate the cost per I/O per second (IOPS) of using small or large drives. Assume that every disk I/O requires an average seek and average rotational delay. Use the optimistic assumption that all devices can be used at 100% of capacity and that the workload is evenly divided between all disks.

Answer

I/O performance is limited by the weakest link in the chain, so we evaluate the maximum performance of each link in the I/O chain for each organization to determine the maximum performance of that organization.

Let's start by calculating the maximum number of IOPS for the CPU, main memory, and I/O bus. The CPU I/O performance is determined by the speed of the CPU and the number of instructions to perform a disk I/O:

$$\text{Maximum IOPS for CPU} = \frac{50 \text{ MIPS}}{10000 \text{ instructions per I/O}} = 5000$$

The maximum performance of the memory system is determined by the memory cycle time, the width of the memory, and the size of the I/O transfers:

$$\text{Maximum IOPS for main memory} = \frac{(1/200 \text{ ns})*8}{8 \text{ KB per I/O}} \approx 5000$$

The I/O bus maximum performance is limited by the bus bandwidth and the size of the I/O:

$$\text{Maximum IOPS for the I/O bus} = \frac{80 \text{ MB/sec}}{8 \text{ KB per I/O}} \approx 10000$$

Thus, no matter which disk is selected, the CPU and main memory limits the maximum performance to no more than 5000 IOPS.

Now its time to look at the performance of the next link in the I/O chain, the SCSI controllers. The time to transfer 8 KB over the SCSI bus is

$$\text{SCSI bus transfer time} = \frac{8 \text{ KB}}{4 \text{ MB/sec}} = 2 \text{ ms}$$

Adding the 2-ms SCSI controller overhead means 4 ms per I/O, making the maximum rate per controller

$$\text{Maximum IOPS per SCSI controller} = \frac{1}{4 \text{ ms}} = 250 \text{ IOPS}$$

All the organizations will use several controllers, so 250 IOPS is not the limit for the whole system.

The final link in the chain is the disks themselves. The time for an average disk I/O is

$$\text{I/O time} = 12 \text{ ms} + \frac{0.5}{3600 \text{ RPM}} + \frac{8 \text{ KB}}{2 \text{ MB/sec}} = 12+8.3+ 4 = 24.3 \text{ ms}$$

so the disk performance is

$$\text{Maximum IOPS (using average seeks) per disk} = \frac{1}{24.3 \text{ ms}} \approx 41 \text{ IOPS}$$

The number of disks in each organization depends on the size of each disk: 100 GB can be either 25 4-GB disks or 100 1-GB disks. The maximum number of I/Os for all the disks is:

$$\text{Maximum IOPS for 25 4-GB disks} \quad = \quad 25 * 41 = 1025$$

$$\text{Maximum IOPS for 100 1-GB disks} \quad = \quad 100 * 41 = 4100$$

Thus, provided there are enough SCSI strings, the disks become the new limit to maximum performance: 1025 IOPS for the 4-GB disks and 4100 for the 1-GB disks.

While we have determined the performance of each link of the I/O chain, we still have to determine how many SCSI buses and controllers to use and how many disks to connect to each controller, as this may further limit maximum performance. The I/O bus is limited to 20 SCSI controllers and the SCSI standard limits disks to 7 per SCSI string. The minimum number of controllers is for the 4-GB disks

$$\text{Minimum number of SCSI strings for 25 4-GB disks} = \frac{25}{7} \text{ or } 4$$

and for 1-GB disks

$$\text{Minimum number of SCSI strings for 100 1-GB disks} = \frac{100}{7} \text{ or } 15$$

We can calculate the maximum IOPS for each configuration:

$$\text{Maximum IOPS for 4 SCSI strings} = 4 * 250 = 1000 \text{ IOPS}$$

$$\text{Maximum IOPS for 15 SCSI strings} = 15 * 250 = 3750 \text{ IOPS}$$

The maximum performance of this number of controllers is slightly lower than the disk I/O throughput, so let's also calculate the number of controllers so they don't become a bottleneck. One way is to find the number of disks they can support per string:

$$\text{Number of disks per SCSI string at full bandwidth} = \frac{250}{41} = 6.1 \text{ or } 6$$

and then calculate the number of strings:

$$\text{Number of SCSI strings for full bandwidth 4-GB disks} = \frac{25}{6} = 4.1 \text{ or } 5$$

$$\text{Number of SCSI strings for full bandwidth 1-GB disks} = \frac{100}{6} = 16.7 \text{ or } 17$$

This establishes the performance of four organizations: 25 4-GB disks with 4 or 5 SCSI strings and 100 1-GB disks with 15 to 17 SCSI strings. The maximum performance of each option is limited by the bottleneck (in boldface):

4-GB disks, 4 strings $= \text{Min}(5000,5000,10000,1025,\mathbf{1000}) = 1000 \text{ IOPS}$

4-GB disks, 5 strings $= \text{Min}(5000,5000,10000,\mathbf{1025},1250) = 1025 \text{ IOPS}$

1-GB disks, 15 strings $= \text{Min}(5000,5000,10000,4100,\mathbf{3750}) = 3750 \text{ IOPS}$

1-GB disks, 17 strings $= \text{Min}(5000,5000,10000,\mathbf{4100},4250) = 4100 \text{ IOPS}$

We can now calculate the cost for each organization:

4-GB disks, 4 strings   = $50,000 + 4*$2,500 + 25 * (4096*$3)   = $367,200

4-GB disks, 5 strings   = $50,000 + 5*$2,500 + 25 * (4096*$3)   = $369,700

1-GB disks, 15 strings = $50,000 + 15*$2,500 + 100 * (1024*$3) = $394,700

1-GB disks, 17 strings = $50,000 + 17*$2,500 + 100 * (1024*$3) = $399,700

Finally, the cost per IOPS for each of the four configurations is $367, $361, $105, and $97, respectively. Calculating maximum number of average I/Os per second assuming 100% utilization of the critical resources, the best cost/performance is the organization with the small disks and the largest number of controllers. The small disks have 3.4 to 3.8 times better cost/performance than the large disks in this example. The only drawback is that the larger number of disks will affect system availability unless some form of redundancy is added (see pages 520–521).

This above example assumed that resources can be used 100%. It is instructive to see what is the bottleneck in each organization.

Example   For the organizations in the last example, calculate the percentage of utilization of each resource in the computer system.

Answer   Figure 9.31 gives the answer.

Resource	4-GB disks, 4 strings	4-GB disks, 5 strings	1-GB disks, 15 strings	1-GB disks, 17 strings
CPU	20%	21%	75%	82%
Memory	20%	21%	75%	82%
I/O bus	10%	10%	38%	41%
SCSI buses	100%	82%	100%	96%
Disks	98%	100%	91%	100%

FIGURE 9.31 The percentage of utilization of each resource given the four organizations in the previous example. Either the SCSI buses or the disks are the bottleneck.

In reality buses cannot deliver close to 100% of bandwidth without severe increase in latency and reduction in throughput due to contention. A variety of rules of thumb have been evolved to guide I/O designs:

No I/O bus should be utilized more than 75% to 80%;

No disk string should be utilized more than 40%;

No disk arm should be seeking more than 60% of the time.

Example   Recalculate performance in the example above using these rules of thumb, and show the utilization of each component. Are there other organizations that follow these guidelines and improve performance?

Answer   Figure 9.31 shows that the I/O bus is far below the suggested guidelines, so we concentrate on the utilization of seek and SCSI bus. The utilization of seek time per disk is

$$\frac{\text{Time of average seek}}{\text{Time between I/Os}} = \frac{12 \text{ ms}}{\dfrac{1}{41 \text{ IOPS}}} = \frac{12}{24} = 50\%$$

which is below the rule of thumb. The biggest impact is on the SCSI bus:

$$\text{Suggested IOPS per SCSI string} = \frac{1}{4 \text{ ms}} * 40\% = 100 \text{ IOPS}.$$

With this data we can recalculate IOPS for each organization:

4-GB disks, 4 strings   = Min(5000,5000,7500,1025,**400**)   = 400 IOPS

4-GB disks, 5 strings   = Min(5000,5000,7500,1025,**500**)   = 500 IOPS

1-GB disks, 15 strings = Min(5000,5000,7500,4100,**1500**) = 1500 IOPS

1-GB disks, 17 strings = Min(5000,5000,7500,4100,**1700**) = 1700 IOPS

Under these assumptions, the small disks have about 3.0 to 4.2 times the performance of the large disks.

Clearly, the string bandwidth is the bottleneck now. The number of disks per string that would not exceed the guideline is

$$\text{Number of disks per SCSI string at full bandwidth} = \frac{100}{41} = 2.4 \text{ or } 2$$

and the ideal number of strings is

$$\text{Number of SCSI strings for full bandwidth 4-GB disks} = \frac{25}{2} = 12.5 \text{ or } 13$$

$$\text{Number of SCSI strings for full bandwidth 1-GB disks} = \frac{100}{2} = 50$$

This suggestion is fine for 4-GB disks, but the I/O bus is limited to 20 SCSI controllers and strings so that becomes the limit for 1-GB disks:

4-GB disks, 13 strings = Min(5000,5000,7500,**1025**,1300) = 1025 IOPS

1-GB disks, 20 strings = Min(5000,5000,7500,4100,**2000**) = 2000 IOPS

We can now calculate the cost for each organization:

4-GB disks, 13 strings = $50,000 + 13*$2,500 + 25 * (4096*$3) = $389,700

1-GB disks, 20 strings = $50,000 + 20*$2,500 + 100 * (1024*$3) = $407,200

In this case the small disks cost 5% more yet have about twice the performance of the large disks. The utilization of each resource is shown in Figure 9.32. It shows that following the rule of thumb of 40% string utilization sets the performance limit in all but one case.

Resource	4-GB disks, 4 strings	4-GB disks, 5 strings	1-GB disks, 15 strings	1-GB disks, 17 strings	4-GB disks, 13 strings	1-GB disks, 20 strings
CPU	8%	10%	30%	34%	21%	40%
Memory	8%	10%	30%	34%	21%	40%
I/O bus	5%	7%	20%	23%	14%	27%
SCSI buses	40%	40%	40%	40%	32%	40%
Disks	39%	49%	37%	41%	100%	49%
Seek utilization	19%	24%	18%	20%	49%	24%
IOPS	400	500	1500	1700	1025	2000

FIGURE 9.32   The percentage of utilization of each resource given the six organizations in this example, which tries to limit utilization of key resources to the rules of thumb given above.

9.9 | Putting It All Together: The IBM 3990 Storage Subsystem

If computer architects were polled to select the leading company in I/O design, IBM would win hands down. A good deal of IBM's mainframe business is commercial applications, known to be I/O intensive. While there are graphic devices and networks that can be connected to an IBM mainframe, IBM's reputation comes from disk performance. It is on this aspect that we concentrate in this section.

The IBM 360/370 I/O architecture has evolved over a period of 25 years. Initially, the I/O system was general purpose, and no special attention was paid to any particular device. As it became clear that magnetic disks were the chief consumers of I/O, the IBM 360 was tailored to support fast disk I/O. IBM's dominant philosophy is to choose latency over throughput whenever it makes a difference. IBM almost never uses a large buffer outside the CPU; their goal is to set up a clear path from main memory to the I/O device so that when a device is ready, nothing can get in the way. Perhaps IBM followed a corollary to the quote on page 526: you can buy bandwidth, but you need to design for latency. As a secondary philosophy, the CPU is unburdened as much as possible to allow the CPU to continue with computation while others perform the desired I/O activities.

The example for this section is the high-end IBM 3090 CPU and the 3990 Storage Subsystem. The IBM 3090, models 3090/100 to 3090/600, can contain one to six CPUs. This 18.5-ns-clock-cycle machine has a 16-way interleaved memory that can transfer eight bytes every clock cycle on each of two (3090/100) or four (3090/600) buses. Each 3090 processor has a 64-KB, 4-way–set-associative, write-back cache, and the cache supports pipelined access taking two cycles. Each CPU is rated about 30 IBM MIPS (see page 78), giving at most 180 MIPS to the IBM 3090/600. Surveys of IBM mainframe installations suggest a rule of thumb of about 4 GB of disk storage per MIPS of CPU power (see Section 9.12).

It is only fair warning to say that IBM terminology may not be self-evident, although the ideas are not difficult. Remember that this I/O architecture has evolved since 1964. While there may well be ideas that IBM wouldn't include if they were to start anew, they are able to make this scheme work, and make it work well.

The 3990 I/O Subsystem Data-Transfer Hierarchy and Control Hierarchy

The I/O subsystem is divided into two hierarchies:

1. Control—This hierarchy of controllers negotiates a path through a maze of possible connections between the memory and the I/O device and controls the timing of the transfer.

2. Data—This hierarchy of connections is the path over which data flows between memory and the I/O device.

After going over each of the hierarchies, we trace a disk read to help understand the function of each component.

For simplicity, we begin by discussing the data-transfer hierarchy, shown in Figure 9.33 (page 548). This figure shows one section of the hierarchy that contains up to 64 large IBM disks; using 64 of the recently announced IBM 3390 disks, this piece could connect to over one trillion bytes of storage! Yet this piece represents only one-sixth of the capacity of the IBM 3090/600 CPU. This ability to expand from a small I/O system to hundreds of disks and terabytes of storage is what gives IBM mainframes their reputation in the I/O world.

The best-known member of the data hierarchy is the *channel*. The channel is nothing more than 50 wires that connect two levels on the I/O hierarchy together. Only 18 of the 50 wires are used for transferring data (8 data plus 1 parity in each direction), while the rest are for control information. For years the maximum data rate was 3 MB per second, but it recently was raised to 4.5 MB per second. Up to 48 channels can be connected to a 3090/100 CPU, and up to

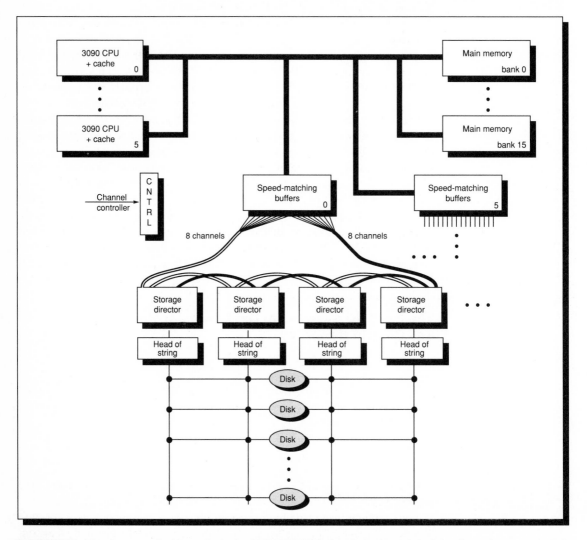

FIGURE 9.33   The data-transfer hierarchy in the IBM 3990 I/O Subsystem. Note that all the channels are connected to all the storage directors. The disks at the bottom represent the quad-ported IBM 3380 disk drives, with the maximum of 64 disks. The collection of disks on the same path to the head-of-string controller is called a *string* .

96 channels to a 3090/600. Because they are "multiprogrammed," channels can actually service several disks. For historical reasons, IBM calls this *block multiplexing*.

Channels are connected to the 3090 main memory via two *speed-matching buffers*, which funnel all the channels into a single port to main memory. Such buffers simply match the bandwidth of the I/O device to the bandwidth of the memory system. There are two 8-byte buffers per channel.

The next level down the data hierarchy is the *storage director*. This is an intermediary device that allows the many channels to talk to many different I/O devices. Four to sixteen channels go to the storage director depending on the model, and two or four paths come out the bottom to the disks. These are called *two-path strings* or *four-path strings* in IBM parlance. Thus, each storage director can talk to any of the disks using one of the strings. At the top of each string is the *head of string*, and all communication between disks and control units must pass through it.

At the bottom of the datapath hierarchy are the disk devices themselves. To increase availability, disk devices like the IBM 3380 provide four paths to connect to the storage director; if one path fails, the device can still be connected.

The redundant paths from main memory to the I/O device not only improve availability, but also can improve performance. Since the IBM philosophy is to avoid large buffers, the path from the I/O device to main memory must remain connected until the transfer is complete. If there were a single hierarchical path from devices to the speed-matching buffer, only one I/O device in a subtree could transfer at a time. Instead, the multiple paths allow multiple devices to transfer simultaneously through the storage director and into memory.

The task of setting up the datapath connection is that of the control hierarchy. Figure 9.34 shows both the control and data hierarchies of the 3990 I/O subsystem. The new device is the I/O processor. The 3090 channel controller and I/O processor are load/store machines similar to DLX, except that there is no memory hierarchy. In the next subsection we see how the two hierarchies work together to read a disk sector.

Tracing a Disk Read in the IBM 3990 I/O Subsystem

The 12 steps below trace a sector read from an IBM 3380 disk. Each of the 12 steps is labeled on a drawing of the full hierarchy in Figure 9.34 (page 550).

1. The user sets up a data structure in memory containing the operations that should occur during this I/O event. This data structure is termed an *I/O control block*, or IOCB, which also points to a list of channel control words (CCWs). This list is called a *channel program*. Normally, the operating system provides the channel program, but some users write their own. The operating system checks the IOCB for protection violations before the I/O can continue.

2.   The CPU executes a START SUBCHANNEL instruction. The actual request
is defined in the channel program. A channel program to read a record might
look like Figure 9.35.

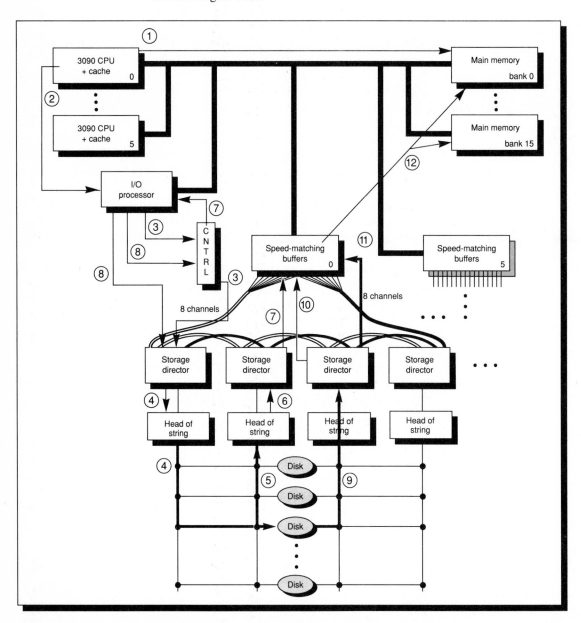

**FIGURE 9.34   The control and data hierarchies in the IBM 3990 I/O Subsystem labeled with the 12 steps to read a
sector from disk.** The only new box over Figure 9.33 (page 548) is the I/O processor.

Location	CCW	Comment
CCW1:	Define Extent	Transfers a 16-byte parameter to the storage director. The channel sees this as a write data transfer.
CCW2:	Locate Record	Transfers a 16-byte parameter to the storage director as above. The parameter identifies the operation (read in this case) plus seek, sector number, and record ID. The channel again sees this as a write data transfer.
CCW3:	Read Data	Transfers the desired disk data to the channel and then to the main memory.

FIGURE 9.35 A channel program to perform a disk read, consisting of three channel command words (CCWs). The operating system checks for virtual memory access violations of CCWs by simulating them to check for violations. These instructions are linked so that only one START SUBCHANNEL instruction is needed.

3. The I/O processor uses the control wires of one of the channels to tell the storage director which disk is to be accessed and the disk address to be read. The channel is then released.

4. The storage director sends a SEEK command to the head-of-string controller and the head-of-string controller connects to the desired disk, telling it to seek to the appropriate track, and then disconnects. The disconnect occurs between CCW2 and CCW3 in Figure 9.35.

Upon completion of these first four steps of the read, the arm on the disk seeks the correct track on the correct IBM 3380 disk drive. Other I/O operations can use the control and data hierarchy while this disk is seeking and the data is rotating under the read head. The I/O processor thus acts like a multiprogrammed system, working on other requests while waiting for an I/O event to complete.

An interesting question arises: When there are multiple uses for a single disk, what prevents another seek from screwing up the works before the original request can continue with the I/O event in progress? The answer is the disk appears busy to the programs in the 3090 between the time a START SUBCHANNEL instruction starts a channel program (step 2) and the end of that channel program. An attempt to execute another START SUBCHANNEL instruction would receive busy status from the channel or from the disk device.

After both the seek completes and the disk rotates to the desired point relative to the read head, the disk reconnects to a channel. To determine the rotational position of the 3380 disk, IBM provides rotational positional sensing (RPS), a feature that gives early warning when the data will rotate under the read head. IBM essentially extends the seek time to include some of the rotation time, thereby tying up the datapath as little as possible. Then the I/O can continue:

5. When the disk completes the seek and rotates to the correct position, it contacts the head-of-string controller.

6. The head-of-string controller looks for a free storage director to send the signal that the disk is on the right track.

7. The storage director looks for a free channel so that it can use the control wires to tell the I/O processor that the disk is on the right track.

8. The I/O processor simultaneously contacts the storage director and I/O device (the IBM 3380 disk) to give the OK to transfer data, and tells the channel controller where to put the information in main memory when it arrives at the channel.

There is now a direct path between the I/O device and memory and the transfer can begin:

9. When the disk is ready to transfer, it sends the data at 3 megabytes per second over a bit-serial line to the storage director.

10. The storage director collects 16 bytes in one of two buffers and sends the information on to the channel controller.

11. The channel controller has a pair of 16-byte buffers per storage director and sends 16 bytes over a 3-MB or 4.5-MB per second, 8-bit-wide datapath to the speed-matching buffers.

12. The speed-matching buffers take the information coming in from all channels. There are two 8-byte buffers per channel that send 8 bytes at a time to the appropriate locations in main memory.

Since nothing is free in computer design, one might expect there to be a cost in anticipating the rotational delay using RPS. Sometimes a free path cannot be established in the time available due to other I/O activity, resulting in an *RPS miss*. An RPS miss means the 3990 I/O Subsystem must either:

- Wait another full rotation—16.7 ms—before the data is back under the head, or

- Break down the hierarchical datapath and start all over again!

Lots of RPS misses can ruin response times.

As mentioned above, the IBM I/O system evolved over many years, and Figure 9.36 shows the change in response time for a few of those changes. The first improvement concerns the path for data after reconnection. Before the System/370-XA, the data path through the channels and storage director (steps 5 through 12) had to be the same as the path taken to request the seek (steps 1 through 4). The 370-XA allows the path after reconnection to be different, and this option is called *dynamic path reconnection* (DPR). This change reduced the time waiting for the channel path and the time waiting for disks (queueing delay), yielding a reduction in the total average response time of 17%. The second change in Figure 9.36 involved a new disk design. Improvements to the microcode control of the 3380D made slight improvements in seek time plus removed a restriction that disk arms that were on the same internal path were prevented from operating at the same time. IBM calls this option *Device Level Select* (DLS). This change reduced internal path delays to 0. This had little impact since there was not much time waiting on internal delays because customers intentionally placed data on disks trying to avoid internal path delays. This second change reduced response time another 9%. The final change was addition of a 32-MB write-through disk cache to a 3380D, called the IBM 3880-23. The disk cache reduced average rotational latency, seek time, and queueing delays, giving another 41% reduction in response time.

One indication of the effectiveness of DPR is the number of disk devices connected to a string. Studies of IBM systems using DPR, which average 16 disk devices per string versus 12 without DPR, suggest dynamic reconnect allows a higher I/O rate with comparable response time [Henly and McNutt 1989].

Summary of the IBM 3990 I/O Subsystem

Goals for I/O systems consist of supporting the following:

- Low cost

- A variety of types of I/O devices

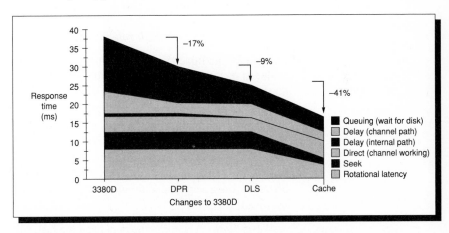

FIGURE 9.36   Changes in response time with improvements in 3380D broken into six categories [Friesenborg and Wicks 1985]. Queueing delay refers to the time when the program waits for another program to finish with the disk. Channel-path delay is the time the operation waits due to the channel path and storage director being busy with another task. Internal-path delay is similar to channel-path delay except it refers to internal paths in the 3380D. Direct means the time the channel path is busy with the operation. Seek time and rotational latency are the standard definitions. Robinson and Blount [1986] report in the study of the 3880-23 that the read hit rate for the 32-MB write-through cache in some large systems averages about 90%, with reads accounting for 92% of the disk accesses.

- A large number of I/O devices at a time

- High performance

- Low latency

Substantial expendability and lower latency are hard to get at the same time. IBM channel-based systems achieve the third and fourth goals by utilizing hierarchical data paths to connect a large number of devices. The many devices and parallel paths allow simultaneous transfers and, thus, high throughput. By avoiding large buffers and providing enough extra paths to minimize delay from congestion, channels offer low-latency I/O as well. To maximize use of the hierarchy, IBM uses rotational positional sensing to extend the time that other tasks can use the hierarchy during an I/O operation.

Therefore, a key to performance of the IBM I/O subsystem is the number of rotational positional misses and congestion on the channel paths. A rule of thumb is that the single-path channels should be no more than 30% utilized and the quad-path channels should be no more than 60% utilized, or too many rotational positional misses will result. This I/O architecture dominates the industry, yet it would be interesting to see what, if anything, IBM would do differently if given a clean slate.

9.10 | Fallacies and Pitfalls

Fallacy: I/O plays a small role in supercomputer design

The goal of the Illiac IV was to be the world's fastest computer. It may not have achieved that goal, but it showed I/O as the Achilles' Heel of high-performance machines. In some tasks, more time was spent in loading data than in computing. Amdahl's Law demonstrated the importance of high performance in all the parts of a high-speed computer. (In fact, Amdahl made his comment in reaction to claims for performance through parallelism made on behalf of the Illiac IV.) The Illiac IV had a very fast transfer rate (60 MB/sec), but very small, fixed-head disks (12-MB capacity). Since they were not large enough, more storage was provided on a separate computer. This led to two ways of measuring I/O overhead:

Warm start—Assuming the data is on the fast, small disks, I/O overhead is the time to load the Illiac IV memory from those disks.

Cold start—Assuming the data is in on the other computer, I/O overhead must include the time to first transfer the data to the Illiac IV fast disks.

Figure 9.37 shows ten applications written for the Illiac IV in 1979. Assuming warm starts, the supercomputer was busy 78% of the time and waiting for I/O 22% of the time; assuming cold starts, it was busy 59% of the time and waiting for I/O 41% of the time.

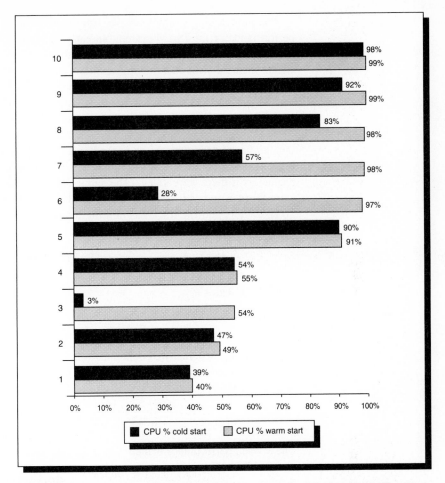

FIGURE 9.37 Feierback and Stevenson [1979] summarized the important Illiac IV applications and the percentage of time spent computing versus waiting for I/O. The arithmetic means of the 10 programs are 78% computing for warm start and 59% computing for cold start.

Pitfall: Moving functions from the CPU to the I/O processor to improve performance.

There are many examples of this pitfall, although I/O processors can enhance performance. A problem inherent with a family of computers is that the migration of an I/O feature usually changes the instruction set architecture or system architecture in a programmer-visible way, causing all future machines to have to live with a decision that made sense in the past. If CPUs are improved in cost/performance more rapidly than the I/O processor (and this will likely be the case) then moving the function may result in a slower machine in the next CPU.

The most telling example comes from the IBM 360. It was decided that the performance of the ISAM system, an early database system, would improve if some of the record searching occurred in the disk controller itself. A key field was associated with each record, and the device searched each key as the disk rotated until it found a match. It would then transfer the desired record. For the disk to find the key, there had to be an extra gap in the track. This scheme is applicable to searches through indices as well as data.

The speed a track can be searched is limited by the speed of the disk and of the number of keys that can be packed on a track. On an IBM 3330 disk the key is typically 10 characters, but the total gap between records is equivalent to 191 characters if there were a key. (The gap is only 135 characters if there is no key, since there is no need for an extra gap for the key.) If we assume the data is also 10 characters and the track has nothing else on it, then a 13165-byte track can contain

$$\frac{13165}{191+10+10} = 62 \text{ key-data records}$$

This performance is

$$\frac{16.7 \text{ ms (1 revolution)}}{62} \approx .25 \text{ ms/key search}$$

In place of this scheme, we could put several key-data pairs in a single block and have smaller inter-record gaps. Assuming there are 15 key-data pairs per block and the track has nothing else on it, then

$$\frac{13165}{135+15*(10+10)} = \frac{13165}{135+300} = 30 \text{ \textbf{blocks} of key-data pairs}$$

The revised performance is then

$$\frac{16.7 \text{ ms (1 revolution)}}{30*15} \approx .04 \text{ ms/key search}$$

Yet as CPUs got faster, the CPU time for a search was trivial. While the strategy made early machines faster, programs that use the search-key operation in the I/O processor run six times slower on today's machines!

Fallacy: Comparing the price of media versus the price of the packaged system.

This happens most frequently when new memory technologies are compared to magnetic disks. For example, comparing the DRAM-chip price to magnetic-disk packaged price in Figure 9.16 (page 518) suggests the difference is less than a factor of 10, but its much greater when the price of packaging DRAM is included. A common mistake with removable media is to compare the media cost not including the drive to read the media. For example, optical media costs only $1 per MB in 1990, but including the cost of the optical drive may bring the price closer to $6 per MB.

Fallacy: The time of an average seek of a disk in a computer system is the time for a seek of one-third the number of cylinders.

This fallacy comes from confusing the way manufacturers market disks with the expected performance and with the false assumption that seek times are linear in distance. The 1/3 distance rule of thumb comes from calculating the distance of a seek from one random location to another random location, not including the current cylinder and assuming there are a large number of cylinders. In the past, manufacturers listed the seek of this distance to offer a consistent basis for comparison. (As mentioned on page 516, today they calculate the "average" by timing all seeks and dividing by the number.) Assuming (incorrectly) that seek time is linear in distance, and using the manufacturers reported minimum and "average" seek times, a common technique to predict seek time is:

$$\text{Time}_{seek} = \text{Time}_{minimum} + \frac{\text{Distance}}{\text{Distance}_{average}} * (\text{Time}_{average} - \text{Time}_{minimum})$$

The fallacy concerning seek time is twofold. First, seek time is **not** linear with distance; the arm must accelerate to overcome inertia, reach its maximum traveling speed, decelerate as it reaches the requested position, and then wait to allow the arm to stop vibrating (settle time). Moreover, in recent disks sometimes the arm must pause to control vibrations. Figure 9.38 (page 558) plots time versus seek distance for an example disk. It also shows the error in the simple seek-time formula above. For short seeks, the acceleration phase plays a larger role than the maximum traveling speed, and this phase is typically modeled as the square root of the distance. Figure 9.39 (page 558) shows accurate formulas used to model the seek time versus distance for two disks.

The second problem is the average in the product specification would only be true if there was no locality to disk activity. Fortunately, there is both temporal and spatial locality (page 403 in Chapter 8): disk blocks get used more than once and disk blocks near the current cylinder are more likely to be used than those farther away. For example, Figure 9.40 (page 559) shows sample measurements of seek distances for two workloads: a UNIX timesharing workload and a business-processing workload. Notice the high percentage of disk accesses to the same cylinder, labeled distance 0 in the graphs, in both workloads.

Thus, this fallacy couldn't be more misleading. The Exercises debunk this fallacy in more detail.

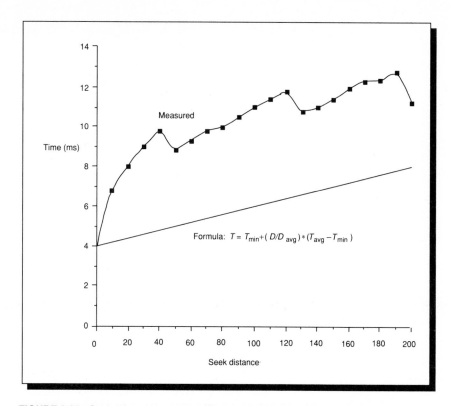

FIGURE 9.38   Seek time versus seek distance for the first 200 cylinders. The Imprimis Sabre 97209 contains 1.2 GB using 1635 cylinders and has the IPI-2 interface [Imprimis 1989]. This is an 8-inch disk. Note that longer seeks can take **less** time than shorter seeks. For example, a 40-cylinder seek takes almost 10 ms, while a 50-cylinder seek takes less than 9 ms.

IBM 3380D			IBM 3380J		
Range for formula		Formulas	Range for formula		Formulas
$\geq$	$\leq$		$\geq$	$\leq$	
1	50	$1.9 + \sqrt{\text{Distance}} - \dfrac{\text{Distance}}{50}$	1	50	$2.48 + \sqrt{\text{Distance}} - \dfrac{\text{Distance}}{20}$
51	100	$8.1 + 0.044 * (\text{Distance}{-}50)$	51	130	$7.28 + 0.0320 * (\text{Distance}{-}50)$
101	500	$10.3 + 0.025 * (\text{Distance}{-}100)$	131	500	$10.08 + 0.0166 * (\text{Distance}{-}130)$
501	884	$20.4 + 0.017 * (\text{Distance}{-}500)$	501	884	$16.00 + 0.0114 * (\text{Distance}{-}500)$

FIGURE 9.39   Formulas for seek time in ms for two IBM disks. Thisquen [1988] measured these disks and proposed these formulas to model them. The two columns on the left show the range of seek distances in cylinders to which each formula applies. Each disk has 885 cylinders, so the maximum seek is 884.

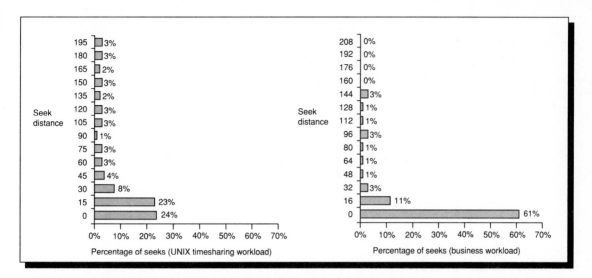

FIGURE 9.40 Sample measurements of seek distances for two systems. The left measurements were taken on a UNIX timesharing system. The right measurements were taken from a business processing application in which the disk seek activity was scheduled. Seek distance of 0 means the access was made to the same cylinder. The rest of the numbers show the collective percentage for distances up between numbers on the y axis. For example, 11% for the bar labeled 16 in the business graph means that the percentage of seeks between 1 and 16 cylinders was 11%. The UNIX measurements stopped at 200 cylinders, but this captured 85% of the accesses. The total was 1000 cylinders. The business measurements tracked all 816 cylinders of the disks. The only seek distances with 1% or greater of the seeks that are not in the graph are 224 with 4% and 304, 336, 512, and 624 each having 1%. This total is 94%, with the difference being small but nonzero distances in other categories. The measurements are courtesy of Dave Anderson of Imprimis.

9.11 | Concluding Remarks

I/O systems are judged by the variety of I/O devices, the maximum number of I/O devices, cost, and performance, measured both in latency and in throughput. These common goals lead to widely varying schemes, with some relying extensively on buffering and some avoiding buffering at all costs. If one is clearly better than the other, it is not obvious today. Perhaps this situation is like the instruction set debates of the 1980s, and the strengths and weaknesses of the alternatives will become apparent in the 1990s.

According to Amdahl's Law, ignorance of I/O will lead to wasted performance as CPUs get faster. Disk performance is growing at 4% to 6% per year, while CPUs are growing at a much faster rate. The future demands for I/O include better algorithms, better organizations, and more caching in a struggle to keep pace.

9.12 | Historical Perspective and References

The forerunner of today's workstations was the Alto developed at Xerox Palo Alto Research Center in 1974 [Thacker et al. 1982]. This machine reversed traditional wisdom, making instruction set interpretation take back seat to the display: the display used half the memory bandwidth of the Alto. In addition to the bit-mapped display, this historic machine had the first Ethernet [Metcalfe and Boggs 1976] and the first laser printer. It also had a mouse, invented earlier by Doug Engelbart of SRI, and a removable cartridge disk. The 16-bit CPU implemented an instruction set similar to the Data General Nova and offered writable control store (see Chapter 5, Section 5.8). In fact, a single microprogrammable engine drove the graphics display, mouse, disks, network, and, when there was nothing else to do, interpreted the instruction set.

The attraction of a personal computer is that you don't have to share it with anyone. This means response time is predictable, unlike timesharing systems. Early experiments in the importance of fast response time were performed by Doherty and Kelisky [1979]. They showed that if computer-system response time increased a second that user think time did also. Thadhani [1981] showed a jump in productivity as computer response times dropped to a second and another jump as they dropped to a half-second. His results inspired a flock of studies, and they supported his observations [IBM 1982]. In fact, some studies were started to disprove his results! Brady [1986] proposed differentiating entry time from think time (since entry time was becoming significant when the two were lumped together) and provided a cognitive model to explain the more than linear relationship between computer response time and user think time.

The ubiquitous microprocessor has inspired not only personal computers in the 1970s, but the current trend to moving controller functions into I/O devices in the late 1980s and 1990s. For example, microcoded routines in a central CPU made sense for the Alto in 1975, but technological changes soon made separate microprogrammable controller I/O devices economical. These were then replaced by the application-specific integrated circuits. I/O devices continued this trend by moving controllers into the devices themselves. These are called *intelligent devices*, and some bus standards (e.g., IPI and SCSI) have been created just for these devices. Intelligent devices can relax the timing constraints by handling many of the low-level tasks and queuing the results. For example, many SCSI-compatible disk drives include a track buffer on the disk itself, supporting read ahead and connect/disconnect. Thus, on a SCSI string some disks can be seeking and others loading their track buffer while one is transferring data from its buffer over the SCSI bus.

Speaking of buses, the first multivendor bus may have been the PDP-11 Unibus in 1970. DEC encouraged other companies to build devices that would plug into their bus, and many companies did. A more recent example is SCSI, which stands for *small computer systems interface*. This bus, originally called SASI, was invented by Shugart and was later standardized by the IEEE. Sometimes buses are developed in academia; the *NuBus* was developed by Steve Ward and his colleagues at MIT and used by several companies. Alas, this open-door policy on buses is in contrast to companies with proprietary buses using patented interfaces, thereby preventing competition from plug-compatible vendors. This practice also raises costs and lowers availability of I/O devices that plug into proprietary buses, since such devices must have an interface designed just for that bus. Levy [1978] has a nice survey on issues in buses.

We must also give a few references to specific I/O devices. Readers interested in the ARPANET should see Kahn [1972]. As mentioned in one of the section quotes, the father of computer graphics is Ivan Sutherland, who received the ACM Turing Award in 1988. Sutherland's Sketchpad system [1963] set the standard for today's interfaces and displays. See Foley and Van Dam [1982] and Newman and Sproull [1979] for more on computer graphics. Scranton, Thompson, and Hunter [1983] were among the first to report the myths concerning seek times and distances for magnetic disks.

Comments on the future of disks can be found in several sources. Goldstein [1987] projects the capacity and I/O rates for IBM mainframe installations in 1995, suggesting that the ratio is no less than 3.7 GB per IBM mainframe MIPS today, and that will grow to 4.5 GB per MIPS in 1995. Frank [1987] speculated on the physical recording density, proposing the MAD formula on disk growth that we used in Section 9.4. Katz, Patterson, and Gibson [1990] survey current high-performance disks and I/O systems and speculate about future systems. The possibility of achieving higher-performance I/O systems using collections of disks is found in papers by Kim [1986], Salem and Garcia-Molina [1986], and Patterson, Gibson, and Katz [1987].

Looking backward rather than forward, the first machine to extend interrupts from detecting arithmetic abnormalities to detecting asynchronous I/O events is credited as the NBS DYSEAC in 1954 [Leiner and Alexander 1954]. The following year the first machine with DMA was operational, the IBM SAGE. Just as today's DMA, the SAGE had address counters that performed block transfers in parallel with CPU operations. The first I/O channel may have been on the IBM 709 in 1957 [Bashe et al. 1981 and 1986]. Smotherman [1989] explores the history of I/O in more depth.

References

ANON ET AL. [1985]. "A measure of transaction processing power," Tandem Tech. Rep. TR 85.2. Also appeared in *Datamation*, April 1, 1985.

BASHE, C. J., W. BUCHHOLZ, G .V. HAWKINS, J .L. INGRAM, AND N. ROCHESTER [1981]. "The architecture of IBM's early computers," *IBM J. of Research and Development* 25:5 (September) 363–375.

BASHE, C. J., L. R. JOHNSON, J. H. PALMER, AND E. W. PUGH [1986]. *IBM's Early Computers*, MIT Press, Cambridge, Mass.

BORRILL, P. L. [1986]. "32-bit buses–An objective comparison," *Proc. Buscon 1986 West,* San Jose, Calif., 138–145.

BRADY, J. T. [1986]. "A theory of productivity in the creative process," *IEEE CG&A* (May) 25–34.

BUCHER, I. V. AND A. H. HAYES [1980]. "I/O Performance measurement on Cray-1 and CDC 7000 computers," *Proc. Computer Performance Evaluation Users Group, 16th Meeting*, NBS 500-65, 245–254.

CHEN, P. [1989]. *An Evaluation of Redundant Arrays of Inexpensive Disks Using an Amdahl 5890*, M. S. Thesis, Computer Science Division, Tech. Rep. UCB/CSD 89/506.

DOHERTY, W. J. AND R. P. KELISKY [1979]. "Managing VM/CMS systems for user effectiveness," *IBM Systems J.* 18:1, 143–166.

FEIERBACK, G AND D. STEVENSON [1979]. "The Illiac-IV," in *Infotech State of the Art Report on Supercomptuers*, Maidenhead, England. This data also appears in D. P. Siewiorek, C. G. Bell, and A. Newell, *Computer Structures: Principles and Examples* (1982), McGraw-Hill, New York, 268–269.

FOLEY, J. D. AND A. VAN DAM [1982]. *Fundamentals of Interactive Computer Graphics*, Addison-Wesley, Reading, Mass.

FRANK, P. D. [1987]. "Advances in Head Technology," presentation at *Challenges in Winchester Technology* (December 15), Santa Clara Univ.

FRIESENBORG, S. E. AND R. J. WICKS [1985]. "DASD expectations: The 3380, 3380-23, and MVS/XA," Tech. Bulletin GG22-9363-02 (July 10), Washington Systems Center.

GOLDSTEIN, S. [1987]. "Storage performance—an eight year outlook," Tech. Rep. TR 03.308-1 (October), Santa Teresa Laboratory, IBM, San Jose, Calif.

HENLY, M. AND B. MCNUTT [1989]. "DASD I/O characteristics: A comparison of MVS to VM," Tech. Rep. TR 02.1550 (May), IBM, General Products Division, San Jose, Calif.

HOWARD, J. H. ET AL. [1988]. "Scale and performance in a distributed file system," *ACM Trans. on Computer Systems* 6:1, 51–81.

IBM [1982]. *The Economic Value of Rapid Response Time*, GE20-0752-0 White Plains, N.Y., 11–82.

IMPRIMIS [1989]. "Imprimis Product Specification, 97209 Sabre Disk Drive IPI-2 Interface 1.2 GB," Document No. 64402302 (May).

KAHN, R. E. [1972]. "Resource-sharing computer communication networks," *Proc. IEEE* 60:11 (November) 1397-1407.

KATZ, R. H., D. A. PATTERSON, AND G. A. GIBSON [1990]. "Disk system architectures for high performance computing," *Proc. IEEE* 78:2 (February).

KIM, M. Y. [1986]. "Synchronized disk interleaving," *IEEE Trans. on Computers* C-35:11 (November).

LEINER, A. L. [1954]. "System specifications for the DYSEAC," *J. ACM* 1:2 (April) 57–81.

LEINER, A. L. AND S. N. ALEXANDER [1954]. "System organization of the DYSEAC," *IRE Trans. of Electronic Computers* EC-3:1 (March) 1–10.

LEVY, J. V. [1978]. "Buses: The skeleton of computer structures," in *Computer Engineering: A DEC View of Hardware Systems Design*, C. G. Bell, J. C. Mudge, and J. E. McNamara, eds., Digital Press, Bedford, Mass.

MABERLY, N. C. [1966]. *Mastering Speed Reading*, New American Library, Inc., New York.

METCALFE, R. M. AND D. R. BOGGS [1976]. "Ethernet: Distributed packet switching for local computer networks," *Comm. ACM* 19:7 (July) 395–404.

NEWMAN, W. N. AND R. F. SPROULL [1979]. *Principles of Interactive Computer Graphics*, 2nd ed., McGraw-Hill, New York.

OUSTERHOUT, J. K. ET AL. [1985]. "A trace-driven analysis of the UNIX 4.2 BSD file system," *Proc. Tenth ACM Symposium on Operating Systems Principles*, Orcas Island, Wash., 15–24.

PATTERSON, D. A., G. A. GIBSON, AND R. H. KATZ [1987]. "A case for redundant arrays of inexpensive disks (RAID)," Tech. Rep. UCB/CSD 87/391, Univ. of Calif. Also appeared in *ACM SIGMOD Conf. Proc.*, Chicago, Illinois, June 1–3, 1988, 109–116.

ROBINSON, B. AND L. BLOUNT [1986]. "The VM/HPO 3880-23 performance results," IBM Tech. Bulletin, GG66-0247-00 (April), Washington Systems Center, Gathersburg, Md.

SALEM, K. AND H. GARCIA-MOLINA [1986]. "Disk striping," *IEEE 1986 Int'l Conf. on Data Engineering*.

SCRANTON, R. A., D. A. THOMPSON, AND D. W. HUNTER [1983]. "The access time myth," Tech. Rep. RC 10197 (45223) (September 21), IBM, Yorktown Heights, N.Y.

SMITH, A. J. [1985]. "Disk cache—miss ratio analysis and design considerations," *ACM Trans. on Computer Systems* 3:3 (August) 161–203.

SMOTHERMAN , M. [1989]. "A sequencing-based taxonomy of I/O systems and review of historical machines," *Computer Architecture News* 17:5 (September) 5–15.

SUTHERLAND, I. E. [1963]. "Sketchpad: A man-machine graphical communication system," *Spring Joint Computer Conf.* 329.

THACKER, C. P., E. M. MCCREIGHT, B. W. LAMPSON, R. F. SPROULL, AND D. R. BOGGS [1982]. "Alto: A personal computer," in *Computer Structures: Principles and Examples*, D. P. Siewiorek, C. G. Bell, and A. Newell, eds., McGraw-Hill, New York, 549–572.

THADHANI, A. J. [1981]. "Interactive user productivity," *IBM Systems J.* 20:4, 407–423.

THISQUEN, J. [1988]. "Seek time measurements," *Amdahl Peripheral Products Division Tech. Rep.* (May).

E X E R C I S E S

9.1 <9.10> [10/25/10] Using the formulas in Figure 9.39 (page 558):

a.   [10] Calculate the seek time for moving the arm one-third of the cylinders for both disks.

b.   [25] Write a program to calculate the "average" seek time by estimating the time for all possible seeks using these formulas and then dividing by the number of seeks.

c.   [10] How close does (a) approximate (b)?

9.2 <9.10> [15/20] Using the formulas in Figure 9.39 (page 558) and the statistics in Figure 9.40 (page 559), calculate the average seek distance and the average seek time on the IBM 3380J. Use the midpoint of a range as the seek distance. For example, use 98 as the seek distance for the entry representing 91–105 in Figure 9.40. For the business workload, just ignore the missing 5% of the seeks. For the UNIX workload, assume the missing 15% of the seeks have an average distance of 300 cylinders.

a.   [15] If you were misled by the fallacy, you might calculate the average distance as 884/3. What is the measured distance for each workload?

b.   [20] The time to seek 884/3 cylinders on the IBM 3380J is about 12.8 ms. What is the average seek time for each workload on the IBM 3380J using the measurements?

9.3 <1.4,8.4,9.4> [20/10/Discussion] Assume the improvements in density of DRAMs and magnetic disks continue as predicted in Figure 1.5 (page 17). Assuming that the improvement in cost per megabyte tracks the density improvements and that 1990 is the start of the 4-megabit DRAM generation, when will the cost per megabyte of DRAM equal the cost per megabyte of magnetic disk given:

■   The cost difference in 1990 is that DRAM is 10 times more expensive.

■   The cost difference in 1990 is that DRAM is 30 times more expensive.

a.   [20] Which generation of DRAM chip—measured in bits per chip—will reach equity for each cost difference assumption? What year will that occur?

b.   [10] What will be the difference in cost in the previous generation?

c.   [Discussion] Do you think the cost difference in the previous generation is sufficient to prevent disks being replaced by DRAMs?

9.4 <9.2> [12/12/12] Assume a workload takes 100 seconds total, with the CPU taking 70 seconds and I/O taking 50 seconds.

a.   [12] Assume that the floating-point unit is responsible for 25 seconds of the CPU time. You are considering a floating-point accelerator that goes five times faster. What is the time of the workload for maximum overlap, scaled overlap, and no overlap?

b.   [12] Assume that seek and rotational delay of magnetic disks are responsible for 10 seconds of the I/O time. You are considering replacing the magnetic disks with solid state disks that will remove all the seek and rotational delay. What is the time of the workload for maximum overlap, scaled overlap, and no overlap?

c.   [12] What is the time of the workload for scaled overlap if you make both changes?

9.5–9.9 Transaction-processing performance. The I/O bus and memory system of a computer are capable of sustaining 100 MB/sec without interfering with the performance of an 80-MIPS CPU (costing $50,000). Here are the assumptions about the software:

■   Each transaction requires 2 disk reads plus 2 disk writes.

■   The operating system uses 15,000 instructions for each disk read or write.

■   The database software executes 40,000 instructions to process a transaction.

■   The transfer size is 100 bytes.

You have a choice of two different types of disks:

■   A 2.5-inch disk that stores 100 MB and costs $500.

■   A 3.5-inch disk that stores 250 MB and costs $1250.

■   Either disk in the system can support on average 30 disk reads or writes per second.

Answer the questions below using the TP-1 benchmark in Section 9.3. Assume that the requests are spread evenly to all the disks, that there is no waiting time due to busy disks, and that the account file must be large enough to handle 1000 TPS according to the benchmark ground rules.

9.5 <9.3,9.4> [20] How many TP-1 transactions per second are possible with each disk organization, assuming that each uses the minimum number of disks to hold the account file?

9.6 <9.3,9.4> [15] What is the system cost per transaction per second of each alternative for TP-1?

9.7 <9.3,9.4> [15] How fast a CPU makes the 100 MB/sec I/O bus a bottleneck for TP-1? (Assume that you can continue to add disks.)

9.8 <9.3,9.4> [15] As manager of MTP (Mega TP), you are deciding whether to spend your development money building a faster CPU or improve the performance of the software. The database group says they can reduce a transaction to 1 disk read and 1 disk write and cut the database instructions per transaction to 30,000. The hardware group can build a faster CPU that sells for the same amount of the slower CPU with the same development budget. (Assume you can add as many disks as needed to get higher performance.) How much faster does the CPU have to be to match the performance gain of the software improvement?

9.9 <9.3,9.4> [15/15] The MTP I/O group was listening at the door during the software presentation. They argue that advancing technology will allow CPUs to get faster without significant investment, but that the cost of the system will be dominated by disks if they don't develop new faster 2.5-inch disks. Assume the next CPU is 100% faster at the same cost and that the new disks have the same capacity as the old ones.

a. [15] Given the new CPU and the old software, what will be the cost of a system with enough old 2.5-inch disks so that they do not limit the TPS of the system ?

b. [15] Now assume you have as many new disks as you had old 2.5 inch disks in the original design. How fast must the new disks be (I/Os per second) to achieve the same TPS rate with the new CPU as the system in part a? What will the system cost?

9.10 <9.4> [20/20/20] Assume that we have the following two magnetic-disk configurations: a single disk and an array of four disks. Each disk has 20 surfaces, 885 tracks per surface with 16 sectors/track, each sector holds 1K bytes, and it revolves at 3600 RPM. Using the seek-time formula, for the IBM 3380D in Figure 9.39 (page 558). The time to switch between surfaces is the same as to move the arm one track. In the disk array all the spindles are synchronized—sector 0 in every disk rotates under the head at the exact same time—and the arms on all four disks are always over the same track. The data is "striped" across all 4 disks, so four consecutive sectors on a single disk system will be spread one sector per disk in the array. The delay of the disk controller is 2 ms per transaction, either for a single disk or for the array. Assume the performance of the I/O system is limited only by the disks and that there is a path to each disk in the array.

Compare the performance in both I/Os per second and megabytes per second of these two disk organizations assuming the following request patterns:

a. [20] Random reads of 4 KB of sequential sectors. Assume the 4 KB are aligned under the same arm on each disk in the array.

b. [20] Reads of 4 KB of sequential sectors where the average seek distance is 10 tracks. Assume the 4 KB are aligned under the same arm on each disk in the array.

c. [20] Random reads of 1 MB of sequential sectors. (If it matters, assume the disk controller allows the sectors to arrive in any order.)

9.11 [20] <9.4> Assume that we have one disk defined as in Exercise 9.9. Assume that we read the next sector after any read and that *all* read requests are one sector in length. We store the extra sectors that were read ahead in a *disk cache*. Assume that the probability of receiving a request for the sector we read ahead at some time in the future (before it must be discarded because the disk-cache buffer fills) is 0.1. Assume that we must still pay the controller overhead on a disk-cache read hit, and the transfer time for the disk cache is 250 ns per word. Is the read-ahead strategy faster? (Hint: Solve the problem in the steady state by assuming that the disk cache contains the appropriate information and a request has just missed.)

9.12–9.14 Assume the following information about our DLX machine:

Loads 2 cycles

Stores 2 cycles

All other instructions are 1 cycle. Use the summary instruction mix information in Figure C.4 in Appendix C on DLX for GCC.

Here are the cache statistics for a write-through cache:

- Each cache block is four words, and the whole block is read on any miss.

- Cache miss takes 13 cycles.

- Write through takes 6 cycles to complete, and there is no write buffer.

Here are the cache statistics for a write-back cache:

- Each cache block is four words, and the whole block is read on any miss.

- Cache miss takes 13 cycles for a clean block and 21 cycles for a dirty block.

- Assume that on a miss, 30% of the time the block is dirty.

Assume that the bus

- is only busy during transfers,

- transfers on average 1 word / clock cycle, and

- must read or write a single word at a time (it is not faster to read or write two at once).

9.12 [20/10/20/20] <9.4,9.5,9.6> Assume that DMA I/O can take place simultaneously with CPU cache hits. Also assume that the operating system can guarantee that there will be no stale-data problem in the cache due to I/O. The sector size is 1 KB.

a.   [20] Assume the cache miss rate is 5%. On the average, what percentage of the bus is used for each cache write policy? This measured is called the *traffic ratio* in cache studies.

b.   [10] If the bus can be loaded up to 80% of capacity without suffering severe performance penalties, how much memory bandwidth is available for I/O for each cache write policy? The cache miss rate is still 5%.

c.   [20] Assume that a disk sector read takes 1000 clock cycles to initiate a read, 100,000 clock cycles to find the data on the disk, and 1000 clock cycles for the DMA to transfer the data to memory. How many disk reads can occur per million instructions executed for each write policy? How does this change if the cache miss rate is cut in half?

d.   [20] Now you can have any number of disks. Assuming ideal scheduling of disk accesses, what is the maximum number of sector reads that can occur per million instructions executed?

9.13 [20/20] <9.4,9.5> Most machines today have a separate frame buffer to update the screen to avoid slowing down the memory system. An interesting issue is the percentage of the memory bandwidth that would be used if there were no frame buffer. Assume that all accesses to the memory are the size of a full cache block and they all take the time of a cache miss. The refresh rate is 60 Hz. Using the information in Section 9.4, calculate the memory traffic for the following graphics devices:

1.   A 340 by 540 black-and-white display.

2.   A 1280 by 1024 color display with 24 bits of color.

3.   A 1280 by 1024 color display using a 256-word color map.

Assume the clock rate of the CPU is 60 MHz.

a.   [20] What percentage of the memory/bus bandwidth do each of the three displays consume?

b.   [20] Suppose instead of the bus and main memory being 32 bits wide that both are 512 bits wide. How long should a memory access take now using the wider bus? What percentage of memory bandwidth is now used by each display?

9.14 [20] <9.4,9.9> The IBM 3990 I/O Subsystem storage director can have a large cache for reads and writes. Assume the cache costs the same as four 3380D disks. What hit rate must the cache achieve to get the same performance as four more 3380D disks? (See Figure 9.15 (page 517) for 3380 performance.) Assume the cache could support 5000 I/Os per second if everything hit the cache.

9.15 [50] <9.3, 9.4> Take your favorite computer and write three programs that achieve the following:

1.   Maximum bandwidth to and from disks

2.   Maximum bandwidth to a frame buffer

3.   Maximum bandwidth to and from the local area network

What is the percentage of the bandwidth that you achieve compared to what the I/O device manufacturer claims? Also record CPU utilization in each case for the programs running separately. Next run all three together and see what percentage of maximum bandwidth you achieve for three I/O devices as well as the CPU utilization. Try to determine why one gets a larger percentage than the others.

9.16 [40] <9.2> The system speedup formulas are limited to one or two types of devices. Derive simple to use formulas for unlimited numbers of devices, using as many different assumptions on overlap that you can handle.

9.17 [Discussion] <9.2> What are arguments for predicting system performance using maximum overlap, scaled overlap, and nonoverlap? Construct scenarios where each one seems most likely and other scenarios where each interpretation is nonsensical.

9.18 [Discussion] <9.11> What are the advantages and disadvantages of a minimal buffer I/O system like that used by IBM versus a maximal buffer I/O system on I/O system cost/performance?

The turning away from the conventional organization came in the middle 1960's, when the law of diminishing returns began to take effect in the effort to increase the operational speed of a computer. . . . Electronic circuits are ultimately limited in their speed of operation by the speed of light . . . and many of the circuits were already operating in the nanosecond range.

Bouknight et al. [1972]

. . . sequential computers are approaching a fundamental physical limit on their potential computational power. Such a limit is the speed of light . . .

A. L. DeCegama, *The Technology of Parallel Processing, Volume I* (1989)

. . . today's machines . . . are nearing an impasse as technologies approach the speed of light. Even if the components of a sequential processor could be made to work this fast, the best that could be expected is no more than a few million instructions per second.

Mitchell [1989]

10 Future Directions

10.1 Introduction

In the first nine chapters we limited ourselves to ideas that have proven themselves in the marketplace. Yet the principles of these chapters can be found in the first paper on stored-program computers. The quotes on the facing page suggest that the days of the traditional computer are numbered. For a dated model of computation it has surely demonstrated its viability! Today it is improving in performance faster than at any time in its history, and the improvement in cost and performance since 1950 has been five orders of magnitude. Had the transportation industry kept pace with these advances, we could travel from San Francisco to New York in one minute for one dollar!

In this last chapter we abandon our conservative perspective and speculate about the future of computer architecture and compilers. The goal of innovative designs is dramatic improvements in cost/performance, or highly scalable performance with good cost/performance. Many of the ideas covered here have led to machines that are beginning to compete in the computer marketplace today. Some of them may not be around for the next edition of this book, while others may need their own chapters.

10.2 | Flynn Classification of Computers

Flynn [1966] proposed a simple model of categorizing all computers. He looked at the parallelism in the instruction and data streams called for by the instructions at the most constrained component of the machine, and placed all computers in one of four categories:

1. *Single instruction stream, single data stream* (SISD, the uniprocessor)

2. *Single instruction stream, multiple data streams* (SIMD)

3. *Multiple instruction streams, single data stream* (MISD)

4. *Multiple instruction streams, multiple data streams* (MIMD)

This is a coarse model, as some machines are hybrids of these categories. Yet in this chapter we stick with this classic model because it is simple, easy to understand, gives a good first approximation, and—perhaps because of ease of understanding—is also the most widely used scheme.

Your first question about the model should be, "Single or multiple compared to what?" A machine that can add a 32-bit number in one clock cycle would seem to have multiple data streams when compared to a bit-serial computer that takes 32 clock cycles for the same operation. Flynn chose popular computers of that day, the IBM 704 and IBM 7090, as the model of SISD, although today any of the machines in Chapter 4 would serve as the example.

Having thus established the reference point for SISD, the next class is SIMD.

10.3 | SIMD Computers—Single Instruction Stream, Multiple Data Streams

The cost of a general multiprocessor is, however, very high and further design options were considered which would decrease the cost without seriously degrading the power or efficiency of the system. The options consist of recentralizing one of the three major components.... Centralizing the [control unit] gives rise to the basic organization of [an]... array processor such as the Illiac IV.

Bouknight et al. [1972]

We have already seen typical instructions for a SIMD machine, yet the machine is not SIMD. The vector instructions of Chapter 7 operate on several data elements within a single instruction, executing in pipelined fashion in a single functional unit. Unlike SIMD, many functional units are not being invoked by a single instruction. A true SIMD would have, say, 64 data streams simultaneously going to 64 ALUs to form 64 sums within the same clock cycle.

The virtues of SIMD are that all the parallel execution units are synchronized and that they all respond to a single instruction from a single PC. From a programmer's perspective, this is close to the already familiar SISD. The original motivation for SIMD was to amortize the cost of the control unit over dozens of execution units. A more recently observed advantage is the reduced size of program memory—SIMD needs only one copy of the code being simultaneously executed, while MIMD needs a copy in every processor. Hence, the cost of program memory for a large number of execution units is less for SIMD.

Like vector machines, real SIMD computers have a mixture of SISD and SIMD instructions. There is a SISD host computer to perform operations such as branches or address calculation that do not need massive parallelism. The SIMD instructions are broadcast to all the execution units, each of which has its own set of registers. Also, as in vector machines, individual execution units can be disabled during a SIMD instruction. Unlike vector machines, massively parallel SIMD machines rely on interconnection or communication networks to exchange data between processing elements.

SIMD works best when vector instructions work best—in dealing with arrays in for-loops. Hence, to have the opportunity for massive parallelism in SIMD there must be massive amounts of data, or *data parallelism*. SIMD is at its weakest in case statements, where each execution unit must perform a different operation on its data, depending on what data it has. The execution units with the wrong data are disabled so that the proper units can continue. Such situations essentially run at $1/n$th performance, where n is the number of cases.

The basic tradeoff in SIMD machines is performance of a processor versus number of processors. The machines in the marketplace today emphasize a large degree of parallelism over performance of the individual processors. The Connection Machine 2, for example, offers 65,536 single bit-wide processors while the ILLIAC IV had 64 64-bit processors.

While MISD fills out Flynn's classification, it is difficult to envision. A single instruction stream is simpler than multiple instruction streams, but multiple instruction streams with multiple data streams are easier to imagine than multiple instructions with a single data stream. A few of the architectures we have covered might be considered MISD: superscalar and VLIW architectures of Chapter 6 (Section 6.8) often have a single data stream and multiple instructions, although these machines have a single program counter. Perhaps closer to the mark are the decoupled architectures (pages 321–322), which have two instruction streams with independent program counters and a single data stream. Systolic architectures, covered in Section 10.6, might also be considered MISD.

While we can find examples of SIMD and MISD, their number is dwarfed by the multitude of MIMD machines.

10.4 | MIMD Computers—Multiple Instruction Streams, Multiple Data Streams

Multis are a new class of computers based on multiple microprocessors. The small size, low cost, and high performance of microprocessors allow design and construction of computer structures that offer significant advantages in manufacture, price-performance ratio, and reliability over traditional computer families.... Multis are likely to be the basis for the next, the fifth, generation of computers.

Bell [1985, 463]

Practically since the first working computer, architects have been striving for the El Dorado of computer design: To compose a powerful computer by simply connecting many existing smaller ones. The user orders as many CPUs as he can afford and gets a commensurate amount of performance. Other advantages of MIMD may be highest absolute performance, faster than the largest uniprocessor, and highest reliability/availability (page 520) via redundancy.

For decades, computer designers have been looking for the missing piece of the puzzle that allows this speedup to happen, as if by magic. People are heard making statements that begin "Now that computers have dropped to such a low price..." or "This new interconnection scheme will overcome the scaling problem, so..." or "As this new programming language becomes widespread...," and end with "MIMDs will (finally) dominate computing."

With so many attempts to use parallelism, there are a few terms that are useful to know when discussing MIMDs. The principal division is that which delineates how information is shared. *Shared-memory* processors offer the programmer a single memory address that all processors can access; cache-coherent multiprocessors are shared-memory machines (see Sections 8.8 and 10.8). Processes communicate through shared variables in memory, with loads and stores capable of accessing any memory location. Synchronization must be available to coordinate processes. An alternative model to sharing data is where processes communicate by sending messages. As an extreme example, processes on different workstations communicate by sending messages over a local area network. This communication distinction is so fundamental that Bell suggests the term *multiprocessor* be limited to MIMDs that can communicate via shared memory, while MIMDs that can only communicate via explicit message passing should be called *multicomputers*. Since a portion of a shared memory could be used for messages, most multiprocessors can efficiently execute message-passing software. A multicomputer might be able to simulate shared memory by sending a message for every load or store, but presumably this would run excruciatingly slowly. Thus, Bell's distinction is based on the underlying hardware and program execution model, reflected in the performance of shared-memory communication, as opposed to the software that might run on a machine. Message-passing docents question the *scalability* of multiprocessors, while shared-memory advocates question the programmability of multicomputers. The next section examines this debate further.

The good news is that after many assaults, MIMD has established a beachhead. Today it is generally agreed that a multiprocessor may be more effective for a timesharing workload than a SISD. No single program takes less CPU time, but more independent tasks can be completed per hour—a throughput versus latency argument. Not only are start-up companies like Encore and Sequent selling small-scale multiprocessors, but the high-end machines from IBM, DEC, and Cray Research are multiprocessors. This means multiprocessors now embody a significant market, responsible for a majority of the mainframes and virtually all supercomputers. The only disappointment to computer architects is that shared memory is practically irrelevant for user programs run on the machine, with the operating system being the only benefactor. The development of a multiprocessor's operating system, particularly its resource manager, is simplified by shared memory.

The bad news is that it remains to be seen how many important applications run faster on MIMDs. The difficulty has not lain in the prices of SISDs, in flaws in topologies of interconnection networks, or in programming languages; but in the lack of applications software that have been reprogrammed to take advantage of many processors to complete important tasks sooner. Since it has been even harder to find applications that can take advantage of many processors, the challenge is greater for large scale MIMDs. When the positive gains from timesharing are combined with the scarcity of highly parallel applications, we can appreciate the predicament facing computer architects designing large-scale MIMDs that do not support timesharing.

But why is this so? Why should it be so much harder to develop MIMD programs than sequential programs? One reason is that it is hard to write MIMD programs that achieve close to linear speedup as the number of processors dedicated to the task increases. As an analogy, think of the communication overhead for a task done by one person versus the overhead for a task done by a committee, especially as the size of the group increases. While n people may have the potential to finish any task n times faster, the communication overhead for the group can prevent it from achieving this; this becomes especially hard as n increases. (Imagine the change in communication overhead going from 10 people to 1,000 people to 1,000,000.) Another reason for the difficulty in writing parallel programs is how much the programmer must know about the hardware. On a uniprocessor, the high-level language programmer writes his program ignoring the underlying machine organization—that's the job of the compiler. For a multiprocessor today, the programmer had better know the underlying hardware and organization if he is to write fast and scalable programs. This intimacy also makes portable parallel programs rare. Though this second obstacle may lessen over time, it is now the biggest challenge facing computer science. Finally, from Chapter 1 comes Amdahl's Law (page 8) to remind us that even small parts of a program must be parallelized to reach the full potential. Thus, coming close to linear speedup involves inventing new algorithms that are inherently parallel.

Example

Suppose you want to achieve linear speedup with 100 processors. What fraction of the original computation can be sequential?

Answer

Amdahl's Law is

$$\text{Speedup} = \frac{1}{(1 - \text{Fraction}_{\text{enhanced}}) + \dfrac{\text{Fraction}_{\text{enhanced}}}{\text{Speedup}_{\text{enhanced}}}}$$

Substituting for the goal of linear speedup with 100 processors gives:

$$100 = \frac{1}{(1 - \text{Fraction}_{\text{enhanced}}) + \dfrac{\text{Fraction}_{\text{enhanced}}}{100}}$$

Solving for percentage converted to enhanced mode:

$$100 - 100 * \text{Fraction}_{\text{enhanced}} + 1 * \text{Fraction}_{\text{enhanced}} = 1$$

$$-99 * \text{Fraction}_{\text{enhanced}} = -99$$

$$\text{Fraction}_{\text{enhanced}} = 1$$

Thus, to achieve linear speedup with 100 processors, **none** of the original computation can be sequential. Put another way, to get a speedup of 99 from 100 processors means the sequential fraction of the original program had to be about 0.0001.

The example above demonstrates the need for new algorithms. This underlines the authors' belief that major successes in using large-scale parallel machines of the 1990s are possible for those who understand applications, algorithms, and architecture.

10.5 | The Roads to El Dorado

Figure 10.1 shows the state of the industry, plotting number of processors versus performance of an individual processor. The massive parallelism question is whether taking the high road or the low road in Figure 10.1 will get us to El Dorado. Currently we don't know enough about parallel programming and applications to be able to quantitatively trade-off number of processors versus performance per processor to achieve the best cost/performance.

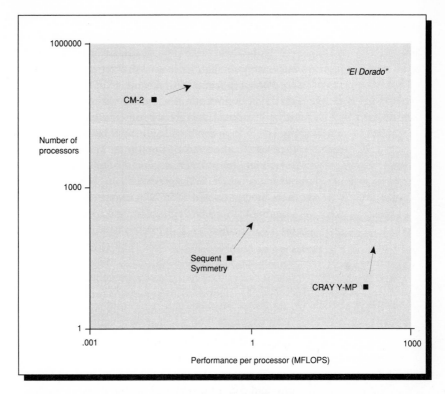

FIGURE 10.1 Danny Hillis, architect of the Connection Machines, has used a figure similar to this to illustrate the multiprocessor industry. (Hillis's x axis was processor width rather than processor performance.) Processor performance on this graph is approximated by the MFLOPS rating of a **single** processor for the DAXPY procedure of the Linpack benchmark for a 1000 x 1000 matrix. Generally, it is easier for programmers when moving to the right , while moving up is easier for the hardware designer because there is more hardware replication. The massive parallelism question is, "Which is the quickest path to the upper right corner?" The computer design question is, "Which has the best cost/performance or is more scalable for equivalent cost/performance?"

It is interesting to note that very different changes are required to improve performance depending on whether you take the low road or the high road in this figure. Since most programs are written in high-level languages, moving along the horizontal direction (increasing performance per processor) is almost entirely a matter of improving the hardware. The applications are unchanged, with compilers adapting them to the more powerful processor. Hence, increasing processor performance versus number of processors is easier for the applications software. Improving performance by moving in the vertical direction (increasing parallelism), on the other hand, may involve significant changes to applications, since programming ten processors may be very different from programming a thousand, and different yet again from programming a million. (But going from

100 to 101 is probably not different.) An advantage of the vertical path to performance is that the hardware may be simply replicated—the processors in particular, but also the hardware of the interconnection switch. Hence, increasing number of processors versus processor performance results in more hardware replication. An advantage of the low road is that it is much more likely that there will be a market at the various points along the way to El Dorado. In addition, those who take the high road must grapple with Amdahl's Law.

This brings us to a fundamental debate about the organization of memory in large-scale machines of the future. The debate unfortunately often centers on a false dichotomy: *shared memory* versus *distributed memory*. Shared memory means a single address space, implying implicit communication. The real opposite to a shared address is *multiple private address spaces,* implying explicit communication. Distributed memory refers to the location of the memory. If physical memory is divided into modules with some placed near each processor (which allows faster access time to that memory), then physical memory is distributed. The real opposite of distributed memory is *centralized memory,* where access time to a physical memory location is the same for all processors.

Clearly shared address versus multiple address and distributed memory versus centralized memory are orthogonal issues: SIMDs or MIMDs can have a shared address and a distributed physical memory or multiple private address spaces and a centralized physical memory (although this last combination would be unusual). Figure 10.2 categorizes several machines by these axes. The proper debates concerning the future are the pros and cons of a single address and the pros and cons of distributed memory.

The single address debate is closely tied to the model of communication, since shared-address machines must offer implicit communication (possibly

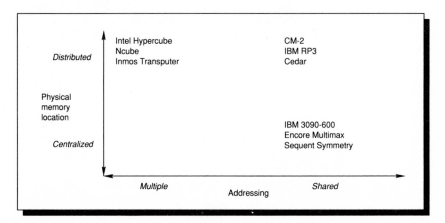

FIGURE 10.2   Parallel processors placed according to centralized versus distributed memory and shared versus multiple addressing. In general it is easier for software for machines on the shared side of the addressing axis and it is easier to build larger-scale machines on the distributed end of the vertical access. These machines in the graph are described in Section 10.11.

part of any memory access) and multiple-address machines must have explicit communication. (It is not quite that simple since some shared-address machines also offer explicit communication in various forms.) "Implicitists" knock "explicitists" for advocating machines that are harder to program when it is already hard to find applications: Why make the programmer's life more difficult when software is the linchpin of large-scale parallelism? One reply is that if memory is distributed, as processors get faster the time to remote memory will be so long—say 50 to 100 clock cycles—the compiler or programmer must be aware he is writing for a large-scale parallel machine no matter which communication scheme is used. Explicit communication also offers the possibility of hiding the cost of communication by overlapping it with computation. The implicitist reply is that using hardware rather than explicit instructions reduces the overhead of communication. Moreover, a single address means processes can use pointers and communicate data only if the pointer is dereferenced, while explicit communication means the data must be sent in the presence of pointers since the data **might** be accessed. The explicitist rebuttal is the owner of the data can send the data, traversing a properly designed network only once, while in shared-memory machines a processor requests the data and then the owner returns it, requiring two trips over the communications network.

Distributed-memory advocates argue that no matter how much caching is placed in front of a single central memory, it has limited bandwidth, and thus, limits the number of processors. Central-memory advocates raise the question of efficiency: If there is not enough parallelism to use many processors, then why distribute memory? Centralists also point out that distributed memory increases the difficulty of programming, since now the programmer or the compiler must decide how to lay out the data in the physical memory modules so as to reduce communication. Hence, distributed memory introduces the concept of data elements being near a processor (the module taking less time to access) or far (in other memory modules).

We can now explain a difficulty of the distributed versus centralized dichotomy. Every processor will likely have a cache, which is in some sense a distributed memory no matter how main memory is organized. Even with caches, the latency of a miss and the effective bandwidth for satisfying cache requests can be improved if data is allocated to the memory module near the appropriate cache. Hence, there is still a distinction between centralized and distributed main memory in the presence of caches.

As you can imagine, these debates continue back and forth, practically interminably. Fortunately, in computer architecture such disagreements are settled by measurements rather than polemics. Thus, time will be the judge of these issues, but your authors will be the judge of a bet inspired by these debates (see page 590 in 10.11).

The real issues for future machines are these: Do problems and algorithms with sufficient parallelism exist? And can people be trained or compilers be written to exploit such parallelism?

10.6 | Special-Purpose Processors

In addition to exploring parallelism, many designers today are exploring special-purpose computers. With the increasing sophistication of *computer-aided design* software and increasing capacity per chip comes the opportunity of quickly building a chip that does one thing well at low cost. Real-time speech recognition and image processing are examples. Such special-purpose devices, or *coprocessors*, frequently act in conjunction with the CPU. There are two types in the coprocessor trend: digital signal processors and systolic arrays.

Digital signal processors (or DSPs) are not derived from the traditional model of computing, and tend to look like horizontal microprogrammed machines (see page 212) or VLIW machines (see pages 322–325). They tend to solve real-time problems, essentially having an infinite-input data stream. There has been little emphasis on compiling from programming languages such as C, but that is starting to change. As DSPs bend to the demands of programming languages, it will be interesting to see how they differ from traditional microprocessors.

Systolic arrays evolved from attempts to get more efficient computing bandwidth from silicon. Systolic arrays can be thought of as a method for designing special-purpose computers to balance resources, I/O bandwidth, and computation. Relying on pipelining, data flows in stages from memory through an array of computation units and back to memory, as suggested in Figure 10.3. Recently, systolic-array research has moved away from many, dedicated special-purpose chips to fewer, more powerful chips that are programmable.

The authors expect an increasing role for special-purpose computers in the 1990s because they offer both higher performance and lower cost for dedicated functions such as real-time speech recognition and image processing. The consumer marketplace seems the most likely candidate, given its high volume and sensitivity to cost.

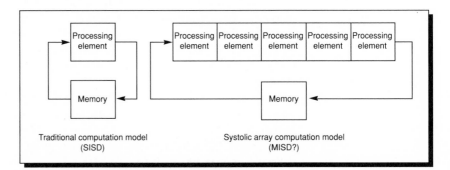

FIGURE 10.3 The systolic architecture gets its name from the heart rhythmically pumping blood. Data arrives at a processing element at regular intervals, where it is modified and passed to the next element, and so on, until it circulates back to memory. Some consider systolic arrays an example of MISD.

10.7 | **Future Directions for Compilers**

Compilers of the future have two challenges on machines of the future:

- Lay out of data to reduce memory hierarchy and communication overhead, and

- Exploitation of parallelism.

Programs of the future will spend a larger percentage of the execution time waiting for the memory hierarchy as the gap grows between the clock cycle time of processors and the access time of main memory (see Figure 8.18, page 427). Compilers that arrange code and data so as to reduce cache misses may lead to larger performance improvements than traditional optimizations of today. Further improvements are possible with the possibility of prefetching data into a cache before it is needed by the program. One interesting proposition is by extending existing programming languages with array operations a programmer can express parallelism with calculations on entire arrays at a time, leaving it up to the compiler to lay out the data into processors to reduce the amount of communication. For example, the proposed extension to FORTRAN 77 called FORTRAN 8X includes array extensions. The hope is that the programmer's task might even be simpler than with SISD machines where array operations must be specified with loops. The range of programs that such a compiler can handle efficiently and the number of hints a programmer must supply on where to place data will determine the practical value of this proposal.

In addition to reducing the costs of memory access and communication, compilers may change performance by factors of two or three by utilizing parallelism available in the processor. Figure 2.25 (page 75) shows the Perfect Club benchmarks operate at only 1% of peak performance, clearly suggesting many opportunities for software. More specifically, the superscalar machines of Chapter 6 (pages 318–320) typically achieve a speedup of less than 2 using today's compilers, even through the potential performance improvement of executing 4 instructions at once is 4. From Chapter 7 we see that vector machines typically achieve a vectorization rate of 40% to 70%, delivering a speedup of 1.5 to 2.5, where a vectorization rate of 90% could achieve a speedup over 5. And current compilers for multiprocessors are considered successful if they achieve a speedup 3 for a single program when the potential from 8 processors is 8. Figure 10.4 (page 582) shows the potential improvement in performance of a larger percentage of the work executing in the higher-performance mode for each of these categories. Since we can expect multiple processors in machines where each processor has vector or superscalar features, the potential speedup of these factors may be multiplied together.

While this opportunity exists for compilers, we do not want to belittle its difficulty. Parallelizing compilers have been under development since 1975 but progress has been slow. These problems are hard, especially for the "dusty deck" challenge of running existing programs. Success has been limited to programs where the parallelism is available in the algorithm and expressed in the program and to machines with a small number of processors. Significant progress may eventually require new programming languages as well as smarter compilers!

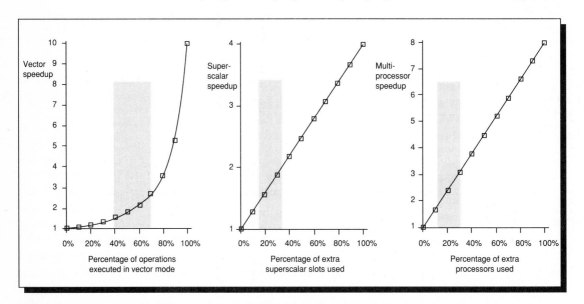

FIGURE 10.4   Potential for performance improvement by compilers transforming more of the computation into the faster mode. The leftmost graph shows the percentage of operations executed in vector mode, while the other graphs show the percentage of the potential speedup in use on average: percentage of four instructions used per cycle in superscalar and percentage of time all eight processors were utilized in the multiprocessor. The gray area shows the range of utilization typically found in programs using current compilers.

10.8 | Putting It All Together: The Sequent Symmetry Multiprocessor

The high performance and low cost of the microprocessor inspired renewed interest in multiprocessors in the 1980s. Several microprocessors can be placed on a common bus because:

they are much smaller than multichip processors,

caches can lower bus traffic, and

coherency protocols can keep caches and memory consistent.

Traffic per processor and the bus bandwidth determine the number of processors in such a multiprocessor.

Several research projects and companies investigated these shared-bus multiprocessors. One example is Sequent Corporation, founded to build multiprocessors based on standard microprocessors, and the UNIX operating system. The first-generation system was the Balance 8000, offered in 1984 with 2 to 12 National 32032 microprocessors, a 32-bit split transaction bus that multiplexed address and data, and one 8-KB, 2-way–set-associative, write-through cache per processor. Each cache watched the bus to maintain coherency using write through with invalidate. (See Sections 8.4, 8.8, and 9.4 for a review of these terms.) The sustained bandwidth of the main memory and bus is 26.7 MB/sec. Two years later Sequent upgraded to the Balance 21000, offering up to 30 National 32032 microprocessors with the same memory system and bus.

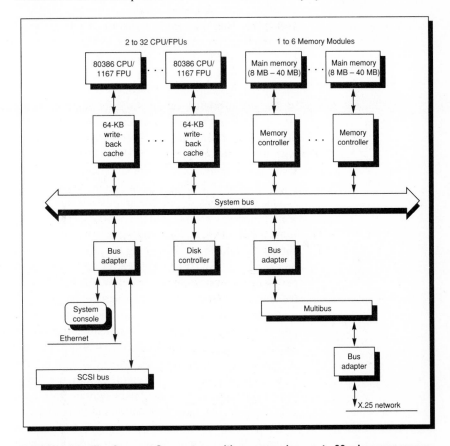

FIGURE 10.5 The Sequent Symmetry multiprocessor has up to 30 microprocessors, each with 64 KB of 2-way set associative, write-back caches connected over the shared system bus. Up to six memory controllers also talk to this 64-bit-wide bus, plus some interfaces for I/O. In addition to a special-purpose disk controller, there is an interface for the system console, Ethernet network, and SCSI I/O bus (see Chapter 9), as well as another interface for Multibus. I/O devices can be attached either to SCSI or to Multibus, as the customer desires. (Although all interfaces are labeled "Bus adapter," each is a unique design.)

In 1986, Sequent began the design of the Symmetry multiprocessor, assuming a microprocessor 300% to 400% faster than the 32032. The goal was to support as many processors as possible using the I/O controllers developed for the Balance system. This meant the bus had to remain compatible, though the new memory and bus system had to deliver roughly 300% to 400% higher bandwidth than the older system.

The goal of higher memory-system bandwidth with a similar bus was attacked on four levels. First, the cache was increased to 64 KB, increasing the hit rate and therefore the effective memory bandwidth as seen by the processor. Second, the cache policy was changed from write through to write back to reduce the number of write operations on the shared bus. To maintain cache coherency with write back, Symmetry uses a write-invalidate scheme (see pages 468–469). The third change was to double the bus width to 64 bits, thereby doubling the bus bandwidth to 53 MB/sec. The final change was to have each memory controller interleave memory as two banks (see Section 8.8), allowing the memory system to match the bandwidth of the wider bus. The memory system can have up to six controllers with up to 240-MB total main memory.

The use of high-level languages and the portability of the UNIX operating system allowed changing instruction sets to the faster Intel 80386. Running at a higher clock rate, with the faster Weitek 1167 floating-point accelerator, **and** with the improved memory system, a single 80386 ran from 214% to 776% faster for floating-point benchmarks and about 375% faster for integer benchmarks. Figure 10.5 (page 583) shows the organization of the Symmetry.

One of the other design constraints was that the new Symmetry boards had to work properly when put into the old Balance systems. Since the new system was to use write back and the old system used write through, the hardware team solved the problem by designing the new caches to support either write through or write back. Lovett and Thakkar [1988] took advantage of that feature to run parallel programs with both policies. Figure 10.6 shows bus utilization versus the number of processors for four parallel programs.

As mentioned above, bus utilization directly corresponds to the number of processors that can be used in such single-bus systems. Write-through caches should have higher bus utilization for the same number of processors since every write must go over the bus; or from a different perspective, the same bus should be able to support more processors if they use write-back caches. Figure 10.6 fulfills our expectations; the buses saturate with fewer than 16 processors with write through, but write back appears to scale to the full size.

There are two components to the bus traffic: normal misses and coherency support. Uniprocessor misses (compulsory, capacity, and conflict) can be reduced by larger caches and by better write policies, but the coherency traffic is a function of the parallel program. The primary benefit of write back for the programs in Figure 10.6 was simply reducing the number of writes on the bus due to the write-back policy, for there were few writes to shared data in these programs.

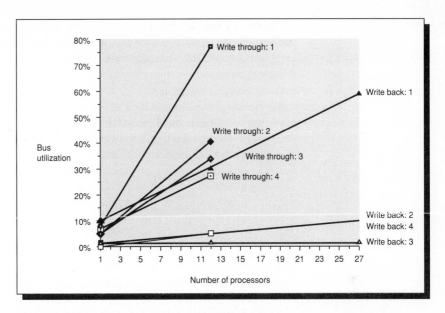

FIGURE 10.6   Comparing the impact of write-through versus write-back cache coherency on bus utilization of the Sequent Symmetry multiprocessor for four parallel benchmarks: (1) Butterfly Switch Simulator, (2) 2D Monte Carlo Simulation, (3) Ray Tracing , and (4) Parallel Linpack Benchmark. Lovett and Thakkar [1988] collected these data with a hardware performance monitor.

Another experiment evaluated the Symmetry as a timeshared (multiprogrammed) multiprocessor running ten independent programs. The experiment ran n copies of the program on n processors. This study found about half the programs started to stray from linearly increasing throughput at 6 to 8 processors with write through, yet with write back it stayed near linear for all but one of the ten programs for up to 28 processors. (The single dud was due to hot spots in the operating system rather than write-back coherency protocol.)

10.9 | Fallacies and Pitfalls

Given the speculative nature of this chapter, it would seem that this section would not be needed. In good conscience, however, we submit two warnings.

Pitfall: Measuring performance of multiprocessors by linear speedup versus execution time.

"Mortar shot" graphs—plotting performance versus number of processors showing linear speedup, a plateau, and then a falling off—have long been used to judge the success of parallel processors. While scalability is one facet of a parallel program, it is not a direct measure of performance. The first question is the power of the processors being scaled: A program that linearly improves performance to equal 100 Intel 8080s may be slower than the sequential version on a workstation. Be especially careful of floating-point–intensive programs, as processing elements without hardware assist may scale wonderfully but have poor collective performance.

Comparing execution times is only fair if you are comparing the best algorithms on each machine. (Of course, you can't subtract time for idle processors when evaluating a multiprocessor, so CPU time is inappropriate for multiprocessors.) Comparing the identical code on two machines may seem fair, but it is not; the parallel program may be slower on a uniprocessor than a sequential version. Sometimes, developing a parallel program will lead to algorithmic improvements, so that comparing the previously best-known sequential program with the parallel code—which seems fair—will not compare equivalent algorithms. To reflect this issue, sometimes the terms *relative speedup* (same program) and *true speedup* (best programs) are used. Results that suggest *super-linear* performance, when a program on *n* processors is more than *n* times faster than the equivalent uniprocessor, give a clue to unfair comparisons.

Fallacy: Amdahl's Law doesn't apply to parallel computers.

In 1987, the head of a research organization claimed that Amdahl's Law (see Section 1.3) had been broken by a MIMD machine. This hardly meant, however, that the law has been overturned for parallel computers; the neglected portion of the program will still limit performance. To try to understand the basis of the media reports, let's see what Amdahl [1967] originally said:

A fairly obvious conclusion which can be drawn at this point is that the effort expended on achieving high parallel processing rates is wasted unless it is accompanied by achievements in sequential processing rates of very nearly the same magnitude. [page 483]

One interpretation of the law was that since portions of every program must be sequential, there is a limit to the useful economic number of processors—say 100. By showing linear speedup with 1000 processors, this interpretation of Amdahl's Law was disproved.

The approach of the researchers was to change the input to the benchmark, so that rather than going 1000 times faster, they essentially computed 1000 times more work in comparable time. For their algorithm the sequential portion of the program was constant independent of the size of the input, and the rest was fully parallel—hence, linear speedup with 1000 processors.

Chapter 2 (see Section 2.2) describes the dangers of letting each experimenter select his own input for benchmarks. We see no reason why varying input is safe for evaluating performance of multiprocessors, nor why Amdahl's Law doesn't apply. What this research does point out is the importance of having benchmarks that are large enough to demonstrate performance of large-scale parallel processors.

10.10 | Concluding Remarks—Evolution Versus Revolution in Computer Architecture

Reading conference and journal articles from the last 20 years can leave one discouraged; so much effort has been expended with so little impact. Optimistically speaking, these papers act as gravel and, when placed logically together, form the foundation for the next generation of computers. From a more pessimistic point of view, if 90% of the ideas disappeared no one would notice.

One reason for this could be called the "von Neumann syndrome." By hoping to invent a new model of computation that will revolutionize computing, researchers are striving to become known as the von Neumann of the 21st century. Another reason is taste: researchers often select problems that no one else cares about. Even if important problems are selected, there is frequently a lack of experimental evidence to convincingly demonstrate the value of the solution. Moreover, when important problems are selected and the solutions are demonstrated, the proposed solutions may be too expensive relative to their

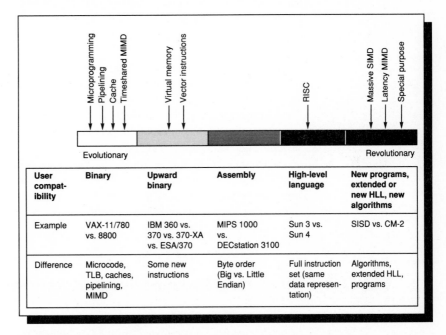

User compat- ibility	Binary	Upward binary	Assembly	High-level language	New programs, extended or new HLL, new algorithms
Example	VAX-11/780 vs. 8800	IBM 360 vs. 370 vs. 370-XA vs. ESA/370	MIPS 1000 vs. DECstation 3100	Sun 3 vs. Sun 4	SISD vs. CM-2
Difference	Microcode, TLB, caches, pipelining, MIMD	Some new instructions	Byte order (Big vs. Little Endian)	Full instruction set (same data represen- tation)	Algorithms, extended HLL, programs

FIGURE 10.7   The evolution-revolution spectrum of computer architecture. The first four columns are distinguished from the last column in that applications and operating systems can be ported from other computers rather than written from scratch. For example, RISC is listed in the middle of the spectrum because user compatibility is only at the level of high-level languages, while microprogramming allows binary compatibility, and latency-oriented MIMDs require changes to algorithms and extending HLLs. Time-shared MIMD means MIMDs justified by running many independent programs at once, while latency MIMD means MIMDs intended to run a single program faster.

benefit. Sometimes this expense is measured as straightforward cost/performance—the performance enhancement does not merit the added cost. More often the expense of innovation is that it is too disruptive to computer users. Figure 10.7 shows what we mean by the *evolution-revolution spectrum* of computer architecture innovation. To the left are ideas that are invisible to the user (presumably excepting better cost, better performance, or both). This is the evolutionary end of the spectrum. At the other end are revolutionary architecture ideas. Those are the ideas that require new applications from programmers who must learn new programming languages and models of computation, and must invent new data structures and algorithms.

Revolutionary ideas are easier to publish than evolutionary ideas, but to be adopted they must have a much higher payoff. Caches are an example of an evolutionary improvement. Within five years after the first publication about caches almost every computer company was designing a machine with a cache. The RISC ideas were nearer to the middle of the spectrum, for it took closer to ten years for most companies to have a RISC product. An example of a revolutionary computer architecture is the Connection Machine. Every program that runs efficiently on that machine was either substantially modified or written especially for it, and programmers need to learn a new style of programming for it. Thinking Machines was founded in 1983, but only a few companies offer that style of machine.

There **is** value in projects that do not affect the computer industry because of lessons that they document for future efforts. The sin is not in having a novel architecture that is not a commercial success; the sin is in not quantitatively evaluating the strengths and weaknesses of the novel ideas. The next section mentions several machines whose primary contribution is documentation of the machine and experience using it.

When contemplating the future—and when inventing your own contributions to the field—remember the evolution-revolution spectrum. Also keep in mind the laws and principles of computer architecture found in the early chapters; these will surely guide computers of the future, just as they have guided computers of the past.

10.11 | Historical Perspective and References

For over a decade prophets have voiced the contention that the organization of a single computer has reached its limits and that truly significant advances can be made only by interconnection of a multiplicity of computers in such a manner as to permit cooperative solution.... Demonstration is made of the continued validity of the single processor approach...

Amdahl [1967, 483]

The quotes at the chapter opening give the classic arguments for abandoning the current form of computing, and Amdahl [1967] gives the classic reply.

Arguments for the advantages of parallel execution can be traced back to 19th century [Menabrea 1842]! Yet the effectiveness of the multiprocessor for reducing latency of individual important programs is still being determined.

The earliest ideas on SIMD-style computers are from Unger [1958] and Slotnick, Borck, and McReynolds [1962]. Slotnick's Solomon design formed the basis of the Illiac IV, perhaps the most infamous of the supercomputer projects. While successful in pushing several technologies useful in later projects, it failed as a computer. Costs escalated from the $8 million estimate in 1966 to $31 million by 1972, despite constructing only a quarter of the planned machine. Actual performance was at best 15 MFLOPS versus initial predictions of 1000 MFLOPS for the full system (see Hord [1982]). Delivered to NASA Ames Research 1972, the computer took three more years of engineering before it was usable. These events slowed investigation of SIMD, with Danny Hillis [1985] resuscitating this style in the Connection Machine: The cost of a program memory for each of 65,636 1-bit processors was prohibitive, and SIMD was the solution.

It is difficult to distinguish the first multiprocessor. The first computer from the Eckert-Mauchly Corporation, for example, had duplicate units to improve availability. Holland [1959] gave early arguments for multiple processors. After several laboratory attempts at multiprocessors, the 1980s first saw successful commercial multiprocessors. Bell [1985] suggests the key was that the smaller size of the microprocessor allowed the memory bus to replace the interconnection network hardware, and that portable operating systems meant multiprocessor projects no longer required the invention of a new operating system. This is the paper in which he defines the terms "multiprocessor" and "multicomputer." Two of the best-documented multiprocessor projects are the C.mmp [Wulf and Bell 1972 and Wulf and Habrison 1978] and Cm* [Swan et al. 1977 and Gehringer, Siewiorek, and Segall 1987]. Recent commercial multiprocessors include the Encore Multimax [Wilson 1987] and the Sequent Symmetry [Lovett and Thakkar 1988]. The Cosmic Cube is an early multicomputer [Seitz 1985]. Recent commercial multicomputers are the Intel Hypercube and the Transputer-based machines [Whitby-Strevens 1985]. Attempts at building a scalable shared-memory multiprocessor include the IBM RP3 [Pfister, Brantley, George, Harvey, Kleinfekder, McAuliffe, Melton, Norton, and Weiss 1985], the NYU Ultracomputer [Schwartz 1980 and Elder, Gottlieb, Kruskal, McAuliffe, Randolph, Snir, Teller, and Wilson 1985], and the University of Illinois Cedar project [Gajksi, Kuck, Lawrie, and Sameh 1983].

There is unbounded information on multiprocessors and multicomputers: Conferences, journal papers, and even books seem to be appearing faster than any single person can absorb the ideas. One good source is the International Conference on Parallel Processing, which has met annually since 1972. Two recent books on parallel computing have been written by Almasi and Gottlieb [1989] and Hockney and Jesshope [1988]. Eugene Miya of NASA Ames has collected an on-line bibliography of parallel-processing papers that contains more than 10,000 entries. To highlight a few papers, he sends out electronic requests every January to ask which papers every serious student in the field should read. After collecting the ballots, he picks the ten papers most frequently recommended and publishes that list. Here is an alphabetical list of the winners: Andrews and Schneider [1983]; Batcher [1974]; Dewitt, Finkel, and Solomon [1984]; Kuhn and Padua [1981]; Lipovski and Tripathi [1977]; Russell [1978]; Seitz [1985]; Swan, Fuller, and Siewiorek [1977]; Treleaven, Brownbridge, and Hopkins [1982]; and Wulf and Bell [1972].

Special-purpose computers predate the stored-program computer. Brodersen [1989] gives a history of signal processing and its evolution to programmable devices. H. T. Kung [1982] coined the term "systolic array" and has been one of the leading proponents of this style of computer design. Recent research has been in the direction of making programmable systolic-array elements and providing a programming environment to simplify the programming task.

Its hard to predict the future, yet Gordon Bell has made two predictions for 1995. The first is that a computer capable of sustaining a TeraFLOPS—one million MFLOPS—will be constructed by 1995, either using a multicomputer with 4K to 32K nodes or a Connection Machine with several million processing elements [Bell 1989]. To put this prediction in perspective, each year the Gordon Bell Prize acknowledges advances in parallelism, including the fastest real program (highest MFLOPS). In 1988, the winner achieved 400 MFLOPS using a CRAY X-MP with four processors and 16 megawords and in 1989 the winner used an eight-processor CRAY Y-MP to run at 1680 MFLOPS. Machines and programs will have to improve by a factor of three each year for the fastest program to achieve 1 TFLOPS in 1995.

The second Bell prediction concerns the number of data streams in super-computers shipped in 1995. Danny Hillis believes that while supercomputers with a small number of data streams may be best sellers, the biggest machines will be machines with many data streams, and these will perform the bulk of the computations. Bell bet Hillis that in the last quarter of calendar year 1995 more sustained MFLOPS will be shipped in machines using few data streams (≤ 100) rather than many data streams (≥ 1000). This bet concerns only supercomputers, defined as machines costing more than $1,000,000 and used for scientific applications. Sustained MFLOPS is defined for this bet as the number of floating-point operations per **month**, so availability of machines affects their rating. The loser must write and publish an article explaining why his prediction failed; your authors will act as judge and jury.

References

ALMASI, G. S. AND A. GOTTLIEB [1989]. *Highly Parallel Computing,* Benjamin/Cummings, Redwood City, Calif.

AMDAHL, G. M. [1967]. "Validity of the single processor approach to achieving large scale computing capabilities," *Proc. AFIPS Spring Joint Computer Conf.* 30, Atlantic City, N. J. (April) 483–485.

ANDREWS, G. R. AND F. B. SCHNEIDER [1983]. "Concept and notations for concurrent programming," *Computing Surveys* 15:1 (March) 3–43.

BATCHER, K. E. [1974]. "STARAN parallel processor system hardware," *Proc. AFIPS National Computer Conference*, 405–410.

BELL, C. G. [1985]. "Multis: A new class of multiprocessor computers," *Science* 228 (April 26) 462–467.

BELL, C. G. [1989]. "The future of high performance computers in science and engineering," *Comm. ACM* 32:9 (September) 1091–1101.

BOUKNIGHT, W. J, S. A. DENEBERG, D. E. MCINTYRE, J. M. RANDALL, A. H. SAMEH, AND D. L. SLOTNICK [1972]. "The ILLIAC IV system," *Proc. IEEE* 60:4, 369–379. Also appears in D. P. Siewiorek, C. G. Bell, and A. Newell, *Computer Structures: Principles and Examples* (1982), 306–316.

BRODERSEN, R. W. [1989]. "Evolution of VLSI signal-processing circuits," *Proc. Decennial Caltech Conf. on VLSI* (March) 43–46, The MIT Press, Pasadena, Calif.

DEWITT, D. J., R. FINKEL, AND M. SOLOMON [1984]. "The CRYSTAL multicomputer: Design and implementation experience, Computer Sciences Tech. Rep. No. 553, University of Wisconsin-Madison, September.

ELDER, J., A. GOTTLIEB, C. K. KRUSKAL, K. P. MCAULIFFE, L. RANDOLPH, M. SNIR, P. TELLER, AND J. WILSON [1985]. "Issues related to MIMD shared-memory computers: The NYU Ultracomputer approach," *Proc. 12th Int'l Symposium on Computer Architecture* (June), Boston, Mass., 126–135.

FLYNN, M. J. [1966]. "Very high-speed computing systems," *Proc. IEEE* 54:12 (December) 1901–1909.

GAJSKI, D., D. KUCK, D. LAWRIE, AND A. SAMEH [1983]. "CEDAR—A large scale multiprocessor," *Proc. Int'l Conf. on Parallel Processing* (August) 524–529.

GEHRINGER, E. F., D. P. SIEWIOREK, AND Z. SEGALL [1987]. *Parallel Processing: The Cm* Experience*, Digital Press, Bedford, Mass.

HILLIS, W. D. [1985]. *The Connection Machine*, The MIT Press, Cambridge, Mass.

HOCKNEY, R. W. AND C. R. JESSHOPE [1988]. *Parallel Computers-2, Architectures, Programming and Algorithms*, Adam Hilger Ltd., Bristol, England and Philadelphia.

HOLLAND, J. H. [1959]. "A universal computer capable of executing an arbitrary number of subprograms simultaneously," *Proc. East Joint Computer Conf.* 16, 108–113.

HORD, R. M. [1982]. *The Illiac-IV, The First Supercomputer,* Computer Science Press, Rockville, Md.

KUHN, R. H. AND D. A. PADUA, EDS. [1981]. *Tutorial on Parallel Processing*, IEEE.

KUNG, H. T. [1982]. "Why systolic architectures?," *IEEE Computer* 15:1, 37–46.

LIPOVSKI, A. G. AND A. TRIPATHI [1977]. "A reconfigurable varistructure array processor," *Proc. 1977 Int'l Conf. of Parallel Processing* (August), 165–174.

LOVETT, T. AND S. THAKKAR [1988]. "The Symmetry multiprocessor system," *Proc. 1988 Int'l Conf. of Parallel Processing*, University Park, Pennsylvania, 303–310.

MENABREA, L. F. [1842]. "Sketch of the analytical engine invented by Charles Babbage," Bibiothèque Universelle de Genève (October).

MITCHELL, D. [1989]. "The Transputer: The time is now," *Computer Design*, RISC supplement, 40–41 (November).

PFISTER, G. F., W. C. BRANTLEY, D. A. GEORGE, S. L. HARVEY, W. J. KLEINFEKDER, K. P. MCAULIFFE, E. A. MELTON, V. A. NORTON, AND J. WEISS [1985]. "The IBM research parallel processor prototype (RP3): Introduction and architecture," *Proc. 12th Int'l Symposium on Computer Architecture* (June), Boston, Mass., 764–771.

RUSSELL, R. M. [1978]. "The Cray-1 computer system," *Comm. ACM* 21:1 (January) 63–72.

SEITZ, C. [1985]. "The Cosmic Cube," *Comm. ACM* 28:1 (January) 22–31.

SLOTNICK, D. L., W. C. BORCK, AND R. C. MCREYNOLDS [1962]. "The Solomon computer," *Proc. Fall Joint Computer Conf.* (December), Philadelphia, 97–107.

SWAN, R. J., A. BECHTOLSHEIM, K. W. LAI, AND J. K. OUSTERHOUT [1977]. "The implementation of the Cm* multi-microprocessor," *Proc. AFIPS National Computing Conf.*, 645–654.

SWAN, R. J., S. H. FULLER, AND D. P. SIEWIOREK [1977]. "Cm*—A modular, multi-microprocessor," *Proc. AFIPS National Computer Conf.* 46, 637–644.

SWARTZ, J. T. [1980]. "Ultracomputers," *ACM Transactions on Programming Languages and Systems* 4:2, 484–521

TRELEAVEN, P. C., D. R. BROWNBRIDGE, and R. P. HOPKINS [1982]. "Data-driven and demand-driven computer architectures," *Computing Surveys*, 14:1 (March) 93–143.

UNGER, S. H. [1958]. "A computer oriented towards spatial problems," *Proc. Institute of Radio Engineers* 46:10 (October) 1744–1750.

VON NEUMANN, J. [1945]. "First draft of a report on the EDVAC." Reprinted in W. Aspray and A. Burks, eds., *Papers of John von Neumann on Computing and Computer Theory* (1987), 17–82, The MIT Press, Cambridge, Mass.

WHITBY-STREVENS C. [1985]. "The transputer," *Proc. 12th Int'l Symposium on Computer Architecture*, Boston, Mass. (June) 292–300.

WILSON, A. W., JR. [1987]. "Hierarchical cache/bus architecture for shared memory multiprocessors," *Proc. 14th Int'l Symposium on Computer Architecture* (June), Pittsburg, Penn., 244–252.

WULF, W. AND C. G. BELL [1972]. "C.mmp—A multi-mini-processor," *Proc. AFIPS Fall Joint Computing Conf.* 41, part 2, 765–777.

WULF, W. AND S. P. HARBISON [1978]. "Reflections in a pool of processors—An experience report on C.mmp/Hydra," *Proc. AFIPS 1978 National Computing Conf.* 48 (June), Anaheim, Calif. 939–951.

EXERCISES

10.1 [Discussion] <10.4> The weakness of SIMD for case statements, as well as the failure of the first machine to popularize SIMD, prevented exploration of SIMD designs while MIMD was still an open frontier. MIMD also has the advantage of riding the wave of improvements in SISD processors. Now that MIMD programming has not succumbed easily to assaults of computer scientists, the issue arises whether the simpler programming model of SIMD might lead it to victory over MIMD for large numbers of processors. It looks as if MIMD programs for thousands of processors will consist of thousands of copies of one program rather than thousands of different programs. Thus, the direction is toward a single **program** with multiple data streams, independent of whether the machine itself is SIMD or MIMD. What trends favor MIMD over SIMD, and vice versa? Be sure to consider utilization of memory and processors (including communication and synchronization).

10.2 [Discussion] <10.3–10.5> It might take approximately 100 clocks to communicate in a massively parallel SIMD or MIMD machine. What hardware techniques might this time? How can you change the architecture or the programming model to make a computer more immune to such delays?

10.3 [Discussion] <10.4,10.8> What must happen before latency-oriented MIMD machines become commonplace?

10.4 [Discussion] <10.6> When do special-purpose processors make sense economically?

10.5 [Discussion] <10.8> Construct a scenario whereby a truly revolutionary architecture—pick your favorite candidate—will play a significant role. Significant is defined as 10% of the computers sold, 10% of the users, 10% of the money spent on computers, or 10% of some other figure of merit.

10.6 [30] <10.2> The CM-2 uses 64K 1-bit processors in SIMD mode. Bit-serial operations can easily be simulated 32 bits one step by a 32-bit-wide SISD, at least for logical operations. The CM-2 takes about 500 ns for such operations. If you have access to a fast SISD, calculate how long add and logical AND take on 64K 1-bit numbers.

10.7 [30] <10.2> Similar to the question above, a popular use of the CM-2 is to operate on 32-bit data using multiple steps with the 64K 1-bit processors. The CM-2 takes about 16 microseconds for a 32-bit AND or add. Simulate this activity on a fast SISD; calculate how long it takes to add and logical AND 64K 32-bit numbers.

10.8–10.12 <2.2,10.4> **If you have access to a few different multiprocessors or multicomputers, performance comparison is the basis of some projects.**

10.8 [50] <2.2,10.4> One argument for super-linear speedup (pages 585–586) is that time spent servicing interrupts or switching contexts is reduced when you have many processors, since only one need service interrupts and there are more processors to be shared by users. Measure the time spent on a workload in handling interrupts or context switching on a uniprocessor versus a multiprocessor. This workload may be a mix of independent jobs for a multiprogramming environment or a single large job. Does the argument hold?

10.9 [50] <2.2,10.4> A multiprocessor or multicomputer is typically marketed using programs that can scale performance linearly with the number of processors. The project would be to port programs written for one machine to the others and measure their absolute performance and how it changes as you change the number of processors. What changes need to be made to improve performance of the ported programs on each machine? What is the ratio of processor performance according to each program?

10.10 [50] <2.2,10.4> Instead of trying to create fair benchmarks, invent programs that make one multiprocessor or multicomputer look terrible compared to the others, and also programs that always make one look better than the others. It would be an interesting result if you couldn't find a program that made one multiprocessor or multicomputer look worse than the others. What are the key performance characteristics of each organization?

10.11 [50] <2.2,10.4> Multiprocessors and multicomputers usually show performance increases as you increase the number of processors, with the ideal being n times speedup for n processors. The goal of this biased benchmark is to make a program that gets worse performance as you add processors. For example, this means that 1 processor on the multiprocessor or multicomputer runs the program fastest, 2 is slower, 4 is slower than 2, and so on. What are the key performance characteristics for each organization that give inverse linear speedup?

10.12 [50] <10.4> Networked workstations can be considered multicomputers, albeit with slow communication relative to computation. Port multicomputer benchmarks to a network using remote procedure calls for communication. How well do the benchmarks scale on the network versus the multicomputer? What are the practical differences between networked workstations and a commercial multicomputer?

The Fast drives out the Slow even if the Fast is wrong.

W. Kahan

by David Goldberg
(Xerox Palo Alto Research Center)

A | Computer Arithmetic

A.1 | Introduction

A tremendous variety of algorithms have been proposed for use in floating-point accelerators. However, actual floating-point chips are usually based on refinements and variations of just a few basic algorithms. In this appendix, we focus on those algorithms. In addition to choosing algorithms for addition, subtraction, multiplication and division, the computer architect must decide whether to go beyond the basics. Should square root be implemented in hardware or software? Should extended precision be implemented? This appendix will give you the background for making these and other decisions.

Our discussion of floating point will focus almost exclusively on the IEEE floating-point standard (IEEE 754) because of its rapidly increasing acceptance. Although floating-point arithmetic involves manipulating exponents and shifting fractions, the bulk of the time in floating-point operations is spent operating on fractions using integer algorithms (but not necessarily using the integer hardware). Thus, after our discussion of floating point, we will take a more detailed look at integer algorithms.

Some good references on computer arithmetic, in order from least to most detailed, are Chapter 7 of Hamacher, Vranesic, and Zaky [1984], Gosling [1980], and Scott [1985].

A.2 | Basic Techniques of Integer Arithmetic

Readers who have studied computer arithmetic before will find most of this section to be review.

Ripple-Carry Addition

The building blocks of an adder that can compute the sum of the n-bit numbers $a_{n-1}\cdots a_1 a_0$ and $b_{n-1}\cdots b_1 b_0$ are *half adders* and *full adders*. The half adder takes two bits a_i and b_i as input and produces a sum bit s_i and a carry bit c_{i+1} as output. Mathematically, $s_i = (a_i + b_i) \bmod 2$, and $c_{i+1} = \lfloor (a_i + b_i)/2 \rfloor$, where $\lfloor \ \rfloor$ is the floor function. As logic equations, $s_i = a_i \overline{b_i} + \overline{a_i} b_i$, and $c_{i+1} = a_i b_i$, where $a_i b_i$ means $a_i \wedge b_i$ and $a_i + b_i$ means $a_i \vee b_i$. The half adder is also called a (2,2) adder, since it takes two inputs and produces two outputs. The full adder is a (3,2) adder and is defined by the logic equations

A.2.1
$$s_i \ = \ a_i \overline{b_i}\,\overline{c_i} + \overline{a_i} b_i \overline{c_i} + \overline{a_i}\,\overline{b_i} c_i + a_i b_i c_i$$

A.2.2
$$c_{i+1} \ = \ a_i b_i + a_i c_i + b_i c_i$$

The input c_i is called the *carry in*, while c_{i+1} is the *carry out*. The principle problem in building an adder for n-bit numbers is propagating the carries. The most obvious way to solve this is with a *ripple-carry adder*, consisting of n full adders, as illustrated in Figure A.1. (In the figures in this appendix the least significant bit is always on the right.) The c_{i+1} output of the ith adder is fed into the c_{i+1} input of the next adder (the $(i + 1)$-th adder) with the lower order carry in c_0 set to 0. Since the low-order carry in is zero, the low-order adder could be a half adder. Later, however, we will see that setting the low-order carry-in bit to 1 is useful for performing subtraction.

From Equation A.2.2, there are two levels of logic involved in computing c_{i+1} from c_i. Thus, if the least significant bit generates a carry, and that carry gets propagated all the way to the last adder, the a_0 signal will pass through $2n$ levels of logic before the final gate can determine whether there is a carry out of the most significant place. In general, the time a circuit takes to produce an output is proportional to the maximum number of logic levels through which a signal travels. However, determining the exact relationship between logic levels and timings is highly technology dependent. Therefore, when comparing adders we will simply compare the number of logic levels in each one. For a ripple-carry adder that operates on n bits, there are $2n$ logic levels. Typical values of n are 32 for integer arithmetic and 53 for double-precision floating point. The ripple-carry adder is the slowest adder, but also the cheapest. It can be built with only n simple cells, connected in a simple, regular way.

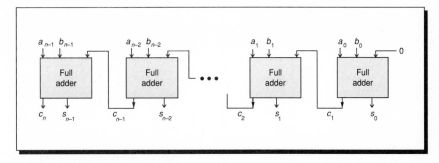

FIGURE A.1   Ripple-carry adder, consisting of *n* full adders. The carry out of one full adder is connected to the carry in of the adder for the next most significant bit. The carries ripple from the least significant bit (on the right) to the most significant bit (on the left).

Because the ripple-carry adder is relatively slow compared to the designs discussed in Section A.8, one might wonder why it is used at all. In technologies like CMOS, even though ripple adders take time $O(n)$, the constant factor is very small. In such cases short ripple adders are often used as building blocks in larger adders.

Radix-2 Multiplication and Division

The simplest multiplier operates on two unsigned numbers, one bit at a time, as illustrated in Figure A.2(a) (page A-4). The numbers to be multiplied are $a_{n-1}a_{n-2}\cdots a_0$ and $b_{n-1}b_{n-2}\cdots b_0$, and they are placed in registers A and B, respectively. Register P is initially zero. There are two parts in each multiply step.

1. If the least significant bit of A is 1, then register B, containing $b_{n-1}b_{n-2}\cdots b_0$, is added to P; otherwise $00\cdots00$ is added to P. The sum is placed back into P.

2. Registers P and A are shifted right, with the low-order bit of P being moved into register A and the rightmost bit of A, which is not used in the rest of the algorithm, being shifted out.

After n steps, the product appears in registers P and A, with A holding the lower-order bits.

The simplest divider also operates on unsigned numbers and produces a bit at a time. A hardware divider is shown in Figure A.2(b). To compute a/b, put a in the A register, b in the B register, 0 in the P register, and then proceed as follows:

1. Shift the register pair (P,A) one bit left.

2. Subtract the content of register B (which is $b_{n-1}b_{n-2}\cdots b_0$) from register P.

3. If the result of step 2 is negative, set the low-order bit of A to 0, otherwise to 1.

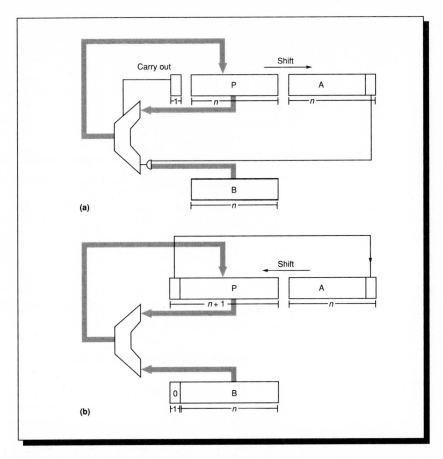

FIGURE A.2   Block diagram of simple multiplier (a) and divider (b) for *n*-bit unsigned integers. Each multiplication step consists of adding the contents of P to either B or 0 (depending on the low-order bit of A), replacing P with the sum, and then shifting both P and A one bit right. Each division step involves first shifting P and A one bit left, subtracting B from P, and if the difference is nonnegative, putting it into P. If the difference is nonnegative, the low-order bit of A is set to 1.

4. If the result of step 2 is negative, restore the old value of P by adding the contents of register B back into P.

After repeating this n times, the A register will contain the quotient, and the P register will contain the remainder. This algorithm is the binary version of the paper-and-pencil method; a numerical example is illustrated in Figure A.3(a) (page A-6).

Notice that the two block diagrams in Figure A.2 are very similar. The main difference is that the register pair (P,A) shifts right when multiplying and left when dividing. By allowing these registers to shift bidirectionally, the same hardware can be shared between multiplication and division.

The division algorithm illustrated in Figure A.3(a) (page A-6) is called *restoring*, because if subtraction by *b* yields a negative result, the P register is restored by adding *b* back in. The restoration step (4 above) can be easily eliminated. To see why, let *r* be the contents of the (P,A) register pair, with a binary point between the low-order bit of P and the high-order bit of A. Then each step of the algorithm computes $2r - b$, putting the high-order word of this difference in P, and the low-order word in A. Suppose the result of a step is negative. Normally, we would add *b* back in (giving 2*r*), shift (giving 4*r*), and then subtract (obtaining $4r - b$). Suppose we didn't restore, but continued with the algorithm. First, shift the unrestored $2r - b$, yielding $4r - 2b$, then add *b*, giving $4r - b$. This is exactly what we would have obtained if we had restored! Thus, the *nonrestoring* algorithm is

If P is negative,

   1a. Shift the register pair (P,A) one bit left.

   2a. Add the contents of register B to P.

Else,

   1b. Shift the register pair (P,A) one bit left.

   2b. Subtract the contents of register B from P.

Finally,

   3. If P is negative, set the low-order bit of A to 0, otherwise set it to 1.

After repeating this *n* times, the quotient is in A. If P is nonnegative, it is the remainder. Otherwise, it needs to be restored (i.e., add *b*), and then it will be the remainder. A numerical example is given in Figure A.3(b). Note that the sign of P must be tested before shifting, since the sign bit can be lost when shifting. However, because of two's complement arithmetic (discussed in the next section), the net result of shifting followed by the appropriate add/subtract operation will be the correct value. This comes about because the result of each step is a number *r* with $|r| \leq b$.

If *a* and *b* are unsigned numbers in the range $0 \leq a,b \leq 2^n - 1$, then the multiplier in Figure A.2 will work if register P is *n* bits long. However, for division, P must be extended to $n + 1$ bits in order to detect the sign of P. Thus the adder must also have $n + 1$ bits.

Why would anyone implement restoring division, which uses the same hardware as nonrestoring division (the control is slightly different) but involves an extra addition? In fact, the usual implementation for restoring division doesn't literally perform an add in step 4. Rather, the sign resulting from the subtraction is tested, and only if the sum is nonnegative is it loaded back into the P register.

As a final point, before beginning to divide, the hardware must check to see if the divisor is zero.

(a)

P	A	
00000	1110	Divide 14 = 1110 by 3 = 11. B always contains 0011
00001	110	step (1): shift
−00011		step (2): subtract
−00010	1100	step (3): result is negative, set quotient bit to 0
00001	1100	step (4): restore
00011	100	step (1): shift
−00011		step (2): subtract
00000	1001	step (3): result is nonnegative, set quotient bit to 1
00001	001	step (1): shift
−00011		step (2): subtract
−00010	0010	step (3): result is negative, set quotient bit 0
00001	0010	step (4): restore
00010	010	step (1): shift
−00011		step (2): subtract
−00001	0100	step (3): result is negative, set quotient bit to 0
00010	0100	step (4): restore. The quotient is 0100 and the remainder is 00010.

(b)

00000	1110	Divide 14 = 1110 by 3 = 11. B always contains 0011
00001	110	step (1b): shift
+11101		step (2b): subtract b (add 2's complement)
11110	1100	step (3): P is negative, so set quotient bit to 0
11101	100	step (1a): shift
+00011		step (2a): add b
00000	1001	step (3): P is nonnegative, so set quotient bit to 1
00001	001	step (1b): shift
+11101		step (2b): subtract b
11110	0010	step (3): P is negative, so set quotient bit to 0
11100	010	step (1a): shift
+00011		step (2a): add b
11111	0100	step (3): P is negative, so set quotient bit to 0
+00011		remainder is negative, so do final restore step
00010		The quotient is 0100 and the remainder is 00010

FIGURE A.3 Numerical example of (a) restoring division and (b) nonrestoring division.

Signed Numbers

There are four methods commonly used to represent signed n-bit numbers: *sign magnitude, two's complement, one's complement,* and *biased.* In the sign-magnitude system, the high-order bit is the sign bit, and the low-order $n-1$ bits are the magnitude of the number. In the two's complement system, a number and its negative add up to 2^n. In one's complement, the negative of a number is obtained by complementing each bit. In a biased system, a fixed bias is picked so that the sum of the bias and the number being represented will always be nonnegative. A number is represented by first adding it to the bias, and then encoding the sum as an ordinary unsigned number.

Example: How is -3 expressed in each of these formats?

Answer: The binary representation of 3 is 0011_2. In signed magnitude, $-0011 = 1011$. In two's complement $0011_2 + 1101_2 = 8$, so $-0011 = 1101$. In one's complement, $-0011 = 1100$. Using a bias of 8, 3 is represented by 1011, and -3 by 0101.

The most widely used system for representing integers, two's complement, is the system we will use here; one's complement is discussed in the Exercises. One reason for the popularity of two's complement is that addition is extremely simple: Simply discard the carry out from the high-order bit. To add $5 + -2$, for example, add 0101 and 1110 to obtain 0011, resulting in the correct value of 3. A useful formula for the value of a two's complement number $a_{n-1}a_{n-2}\cdots a_1 a_0$ is

A.2.3
$$-a_{n-1}2^{n-1} + a_{n-2}2^{n-2} + \cdots + a_1 2^1 + a_0$$

Overflow occurs when the result of the operation does not fit in the representation being used. For example, if unsigned numbers are being represented using four bits, then $6 = 0110_2$, and $11 = 1011_2$. Their sum (17) overflows because its binary equivalent (10001_2) doesn't fit into four bits. For unsigned numbers, detecting overflow is easy; it occurs exactly when there is a carry out of the most significant bit. For two's complement, things are trickier: Overflow occurs exactly when the carry into the high-order bit is different from the (to be discarded) carry out of the high-order bit. In the example of $5 + -2$ above, a 1 is carried both into and out of the leftmost bit, avoiding overflow.

Negating a two's complement number involves complementing each bit and then adding 1. For instance, to negate 0011, complement it to get 1100 and then add 1 to get 1101. Thus, to implement $a - b$ using an adder, simply feed a and $\overline{b}$ (where $\overline{b}$ is the number obtained by complementing each bit of b) into the adder, and set the low-order, carry-in bit to 1. This explains why the rightmost adder in Figure A.1 is a full adder.

Multiplying two's complement numbers is not quite as simple as adding them. The obvious approach is to convert both operands to be nonnegative, do an unsigned multiplication, and then (if the original operands were of opposite signs) negate the result. Although this is conceptually simple, it requires extra time and hardware. Here is a better approach: Suppose that we are multiplying a times b using the hardware shown in Figure A.2(a) (page A-4). Register A is loaded with the number a; B is loaded with b. Since the contents of register B is always b, we will use B and b interchangeably. The first thing to do when multiplying two's complement numbers is to ensure that when P is shifted, it is shifted arithmetically; that is, the bit shifted into the high-order bit of P should be the sign bit of P. Note that our n-bit–wide adder will now be adding n-bit two's complement numbers between -2^{n-1} and $2^{n-1} - 1$.

Next, suppose a is negative. The method for handling this case is called *Booth recoding*. Booth recoding is a very basic technique in computer arithmetic and will play a key role in Section A.9. Observe that multiplying by 0111_2 is the same as multiplying by $1000_2 - 1$. To perform this multiplication, subtract b from register P in the first multiplication cycle. Add zero in the second and third cycles. In the fourth cycle, add b. To apply this technique to a negative multiplier like $-4 = 1100_2$, think of it as an unsigned number and write it as $10000_2 - 0100_2$. If the multiplication algorithm only involves n steps ($n = 4$ in this case), the 10000_2 term is ignored, and we end up subtracting $0100_2 = 4$ times the multiplier—exactly the right answer. The advantage of Booth recoding is that it works equally well for positive and negative multipliers. To deal with negative values of a, then, all that is required is to sometimes subtract b from P, instead of either adding b or 0 to P. Here are the precise rules: If the initial content of A is $a_{n-1} \cdots a_0$, then at the ith multiply step, the low-order bit of register A is a_i, and

1. If $a_i = 0$ and $a_{i-1} = 0$ then add 0.

2. If $a_i = 0$ and $a_{i-1} = 1$ then add B.

3. If $a_i = 1$ and $a_{i-1} = 0$ then subtract B.

4. If $a_i = 1$ and $a_{i-1} = 1$ then add 0.

For the first step, when $i = 0$, take a_{i-1} to be 0.

Example: When multiplying -6 times -5, what is the sequence of values in the (P,A) register pair?

Answer: Initially, P is zero and A holds $-6 = 1010_2$. From Figure A.4, in the first step 0 is added to P giving (P,A) = 0000 1010. After shifting (P,A) = 0000 0101. In the next step, Figure A.4 shows that 0101 is added to P giving (P,A) = 0101 0101. Continuing, (P,A) = 0010 1010, 1101 1010, 1110 1101, 0011 1101, and finally 0001 1110.

The four cases above can be restated as saying that in the ith step you should add $(a_{i-1} - a_i)$B to P. With this observation, it is easy to verify that these rules work, because the result of all the additions is

$$\sum_{i=0}^{n-1} b(a_{i-1} - a_i)2^i = b(-a_{n-1}2^{n-1} + a_{n-2}2^{n-2} + \cdots + a_1 2 + a_0)$$

From Equation A.2.3 (page A-7), the quantity in parenthesis is the value of A as a two's complement number.

The simplest way to implement the rules for Booth recoding is to extend the A register one bit to the right so that this new bit will contain a_{i-1}. Unlike the naive method of inverting any negative operands, this technique doesn't require extra steps or any special casing for negative operands. It has only a slightly more complicated control logic. If the multiplier is being shared with a divider, there will already be the capability for subtracting b, rather than adding it. To summarize, a simple method for handling two's complement multiplication is to pay attention to the sign of P when shifting it right, and to save the most recently shifted off bit of A to use in deciding whether to add or subtract b from P.

The reason for the term "recoding" is as follows. Consider representing numbers using 1, 0, and $\overline{1}$ where $\overline{1}$ represents -1; as an example, this allows us to also represent (recode) 0111 as $100\overline{1}$. Imagine a multiplication algorithm that worked as follows: Put a recoded number into the A register. If the low-order bit of A is 1, then add B. If it is $\overline{1}$, then subtract B. If the low-order bit of A is 0, then add 0. This imaginary algorithm has exactly the same effect as the Booth recoding method given above.

Booth recoding is usually the best method for designing hardware that operates on signed numbers. For hardware that doesn't directly implement it, however, performing Booth recoding in software or microcode is usually too slow, due to the conditional tests and branches. If the hardware supports arithmetic shifts (so that negative b is handled correctly), then the following

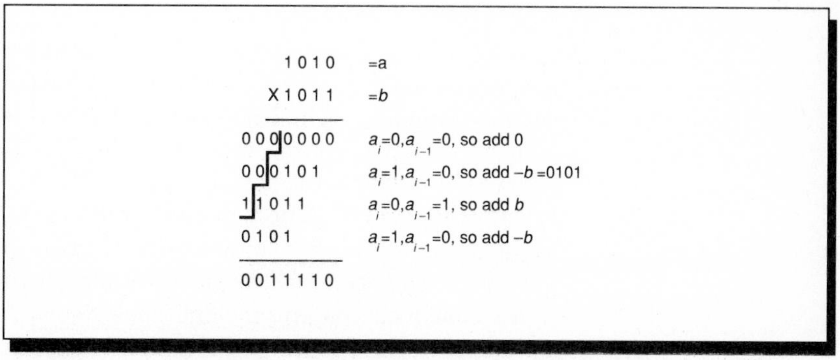

FIGURE A.4. **Multiplication of $a = -6$ by $b = -5$ to get 30 using Booth recoding.** The digits to the left of the jagged line are the sign-extended digits.

method can be used. Treat the multiplier a as if it were an unsigned number, and perform $n-1$ multiply steps. If $a < 0$ (in which case there will be a 1 in the low-order bit of the A register at this point), then subtract b from P; otherwise ($a \geq 0$) neither add nor subtract. In either case, do a final shift (for a total of n shifts) to get the low-order bit of the product into the low-order position of A. This works because it amounts to multiplying b by $-a_{n-1}2^{n-1} + \cdots + a_1 2 + a_0$, which is the value of $a_{n-1} \cdots a_0$ as a two's complement number by Equation A.2.3. If the hardware doesn't support arithmetic shift, then converting the operands to be nonnegative is probably the best approach.

Two final remarks: A good way to test a signed-multiply routine is to try $-2^{n-1} \times -2^{n-1}$, since this is the only case that produces a $2n-1$ bit result. Unlike multiplication, division is usually performed in hardware by converting the operands to be nonnegative and then doing an unsigned divide; because division is substantially slower (and less frequent) than multiplication, the extra time used to manipulate the signs has less impact than it does on multiplication.

Systems Issues

When designing an instruction set, there are a number of issues related to integer arithmetic that need to be resolved. Several of them are discussed here.

First, what should be done about integer overflow? This situation is complicated by the fact that detecting overflow is different depending on whether the operands are signed or unsigned integers. Consider signed arithmetic first. There are three approaches: Set a bit on overflow, trap on overflow, or do nothing on overflow. In the last case, software has to check whether or not an overflow occurred. The most convenient solution for the programmer is to have an enable bit. If this bit is turned on, then overflow causes a trap. If it is turned off, then overflow sets a bit. The advantage of this approach is that both trapping and nontrapping operations require only one instruction. Furthermore, as we will see in Section A.7, this is analogous to how the IEEE floating-point standard handles floating-point overflow. Figure A.5 shows how some common machines treat overflow.

What about unsigned addition? Notice that none of the architectures in Figure A.5 trap on unsigned overflow. The reason for this is that the primary use of unsigned arithmetic is in manipulating addresses. It is convenient to be able to subtract from an unsigned address by adding. For example, when $n = 4$, we can subtract 2 from the unsigned address $10 = 1010_2$ by adding $14 = 1110_2$. Even though $1010_2 + 1110_2$ sums to the answer we wanted ($1000_2 = 8$), this operation has an unsigned overflow. In other words, addresses are treated as both signed and unsigned numbers, making an overflow trap useless for address calculations.

A second issue concerns multiplication. Should the result of multiplying two n-bit numbers be a $2n$-bit result, or should multiplication just return the low-order n bits, signaling overflow if the result doesn't fit in n bits? The argument in favor of an n-bit result is that in virtually all high-level languages, multiplication is an operation whose arguments are integer variables and whose result is an integer variable of the same type. Therefore, there is no way to generate code that utilizes a double-precision result. The argument in favor of a $2n$-bit result is that it can be used by an assembly language routine to speed up multiplication of multiple-precision integers substantially (by about a factor of 3).

A third issue concerns machines that want to execute one instruction every cycle. It is rarely practical to perform a multiplication or division in the same amount of time that an addition or register–register move takes. There are three possible approaches to this problem. The first is to have a single-cycle *multiply-step* instruction. This might do one step of the Booth algorithm. The second approach is to do integer multiplication in the floating-point unit and have it be part of the floating-point instruction set. (This is what DLX does.) The third approach is to have an autonomous unit in the CPU do the multiplication. In this case, the result can either be guaranteed to be delivered in a fixed number of cycles—and the compiler charged with waiting the proper amount of time—or there can be an interlock. The same comments apply to division as well. As examples, the SPARC has a multiply-step instruction but no divide-step instruction, and the MIPS R3000 has an autonomous unit that does multiplication and division (see Section E-6 for new extensions to SPARC for arithmetic). The designers of the HP Precision Architecture did an especially thorough job of analyzing the frequency of the operands for multiplication and division, and based their multiply and divide steps accordingly. (See Magenheimer et al. [1988] for details.)

A potential pitfall worth mentioning concerns multiple-precision addition. Many instruction sets offer a variant of the ADD instruction that adds three operands: two n-bit numbers together with a third single-bit number. This third number is the carry from the previous addition. Since the multiple-precision number will typically be stored in an array, it is important to be able to increment the array pointer without destroying the carry bit.

Machine	Trap on signed overflow?	Trap on unsigned overflow?	Set bit on signed overflow?	Set bit on unsigned overflow?
VAX	If enable is on	No	Yes. ADD sets V bit.	Yes. ADD sets C bit.
IBM 370	If enable is on	No	Yes. ADD sets cond code.	Yes. Logical ADD sets cond code.
Intel 8086	No	No	Yes. ADD sets V bit.	Yes. ADD sets C bit.
MIPS R3000	There are 2 ADD instructions: one always traps, the other never does.	No	No. Software must deduce it from sign of operands and result.	
SPARC	No	No	ADDCC sets V bit. ADD does not.	ADDCC sets C bit. ADD does not.

FIGURE A.5 Summary of how various machines handle integer overflow. Both the 8086 and SPARC have an instruction that traps if the V bit is set, so the cost of trapping on overflow is one extra instruction.

A.3 | Floating Point

Introduction

Many applications require numbers that aren't integers. There are a number of ways that nonintegers can be represented. One is to use *fixed point*; that is, use integer arithmetic and simply imagine the binary point somewhere other than just to the right of the least significant digit. Adding two such numbers can be done with an integer add, whereas multiplication requires some extra shifting. Other representations that have been proposed involve storing the logarithm of a number and doing multiplication by adding the logarithms, or using a pair of integers (a,b) to represent the fraction a/b. However, there is only one noninteger representation that has gained widespread use, and that is the floating-point representation. In this system, a computer word is divided into two parts, an exponent and a significand. As an example, an exponent of -2 and significand of 1.5 might represent the number $1.5 \times 2^{-2} = 0.375$. The advantages of standardizing a particular representation are obvious. Numerical analysts can build up high-quality software libraries, computer designers can develop techniques for implementing high-performance hardware, and hardware vendors can build standard accelerators. Given the predominance of the floating-point representation, it appears unlikely that any other representation will come into widespread use.

A key fact about floating-point instructions is that their semantics are not as clear cut as the semantics of the rest of the instruction set, and in the past the behavior of floating-point operations varied considerably from one computer family to the next. The variations involved such things as the number of bits allocated to the exponent and significand, the range of exponents, how rounding was carried out, and the actions taken on exceptional conditions like underflow and overflow. Computer architecture books used to dispense advice on how to deal with all these details, but fortunately this is no longer necessary. That's because the computer industry is rapidly converging on the format specified by IEEE standard 754-1985. The advantages of using a standard variant of floating point are similar to those for using floating point over other noninteger representations. In this chapter we will discuss only the IEEE version of floating point. For further reading see IEEE [1985], Cody et al. [1984], Cody [1988], and Goldberg [1989].

Overview of the IEEE Standard

Probably the most notable feature of the standard is that it requires computation to continue in the face of exceptional conditions, such as dividing by zero or taking the square root of a negative number. The result of taking the square root of a negative number is a *NaN* (*Not a Number*), a bit pattern that does not represent an ordinary number. As an example of how NaNs might be useful, consider the code for a zero finder that takes a function F as an argument and evaluates F at various points to determine a zero for it. If the zero finder accidentally probes outside the valid values for F, F may well cause an exception. Writing a zero finder that deals with this case is highly language and operating-system dependent, because it relies on how the operating system reacts to exceptions and how this reaction is mapped back into the programming language. In IEEE arithmetic it is easy to write a zero finder that handles this situation and runs on many different systems. After each evaluation of F, it simply checks to see if F has returned a NaN; if so, it knows it has probed outside the domain of F.

Because of the rules for performing arithmetic with NaNs, writing floating-point subroutines that can accept NaN as an argument rarely requires any special case checks. Suppose that arccos is computed in terms of arctan, using the formula arccos $x = 2\arctan(\sqrt{(1-x)/(1+x)}\,)$. If arctan handles an argument of NaN properly, arccos will automatically do so too. That's because the IEEE standard specifies that when an argument of an operation is a NaN, the result should be a NaN. Therefore if x is a NaN, $1 + x$, $1 - x$, $(1 + x)/(1 - x)$ and $\sqrt{(1-x)/(1+x)}$ will also be NaNs. No checking for NaNs is required.

While the result of $\sqrt{-1}$ is a NaN, the result of $1/0$ is not a NaN, but $+\infty$, which is another special value. The standard defines arithmetic on infinities (including $-\infty$) using rules such as $1/\infty = 0$. The formula arccos $x = 2\arctan(\sqrt{(1-x)/(1+x)})$ illustrates how infinity arithmetic can be used. Since $\arctan x$ asymptotically approaches $\pi/2$ as x approaches ∞, it is natural to define $\arctan(\infty) = \pi/2$, in which case arccos(-1) will automatically be computed correctly as $2\arctan(\infty) = \pi$.

Another feature of the IEEE standard with implications for hardware is the rounding rule. When operating on two floating-point numbers, the result is usually a number that cannot be exactly represented as another floating-point number. For example, in a floating-point system using base 10 and two significant digits, $2.1 \times 0.5 = 1.05$. This needs to be rounded to two digits. Should it be rounded to 1.0 or 1.1? In the IEEE standard, such halfway cases are rounded to the number whose low-order digit is even. That is, 1.05 rounds to 1.0, not 1.1. The standard actually has four *rounding modes*. The default is *round to nearest*, which rounds to an even number in the case of ties. The other modes are round toward 0, round toward $+\infty$ and round toward $-\infty$.

The standard specifies four precisions: *single*, *single extended*, *double*, and *double extended*. The properties of these precisions are summarized in Figure A.6 (page A-14). Implementations are not required to have all four precisions, but are encouraged to support either the combination of single and single extended or all of single, double, and double extended. Let us consider single precision in more detail. Single-precision numbers are represented using 32 bits: 1 for the sign, 8 for the exponent, and 23 for the fraction. The exponent is a signed number represented using the bias method (as explained in Section A.2 above) with a bias of 127. We will always use the term *exponent field* to mean the unsigned number contained in bits one through nine and *exponent* to mean the power to which two is to be raised. (In the standard these are called the "biased exponent" and the "unbiased exponent," respectively.) The fraction represents a number less than one, but the *significand* of the floating-point number is one plus the fraction part. In other words, if e is the value of the exponent field and f is the value of the fraction field, the number being represented is $1.f \times 2^{e-127}$.

Example:

What single-precision number does the following 32-bit word represent?

$$1 \quad 10000001 \quad 01000000000000000000000$$

Answer:

Considered as an unsigned number, the exponent field is 129, making the value of the exponent $129 - 127 = 2$. The fraction part is $.01_2 = .25$, making the significand 1.25. Thus, this bit pattern represents the number $-1.25 \times 2^2 = -5$.

The fractional part of a floating-point number (.25 in the example above) must not be confused with the significand, which is one plus the fractional part. The leading 1 in the significand $1.f$ does not appear in the representation; that is, the leading bit is implicit. When performing arithmetic on IEEE format numbers, the fraction part normally needs to be *unpacked,* which is to say the implicit one needs to be made explicit.

In Figure A.6, the range of exponents for single precision is −126 to 127; accordingly, the exponent field ranges from 1 to 254. The exponent fields of 0 and 255 are used to represent special values. When the exponent field is 255, a zero fraction field represents infinity, and a nonzero fraction field represents a NaN. Thus, there is an entire family of NaNs. When the exponent and fraction fields are zero, then the number represented is zero. Because ordinary numbers always have a significand greater than or equal to 1—and are thus never zero—a special convention such as this is required to represent zero.

A zero exponent field and nonzero fraction part represent a *denormal* number, also sometimes called a *subnormal* number. These numbers make up the most controversial part of the standard. Later, in the discussion of multiplication, we will see why they are difficult to implement in hardware. In many floating-point systems if E_{min} is the smallest exponent, a number less than $1.0 \times 2^{E_{min}}$

	Single	Single extended	Double	Double extended
p (bits of precision)	24	≥ 32	53	≥ 64
E_{max}	127	≥ 1023	1023	≥ 16383
E_{min}	−126	≤ -1022	−1022	≤ -16382
Exponent bias	127		1023	

FIGURE A.6   Format parameters for the IEEE 754 floating-point standard. The first row gives the number of bits in the significand. The blank boxes are unspecified parameters.

cannot be represented, and a floating-point operation that results in a number less than this is simply flushed to zero. In the IEEE standard, on the other hand, numbers less than $1.0 \times 2^{E\min}$ are represented by shifting their fraction part to the right. This is called *gradual underflow*. Thus, as numbers decrease in magnitude below $2^{E\min}$, they gradually lose their significance and are only represented by zero when all their significance has been shifted out. For example, in base 10 with 4 significant figures, let $x = 1.234 \times 2^{E\min}$. Then $x/10 = 0.123 \times 10^{E\min}$, having lost a digit of precision; $x/100$ and $x/1000$ have even less precision, while $x/10000$ is finally small enough to be rounded to zero. Denormalized numbers are implemented by having a word with a zero exponent field represent the number $0.f \times 2^{E\min}$. One of the advantages of gradual underflow is that when it is used, if $x \neq y$, then $x - y \neq 0$. In a flush-to-zero system, this is not always true.

The primary reason why the IEEE standard, like most other floating-point formats, uses biased exponents is that it means nonnegative numbers are ordered in the same way as integers. That is, the magnitude of floating-point numbers can be compared using an integer comparator. Another (related) advantage is that zero is represented by a word of all zeros. The down side of biased exponents is that adding them is slightly awkward, because it requires that the bias be subtracted from their sum.

As the IEEE standard becomes more widespread, it will become easier to port software and to write portable libraries that deal with floating-point exceptions. But the standard also has some drawbacks:

1. It was originally intended for microprocessors, so the requirements of high-performance implementations were not given high priority.

2. The standard contains optional parts. This results in difficult decisions for implementors—which parts should they implement?—and for portable software writers—should they avoid using any of the optional parts of the standard?

3. Gradual underflow has usually been implemented in a way that is orders of magnitude slower than flush to zero, so users often disable it.

4. There is as yet no industrial-strength, public-domain, IEEE floating-point test suite.

Although the standard may ultimately improve the quality of floating-point libraries, this has yet to happen because of the large base of VAXes, IBM/370s, and Crays, as well as the fact that there is no corresponding standard for how to access its features in software. On the other hand, both DEC and IBM have recently introduced machines that use IEEE arithmetic.

Some final comments on the standard:

1. Unlike most standards, IEEE 754 did not ratify or refine any existing system. Although most of the features of the standard appeared in at least one previous computer system, it is substantially different from what was current practice at the time.

2. The standard says nothing about integer arithmetic or about transcendental functions (sin, cos, exp, and so forth). In particular, it says nothing about the accuracy that transcendentals should have, and it says nothing about the exceptional values of transcendentals, such as 0^0.

3. It is intended that a computer **system**—that is, some combination of hardware and software—will implement the standard. Thus, there is nothing wrong with designing hardware that does not completely implement the standard, as long as there is some way for software to provide what the hardware does not. In fact, the best design may well involve having rare cases handled by software.

A.4 | Floating-Point Addition

There are two differences between floating-point arithmetic and integer arithmetic: An exponent field must be manipulated, in addition to the fraction field, and the result of a floating-point operation usually has to be rounded in order to be represented by another floating-point number of the same precision.

Rounding

The IEEE standard specifies that the result of an arithmetic operation should be the same as it would be if computed exactly and then rounded using the current rounding mode. The most difficult mode to implement is the default mode—round toward the nearest value (and round halfway cases to even). The naive approach to complying with the IEEE standard is to compute the sum exactly and then round. This would be quite expensive, since it would require a very long adder. To see how to satisfy the standard with less hardware, we will consider some examples.

There are two ways that rounding can occur during addition. For purposes of illustration we will use base 10, which is more natural for humans, and three significant digits. The first case requires rounding due to carry out on the left, as illustrated in Figure A.7(a). The second case requires rounding due to unequal exponents, as in Figure A.7(b). Figure A.7(c) shows that it is possible for both situations to occur simultaneously. In each of these cases, the sum must be computed to more than three places in order to perform rounding. In one case—when subtracting nearby numbers, as in Figure A.7(d)—the sum must be computed to more than three places, even though no rounding occurs. By temporarily ignoring the round-to-even requirement, each of these examples can be implemented with a four-digit-wide adder (that is, using one additional digit). Thus, in Figure A.7(b) the rightmost 6 of 2.56 can simply be dropped before adding. But there is one case, shown in Figure A.7(e), in which four digits are not enough. If the low-order digit of .0376 were shifted off, the answer would have been .973 instead of .972. However, it is easy to check (disregarding round to even) that two extra digits are always enough. These extra digits are called the *guard* and *round* digits.

The round-to-even rule introduces an extra complication. Figure A.7(f) shows an example with five significant digits. It might appear at first that one needs to keep double the number of digits to perform round to even, as the rightmost 1 in 2.5001 determines whether the result will be 4.5676 or 4.5677.

Upon a little reflection one can see that it is only necessary to know whether or not there are any nonzero digits past the guard and round positions. This information can be stored in a single bit, usually called the *sticky bit*, which is implemented by examining each digit as it is shifted off. As soon as a nonzero digit appears, the sticky bit is set on and remains stuck on. To implement round to even, simply append the sticky bit to the right of the round digit just before rounding.

a)
$$2.34 \times 10^2$$
$$+8.51 \times 10^2$$
$$\overline{10.85 \times 10^2} \qquad \text{rounds to } 1.08 \times 10^3$$

b)
$$2.34 \times 10^2 \qquad\qquad 2.34 \times 10^2$$
$$+2.56 \times 10^0 \qquad\qquad +.0256 \times 10^2$$
$$\qquad\qquad\qquad \overline{2.3656 \times 10^2} \quad \text{rounds to } 2.37 \times 10^2$$
$$\qquad\qquad\qquad\qquad gr$$

c)
$$9.51 \times 10^2$$
$$+.642 \times 10^2$$
$$\overline{10.152 \times 10^2} \qquad \text{rounds to } 1.02 \times 10^3$$
$$\quad g$$

d)
$$1.47 \times 10^2$$
$$-.876 \times 10^2$$
$$\overline{.594 \times 10^2}$$
$$\quad g$$

e)
$$1.01 \times 10^2$$
$$-.0376 \times 10^2$$
$$\overline{.9724 \times 10^2} \qquad \text{rounds to } .972 \times 10^2$$
$$\quad gr$$

f)
$$4.5674 \times 10^0 \qquad\qquad 4.5674$$
$$2.5001 \times 10^{-4} \qquad\qquad +.00025001$$
$$\qquad\qquad\qquad \overline{4.56765001} \qquad \text{rounds to } 4.5677$$
$$\qquad\qquad\qquad\quad gr$$

FIGURE A.7 Examples of rounding. In (a) there is rounding because of carry out on the left and in (b) because of unequal exponents, whereas in (c) both occur. Example (d) shows that one extra place must be kept even if there is no rounding, while (e) shows the situation in which two extra digits are needed. Finally (f), where $p = 5$, illustrates why a sticky bit is necessary to perform round to even. The letters g and r are placed under the guard and round digits.

The Addition Algorithm

The notations e_i and s_i are used here for the exponent and significand fields of the floating-point number a_i. This means that the floating-point number has been unpacked and that s_i has an explicit leading bit. The basic procedure for adding two floating-point numbers a_1 and a_2 is straightforward and involves five steps.

1. If $e_1 < e_2$, swap the operands so that the difference of the exponents satisfies $d = e_1 - e_2 \geq 0$. Tentatively set the exponent of the result to e_1.

2. Shift s_2 by $d = e_1 - e_2$ places to the right. More precisely, put s_2 into a p-bit register and then extend that register MIN(2,d) bits to the right. Shift s_2 d places to the right. If $d > 2$, set the sticky bit to the logical OR of the $d-2$ bits that are shifted out of the extended register. Of the two extended bits, the most significant is the guard bit; the least significant is the round bit.

3. Append the sticky bit to s_2, and then add the two signed-magnitude fraction fields in a $p + 3$ bit adder. Call this preliminary sum S.

4. If there was a carry out from the most significant place in the previous step, shift the magnitude of S right by one. Otherwise, shift it left until it is normalized. Adjust the exponent of the result accordingly. The round bit is now set to the $(p + 1)$-st bit of the magnitude of S, and the sticky bit to the logical OR of all the bits to the right of the round bit.

5. Round the result using Figure A.8. If a table entry is nonempty, add 1 to the magnitude of S. Thus, if $S \geq 0$, you will be computing $S + 1$, otherwise $S - 1$.

   The guard and round bits before shifting are marked in each of the examples of Figure A.7 (page A-17).

Example: Show how the addition algorithm proceeds on the operands of Figure A.7(f) when round to nearest is in effect.

Answer: In step 1, $e_1 = 0 > e_2 = -3$, so $d = 3$ and no swapping is necessary. In step 2, $g = 5$, $r = 0$, and sticky is the OR of 0, 0, and 1; hence, sticky is 1. In step 3 the numbers to be added are 4.5674 and 0.0002501, so the preliminary sum is $S = 4.5676501$. In step 4 there is no carry out, so d is still 3. The round bit is 5, and the sticky bit is $1 = 0 \lor 1$. In step 5, consulting the table tells us that because round and sticky are both nonzero, we must add 1 to the fifth digit of S, changing S from 45676 to $45676 + 1 = 45677$.

   Step 3 involves adding sign-magnitude numbers, and itself has three steps:

3a. Convert any negative numbers to two's complement.

3b. Perform a $(p + 4)$-bit two's complement addition ($p + 3$ bits of magnitude, 1 bit for the sign).

3c. If the result is negative, perform another two's complementation to put the result back into sign-magnitude form.

As is apparent from this, addition is quite a complicated operation. Here is one trick that can speed it up. A pair of numbers will only need to be variably shifted once, in either step 2 or step 4, but not in both. The reason is simple: If $|e_1 - e_2| > 1$, then step 4 can require a shift of at most one place. And if $|e_1 - e_2| \le 1$, then step 2 obviously requires a shift of at most one step. A non-pipelined adder can exploit this and reduce the number of steps from five to four. An adder that uses each of the above steps as a pipeline stage can also use this reduction, though it requires duplicating the shifter and adder.

Step 3 can be time consuming, because it can involve as many as four additions: two to negate both operands (two's complementation done by performing a bitwise complementation followed by adding 1), a third for the addition itself, and then a fourth to negate the result. There are a number of ways to speed up this step. We have already seen that 1 can be added to a sum essentially for free by setting the low-order, carry-in bit of the adder to 1. If both operands are negative, we can set their sign bits to zero, remembering to negate the result. The add required when negating the result can be combined with the rounding step (which must be prepared to do an add anyway).

The rounding step requires a second full-precision add in addition to the one in step 3. It is possible to combine these into a single add. Observe that at the end of step 2, the g, r, and s bits are known; thus it is also known whether or not to round up, adding 1 to the pth most significant bit. What is not known is the position of the pth most significant bit, since its location depends on the result of the add in step 3; when adding numbers of the same sign, that position is determined by whether there is a carry out of the most significant bit. Therefore, the way to eliminate step 5 is to add in the round-up bit (if necessary) as part of step 3. Because the position is unknown, two versions of step 3 must be performed using two adders in parallel. Each adder assumes one of the two possibilities for the position where the round-up bit goes. This technique for reducing the number of addition steps is used on the Intel 860 [Kohn 1989]. When rounding, there is one complication that can arise: The addition of 1 could cause a carry out of the high-order bit. This case occurs only when the value of S is $11\cdots11$.

Rounding mode	$S \ge 0$	$S < 0$
$-\infty$		$+1$ if $r \vee s$
$+\infty$	$+1$ if $r \vee s$	
0		
Nearest	$+1$ if $r \wedge \bar{s} \wedge p_0$ or $r \wedge s$	$+1$ if $r \wedge \bar{s} \wedge p_0$ or $r \wedge s$

FIGURE A.8 Rules for implementing the IEEE rounding modes. Blank boxes mean that the p most significant bits of the preliminary sum S are the actual sum bits. If the condition in the box is true, add 1 to the pth most significant bit of S. The symbols r and s represent the round and sticky bits, while p_0 is the pth most significant bit of S.

Denormalized Numbers

Very little changes in the above description if one of the inputs is a denormal number. There must be a test to see if the exponent field is 0. If it is, then when unpacking the significand there will not be a leading 1. By setting the exponent field to 1 when unpacking a denormal, the shifting rules in steps 1–5 are still correct.

In order to deal with denormalized outputs, step 4 must be modified slightly. The value in the P register is shifted left until P is normalized, or until the exponent becomes E_{min} (that is, the exponent field becomes 1). If the exponent is E_{min}, and if after rounding, the high-order bit of P is 1, then the result is a normalized number and should be packed in the usual way, by omitting the 1. If, on the other hand, the high-order bit is 0, the result is denormal, and when the result is unpacked the exponent field must be set to 0.

Incidentally, detecting overflow is very easy. It can only happen if step 4 involves a shift right, and if the exponent field at that point is bumped up to 255 in single precision (or 2047 for double precision), or if this occurs after rounding.

Detecting underflow is complicated by the fact that it depends on whether there is a user trap handler. The IEEE standard specifies that if user trap handlers are enabled, the system must trap if the result is denormal. On the other hand, if trap handlers are disabled, then the underflow flag is set only if there is a loss of accuracy—that is, if the result must be rounded. The rationale for this is that if no accuracy is lost on an underflow, there is no point in setting a warning flag. But if a trap handler is enabled, the user might be trying to simulate flush-to-zero and should therefore be notified whenever a result dips below $1.0 \times 2^{E_{min}}$. This discussion is relevant for addition in that an addition or subtraction resulting in a denormal number will always be exact; because no accuracy can be lost to underflow, there is no need to set the underflow flag.

A.5 | Floating-Point Multiplication

Floating-point multiplication is much like integer multiplication. Because floating-point numbers are stored in sign-magnitude form, the multiplier need only deal with unsigned numbers (although we have seen that Booth recoding handles signed two's complement numbers painlessly). If the fractions are unsigned p-bit numbers, then the product can have as many as $2p$ bits and must be rounded to a p-bit number. Besides multiplying the fraction parts, the exponent fields must be added, and the bias then subtracted from their sum.

Here is a straightforward method of handling rounding using the multiplier of Figure A.2 (page A-4): Multiply the two fractions to obtain a $2p$-bit product in the (P,A) registers. During the multiplication, the first $p - 2$ times a bit is shifted into the A register, OR it into the sticky bit. After the end of all the multiply steps, the high-order bit of A is the guard bit, and the second high-order bit is the round bit. There are two cases:

1. The high-order bit of P is 0. Shift P left 1 bit, shifting in the g bit from A. Shifting the rest of A is not necessary.

2. The high-order bit of P is 1. Set $s := s \vee r$ and $r := g$, and add 1 to the exponent.

Now use the rules in Figure A.8 (page A-19) to round the result, adding the 1 (if necessary) into the low-order bit of P. The fraction (in unpacked form) is in the P register. Recall that the rounding operation can cause a carry out of the most significant bit. A good discussion of more efficient ways to implement rounding is in Santoro, Bewick, and Horowitz [1989].

Detecting overflow and underflow is slightly tricky. Consider the case of single precision. The exponent fields must be added together with -127. If the addition is done in a 10-bit adder, $-127 = 1110000001_2$, and overflow occurs when the high-order bits of the sum are 01 or if the sum is 0011111111. Underflow occurs when the high-order bits are 11 or the sum is 0000000000. Alternatively, the addition can be done using only an 8-bit adder. Simply add both exponents and $-127 = 10000001_2$. If the high-order bits of the exponent fields are different, no over/underflow is possible. If the high-order bits are both 1, the result has overflowed if it has 0 in the high-order bit or if it is 1111111. If both the exponents have high-order bits of zero, underflow has occurred if the sum has a high-order bit of 1, or if the sum is 00000000.

Denormals

From the description of the multiplication algorithm, one can see that after doing an integer multiplication on the fractions, the final result is obtained with at most one shift. With denormals, the situation changes completely. Suppose the input is normalized, but the output is denormal, so that in single precision the product has an exponent e with $e < -126$. Then the result must be shifted right by $-e - 126$ places. This requires extra hardware (a barrel shifter that wouldn't otherwise be needed) and extra time. The situation with denormal inputs isn't any better, because even if the final result is a normalized number, a variable shift is still required. Thus, high-performance, floating-point multipliers often do not handle denormalized numbers, but instead trap, letting software handle them. There are a few practical codes that generate many underflows, even when working properly, and these programs usually run quite a bit slower on systems that require denormals to be processed by a trap handler.

One procedure followed by some floating-point units is to have the multiplier deliver denormalized outputs in *wrapped* form. That is, the fraction part is normalized, and the exponent is wrapped around to a large positive number. This is exactly the result when following the multiplication algorithm for normalized numbers given above. Since the addition unit must have a barrel shifter, it is usually straightforward to provide a way to convert wrapped numbers into their correct denormalized form by passing them through the adder. However, if a trap handler has to intervene in order to send wrapped numbers into the adder, multiplication will still be slowed down substantially.

There are some fine points that occur when a multiplication results in a denormal number. Consider the simple case of a base 2 floating-point system with 3-bit significands (hence two bits of fraction). The exact result of 1.11×2^{-2} multiplied by $1.11 \times 2^{E\min}$ is $0.110001 \times 2^{E\min}$. If the rounding mode is round toward plus infinity, the rounded result is the normal number $1.00 \times 2^{E\min}$. Should underflow be signaled? Signaling underflow means that one is using the *before rounding* rule, because the result was denormal before rounding. Not signaling underflow means that one is using the *after rounding* rule, because the result is normalized after rounding. The IEEE standard provides for choosing either rule; however, the one chosen must be used consistently for all operations.

As mentioned in the addition section, the trap handler, if there is one, should be called whenever the result is denormal. If there is no trap handler, the underflow exception is signaled only when the result is denormal and inexact. Normally, inexact means there was a result that couldn't be represented exactly and had to be rounded. Consider again the example of $(1.11 \times 2^{-2}) \times (1.11 \times 2^{E\min}) = 0.110001 \times 2^{E\min}$, with round to nearest in effect. The delivered result is $0.11 \times 2^{E\min}$, which had to be rounded, causing inexact to be signaled. But is it correct to also signal underflow? Gradual underflow loses significance because the exponent range is bounded. If the exponent range were unbounded, the delivered result would be $1.10 \times 2^{E\min-1}$, exactly the same answer obtained with gradual underflow. The fact that denormalized numbers have fewer bits in their significand than normalized numbers therefore doesn't make any difference in this case. The commentary to the standard [Cody et al. 1984] encourages this as the criterion for setting the underflow flag. That is, it should be set whenever the delivered result is different from what would be delivered in a system with the same fraction size, but with a very large exponent range. However, owing to the difficulty of implementing this scheme, the standard allows setting the underflow flag whenever the result is denormal and different from the infinitely precise result.

Precision of Multiplication

In the discussion of integer multiplication, we mentioned that designers must decide whether to deliver the low-order word of the product or the entire product. A similar issue arises in floating-point multiplication, where the exact product can be rounded to the precision of the operands or to the next higher precision. In the case of integer multiplication, none of the standard high-level languages contains a construct that would generate a "single times single gets double" instruction. The situation is different for floating point. Not only do many languages allow assigning the product of two single-precision variables to a double-precision one, but the construction can also be exploited by numerical algorithms. The best-known case is using iterative refinement to solve linear systems of equations.

A.6 | Division and Remainder

Iterative Division

We earlier discussed an algorithm for integer division. Converting it into a floating-point division algorithm is similar to converting the integer multiplication algorithm into floating point. If the numbers to be divided are $s_1 2^{e_1}$ and $s_2 2^{e_2}$ then the divider will compute s_1/s_2, and the final answer will be this quotient multiplied by $2^{e_1 - e_2}$. Referring to Figure A.2(b) (page A-4), the alignment of operands is slightly different from integer division. Load s_2 into b and $s_1/2$ into P so that s_1 is shifted right one bit. Then the integer algorithm for division can be used, and the result will be of the form $q_0.q_1 \cdots$. For floating-point division, the A register is not needed to hold the operands. To round, simply compute two additional quotient bits (guard and round) and use the remainder as the sticky bit. The guard digit is necessary because the first quotient bit might be zero. However, since the numerator and denominator are both normalized, it is not possible for the two most significant quotient bits to be zero.

There is a different approach to division, based on iteration. An actual machine that uses this algorithm will be discussed in Section A.10. First, we will describe the two main iterative algorithms and then discuss the pros and cons of iteration compared to the direct algorithms. There is a general technique for constructing iterative algorithms, called *Newton's iteration*, shown in Figure A.9.

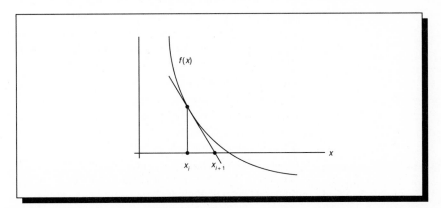

FIGURE A.9 Newton's iteration for zero finding. If x_i is an estimate for a zero of f, then x_{i+1} is a better estimate. To compute x_{i+1}, find the intersection of the x axis with the tangent line to f at x_i.

First, cast the problem in the form of finding the zero of a function. Then, starting from a guess for the zero, approximate the function by its tangent at that guess and form a new guess based on where the tangent has a zero. If x_i is a guess at a zero, then the tangent line has the equation

$$y - f(x_i) = f'(x_i)(x - x_i)$$

This equation has a zero at

A.6.1
$$x = x_{i+1} = x_i - \frac{f(x_i)}{f'(x_i)}$$

To recast division as finding the zero of a function, consider $f(x) = 1/x - b$. Since the zero of this function is at $1/b$, applying Newton's iteration to it will give an iterative method of computing $1/b$ from b. Using $f'(x) = -1/x^2$, Equation A.6.1 becomes

A.6.2
$$x_{i+1} = x_i - \frac{1/x_i - b}{-1/x_i^2} = x_i + x_i - x_i^2 b = x_i(2 - x_i b)$$

Thus, we could implement computation of a/b using the following method:

1. Scale b to lie in the range $1 \leq b < 2$ and get an approximate value of $1/b$ (call it x_0) using a table lookup.

2. Iterate $x_{i+1} = x_i(2 - x_i b)$ until reaching an x_n that is accurate enough.

3. Compute ax_n and reverse the scaling done in step 1.

Here are some more details. How many times will step 2 have to be iterated? To say that x_i is accurate to p bits means that $(x_i - 1/b)/(1/b) = 2^{-p}$, and a simple algebraic manipulation shows $(x_{i+1} - 1/b)/(1/b) = 2^{-2p}$. Thus the number of correct bits doubles at each step. Newton's iteration is **self-correcting** in the sense that making an error in x_i doesn't really matter. That is, it treats x_i as a guess at $1/b$ and returns x_{i+1} as an improvement on it (roughly doubling the digits). One thing that would cause x_i to be in error is rounding error. More importantly, however, in the early iterations we can take advantage of the fact that we don't expect many correct bits by performing the multiplication in reduced precision, thus gaining speed without sacrificing accuracy. Some other applications of Newton's iteration are discussed in the Exercises.

The second iterative division method is sometimes called *Goldschmidt's algorithm*. It is based on the idea that to compute a/b, you should multiply the numerator and denominator by a number r with $rb \approx 1$. In more detail, let $x_0 = a$ and $y_0 = b$. At each step compute $x_{i+1} = r_i x_i$ and $y_{i+1} = r_i y_i$. Then the quotient $x_{i+1}/y_{i+1} = x_i/y_i = a/b$ is constant. If we pick r_i so that $y_i \to 1$, then $x_i \to a/b$, so the x_i converge to the answer we want. This same idea can be used to compute other functions. For example, to compute the square root of a, let $x_0 = a$ and $y_0 = a$, and at each step compute $x_{i+1} = r_i^2 x_i$, $y_{i+1} = r_i y_i$. Then $x_{i+1}/y_{i+1}^2 = x_i/y_i^2 = 1/a$, so if the r_i are chosen to drive $x_i \rightarrow 1$, then $y_i \rightarrow \sqrt{a}$. This technique is used to compute square roots on the TI 8847.

Returning to Goldschmidt's division algorithm, set $x_0 = a$ and $y_0 = b$, and write $b = 1 - \delta$, where $|\delta| < 1$. If we pick $r_0 = 1 + \delta$, then $y_1 = r_0 y_0 = 1 - \delta^2$. We next pick $r_1 = 1 + \delta^2$, so that $y_2 = r_1 y_1 = 1 - \delta^4$, and so on. Since $|\delta| < 1$, $y_i \rightarrow 1$. With this choice of r_i, the x_i will be computed as $x_{i+1} = r_i x_i = (1 + \delta^{2^i})x_i = (1 + (1-b)^{2^i})x_i$, or

A.6.3
$$x_{i+1} = a[1 + (1-b)][1 + (1-b)^2][1 + (1-b)^4]\cdots[1 + (1-b)^{2^i}]$$

There appear to be two problems with this algorithm. First, convergence is slow when b is not near 1 (that is, δ is not near 0); and second, the formula isn't self-correcting—since the quotient is being computed as a product of independent terms, an error in one of them won't get corrected. To deal with slow convergence, if you want to compute a/b, look up an approximate inverse to b (call it b'), and run the algorithm on ab'/bb'. This will converge rapidly since $bb' \approx 1$.

To deal with the self-correction problem, the computation should be run with a few bits of extra precision to compensate for rounding errors. However, Goldschmidt's algorithm does have a weak form of self-correction, in that the precise value of the r_i does not matter. Thus, in the first few iterations, you can choose r_i to be a truncation of $1 + \delta^{2^i}$ which may make these iterations run faster without affecting the speed of convergence. If r_i is truncated, then y_i is no longer exactly $1 - \delta^{2^i}$, so Equation A.6.3 can no longer be used, but it is easy to organize the computation so that it does not depend on the precise value of r_i. With these changes, Goldschmidt's algorithm is as follows (the notes in brackets show the connection with our earlier formulas).

1. Scale a and b so that $1 \leq b < 2$.

2. Look up an approximation to $1/b$ (call it b') in a table.

3. Set $x_0 = ab'$ and $y_0 = bb'$.

4. Iterate until x_i is close enough to a/b :

   $r \approx 2 - y$ [if $y_i = 1 + \delta_i$, then $r \approx 1 - \delta_i$]

   $y = y \times r$ [$y_{i+1} = y_i \times r \approx 1 - \delta_i^2$]

   $x = x \times r$ [$x_{i+1} = x_i \times r$]

The two iteration methods are related. Suppose in Newton's method that we unroll the iteration and compute each term x_{i+1} directly in terms of b, instead of recursively in terms of x_i. By carrying out this calculation, we discover that

$$x_{i+1} = x_0(2 - x_0 b)(1 + (x_0 b - 1)^2)(1 + (x_0 b - 1)^4) \cdots (1 + (x_0 b - 1)^{2^i})$$

This formula is of a very similar form to Equation A.6.3 when $a = 1$. In fact, if the iterations were done to infinite precision, the two methods would yield exactly the same sequence x_i.

The advantage of iteration is that it doesn't require special divide hardware, but can instead use the multiplier (which, however, requires extra control). Further, on each step, it delivers twice as many digits as in the previous step— unlike ordinary division, which produces a fixed number of digits at every step. There are two disadvantages with inverting by iteration. The first is that the IEEE standard requires division to be correctly rounded, but iteration only delivers a result that is close to the correctly rounded answer. In the case of Newton's iteration, which computes $1/b$ instead of a/b directly, there is an additional problem. Even if $1/b$ was correctly rounded, there is no guarantee that a/b will be. Take 5/7 as an example: To two digits of accuracy 1/7 is 0.14, and 5×0.14 is 0.70, but 5/7 is 0.71. The second disadvantage is that iteration does not give a remainder. This is especially troublesome if the floating-point divide hardware is being used to perform integer division, since a remainder operation is present in almost every high-level language.

Traditional folklore has held that the way to get a correctly rounded result from iteration is to compute $1/b$ to slightly more than $2p$ bits, compute a/b to slightly more than $2p$ bits, and then round to p bits. However, there is a faster way, which apparently was first implemented on the TI 8847. In this method, a/b is computed to about six extra bits of precision, giving a preliminary quotient q. By comparing qb with a (again with only six extra bits), it is possible to quickly decide whether q is correctly rounded or whether it needs to be bumped up or down by 1 in the least significant place. This algorithm is explored further in the Exercises.

One factor to take into account when deciding on division algorithms is the relative speed of division and multiplication. Since division is more complex than multiplication, it will run more slowly. As a general rule of thumb, division algorithms should try to achieve a speed that is about one-third that of multiplication. One argument in favor of this rule is that there are real programs (such as some versions of Spice) where the ratio of division to multiplication is 1:3. Another place where a factor of three arises is in the standard iterative method for computing square root. This method involves one division per iteration, but can be replaced by one using three multiplications. This is discussed in the Exercises.

Floating-Point Remainder

For nonnegative integers, integer division and remainder satisfy

$$a = (a \text{ DIV } b)b + a \text{ REM } b, \ 0 \le a \text{ REM } b < b$$

A floating-point remainder x REM y can be similarly defined as $x = \text{INT}(x/y)y + x$ REM y. How should x/y be converted to an integer? The IEEE remainder function uses the round-to-even rule. That is, pick $n = \text{INT}(x/y)$ so that $|x/y - n| \leq 1/2$. If two different n satisfy this relation, pick the even one. Then REM is defined to be $x - yn$. Unlike integers where $0 \leq a$ REM $b < b$, for floating-point numbers $|x \text{ REM } y| \leq y/2$. Although this defines REM precisely, it is not a practical operational definition, because n can be huge. In single precision, n could be as large as $2^{127}/2^{-126} = 2^{253} \approx 10^{76}$.

There is a natural way to compute REM if a direct division algorithm is used. Proceed as if you were computing x/y. If $x = s_1 2^{e_1}$ and $y = s_2 2^{e_2}$ and the divider is as in Figure A.2(b) (page A-4), then load s_1 into P and s_2 into B. After $e_1 - e_2$ division steps, the P register will hold a number r of the form $x - yn$ satisfying $0 \leq r < y$. The IEEE remainder is then either r or $r - y$. It is only necessary to keep track of the last quotient bit produced, which is needed in order to resolve halfway cases. Unfortunately, $e_1 - e_2$ can be a lot of steps, and floating-point units typically have a maximum amount of time they are allowed to spend on one instruction. Thus, it is usually not possible to implement REM directly. None of the chips discussed in Section A.10 implement REM, but they could by providing a remainder-step instruction—this is what is done on the Intel 8087 family. A remainder step takes as arguments two numbers x and y, and performs divide steps until either the remainder is in P, or else n steps have been performed, where n is a small number, such as the number of steps required for division in the highest supported precision. The REM driver calls the REM-step instruction $\lfloor (e_1 - e_2)/n \rfloor$ times, initially using x as the numerator, but then replacing it with the remainder from the previous REM step. It is useful if the REM-step instruction returns the low-order three bits of the quotient, since when doing trigonometric argument reduction to the interval $(0, \pi/4)$, you need to know the value of n mod 8 in order to know what quadrant you are in.

Currently, most of the fastest floating-point chips don't implement remainder, even though it is a required part of the IEEE standard. Since the standard allows implementations to be a combination of hardware and software, the REM operation could be implemented entirely in software. However, availability of the REM-step instruction would make computing REM much simpler. Is a REM-step instruction worth it? For two reasons this situation is difficult to decide on the basis of frequency data. First, because REM is peculiar to the IEEE standard, few people are currently using it. Testing the demand for REM is somewhat like trying to estimate the demand for a new product. Second, the main benefit from REM is not an increase in performance, but rather an increase in accuracy, and it is not easy to quantify the value of accuracy. What we will do here is simply present the primary application of REM, which is argument reduction for periodic functions, like sin and cos.

There are some subtle issues involved in argument reduction. To simplify things, imagine that we are working in base 10 with 5 significant figures, and consider computing $\sin x$. Suppose that $x = 7$. Then we reduce by $\pi = 3.1416$

and compute $\sin(7) = \sin(7 - 2 \times 3.1416) = \sin(0.7168)$ instead. But suppose we want to compute $\sin(2.0 \times 10^5)$. Then $2 \times 10^5/3.1416 = 63661.8$, which in our 5-place system comes out to be 63662. Since multiplying 3.1416 times 63662 gives 200000.5392, which rounds to 2.0000×10^5, argument reduction reduces 2 $\times 10^5$ to 0, which is not even close to being correct. The problem is that our 5-place system does not have the precision to do correct argument reduction. Suppose we had the REM operator. Then we could compute 2×10^5 REM 3.1416 and get $-.5392$. However, this is still not correct because we used 3.1416, which is an approximation for π. The value of 2×10^5 REM π is $-.071513$. The difficulty is that we subtracted two nearby numbers, 2×10^5 and 63662×3.1416, where 63662×3.1416 was slightly in error due to approximating π. Even though REM has the effect of performing the subtraction exactly, all the significant figures in 63662×3.1416 canceled, leaving behind only rounding error.

Traditionally, there have been two approaches to computing periodic functions with large arguments. The first is to return an error for their value when x is large. The second is to store π to a very large number of places and do exact argument reduction. The REM operator is not much help in either of these situations. There is a third approach that has been used in some math libraries, such as the Berkeley UNIX 4.3bsd release. In these libraries, π is computed to the nearest floating-point number. Let's call this machine π, and denote it by π'. Then when computing $\sin x$, reduce x using x REM π'. As we saw in the above example, x REM π' is quite different from x REM π, so that computing $\sin x$ as $\sin(x$ REM $\pi')$ will not give the exact value of $\sin x$. However, computing trigonometric functions in this fashion has the property that all familiar identities (such as $\sin^2 x + \cos^2 x = 1$) are true to within a few rounding errors. Thus, using REM together with machine π provides a simple method of computing trigonometric functions that is accurate for small arguments and still useful for large arguments in most applications.

A.7 | Precisions and Exception Handling

Precisions

Implementations of the IEEE standard are only required to support single precision. Thus, the computer designer must make a choice about what other precisions to support. Because of the widespread use of double precision in scientific computing, double precision is almost always implemented.

Double-extended precision is more problematic. Although the Motorola 68882 and Intel 387 coprocessors implement extended precision, most of the more recently designed, high-performance floating-point chips do not implement extended precision. Among the reasons are that the 80-bit width of extended precision is awkward for 64-bit buses and registers, and that many high-level languages do not give the user access to extended precision. However, extended precision is very useful to writers of mathematical software. As an example, consider writing a library routine to compute the length of a vector in the plane $\sqrt{x^2 + y^2}$. If x is larger than $2^{E_{max}/2}$, then computing this in the obvious way will overflow. This means that either the allowable exponent range for this subroutine will be cut in half, or a more complex algorithm using scaling will have to be employed. But if extended precision is available, then the simple algorithm will work. Computing the length of a vector is a simple task, and it is not difficult to come up with an algorithm that doesn't overflow. However, there are more complex problems for which extended precision means the difference between a simple, fast algorithm and a much more complex one. One of the best examples of this is binary/decimal conversion. An efficient algorithm for binary-to-decimal conversion that makes essential use of extended precision is very readably presented in Coonen [1984]. This algorithm is also briefly sketched in Goldberg [1989]. Computing accurate values for transcendental functions is another example of a problem that is made much easier if extended precision is present.

One very important fact about precision concerns *double rounding*. To illustrate in decimal, suppose that we want to compute 1.9×0.66, and that single precision is two digits, while extended precision is three digits. The exact result of the product is 1.254. Rounded to extended precision, the result is 1.25. When further rounded to single precision, we get 1.2. However, the result of 1.9×0.66 correctly rounded to single precision is 1.3. Thus, rounding twice may not produce the same result as rounding once. Suppose you want to build hardware that only does double-precision arithmetic. Can you simulate single precision by computing first in double precision and then rounding to single? The above example suggests that you can't. However, double rounding is not always dangerous. In fact, the following rule is true (although it is not easy to prove).

> *If x and y have p-bit significands, and $x + y$ is computed exactly and then rounded to q places, a second rounding to p places will not change the answer if $p \leq (q-1)/2$. This is true not only for addition, but also for multiplication, division, and square root.*

In our example above, $q = 3$, and $p = 2$, so $2 \leq (3-1)/2$ is not true. On the other hand, for IEEE arithmetic, double precison has $p = 53$, and single precision is $p = 24 \leq (q-1)/2 = 26$. Thus, single precision can be implemented by computing in double precision (that is, computing the answer exactly and then rounding to double) and then rounding to single precision.

The standard requires implementations to provide versions of addition, subtraction, multiplication, division, and remainder that take two operands of the same precision and produce a result of that precision. It also recommends that implementations allow operations that take operands of two different precisions and return a result whose precision is at least as wide as the widest operand. The standard allows implementations to combine two operands and return a result in a higher precision. Remember that the result of an operation is the exact result rounded to the destination precision. What the standard does not allow is combining two operands and returning a result in a lower precision. Although at first this may seem like a minor restriction, consider again the problem of computing $\sqrt{x^2 + y^2}$. If x and y are double, then you might like to compute $x^2 + y^2$ in extended precision and then compute a square root that takes an extended-precision argument and returns a double-precision answer. But this is not allowed by the standard.

There is a related issue. The standard permits combining two extended variables to produce a result that is stored in extended format, but rounded to double precision. However, this doesn't help in the square root example, because the result of the square root must still be explicitly converted from an extended format to a double-precision format.

Exceptions

The IEEE standard defines five exceptions: underflow, overflow, divide by zero, inexact, and invalid. By default, when these exceptions occur, they merely set a flag and the computation continues. The flags are *sticky*, meaning that once set they remain set until explicitly cleared. The standard strongly encourages implementations to provide a trap-enable bit for each exception. When an exception with an enabled trap handler occurs, a user trap handler is called, and the value of the associated exception flag is undefined.

The underflow, overflow, and divide-by-zero exceptions are found in most other systems. The *inexact exception* is peculiar to IEEE arithmetic and occurs when either the result of an operation must be rounded or when it overflows. In fact, since 1/0 and an operation that overflows both deliver ∞, the exception flags must be consulted to distinguish between them. The inexact exception is an unusual "exception," in that it is not really an exceptional condition because it occurs so frequently. Thus, enabling a trap handler for inexact will most likely have a severe impact on performance. The *invalid exception* is for things like $\sqrt{-1}$, 0/0 or $\infty - \infty$, which don't have any natural value as a floating-point number or as $\pm\infty$. Thus, 1/0 causes a divide by zero exception and delivers ∞, whereas 0/0 causes an invalid exception and delivers a NaN. There is a twist in IEEE underflow, because it is not always signaled when numbers fall below $1.0 \times 2^{E_{min}}$. If a user trap handler is not installed, then underflow is signaled only if the result of an operation is below $2^{E_{min}}$ and is inexact.

The IEEE standard assumes that when a trap occurs, it is possible to identify the operation that trapped and its operands. On machines with pipelining, or machines with multiple arithmetic units, when an exception occurs, it may not be enough to simply have the trap handler examine the program counter. Hardware support may be necessary in order to identify exactly which operation trapped. Another problem is illustrated by the following program fragment.

```
X = Y * Z;
Z = A + B;
```

These two instructions might well be executed in parallel. If the multiply traps, its argument Z could already have been overwritten by the addition, especially since addition is usually faster than multiplication. Computer systems that support trapping in the IEEE standard must provide some way to save the value of Z, either in hardware or by having the compiler avoid such a situation in the first place.

One approach to this problem, used in the MIPS R3010, is to treat floating-point exceptions similarly to page-fault exceptions. If an instruction that assigns a memory location to a register causes a page fault, the execution of the instruction must stall before it clobbers the register because (for example) that very register might be used to reference the memory that faulted. The key to making this work is that the memory address is computed early in the instruction cycle, before the instruction actually writes anything. A similar trick can be done with floating-point operations. An instruction that may cause an exception can be identified early in the instruction cycle. For example, an addition can overflow only if one of the operands has an exponent of E_{max}, and so on. This early check is conservative: It might flag an operation that doesn't actually cause an exception. However, if such false positives are rare, then this technique will have excellent performance. When an instruction is tagged as being possibly exceptional, special code in a trap handler can compute it without destroying any state. Remember that all these problems occur only when trap handlers are enabled. Otherwise, setting the exception flags during normal processing is straightforward.

There is a subtlety that should be mentioned that involves the underflow trap. When there is no underflow trap handler, the result of an operation that involves an underflow is a denormal number. When there is a trap handler, it is provided with the result of the operation with the exponent wrapped around. Now there is a potential double-rounding problem. If the rounding mode is round toward nearest, when there is a trap handler the result is correctly rounded to p significant bits. If there is no trap handler, the result is rounded to less than p bits, depending on how many leading zeros the denormal number has. If the trap handler wants to return the denormal result, it can't just round its argument, because that might lead to a double-rounding error. Thus, the trap handler must be passed at least one extra bit of information if it is to be able to deliver the correctly rounded result.

A.8 | Speeding Up Integer Addition

The previous section showed that there are many steps that go into implementing floating-point operations. However, each floating-point operation eventually reduces to an integer operation. Thus, increasing the speed of integer operations will also lead to faster floating point.

Integer addition is the simplest operation and the most important. Even for programs that don't do explicit arithmetic, addition must be performed to increment the program counter and to do address calculations. Despite the simplicity of addition, there isn't a single best way to perform high-speed addition. We will discuss three techniques that are in current use: carry lookahead, carry skip, and carry select.

Carry Lookahead

An n-bit adder is just a combinational circuit. It can therefore be written by a logic formula whose form is a sum of products and can be computed by a circuit with two levels of logic. How does one figure out what this circuit looks like? Recall from Equation A.2.1 that the formula for the ith sum bit is

A.8.1
$$s_i = a_i \overline{b_i}\overline{c_i} + \overline{a_i}b_i\overline{c_i} + \overline{a_i}\overline{b_i}c_i + a_ib_ic_i$$

The problem with this formula is that although we know the values of a_i and b_i—they are inputs to the circuit—we don't know c_i. So our goal is to write c_i in terms of a_i and b_i. To accomplish this, we first rewrite Equation A.2.2 (page A-2) as

A.8.2
$$c_{i+1} = g_i + p_ic_i, \quad g_i = a_ib_i, \quad p_i = a_i + b_i$$

Here is the reason for the symbols p and g: If g_i is true, then c_{i+1} is certainly true, so a carry is *generated*. Thus, g is for generate. If p_i is true, then if c_i is true, it is *propagated* to c_{i+1}. Start with Equation A.8.1 and use Equation A.8.2 to replace c_i with $g_{i-1} + p_{i-1}c_{i-1}$. Then, use Equation A.8.2 with $i-1$ in place of i, to replace c_{i-1} with c_{i-2}, and so on. This gives the result

A.8.3
$$c_{i+1} = g_i + p_i g_{i-1} + p_ip_{i-1}g_{i-2} + \cdots + p_ip_{i-1}\cdots p_1 g_0 + p_ip_{i-1}\cdots p_1p_0c_0$$

An adder that computes carries using Equation A.8.3 is called a *carry-lookahead adder,* or CLA adder. A CLA adder requires one logic level to form p and g, two levels to form the carries, and two for the sum, for a grand total of five logic levels. This is a vast improvement over the $2n$ levels required for the ripple-carry adder.

Unfortunately, as is evident from Equation A.8.3 or from Figure A.10, a carry-lookahead adder on n bits requires a fan-in of $n+1$ at the OR gate as well as at the rightmost AND gate. Also, the p_{n-1} signal must drive n AND gates. In addition, the rather irregular structure and many long wires of Figure A.10 make it impractical to build a full carry-lookahead adder when n is large.

However, we can use the carry-lookahead idea to build an adder that has about $\log_2 n$ logic levels (substantially less than the $2n$ required by a ripple-carry adder), and yet has a simple, regular structure. The idea is to build up the p's and g's in steps. We have already seen that

$$c_1 = g_0 + c_0p_0$$

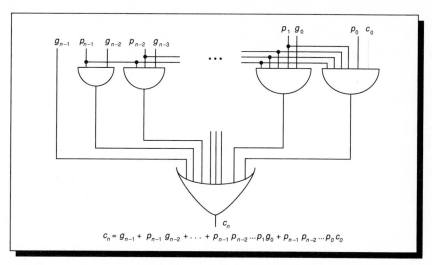

$$c_n = g_{n-1} + p_{n-1}\, g_{n-2} + \cdots + p_{n-1}\, p_{n-2} \cdots p_1 g_0 + p_{n-1}\, p_{n-2} \cdots p_0 c_0$$

FIGURE A.10 Pure carry-lookahead circuit for computing the carry out c_n of an n-bit adder.

This says there is a carry out of the 0th position (c_1) if there is either a carry generated in the 0th position, or if there is a carry into the 0th position and the carry propagates. Similarly,

$$c_2 = G_{01} + P_{01}c_0$$

G_{01} means there is a carry generated out of the block consisting of the first two bits. P_{01} means that a carry propagates through this block. P and G have the following logic equations:

$$G_{01} \;=\; g_1 + p_1 g_0$$

$$P_{01} \;=\; p_1 p_0$$

More generally, for any j with $i < j, j + 1 < k$, we have the recursive relations

A.8.4
$$c_{k+1} \;=\; G_{ik} + P_{ik}c_i$$

A.8.5
$$G_{ik} \;=\; G_{j+1,k} + P_{j+1,k}G_{ij}$$

A.8.6
$$P_{ik} \;=\; P_{ij}P_{j+1,k}$$

Equation A.8.5 says that a carry is generated out of the block consisting of bits i through k inclusive if it is generated in the high-order part of the block ($j + 1, k$) or if it is generated in the low-order (i,j) part of the block and then propagated through the high part. These equations will also hold for $i \leq j < k$ if we set $G_{ii} = g_i$ and $P_{ii} = p_i$.

Example:

Express P_{03} and G_{03} in terms of p's and g's.

Answer:

Using A.8.6, $P_{03} = P_{01}P_{23} = P_{00}P_{11}P_{22}P_{33}$. Since $P_{ii} = p_i$, $P_{03} = p_0 p_1 p_2 p_3$. For G_{03}, Equation A.8.5 says $G_{03} = G_{23} + P_{23}G_{01} = (G_{33} + P_{33}G_{22}) + (P_{22}P_{33})(G_{11} + P_{11}G_{00}) = g_3 + p_3 g_2 + p_3 p_2 g_1 + p_3 p_2 p_1 g_0$.

With these preliminaries out of the way, we can now show the design of a practical CLA adder. The adder consists of two parts. The first part computes various values of P and G from p_i and g_i, using Equations A.8.5 and A.8.6; the second part uses these P and G values to compute all the carries via Equation A.8.4. The first part of the design is in Figure A.11. At the top of the diagram, input numbers $a_7 \cdots a_0$ and $b_7 \cdots b_0$ are converted to p's and g's using cells of type 1. Then various P's and G's are generated by combining cells of type 2 in a binary-tree structure. The second part of the design is shown in Figure A.12. By feeding c_0 in at the bottom of this tree, all the carry bits come out the top. Each cell must know a pair of (P,G) values in order to do the conversion, and the value it needs is written inside the cells. Now compare Figure A.11 and Figure A.12. There is a one-to-one correspondence between cells, and the value of (P,G) needed by the carry-generating cells is exactly the value known by the

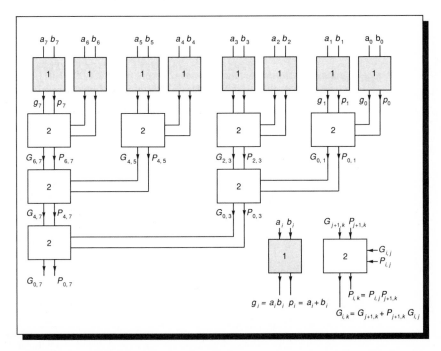

FIGURE A.11 First part of carry-lookahead tree. As signals flow from the top to the bottom, various values of P and G are computed.

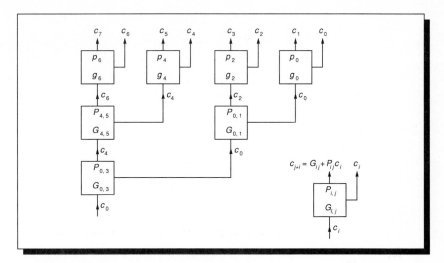

FIGURE A.12 Second part of carry-lookahead tree. Signals flow from the bottom to the top, combining with P and G to form the carries.

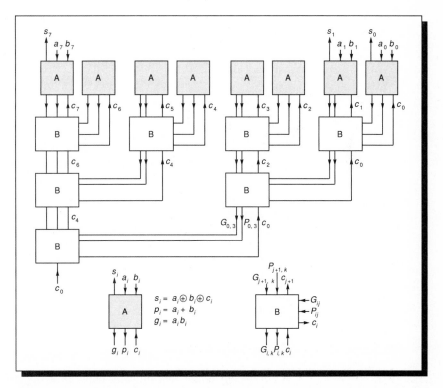

FIGURE A.13 Complete carry-lookahead tree adder. This is the combination of Figures A.11 and A.12. The numbers to be added enter at the top, flow to the bottom to combine with c_0, and then flow back up to compute the sum bits.

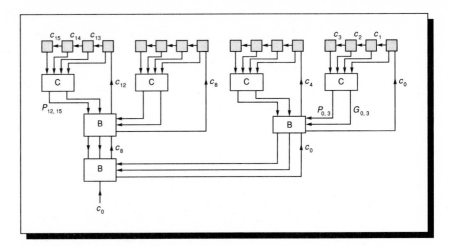

FIGURE A.14   Combination of CLA adder and ripple-carry adder. In the top row, carries ripple within each group of four boxes.

corresponding (P,G) generating cells. The combined cell is shown in Figure A.13. The numbers to be added flow into the top and downward through the tree, combining with c_0 at the bottom and flowing back up the tree to form the carries. Note that there is one thing missing from Figure A.13: a small piece of extra logic to compute c_8 for the carry out of the adder.

The bits in a CLA must pass through about $\log_2 n$ logic levels, compared with $2n$ for a ripple-carry adder. This is a substantial speed improvement, especially for a large n. Whereas the ripple-carry adder had n cells, however, the CLA adder has $2n$ cells, although in our layout they will take $n \log n$ space. The point is that a small investment in size pays off in a dramatic improvement in speed.

There are a number of technology-dependent modifications that can improve CLA adders. For example, if each node of the tree has three inputs instead of two, then the height of the tree will decrease from $\log_2 n$ to $\log_3 n$. Of course, the cells will be more complex and thus might operate more slowly, negating the advantage of the decreased height. For technologies where rippling works well, a hybrid design might be better. This is illustrated in Figure A.14. Carries ripple between adders at the top level, while the "B" boxes are the same as in Figure A.13. This design will be faster if the time to ripple between four adders is faster than the time it takes to traverse a level of "B" boxes.

Carry-Skip Adders

A *carry-skip adder* sits midway between a ripple-carry adder and a carry-lookahead adder, both in terms of speed and cost. (A carry-skip adder is not called a CSA, as that name is reserved for carry-save adders.) The motivation for this adder comes from examining the equations for P and G. For example,

$$P_{03} = p_0 p_1 p_2 p_3$$

$$G_{03} = g_3 + p_3 g_2 + p_3 p_2 g_1 + p_3 p_2 p_1 g_0$$

Computing P is much simpler than computing G, and a carry-skip adder only computes the P's. Such an adder is illustrated in Figure A.15. Carries begin rippling simultaneously through each block. If any block generates a carry, then the carry out of a block will be true, even though the carry in to the block may not be correct yet. If at the start of each add operation the carry in to each block is zero, then no spurious carry outs will be generated. Thus, the carry out of each block can thus be thought of as if it were the G signal. Once the carry out from the least significant block is generated, it not only feeds into the next block, but is also fed through the AND gate with the P signal from that next block. If the carry out and P signals are both true, then the carry **skips** the second block and is ready to feed into the third block, and so on. The carry-skip adder is only practical if the carry in signals can be easily cleared at the start of each operation—for example by precharging in CMOS.

To analyze the speed of a carry-skip adder, let's assume that it takes one time unit for a signal to pass through two logic levels. Then it will take k time units for a carry to ripple across a block of size k, and it will take one time unit for a carry to skip a block. The longest signal path in the carry-skip adder starts with a carry being generated at the 0th position. Then it takes k time units to ripple through the first block, $n/k - 2$ time units to skip blocks, and k more to ripple through the last block. To be specific: If we have a 20-bit adder broken into groups of 4 bits, it will take 11 time units to perform an add. Suppose we keep the least significant block at 4 bits, but combine the next two blocks into a single 8-bit block. Then the time of the adder drops to 10 time units. However, if we had combined three blocks instead of two, then the time to ripple through this 3-block unit (12 bits in all) would dominate the time to add. However, the general principle is important: For a carry-skip adder, making the interior blocks larger will speed up the adder. In fact, the same idea of varying the block sizes can sometimes speed up other adder designs as well. Because of the large amount of rippling, a carry-skip adder is most appropriate for technologies where rippling is fast.

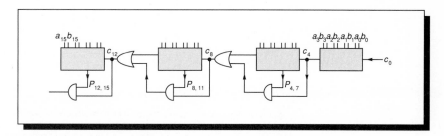

FIGURE A.15 Carry-skip adder.

Carry-Select Adder

A *carry-select adder* works on the following principle: Two additions are performed in parallel, one assuming the carry in is zero and the other assuming the carry in is one. When the carry in is finally known, the correct sum (which has been precomputed) is simply selected. An example of such a design is shown in Figure A.16. An 8-bit adder is divided into two halves, and the carry out from the lower half is used to select the upper half. If each block is computing its sum using rippling (a linear-time algorithm), then the design in Figure A.16 is twice

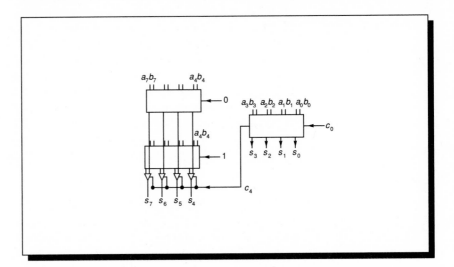

FIGURE A.16 Simple carry-select adder. At the same time that the sum of the low-order four bits are being computed, the high-order bits are being computed twice in parallel: once assuming that $c_4 = 0$, and once assuming $c_4 = 1$.

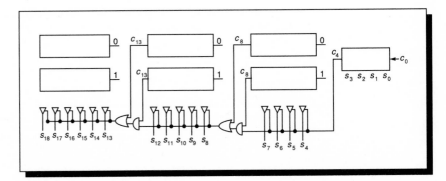

FIGURE A.17 Carry-select adder. As soon as the carry out of the rightmost block is known, it is used to select the other sum bits.

as fast at 50% more cost. However, note that the c_4 signal must drive many muxes, which may be very slow in some technologies. Instead of dividing the adder into halves, it could be divided into quarters for a still further speedup. This is illustrated in Figure A.17. If it takes k time units for a block to add k-bit numbers, and if it takes one time unit to compute the mux input from the two carry-out signals, then for optimal operation each block should be one bit wider than the next, as shown in Figure A.17. Therefore, as in the carry-skip adder, the best design involves variable-sized blocks.

As a summary of this section, the asymptotic time and space requirements for the different adders are given in Figure A.18. These different adders shouldn't be thought of as disjoint choices, but rather as building blocks to be used in constructing an adder. The utility of these different building blocks is highly dependent on the technology used. For example, the carry-select adder works well when a signal can drive many muxes, and the carry-skip adder is attractive in technologies where signals can be cleared at the start of each operation. Knowing the asymptotic behavior of adders is useful in understanding them, but relying too much on that behavior is a pitfall. The reason is that asymptotic behavior is only important as n grows very large. But n for an adder is the bits of precision, and double precision today is the same as it was twenty years ago—about 53 bits. Although it is true that as computers get faster, computations get longer—and thus have more rounding error, which in turn requires more precision—this effect grows very slowly with time.

	Time	Space
Ripple	$O(n)$	$O(n)$
CLA	$O(\log n)$	$O(n \log n)$
Carry skip	$O(\sqrt{n})$	$O(n)$
Carry select	$O(\sqrt{n})$	$O(n)$

FIGURE A.18   **Asymptotic time and space requirements for four different types of adders.**

A.9 | Speeding Up Integer Multiplication and Division

The multiplication and division algorithms presented in Section A.2 are fairly slow, producing one bit per cycle (although that cycle might be a fraction of the CPU instruction cycle time). In this section we discuss various techniques for higher performance multiplication and division.

Shifting Over Zeros

Shifting over zeros is a technique that is not currently used much, but is instructive to consider. It is distinguished by the fact that its execution time is operand dependent. Its lack of use is primarily attributable to its failure to offer enough speedup over bit-at-a-time algorithms. In addition, pipelining, synchronization with the CPU, and good compiler optimization are difficult with algorithms that run in variable time. In multiplication, the idea behind shifting over zeros is to add logic that detects when the low-order bit of the A register is zero (see Figure A.2(a)) and, if so, skip the addition step and proceed directly to the shift step—hence the term *shifting over zeros*. This technique becomes more useful if the number of zeros in the A operand can be increased. The Exercises discuss how well Booth recoding does in increasing zeros.

What about shifting for division? In nonrestoring division, an ALU operation (either an addition or subtraction) is performed at every step, so that there appears to be no opportunity for skipping an operation. But think about division this way: To compute a/b, subtract multiples of b from a, and then report how many subtractions were done. At each stage of the subtraction process the remainder must fit into the P register of Figure A.2(b) (page A-4). In the case when the remainder is a small positive number, you normally subtract b; but suppose instead you only shifted the remainder and subtracted b the next time. As long as the remainder was sufficiently small (its high-order bit 0), after shifting it still would fit into the P register, and no information would be lost. However, this method does require changing the way we keep track of the number of times b has been subtracted from a. This idea usually goes under the name of *SRT division*, for Sweeney, Robertson, and Tocher, who independently proposed algorithms of this nature. The main extra complication of SRT division is that the quotient bits cannot be determined immediately from the sign of P at each step, as it can be in ordinary nonrestoring division.

More precisely, to divide a by b where a and b are n-bit numbers, load a and b into the A and B registers, respectively, of Figure A.2 (page A-4).

1. If B has k leading zeros when expressed using n bits, shift all the registers left k bits. After this shift, since b has $n+1$ bits, its most significant bit will be 0, and its second-most-significant bit will be 1.

2. For $i = 0, n-1$ do

    If the top three bits of P are equal, set $q_i = 0$ and shift (P,A) one bit left.

    If the top three bits of P are not all equal and P is negative, set $q_i = \overline{1}$, shift (P,A) one bit left, and add B.

    Otherwise set $q_i = 1$, shift (P,A) one bit left, and subtract B

    Endloop

3. If the final remainder is negative, correct the remainder by adding B, and correct the quotient by subtracting 1 from q_0. Finally, the remainder must be shifted k bits right, where k is the initial shift.

A numerical example is given in Figure A.19. Although we are discussing integer division, it helps in explaining the algorithm to move the binary point from the right of the least significant bit to the left of the most significant bit. Thus if $n = 4$ and the operation is 9/4, the A register holds 0.1001 and (remembering that the B register has $n + 1$ bits), the B register holds 0.0100.

Since this changes the binary point in both the numerator and denominator, the quotient is not affected. The remainder being a two's complement number, a P register of 1.1110_2 represents $-1/8$. With this convention, the P register holds numbers satisfying $-1 \leq P < 1$. The first step of the algorithm shifts b so that $b \geq 1/2$. As before, let r be the value of the (P,A) pair. Our rule for which ALU operation to perform is this: If $-1/4 \leq r < 1/4$ (true whenever the top three bits of P are equal), then compute $2r$ by shifting (P,A) left one bit; else if $r < 0$ (and hence $r < -1/4$, since otherwise it would have been eliminated by the first condition), then compute $2r + b$ by shifting and then adding, else $r \geq 1/4$ and subtract b from $2r$. Using $b \geq 1/2$, it is easy to check that these rules keep $-1/2 \leq r < 1/2$. For nonrestoring division, we only have $|r| \leq b$, and we need P to be $n + 1$ bits wide. But for SRT division, the bound on r is tighter, namely $-1/2 \leq r < 1/2$. Thus, we can save a bit by eliminating the high-order bit of P (and b and the adder). In particular, the test for equality of the top three bits of P becomes a test on just two bits.

P	A	
00000	1000	B contains 0011, so shift all registers left two places
00010	0000	B now contains 1100. Top bits of P are equal, so shift and set $q_0 = 0$
00100	0000	Top bits are not equal, so set $q_1 = 1$
01000	0000	shift and
+10100		subtract B
11100	0000	Top bits equal, so shift and set $q_2 = 0$
11000	0000	Top bits are unequal, so set $q_3 = -1$
10000	0000	shift and
+01100		add B
11100		Remainder is negative, so restore it and subtract 1 from q_0
+01100		
01000		This must be shifted right two places to give remainder
		Remainder $= 10, q = 010\bar{1} - 1 = 0010$

FIGURE A.19 SRT division of 1000/0011.

The algorithm might change slightly in an implementation of SRT division. After each ALU operation, the P register can be shifted as many places as necessary to make either P ≥ 1/4 or P < −1/4. By shifting k places, k quotient bits are set equal to zero all at once. For this reason SRT division is sometimes described as one that keeps the remainder normalized to $|r| \geq 1/4$.

Notice that the value of the quotient bit computed in a given step is based on which operation is performed in that step (which in turn depends on the result of the operation from the previous step). This is in contrast to nonrestoring division, where the quotient bit computed in ith step depends on the result of the operation in the same step. This difference is reflected in the fact that when the final remainder is negative, the last quotient bit must be adjusted in SRT division, but not in nonrestoring division. However, the key fact about the quotient bits in SRT division is that they can include $\bar{1}$. Therefore the quotient bits can't be stored in the low-order bits of the A register; furthermore, the quotient must be converted to ordinary two's complement in a full adder. A common way to do this is to accumulate the positive quotient bits in one register and the negative quotient bits in another, and then subtract the two registers after all the bits are known. Because there is more than one way to write a number in terms of the digits −1, 0, 1, SRT division is said to use a *redundant* quotient representation.

The differences between SRT division and ordinary nonrestoring division can be summarized as follows:

1. ALU decision rule: In nonrestoring division, it is determined by the sign of P; in SRT, it is determined by the two most significant bits of P.

2. Quotient determination: In nonrestoring division, it is immediate from the signs of P; in SRT, it must be computed in a full n-bit adder.

3. Speed: SRT division will be faster on operands that produce zero quotient bits.

Speeding Up Multiplication with a Single Adder

As mentioned before, shifting-over techniques are not used much in current hardware. We now discuss some methods that are in more widespread use. Methods that increase the speed of multiplication can be divided into two classes: those that use a single adder and those that use multiple adders. Let's first discuss techniques that use a single adder.

In the discussion of addition we noted that, because of carry propagation, it is not practical to perform addition with two levels of logic. Using the cells of Figure A.13, adding two 64-bit numbers will require a trip through seven cells to compute the P's and G's, and seven more to compute the carry bits, which will require at least 28 logic levels. Each multiplication step will require a trip through this adder. A way to avoid this computation in each step is to use *carry-save adders* (CSA). A carry-save adder is simply n independent full adders. A

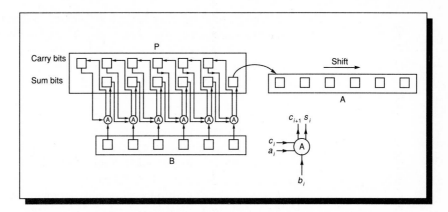

FIGURE A.20 Carry-save multiplier. Each circle represents a (3,2) adder working independently. At each step, the only bit of P that needs to be shifted is the low-order sum bit.

multiplier using such an adder is illustrated in Figure A.20. Each circle marked "A" is a single-bit full adder, and each box represents one bit of a register. Each addition operation results in a pair of bits, stored in the sum and carry parts of P. Since each add is independent, only two logic levels are involved in the add—a vast improvement over 28.

To operate the multiplier in Figure A.20, load the sum and carry bits of P with zero and perform the first ALU operation. (If Booth recoding is used, it might be a subtraction rather than an addition.) Then shift the low-order sum bit of P into A, as well as shifting A itself. The $n - 1$ high-order bits of P don't need to be shifted because on the next cycle the sum bits are fed into the next lower order adder. Each addition step is dramatically increased in speed, since each add cell is working independently of the others, and no carry is propagated. There are two drawbacks to carry-save adders. First, they require more hardware because there must be a copy of register P to hold the carry outputs of the adder. Second, after the last step, the high-order word of the result must be fed into an ordinary adder to combine the sum and carry parts. This could be accomplished by feeding the output of P into the adder used to perform the addition operation. Multiplying with a carry-save adder is sometimes called redundant multiplication because P is represented using two registers. Since there are many ways to represent P as the sum of two registers, this representation is redundant. The term *carry-propagate adder* (CPA) is used to denote an adder that is not a CSA. A propagate adder may propagate its carries using ripples, carry lookahead, or some other method.

Another way to speed up multiplication without using extra adders is to examine k low-order bits of A at each step, rather than just one bit. This is often called *higher-radix multiplication*. As an example, suppose that $k = 2$. If the pair of bits is 00, add 0 to P, and if it is 01, add B. If it is 10, simply shift b one bit left before adding it to P. Unfortunately, if the pair is 11, it appears we would have to compute $b + 2b$. But this can be avoided by using a higher-radix version of Booth recoding. Imagine A as a base 4 number: When the digit 3 appears, change it to $\overline{1}$ and add 1 to the next higher digit to compensate. The name for this technique, *overlapping triplets*, comes from the fact that it looks at 3 bits to determine what multiple of b to use, whereas ordinary Booth recoding looks at 2 bits.

The precise rules for overlapping triplets are given in Figure A.21. Besides having more complex control logic, this technique also requires that the P register be one bit wider to accommodate the possibility of $2b$ or $-2b$ being added to it. It is also possible to use a radix-8 (or even higher) version of Booth recoding. In that case, however, it will be necessary to use the multiple 3B as a potential summand. Radix-8 multipliers normally compute 3B once and for all at the beginning of a multiplication operation.

Current pair		Previous	Multiple
$i + 1$	i	$i - 1$	
0	0	0	0
0	0	1	$+b$
0	1	0	$+b$
0	1	1	$+2b$
1	0	0	$-2b$
1	0	1	$-b$
1	1	0	$-b$
1	1	1	0

FIGURE A.21   Multiples of b to use for radix-4 Booth recoding. For example, if the two low-order bits of the A register are both 1, and the last bit to be shifted out of the A register was 0, then the correct multiple is $-b$, obtained from the second to last row of the table.

Faster Multiplication with Many Adders

If the space for many adders is available, then multiplication speed can be improved. Figure A.22 shows a block diagram of a simple *array multiplier* for multiplying two 8-bit numbers using seven CSAs and one propagate adder. As it still takes eight additions to compute the product, the latency of computing a product is not dramatically different from using a single carry-save adder. However, with the hardware in Figure A.22, multiplication can be pipelined, increasing the total throughput. On the other hand, although this level of pipelining is sometimes used in array processors, it is not used in any of the single-chip, floating-point accelerators discussed in Section A.10. Pipelining is discussed in general in Chapter 6 and by Kogge [1981] in the context of multipliers.

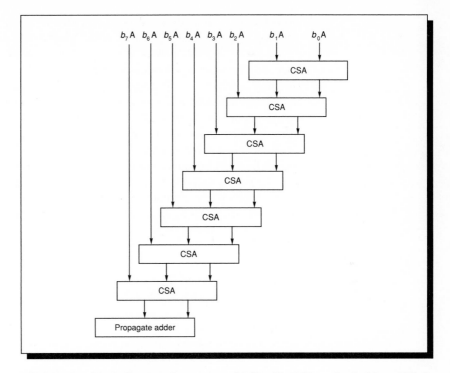

FIGURE A.22   Block diagram of an array multiplier. The 8-bit number in A is multiplied by $b_7 b_6 \cdots b_0$. Each box marked "CSA" is a carry-save adder.

With the technology of 1990, it is not possible to fit an array large enough to multiply two double-precision numbers on a single chip and have space left over for the other arithmetic operations. Thus, a popular design is to use a two-pass arrangement such as the one shown in Figure A.23 (page A-46). The first pass through the array "retires" four bits of B. Then the result of this first pass is fed back into the top to be combined with the next four summands. The result of this second pass is then fed into a CPA. This design, however, loses the ability to be pipelined.

If arrays require as many addition steps as the much cheaper arrangement in Figure A.2, why are they so popular? First of all, using an array has a smaller latency than using a single adder—because the array is a combinational circuit, the signals flow through it directly without being clocked. Although the two-pass adder of Figure A.23 would normally still use a clock, the cycle time for passing through k arrays can be less than k times the clock that would be needed for a design like the one in Figure A.2. Secondly, the array is amenable to various schemes for further speedup. One of them is shown in Figure A.24 (page A-47). The idea of this design is that two adds proceed in parallel or, to put it another way, each stream passes through only half the adders. Thus, it runs at almost twice the speed of the multiplier in Figure A.22. This *even/odd* multiplier is popular in VLSI because of its regular structure. Arrays can also be speeded up using asynchronous logic. One of the reasons why the multiplier of Figure A.2 (page A-4) needs a clock is to keep the output of the adder from feeding back into the input of the adder before the output has fully stabilized. Thus, if the array in Figure A.23 is long enough so that no signal can propagate from the top through the bottom in the time it takes for the first adder to stabilize, it may be possible to avoid clocks altogether. Williams et al. [1987] discusses a design using this idea, although it is for dividers instead of for multipliers.

The techniques of the previous paragraph still have a multiply time of O(n), but the time can be reduced to log n using a tree. The simplest tree would combine pairs of summands $b_0A \cdots b_{n-1}A$, cutting the number of summands from n to $n/2$. Then these $n/2$ numbers would be added in pairs again, reducing to $n/4$, and so on, and resulting in a single sum after log n steps. However, this simple binary-tree idea doesn't map into full (3,2) adders, which reduce three inputs to two rather than reducing two inputs to one. A tree that does use full adders, known as a *Wallace tree*, is shown in Figure A.25. When computer arithmetic units were built out of MSI parts, a Wallace tree was the design of choice for high-speed multipliers. There is, however, a problem with implementing them in VLSI.

Figures A.22–A.24 are sufficiently concise that it may be hard to visualize all the adders involved in an array multiplier. Figure A.26 (page A-49) shows each individual adder in a 4-bit array multiplier. Figure A.26(b) shows the inputs to the circuit, and Figure A.26(c) shows how those inputs are connected by adders.

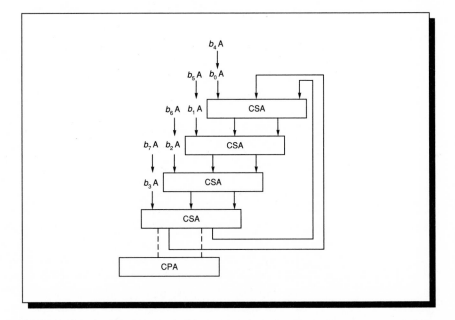

FIGURE A.23   Multipass array multiplier. Multiplies two 8-bit numbers with about half the hardware of that in Figure A.22. At the end of the second pass, the bits flow into the CPA.

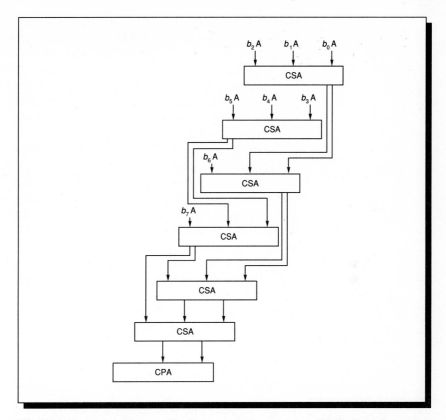

FIGURE A.24 Even/odd array. The first two adders work in parallel. Their results are fed into the third and fourth adders, which also work in parallel, and so on.

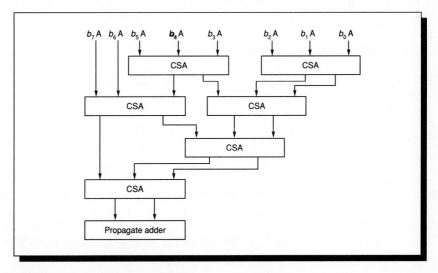

FIGURE A.25 Wallace-tree multiplier.

Each row of adders in A.26(c) corresponds to a single box in A.26(a). In actual implementation the array would be laid out as a square, not "twisted" as shown in the picture. (Lining up bits of the same significance in the same column makes the picture easier to understand.) If you try to fill in all the adders and paths for the Wallace tree of Figure A.25 (page A-47), you will discover that it does not have the nice, regular structure of Figure A.26. This is why VLSI designers have often chosen to use other $\log n$ designs such as the *binary-tree multiplier*, which is discussed next.

The problem with adding summands in a binary tree is that of coming up with a (2,1) adder that combines two digits and produces a single-sum digit. Because of carries, this isn't possible using binary notation, but it can be done with some other representation. We will use the *signed-digit representation* 1, $\bar{1}$, and 0, which we used previously to understand Booth's algorithm. This representation has two costs. First, it takes two bits to represent each signed digit. Second, the algorithm for adding two signed-digit numbers a_i and b_i is complex and requires examining $a_i a_{i-1} a_{i-2}$ and $b_i b_{i-1} b_{i-2}$. Although this means you must look two bits back, in binary addition you might have to look an arbitrary number of bits back (because of carries).

We can describe the algorithm for adding two signed-digit numbers as follows. First, compute sum and carry bits s_i and c_{i+1} using the table in Figure A.27. Then compute the final sum as $s_i + c_i$. The tables are set up so that this final sum does not generate a carry.

Example: What is the sum of the signed-digit numbers $1\bar{1}0$ and 001 ?

Answer: The two low-order bits sum to $0 + 1 = 1\bar{1}$, the next pair sums to $\bar{1} + 0 = 0\bar{1}$, and the high-order pair sums to $1 + 0 = 01$, so the sum is $1\bar{1} + 0\bar{1}0 + 0100 = 10\bar{1}$.

This, then, defines a (2,1) adder. With this in hand, we can use a straightforward binary tree to perform multiplication. In the first step it adds $b_0 A + b_1 A$ in parallel with $b_2 A + b_3 A$, $\cdots$, $b_{n-2} A + b_{n-1} A$. The next step adds the results of these sums in pairs, and so on. Although the final sum must be run through a carry-propagate adder to convert it from signed-digit form to two's complement, this final add step is necessary in any multiplier using CSAs.

To summarize, both Wallace trees and signed-digit trees are $\log n$ multipliers. The Wallace tree uses the fewer gates but is harder to lay out. The signed-digit tree has a more regular structure, but requires two bits to represent each digit and has more complicated add logic. As with adders, it is possible to combine different multiply techniques. For example, Booth recoding and arrays can be combined. In Figure A.22 (page A-45) instead of having each input be $b_i A$, we could have it be $b_i b_{i-1} A$, and in order to avoid having to compute the multiple $3b$, we can use Booth recoding.

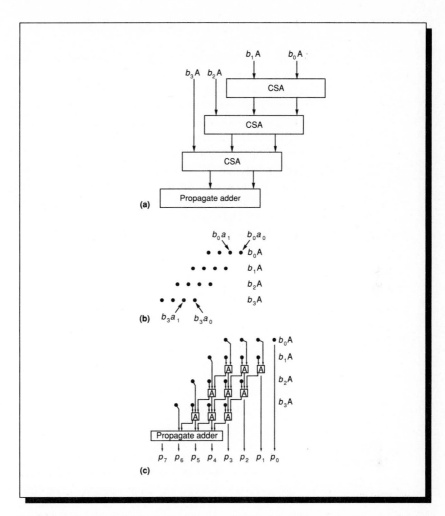

FIGURE A.26 Block diagram of an array multiplier (a); the inputs to the array (b); the array expanded to show all the adders (c).

$$
\begin{array}{ccccccc}
1 & 1 & \bar{1} & 0 & 1\ x & & \bar{1}\ x \\
\underline{+\,1} & \underline{+\,\bar{1}} & \underline{+\,\bar{1}} & \underline{+\,0} & \underline{+\,0\ y} & & \underline{+\,0\ y} \\
1\,0 & 0\,0 & \bar{1}\,0 & 0\,0 & 1\,\bar{1} & \text{if } x\ge0 \text{ and } y\ge0 & 0\,\bar{1} & \text{if } x\ge0 \text{ and } y\ge0 \\
& & & & 0\,1 & \text{otherwise} & \bar{1}\,1 & \text{otherwise}
\end{array}
$$

FIGURE A.27 Signed-digit addition table. The leftmost sum shows that when computing 1 + 1, the sum bit is 0 and the carry bit is 1.

Faster Division with One Adder

The two techniques for speeding up multiplication with a single adder were carry-save adders and higher-radix multiplication. There is a difficulty when trying to utilize these approaches to speed up nonrestoring division. The problem with CSAs is that at the end of each cycle the value of P, since it is in carry-save form, is not known exactly. In particular, the sign of P is uncertain, yet it is the sign of P that is used to compute the quotient digit and decide on the next ALU operation. When a higher radix is used, the problem is deciding what value to subtract from P. In the paper-and-pencil method, you have to guess the quotient digit. In binary division there are only two possibilities; we were able to finesse the problem by initially guessing one and then adjusting the guess based on the sign of P. This doesn't work in higher radices because there are more than two possible quotient digits, rendering quotient selection potentially quite complicated: You would have to compute all the multiples of b and compare them to P.

Both the carry-save technique and higher-radix division can be made to work if we use a redundant quotient representation. Recall from our discussion of SRT division that by allowing the quotient digits to be -1, 0, or 1, there is often a choice of which one to pick. The idea in the previous algorithm was to choose zero whenever possible because that meant an ALU operation could be skipped. In carry-save division, the idea is that because the remainder (P register) is not known exactly (being stored in carry-save form), the exact quotient digit is also not known. But thanks to the redundant representation, the remainder doesn't have to be known precisely in order to pick a quotient digit. This is illustrated in Figure A.28, where the x axis represents r_i, the contents of the (P,A) register pair after i steps. The line labeled $q_i = 1$ shows the value that r_{i+1} would be if we choose $q_i = 1$, and similarly for the lines $q_i = 0$ and $q_i = -1$. We can choose any value for q_i, as long as $r_{i+1} = r\mathrm{P}_i - q_i\mathrm{B}$ satisfies $|r_{i+1}| \leq \mathrm{B}$. The allowable ranges are shown in the right half of Figure A.28. Thus we only need to know r precisely enough to decide in which range in Figure A.28 it lies.

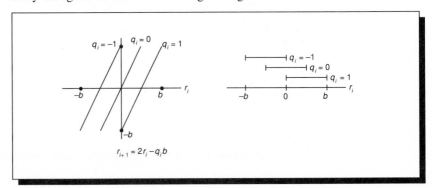

FIGURE A.28 Quotient selection for radix-2 division. The x axis represents the i th remainder, which is the quantity in the (P,A) register pair. The y axis shows the value of the remainder after one additional divide step. Each bar on the right-hand graph gives the range of r_i values for which it is permissible to select the associated value of q_i.

This is the basis for using carry-save adders. Look at the high-order bits of the carry-save adder and sum them in a propagate adder. Then use this approximation of r to compute q_i, usually by means of a lookup table. The same technique works for higher-radix division (whether or not a carry-save adder is used). The high-order bits P can be used to index a table that gives one of the allowable quotient digits.

The design challenge when building a high-speed SRT divider is figuring out how many bits of P and B need to be examined. For example, suppose that we take a radix of 4, use quotient digits of $2, 1, 0, \overline{1}, \overline{2}$, but have a propagate adder. How many bits of P and B need to be examined? Deciding this involves two steps. For ordinary radix-2 nonrestoring division, because at each stage $|r| \leq b$, the P buffer won't overflow. But for radix 4, $r_{i+1} = 4r_i - q_i b$ is computed at each stage, and if r_i is near b, then $4r_i$ will be near $4b$, and even the largest quotient digit will not bring r back to the range $|r_{i+1}| \leq b$. In other words, the remainder might grow without bound. However, restricting $|r_i| \leq 2b/3$ makes it easy to check that r_i will stay bounded.

After figuring out the bound that r_i must satisfy, we can draw the diagram in Figure A.29, which is analogous to Figure A.28. If r_i is between $(1/12)b$ and $(5/12)b$, we can pick $q = 1$, and so on. Or to put it another way, if r/b is between $1/12$ and $5/12$, we can pick $q = 1$. Suppose we look at 4 bits of P and 4 bits of b, and the high bits of P (not counting the $(n + 1)$-st sign bit) are $0011xxx\cdots$, while the high bits of b are $1001xxx\cdots$. To simplify calculation, imagine the binary point at the left end of each register. Since we truncated, r (the value of P concatenated with A) could have a value from $.0011$ to $.0100$, and b could have a value from $.1001$ to $.1010$. Thus r/b could be as small as $.0011/.1010$ or as large as $.0100/.1001$. But $.0011_2/.1010_2 = 3/10 < 1/3$ would require a quotient bit of 1, while $.0100_2/.1001_2 = 4/9 > 5/12$ would require a quotient bit of 2. In other words, 4 bits of P and 4 bits of b aren't enough to pick a quotient bit. It turns out that 5 bits of P and 4 bits of b are enough. This can be verified by writing a simple program that checks all the cases.

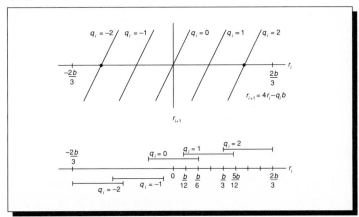

FIGURE A.29 Quotient selection for radix-4 division.

Example: Suppose that the radix is 4 and the quotient digits are 2, 1, 0,$\overline{1}$, $\overline{2}$, but this time a CSA is used instead of a propagate adder. How many bits of the P and B registers need to be examined?

Answer: Once again $|r_i| \leq 2b/3$, and the ranges of the q_i are still as in Figure A.29. If the top 4 bits of the sum part and the carry part of P are respectively 0010 and 0001, then the sum part ranges from 0010 to 0011 and the carry part from 0001 to 0010. Accordingly, the true value of r ranges from 0010 + 0001 = 0011 to 0011 + 0010 = 0101. Given, therefore, a CPA that adds the top 4 bits of the carry and sum parts of P, and a sum of 0011, the true sum will be anywhere from 0011 to 0101. A program that checks all the cases will show that 6 bits of P and 4 bits of b are needed to predict a quotient digit. The result of such a program is shown in Figure A.30. For example, if b is 1001$xxx\cdots$ and r is 001101$xxx\cdots$, then the top 4 bits of b are 9 and the top 6 bits of r are 13, making the quotient digit 1. But if r were $001110_2 = 14$, the quotient digit would have to be 2.

b	Range of P		q	b	Range of P		q
8	−21	−14	−2	12	−32	−20	−2
8	−13	−5	−1	12	−20	−7	−1
8	−5	3	0	12	−8	6	0
8	3	11	1	12	5	18	1
8	12	21	2	12	18	32	2
9	−24	−16	−2	13	−34	−21	−2
9	−15	−6	−1	13	−21	−7	−1
9	−6	4	0	13	−8	6	0
9	4	13	1	13	5	19	1
9	14	24	2	13	19	34	2
10	−26	−17	−2	14	−37	−22	−2
10	−16	−6	−1	14	−23	−7	−1
10	−6	4	0	14	−9	7	0
10	4	14	1	14	5	21	2
10	15	26	2	14	20	37	2
11	−29	−18	−2	15	−40	−24	−2
11	−18	−6	−1	15	−25	−8	−1
11	−7	5	0	15	−10	8	0
11	4	16	1	15	6	23	1
11	16	29	2	15	22	40	2

FIGURE A.30 Quotient digits for radix-4 SRT division with a CSA. The top row says that if the high-order 4 bits of b are $1000_2 = 8$, and if the top 6 bits of P are between $110010_2 = -14$ and $10101_2 = -21$, then the quotient digit is −2.

Although these are simple cases, all SRT analyses proceed in the same way. First compute the range of r_i, then plot r_i against r_{i+1} to find the quotient ranges, and finally write a program to compute how many bits are necessary. (It is sometimes also possible to compute the required number of bits analytically.) Two final comments about high-radix SRT division are in order. First, Figure A.30 is not symmetrical. Thus, for a radix-4 CSA divider, the lookup table needs not only 6 bits of P, but also the sign of P. Second, the quotient lookup table has a fairly regular structure. This means it is usually cheaper to encode it as a PLA rather than in ROM.

A.10 | Putting It All Together

In this section, we will compare the Weitek 3364, the MIPS R3010, and the Texas Instruments 8847 (see Figures A.31 and A.32, pages A-54–A-55). In many ways, these are ideal chips to compare. They each implement the IEEE standard for addition, subtraction, multiplication, and division on a single chip. All were introduced in 1988 and run with a cycle time of about 40 nanoseconds. However, as we will see, they use quite different algorithms. The Weitek chip is well described in Birman et al. [1988], the MIPS chip is described in less detail in Rowen, Johnson, and Ries [1988], and the details of the TI chip have yet to be published.

There are a number of things that these three chips have in common. They perform addition and multiplication in parallel, and they implement neither extended precision nor the IEEE remainder operation. We discussed earlier how an efficient REM could be provided in software if only chips would implement a remainder-step function. The designers of these chips probably decided not to

	MIPS R3010	Weitek 3364	TI 8847
Clock cycle time (ns)	40	50	30
Size (mil^2)	114,857	147,600	156,180
Transistors	75,000	165,000	180,000
Pins	84	168	207
Power (watts)	3.5	1.5	1.5
Cycles/add	2	2	2
Cycles/mult	5	2	3
Cycles/divide	19	17	11
Cycles/sq root	–	30	14

FIGURE A.31 **Summary of the three floating-point chips discussed in this section.** The cycle times are for production parts available in June 1989. The cycle counts are for double-precision operations.

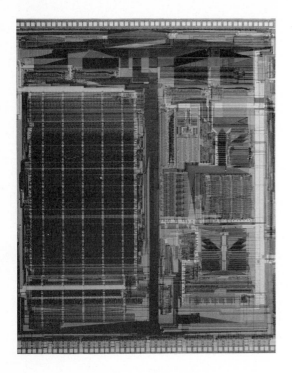

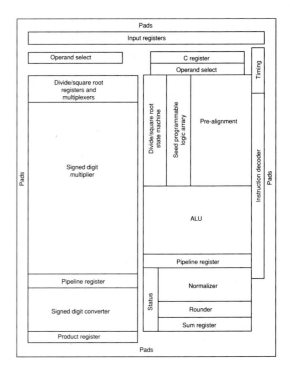

			Pads			
			Input registers			
Operand select				C register		Timing
				Operand select		
Divide/square root registers and multiplexers		Divide/square root state machine	Seed programmable logic array	Pre-alignment		Instruction decoder
Signed digit multiplier						
			ALU			
			Pipeline register			
Pipeline register		Status	Normalizer			
Signed digit converter			Rounder			
			Sum register			
Product register						
			Pads			

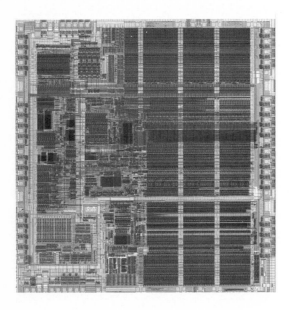

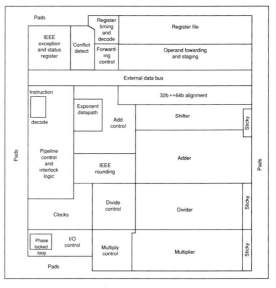

Pads				Register file		
IEEE exception and status register	Conflict detect	Register timing and decode		Register file		
		Forwarding control		Operand forwarding and staging		
		External data bus				
Instruction		Exponent datapath		32b ↔64b alignment		
decode			Add control	Shifter		Sticky
Pipeline control and interlock logic		IEEE rounding		Adder		Pads
		Divide control		Divider		Sticky
Clocks						
Phase locked loop	I/O control	Multiply control		Multiplier		Sticky
		Pads				

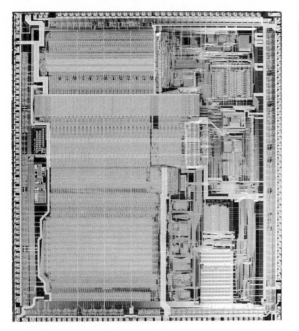

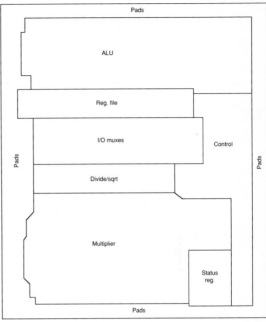

FIGURE A.32 Chip layout. In the left-hand column are the photomicrographs; the right-hand column shows the corresponding floor plans. Top left is the TI 8847, bottom left is the MIPS R3010, and above is the Weitek 3364.

provide extended precision because the most influential users are those who run portable codes, which can't rely on extended precision. However, as we have seen, extended precision can make for faster and simpler math libraries.

A summary of the three chips is given in Figures A.31 (page A-53) and A.32. Note that a higher transistor count generally leads to smaller cycle counts. Comparing the cycles/op numbers needs to be done carefully because the figures for the MIPS chip are those for a complete system (R3000/3010 pair), while the Weitek and TI numbers are for standalone chips, and are usually larger when used in a complete system.

The MIPS chip has the fewest transistors of the three. This is reflected in the fact that it is the only chip of the three that does not have any pipelining or hardware square root. Further, the multiplication and addition operations are not completely independent because they share the carry-propagate adder that performs the final rounding (as well as the rounding logic). Addition on the R3010 uses a mixture of ripple, CLA, and carry select. A carry-select adder is used in the fashion of Figure A.16 (page A-38). Within each half, carries are propagated using a hybrid ripple-CLA scheme of the type indicated in Figure A.14. However, this is further tuned by varying the size of each block, rather than having each fixed at four bits (as they are in Figure A.14 on page A-36). The multiplier is midway between the designs of Figures A.2 (page A-4) and A.22 (page A-45). It has an array just large enough so that output can be fed back into the input without having to be clocked. Also, it uses radix-4 Booth recoding and the even-odd technique of Figure A.24 (page A-47). The R3010 can do a divide and multiply in parallel (like the Weitek chip but unlike the TI chip). The divider is a radix-4 SRT method with quotient digits -2, -1, 0, 1, and 2, and is similar to that described in Taylor [1985]. Double-precision division is about four times slower than multiplication. The R3010 shows that for chips using an $O(n)$ multiplier, an SRT divider can operate fast enough to keep a reasonable ratio between multiply and divide.

The Weitek 3364 has independent add, multiply, and divide units, and also uses radix-4 SRT division. However, the add and multiply operations on the Weitek chip are pipelined. The three addition stages are (1) exponent compare, (2) add followed by shift (or vice versa), and (3) final rounding. Stages (1) and (3) take only a half-cycle, allowing the whole operation to be done in two cycles, even though there are three pipline stages. The multiplier uses an array of the style of Figure A.23 but uses radix-8 Booth recoding, which means it must compute 3 times the multiplier. The three multiplier pipeline stages are (1) compute $3b$, (2) pass through array, and (3) final carry-propagation add and round. Single precision passes through the array once, double precision twice. Like addition, the latency is two cycles. The Weitek chip uses an interesting addition algorithm. It is a variant on the carry-skip adder pictured in Figure A.15 (page A-37). However P_{ij}, which is the logical AND of many terms, is computed by rippling, performing one AND per ripple. Thus, while the carries propagate left within a block, the value of P_{ij} is propagating right within the next block, and the block sizes are chosen so that both waves complete at the same time. Unlike the MIPS chip, the 3364 has hardware square root, which shares the divide hardware. The ratio of double-precision multiply to divide is 2:17. The large disparity between multiply and divide is due to the fact that multiplication uses radix-8 Booth recoding, while division uses a radix-4 method. In the MIPS R3010, multiplication and division use the same radix.

The notable feature of the TI 8847 is that it does division by iteration (using the Goldschmidt algorithm discussed in Section A.6). This improves the speed of division (the ratio of multiply to divide is 3:11), but means that multiplication and division cannot be done in parallel as on the other two chips. Addition has a two-stage pipeline. Exponent compare, fraction shift, and fraction addition are done in the first stage, normalization and rounding in the second stage. Multiplication uses a binary tree of signed-digit adders and has a three-stage pipeline. The first stage passes through the array retiring half the bits, the second stage passes through the array a second time, and the third stage converts from signed-digit form to two's complement. Since there is only one array, a new multiply operation can only be initiated in every other cycle. However, by slowing down the clock, two passes through the array can be made in a single cycle. In this case, a new multiplication can be initiated in each cycle. The 8847 adder uses a carry-select algorithm rather than carry lookahead. As mentioned in Section A.6, the TI carries 60 bits of precision in order to do correctly rounded division.

These three chips illustrate the different tradeoffs made by designers with similar constraints. One of the most interesting things about these chips is the diversity of their algorithms. Each uses a different add algorithm, as well as a different multiply algorithm. In fact, Booth recoding is the only technique that is universally used by all the chips.

A.11 | Fallacies and Pitfalls

Fallacy: Underflows rarely occur in actual floating-point application code.

Although most codes rarely underflow, there are actual codes that underflow frequently. SDRWAVE [Kahaner 1988], which solves a one-dimensional wave equation, is one such example. This program underflows quite frequently, even when functioning properly. Measurements on one machine show that adding hardware support for gradual underflow would cause SDRWAVE to run about 50% faster.

Fallacy: Conversions between integer and floating point are rare.

In fact, in Spice they are as frequent as divides. The assumption that conversions are rare leads to a mistake in the SPARC instruction set, which does not provide an instruction to move from integer registers to floating-point registers.

Pitfall: Don't increase the speed of a floating-point unit without increasing its memory bandwidth.

A typical use of a floating-point unit is to add two vectors to produce a third vector. If these vectors consist of double-precision numbers, then each floating-point add will use three operands of 64 bits each, or 24 bytes of memory. The memory bandwidth requirements are even greater if the floating-point unit can perform addition and multiplication in parallel (as most do).

Pitfall: $-x$ is not the same as $0 - x$.

This is a fine point in the IEEE standard that has tripped up some designers. Because floating-point numbers use the sign/magnitude system, there are two zeros, $+0$ and -0. The standard says that $0 - 0 = +0$, whereas $-(0) = -0$. Thus $-x$ is not the same as $0 - x$ when $x = 0$.

A.12 | Historical Perspective and References

The earliest computers used fixed point rather than floating point. In "Preliminary Discussion of the Logical Design of an Electronic Computing Instrument," Burks, Goldstine, and von Neumann put it like this:

There appear to be two major purposes in a "floating" decimal point system both of which arise from the fact that the number of digits in a word is a constant fixed by design considerations for each particular machine. The first of these purposes is to retain in a sum or product as many significant digits as possible and the second of these is to free the human operator from the burden of estimating and inserting into a problem "scale factors" — multiplicative constants which serve to keep numbers within the limits of the machine.

There is, of course, no denying the fact that human time is consumed in arranging for the introduction of suitable scale factors. We only argue that the time so consumed is a very small percentage of the total time we will spend in preparing an interesting problem for our machine. The first advantage of the floating point is, we feel, somewhat illusory. In order to have such a floating point, one must waste memory capacity which could otherwise be used for carrying more digits per word. It would therefore seem to us not at all clear whether the modest advantages of a floating binary point offset the loss of memory capacity and the increased complexity of the arithmetic and control circuits. [Bell and Newell 1971, 97]

This enables us to see things from the perspective of early computer designers, who believed that saving computer time and memory were more important than saving programmer time.

The original papers introducing the Wallace tree, Booth recoding, SRT division, overlapped triplets, and so on, are reprinted in Swartzlander [1980]. A good explanation of an early machine (the IBM 360/91) that used a pipelined Wallace tree, Booth recoding, and iterative division is in Anderson et al. [1967]. A discussion of the average time for single-bit SRT division is in Freiman [1961]; this is one of the few interesting historical papers that does not appear in Swartzlander.

The standard book of Mead and Conway [1980] discouraged the use of CLAs as not being cost effective in VLSI. Brent and Kung [1982] was an important paper that helped combat that view. An example of a detailed layout for CLAs can be found in Ngai and Irwin [1985] or in Weste and Eshraghian [1985]. Takagi, Yasuura, and Yajima [1985] provides a detailed description of a signed-digit–tree multiplier.

Although the IEEE standard is being widely adopted, there are still three other important floating-point systems in use: the IBM/370, the DEC VAX, and the Cray. We will briefly discuss these older formats. The VAX format is closest to the IEEE standard. Its single-precision format (F format) is like IEEE single precision in that it has a hidden bit, 8 bits of exponent, and 23 bits of fraction. However, it does not have a sticky bit, which causes it to round halfway cases up instead of to even. The VAX has a slightly different exponent range than IEEE single: E_{min} is −128 rather than −126 as in IEEE, and E_{max} is 126 instead of 127. The main differences between VAX and IEEE are the lack of special values and gradual underflow. The VAX has a reserved operand, but it works like a signaling NaN: it traps whenever it is referenced. Originally, the VAX's double precision (D format) also had 8 bits of exponent. However, as this is too small for many applications, a G format was added; like the IEEE standard, this format has 11 bits of exponent. The VAX also has an H format, which is 128 bits long.

The IBM/370 floating-point format uses base 16 rather than base 2. This means it cannot use a hidden bit. In single precision, it has 7 bits of exponent and 24 bits (6 hex digits) of fraction. Thus, the largest representable number is $16^{2^7} = 2^4 \times 2^7 = 2^{2^9}$, compared with 2^{2^8} for IEEE. However, a number that is normalized in the hexadecimal sense only needs to have a nonzero leading digit. When interpreted in binary, the three most significant bits could be zero. Thus, there are potentially fewer than 24 bits of significance. The reason for using the higher base was to minimize the amount of shifting required when adding floating-point numbers. However, this is less significant in current machines, where the floating-point add time is usually fixed independent of the operands. Another difference between 370 arithmetic and IEEE arithmetic is that the 370 has neither a round digit nor a sticky digit, which effectively means that it truncates rather than rounds. Thus, in many computations, the result will systematically be too small. Unlike the VAX and IEEE arithmetic, every bit pattern is a valid number. Thus, library routines must establish conventions for what to return in case of errors. In the IBM FORTRAN library, for example, $\sqrt{-4}$ returns 2!

Arithmetic on Cray computers is interesting because it is driven by a motivation for the highest possible floating-point performance. It has a 15-bit exponent field and a 48-bit fraction field. Addition on Cray computers does not have a guard digit, and multiplication is even less accurate than addition. Thinking of multiplication as a sum of p numbers, each $2p$ bits long, what Cray computers do is to drop the low-order bits of each summand. Thus, analyzing the exact error characteristics of the multiply operation is not easy. Reciprocals are computed using iteration, and division of a by b is done by multiplying a times $1/b$. The errors in multiplication and reciprocation combine to make the last three bits of a divide operation unreliable. At least Cray computers serve to keep numerical analysts on their toes!

The IEEE standardization process began in 1977, inspired mainly by W. Kahan, and is based partly on Kahan's work with the IBM 7094 at the University of Toronto [Kahan 1968]. The standardization process was a lengthy affair, with gradual underflow causing the most controversy. (According to Cleve Moler, visitors to the U.S. were advised that the sights not to be missed were Las Vegas, the Grand Canyon, and the IEEE standards committee meeting.) The standard was finally approved in 1985. The Intel 8087 was the first major commercial IEEE implementation and appeared in 1981, before the standard was finalized. It contains features that were eliminated in the final standard, such as projective bits. According to Kahan, the length of double-extended precision was based on what could be implemented in the 8087. Although the IEEE standard was not based on any existing floating-point system, most of its features were present in some other system. For example the CDC 6600 reserved special bit patterns for INDEFINITE and INFINITY, while the idea of denormal numbers appears in Goldberg [1967] as well as in Kahan [1968]. Kahan was awarded the 1989 Turing prize in recognition of his work on floating point.

References

ANDERSON, S. F., J. G. EARLE, R. E. GOLDSCHMIDT, AND D. M. POWERS [1967]. "The IBM System/360 Model 91: Floating-point execution unit," *IBM J. Research and Development* 11, 34–53. Reprinted in [Swartzlander 1980].

> *Good description of an early high-performance floating-point unit that used a pipelined Wallace-tree multiplier and iterative division.*

ATKINS, D. E. [1968]. "Higher-radix division using estimates of the divisor and partial remainders," *IEEE Trans. on Computers* C-17:10, 925–934. Reprinted in [Swartzlander 1980].

> *This is the standard reference for high-radix SRT division.*

BELL, C. G. AND A. NEWELL, [1971]. *Computer Structures: Readings and Examples,* McGraw-Hill, New York.

BIRMAN, M., G. CHU, L. HU, J. MCLEOD, N. BEDARD, F. WARE, L. TORBAN, AND C. M. LIM [1988]. "Design of a high-speed arithmetic datapath," *Proc. ICCD: VLSI Computers and Processors,* 214–216.

> *Fairly detailed description of the Weitek 3364 floating-point chip.*

BRENT, R. P. AND H. T. KUNG [1982] "A regular layout for parallel adders," *IEEE Trans. on Computers* C-31, 260–264.

> *This is the paper that popularized CLA adders in VLSI.*

BURKS, A. W., H. H. GOLDSTINE, AND J. VON NEUMANN, [1946]. *Preliminary Discussion of the Logical Design of an Electronic Computing Instrument.*

CODY, W. J. [1988]. "Floating point standards: Theory and practice," in *Reliability in Computing: The Role of Interval Methods in Scientific Computing,* R. E. Moore, (ed.), Academic Press, Boston, Mass., 99–107.

> *Presents a status of hardware and software implementations of the standard.*

CODY, W. J., J. T. COONEN, D. M. GAY, K. HANSON, D. HOUGH, W. KAHAN, R. KARPINSKI, J. PALMER, F. N. RIS, AND D. STEVENSON [1984]. "A proposed radix- and word-length-independent standard for floating-point arithmetic," *IEEE Micro* 4:4, 86–100.

> *Contains a draft of the 854 standard, which is more general than 754. The significance of this article is that it contains commentary on the standard, most of which is equally relevant to 754.*

COONEN, J. [1984]. *Contributions to a Proposed Standard for Binary Floating-Point Arithmetic,* Ph.D. Thesis, Univ. of Calif., Berkeley.

> *The only detailed discussion of how rounding modes can be used to implement efficient binary decimal conversion.*

FREIMAN, C. V. [1961]. "Statistical analysis of certain binary division algorithms," *Proc. IRE* 49:1, 91–103.

> *Contains an analysis of the performance of shifting-over-zeros SRT division algorithm.*

GOLDBERG, D. [1989]. "Floating-point and computer systems," *Xerox Tech. Rep.* CSL-89-9. A version of this paper will appear in *Computing Surveys.*

> *Contains an in-depth tutorial on the IEEE standard from the software point of view.*

GOLDBERG, I. B. [1967]. "27 bits are not enough for 8-digit accuracy," *Comm. ACM* 10:2, 105–106.

> *This paper proposes using hidden bits and gradual underflow.*

GOSLING, J. B. [1980]. *Design of Arithmetic Units for Digital Computers,* Springer-Verlag NewYork, Inc., New York.

> *A concise, well-written book, although it focuses on MSI designs.*

HAMACHER, V. C., Z. G. VRANESIC, AND S. G. ZAKY [1984]. *Computer Organization,* 2nd ed., McGraw-Hill, New York.

> *Introductory computer architecture book with a good chapter on computer arithmetic.*

HWANG, K. [1979]. *Computer Arithmetic: Principles, Architecture, and Design,* Wiley, New York.

> *This book contains the widest range of topics of the computer arithmetic books.*

IEEE [1985]. "IEEE standard for binary floating-point arithmetic," *SIGPLAN Notices* 22:2, 9–25.

> *IEEE 754 is reprinted here.*

KAHAN, W. [1968]. "7094-II system support for numerical analysis," *SHARE Secretarial Distribution* SSD-159.

> *This system had many features that were incorporated into the IEEE floating-point standard.*

KAHANER, D. K. [1988]. "Benchmarks for 'real' programs," *SIAM News* (November).

> *The benchmark presented in this article turns out to cause many underflows.*

KNUTH, D. [1981]. *The Art of Computer Programming,* vol II, 2nd ed., Addison-Wesley, Reading, Mass.

> *Has a section on the distribution of floating-point numbers.*

KOGGE, P. [1981]. *The Architecture of Pipelined Computers,* McGraw-Hill, New York.

> *Has brief discussion of pipelined multipliers.*

KOHN, L. AND S.-W. FU, [1989]. "A 1,000,000 transistor microprocessor," *IEEE Int'l Solid-State Circuits Conf.,* 54–55.

  A brief overview of the Intel 860, whose floating-point addition algorithm is discussed in Section A.4.

MAGENHEIMER, D. J., L. PETERS, K. W. PETTIS, AND D. ZURAS, [1988]. "Integer multiplication and division on the HP Precision Architecture," *IEEE Trans. on Computers* 37:8, 980–990.

  Rationale for the integer- and divide-step instructions in the Precision architecture.

MEAD, C. AND L. CONWAY [1980]. *Introduction to VLSI Systems,* Addison-Wesley, Reading, Mass.

NGAI, T-F. AND M. J. IRWIN [1985]. "Regular, area-time efficient carry-lookahead adders," *Proc. Seventh IEEE Symposium on Computer Arithmetic,* 9–15.

  Describes a CLA adder like that of Figure A.13, where the bits flow up and then come back down.

PENG, V., S. SAMUDRALA, AND M. GAVRIELOV [1987]. "On the implementation of shifters, multipliers, and dividers in VLSI floating point units," *Proc. Eighth IEEE Symposium on Computer Arithmetic,* 95–102.

  Highly recommended survey of different techniques actually used in VLSI designs.

ROWEN, C., M. JOHNSON, and P. RIES [1988]. "The MIPS R3010 floating-point coprocessor," *IEEE Micro* 53–62 (June).

SANTORO, M. R., G. BEWICK, and M. A. HOROWITZ [1989]. "Rounding algorithms for IEEE multipliers," *Proc. Ninth IEEE Symposium on Computer Arithmetic,* 176–183.

  A very readable discussion of how to efficiently implement rounding for floating-point multiplication.

SCOTT, N. R. [1985]. *Computer Number Systems and Arithmetic,* Prentice-Hall, Englewood Cliffs, N.J.

SWARTZLANDER, E., ED. [1980]. *Computer Arithmetic,* Dowden, Hutchison and Ross (distributed by Van Nostrand, New York).

  A collection of historical papers.

TAKAGI, N., H. YASUURA, AND S. YAJIMA [1985]."High-speed VLSI multiplication algorithm with a redundant binary addition tree," *IEEE Trans. on Computers* C-34:9, 789–796.

  A discussion of the binary-tree signed multiplier that was the basis for the design used in the TI 8847.

TAYLOR, G. S. [1981]. "Compatible hardware for division and square root," *Proc. Fifth IEEE Symposium on Computer Arithmetic,* 127–134.

  Good discussion of a radix-4 SRT division algorithm.

TAYLOR, G. S. [1985]. "Radix 16 SRT dividers with overlapped quotient selection stages," *Proc. Seventh IEEE Symposium on Computer Arithmetic,* 64–71.

  Describes a very sophisticated high-radix division algorithm.

WESTE, N. AND K. ESHRAGHIAN [1985]. *Principles of CMOS VLSI Design,* Addison-Wesley, Reading, Mass.

  This textbook has a section on the layouts of various kinds of adders.

WILLIAMS, T. E., M. HOROWITZ, R. L. ALVERSON, AND T. S. YANG [1987]. "A self-timed chip for division," *Advanced Research in VLSI, Proc. 1987 Stanford Conf.,* The MIT Press, Cambridge, Mass.

  Describes a divider that tries to get the speed of a combinational design without using the area that would be required by one.

EXERCISES

A.1 [15/15/20] <A.3> Represent the following numbers as single-precision and double-precision IEEE floating-point numbers.

a.   [15] 10

b.   [15] 10.5

c.   [20] 0.1

A.2 [10/15/20] <A.8> Complete the details of the block diagrams for the following adders.

a.   [10] In Figure A.11, show how to implement the "1" and "2" boxes in terms of AND and OR gates.

b.   [15] In Figure A.14, what signals need to flow from the adder cells in the top row into the "C" cells? Write the logic equations for the "C" box.

c.   [20] Show how to extend the block diagram in A.13 so it will produce the carry-out bit c_8.

A.3 [15/15] <A.4> Floating-point addition.

a.   [15] In a decimal system with $p = 5$, compute $-4.5673 + 4.9999 \times 10^{-5}$ assuming round to nearest. Give the value of the guard and round digits, and the sticky bit.

b.   [15] What is the value of the sum for the other three rounding modes?

A.4 [15] <A.3> Show that if gradual underflow is not used, then it is no longer true that $x \neq y$ if and only if $x - y \neq 0$.

A.5 [25] <A.9> Write out the analogue of Figure A.21 for radix-8 Booth recoding.

A.6 [15] <A.3> Is the ordering of nonnegative floating-point numbers the same as integers when denormalized numbers are also considered? What if the denormalized numbers are represented using the wrapped representation mentioned in Section A.5?

A.7 [25/10] <A.2> One's complement.

a.   [25] When adding two's complement numbers, you discard the carry out from the most significant bit. Show that in one's complement, you must add the carry back into the low end.

b.   [10] Find the rule for detecting overflow in one's complement.

A.8 [15] <A.2> Equations A.2.1 and A.2.2 are for adding two n-bit numbers. Derive similar equations for subtraction, where there will be a borrow instead of a carry.

A.9 [15/20] <A.2> More one's complement.

a. [15] A complication that arises with one's complement arithmetic is that zero has two representations. Show that even if the negative form of zero is never an input, the adder in Equation A.2.1 (with c_0 the end around carry) can still produce a negative zero.

b. [20] Use the fact that $a + b = a - (-b)$ together with the subtractor circuit of the previous problem to derive a different one's complement adder. Can this adder ever produce negative zero?

A.10 [20] <A.2> On a machine that doesn't detect integer overflow in hardware, show how you would detect overflow on a signed addition operation in software.

A.11 [25] <A.9> In the array of Figure A.23, the fact that an array can be pipelined is not exploited. Can you come up with a design that feeds the output of the bottom CSA into the bottom CSAs instead of the top one, and that will run faster than the arrangement of Figure A.23?

A.12 [15] <A.9> For ordinary Booth recoding, the multiple of b used in the ith step is simply $a_{i-1} - a_i$. Can you find a similar formula for radix-4 Booth recoding (overlapped triplets)?

A.13 [25/15/30] <A.9> Shifting-over-zeros multiplication.

a. [25] Does Booth recoding always increase the number of zeros in a number? Can it ever decrease the number of zeros?

b. [15] Given the number $a_{n-1}\cdots a_0$, define $c_0 = 0$, and define c_i to be the carry out from adding a_i, a_{i-1}, and c_{i-1}. Then *modified Booth recoding* gives a number with digits $A_i = a_i + c_i - 2c_{i+1}$. What is the recoding of 01101?

c. [30] Show that modified Booth recoding never decreases the number of zeros.

A.14 [20/15/20/15/20/15] <A.6> Iterative square root.

a. [20] Use Newton's method to derive an iterative algorithm for square root. The formula will involve a division.

b. [15] What is the fastest way you can think of to divide a floating-point number by 2?

c. [20] If division is slow, then the iterative square root routine will also be slow. Use Newton's method on $f(x) = 1/x^2 - a$ to derive a method that doesn't use any divisions.

d. [15] Assume that the ratio division by 2 : floating-point add : floating-point multiply is 1:2:4. What ratios of multiplication time to divide time makes each iteration step in the method of Part c faster than each iteration in the method of Part a?

e. [20] When using the method of Part a, how many bits need to be in the initial guess in order to get double-precision accuracy after 3 iterations? (You may ignore rounding error.)

f. [15] Suppose that when Spice runs on the TI 8847, it spends 16.7% of its time in the square root routine (this percentage has been measured on other machines). Using the values in Figure A.31 and assuming 3 iterations, how much slower would Spice run if square root was implemented in software using the method of Part a?

A.15 [30/10] <A.2> This problem presents an algorithm for adding signed-magnitude numbers. If A and B are integers of opposite signs, let a and b be their magnitudes.

a. [30] Show that the following rules for manipulating the unsigned numbers a and b gives $A + B$

   1. Complement one of the operands.

   2. Using end around carry (as in the one's complement adder of problem A.7) add the complemented operand and the other (uncomplemented) one.

   3. If there was a carry out, the sign of the result is the sign associated with the uncomplemented operand.

   4. Otherwise, if there was no carry out, complement the result, and give it the sign of the complemented operand.

b. [10] <A.4> In our discussion of floating-point add, we suggested that when the result is negative the +1 needed to do two's complement be done in the rounding unit. Use the result of Part A to devise a floating-point adder that doesn't require this.

A.16 [15] <A.7> Our example that showed that double rounding can give a different answer from rounding once used the round-to-even rule. If halfway cases are rounded up, is double rounding still dangerous?

A.17 [15/30] <A.9> The text discussed radix-4 SRT division with quotient digits of -2, -1, 0, 1, 2. Suppose that 3 and -3 are also allowed as quotient digits.

a. [15] What relation replaces $|r_i| \leq 2b/3$?

b. [30] How many bits of b and P do you need to examine ?

A.18 [25] <A.6,A.9> The discussion of the remainder-step instruction assumed that division was done using a bit-at-a-time algorithm. What would have to change if division was implemented using a higher-radix method?

A.19 [20/20/25/25/20] <A.3> Signed-logarithm representation.

a. [20] Suppose you want to represent a number x by its sign and $\log|x|$. Then if $\log|x|$ is to be nonnegative, x must be ≥ 1. You can allow smaller x if you represent x by $\log k|x|$ for some constant k. Use 0 if $k|x| < 1$. Now $\log k|x|$ will not be an integer, but it can be represented as a fixed-point number. If we put the binary point m bits to the left of the least significant bit, write down formulas for converting x to signed-logarithm form and back.

b. [20] Give the rules for multiplication and division.

c. [25] Show that no matter what base of logs is used, this system cannot exactly represent all of 1, 2, and 3.

d. [25] Show how to implement addition using a table containing 2^{p-1} entries of $p-1$ bits each, where the signed logarithm number is stored in a p-bit register.

e. [20] Show that for numbers which are exactly representable in this system, multiplication is exact, addition is not, but $a(b + c) = ab + ac$ exactly (when there is no over/underflow).

A.20 [20/10] <A.8> Carry-skip adders.

a. [20] Assuming that time is proportional to logic levels, what (fixed) block size gives the fastest addition for an adder of some fixed total length?

b. [10] Explain why the carry-skip adder takes time $\sqrt{n}$.

A.21 [Discussion] In the MIPS approach to exception handling, you need a test for determining whether two floating-point operands could cause an exception. This should be fast and also not have too many false positives. Can you come up with a practical test? The performance cost of your design will depend on the distribution of floating-point numbers. This is discussed in Knuth [1981] and Swartzlander [1980].

A.22 [35] <A.8> The simplest carry-select adder replaces an n-bit adder with $n/2$ bit adders and a mux. A more complex carry-select adder would use $n/4$-bit adders and more muxes. Can you design an adder that uses muxes and 1-bit adders and runs in O(log n) time? Such an adder is called a *conditional-sum adder*.

A.23 [10/15/20/15/15] <A.6> Correctly rounded iterative division. Let a and b be floating-point numbers with p-bit significands ($p = 53$ in double precision). Let q be the exact quotient $q = a/b$. Suppose that $\bar{q}$ is the result of an iteration process, that $\bar{q}$ has a few extra bits of precision, and that $0 < q - \bar{q} < 2^{-p}$.

a. [10] If x is a floating-point number, and $1 \le x < 2$, what is the next representable number after x?

b. [15] Show how to compute q' from $\bar{q}$, where q' has $p + 1$ bits of precision and $|q - q'| < 2^{-p}$.

c. [20] Assuming round to nearest, show that the correctly rounded quotient is either q', $q' - 2^{-p}$, or $q' + 2^{-p}$.

d. [15] Give rules for computing the correctly rounded quotient from q' based on the low-order bit of q' and the sign of $a - bq'$.

e. [15] Solve Part c for the other three rounding modes.

B Complete Instruction Set Tables

B.1 | VAX User Instruction Set

The following tables include all the VAX user instructions; the system instructions are not included.

The underscore following the instruction name implies that the instruction will operate upon any data type contained in the parentheses following that instruction. The data type abbreviations are:

B	= byte (8 bits)	F	= F_floating (32 bits)
W	= word (16 bits)	D	= D_floating (64 bits)
L	= longword (32 bits)	G	= G_floating (64 bits)
Q	= quadword (64 bits)	H	= H_floating (128 bits)
O	= octaword (128 bits)		

Integer and Floating-Point Logical and Arithmetic Instructions

Instruction	Description
ADAWI	Add aligned word interlocked
ADD_2	Add (B,W,L,F,D,G,H) 2 operand
ADD_3	Add (B,W,L,F,D,G,H) 3 operand
ADWC	Add with carry
ASH_	Arithmetic shift (L,Q)
BIC_2	Bit clear (B,W,L) 2 operand
BIC_3	Bit clear (B,W,L) 3 operand
BICPSW	Bit clear processor status word
BIS_2	Bit set (B,W,L) 2 operand
BIS_3	Bit set (B,W,L) 3 operand
BISPSW	Bit set processor status word
BIT_	Bit test (B,W,L)
CLR_	Clear (B,W,L=F,Q=D=G,O=H)
CVT_	Convert (B,W,L,F,D,G,H)(B,W,L,F,D,G,H) except BB, WW, LL, FF, DD, GG, HH, DG, and GD
CVTR_L	Convert rounded (F,D,G,H) to longword
CMP_	Compare (B,W,L,F,D,G,H)
DEC_	Decrement (B,W,L)
DIV_2	Divide (B,W,L,F,D,G,H) 2 operand
DIV_3	Divide (B,W,L,F,D,G,H) 3 operand
EDIV	Extended divide
EMOD_	Extended modulus (F,D,G,H)
EMUL	Extended multiply

Instruction	Description
INC_	Increment (B,W,L)
INDEX	Compute index
MCOM_	Move complemented (B,W,L)
MNEG_	Move negated (B,W,L,F,D,G,H)
MOVA_	Move address (B,W,L=F,Q=D=G,O=H)
MOV_*	Move (B,W,L,F,D,G,H,Q,O)**—general move between two operands
MOVPSL	Move from processor status longword
MOVZ_	Move zero-extended (BW,BL,WL)
MUL_2	Multiply (B,W,L,F,D,G,H) 2 operand
MUL_3	Multiply (B,W,L,F,D,G,H) 3 operand
POLY_	Polynomial evaluation (F,D,G,H)
POPR	Pop registers from stack
PUSHA_	Push address (B,W,L=F,Q=D=G,O=H) on stack
PUSHL	Push longword on stack
PUSHR	Push registers on stack
ROTL	Rotate longword
SBWC	Subtract with carry
SUB_2	Subtract (B,W,L,F,D,G,H) 2 operand
SUB_3	Subtract (B,W,L,F,D,G,H) 3 operand
TST_	Test (B,W,L,F,D,G,H)
XOR_2	Exclusive or (B,W,L) 2 operand
XOR_3	Exclusive or (B,W,L) 3 operand

Branch, Jump, and Procedure Call Instructions

Instruction	Description
ACB_	Add, compare and branch (B,W,L.F,D,G,H)
AOBLEQ	Add one and branch less than or equal
AOBLSS	Add one and branch less than
BB_	Branch on bit (set, clear)
BBS_	Branch on bit (set, clear) and (set, clear) bit
BB_I	Branch on bit set (clear) and set (clear) bit interlocked
BCC	Branch carry cleared
BCS	Branch carry set
BEQL	Branch equal
BEQLU	Branch equal unsigned
BGEQ	Branch greater than or equal
BGEQU	Branch greater than or equal unsigned
BGTR	Branch greater than

Instruction	Description
BGTRU	Branch greater than unsigned
BLB_	Branch on low bit (set, clear)
BLEQ	Branch less than or equal
BLEQU	Branch less than or equal unsigned
BLSS	Btranch less than
BLSSU	Branch less than unsigned
BNEQ	Branch not equal
BNEQU	Branch not equal unsigned
BR_	Jump with (B,W) displacement
BSB_	Branch to subroutine with (B,W) displacement
BV_	Branch overflow (set,clear)
CALLG	Call procedure with general argument list
CALLS	Call procedure with stack argument list
CASE_	Case on (B,W,L)
JMP	Jump
JSB	Jump to subroutine
RET	Return from procedure
RSB	Return from subroutine
SOBGEQ	Subtract one and branch greater than or equal
SOBGTR	Subtract one and branch greater than

Decimal and String Instructions

Instruction	Description
ADDP4	Add packed 4 operand
ADDP6	Add packed 6 operand
ASHP	Arithmetic shift packed and round
CMPC3	Compare characters 3 operand
CMPC5	Compare characters 5 operand
CMPP3	Compare packed 3 operand
CMPP4	Compare packed 4 operand
CRC	Calculate cyclic redundancy check
CVTLP	Convert long to packed
CVTPL	Convert packed to long
CVTPT	Convert packed to trailing
CVTTP	Convert trailing to packed
CVTPS	Convert packed to separate
CVTSP	Convert separate to packed
DIVP	Divide packed
EDITPC	Edit packed to character string

Instruction	Description
LOCC	Locate character
MATCHC	Match characters
MOVC3	Move character 3 operand
MOVC5	Move character 5 operand
MOVP	Move packed
MOVTC	Move translated characters
MOVTUC	Move translated until character
MULP	Multiply packed
SCANC	Scan characters
SKPC	Skip character
SPANC	Span characters
SUBP4	Subtract packed 4 operand
SUBP6	Subtract packed 6 operand

Variable-Length Bit Field Instructions

Instruction	Description
CMPV	Compare field
CMPZV	Compare zero-extended field
EXTV	Extract field
EXTZV	Extract zero-extended field
INSV	Insert field
FFS	Find first set
FFC	Find first clear

Queue Instructions

Instruction	Description
INSQHI	Insert entry into queue at head, interlocked
INSQTI	Insert entry into queue at tail, interlocked
INSQUE	Insert entry in queue
REMQHI	Remove entry from queue at head, interlocked
REMQTI	Remove entry from queue at tail, interlocked
REMQUE	Remove entry from queue

B.2 | System/360 Instruction Set

The 360 instruction set is shown in the following tables, organized by instruction type and format. System/370 contains 15 additional user instructions.

Integer/Logical and Floating-Point R–R Instructions

The * indicates the instruction is floating point, and may be either D (double precision) or E (single precision).

Instruction	Description
ALR	Add logical register
AR	Add register
A*R	FP addition
CLR	Compare logical register
CR	Compare register
C*R	FP compare
DR	Divide register
D*R	FP divide
H*R	FP halve
LCR	Load complement register
LC*R	Load complement
LNR	Load negative register
LN*R	Load negative
LPR	Load positive register
LP*R	Load positive
LR	Load register
L*R	Load FP register
LTR	Load and test register
LT*R	Load and test FP register
MR	Multiply register
M*R	FP multiply
NR	And register
OR	Or register
SLR	Subtract logical register
SR	Subtract register
S*R	FP subtraction
XR	Exclusive or register

Branches and Status Setting R–R Instructions

These are R–R format instructions that either branch or set some system status; several of them are privileged and legal only in supervisor mode.

Instruction	Description
BALR	Branch and link
BCTR	Branch on count
BCR	Branch/condition
ISK	Insert key
SPM	Set program mask
SSK	Set storage key
SVC	Supervisor call

Integer/Logical and Floating-Point Instructions— RX Format

These are all RX format instructions. The symbol "+" means either a word operation (and then stands for nothing) or H (meaning halfword); for example, A+ stands for the two opcodes A and AH. The symbol "*" is D or E standing for double- or single-precision floating point.

Instruction	Description
A+	Add
A*	FP add
AL	Add logical
C+	Compare
C*	FP compare
CL	Compare logical
D	Divide
D*	FP divide
L+	Load
L*	Load FP register
M+	Multiply
M*	FP multiply
N	And
O	Or
S+	Subtract
S*	FP subtract
SL	Subtract logical
ST+	Store
ST*	Store FP register
X	Exclusive or

Branches and Special Loads and Stores—RX format

Instruction	Description
BAL	Branch and link
BC	Branch condition
BCT	Branch on count
CVB	Convert-binary
CVD	Convert-decimal
EX	Execute
IC	Insert character
LA	Load address
STC	Store character

RS and SI Format Instructions

These are the RS and SI format instructions. The symbol "*" may be A (arithmetic) or L (logical).

Instruction	Description
BXH	Branch/high
BXLE	Branch/low-equal
CLI	Compare logical immediate
HIO	Halt I/O
LPSW	Load PSW
LM	Load multiple
MVI	Move immediate
NI	And immediate
OI	Or immediate
RDD	Read direct
SIO	Start I/O
SL*	Shift left A/L
SLD*	Shift left double A/L
SR*	Shift right A/L
SRD*	Shift right double A/L
SSM	Set system mask
STM	Store multiple
TCH	Test channel
TIO	Test I/O
TM	Test under mask
TS	Test and set
WRD	Write direct
XI	Exclusive or immediate

SS Format Instructions

These are all decimal or string instructions.

Instruction	Description
AP	Add packed
CLC	Compare logical chars
CP	Compare packed
DP	Divide packed
ED	Edit
EDMK	Edit and mark
MP	Multiply packed
MVC	Move character
MVN	Move numeric
MVO	Move with offset
MVZ	Move zone
NC	And characters
OC	Or characters
PACK	Pack (Character → decimal)
SP	Subtract packed
TR	Translate
TRT	Translate and test
UNPK	Unpack
XC	Exclusive or characters
ZAP	Zero and add packed

B.3 | 8086 Instruction Set

These charts contain the instruction set of the 8086; floating-point instructions that are neither included nor used by the 8086 benchmarks are not included.

Arithmetic and Logical Instructions

Instruction	Description
AAA	ASCII adjust after addition
AAD	ASCII adjust before division
AAM	ASCII adjust after multiplication
AAS	ASCII adjust after subtraction
ADC	Add with carry
ADD	Integer addition
AND	Logical and
CBW/CWD/CDQ	Convert byte to word/word to dword/dword to quad
CLC	Clear the carry flag
CLD	Clear the direction flag
CLI	Clear the interrupt flag
CMC	Complement the carry flag
CMP	Compare
DAA	Decimal adjust after addition
DAS	Decimal adjust after subtraction
DEC	Decrement
DIV	Unsigned divide
IDIV	Signed divide
IMUL	Signed multiplication
INC	Increment
MUL	Unsigned multiplication
NEG	Negate
NOT	Not
OR	Inclusive or
RCL	Rotate through carry left
RCR	Rotate through carry right
ROL	Rotate left
ROR	Rotate right
SAL/SHL	Shift arithmetic left
SAR	Shift arithmetic right
SBB	Subtract with borrow
SHR	Shift logical right
STC	Set carry flag
STD	Set direction flag
STI	Set interrupt flag
SUB	Subtract
TEST	Logical compare
XOR	Exclusive or

Control Instructions

Instruction	Description
CALL	Call procedure (intrasegment)
CALL	Call procedure (intersegment)
HLT	Halt
INT	Call to interrupt procedure
INTO	On overflow call interrupt procedure
IRET	Interrupt return
JB/JNAE/JC	Jump below
JBE/JNA	Jump below or equal
JCXZ/JECXZ	Jump CX/ECX zero
JE/JZ	Jump equal
JL/JNGE	Jump less
JLE/JNG	Jump less or equal
JMP	Jump (intrasegment)
JMPF	Jump (intersegment)
JNB/JAE/JNC	Jump not below
JNBE/JA	Jump not below or equal
JNE/JNZ	Jump not equal
JNL/JCE	Jump not less
JNLE/JG	Jump not less or equal
JNO	Jump no overflow
JNP/JPO	Jump not parity
JNS	Jump not sign
JO	Jump overflow
JP/JPE	Jump parity
JS	Jump sign
LOCK	Bus lock
RET	Return (intrasegment)
RETF	Return (intersegrnent)

Data Transfer Instructions

Instruction	Description
IN	Input from a port
LAHF	Load flags into AH register
LDS	Load pointer to DS
LEA	Load effective address
LES	Load pointer to ES
LOCK	Bus lock
MOV	Move
OUT	Output to a port
POP	Pop off stack
POPF/POPFD	Pop from stack into flags
PUSH	Push onto stack
PUSH	Push segment register onto the stack
PUSHF/PUSHFD	Push flags onto stack
SAHF	Store AH register into flags
XCHC	Exchange
XLAT/XLATB	Table lookup translation

String Instructions

Instruction	Description
CMPS/CMPSB/CMPSW/CMPSD	Compare string
LODS/LODSB/LODSW/LODSD	Load string
MOVS/MOVSB/MOVSW/MOVSD	Move string
REP	Repeat
REPE/REPZ	Repeat while equal
REPNE/REPNZ	Repeat while not equal
SCAS/SCASB/SCASW/SCASD	Scan string
STOS/STOSB/STOSW/STOSD	Store string

C Detailed Instruction Set Measurements

C.1 | VAX Detailed Measurements

Instruction	GCC	Spice	TeX	COBOLX	Average
Control	**30%**	**18%**	**30%**	**25%**	**26%**
Conditional Branch	20%	13%	19%	18%	17%
BRB,BRW	6%	3%	4%	5%	5%
CALLS,CALLG	2%	1%	4%	0%	2%
RET	2%	1%	4%	0%	2%
JMP				2%	1%
Arithmetic, logical	**40%**	**23%**	**33%**	**24%**	**30%**
CMP*	12%	5%	11%	9%	9%
ADDL_	5%	12%	4%		5%
INCL	3%		3%	5%	3%
MOVA*	1%	3%	4%	2%	3%
TSTL	4%	2%	3%		2%
CLRL	3%	1%	2%	3%	2%
SUB*_	3%	1%	3%		2%
CVT*L	6%			0%	2%
ASHL	3%		3%	0%	2%
MULL_	0%			5%	1%
Data transfer	**19%**	**15%**	**28%**	**4%**	**16%**
MOVL	15%	9%	17%	4%	11%
PUSHL	3%		7%		2%
MOVQ		6%			1%
MOVZ*L	1%		4%		1%
Floating point	**0%**	**23%**	**0%**	**0%**	**6%**
MULD_		9%			2%
SUBD_		6%			1%
ADDD_		6%			1%
DIVD_		3%			1%
CMPD		2%			
Decimal, string	**0%**	**0%**	**1%**	**38%**	**10%**
CVTTP,CVTPT				19%	5%
MOVC3,MOVC5			1%	9%	2%
ADDP4				6%	1%
CMPP_				2%	1%
CMPC3				2%	1%
Totals	**88%**	**79%**	**92%**	**88%**	**87%**

FIGURE C.1   Instructions responsible for more than 1.5% of the dynamic executions in any benchmark. The instructions are broken into five classes, printed in boldface. The data in those rows give the total frequency for the operations in that class. Cells representing a contribution of 1% or less are empty, except the average column can have an entry of 1%. Because of rounding, the average can differ from what might appear to be correct if based on the figures in the individual columns.

C.2 360 Detailed Measurements

Instruction	PLIC	FORTGO	PLIGO	COBOLGO	Average
Control	**32%**	**13%**	**5%**	**16%**	**16%**
BC, BCR	28%	13%	5%	14%	15%
BAL, BALR	3%			2%	1%
Arithmetic, logical	**29%**	**35%**	**29%**	**9%**	**26%**
A, AR	3%	17%	21%		10%
SR	3%	7%			3%
SLL		6%	3%		2%
LA	8%	1%	1%		2%
CLI	7%				2%
NI				7%	2%
C	5%	4%	4%	0%	3%
TM	3%	1%		3%	2%
MH			2%		1%
Data transfer	**17%**	**40%**	**56%**	**20%**	**33%**
L, LR	7%	23%	28%	19%	19%
MVI	2%		16%	1%	5%
ST	3%		7%		3%
LD		7%	2%		2%
STD		7%	2%		2%
LPDR		3%			1%
LH	3%				1%
IC	2%				1%
LTR		1%			0%
Floating point		**7%**			**2%**
AD		3%			1%
MDR		3%			1%
Decimal, string	**4%**			**40%**	**11%**
MVC	4%			7%	3%
AP				11%	3%
ZAP				9%	2%
CVD				5%	1%
MP				3%	1%
CLC				3%	1%
CP				2%	1%
ED				1%	0%
Total	**82%**	**95%**	**90%**	**85%**	**88%**

FIGURE C.2 (See previous page.) Distribution of instruction execution frequencies for the four 360 programs. All instructions with a frequency of execution greater than 1.5% are included. Immediate instructions, which operate on only a single byte, are included in the section that characterizes their operation, rather than with the long character-string versions of the same operation. By comparison, the average frequencies for the major instruction classes of the VAX are 23% (control), 28% (arithmetic), 29% (data transfer), 7% (floating point), and 9% (decimal). Once again, a 1% entry in the average column can occur because of entries in the constituent columns.

C.3 | Intel 8086 Detailed Measurements

Instruction	Turbo C	MASM	Lotus	Average
Control	**21%**	**20%**	**32%**	**24%**
Conditional jumps	10%	12%	9%	10%
CALL, CALLF	4%	3%	5%	4%
RET, RETF	4%	3%	5%	4%
LOOP			12%	4%
JMP	3%	2%	2%	2%
Arithmetic, logical	**23%**	**24%**	**26%**	**25%**
CMP	8%	9%	5%	7%
SAL, SHR, RCR	2%	1%	11%	5%
ADD	3%	2%	3%	3%
OR, XOR	4%	2%	2%	3%
INC, DEC	3%	4%	3%	3%
SUB	2%	3%		2%
CBW	1%	1%		1%
TEST		2%	2%	1%
Data transfer	**49%**	**46%**	**30%**	**42%**
MOV	29%	31%	21%	27%
LES	6%	2%		3%
PUSH	10%	8%	4%	7%
POP	5%	6%	5%	5%
Totals	**93%**	**90%**	**88%**	**90%**

FIGURE C.3 The instructions responsible for more than 1.5% of the executions on any of the three benchmarks Some very similar instructions were combined for simplicity. Although MASM makes some use of string operations, the frequency is too low to make the table.

C.4 | DLX Detailed Instruction Set Measurements

Instruction	GCC	Spice	TeX	US Steel	Average
Control	**21%**	**5%**	**7%**	**23%**	**14%**
B--Z	19%	2%	7%	16%	11%
J	2%	3%		3%	2%
JAL				2%	0%
JR				2%	0%
Arithmetic, logical	**37%**	**28%**	**41%**	**49%**	**39%**
ADDU, ADDUI	17%	16%	20%	27%	20%
LHI	2%	7%	10%	3%	5%
SLL	5%	5%	5%	4%	5%
LI	4%		4%	6%	4%
S--, S--I	5%		3%	3%	3%
AND, ANDI	2%			3%	1%
SRA	2%			2%	1%
OR, ORI				2%	1%
Data transfer	**28%**	**35%**	**33%**	**10%**	**26%**
LW	18%	8%	19%	5%	13%
SW	10%	2%	12%	5%	7%
LBU			2%		1%
LD		14%			4%
SD		6%			1%
MOVFP2I, MOVI2FP		5%			1%
Floating point	**0%**	**15%**	**0%**	**0%**	**4%**
FMUL		5%			1%
FADD		4%			1%
FSUB		3%			1%
FDIV		3%			1%
Totals	**85%**	**83%**	**82%**	**82%**	**83%**

FIGURE C.4   Instruction mixes for GCC, Spice, TeX, and the U.S. Steel COBOL benchmark. Some instructions were combined, both in the interest of space and because the combined class more correctly reflects what the processor is doing. The instruction class "B--Z" includes all conditional branches (which are all compares to zero). The class "S--,S--I" includes all set conditional instructions, both immediate and register–register. Immediate operations have been combined with the non-immediate class for all operations except loads, where they are distinctly different. Again, a blank space means that the instruction is not responsible for more than 1.5% of the executions, and the average may appear at 1% or less because the instruction is not used by all benchmarks.

D

Time Versus Frequency
Measurements

D.1 | Time Distribution on the VAX-11/780

We know from Chapters 2 and 3 that measuring instruction counts alone can be misleading. In this appendix we will examine the time distributions for some programs running on these four machines. For the 360, the 8086, and DLX, we will show the time distribution averaged over the three programs in the graph format used earlier. For the VAX, we will use measurements reported in Clark and Levy [1982] (see References in Chapter 4).

Figure D.1 shows the distribution of instruction executions, both by time and by frequency of occurrence. These data were measured by Emer and reported by Clark and Levy for a VAX-11/780 running VMS with multiple users doing three primary tasks:

1. Updating indexed files

2. Executing a matrix multiplication routine

3. Doing program development, including editing, compiling, and debugging

Figure D.1 includes any user instruction that accounts for more than 1% of the instruction executions or more than 1% of execution time. There are 26 instructions that fit this description, and together they account for 59% of the executions and 58% of the time. The measured data include the operating system and file system overhead.

Time distributions are particularly important on architectures like the VAX, where the number of cycles for an instruction may vary from one or two up to tens or hundreds.

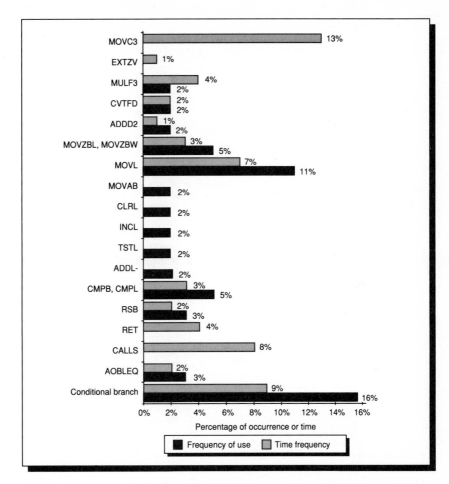

FIGURE D.1 Time and frequency distribution for a multiuser workload on a VAX-11/780 running VMS. This data includes all user instructions that are responsible for more than 1% of either the instruction executions or the execution time. (Two operating system instructions (REI and MTPR), each of which accounts for about 1% of the execution time, are not included.) The absence of an execution-frequency bar or time-frequency bar for an entry (such as MOVC3 or TSTL) means that the time frequency or execution-time frequency is below 1% (not that it is 0!). Clark and Levy [1982] commented that the large percentage of time consumed by the MOVC3 in the time distribution is somewhat abnormal for a nonbusiness workload and has not been observed in other measurements on the 11/780.

D.2 | Time Distribution on the IBM 370/168

Figure D.2 shows the time distribution on an IBM 370/168 for the same programs we discussed in Chapter 4 and included in Figure 4.28 (page 175). All instructions that are responsible for more than 1.5% of the execution frequency and the execution time for at least one program are included. Several

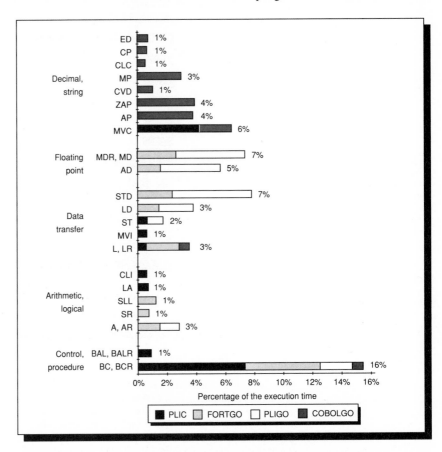

FIGURE D.2   Time distribution for the four programs discussed in Chapter 4 running on an IBM 370/168. The corresponding data on execution frequency appears in Figure 4.28 (page 175), or in table form in Figure C.2. Any instruction with greater than 1.5% frequency in the time distribution and in the execution-count distribution is included in this chart. Shustek [1978] (see References in Chapter 4) computed these numbers using a model of the 370/168 CPU. The model predicts the execution time for the programs and has an overall accuracy for each program of about 99% except on PLIGO, where it has an 8% error.

instructions appeared in the time distribution that were not in the frequency distribution, where their occurrence was too low. These instructions, which are not in Figure 4.28, are

TRT—Translate and test, a string instruction used by the PL/I compiler, most likely to scan the input source; takes 5.4% of the time in that program.

DP—Divide packed, a low frequency but long-running instruction that takes 18.7% of the time in COBOLGO.

DDR—Divide double register, a floating-point divide, infrequent but long running at 5.2% of the FORTGO execution time.

LM and STM—Load multiple and store multiple, with frequencies just below 1%, are somewhat slower than the average instruction; thus, they take 3% to 4% of the cycles in PLIGO.

BCT,BXLE—Loop branches that involve incrementing counts or doing other compares; BCT consumes about 2% of the time in PLIC, and BXLE consumes 3.5% in FORTGO.

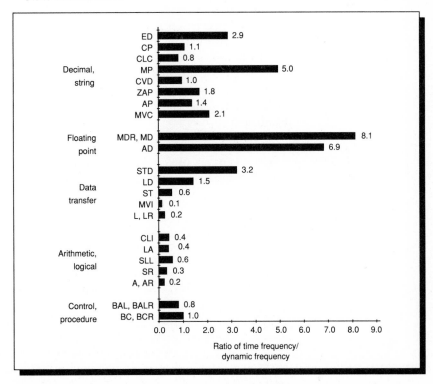

FIGURE D.3 Time frequency (percent of cycles doing this instruction as measured on an IBM 370/168) divided by dynamic frequency (percent of executions for this instruction). The programs are those in Chapter 4. This data is obtained directly from Figures 4.28 (page 175) and Figure D.2. This clearly shows that the floating-point instructions are the most expensive.

Several of the simpler but lower-frequency data transfer and ALU instructions that appeared in the frequency distribution do not appear in the time distribution because they constitute a very small percentage of the execution time. In total, the instructions shown in Figure D.2 account for 89% of the instruction executions and 72% of the execution time.

Figure D.3 gives the average execution time divided by the average frequency for those instructions that appear in both distributions. This measurement is a ratio that indicates the relative cost of an instruction. For example, an instruction that is responsible for 10% of the executions and 10% of the execution time will have a ratio of 1:1, or a cost factor of 1, and a CPI equal to the average CPI on the machine.

D.3 | Time Distribution on an 8086 in an IBM PC

Figure D.4 continues our examination of time distribution by looking at the top time-consuming instructions on the 8086 for the same programs as measured in Chapter 4. These curves look very similar to those in Figure 4.32 (page 178), the frequency distribution for the 8086 (shown in table form in Figure C.3, page C-4). Two arithmetic and logical instructions, CBW and SUB, that appeared in the frequency distribution do not appear in the top of the execution-time distribution. Additionally, there are four instructions that have a significant contribution to the time frequency but are not in the execution-frequency distribution:

- String instructions SCAS (a string search) and MOVS (a string move). Both instructions are used in MASM, where they account for 8% and 7% of the execution time, respectively. MOVS is also used in Lotus, where it accounts for 6.6% of the program's execution time.

- Integer multiply and divide ML16 and DV16. These are used in Lotus, where they respectively account for 10% and 4% of the program's execution time.

Together, the instructions in Figure D.4 are responsible for 87% of the instruction executions and 85% of the execution time.

Figure D.5 shows the ratio of execution time to execution frequency in the same fashion used for the IBM 360. Calls, returns, and loading a segment register consume a larger percentage of the execution time relative to their dynamic occurrence. However, the overall execution time profile of the 8086 is much closer to the execution frequency profile—the correspondence is often 1:1, and never as high as 1:2. This is primarily because the variation in CPI among instructions is small compared to an overall average CPI of 14.1. The long-running instructions that do not even appear in the frequency counts but are major consumers of execution time (and would have a high CPI) are the string instructions and integer multiply and divide.

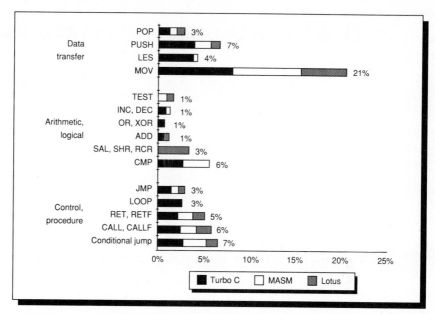

FIGURE D.4   The 8086 time distribution as measured on an IBM PC running MS-DOS. The format and data are the same as in Figure 4.32 (page 178).

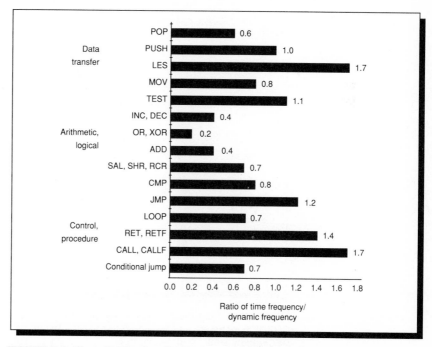

FIGURE D.5   Time distribution divided by frequency distribution for the 8086. This data is directly derived from Figures 4.32 (page 178) and D.4. The distribution is remarkably flatter than that for the IBM 360 or the VAX.

D.4 | Time Distribution on a DLX Relative

To obtain a time distribution for DLX, we turn to the DECstation 3100, which has an instruction set architecture very similar to DLX (see Appendix E). The time distribution on the DECstation 3100 for the same programs measured in Chapter 4 (Figure 4.34 on page 181 and in table form in Figure C.4 is shown in Figure D.6. Figure D.6 includes all instructions that contribute more than 1% to the execution time. In total, these instructions account for 81% of all instruction executions and 97% of the execution time.

This time distribution is by far the closest to the frequency distribution. This is because under ideal conditions almost all instructions in DLX can take one cycle; only the LD and SD instructions must take two cycles. Of course, these perfect conditions never arise. The average CPI using the DECstation 3100 as a base is about 1.6 for GCC, TeX, and COBOLX, and about 2.1 for Spice.

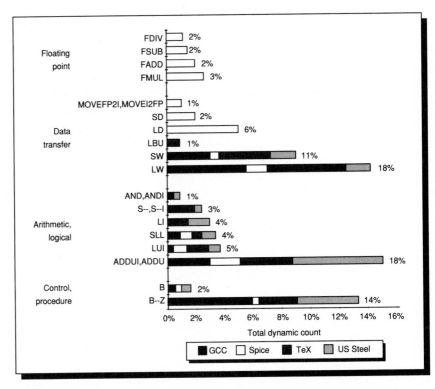

FIGURE D.6 The time distribution for our three benchmarks plus the US Steel COBOL benchmark as they would run on DLX using the CPI measurements from a DECstation 3100.

Figure D.7 shows contribution to execution time over contribution to execution frequency for the top instructions. Like the 360 and 8086 charts, a value above 1 indicates that this instruction has a higher CPI than the average instruction. Remember, though, that the ratio does not indicate the CPI for the instruction. However, we can use this figure to find the CPI for an instruction, given the base CPI for a specific program.

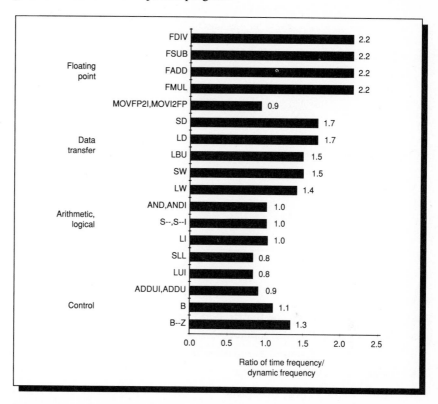

FIGURE D.7 Time frequency divided by execution frequency for DLX as measured using the time data from Figure D.6 and the frequency data from Figure 4.34 (page 181). The integer register–floating-point register moves are inexpensive, since they are really register–register operations. Surprisingly, the double-precision memory references are **not** twice as expensive as the 32-bit loads and stores. Can you hypothesize why based on the discussions of pipelining and cache design?

RISC: any computer announced after 1985.

Steven Przybylski (a designer of the Stanford MIPS)

Survey of RISC Architectures

Introduction

We cover four examples of Reduced Instruction Set Computer (RISC) architectures in this appendix:

- Intel 860;
- MIPS R3000/R3010 (plus a section on MIPS II, used in the R6000);
- Motorola M88000; and
- SPARC, developed originally by Sun Microsystems.

We also include DLX, the instruction set architecture invented for this book. (A review of DLX can be found in the back inside cover or in pages 160–167 of Chapter 4.) Characteristics of these architectures are found in Figure E.1.

There has never been another class of computers that were so similar. This similarity allows the presentation of four architectures at once, with DLX thrown in for good measure! After presenting the addressing modes and instruction formats, the instructions are presented in three steps:

- Instructions found in DLX;
- Instructions not found in DLX but found in two or more architectures; and
- The unique instructions and characteristics of each architecture.

We conclude with a speculation about the future directions for RISCs.

	DLX	**i860**	**MIPS**	**M88000**	**SPARC**
Date announced	1990	1989	1986	1988	1987
Instruction size (bits)	32	32	32	32	32
Address space (size, model)	32 bits, flat	32 bits, flat	32 bits, flat	32 bits, flat	32 bits, flat
Data alignment	Aligned	Aligned	Aligned	Aligned	Aligned
Data addressing modes	1	2	1	3	2
Protection	Page	Page	Page	Page	Page
Page size	4 KB	4 KB	4 KB	4 KB	4–64 KB
I/O	Memory mapped	Memory mapped	Memory mapped	Memory mapped	Memory mapped
Integer registers (size, model, number)	31 GPR x 32 bits	31 GPR x 32 bits	31 GPR x 32 bits	31 GPR x 32 bits	31 GPR x 32 bits
Separate floating-point registers	32 x 32 or 16 x 64 bits	30 x 32 or 15 x 64 bits	16 x 32 or 16 x 64 bits	0	32 x 32 or 16 x 64
Floating-point format	IEEE 754 single, double	IEEE 754 single, double	IEEE 754 single, double	IEEE 754 single, double	IEEE 754 single,double

FIGURE E.1 Summary of five recent architectures. Except for number of data address modes and some instruction set details, the integer instruction sets of these architectures of the late 1980s are identical. Contrast this to Figure E.13, page E-23.

E.2 Addressing Modes and Instruction Formats

Figure E.2 shows the data addressing modes supported by each architecture. Since all have one register that always has the value 0—in fact, it is r0 in every architecture—the absolute address mode with limited range can be synthesized using r0 as the base in displacement addressing. Similarly, register-indirect addressing is synthesized by using displacement addressing with an offset of 0. Simplified addressing modes is one distinguishing feature between these and prior architectures.

Addressing mode	**DLX**	**i860**	**MIPS**	**M88000**	**SPARC**
Register + offset (displacement or based)	√	√	√	√	√
Register + register (indexed)	--	√	--	√	√
Register + scaled register (scaled)	--	--	--	√	--

FIGURE E.2 Summary of data addressing modes. (These addressing modes are explained in Section 3.4, pages 94–103) While the i860 does have indexed data addressing for all loads and floating-point stores, it is not available for integer stores.

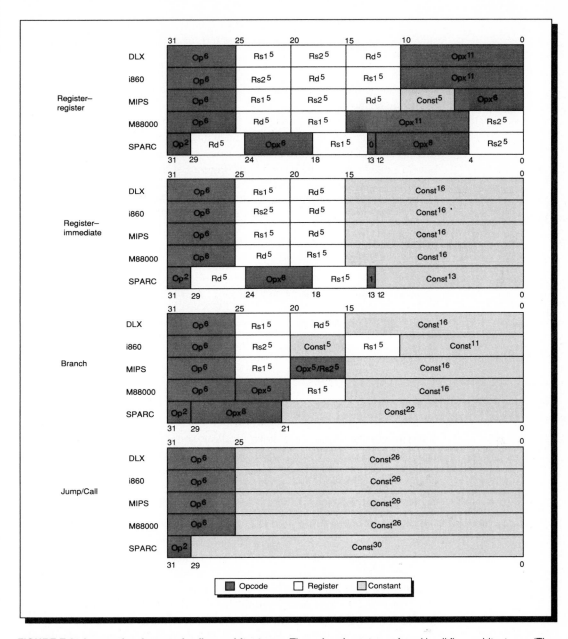

FIGURE E.3 Instruction formats for five architectures. These four formats are found in all five architectures. (The superscript notation in this figure means something different from our standard notation; it shows the width of a field in bits.) While the register fields are located in similar pieces of the instruction, beware that the destination and two source fields are scrambled. Here are the meanings of the abbreviations: Op = the main opcode, Opx =an opcode extension, Rd = the destination register, Rs1 = source register 1, Rs2 = source register 2, and Const = a constant (used as an immediate or as an address). The main variation for the M88000 is register–immediate format when the operation doesn't need a full 16-bit immediate: an opcode extension field is placed in the upper bits of the constant field. The variation for the i860 is using Rs1 in the Branch format to specify a 5-bit constant as well as a register.

References to code are normally PC-relative, although register indirect is supported for returning from procedures and for case statements. One variation is that PC-relative branch addresses in everything but DLX are shifted left 2 bits before being added to the PC, thereby increasing the branch distance. This works because the length of all instructions is one word and instructions must be word aligned in memory.

Figure E.3 (page E-3) shows the format of instructions, which includes the size of the address in the instructions. Each instruction set architecture uses these four primary instruction formats. The primary differences are subtle, concerning how to extend constant fields to 32 bits. Figure E.4 shows the variations.

Format: instruction category	DLX	i860	MIPS	M88000	SPARC
Branch: all	Sign	Sign	Sign	Sign	Sign
Jump/Call: all	Sign	Sign	--	Sign	Sign
Register–immediate: data transfer	Sign	Sign	Sign	Zero	Sign
Register–immediate: arithmetic	Sign	Sign	Sign	Zero	Sign
Register–immediate: logical	Sign	Zero	Zero	Zero	Sign

FIGURE E.4 Summary of constant extension. The constant in the Jump and Call instructions of MIPS are not sign extended since they only replace the lower 28 bits of the PC, leaving the upper 4 bits unchanged.

E.3 | Instructions: The DLX Subset

The similarities of each architecture allow simultaneous descriptions of the architectures, starting with the operations equivalent to DLX.

DLX Instructions

Almost every instruction found in DLX instructions is found in the other architectures, as Figure E.5 shows. (For reference, definitions of the DLX instructions are found on pages 160 to 167 of Chapter 4 and the back inside cover.) Instructions are listed under four categories: "Data transfer," "Arithmetic, logical," "Control," and "Floating point." A fifth category in the figure shows conventions for register usage and pseudoinstructions on each architecture. If a DLX instruction requires a short sequence of instructions, these instructions are separated by semicolons in Figure E.5. (To avoid confusion, the destination register will **always** be the leftmost operand in this appendix, independent of the notation normally used with each architecture.)

Every architecture must have a scheme for compare and conditional branch, but even with all the similarities, each of these architectures has found a different way to perform the operation. The advantages and disadvantages of the general options are found on pages 105–109 of Chapter 3.

Instruction name	DLX	i860	MIPS	M88000	SPARC
Data transfer (Instruction formats)	**R–I**	**R–I, R–R**	**R–I**	**R–I, R–R**	**R–I, R–R**
Load byte signed	LB	LD.B	LB	LD.B	LDSB
Load byte unsigned	LBU	LD.B; AND ...,x00FF,...	LBU	LD.BU	LDUB
Load halfword signed	LH	LD.S	LH	LD.H	LDSH
Load halfword unsigned	LHU	LD.S; AND ...,xFFFF...	LHU	LD.HU	LDUH
Load word	LW	LD.L	LW	LD	LD
Load SP float	LF	FLD.L	LWC1	LD	LDF
Load DP float (see E.5 for MIPS)	LD	FLD.D	LWC1 Rd; LWC1 Rd+1	LD.D	LDDF
Store byte	SB	ST.B	SB	ST.B	STB
Store halfword	SH	ST.S	SH	ST.H	STH
Store word	SW	ST.L	SW	ST	ST
Store SP float	SF	FST.L	SWC1	ST	STF
Store DP float (see E.5 for MIPS)	SD	FST.D	SWC1 Rd; SWC1 Rd+1	ST.D	STDF
Read, write special registers	MOVS2I, MOVI2S	LD.C, ST.C	MF_, MT_	LDCR,FLDCR STCR,FSTCR	RD, LDFSR, WR, STFSR
Move int. to FP reg.	MOVI2FP	IXFR	MFC1	not applicable	ST;LDF,
Move FP to int. reg.	MOVFP2I	FXFR	MTC1	not applicable	STF;LD
Arithmetic, logical (Instruction formats)	**R–R, R–I**	**R–R, R–I**	**R–R, R–I**	**R–R, R–I**	**R–R, R–I**
Add	ADDU,ADDUI	ADD,ADDU	ADDU,ADDIU	ADDU	ADD
Add (trap if overflow)	ADD,ADDI	ADD; INTOVR	ADD,ADDI	ADD	ADDcc; TVS
Sub	SUBU,SUBUI	SUB,SUBU	SUBU	SUBU	SUB
Sub (trap if overflow)	SUB,SUBI	SUB; INTOVR	SUB	SUB	SUBcc; TVS
Multiply (see E.6 for SPARC)	MULTU, MULTUI	FMLOW	MULT, MULTU	MUL	MULScc;....; MULScc
Multiply (trap if ovf)	MULT,MULTI	--	--	--	-- (see E.6)
Divide	DIVU,DIVUI	--	DIV,DIVU	DIV,DIVU	-- (see E.6)
Divide (trap if ovf)	DIV,DIVI	--	--	--	-- (see E.6)
And	AND,ANDI	AND	AND,ANDI	AND	AND
Or	OR,ORI	OR	OR,ORI	OR	OR
Xor	XOR,XORI	XOR	XOR,XORI	XOR	XOR
Load high part reg.	LHI	OR.H ...,r0,...	LUI	OR.U ...,r0,...	SETHI (B fmt.)
Shift left logical	SLL,SLLI	SHL	SLLV,SLL	MAK	SLL
Shift right logical	SRL,SRLI	SHR	SRLV,SRL	EXTU	SRL
Shift right arithmetic	SRA,SRAI	SHRA	SRAV,SRA	EXT	SRA
Compare	S-($<,>,\leq,\geq,=,\neq$)	SUB r0,...	SLT,SLTU, SLTI,SLTIU	CMP	SUBcc r0,...

Instruction Name	DLX	i860	MIPS	M88000	SPARC
Control (Instruction formats)	**B, J/C**	**B, J/C**	**B, J/C**	**B, J/C**	**B, J/C**
Branch on integer compare	BEQ,BNE	BC.T,BNC.T, BTE,BTNE	BEQ,BNE,B_Z $(<,>,\le,\ge)$	BB1.N,BB0.N, BCND.N	Bicc $(<,>,\le,\ge,=,\ne)$
Branch on floating-point compare	BFPT,BFPF	BC.T,BNC.T	BC1T,BC1F	BB1.N,BB0.N, BCND.N	FBfcc $(<,>,\le,\ge,=,...)$
Jump, jump register	J,JR	BR, BRI	J,JR	BR.N,JMP.N	B, JMPL r0,...
Call, call register	JAL,JALR	CALL, CALLI	JAL,JALR	BSR.N,JSR.N	CALL,JMPL
Trap	TRAP	TRAP	BREAK	TCND, TB0	Ticc
Return from interrupt	RFE	BRI *(trap bits≠0)*	JR; RFE	RTE	RETT
Floating point (Instruction formats)	**R–R**	**R–R**	**R–R**	**R–R**	**R–R**
Add single, double	ADDF, ADDD	FADD.SS, FADD.DD	ADD.S, ADD.D	FADD.SSS, FADD.DDD	FADDS, FADDD
Sub single, double	SUBF, SUBD	FSUB.SS, FSUB.DD	SUB.S, SUB.D	FSUB.SSS, FSUB.DDD	FSUBS, FSUBD
Mult single, double	MULF, MULD	FMUL.SS, FMUL.DD	MUL.S, MUL.D	FMUL.SSS, FMUL.DDD	FMULS, FMULD
Div single, double	DIVF, DIVD	--, --	DIV.S, DIV.D	FDIV.SSS, FDIV.DDD	FDIVS, FDIVD
Compare	_F, _D $(<,>,\le,\ge,=,...)$	PF_.SS, PF_.DD $(>,\le,=)$	C_.S, C_.D $(<,>,\le,\ge,=,...)$	FCMP.SS, FCMP.DD	FCMPS, FCMPD
Move R–R	MOVF	FIADD.SS ...,f0,	MOV.S	ADD ...,r0,...	FMOVS
Convert (single,double,integer) to (single,double,integer)	CVTF2D, CVTD2F, CVTF2I, CVTD2I, CVTI2F, CVTI2D	FADD.SD ..f0.., FADD.DS ..f0.., FIX.SS, FIX.DS, --, --	CVT.S.D, CVT.D.S, CVT.S.W, CVT.D.W, CVT.W.S, CVT.W.D	FADD.SSD r0, --, INT.SS, INT.SD, FLT.SS, FLT.DS	FSTOD, FDTOS, FSTOI, FDTOI, FITOS, FITOD
Conventions					
Register with value 0	r0	r0	r0	r0	r0
Return address reg.	r31	r1	r31	r1	r31
Noop	ADD r0,r0,r0	SHL r0,r0,r0	SLL r0,r0,r0	OR r0,r0,r0	SETHI r0,0
Move R–R integer	ADD ...,r0,...	SHL ...,r0,...	ADD ...,r0,...	OR ...,r0,...	OR ...,r0,...
Operand order	OP Rd,Rs1,Rs2	OP Rs1,Rs2,Rd	OP Rd,Rs1,Rs2	OP Rd,Rs1,Rs2	OP Rs1,Rs2,Rd

FIGURE E.5 Instructions equivalent to DLX. Dashes mean the operation is not available in that architecture, or not synthesized in a few instructions. Such a sequence of instructions is shown separated by semicolons. If there are several choices of instructions equivalent to DLX, they are separated by commas. Finally, "not applicable" means that while this operation is not directly available, other changes in the architecture means it wouldn't make sense. This later category is for the M88000, since integer and floating-point instructions sharing the same registers means separate floating-point move instructions are unnecessary. Note that in the "Arithmetic, logical" category DLX and MIPS use separate instruction mnemonics to indicate an immediate operand, while the i860, M88000, and SPARC offer immediate versions of these instructions but use a single mnemonic. (Of course these are separate opcodes!) Both MIPS and SPARC have new instructions that were not implemented in the first machine and that apply to some of these cases: see Sections E.5 and E.6.

Compare and Conditional Branch

SPARC uses the traditional four condition code bits stored in the program status word: Negative, Zero, Carry, and Overflow. They can be set on any arithmetic or logical instruction, but unlike earlier architectures this setting is optional on each instruction. This leads to fewer problems in pipelined implementation (page 334 in Chapter 6). While condition codes can be set as a side effect of an operation, explicit compares are synthesized with a subtract using r0 as the destination. Floating point uses separate condition codes to encode the IEEE 754 conditions, requiring a floating-point compare instruction. SPARC conditional branches test condition codes to determine all possible unsigned and signed relations.

MIPS uses the contents of registers to evaluate conditional branches. Any two registers can be compared for equality (BEQ) or inequality (BNE) and then the branch is taken if the condition holds. The set-on-less-than instructions (SLT,SLTI, SLTU,SLTIU) compare two operands and then set the destination register to 1 if less and to 0 otherwise. These instructions are enough to synthesize the full set of relations. Because of the popularity of comparisons to 0, MIPS includes special compare-and-branch instructions for all such comparisons: greater than or equal to zero (BGEZ), greater than zero (BGTZ), less than or equal to zero (BLEZ), and less than zero (BLTZ). Of course, equal and not equal to zero can be synthesized using r0 with BEQ and BNE. Like SPARC, MIPS uses a condition code for floating point with separate floating-point compare and branch instructions.

The M88000 also uses registers to evaluate conditions and optimizes compare to 0 with a separate set of compare-and-branch instructions (BCND.N). Comparison of arbitrary operands differs. MIPS offers several compare instructions to set the register to 0 or 1 depending on the selected condition, but the M88000 uses a single instruction (CMP) and sets 10 bits of the destination register showing the relationship of the two operands. These bits represent equality (=, ≠) plus all relations for signed (<, ≤, >, ≥) and unsigned (<, ≤, >, ≥) operands. Instructions that branch if a bit in a register is 1 (BB1.N) or 0 (BB0.N) complete the conditional branch set. (Another option is using EXTU with CMP to set a register to 0 or 1 and then using BCND.N. Using EXT instead of EXTU sets a register to 0 or −1, if so desired.) Since there is a common register set for integer and floating point, floating-point compare uses the same scheme: set bits of a register and branch based on the result using BB1.N or BB0.N.

The Intel i860 uses condition codes for branches like SPARC, except that the i860 condition codes are set implicitly as part of every integer arithmetic or logical instruction. Also unlike SPARC, the i860 uses just two bits of conditions: OF and CC. OF is set only by the integer add and subtract instructions, and is used to indicate overflow. There is no conditional branch instruction to test this bit, but the INTOVR instruction will cause a trap if the bit is set. The CC bit is set or cleared depending on the operation. The logical instructions (AND,OR,XOR) set CC if the result is 0. The unsigned arithmetic instructions (ADDU,SUBU) set CC if there is a carry out of the most significant bit. Signed subtract (SUBS) sets CC if Rs2 > Rs1, while signed add (ADDS) sets CC if Rs2 is less than the two's complement of Rs1. Floating-point comparison instructions set CC if the condition tested is true: greater than (PFGT), less than or equal (PFLE), or equal (PFEQ).

The i860 conditional branch instructions (BC.T and BNC.T) test CC and branch depending on whether CC is 1 or 0. The i860 also has conditional branch instructions based on equality of two operands: BTE jumps if they are equal and BTNE jumps if they are not.

Figure E.6 summarizes the four schemes used for conditional branches.

	DLX	i860	MIPS	M88000	SPARC
Number of condition code bits (integer and FP)	1 FP	1 both, 1 integer	1 FP	--	4 integer, 2 FP
Basic compare instructions (integer and FP)	1 integer, 1 FP	1 FP	1 integer, 1 FP	1 integer, 1 FP	1 FP
Basic branch instructions (integer and FP)	1 integer, 1 FP	1 both, 1 integer	2 integer, 1 FP	1 both, 1 integer	1 integer, 1 FP
Compare register with register/const and branch	=,≠	=,≠	=,≠	--	--
Compare register to zero and branch	=,≠	=,≠	=,≠,<,≤,>,≥	=,≠,<,≤,>,≥	--

FIGURE E.6 Summary of five approaches to conditional branches. Integer compare on the i860 and SPARC is synthesized with an arithmetic instruction that sets the condition codes using r0 as the destination.

Integer Multiply and Divide

Multiply and divide are usually implemented as multicycle instructions and are thus not a good match for the single-cycle execution goal of the rest of the integer instructions, requiring separate integration into the pipeline. Each architecture takes a different approach to integer multiply and divide as well as conditional branch. The i860 uses the same scheme as DLX: there is a floating-point instruction (FMLOW) that treats the contents of two floating-point registers as integers, leaving a 32-bit result in the lower 32 bits of a double-precision pair of floating-point registers. Programs do integer divide using i860 floating-point instructions. (Floating-point divide uses Newton-Raphson iteration; see pages E-19–E-20.)

The combined integer and floating-point register file allows the M88000 to use the floating-point unit to perform integer multiply and divide, as the operands do not have to be moved to and from the floating-point registers. The one complication in the first version of the architecture, the MC88100, is a negative dividend or negative divisor results in a trap. Software then makes the operands positive, uses the divide instruction, and then complements the quotient (if necessary). A zero divisor traps as well, as we would hope.

In the MIPS architecture the 64-bit product of an integer multiply or the quotient/remainder of an integer divide is placed in a special registers HI and LO. This computation is treated as an independent unit executing in parallel with the integer and floating-point units. The appropriate result is transferred to the correct register with a MFHI or MFLO instruction. Attempts to read the registers before the computation is complete stalls the processor. There is no trap for overflow or divide by zero. These are typically checked by explicit integer instructions that execute in parallel with the divide. (See Section E.5 for architectural extensions not implemented in the first MIPS machines.)

SPARC provides a multiply step instruction. When used in a loop it calculates a full 64-bit product using the special register Y. It is loaded with the multiplier and receives the least significant word of the product. Magenheimer, Peters, Pettis, and Zuras [1988] measured the size of operands in multiplies and divides to show how well the multiply step would work. Using this data for C programs, Muchnick [1988] found that by making special cases the average multiply by a constant takes 6 clock cycles and multiply of variables takes 24 clock cycles. There is no divide step in the SPARC. (See Section E.6 for architectural extensions not implemented in the first SPARC machines.)

E.4 | Instructions: Common Extensions to DLX

Figure E.7 (pages E-10–E-11) lists instructions not found in Figure E.5 (pages E-5–E-6) in the same four categories. Instructions are put in this list if they appear in more than one of the four architectures. The instructions are defined using the hardware description language, which is described on the page facing the inside back cover and on pages 160–167 of Chapter 4.

While most of the categories are self-explanatory, a few bear comment:

- The "Atomic swap" row means a primitive that can exchange a register with memory without interruption. This is useful for operating system semaphores in uniprocessors as well as for multiprocessor synchronization (see pages 471–473 of Chapter 8.)

- In the "Endian" row, "Big or Little" means there is a bit in the program status register that allows the processor to act either as Big Endian or Little Endian. This can be accomplished by simply complementing some of the least significant bits of the address in data transfer instructions.

- The "Coprocessor operations" row lists several categories that allow for the processor to be extended with special-purpose hardware.

- The "Implicit conversions" row under "Floating point" means that floating-point operands in these architectures do not have to all be the same size, and the floating-point unit performs a conversion as part of the operation. The i860 allows for two single-precision operands to produce a double-precision result while the M88000 allows for any combination of single and double precisions for each of the three operands.

One difference that needs a longer explanation is the optimized branches. Figure E.8 (page E-12) shows the options. The i860 and M88000 offer branches that take effect immediately, like branches on earlier architectures. This avoids executing NOPs when there is no instruction to fill the delay slot. SPARC provides a version of delayed branch that makes it easier to fill the delay slot. The "annulling" branch executes the instruction in the delay slot only if the branch is taken; otherwise the instruction is annulled. This means the instruction at the target of the branch can safely be copied into the delay slot since it will only be executed if the branch is taken. The restrictions are that the target is not another branch and that the target is known at compile time. SPARC also offers a nondelayed jump because an unconditional branch with the annul bit set does **not** execute the following instruction.

After covering the similarities, we will cover the unique features of each architecture, ordering them by length of description of the unique features from shortest to longest.

Name	Definition	i860	MIPS	M88000	SPARC
Data transfer					
Atomic swap R/M (for semaphores)	Temp←Rd; Rd← Mem[x]; Mem[x]←Temp	`LOCK;LD.L;` `UNLOCK; ST.L;`	-- (see E.5)	`XMEM,` `XMEMBU`	`SWAP`
Load double integer	Rd←Mem[x]; Rd+1←Mem[x+4]	--	--	`LD.D`	`LDD`
Store double integer	Mem[x]←Rd; Mem[x+4]←Rd+1	--	--	`ST.D`	`STD`
Load coprocessor	Coprocessor←Mem[x]	--	`LWCi`	--	`LDC`
Store coprocessor	Mem[x]←Coprocessor	--	`SWCi`	--	`STC`
Endian	(Big/Little Endian?)	Big or Little	Big or Little	Big or Little	Big
Cache flush	(Flush cache block at this address)	`FLUSH`	-- (see E.5)	--	`FLUSH`
Arithmetic, logical					
Support for multi-word integer add	CarryOut,Rd ← Rs1 + Rs2 + OldCarryOut	`ADDU;BNC;` `ADDU ...,...,#1`	`ADDU;SLTU;` `ADDU`	`ADDU.CIO`	`ADDXcc`
Support for multi-word integer sub	CarryOut,Rd ← Rs1 − Rs2 + OldCarryOut	`SUBU;BNC;` `ADDU ....,...,#1`	`SUBU;SLTU;` `SUBU`	`SUBU.CIO`	`SUBXcc`
And not	Rd ← Rs1 & !(Rs2)	`ANDNOT`	--	`AND.C` *(R–R)*	`ANDN`
Or not	Rd ← Rs1 | !(Rs2)	--	--	`OR.C` *(R–R)*	`ORN`
Xor not	Rd ← Rs1 ^ !(Rs2)	--	--	`XOR.C` *(R–R)*	`XNOR`

	Definition	i860	MIPS	M88000	SPARC
Arithmetic, logical *(continued)*					
And high immediate	$Rd_{0..15} \leftarrow Rs1_{0..15}$ & (Const<<16); $Rd_{16..31} \leftarrow 0$	ANDH *(R–I)*	--	AND.U *(R–I)*	--
Or high immediate	$Rd_{0..15} \leftarrow Rs1_{0..15}$ | (Const<<16); $Rd_{16..31} \leftarrow 0$	ORH *(R–I)*	--	OR.U *(R–I)*	--
Xor high immediate	$Rd_{0..15} \leftarrow Rs1_{0..15}$ ^ (Const<<16); $Rd_{16..31} \leftarrow 0$	XORH *(R–I)*	--	XOR.U *(R–I)*	--
Coprocessor operations	(Defined by coprocessor)	--	COPi	--	CPop
Control					
Optimized delayed branches	(Branch not always delayed)	BC,BNC	--	BB1,BB0, BCND	Bicc,A
Optimized floating-point branches	(Branch not always delayed)	BC,BNC	--	BB1,BB0, BCND	Bfcc,A
Conditional trap	if (COND) {R31←PC; PC ←0..0#i}	--	-- (see E.5)	TB1, TB0, TCND	Ticc
Branch on coprocessor	if (CoProc COND) {PC ←PC+Const}	--	BCiT,BCiF	--	Bccc
No. control regs.	Misc. regs (virtual memory, interrupts,...)	6	12	32	7
Floating point					
Negate	Fd ← Fs ^ x80000000	--	NEG.S, NEG.D	XOR.U 8000	NEGS
Absolute value	Fd ← Fs & x7FFFFFFF	--	ABS.S, ABS.D	AND.U 7FFF	ABSS
Truncate to integer	Fd ← unrounded integer part of Fs	FTRUNC.SS, FTRUNC.DS	--	TRNC.SS, TRNC.SD	--
Implicit conversions	(Convert as part of operation)	_.SD (2 single operands, 1 double result)	--	_.SSD,_.SDS, _.SDD,_.DSS, _.DSD._.DDS (all combinations)	--

FIGURE E.7 Instructions not found in DLX but found in two or more of the four architectures. Both MIPS and SPARC have new instructions that were not implemented in the first machine and that apply to some of these cases: see Sections E.5 and E.6.

	Delayed branch	(Plain) Branch	Annulling delayed branch
Found in architectures	All 5 RISCs	i860, M88000	SPARC
Execute following instruction	Always	Only if branch **not** taken	Only if branch taken

FIGURE E.8 When the instruction following the branch is executed for three types of branches.

E.5 | Instructions Unique to MIPS

Starting with data transfer instructions, MIPS is unlike the others since the architecture requires that the instruction following a load does not refer to the value being loaded. The MIPS Assembler inserts a NOOP instruction if this situation occurs.

Nonaligned Data Transfers

The other unique feature of MIPS data transfer is special instructions to handle misaligned words in memory. A rare event in most programs, it is included for COBOL programs where the programmer can force misalignment by declarations. While all these architectures trap if you try to load a word or store a word to a misaligned address, on all architectures misaligned words can be accessed without traps by using 4 load byte instructions and then assembling the result using shifts and logical ORs. The MIPS load and store word left and right instructions (LWL, LWR, SWL, SWR) allow this to be done in just 2 instructions: LWL loads the left portion of the register and LWR loads the right portion of the register. SWL and SWR do the corresponding stores. Figure E.9 shows how they work. Unlike other loads, a LWL followed by a LWR does not require a NOOP even though both will specify the same register since fields do not overlap.

TLB Instructions

TLB misses are handled in software in the MIPS R2000, so the instruction set also has instructions for manipulating the registers of the TLB (see pages 437–438 and 443–445 in Chapter 8 for more on TLBs.) These registers are considered part of the "system coprocessor" and thus can be accessed by the instructions that move between coprocessor registers and integer registers. The contents of a TLB entry are read by loading via Read Indexed TLB Entry (TLBR) and written using either Write Indexed TLB Entry (TLBWI) or Write Random TLB Entry (TLBWR). The TLB contents are searched using Probe TLB for Matching Entry (TLBP).

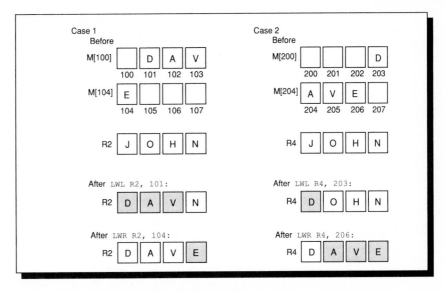

FIGURE E.9 MIPS instructions for unaligned word reads. This figure assumes operating in Big Endian mode. Case (1) first loads the 3 bytes 101,102, and 103 into the left of R2 leaving the least significant byte undisturbed. The following LWR simply loads byte 104 into the least significant byte of R2 leaving the other bytes of the register unchanged using LWL. Case (2) first loads byte 203 into the most significant byte of R4 and the following LWR loads the other 3 bytes of R4 from memory bytes 204, 205, and 206. LWL reads the word with the first byte from memory, shifts to the left to discard the unneeded byte(s), and changes only those bytes in Rd. The byte(s) transferred are from the first byte until the lowest-order byte of the word. The following LWR addresses the last byte, right shifts to discard the unneeded byte(s), and finally changes only those bytes of Rd. The byte(s) transferred are from the last byte up to the highest-order byte of the word. Store word left (SWL) is simply the inverse of LWL, and store word right (SWR) is the inverse of LWR. Changing to Little Endian mode flips which bytes are selected and discarded. (If big/little–left/right–load/store seems confusing, don't worry, it works!)

Remaining Instructions

Below is a list of the remaining unique details of the MIPS architecture:

- *NOR:* This logical instruction calculates !(Rs1 | Rs2).

- *Constant shift amount:* Nonvariable shifts use the 5-bit constant field shown in the register–register format in Figure E.3.

- *SYSCALL:* This special trap instruction is used to invoke the operating system.

- *Move to/from control registers:* CTCi and CFCi move between the integer registers and control registers.

- *Limited single-precision registers:* Although the 32 floating-point registers can be addressed individually for loads and stores, single-precision operands for floating-point operations can use only the 16 even floating-point registers.

- *Jump/Call not PC-relative:* The 26-bit address of jumps and calls is not added to the PC. It is shifted left 2 bits and replaces the lower 28 bits of the PC. This would only make a difference if the program was located near a 256-MB boundary.

- *Conditional procedure call instructions*: BGEZAL saves the return address and branches if the contents of Rs1 is greater than or equal to zero, and BLTZAL does the same for less than zero. The purpose of these instructions is to get a PC-relative call.

There is no specific provision in the MIPS architecture for floating-point execution to proceed in parallel with integer execution, but the MIPS implementations of floating point allow this to happen by checking to see if arithmetic interrupts are possible early in the cycle; normally interrupts are not possible and integer and floating point operate in parallel (see page A-31 in Appendix A).

MIPS II

With the announcement of the R6000 came a set of extensions to the original MIPS architecture described above. Here are the additions of MIPS II:

- *Interlocked loads:* The MIPS II Assembler need not insert a NOP after a load if there is a dependency on the following instruction, as the hardware will automatically stall.

- *Branch likely:* Equivalent to the SPARC annulled branches, this instruction executes the instruction in the delay slot only if the branch is taken.

- *Load double floating point and store double floating point:* MIPS II takes a single instruction to load or store double-precision floating-point numbers.

- *SQRT:* Single- and double-precision floating-point square root are added to the floating-point operations.

- *Conditional trap instructions:* These match the conditional branch instructions, except they are not delayed: When the trap is taken, the following instruction is **not** executed. These instructions are useful for range checking, popular in Ada.

E.6 | Instructions Unique to SPARC

Register Windows

The primary unique feature of SPARC is register windows (pages 450–453 of Chapter 8), used to reduce the register save/restore overhead of procedure calls and returns. SPARC can have between 2 and 32 windows, using 8 registers each for the globals, locals, incoming parameters, and outgoing parameters (see Figure 8.34 page 452.) (Given each window has 16 unique registers, an implementation of SPARC can have as few as 40 physical registers and as many as 520, although most have 128 to 136, so far.) Rather than tie window changes with call and return instructions, SPARC has the separate instructions SAVE and RESTORE. SAVE is used to "save" the caller's window by pointing to the next window of registers in addition to performing an add instruction. The trick is that the source registers are from the caller's window of the addition operation while the destination register is in the callee's window. SPARC compilers typically use this instruction for changing the stack pointer to allocate local variables in a new stack frame. RESTORE is the inverse of SAVE, bringing back the caller's window while acting as an add instruction, with the source registers from the callee's window and the destination register in the caller's window. This automatically deallocates the stack frame. Compilers can also make use of it for generating the callee's final return value. Unlike earlier register window architectures, SPARC uses a Window Invalid Mask, which is used in real-time applications, that allows the windows to be partitioned between different processes.

Another data transfer feature is alternate space option for loads and stores. This simply allows the memory system to identify memory accesses to input/output devices, or to control registers for devices such as the cache and memory-management unit.

Support for LISP and Smalltalk

The primary remaining arithmetic feature is tagged addition and subtraction. The designers of SPARC spent some time thinking about languages like LISP and Smalltalk, and this influenced some of the features of SPARC already discussed: register windows, conditional trap instructions, calls with 32-bit instruction addresses, and multiword arithmetic (see Taylor [1986] and Ungar [1984]). A small amount of support is offered for tagged data types with operations for addition, subtraction, and hence comparison. The two least significant bits indicate whether the operand is an integer (coded as 00), so TADDcc and TSUBcc set the overflow bit if either operand is not tagged as integer or if the result is too large. A subsequent conditional branch or trap instruction can decide what to do. (If the operands are not integers, software recovers the operands, checks the types of the operands, and invokes the correct operation based on those types.) Two other versions of these instructions make the conditional trap unnecessary, as `TADDccTV` and `TSUBccTV` trap if the overflow is set. It turns out that the misaligned memory access trap can also be put to use for tagged data, since loading from a pointer with the wrong tag can be an invalid access. Figure E.10 shows both types of tag support.

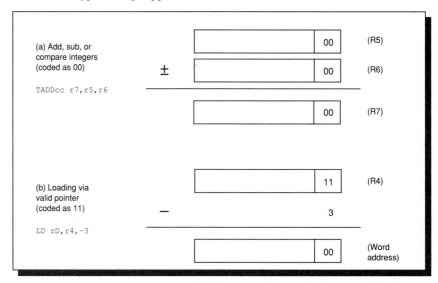

FIGURE E.10 SPARC uses the two least significant bits to encode different data types for the tagged arithmetic instructions. (a) shows integer arithmetic, which takes a single cycle as long as the operands and the result are integers. (b) shows that the misaligned trap can be used to catch invalid memory accesses, such as trying to use an integer as a pointer. For languages with paired data like LISP, an offset of –3 can be used to access the even word of a pair (CAR) and +1 can be used for the odd word of a pair (CDR).

Overlapped Integer and Floating-Point Operations

SPARC allows floating-point instructions to overlap execution with integer instructions. To recover from an interrupt during such a situation, SPARC has a queue of pending floating-point instructions and their addresses. `STDFQ` allows the processor to empty the queue. The second floating-point feature is the inclusion of floating-point square root instructions `FSQRTS` and `FSQRTD`.

Remaining Instructions

The remaining unique features of SPARC are:

- *JMPL* uses Rd to specify the return address register, so specifying `r31` makes it similar to `JALR` in DLX and specifying `r0` makes it like `JR`.

- *LDSTUB* loads the value of the byte into Rd and then stores FF_{16} into the addressed byte. This instruction can be used to implement a semaphore.

- *LDDC and STDC* provide load double and store double for the coprocessor.

- *UNIMP* causes an unimplemented instruction interrupt. Muchnick [1988] explains how this is used for proper execution of aggregate returning procedures in C.

Finally, SPARC includes opcodes for instructions that are emulated in software on early implementations. SPARC application programs generally call dynamically linked library routines to perform these operations, but the opcodes would result in a trap if executed. The instructions are:

- *Signed and unsigned integer multiply and divide*, with both operands and the results being integer registers. The extra 32 bits of a product and the 32-bit remainder of a divide are placed in the Y register.

- *Quadruple precision floating-point arithmetic*, allowing the floating-point registers to act as eight 128-bit registers.

- *Multiple precision floating-point results for multiply*, meaning two single-precision operands can result in a double-precision product and two double-precision operands can result in a quadruple-precision product. These instructions can be useful in complex arithmetic and some models of floating-point calculations.

E.7 | Instructions Unique to M88000

The most distinguishing feature of the M88000 is the single set of 32 registers for both integer and floating-point operations. This simplifies the instruction set at the cost of fewer registers for floating-point programs.

Bit Instructions

The next feature unique to the M88000 is a full set of bit-field instructions, shown in Figure E.11 (page E-18). (While we usually number the most significant bit 0, in this table we follow Motorola's notation, which numbers the most significant bit 31 and the least significant bit 0.) Bit-field instructions need an extra operand to specify the width of the field in addition to the destination register, source register, and beginning of the bit field. This 5-bit width field is located next to the bit field in source 2. The M88000 encodes a width of 0 to mean the full 32-bit value, hence the traditional shift instructions (SLL, SRL, SRA) are simply the corresponding bit-field instructions (MAK, EXTU, EXT) with 0 in the width field.

Name	Instruction	Notation
CLR	Clear bit field	$Rd_{(o+w)..(o+1)} \leftarrow 0^w$
SET	Set bit field	$Rd_{(o+w)..(o+1)} \leftarrow 1^w$
EXT	Extract signed bit field	if (w==0) {Rd ← $Rs1_{31}^o$ ## (Rs1 >> o) } else {Rd ← $(Rs1_{(o+w)})^o$ ## ($Rs1_{(o+w)..(o+1)}$ >> o) }
EXTU	Extract unsigned bit field	if (w==0) {Rd ← 0° ## (Rs1 >> o) } else {Rd ← 0° ## ($Rs1_{(o+w)..(o+1)}$ >> o) }
MAK	Make bit field	if (w==0) {Rd ← Rs1 << o} else {$Rd_{(o+w)..(o+1)}$ ← $Rs1_{(w-1)..0}$ }
ROT	Rotate right	Rd ← $Rs1_{(o-1)..0}$ ## $Rs1_{31..o}$
FF0	Find first bit clear	for (i=31;$Rs2_i$==0||i<0;i ← i-1); /* loop until = 0*/ if(i<0) {Rd ← 32} else {Rd ← i}
FF1	Find first bit set	for (i=31;$Rs2_i$==1||i<0;i ← i-1); /* loop until =1 */ if(i<0) {Rd ← 32} else {Rd ← i}

FIGURE E.11 The M88000 bit-field instructions. The bit offset, o, is the least significant five bits of the second operand and the bit-field width, w, is the five bits next to the offset. The subscript notation specifies a bit field while the superscript notation means replicate the bit that many times. Note that in this table, bit 31 refers to the most significant bit, and 0 refers to the least significant bit.

Remaining Instructions

The final unique instructions are load address (LDA), MASK, round to nearest integer (NINT), trap on bounds (TBND), and exchange control register (XCR):

- LDA loads Rd with the effective address rather than the data in memory. The only time this is different from ADDU is for scaled addressing of nonbyte data.

- MASK is simply another case of logical AND immediate: This instruction clears the other half of the word while AND immediate leaves it undisturbed. Thus, ANDI in DLX is arguably closer to MASK than to AND immediate in the M88000.

- NINT differs from INT in that it rounds to the nearest integer no matter how the rounding modes are set (see Appendix A, pages A-16 to A-17).

- TBND traps if Rs1 > Rs2, treating them as unsigned numbers (see page 239 in Chapter 5 for an explanation of how an unsigned comparison can check two signed bounds at once).

- XCR exchanges a control register with an integer register.

In addition to instructions, here are a few features that distinguish the M88000:

- Double-length operations use Rn and Rn+1 rather than an even-odd register pair. This gives the M88000 more flexibility in register allocation, which is important given the lack of floating-point registers.

- The first implementation, the MC88100, allows all multicycle instructions to overlap execution with following instructions unless there is a data hazard (see pages 264–265 in Chapter 6). Also, all floating-point instructions except divide are pipelined, taking just one cycle to issue single-precision operations and two cycles to issue double-precision operations. The 88000 provides a set of shadow registers (see Section 5.6) for floating-point operands to help software handle both precise and imprecise interrupts (see Motorola [1988]).

- There are special data transfers, identified by appending .USR to the instructions, that allow access to the user's data while in supervisor mode.

E.8 | Instructions Unique to i860

The i860 has many unique features. Before covering the special extensions for graphics and high-performance floating point, let's cover the traditional areas.

The unique data transfers are for floating point only. The i860 provides 128-bit loads (FLD.Q) and stores (FST.Q) of pairs of 64-bit floating-point registers. It also provides an optional addressing mode on all floating-point loads and stores: the effective address (sum of Rs1/Const and Rs2) is stored back into Rs2. One unique characteristic is that the i860 seems to run out of opcode bits for load instructions because it uses the least significant bit to distinguish load halfword from load word. This works fine for the register–register format since bit 0 is an opcode extension field in this format, but in register–immediate format this is the least significant bit of the constant field. To avoid crazy addressing problems, this bit is cleared when used as an address. This prevents having an odd value in an index register that is corrected by an odd byte address in the constant field for halfword and word data transfers (see E.10(b) on page E-16 for a reason this is useful.)

The only unique arithmetic logical instruction is a double-length shift-right logical (SHRD). Rs1 and Rs2 are shifted right as a pair and then the 32 least significant bits are placed into Rd. Since there is no room in the instruction to specify the shift amount, SHRD uses the shift amount from the last SHR instruction. This value is saved in the 5-bit SC field of the program status word. By the way, SHRD can be used to perform a 32-bit rotate by having Rs1 and Rs2 specify the same register.

The i860 control instructions include a loop instruction called BLA. This instruction both performs an add and a conditional branch. Since it is likely that another instruction in the loop would change the condition code, the i860 has a special loop condition code (LCC) just for this instruction. BLA performs Rd ← Rs1+Rs2 and branches if LCC equals 1. In addition, BLA sets the LCC for the next time through the loop if Rs2 ≥ –Rs1 and clears it otherwise. (LCC is set just the opposite of how ADDS sets CC.)

While i860 does not have floating-point divide, it does have a floating-point reciprocal instruction (FRCP). Used with Newton-Raphson iteration (pages A-23–A-24 of Appendix A), this calculates divide that disagrees with the IEEE floating-point standard (IEEE 754) in the 2 least significant bits. Intel offers software to produce the correctly rounded result at twice the cycle count. A similar instruction, FRSQR, calculates a reciprocal step for square root. The floating-point instructions also include 64-bit integer addition and subtraction (FIADD.DD and FISUB.DD) using the floating-point registers.

This covers the unique features in the traditional categories, so let's describe the new categories of the i860.

Graphics Instructions

The graphics or *pixel* instructions of i860 operate on 64 bits of data at a time, with each word representing several pixels. Pixel instructions are intended to be useful in graphics operations such as hidden surface elimination (see page 525 in Chapter 9), distance interpolation, and three-dimensional shading using intensity interpolation. These special-purpose instructions are not simple to understand, so interested readers should refer to the manual for details.

The overview of the operations is that two bits in the program status word determine the size of the pixels in a 64-bit word. Pixels can be 8-, 16-, or 32-bits wide, with each size containing fields representing intensity of the primary colors red, blue, and green. Some pixel instructions work with a 64-bit accumulator called the MERGE register, useful in collecting the results of a series of calculations on pixels. In addition to "merge" instructions (FADDP and FADDZ), the i860 has instructions for z buffers (page 525) that compare two sets of four 16-bit (FZCHKS) or two 32-bit (FZCHKL) values, storing the smaller values in the 64-bit destination register and setting bits indicating which was smaller in the program status word. Pixel-store instructions (PST) then use those bits to selectively store only those pixels that were smaller. Finally, the FORM instruction is used to move the MERGE register into a floating-point register and then clear MERGE.

Pipelined Mode

For higher performance, the i860 offers pipelined versions of all the floating-point and pixel instructions. One model for these instructions is to use them to build vector primitives, allowing procedures to be written to implement vector operations (see Chapter 7). The hope is that existing vectorizing compilers could invoke these more efficient procedures. Another model, used by compilers currently under development at Intel's behest, tries to compile directly into these instructions for both vector and nonvector codes.

In *pipelined mode,* an instruction is launched every cycle, but unlike other pipelined machines, there is no hardware to remember where the results are to be stored. Basically, the instruction issuing at the stage the pipeline completes specifies the destination! There are four independent pipelines in the i860, and each pipeline advances only when the next instruction of that type is executed. Figure E.12 shows the i860 pipelines, the number of pipeline stages, and instructions that advance each pipeline. Thus, the source fields and opcode specify the operation to be launched while the destination field specifies the register to be loaded by an instruction of the same type that is in the final stage at this cycle.

Pipeline	No. of Stages	Instructions using pipeline
FP multiplier	3 (single operands) 2 (double operands)	`PFMUL`
FP adder	3	`PFADD, PFSUB, PFGT, PFLE,` `PFEQ, PFIX, PFTRUNC`
FP load	3	`PFLD`

Graphics	1	`PFIADD, PFISUB, PFZCHKS,`
		 `PFZCHKL, PFADDP, PFADDZ,`
		 `PFORM`

FIGURE E.12 i860 pipelines, including the number of pipeline stages and instructions. All adder and multiplier instructions allow single-precision operands with single-precision results (.SS), single operands with double results (.SD), and double-precision operands with double-precision results (.DD). Since the number of stages differs for multiply depending on single or double, Intel recommends not mixing precisions involving multiplication.

For example, look at the sequence below for the floating-point adder pipeline (assume the operands are specified with the result on the left):

```
PFADD.SS    F4,  F2,  F3       ;Single Prec. Add
PFSUB.DD    F10, F8,  F6       ;Double Prec. Sub
PFMUL.DD    F16, F12, F14      ;Double Prec. Mul
PFADD.SS    F19, F17, F18      ;Single Prec. Add
PFADD.SS    F22, F20, F21      ;Single Prec. Add
```

The floating-point adder pipeline is three stages, so the first instruction launches a floating-point add of F2 and F3, but F4 is loaded from the operation in the adder pipeline launched three instructions earlier. The multiply in this sequence does not advance the adder pipeline, so the third adder pipeline instruction following the first instruction (one subtract and two adds) is the final instruction in the sequence, meaning that F22 ← F2+F3.

The load pipeline has an interesting interaction with the data cache. As long as the data is in the cache, it is fetched from the cache. On a miss the data is fetched from memory, but the cache is not updated with the new data. This policy prevents operations on large data structures from filling the cache with data that will not be reused and throwing out data that would be reused. The programmer must decide on whether to use scalar loads (FLD) or pipelined loads (PFLD), depending on whether the data is likely to be reused or not.

Scalar instructions will normally empty the pipeline. (The exception is the load pipeline because FLD or LD don't empty it.) Thus, before executing a scalar floating-point instruction there must be a sequence of dummy pipelined instructions that store the results away. For example, there is no pipelined version of the floating-point instruction used for integer multiply (FMLOW), so the pipeline must be drained if an integer multiply is needed during a floating-point calculation.

Summarizing pipelined mode on the i860, the advantages are

- Pipeline control is simple (basically it is done in software).

- It doesn't need many registers, since they are not reserved during the operation.

The disadvantages are:

- Operations must be performed to empty the pipeline.

- The interrupt mechanism is complicated, taking longer to recover the state.

- Sometimes the pipeline is hard to use.

- Code size may mushroom (this has not yet been quantified).

Add/Sub and Multiply

To squeeze even more performance from the floating-point unit, the i860 has pipelined instructions that simultaneously perform an add and multiply (PFAM and PFMAM) or a subtract and multiply (PFSM and PFMSM), advancing the pipelines of both the add and multiply units. Since each instruction needs 4 sources and 2 destinations, the i860 has three registers that can also be used in addition to the three floating-point registers specified in the instruction. The registers KI and KR, optionally loaded from Rs1, can be sources for the multiplier, and register T can be a destination of the multiplier or a source for the adder. The final stage of adder pipeline and multiplier pipeline can also be sources. Four bits in each instruction specify a variety of combinations of the operands and the operations.

Dual Instruction Mode

Finally, the i860 allows an integer and a floating-point instruction to be fetched and executed simultaneously. This long instruction word or superscalar form of operation (pages 318–322 in Chapter 6) is called *dual-instruction mode* in the i860. Simultaneous execution occurs in this mode when the upper instruction of an aligned doubleword is an integer instruction and the lower is a floating-point instruction with the "D" bit set (bit 9 = 1). Entering or exiting the mode is delayed: When the i860 finds an instruction with the D bit set, it executes one more instruction before entering dual-instruction mode; and, similarly, when the i860 is in dual-instruction mode and finds a D bit not set, it executes one more pair before going to sequential execution.

Clearly, highest performance comes when the i860 is in both dual-instruction and pipelined modes.

E.9 | Concluding Remarks

This appendix covers the addressing modes, instruction formats, and all instructions found in four recent architectures. While the later sections concentrate on the differences, it would not be possible to cover four architectures in these few pages if there were not so many similarities. In fact, we would guess that more than 90% of the instructions executed for any of these architectures would be found in Figure E.3 (page E-3). To illustrate this homogeneity, Figure E.13 gives a summary for four architectures from the 1970s similar to Figure E.1 (page E-2). (Imagine trying to write a single appendix in this style for those architectures.) In the history of computing, there has never been such widespread agreement on computer architecture.

	IBM 360/370	Intel 8086	Motorola 68000	DEC VAX
Date announced	1964/1970	1978	1980	1977
Instruction size(s) (bits)	16, 32, 48	8,16,24,32, 40,48	16,32,48, 64,80	8,16,24,32, ..., 432
Addressing (size, model)	24 bits, flat	4+16 bits, segmented	24 bits, flat	32 bits, flat
Data aligned?	Yes 360/ No 370	No	16-bit aligned	No
Data addressing modes	4	5	9	≥ 14
Protection	Page	None	Optional	Page
Page size	4 KB	--	0.25 to 32 KB	0.5 KB
I/O	Opcode	Opcode	Memory mapped	Memory mapped
Integer registers (size, model, number)	16 GPR x 32 bits	8 dedicated data x 16 bits	8 data & 8 address x 32 bits	15 GPR x 32 bits
Separate floating-point registers	4 x 64 bits	Optional: 8 x 80 bits	Optional: 8 x 80 bits	0
Floating-point format	IBM	IEEE 754 single, double, extended	IEEE 754 single, double, extended	DEC

FIGURE E.13 Summary of four 1970s architectures. Unlike the architectures in Figure E.1 (page E-2), there is little agreement between these architectures in any category. (See Chapter 4 for more details on the 370, 8086, and VAX.)

This style of architectures cannot remain static, however. One hard lesson is that address space must grow, so the 32-bit size of all these architectures must expand for them to survive. In terms of their implementation, we expect all to offer superscalar execution of 2 to 4 instructions per cycle. The hardware technology will go beyond the current CMOS VLSI and ECL to BiCMOS, and possibly even Gallium Arsenide. Our guess is that all of them will grow beyond the current market of workstations and peripheral controllers to minicomputers, mainframes, and even supercomputers, with increasing numbers of processors per computer class.

E.10 | References

INTEL [1989]. *i860 64-Bit Microprocessor Programmer's Reference Manual.*

KANE, G. [1988]. *MIPS RISC Architecture,* Prentice-Hall, Englewood Cliffs, N. J.

MOTOROLA [1988]. *MC88100 RISC Microprocessor User's Manual.*

MAGENHEIMER, D. J., L. PETERS, K. W. PETTIS AND D. ZURAS [1988]. "Integer multiplication and division on the HP Precision Architecture," *IEEE Trans. on Computers,* 37:8, 980–990.

MUCHNICK, S. S. [1988]. "Optimizing compilers for SPARC," *Sun Technology* (Summer) 1:3, 64–77.

SUN MICROSYSTEMS [1989]. *The SPARC Architectural Manual,* Version 8, Part No. 800-1399-09, August 25, 1989.

TAYLOR, G., P. HILFINGER, J. LARUS, D. PATTERSON, AND B. ZORN [1986]. "Evaluation of the SPUR LISP architecture," *Proc. 13th Symposium on Computer Architecture* (June), Tokyo.

UNGAR, D., R. BLAU, P. FOLEY, D. SAMPLES, AND D. PATTERSON [1984]. "Architecture of SOAR: Smalltalk on a RISC," *Proc. 11th Symposium on Computer Architecture* (June), Ann Arbor, Mich., 188–197.

References

The following is a compilation of all the references listed in the reference section of each chapter. The page number of where each reference appears in the book is in parentheses after the reference.

ADAMS, T. AND R. ZIMMERMAN [1989]. "An analysis of 8086 instruction set usage in MS DOS programs," *Proc. Third Symposium on Architectural Support for Programming Languages and Systems* (April) Boston, 152–161. (p. 188)

AGARWAL, A. [1987]. *Analysis of Cache Performance for Operating Systems and Multiprogramming*, Ph.D. Thesis, Stanford Univ., Tech. Rep. No. CSL-TR-87-332 (May). (p. 487)

AGARWAL, A., R. L. SITES, AND M. HOROWITZ [1986]. "ATUM: A new technique for capturing address traces using microcode," *Proc. 13th Annual Symposium on Computer Architecture* (June 2–5), Tokyo, Japan, 119–127. (p. 486)

AGERWALA, T. AND J. COCKE [1987]. "High performance reduced instruction set processors," IBM Tech. Rep. (March). (p. 340)

ALEXANDER, W. G. AND D. B. WORTMAN [1975]. "Static and dynamic characteristics of XPL programs," *Computer* 8:11 (November) 41–46. (pp. 130, 187)

ALLIANT COMPUTER SYSTEMS CORP. [1987]. *Alliant FX/Series: Product Summary* (June), Acton, Mass. (p. 395)

ALMASI, G. S. AND A. GOTTLIEB [1989]. *Highly Parallel Computing,* Benjamin/Cummings, Redwood City, Calif. (p. 589)

AMDAHL, G. M. [1967]. "Validity of the single processor approach to achieving large scale computing capabilities," *Proc. AFIPS Spring Joint Computer Conf.* 30, Atlantic City, N. J. (April) 483–485. (pp. 26, 588)

AMDAHL, G. M., G. A. BLAAUW, AND F. P. BROOKS, JR. [1964]. "Architecture of the IBM System/360," *IBM J. Research and Development* 8:2 (April) 87–101. (pp. 127, 186)

ANDERSON, D. W., F. J. SPARACIO, AND R. M. TOMASULO [1967]. "The IBM 360 Model 91: Machine philosophy and instruction handling," *IBM J. of Research and Development* 11:1 (January) 8–24. (p. 339)

ANDERSON, S. F., J. G. EARLE, R. E. GOLDSCHMIDT, AND D. M. POWERS [1967]. "The IBM System/360 Model 91: Floating-point execution unit," *IBM J. Research and Development* 11, 34–53. Reprinted in [Swartzlander 1980]. (p. A-59)

ANDREWS, G. R. AND F. B. SCHNEIDER [1983]. "Concept and notations for concurrent programming," *Computing Surveys* 15:1 (March) 3–43. (p. 590)

ANON ET AL. [1985]. "A measure of transaction processing power," Tandem Tech. Rep. TR 85.2. Also appeared in *Datamation*, April 1, 1985. (p. 511)

ARCHIBALD, J. AND J.-L. BAER [1986]. "Cache coherence protocols: Evaluation using a multiprocessor simulation model," *ACM Trans. on Computer Systems* 4:4 (November) 273–298. (p. 487)

ATANASOFF, J. V. [1940]. "Computing machine for the solution of large systems of linear equations," Internal Report, Iowa State University. (p. 24)

ATKINS, D. E. [1968]. "Higher-radix division using estimates of the divisor and partial remainders," *IEEE Trans. on Computers* C-17:10, 925–934. Reprinted in [Swartzlander 1980]. (p. A-60)

BAER, J.-L. AND E.-H. WANG [1988]. "On the inclusion property for multi-level cache hierarchies," *Proc. 15th Annual Symposium on Computer Architecture* (May–June), Honolulu, 73–80. (p. 487)

BAKOGLU, H. B., G. F. GROHOSKI, L. E. THATCHER, J. A. KAHLE, C. R. MOORE, D. P. TUTTLE, W. E. MAULE, W. R. HARDELL, D. A. HICKS, M. NGUYEN PHU, R. K. MONTOYE, W. T. GLOVER , AND S. DHAWAN [1989]. "IBM second-generation RISC machine organization," *Proc. Int'l Conf. on Computer Design, IEEE* (October) Rye, N.Y., 138–142. (p. 340)

BANERJEE, U. [1979]. *Speedup of Ordinary Programs*, Ph.D. Thesis, Dept. of Computer Science, Univ. of Illinois at Urbana-Champaign (October). (p. 395)

BARTON, R. S. [1961]. "A new approach to the functional design of a computer," *Proc. Western Joint Computer Conf.*, 393–396. (p. 127)

BASHE, C. J., L. R. JOHNSON, J. H. PALMER, AND E. W. PUGH [1986]. *IBM's Early Computers*, MIT Press, Cambridge, Mass. (p. 561)

BASHE, C. J., W. BUCHHOLZ, G .V. HAWKINS, J .L. INGRAM, AND N. ROCHESTER [1981]. "The architecture of IBM's early computers," *IBM J. of Research and Development* 25:5 (September) 363–375. (p. 561)

BATCHER, K. E. [1974]. "STARAN parallel processor system hardware," *Proc. AFIPS National Computer Conf.*, 405–410. (p. 590)

BELL , C. G. AND W. D. STRECKER [1976]. "Computer structures: What have we learned from the PDP-11?," *Proc. Third Annual Symposium on Computer Architecture* (January), Pittsburgh, Penn., 1–14. (p. 485)

BELL, C. G. [1984]. "The mini and micro industries," *IEEE Computer* 17:10 (October) 14–30. (p. 27)

BELL, C. G. [1985]. "Multis: A new class of multiprocessor computers," *Science* 228 (April 26) 462–467. (p. 589)

BELL, C. G. [1989]. "The future of high performance computers in science and engineering," *Comm. ACM* 32:9 (September) 1091–1101. (p. 590)

BELL, C. G. AND A. NEWELL, [1971]. *Computer Structures: Readings and Examples,* McGraw-Hill, New York. (p. A-58)

BELL, C. G., J. C. MUDGE, AND J. E. MCNAMARA [1978]. *A DEC View of Computer Engineering,* Digital Press, Bedford, Mass. (p. 80)

BELL, C. G., R. CADY, H. MCFARLAND, B. DELAGI, J. O'LAUGHLIN, R. NOONAN, AND W. WULF [1970]. "A new architecture for mini-computers: The DEC PDP-11," *Proc. AFIPS SJCC*, 657–675. (p. 127)

BERRY, M., D. CHEN, P. KOSS, D. KUCK [1988]. "The Perfect Club benchmarks: Effective performance evaluation of supercomputers," CSRD Report No. 827 (November), Center for Supercomputing Research and Development, University of Illinois at Urbana-Champaign. (p. 80)

BIRMAN, M., G. CHU, L. HU, J. MCLEOD, N. BEDARD, F. WARE, L. TORBAN, AND C. M. LIM [1988]. "Design of a high-speed arithmetic datapath," *Proc. ICCD: VLSI Computers and Processors,* 214–216. (p. A-53)

BLAKKEN, J. [1983]. "Register windows for SOAR," in *Smalltalk On A RISC: Architectural Investigations,* Proc. of CS 292R (April) 126–140. (p. 451)

BLOCH, E. [1959]. "The engineering design of the Stretch computer," *Proc. Fall Joint Computer Conf.,* 48–59. (p. 338)

BORRILL, P. L. [1986]. "32-bit buses—An objective comparison," *Proc. Buscon 1986 West,* San Jose, Calif., 138–145. (p. 533)

BOUKNIGHT, W. J, S. A. DENEBERG, D. E. MCINTYRE, J. M. RANDALL, A. H. SAMEH, AND D. L. SLOTNICK [1972]. "The Illiac IV system," *Proc. IEEE* 60:4, 369–379. Also appears in D. P. Siewiorek, C. G. Bell, and A. Newell, *Computer Structures: Principles and Examples* (1982), 306–316. (p. 570)

BRADY, J. T. [1986]. "A theory of productivity in the creative process," *IEEE CG&A* (May) 25–34. (p. 560)

BRENT, R. P. AND H. T. KUNG [1982] "A regular layout for parallel adders," *IEEE Trans. on Computers* C-31, 260–264. (p. A-59)

BRODERSEN, R. W. [1989]. "Evolution of VLSI signal-processing circuits," *Proc. Decennial Caltech Conf. on VLSI* (March) 43–46, The MIT Press, Pasadena, Calif. (p. 590)

BUCHER, I. Y. [1983]. "The computational speed of supercomputers," *Proc. SIGMETRICS Conf. on Measuring and Modeling of Computer Systems,* ACM (August) 151–165. (p. 395)

BUCHER, I. Y. AND A. H. HAYES [1980]. "I/O Performance measurement on Cray-1 and CDC 7000 computers," *Proc. Computer Performance Evaluation Users Group, 16th Meeting,* NBS 500-65, 245–254. (p. 562)

BUCHOLTZ, W. [1962]. *Planning a Computer System: Project Stretch,* McGraw-Hill, New York. (p. 338)

BURKS, A. W., H. H. GOLDSTINE, AND J. VON NEUMANN [1946]. "Preliminary discussion of the logical design of an electronic computing instrument," Report to the U.S. Army Ordnance Department, p. 1; also appears in *Papers of John von Neumann,* W. Aspray and A. Burks, eds., The MIT Press, Cambridge, Mass. and Tomash Publishers, Los Angeles, Calif., 1987, 97–146. (p. 24)

CALLAHAN, D., J. DONGARRA, AND D. LEVINE [1988]. "Vectorizing compilers: A test suite and results," *Supercomputing '88,* ACM/IEEE (November), Orlando, Fla., 98–105. (p. 377)

CASE, R. P. AND A. PADEGS [1978]. "The architecture of the IBM System/370," *Comm. ACM* 21:1, 73–96. Also appears in D. P. Siewiorek, C. G. Bell, and A. Newell, *Computer Structures: Principles and Examples* (1982), McGraw-Hill, New York, 830–855. (pp. 186, 485)

CENSIER, L. M. AND P. FEAUTRIER [1978]. "A new solution to the coherence problem in multicache systems," *IEEE Trans. on Computers* C-27:12 (December) 1112–1118. (p. 487)

CHAITIN, G. J., M. A. AUSLANDER, A. K. CHANDRA, J. COCKE, M. E. HOPKINS, AND P. W. MARKSTEIN [1982]. "Register allocation via coloring," *Computer Languages* 6, 47–57. (p. 130)

CHARLESWORTH, A. E. [1981]. "An approach to scientific array processing: The architecture design of the AP-120B/FPS-164 family," *Computer* 14:12 (December) 12–30. (p. 340)

CHEN, P. [1989]. *An Evaluation of Redundant Arrays of Inexpensive Disks Using an Amdahl 5890,* M. S. Thesis, Computer Science Division, Tech. Rep. UCB/CSD 89/506. (p. 507)

CHEN, S. [1983]. "Large-scale and high-speed multiprocessor system for scientific applications," *Proc. NATO Advanced Research Work on High Speed Computing* (June); also in K. Hwang, ed., "Supercomputers: Design and applications," *IEEE* (August) 1984. (p. 394)

CHEN, T. C. [1980]. "Overlap and parallel processing" in *Introduction to Computer Architecture,* H. Stone, ed., Science Research Associates, Chicago, 427–486. (p. 339)

CHOW, F. C. [1983]. *A Portable Machine-Independent Global Optimizer—Design and Measurements,* Ph. D. Thesis, Stanford Univ. (December). (p. 130)

CHOW, F. C. AND J. L. HENNESSY [1984]. "Register allocation by priority-based coloring," *Proc. SIGPLAN '84 Compiler Construction (ACM SIGPLAN Notices* 19:6, June) 222–232. (p. 130)

CHOW, F., M. HIMELSTEIN, E. KILLIAN, AND L. WEBER [1986]. "Engineering a RISC compiler system," *Proc. COMPCON* (March), San Francisco, 132–137. (p. 197)

CLARK, D. W. [1983]. "Cache performance of the VAX-11/780," *ACM Trans. on Computer Systems* 1:1, 24–37. (p. 486)

CLARK, D. W. [1987]. "Pipelining and performance in the VAX 8800 processor," *Proc. Second Conf. on Architectural Support for Programming Languages and Operating Systems,* IEEE/ACM (March), Palo Alto, Calif., 173–177. (p. 272)

CLARK, D. W. AND H. LEVY [1982]. "Measurement and analysis of instruction set use in the VAX-11/780," *Proc. Ninth Symposium on Computer Architecture* (April), Austin, Tex., 9–17. (p. 188)

CLARK, D. W. AND J. S. EMER [1985]. "Performance of the VAX-11/780 translation buffer: Simulation and measurement," *ACM Trans. on Computer Systems* 3:1, 31–62. (p. 486)

CLARK, D. W. AND W. D. STRECKER [1980]. "Comments on 'the case for the reduced instruction set computer'," *Computer Architecture News* 8:6 (October) 34–38. (p. 130)

CLARK, D. W., P. J. BANNON, AND J. B. KELLER [1988]. "Measuring VAX 8800 performance with a histogram hardware monitor," *Proc. 15th Annual Symposium on Computer Architecture* (May–June), Honolulu, Hawaii, 176–185. (pp. 213, 486)

COCKE, J. AND J. T. SCHWARTZ [1970]. *Programming Languages and Their Compilers,* Courant Institute, New York Univ., New York City. (p. 130)

COCKE, J., AND J. MARKSTEIN [1980]. "Measurement of code improvement algorithms," *Information Processing* 80, 221–228. (p. 130)

CODD, E. F. [1962]. "Multiprogramming," in F.L. Alt and M. Rubinoff, *Advances in Computers,* vol. 3, Academic Press, New York, 82. (p. 241)

CODY, W. J. [1988]. "Floating point standards: Theory and practice," in *Reliability in Computing: The Role of Interval Methods in Scientific Computing,* R. E. Moore, (ed.), Academic Press, Boston, Mass., 99–107. (p. A-12)

CODY, W. J., J. T. COONEN, D. M. GAY, K. HANSON, D. HOUGH, W. KAHAN, R. KARPINSKI, J. PALMER, F. N. RIS, AND D. STEVENSON [1984]. "A proposed radix- and word-length-independent standard for floating-point arithmetic," *IEEE Micro* 4:4, 86–100. (p. A-12)

COHEN, D. [1981]. "On holy wars and a plea for peace," *Computer* 14:10 (October) 48–54. (p. 95)

COLWELL, R. P, C. Y. HITCHCOCK, III, E. D. JENSEN, H. M. B. SPRUNT, AND C. P. KOLLAR, [1985]. "Computers, complexity, and controversy," *Computer* 18:9 (September) 8–19. (p. 125)

COLWELL, R. P., R. P. NIX, J. J. O'DONNELL, D. B. PAPWORTH, AND B. K. RODMAN [1987]. "A VLIW architecture for a trace scheduling compiler," *Proc. Second Conf. on Architectural Support for Programming Languages and Operating Systems,* IEEE/ACM (March), Palo Alto, Calif., 180–192. (p. 340)

CONTI, C., D. H. GIBSON, AND S. H. PITKOWSKY [1968]. "Structural aspects of the System/360 Model 85, part I: General organization," *IBM Systems J.* 7:1, 2–14. (pp. 77, 486)

COONEN, J. [1984]. *Contributions to a Proposed Standard for Binary Floating-Point Arithmetic,* Ph.D. Thesis, Univ. of Calif., Berkeley. (p. A-29)

CRAWFORD, J. H AND P. P. GELSINGER [1987]. *Programming the 80386,* Sybex, Alameda, Calif. (pp. 188, 446)

CURNOW, H. J. AND B. A. WICHMANN [1976]. "A synthetic benchmark," *The Computer J.* 19:1. (p.77)

DAVIDSON, E. S. [1971]. "The design and control of pipelined function generators," *Proc. Conf. on Systems, Networks, and Computers,* IEEE (January), Oaxtepec, Mexico, 19–21. (p. 339)

DAVIDSON, E. S., A. T. THOMAS, L. E. SHAR, AND J. H. PATEL [1975]. "Effective control for pipelined processors," *COMPCON, IEEE* (March), San Francisco, 181–184. (p. 339)

DEHNERT, J. C., P. Y.-T. HSU, AND J. P. BRATT [1989]. "Overlapped loop support on the Cydra 5," *Proc. Third Conf. on Architectural Support for Programming Languages and Operating Systems* (April), IEEE/ACM, Boston, 26–39. (p. 340)

DEROSA, J., R. GLACKEMEYER, AND T. KNIGHT [1985]. "Design and implementation of the VAX 8600 pipeline," *Computer* 18:5 (May) 38–48. (p. 328)

DEWITT, D. J., R. FINKEL, AND M. SOLOMON [1984]. "The CRYSTAL multicomputer: Design and implementation experience, Computer Sciences Tech. Rep. No. 553, University of Wisconsin-Madison, September. (p. 590)

DIGITAL EQUIPMENT CORPORATION [1987]. *Digital Technical J.* 4 (March), Hudson, Mass. (This entire issue is devoted to the VAX 8800 processor.) (p. 341)

DITZEL, D. R. [1981]. "Reflections on the high-level language Symbol computer system," *Computer* 14:7 (July) 55–66. (p. 129)

DITZEL, D. R. AND D. A. PATTERSON [1980]. "Retrospective on high-level language computer architecture," in *Proc. Seventh Annual Symposium on Computer Architecture,* La Baule, France (June) 97–104. (p. 130)

DITZEL, D. R. AND H. R. MCLELLAN [1987]. "Branch folding in the CRISP microprocessor: Reducing the branch delay to zero," *Proc. 14th Symposium on Computer Architecture* (June), Pittsburgh, 2–7. (p. 339)

DITZEL, D. R., AND H. R. MCLELLAN [1982]. "Register allocation for free: The C machine stack cache," *Symposium on Architectural Support for Programming Languages and Operating Systems* (March 1–3), Palo Alto, Calif., 48–56. (p. 487)

DOHERTY, W. J. AND R. P. KELISKY [1979]. "Managing VM/CMS systems for user effectiveness," *IBM Systems J.* 18:1, 143–166. (p. 560)

DONGARRA, J. J. [1986]. "A survey of high performance computers," *COMPCON, IEEE* (March) 8–11. (p. 394)

EARLE, J. G. [1965]. "Latched carry-save adder," *IBM Technical Disclosure Bull.* 7 (March) 909–910. (p. 254)

EGGERS, S. [1989]. *Simulation Analysis of Data Sharing in Shared Memory Multiprocessors ,* Ph.D. Thesis, Univ. of California, Berkeley, Computer Science Division Tech. Rep. UCB/CSD 89/501 (April). (p. 487)

ELDER, J., A. GOTTLIEB, C. K. KRUSKAL, K. P. MCAULIFFE, L. RANDOLPH, M. SNIR, P. TELLER, AND J. WILSON [1985]. "Issues related to MIMD shared-memory computers: The NYU Ultracomputer approach," *Proc. 12th Int'l Symposium on Computer Architecture* (June), Boston, Mass., 126–135. (p. 589)

ELLIS, J. R., J. A. FISHER, J. C. RUTTENBERG, AND A. NICHOLAU [1984]. "Parallel processing: A smart compiler and a dumb machine," *Proc. SIGPLAN Conf. on Compiler Construction* (June), Montreal, Canada, 37–47. (p. 340)

ELSHOFF, J. L. [1976]. "An analysis of some commercial PL/I programs," *IEEE Trans. on Software Engineering* SE-2 2 (June) 113–120. (p. 130)

EMER, J. S. AND D. W CLARK [1984]. "A characterization of processor performance in the VAX-11/780," *Proc. 11th Symposium on Computer Architecture* (June), Ann Arbor, Mich., 301–310. (pp. 189, 213, 342, 486)

E•SUN MICROSYSTEMS [1989]. *The SPARC Architectural Manual*, Version 8, Part No. 800-1399-09, August 25, 1989.

FABRY, R. S. [1974]. "Capability based addressing," *Comm. ACM* 17:7 (July) 403–412. (p. 485)

FAZIO, D. [1987]. "It's really much more fun building a supercomputer than it is simply inventing one," *COMPCON, IEEE* (February) 102-105. (p. 394)

FEIERBACK, G AND D. STEVENSON [1979]. "The Illiac-IV," in *Infotech State of the Art Report on Supercomptuers*, Maidenhead, England. This data also appears in D. P. Siewiorek, C. G. Bell, and A. Newell, *Computer Structures: Principles and Examples* (1982), McGraw-Hill, New York, 268–269. (p. 556)

FISHER, J. A. [1983]. "Very long instruction word architectures and ELI-512," *Proc. Temth Symposium on Computer Architecture* (June), Stockholm, Sweden. (p. 340)

FLEMMING, P. J. AND J. J. WALLACE [1986]. "How not to lie with statistics: The correct way to summarize benchmarks results," *Comm. ACM* 29:3 (March) 218–221. (p. 78)

FLYNN, M. J. [1966]. "Very high-speed computing systems," *Proc. IEEE* 54:12 (December) 1901–1909. (pp. 351, 591)

FOLEY, J. D. AND A. VAN DAM [1982]. *Fundamentals of Interactive Computer Graphics*, Addison-Wesley, Reading, Mass. (p. 561)

FOSTER, C. C. AND E. M. RISEMAN [1972]. "Percolation of code to enhance parallel dispatching and execution," *IEEE Trans. on Computers* C-21:12 (December) 1411–1415. (p. 340)

FOSTER, C. C., R. H. GONTER, AND E. M. RISEMAN [1971]. "Measures of opcode utilization," *IEEE Trans. on Computers* 13:5 (May) 582–584. (p. 129)

FRANK, P. D. [1987]. "Advances in Head Technology," presentation at *Challenges in Winchester Technology* (December 15), Santa Clara Univ. (p. 561)

FRANK, S. J. [1984]. "Tightly coupled multiprocessor systems speed memory access times," *Electronics* 57:1 (January) 164–169. (p. 487)

FREIMAN, C. V. [1961]. "Statistical analysis of certain binary division algorithms," *Proc. IRE* 49:1, 91–103. (p. A-59)

FRIESENBORG, S. E. AND R. J. WICKS [1985]. "DASD expectations: The 3380, 3380-23, and MVS/XA," Tech. Bulletin GG22-9363-02 (July 10), Washington Systems Center. (p. 554)

FULLER, S. H. [1976]. "Price/performance comparison of C.mmp and the PDP-11," *Proc. Third Annual Symposium on Computer Architecture* (Texas, January 19–21), 197–202. (p. 80)

FULLER, S. H. AND W. E. BURR [1977]. "Measurement and evaluation of alternative computer architectures," *Computer* 10:10 (October) 24–35. (p. 78)

GAGLIARDI, U. O. [1973]. "Report of workshop 4–software-related advances in computer hardware," *Proc. Symposium on the High Cost of Software*, Menlo Park, Calif., 99–120. (p. 129)

GAJSKI, D., D. KUCK, D. LAWRIE, AND A. SAMEH [1983]. "CEDAR—A large scale multiprocessor," *Proc. Int'l Conf. on Parallel Processing* (August) 524–529. (p. 589)

GARNER, R., A. AGARWAL, F. BRIGGS, E. BROWN, D. HOUGH, B. JOY, S. KLEIMAN, S. MUNCHNIK, M. NAMJOO, D. PATTERSON, J. PENDLETON, AND R. TUCK [1988]. "Scaleable processor architecture (SPARC)," *COMPCON, IEEE* (March), San Francisco, 278–283. (p. 190)

GEHRINGER, E. F., D. P. SIEWIOREK, AND Z. SEGALL [1987]. *Parallel Processing: The Cm* Experience*, Digital Press, Bedford, Mass. (p. 587)

GIBSON, D. H. [1967]. "Considerations in block–oriented systems design," *AFIPS Conf. Proc.* 30, SJCC, 75–80. (p. 486)

GIBSON, J. C. [1970]. "The Gibson mix," Rep. TR. 00.2043, IBM Systems Development Division, Poughkeepsie, N.Y. (Research done in 1959.) (p. 77)

GOLDBERG, D. [1989]. "Floating-point and computer systems," *Xerox Tech. Rep.* CSL-89-9. A version of this paper will appear in *Computing Surveys*. (p. A-29)

GOLDBERG, I. B. [1967]. "27 bits are not enough for 8-digit accuracy," *Comm. ACM* 10:2, 105–106. (p. A-60)

GOLDSTEIN, S. [1987]. "Storage performance—an eight year outlook," Tech. Rep. TR 03.308-1 (October), Santa Teresa Laboratory, IBM, San Jose, Calif. (p. 561)

GOLDSTINE, H. H. [1972]. *The Computer: From Pascal to von Neumann,* Princeton University Press, Princeton, N.J. (p. 25)

GOODMAN, J. R. [1983]. "Using cache memory to reduce processor memory traffic," *Proc. Tenth Annual Symposium on Computer Architecture* (June 5–7), Stockholm, Sweden, 124–131. (p. 487)

GOODMAN, J. R. and M.-C. Chiang [1984]. "The use of static column RAM as a memory hierarchy," *Proc. 11th Annual Symposium on Computer Architecture* (June 5–7), Ann Arbor, Mich., 167–174. (p. 488)

GOSLING, J. B. [1980]. *Design of Arithmetic Units for Digital Computers,* Springer-Verlag NewYork, Inc., New York. (p. A-61)

GRAY, W. P. [1989]. Memorandum of Decision, No. C-84-20799-WPG, U.S. District Court for the Northern District of California (February 7, 1989). (p. 244)

GROSS, T. R. [1983]. *Code Optimization of Pipeline Constraints,* Ph.D. Thesis (December), Computer Systems Lab., Stanford Univ. (p. 342)

HALBERT, D. C. AND P. B. KESSLER [1980]. "Windows of overlapping register frames," *CS 292R Final Reports* (June) 82–100. (p. 489)

HAMACHER, V. C., Z. G. VRANESIC, AND S. G. ZAKY [1984]. *Computer Organization,* 2nd ed., McGraw-Hill, New York. (p. A-61)

HAUCK, E. A., AND B. A. DENT [1968]. "Burroughs' B6500/B7500 stack mechanism," *Proc. AFIPS SJCC,* 245–251. (p. 131)

HENLY, M. AND B. MCNUTT [1989]. "DASD I/O characteristics: A comparison of MVS to VM," Tech. Rep. TR 02.1550 (May), IBM, General Products Division, San Jose, Calif. (pp. 80, 562)

HENNESSY, J. [1984]. "VLSI processor architecture," *IEEE Trans. on Computers* C-33:11 (December) 1221–1246. (p. 190)

HENNESSY, J. [1985]. "VLSI RISC processors," *VLSI Systems Design* VI:10 (October) 22–32. (p. 191)

HENNESSY, J. L. AND T. R. GROSS [1983]. "Postpass code optimization of pipeline constraints," *ACM Trans. on Programming Languages and Systems* 5:3 (July) 422–448. (p. 342)

HENNESSY, J., N. JOUPPI, F. BASKETT, AND J. GILL [1981]. "MIPS: A VLSI processor architecture," *Proc. CMU Conf. on VLSI Systems and Computations* (October), Computer Science Press, Rockville, Md. (p. 191)

HENNESSY, J. L., N. JOUPPI, F. BASKETT, T. R. GROSS, AND J. GILL [1982]. "Hardware/software tradeoffs for increased performance," *Proc. Symposium on Architectural Support for Programming Languages and Operating Systems* (March), 2–11. (p. 131)

HENNESSY, J. [1984]. "VLSI processor architecture," *IEEE Trans. on Computers* C-33:11 (December) 1221–1246. (p. 189)

HILL, M. D. [1987]. *Aspects of Cache Memory and Instruction Buffer Performance*, Ph.D. Thesis, Univ. of California at Berkeley Computer Science Division, Tech. Rep. UCB/CSD 87/381 (November). (p. 489)

HILL, M. D. [1988]. "A case for direct mapped caches," *Computer* 21:12 (December) 25–40. (p. 489)

HILLIS, W. D. [1985]. *The Connection Machine,* The MIT Press, Cambridge, Mass. (p. 591)

HINTZ, R. G. AND D. P. TATE [1972]. "Control data STAR-100 processor design," *COMPCON, IEEE* (September) 1–4. (p. 396)

HOCKNEY, R. W. AND C. R. JESSHOPE [1988]. *Parallel Computers-2, Architectures, Programming and Algorithms,* Adam Hilger Ltd., Bristol, England and Philadelphia. (p. 591)

HOLLAND, J. H. [1959]. "A universal computer capable of executing an arbitrary number of subprograms simultaneously," *Proc. East Joint Computer Conf.* 16, 108–113. (p. 591)

HOLLINGSWORTH, W., H. SACHS AND A. J. SMITH [1989]. "The Clipper processor: Instruction set architecture and implementation," *Comm. ACM* 32:2 (February), 200–219. (p. 80)

HORD, R. M. [1982]. *The Illiac-IV, The First Supercomputer,* Computer Science Press, Rockville, Md. (p. 591)

HOWARD, J. H. ET AL. [1988]. "Scale and performance in a distributed file system," *ACM Trans. on Computer Systems* 6:1, 51–81. (p. 512)

HUGUET, M. AND T. LANG [1985]. "A reduced register file for RISC architectures," *Computer Architecture News* 13:4 (September) 22–31. (p. 489)

HWANG, K. [1979]. *Computer Arithmetic: Principles, Architecture, and Design,* Wiley, New York. (p. A-61)

HWU, W.-M. AND Y. PATT [1986]. "HPSm, a high performance restricted data flow architecture having minimum functionality," *Proc. 13th Symposium on Computer Architecture* (June), Tokyo, 297–307. (p. 339)

IBM [1982]. *The Economic Value of Rapid Response Time,* GE20-0752-0 White Plains, N.Y., 11–82. (p. 560)

IEEE [1985]. "IEEE standard for binary floating-point arithmetic," *SIGPLAN Notices* 22:2, 9–25. (p. A-12)

IMPRIMIS [1989]. "Imprimis Product Specification, 97209 Sabre Disk Drive IPI-2 Interface 1.2 GB," Document No. 64402302 (May). (p. 558)

INTEL [1989]. *i860 64-Bit Microprocessor Programmer's Reference Manual.* (E-24)

JORDAN, K. E. [1987]. "Performance comparison of large-scale scientific computers: Scalar main-frames, mainframes with vector facilities, and supercomputers," *Computer* 20:3 (March) 10–23. (p. 395)

JOUPPI N. P. AND D. W. WALL [1989]. "Available instruction-level parallelism for superscalar and superpipelined machines," *Proc. Third Conf. on Architectural Support for Programming Languages and Operating Systems,* IEEE/ACM (April), Boston, 272–282. (p. 340)

KAHAN, W. [1968]. "7094-II system support for numerical analysis," *SHARE Secretarial Distribution* SSD-159. (p. A-60)

KAHANER, D. K. [1988]. "Benchmarks for 'real' programs," *SIAM News* (November). (p. A-57)

KAHN, R. E. [1972]. "Resource-sharing computer communication networks," *Proc. IEEE* 60:11 (November) 1397–1407. (p. 561)

KANE, G. [1986]. *MIPS R2000 RISC Architecture,* Prentice Hall, Englewood Cliffs, N.J. (p. 190)

KANE, G. [1988]. *MIPS RISC Architecture,* Prentice-Hall, Englewood Cliffs, N. J. (E-24)

KATZ, R. H., D. A. PATTERSON, AND G. A. GIBSON [1990]. "Disk system architectures for high performance computing," *Proc. IEEE* 78:2 (February). (p. 561)

KATZ, R. H., S. EGGERS, D. A. WOOD, C. PERKINS, AND R. G. SHELDON [1985]. "Implementing a cache consistency protocol," *Proc. 12th Annual Symposium on Computer Architecture*, 276–283. (p. 487)

KELLER R. M. [1975]. "Look-ahead processors," *ACM Computing Surveys* 7:4 (December) 177–195. (p. 339)

KELLY, E. [1988]. "'SCRAM Cache' in Sun-4/110 beats traditional caches," *Sun Technology* 1:3 (Summer) 19–21. (p. 487)

KILBURN, T., D. B. G. EDWARDS, M. J. LANIGAN, F. H. SUMNER [1962]. "One-level storage system," *IRE Transactions on Electronic Computers* EC-11 (April) 223–235. Also appears in D. P. Siewiorek, C. G. Bell, and A. Newell, *Computer Structures: Principles and Examples* (1982), McGraw-Hill, New York, 135–148. (pp. 26, 487)

KIM, M. Y. [1986]. "Synchronized disk interleaving," *IEEE Trans. on Computers* C-35:11 (November). (p. 561)

KNUTH, D. [1981]. *The Art of Computer Programming,* vol II, 2nd ed., Addison-Wesley, Reading, Mass. (p. A-61)

KNUTH, D. E. [1971]. "An empirical study of FORTRAN programs," *Software Practice and Experience,* Vol. 1, 105–133. (p. 27)

KOGGE, P. M. [1981]. *The Architecture of Pipelined Computers,* McGraw-Hill, New York. (pp. 339, A-44)

KOHN, L. AND S.-W. FU, [1989]. "A 1,000,000 transistor microprocessor," *IEEE Int'l Solid-State Circuits Conf.,* 54–55. (p. A-19)

KROFT, D. [1981]. "Lockup-free instruction fetch/prefetch cache organization," *Proc. Eighth Annual Symposium on Computer Architecture* (May 12–14), Minneapolis, Minn., 81–87. (p. 487)

KUCK, D., P. P. BUDNIK, S.-C. CHEN, D. H. LAWRIE, R. A. TOWLE, R. E. STREBENDT, E. W. DAVIS, JR., J. HAN, P. W. KRASKA, Y. MURAOKA [1974]. "Measurements of parallelism in ordinary FORTRAN programs," *Computer* 7:1 (January) 37–46. (p. 395)

KUHN, R. H. AND D. A. PADUA, EDS. [1981]. *Tutorial on Parallel Processing*, IEEE. (p. 590)

KUNG, H. T. [1982]. "Why systolic architectures?," *IEEE Computer* 15:1, 37–46. (p. 590)

KUNKEL, S. R. AND J. E. SMITH [1986]. "Optimal pipelining in supercomputers," *Proc. 13th Symposium on Computer Architecture* (June), Tokyo, 404–414. (p. 339)

LAM, M. [1988]. "Software pipelining: An effective scheduling technique for VLIW machines," *SIGPLAN Conf. on Programming Language Design and Implementation,* ACM (June), Atlanta, Ga., 318–328. (p. 340)

LAMPSON, B. W. [1982]. "Fast procedure calls," *Symposium on Architectural Support for Programming Languages and Operating Systems* (March 1–3), Palo Alto, Calif., 66–75. (p. 487)

LARSON, JUDGE E. R. [1973]. "Findings of Fact, Conclusions of Law, and Order for Judgment," File No. 4–67, Civ. 138, *Honeywell v. Sperry Rand and Illinois Scientific Development,* U.S. District Court for the District of Minnesota, Fourth Division (October 19). (p. 24)

LEE, R. [1989]. "Precision architecture," *Computer* 22:1 (January) 78–91. (p. 190)

LEINER, A. L. [1954]. "System specifications for the DYSEAC," *J. ACM* 1:2 (April) 57–81. (p. 561)

LEINER, A. L. AND S. N. ALEXANDER [1954]. "System organization of the DYSEAC," *IRE Trans. of Electronic Computers* EC-3:1 (March) 1–10. (p. 561)

LEVY, H. M. AND R. H. ECKHOUSE, JR. [1989]. *Computer Programming and Architecture: The VAX,* 2nd ed., Digital Press, Bedford, Mass. 358–372. (pp. 188, 243)

LEVY, J. V. [1978]. "Buses: The skeleton of computer structures," in *Computer Engineering: A DEC View of Hardware Systems Design,* C. G. Bell, J. C. Mudge, and J. E. McNamara, eds., Digital Press, Bedford, Mass. (p. 561)

LINCOLN, N. R. [1982]. "Technology and design tradeoffs in the creation of a modern supercomputer," *IEEE Trans. on Computers* C-31:5 (May) 363–376. (p. 393)

LIPOVSKI, A. G. AND A. TRIPATHI [1977]. "A reconfigurable varistructure array processor," *Proc. 1977 Int'l Conf. of Parallel Processing* (August), 165–174. (p. 590)

LIPTAY, J. S. [1968]. "Structural aspects of the System/360 Model 85, part II: The cache," *IBM Systems J.* 7:1, 15–21. (p. 486)

LOVETT, T. AND S. THAKKAR [1988]. "The Symmetry multiprocessor system," *Proc. 1988 Int'l Conf. of Parallel Processing,* University Park, Pennsylvania, 303–310. (p. 589)

LUBECK, O., J. MOORE, AND R. MENDEZ [1985]. "A benchmark comparison of three supercomputers: Fujitsu VP-200, Hitachi S810/20, and CRAY X-MP/2," *Computer* 18:12 (December) 10–24. (pp. 75, 395)

LUNDE, A. [1977]. "Empirical evaluation of some features of instruction set processor architecture," *Comm. ACM* 20:3 (March) 143–152. (p. 129)

MABERLY, N. C. [1966]. *Mastering Speed Reading,* New American Library, Inc., New York. (p. 513)

MAGENHEIMER, D. J., L. PETERS, K. W. PETTIS AND D. ZURAS [1988]. "Integer multiplication and division on the HP Precision Architecture," *IEEE Trans. on Computers,* 37:8, 980–990. (p. E-9)

MAGENHEIMER, D. J., L. PETERS, K. W. PETTIS, AND D. ZURAS, [1988]. "Integer multiplication and division on the HP Precision Architecture," *IEEE Trans. on Computers* 37:8, 980–990. (p. A-11)

MCCALL, K. [1983]. "The Smalltalk-80 benchmarks," *Smalltalk 80: Bits of History, Words of Advice,* G. Krasner, ed., Addison-Wesley, Reading, Mass., 153–174. (p. 451)

MCCREIGHT, E. [1984]. "The Dragon computer system: An early overview," Tech. Rep. Xerox Corp. (September). (p. 487)

MCFARLING, S. [1989]. "Program optimization for instruction caches," *Proc. Third Int'l Conf. on Architectural Support for Programming Languages and Operating Systems* (April 3–6), Boston, Mass., 183–191. (p. 496)

MCFARLING, S. AND J. HENNESSY [1986]. "Reducing the cost of branches," *Proc. 13th Symposium on Computer Architecture* (June), Tokyo, 396–403. (p. 340)

MCKEEMAN, W. M. [1967]. "Language directed computer design," *Proc. 1967 Fall Joint Computer Conf.,* Washington, D.C., 413–417. (p. 128)

MCKEVITT, J., ET AL. [1977]. *8086 Design Report,* internal memorandum. (p. 229)

MCMAHON, F. M. [1986]. "The Livermore FORTRAN kernels: A computer test of numerical performance range," Tech. Rep. UCRL-55745, Lawrence Livermore National Laboratory, Univ. of California, Livermore, Calif. (December). (p. 78)

MEAD, C. AND L. CONWAY [1980]. *Introduction to VLSI Systems,* Addison-Wesley, Reading, Mass. (p. A-59)

MENABREA, L. F. [1842]. "Sketch of the analytical engine invented by Charles Babbage," Bibiothèque Universelle de Genève (October). (p. 589)

METCALFE, R. M. AND D. R. BOGGS [1976]. "Ethernet: Distributed packet switching for local computer networks," *Comm. ACM* 19:7 (July) 395–404. (p. 560)

MEYERS, G. J. [1978]. "The evaluation of expressions in a storage-to-storage architecture," *Computer Architecture News* 7:3 (October), 20–23. (p. 127)

MEYERS, G. J. [1982]. *Advances in Computer Architecture,* 2nd ed., Wiley, N.Y. (p. 129)

MIRANKER, G. S., J. RUBENSTEIN, AND J. SANGUINETTI [1988]. "Squeezing a Cray-class supercomputer into a single-user package," *COMPCON, IEEE* (March) 452–456. (p. 395)

MITCHELL, D. [1989]. "The Transputer: The time is now," *Computer Design,* RISC supplement, 40–41 (November). (p. 570)

MIURA, K. AND K. UCHIDA [1983]. "FACOM vector processing system: VP100/200," *Proc. NATO Advanced Research Work on High Speed Computing* (June); also in K. Hwang, ed., "Supercomputers: Design and applications," *IEEE* (August 1984) 59–73. (p. 394)

MOORE, B., A. PADEGS, R. SMITH, AND W. BUCHOLZ [1987]. "Concepts of the System/370 vector architecture," *Proc. 14th Symposium on Computer Architecture* (June), ACM/IEEE, Pittsburgh, Pa., 282–292. (p. 394)

MORSE, S., B. RAVENAL, S. MAZOR, AND W. POHLMAN [1980]. "Intel Microprocessors—8008 to 8086," *Computer* 13:10 (October). (p. 188)

MOTOROLA [1988]. *MC88100 RISC Microprocessor User's Manual.* (E-19)

MOUSSOURIS, J., L. CRUDELE, D. FREITAS, C. HANSEN, E. HUDSON, S. PRZYBYLSKI, T. RIORDAN, AND C. ROWEN [1986]. "A CMOS RISC processor with integrated system functions," *Proc. COMPCON, IEEE* (March), San Francisco. (p. 189)

MUCHNICK, S. S. [1988]. "Optimizing compilers for SPARC," *Sun Technology* (Summer) 1:3, 64–77. (p. E-9)

NEWMAN, W. N. AND R. F. SPROULL [1979]. *Principles of Interactive Computer Graphics*, 2nd ed., McGraw-Hill, New York. (p. 561)

NGAI, T-F. AND M. J. IRWIN [1985]. "Regular, area-time efficient carry-lookahead adders," *Proc. Seventh IEEE Symposium on Computer Arithmetic*, 9–15. (p. A-59)

NICHOLAU, A. AND J. A. FISHER [1984]. "Measuring the parallelism available for very long instruction word architectures," *IEEE Trans. on Computers* C-33:11 (November) 968–976. (p. 340)

OUSTERHOUT, J. K. ET AL. [1985]. "A trace-driven analysis of the UNIX 4.2 BSD file system," *Proc. Tenth ACM Symposium on Operating Systems Principles*, Orcas Island, Wash., 15–24. (p. 538)

PADUA, D. AND M. WOLFE [1986]. "Advanced compiler optimizations for supercomputers," *Comm. ACM* 29:12 (December) 1184–1201. (p. 395)

PAPAMARCOS, M. AND J. PATEL [1984]. "A low coherence solution for multiprocessors with private cache memories," *Proc. of the 11th Annual Symposium on Computer Architecture* (June), Ann Arbor, Mich., 348–354. (p. 487)

PATTERSON, D. A. [1983]. "Microprogramming," *Scientific American* 248:3 (March), 36–43. (p. 244)

PATTERSON, D. A. [1985]. "Reduced Instruction Set Computers," *Comm. ACM* 28:1 (January) 8–21. (p. 189)

PATTERSON, D. A. AND C. H. SEQUIN [1981]. "Lockup-free instruction fetch/prefetch cache organization," *Proc. Eighth Annual Symposium on Computer Architecture* (May 12–14), Minneapolis, Minn., 443–458. (p. 487)

PATTERSON, D. A. AND D. R. DITZEL [1980]. "The case for the reduced instruction set computer," *Computer Architecture News* 8:6 (October), 25–33. (pp. 130, 189)

PATTERSON, D. A., G. A. GIBSON, AND R. H. KATZ [1987]. "A case for redundant arrays of inexpensive disks (RAID)," Tech. Rep. UCB/CSD 87/391, Univ. of Calif. Also appeared in *ACM SIGMOD Conf. Proc.*, Chicago, Illinois, June 1–3, 1988, 109–116. (p. 561)

PENG, V., S. SAMUDRALA, AND M. GAVRIELOV [1987]. "On the implementation of shifters, multipliers, and dividers in VLSI floating point units," *Proc. Eighth IEEE Symposium on Computer Arithmetic*, 95–102. (p. A-62)

PFISTER, G. F., W. C. BRANTLEY, D. A. GEORGE, S. L. HARVEY, W. J. KLEINFEKDER, K. P. MCAULIFFE, E. A. MELTON, V. A. NORTON, AND J. WEISS [1985]. "The IBM research parallel processor prototype (RP3): Introduction and architecture," *Proc. 12th Int'l Symposium on Computer Architecture* (June), Boston, Mass., 764–771. (p. 589)

PHISTER, M., JR. [1979]. *Data Processing Technology and Economics,* 2nd ed., Digital Press and Santa Monica Publishing Company. (p. 80)

PRZYBYLSKI, S. A. [1990]. *Cache Design: A Performance-Directed Approach,* Morgan Kaufmann Publishers, San Mateo, Calif. (p. 487)

PRZYBYLSKI, S. A., M. HOROWITZ, AND J. L. HENNESSY [1988]. "Performance tradeoffs in cache design," *Proc. 15th Annual Symposium on Computer Architecture* (May–June), Honolulu, Hawaii, 290–298. (p. 481)

RADIN, G. [1982]. "The 801 minicomputer," *Proc. Symposium Architectural Support for Programming Languages and Operating Systems* (March), Palo Alto, Calif. 39–47. (p. 189)

RAMAMOORTHY, C. V. AND H. F. LI [1977]. "Pipeline architecture," *ACM Computing Surveys* 9:1 (March) 61–102. (p. 339)

REDMOND, K. C. AND T. M. SMITH [1980]. *Project Whirlwind—The History of a Pioneer Computer,* Digital Press, Boston, Mass. (p. 25)

REIGEL, E. W., U. FABER, AND D. A. FISCHER, [1972]. "The Interpreter—a microprogrammable building block system," *Proc. AFIPS 1972 Spring Joint Computer Conf.* 40, 705–723. (p. 244)

ROBERTS, D., G. TAYLOR, AND T. LAYMAN [1990]. "An ECL RISC microprocessor designed for two-level cache," *IEEE COMPCON* (February). (p. 487)

ROBINSON, B. AND L. BLOUNT [1986]. "The VM/HPO 3880-23 performance results," IBM Tech. Bulletin, GG66-0247-00 (April), Washington Systems Center, Gathersburg, Md. (p. 553)

ROWEN, C., M. JOHNSON, and P. RIES [1988]. "The MIPS R3010 floating-point coprocessor," *IEEE Micro* 53–62 (June). (p. A-53)

RUSSELL, R. M. [1978]. "The CRAY-1 computer system," *Comm. ACM* 21:1 (January) 63–72. (pp. 393, 590)

RYMARCZYK, J. [1982]. "Coding guidelines for pipelined processors," *Proc. Symposium on Architectural Support for Programming Languages and Operating Systems,* IEEE/ACM (March), Palo Alto, Calif., 12–19. (p. 339)

SALEM, K. AND H. GARCIA-MOLINA [1986]. "Disk striping," *IEEE 1986 Int'l Conf. on Data Engineering.* (p. 561)

SAMPLES, A. D. AND P. N. HILFINGER [1988]. "Code reorganization for instruction caches," Tech. Rep. UCB/CSD 88/447 (October), Univ. of Calif., Berkeley. (p. 496)

SANTORO, M. R., G. BEWICK, and M. A. HOROWITZ [1989]. "Rounding algorithms for IEEE multipliers," *Proc. Ninth IEEE Symposium on Computer Arithmetic,* 176–183. (p. A-21)

SCHNECK, P. B. [1987]. *Supercomputer Architecture,* Kluwer Academic Publishers, Norwell, Mass. (p. 394)

SCOTT, N. R. [1985]. *Computer Number Systems and Arithmetic,* Prentice-Hall, Englewood Cliffs, N.J. (p. A-1)

SCRANTON, R. A., D. A. THOMPSON, AND D. W. HUNTER [1983]. "The access time myth," Tech. Rep. RC 10197 (45223) (September 21), IBM, Yorktown Heights, N.Y. (p. 561)

SEITZ, C. [1985]. "The Cosmic Cube," *Comm. ACM* 28:1 (January) 22–31. (p. 590)

SHURKIN, J. [1984]. *Engines of the Mind: A History of the Computer*, W. W. Norton, New York. (p. 25)

SHUSTEK, L. J. [1978]. "Analysis and performance of computer instruction sets," Ph.D. Thesis (May), Stanford Univ., Stanford, Calif. (p. 187)

SITES, R. [1979]. *Instruction Ordering for the CRAY-1 Computer,* Tech. Rep. 78-CS-023 (July), Dept. of Computer Science, Univ. of Calif., San Diego. (p. 339)

SITES, R. L., [1979]. "How to use 1000 registers," *Caltech Conf. on VLSI* (January). (p. 487)

SLATER, R. [1987]. *Portraits in Silicon,* The MIT Press, Cambridge, Mass. (p. 25)

SLOTNICK, D. L., W. C. BORCK, AND R. C. MCREYNOLDS [1962]. "The Solomon computer," *Proc. Fall Joint Computer Conf.* (December), Philadelphia, 97–107. (p. 589)

SMITH, A. AND J. LEE [1984]. "Branch prediction strategies and branch target buffer design," *Computer* 17:1 (January) 6–22. (p. 339)

SMITH, A. J. [1982]. "Cache memories," *Computing Surveys* 14:3 (September) 473–530. (p. 486)

SMITH, A. J. [1985]. "Disk cache—miss ratio analysis and design considerations," *ACM Trans. on Computer Systems* 3:3 (August) 161–203. (p. 538)

SMITH, A. J. [1986]. "Bibliography and readings on CPU cache memories and related topics," *Computer Architecture News* (January) 22–42. (p. 486)

SMITH, B. J. [1981]. "Architecture and applications of the HEP multiprocessor system," *Real-Time Signal Processing IV* 298 (August) 241–248. (p. 395)

SMITH, J. E. [1981]. "A study of branch prediction strategies," *Proc. Eighth Symposium on Computer Architecture* (May), Minneapolis, 135–148. (p. 339)

SMITH, J. E. [1984]. "Decoupled access/execute computer architectures," *ACM Trans. on Computer Systems* 2:4 (November), 289–308. (p. 340)

SMITH, J. E. [1988]. "Characterizing computer performance with a single number," *Comm. ACM* 31:10 (October) 1202–1206. (p. 78)

SMITH, J. E. [1989]. "Dynamic instruction scheduling and the Astronautics ZS-1," *Computer* 22:7 (July) 21–35. (p. 340)

SMITH, J. E. AND A. R. PLEZKUN [1988]. "Implementing precise interrupts in pipelined processors," *IEEE Trans. on Computers* 37:5 (May) 562–573. (p. 339)

SMITH, J. E. AND J. R. GOODMAN [1983]. "A study of instruction cache organizations and replacement policies," *Proc. Tenth Annual Symposium on Computer Architecture* (June 5–7), Stockholm, Sweden,, 132–137. (p. 490)

SMITH, J. E., G. E. DERMER, B. D. VANDERWARN, S. D. KLINGER, C. M. ROZEWSKI, D. L. FOWLER, K. R. SCIDMORE, J. P. LAUDON [1987]. "The ZS-1 central processor," *Proc. Second Conf. on Architectural Support for Programming Languages and Operating Systems,* IEEE/ACM (March), Palo Alto, Calif., 199–204. (p. 340)

SMITH, M. D., M. JOHNSON, AND M. A. HOROWITZ [1989]. "Limits on multiple instruction issue," *Proc. Third Conf. on Architectural Support for Programming Languages and Operating Systems,* IEEE/ACM (April), Boston, Mass., 290–302. (p. 341)

SMITH, W. R., R. R. RICE, G. D. CHESLEY, T. A. LALIOTIS, S. F. LUNDSTROM, M. A. CHALHOUN, L. D. GEROULD, AND T. C. COOK [1971]. "SYMBOL: A large experimental system exploring major hardware replacement of software," *Proc. AFIPS Spring Joint Computer Conf.,* 601–616. (p. 129)

SMOTHERMAN , M. [1989]. "A sequencing-based taxonomy of I/O systems and review of historical machines," *Computer Architecture News* 17:5 (September) 5–15. (pp. 241, 561)

SOHI, G. S., AND S. VAJAPEYAM [1989]. "Tradeoffs in instruction format design for horizontal architectures," *Proc. Third Conf. on Architectural Support for Programming Languages and Operating Systems,* IEEE/ACM (April), Boston, Mass. 15–25. (p. 341)

SPEC [1989]. "SPEC Benchmark Suite Release 1.0," October 2, 1989. (p. 48)

SPORER, M., F. H. MOSS AND C. J. MATHAIS [1988]. "An introduction to the architecture of the Stellar Graphics supercomputer," *COMPCON, IEEE* (March) 464–467. (p. 395)

STERN, N. [1980]. "Who invented the first electronic digital computer," *Annals of the History of Computing* 2:4 (October) 375–376. (p. 24)

STRAPPER, C. H. [1989]. "Fact and fiction in yield modelling," Special Issue of the *Microelectronics Journal* entitled *Microelectronics into the Nineties*, Oxford, UK; Elsevier (May). (p. 80)

STRAPPER, C. H., F. H. ARMSTRONG, AND K. SAJI [1983]. "Integrated circuit yield statistics," *Proc. IEEE* 71:4 (April) 453–470. (p. 80)

STRECKER, W. D. [1976]. "Cache memories for the PDP-11?," *Proc. Third Annual Symposium on Computer Architecture* (January), Pittsburgh, Penn., 155–158. (pp. 187, 486)

STRECKER, W. D. [1978]. "VAX-11/780: A virtual address extension to the PDP-11 family," *Proc. AFIPS National Computer Conf.* 47, 967-980. (128, 187)

STRECKER, W. D. AND C. G. BELL [1976]. "Computer structures: What have we learned from the PDP-11?," *Proc. Third Symposium on Computer Architecture.* (p. 187)

SUTHERLAND, I. E. [1963]. "Sketchpad: A man-machine graphical communication system," *Spring Joint Computer Conf.* 329. (p. 561)

SWAN, R. J., A. BECHTOLSHEIM, K. W. LAI, AND J. K. OUSTERHOUT [1977]. "The implementation of the Cm* multi-microprocessor," *Proc. AFIPS National Computing Conf.,* 645–654. (p. 589)

SWAN, R. J., S. H. FULLER, AND D. P. SIEWIOREK [1977]. "Cm*—A modular, multi-microprocessor," *Proc. AFIPS National Computer Conf.* 46, 637–644. (p. 590)

SWARTZ, J. T. [1980]. "Ultracomputers," *ACM Transactions on Programming Languages and Systems* 4:2, 484–521 (p. 592)

SWARTZLANDER, E., ED. [1980]. *Computer Arithmetic,* Dowden, Hutchison and Ross (distributed by Van Nostrand, New York). (p. A-59)

TAKAGI, N., H. YASUURA, AND S. YAJIMA [1985]."High-speed VLSI multiplication algorithm with a redundant binary addition tree," *IEEE Trans. on Computers* C-34:9, 789–796. (p. A-59)

TANENBAUM, A. S. [1978]. "Implications of structured programming for machine architecture," *Comm. ACM* 21:3 (March) 237–246. (p. 128)

TANG, C. K. [1976]. "Cache system design in the tightly coupled multiprocessor system," *Proc. 1976 AFIPS National Computer Conf.*, 749–753. (p. 487)

TAYLOR, G. S. [1981]. "Compatible hardware for division and square root," *Proc. Fifth IEEE Symposium on Computer Arithmetic,* 127–134. (p. A-62)

TAYLOR, G. S. [1985]. "Radix 16 SRT dividers with overlapped quotient selection stages," *Proc. Seventh IEEE Symposium on Computer Arithmetic,* 64–71. (p. A-56)

TAYLOR, G. S., P. N. HILFINGER, J. R. LARUS, D. A. PATTERSON, AND B. G. ZORN [1986]. "Evaluation of the SPUR Lisp architecture," *Proc. 13th Annual Symposium on Computer Architecture* (June 2–5), Tokyo, Japan, 444–452. (pp. 189, 451)

TAYLOR, G., P. HILFINGER, J. LARUS, D. PATTERSON, AND B. ZORN [1986]. "Evaluation of the SPUR LISP architecture," *Proc. 13th Symposium on Computer Architecture (*June), Tokyo. (p. E-15)

THACKER, C. P. AND L. C. STEWART [1987]. "Firefly: a multiprocessor workstation," *Proc. Second Int'l Conf. on Architectural Support for Programming Languages and Operating Systems,* Palo Alto, Calif., 164–172. (p. 487)

THACKER, C. P., E. M. MCCREIGHT, B. W. LAMPSON, R. F. SPROULL, AND D. R. BOGGS [1982]. "Alto: A personal computer," in *Computer Structures: Principles and Examples,* D. P. Siewiorek, C. G. Bell, and A. Newell, eds., McGraw-Hill, New York, 549–572. (p. 560)

THADHANI, A. J. [1981]. "Interactive user productivity," *IBM Systems J.* 20:4, 407–423. (p. 560)

THISQUEN, J. [1988]. "Seek time measurements," *Amdahl Peripheral Products Division Tech. Rep.* (May). (p. 558)

THORLIN, J. F. [1967]. "Code generation for PIE (parallel instruction execution) computers," *Spring Joint Computer Conf.* (April), Atlantic City, N.J. (p. 339)

THORNTON, J. E. [1964]. "Parallel operation in Control Data 6600," *Proc. AFIPS Fall Joint Computer Conf.* 26, part 2, 33–40. (pp. 128, 339)

THORTON, J. E. [1970]. *Design of a Computer, the Control Data 6600,* Scott, Foresman, Glenview, Ill. (p. 339)

TJADEN, G. S. AND M. J. FLYNN [1970]. "Detection and parallel execution of independent instructions," *IEEE Trans. on Computers* C-19:10 (October) 889–895. (p. 340)

TOMASULO, R. M. [1967]. "An efficient algorithm for exploring multiple arithmetic units," *IBM J. of Research and Development* 11:1 (January) 25–33. (p. 339)

TRELEAVEN, P. C., D. R. BROWNBRIDGE, and R. P. HOPKINS [1982]. "Data-driven and demand-driven computer architectures," *Computing Surveys,* 14:1 (March) 93–143. (p. 590)

TROIANI, M., S. S. CHING, N. N. QUAYNOR, J. E. BLOEM, AND F. C. COLON OSORIO [1985]. "The VAX 8600 I Box, a pipelined implementation of the VAX architecture," *Digital Technical J.* 1 (August) 4–19. (p. 328)

TUCKER, S. G. [1967]. "Microprogram control for the System/360," *IBM Systems Journal* 6:4, 222–241. (p. 242)

UNGAR, D. M. [1987]. *The Design of a High Performance Smalltalk System*, The MIT Press Distinguished Dissertation Series, Cambridge, Mass. (p. 451)

UNGAR, D., R. BLAU, P. FOLEY, D. SAMPLES, AND D. PATTERSON [1984]. "Architecture of SOAR: Smalltalk on a RISC," *Proc. 11th Symposium on Computer Architecture* (June), Ann Arbor, Mich., 188–197. (p. 189)

UNGAR, D., R. BLAU, P. FOLEY, D. SAMPLES, AND D. PATTERSON [1984]. "Architecture of SOAR: Smalltalk on a RISC," *Proc. 11th Symposium on Computer Architecture* (June), Ann Arbor, Mich., 188–197. (p. E-15)

UNGER, S. H. [1958]. "A computer oriented towards spatial problems," *Proc. Institute of Radio Engineers* 46:10 (October) 1744–1750. (p. 589)

VON NEUMANN, J. [1945]. "First draft of a report on the EDVAC." Reprinted in W. Aspray and A. Burks, eds., *Papers of John von Neumann on Computing and Computer Theory* (1987), 17–82, The MIT Press, Cambridge, Mass. (p. 592)

WAKERLY, J. [1989]. *Microcomputer Architecture and Programming,* J. Wiley, New York. (p. 188)

WANG, E.-H., J.-L. BAER, AND H. M. LEVY [1989]. "Organization and performance of a two-level virtual-real cache hierarchy," *Proc. 16th Annual Symposium on Computer Architecture* (May 28–June 1), Jerusalem, Israel, 140–148. (p. 487)

WATANABE, T. [1987]. "Architecture and performance of the NEC supercomputer SX system," *Parallel Computing* 5, 247–255. (p. 394)

WATERS, F., ED. [1986]. *IBM RT Personal Computer Technology,* IBM, Austin, Tex., SA 23-1057. (p. 190)

WATSON, W. J. [1972]. "The TI ASC–A highly modular and flexible super computer architecture," *Proc. AFIPS Fall Joint Computer Conf.,* 221–228. (p. 393)

WEICKER, R. P. [1984]. "Dhrystone: A synthetic systems programming benchmark," *Comm. ACM* 27:10 (October) 1013–1030. (p. 47)

WEISS, S. AND J. E. SMITH [1984]. "Instruction issue logic for pipelined supercomputers," *Proc. 11th Symposium on Computer Architecture* (June), Ann Arbor, Mich., 110–118. (p. 339)

WEISS, S. AND J. E. SMITH [1987]. "A study of scalar compilation techniques for pipelined super-computers," *Proc. Second Conf. on Architectural Support for Programming Languages and Operating Systems* (March), IEEE/ACM, Palo Alto, Calif., 105–109. (p. 340)

WESTE, N. AND K. ESHRAGHIAN [1985]. *Principles of CMOS VLSI Design,* Addison-Wesley, Reading, Mass. (p. A-59)

WHITBY-STREVENS C. [1985]. "The transputer," *Proc. 12th Int'l Symposium on Computer Architecture*, Boston, Mass. (June) 292–300. (p. 589)

WICHMANN, B. A. [1973]. *Algol 60 Compilation and Assessment*, Academic Press, New York. (p. 46)

WIECEK, C. [1982]. "A case study of the VAX 11 instruction set usage for compiler execution," *Proc. Symposium on Architectural Support for Programming Languages and Operating Systems* (March), IEEE/ACM, Palo Alto, Calif., 177–184. (p. 188)

WILKES, M. [1965]. "Slave memories and dynamic storage allocation," *IEEE Trans. Electronic Computers* EC-14:2 (April) 270–271. (p. 486)

WILKES, M. V. [1953]. "The best way to design an automatic calculating machine," in *Manchester University Computer Inaugural Conf.*, 1951, Ferranti, Ltd., London. (Not published until 1953.) Reprinted in "The Genesis of Microprogramming" in *Annals of the History of Computing* 8:116. (p. 241)

WILKES, M. V. [1982]. "Hardware support for memory protection: Capability implementations," *Proc. Symposium on Architectural Support for Programming Languages and Operating Systems* (March 1–3), Palo Alto, Calif., 107–116. (pp. 107, 486)

WILKES, M. V. [1985]. *Memoirs of a Computer Pioneer*, The MIT Press, Cambridge, Mass. (pp. 25, 241)

WILKES, M. V. AND J. B. STRINGER [1953]. "Microprogramming and the design of the control circuits in an electronic digital computer," *Proc. Cambridge Philosophical Society* 49:230–238. Also reprinted in D. P. Siewiorek, C. G. Bell, and A. Newell, *Computer Structures: Principles and Examples* (1982), McGraw-Hill, New York, 158–163, and in "The Genesis of Microprogramming" in *Annals of the History of Computing* 8:116. (p. 248)

WILKES, M. V. AND W. RENWICK [1949]. *Report of a Conf. on High Speed Automatic Calculating Machines,* Cambridge, England. (p. 88)

WILKES, M. V., D. J. WHEELER, AND S. GILL [1951]. *The Preparation of Programs for an Electronic Digital Computer*, Addison-Wesley Press, Cambridge, Mass. (p. 24)

WILLIAMS, T. E., M. HOROWITZ, R. L. ALVERSON, AND T. S. YANG [1987]. "A self-timed chip for division," *Advanced Research in VLSI, Proc. 1987 Stanford Conf.*, The MIT Press, Cambridge, Mass. (p. A-46)

WILSON, A. W., JR. [1987]. "Hierarchical cache/bus architecture for shared memory multiprocessors," *Proc. 14th Int'l Symposium on Computer Architecture* (June), Pittsburg, Penn., 244–252. (p. 589)

WULF, W. [1981]. "Compilers and computer architecture," *Computer* 14:7 (July) 41–47. (p. 130)

WULF, W. A., R. LEVIN AND S. P. HAREISON [1981]. *Hydra/C.mmp: An Experimental Computer System,* McGraw-Hill, New York. (p. 485)

WULF, W. AND C. G. BELL [1972]. "C.mmp—A multi-mini-processor," *Proc. AFIPS Fall Joint Computing Conf.* 41, part 2, 765–777. (p. 590)

WULF, W. AND S. P. HAREISON [1978]. "Reflections in a pool of processors—An experience report on C.mmp/Hydra," *Proc. AFIPS 1978 National Computing Conf.* 48 (June), Anaheim, Calif. 939–951. (p. 589)

Index

Hardware Description Notation (and some standard C operators)

Notation	Meaning	Example	Meaning
$\leftarrow$	Data transfer. Length of the transfer is given by the destination's length; the length is specified when not clear.	R1$\leftarrow$R2;	Transfer contents of R2 to R1. Registers have a fixed length, so transfers shorter than the register size must indicate which bits are used.
M	Array of memory accessed in bytes. The starting address for a transfer is indicated as the index to the memory array.	R1$\leftarrow$M[x];	Place contents of memory location x into R1. If a transfer starts at M[i] ˋand requires 4 bytes, the transferred bytes are M[i],M[i+1],M[i+2], and M[i+3].
$\leftarrow_n$	Transfer an *n*-bit field, used whenever length of transfer is not clear.	M[y]$\leftarrow_{16}$M[x];	Transfer 16 bits starting at memory location x to memory location y. The length of the two sides should match.
X_n	Subscript selects a bit.	R1$_0\leftarrow$0;	Change sign bit of R1 to 0. (Bits are numbered from MSB starting at 0.)
$X_{m..n}$	Subscript selects a bit field.	R3$_{24..31}\leftarrow$M[x];	Moves contents of memory location x into low-order byte of R3.
X^n	Superscript replicates a field.	R3$_{0..23}\leftarrow0^{24}$;	Sets high-order three bytes of R3 to 0.
##	Concatenates two fields.	R3$\leftarrow0^{24}$ ## M[x]	Moves contents of location x into low byte of R3; clears upper three bytes.
		F2##F3$\leftarrow_{64}$M[x];	Moves 64 bits from memory starting at location x; first 32 bits go into F2, second 32 into F3.
$*$, &	Dereference a pointer; get the address of a variable.	P*$\leftarrow$&x;	Assign to object pointed to by p the address of the variable x.
<<,>>	C logical shifts (left,right)	R1 << 5	Shift R1 left 5 bits.
==,!=,>, <,>=,<=	C relational operators: equal, not equal, greater, less, greater or equal, less or equal	(R1==R2) & (R3!=R4)	True if the contents of R1 equal the contents of R2 and the contents of R3 do not equal the contents of R4.
&,|, ^, !	C bitwise logical operations: and, or, exclusive or, and complement.	(R1 & (R2 | R3))	Bitwise and of R1 and the bitwise or of R2 and R3.

DLX Pipeline Structure

Stage	ALU instruction	Load or store instruction	Branch instruction
IF	IR$\leftarrow$Mem[PC]; PC$\leftarrow$PC+4;	IR$\leftarrow$Mem[PC]; PC$\leftarrow$PC+4;	IR$\leftarrow$Mem[PC]; PC$\leftarrow$PC+4;
ID	A$\leftarrow$Rs1; B$\leftarrow$Rs2; PC1$\leftarrow$PC IR1$\leftarrow$IR	A$\leftarrow$Rs1; B$\leftarrow$Rs2; PC1$\leftarrow$PC IR1$\leftarrow$IR	A$\leftarrow$Rs1; B$\leftarrow$Rs2; PC1$\leftarrow$PC IR1$\leftarrow$IR
EX	ALUoutput$\leftarrow$A *op* B; or ALUoutput$\leftarrow$A *op* ((IR1$_{16}$)^{16}##IR1$_{16..31}$);	DMAR$\leftarrow$ A+ ((IR1$_{16}$)^{16}##IR1$_{16..31}$); SMDR$\leftarrow$ B;	ALUoutput$\leftarrow$PC1 + ((IR1$_{16}$)^{16}##IR1$_{16..31}$); cond$\leftarrow$(Rs1 *op* 0);
MEM	ALUoutput1$\leftarrow$ ALUoutput	LMDR$\leftarrow$Mem[DMAR]; or Mem[DMAR]$\leftarrow$SMDR;	if (cond) PC$\leftarrow$ALUoutput;
WB	Rd$\leftarrow$ALUoutput1;	Rd$\leftarrow$LMDR;	